microsoft® office word®

A Professional Approach

WORD 2007

Deborah Hinkle

McGraw-Hill
Higher Education

Boston   Burr Ridge, IL   Dubuque, IA   New York   San Francisco   St. Louis
Bangkok   Bogotá   Caracas   Kuala Lumpur   Lisbon   London   Madrid   Mexico City
Milan   Montreal   New Delhi   Santiago   Seoul   Singapore   Sydney   Taipei   Toronto

McGraw-Hill
Higher Education

MICROSOFT® OFFICE WORD® 2007: A PROFESSIONAL APPROACH
Published by McGraw-Hill, a business unit of The McGraw-Hill Companies, Inc., 1221 Avenue
of the Americas, New York, NY, 10020. Copyright © 2008 by The McGraw-Hill Companies, Inc.
All rights reserved. No part of this publication may be reproduced or distributed in any form
or by any means, or stored in a database or retrieval system, without the prior written consent of
The McGraw-Hill Companies, Inc., including, but not limited to, in any network or other
electronic storage or transmission, or broadcast for distance learning.

Some ancillaries, including electronic and print components, may not be available to customers
outside the United States.

This book is printed on acid-free paper.

1 2 3 4 5 6 7 8 9 0 DOW/DOW 0 9 8 7

ISBN   978-0-07-351919-7 (student edition)
MHID   0-07-351919-7 (student edition)
ISBN   978-0-07-329464-3 (annotated instructor's edition)
MHID   0-07-329464-0 (annotated instructor's edition)

Publisher: *Linda Schreiber*
Associate sponsoring editor: *Janna Martin*
Developmental editor: *Alaina Grayson*
Marketing manager: *Sarah Wood*
Media producer: *Marc Mattson*
Senior project manager: *Rick Hecker*
Production supervisor: *Janean A. Utley*
Designer: *Marianna Kinigakis*
Senior photo research coordinator: *Jeremy Cheshareck*
Media project manager: *Mark A. S. Dierker*
Cover design: *Asylum Studios*
Interior design: *JoAnne Schopler, Graphic Visions*
Typeface: *10.5/13 New Aster*
Compositor: *Aptara*
Printer: *R. R. Donnelley*

Library of Congress Cataloging-in-Publication Data

Hinkle, Deborah A.
   Microsoft Office Word 2007 : a professional approach / Deborah Hinkle.
      p. cm.
   Includes index.
   ISBN-13: 978-0-07-351919-7 (student edition : alk. paper)
   ISBN-10: 0-07-351919-7 (student edition : alk. paper)
   ISBN-13: 978-0-07-329464-3 (annotated instructor's edition : alk. paper)
   ISBN-10: 0-07-329464-0 (annotated instructor's edition : alk. paper)
      1. Microsoft Word. 2. Word processing. I. Title.
Z52.5.M52.H563 2008
005.52--dc22
                                                                2007012662

www.mhhe.com

contents

WORD

Unit 1 *Basic Skills*

Unit 2   Paragraph Formatting, Tabs, and Advanced Editing

Unit 3 *Page Formatting*

Unit 4 *Tables and Columns*

Unit 5 *Graphics and Charts*

Unit 6 *Advanced Topics*

Unit 7 Long Documents and Document Sharing

What Does This Logo Mean?

It means this courseware has been approved by the Microsoft Office Certification Program to be among the finest available for learning *Microsoft Office Word 2007*. It also means that if you complete and fully understand this courseware, you will be prepared to take an exam certifying your proficiency in this application.

What Is a Microsoft Certified Application Specialist?

A Microsoft Certified Application Specialist is an individual who has passed exams that certify his or her skills in one or more of the Microsoft Office desktop applications such as Microsoft Word, Microsoft Excel, Microsoft PowerPoint, Microsoft Outlook, or Microsoft Access. The Microsoft Certified Application Specialist Program is the only program in the world approved by Microsoft for testing proficiency in Microsoft Office desktop applications. This testing program can be a valuable asset in any job search or career advancement.

More Information

To learn more about becoming a Microsoft Certified Application Specialist, visit www.microsoft.com/officespecialist.

The availability of Microsoft Office certification exams varies by application, application version, and language. Visit the site listed above for exam availability.

preface

Microsoft Office Word 2007: A Professional Approach is written to help you master Microsoft Word. The text takes you step by step through the Word features that you are likely to use in both your personal and business life.

Case Study

Learning the features of Word is one component of the text, and applying what you learn is another component. A case study was created to offer the opportunity to learn Word in a realistic business context. Take the time to read the case study about Campbell's Confections, a fictional business located in Grove City, Pennsylvania. All the documents for this course relate to Campbell's Confections.

Organization of the Text

The text includes seven units, and each unit is divided into lessons. There are twenty-five lessons, each self-contained but building on previously learned procedures. This building-block approach, together with the case study and the following features, enables you to maximize the learning process.

Features of the Text

- Objectives are listed for each lesson.
- Required skills for the Microsoft Certification Exam are listed for each lesson.
- The estimated time required to complete each lesson up to the Lesson Applications section is stated.
- Within a lesson, each heading corresponds to an objective.
- Easy-to-follow exercises emphasize learning by doing.
- Key terms are italicized and defined as they are encountered.
- Extensive graphics display screen contents.
- Ribbon commands and keyboard keys are shown in the text when used.
- Large buttons in the margins provide easy-to-see references.
- Lessons contain important notes, useful tips, and helpful reviews.
- The Lesson Summary reviews the important concepts taught in the lesson.
- The Command Summary lists the commands taught in the lesson.
- Concepts Review includes true/false, short answer, and critical thinking questions that focus on lesson content.
- Skills Review provides skill reinforcement for each lesson.
- Lesson Applications apply your skills in a more challenging way.
- On Your Own exercises apply your skills creatively.
- Unit Applications give you the opportunity to practice the skills you learn throughout a unit.
- An Appendix includes Proofreaders' Marks, Standard Forms for Business Documents, Microsoft Certified Application Specialist standards, a Glossary, and an Index.

Microsoft Certified Application Specialist Program

The Microsoft Certified Application Specialist program offers certification for Office Word 2007, Office Excel 2007, Office Outlook 2007, Office PowerPoint 2007, Office Access 2007, and Windows Vista. This certification can be a valuable asset in any job search. For more information about this Microsoft program, go to www.microsoft.com/officespecialist. For a complete listing of the skills for the Office Word 2007 Certification Exam and a correlation to the lessons in the text, see Appendix C, "Microsoft Certified Application Specialist."

Professional Approach Web Site

Visit the Professional Approach Web site at www.mhhe.com/pas07 to access a wealth of additional materials.

Conventions Used in the Text

This text uses a number of conventions to help you learn the program and save your work.

- Text to be keyed appears either in **red** or as a separate figure.
- Filenames appear in **boldface**.
- Options that you choose from tabs and dialog boxes, but that aren't buttons, appear in green; for example, "Choose **Print** from the Office menu."
- You're asked to save each document with your initials followed by the exercise name. For example, an exercise might end with this instruction: "Save the document as *[your initials]*5-12." Documents are saved in folders for each lesson.

If You Are Unfamiliar with Windows

If you are not familiar with Windows, review the "Windows Tutorial" available in the textbook or on the Professional Approach Web site at www.mhhe.com/pas07 before beginning Lesson 1. This tutorial provides a basic overview of Microsoft's operating system and shows you how to use the mouse. You might also want to review "File Management" on the Professional Approach Web site to get more comfortable with files and folders.

Screen Differences

As you practice each concept, illustrations of the screens help you follow the instructions. Don't worry if your screen is different from the illustration. These differences are due to variations in system and computer configurations.

installation requirements

You'll need Microsoft Word 2007 to work through this textbook. Word 2007 needs to be installed on the computer's hard drive or on a network. Use the following checklists to evaluate installation requirements.

Hardware

- Computer with 500MHz or higher processor and at least 256MB of RAM
- CD-ROM or DVD drive
- 1.5GB or more of hard disk space for a "Student" Office installation
- 1024 × 768 or higher-resolution video monitor
- Printer (laser or ink-jet recommended)
- Mouse
- Modem or other Internet connection

Software

- Word 2007 (from Microsoft Office 2007)
- Windows XP with Service Pack 2 or later, or Windows Vista or later operating system
- Browser and Internet access

FEATURE	USE	HOW TO INSTALL/USE
Student template files	Build a new document based on template.	Copy template files to C:\Users\UserName\AppData\Roaming\Microsoft\Templates for files to appear on the My Templates tab of the New dialog box.
Clip art, additional	Use clip art related to the case.	Copy image files to any usable folder.
Templates	Build a new document based on template.	Part of typical installation; files are in C:\Program Files\Microsoft Office 11\Templates\1033.
Internet functionality	Use online help, use online Template Gallery, use additional research tools, view Web pages.	Specific to classroom.
Language tools	Use thesaurus and translation tools in the Research task pane.	Part of a typical installation for Office 2007 Professional. Install when prompted at first use. May require installation CD.

FEATURE	USE	HOW TO INSTALL/USE
Visual Basic Editor	View, edit, and save macros.	Part of a typical installation for Office 2007 Professional. Install when prompted. May require installation CD.
Digital Signature	Create a digital signature.	Part of a typical installation for Office 2007 Professional. Listed at Microsoft Office Button, Prepare.
XPS/PDF Add-in	Save files in XPS or PDF format.	
Compatibility Checker	Save files in XLS format.	Part of a typical installation for Office 2007 Professional.

If you are not familiar with Windows, review this "Windows Tutorial" carefully. You will learn how to

- Use a mouse.
- Start Windows.
- Use the taskbar, menus, Ribbon, dialog boxes, and other important aspects of Windows.

NOTE

All examples in this tutorial refer specifically to Windows Vista. If you are using any other version of Windows, your screen might differ slightly from the images shown in this tutorial. However, because most basic features are common to all versions of Windows, this tutorial should be helpful to you no matter which version of Windows you use.

If you are familiar with Windows but need help navigating Windows files and folders, refer to the section "File Management." There you will find information on how Windows stores information and how to use Windows Explorer, a tool for managing files and folders.

Computers differ in the ways they can be set up. In most cases, when you turn on your computer, Windows loads automatically and the Windows log-on screen appears. When you see the Windows log-on screen, you need to log on and key a password. In order to log on, you need to know how to use the mouse, a device attached to your computer.

Using the Mouse

A *mouse* is a pointing device that is typically attached to your computer. Optical versions, which are not attached, are also available. The mouse is your access to the computer screen, allowing you to accomplish specific tasks. It operates through a pointer, a screen object you use to point to objects on the computer screen. The normal shape for the mouse cursor is an arrow. To move the pointer arrow on the screen, you roll the mouse on any flat object, or on a mouse pad, which has a smooth surface designed for easy mouse rolling. Although you can use the keyboard with Windows, you will probably find yourself using the mouse most of the time.

To use the mouse to point to an object on the computer screen:

1. Turn on the computer (if it is not on already). Windows loads, and the log-on screen appears. The screen includes a log-on name and picture assigned to you by your instructor.

To log on, you need to move the mouse pointer to the log-on name that was assigned. The pointer on the computer screen mirrors the actions made by the mouse when you roll it. Place your hand over the mouse and roll it to the left. The pointer on the screen moves to the left.

2. Roll the mouse to the right, and watch the pointer on the screen move to the right.
3. Practice rolling the mouse in all directions.
4. Roll your mouse to the edge of the pad, and then lift it up and place it back in the middle of the pad. Try it now to see how it works. When you feel that you can control the mouse position on the screen, roll the mouse to the name you have been assigned.

To log on, you will need to click the name to select it. Mouse clicks are covered in the next section; instructions for logging onto Windows Vista are covered in succeeding sections.

Clicks and Double-Clicks

A mouse typically has two buttons at the front (the edge of the mouse where the cord attaches)—one on the left (primary) and one on the right (secondary). A mouse might also have a center button or a wheel.

Single-click actions with the mouse are used to position the pointer at a specific screen location. To perform a single click:

1. Roll the mouse around on the mouse pad until the pointer on the screen is over an object on the screen. Remember that the direction in which you move the mouse on the pad represents the pointer's movement on the screen.

2. Press and release the left mouse button once. Pressing and releasing the mouse button is referred to as a *click*. The computer tells you that the action has been performed when the object you click is *highlighted* (typically, the color of the selected object changes) to indicate to you that it has been *selected*. In Windows, you often need to select an object before you can perform an action. For example, you usually need to select an object before you can copy it.

Pressing and releasing the mouse button twice is referred to as a *double-click*. When you double-click an object on the screen, it is selected—the object is highlighted—and an action is performed. For example:

NOTE

Whenever you are told to "click" or "double-click" an object on the computer screen, use the left mouse button.

- When you double-click a folder, it is highlighted and opens to a window showing the items the folder contains.

- When you double-click a word in a text file, it is selected for a future action. In a text file, the pointer becomes an I-beam for selecting text in the document.

Selecting and Highlighting

You can also select a larger object such as a picture or a block of text by using the mouse.

1. Position the pointer on one side of the object, and hold down the left mouse button.

2. Roll the mouse until the pointer reaches the other side of the object.

3. Release the mouse button. The selected object is highlighted.

Drag and Drop—Moving an Object Using the Mouse

You can use the mouse to move an object on the screen to another screen location. In this operation, you select an object and drag the mouse to move the selected object, such as an icon. The operation is known as *drag and drop*.

1. Using the mouse, move the pointer over the object you want to drag.
2. Perform a single-click action by pressing the left mouse button but keep it pressed down. The selected object will be highlighted.
3. With the left mouse button still depressed, roll the mouse until the pointer and selected object are placed at the desired new location.
4. Release the mouse button to drop the object. The object is now positioned at the new location.

Using the Right Mouse Button

Pressing and quickly releasing the right mouse button is referred to as a *right-click*. Although the right mouse button is used less frequently, using it can be a real time-saver. When you right-click an icon, a *shortcut menu* appears with a list of commands. The list of commands displayed varies for each icon or object.

As you progress in this tutorial, you will become familiar with the terms in Table 1, describing the actions you can take with a mouse.

TABLE 1 Mouse Terms

TERM	DESCRIPTION
Point	Roll the mouse until the tip of the pointer is touching the desired object on the computer screen.
Click	Quickly press and release the left mouse button. Single-clicking selects objects.
Double-click	Quickly press and release the left mouse button twice. Double-clicking selects an object and performs an action such as opening a folder.
Drag	Point to an object on screen, hold down the left mouse button, and roll the mouse until the pointer is in position. Then release the mouse button (drag and drop).
Right-click	Quickly press and release the right mouse button. A shortcut menu appears.
Select	When working in Windows, you must first select an object in order to work with it. Many objects are selected with a single click. However, depending on the size and type of object to be selected, you may need to roll the mouse to include an entire area: Holding down the left mouse button, roll the mouse so that the pointer moves from one side of an object to another. Then release the mouse button.

Pointer Shapes

As you perform actions on screen using the mouse, the mouse pointer changes its shape, depending on where it is located and what operation you are performing. Table 2 shows the most common types of mouse pointers.

TABLE 2 Frequently Used Mouse Pointers

SHAPE	NAME	DESCRIPTION
	Pointer	Used to point to objects.
	I-Beam	Used in typing, inserting, and selecting text. When the I-beam is moved to a selected location, it turns into a blinking bar.
	Two-pointed arrow	Used to change the size of objects or windows.
	Four-pointed arrow	Used to move objects.
	Busy	Indicates the computer is processing a command. While the busy or working in background pointer is displayed, it is best to wait rather than try to continue working. Note: Some of the working in background actions will not allow you to perform other procedures until processing is completed.
	Working in background	
	Hand	Used to select a *link* in Windows' Help or other programs.

Starting Windows: The Log-on Screen

The Windows Vista log-on screen allows several people to use the same computer at different times. Each person is assigned a user account that determines which files and folders you can access and your personal preferences, such as your desktop background. Each person's files are hidden from the others using the computer. However, users may share selected files using the Public folder. The log-on screen lists each user allocated to the computer by name.

If the administrator has added your name to a given computer, the log-on screen will include your name. If the computers are not assigned to specific individuals, you may find a box for Guest or for a generic user. If your computer is on a network, your instructor might need to provide you with special start-up instructions.

After you have logged on to Windows Vista, the desktop is the first screen you will see. It is your on-screen work area. All the elements you need to start working with Windows appear on the desktop.

1. If you have not already turned on the computer, do so now to begin the Windows Vista loading process. The Windows log-on screen appears.

NOTE

On some computers, the log-on screen does not appear automatically. You might have to press the following keys, all at once, and then quickly release them: Ctrl + Alt + Delete .

2. Click your name to select it. The Password box appears with an I-beam in position ready for you to type your password.

3. Type your password.

4. Click the arrow icon to the right of the box. If you have entered the password correctly, the Windows desktop appears. If you made an error, the Password box returns for you to type the correct password.

The Windows Desktop

The Desktop includes the Start button, taskbar, and sidebar. You may also see icons on the desktop that represent folders, programs, or other objects. You can add and delete icons from the desktop as well as change the desktop background. The Start button is your entry into Vista functions.

Figure 1
Windows Vista
Desktop

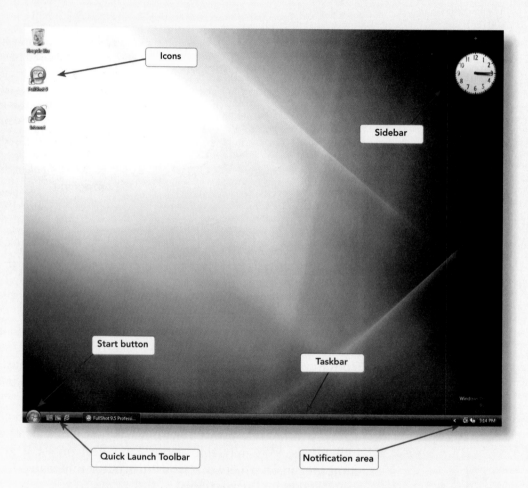

Using the Start Menu

Click the taskbar Start button to open the Start menu. You can also press the Windows logo key on the keyboard to open the Start menu. Use the Start menu to launch programs, adjust computer settings, search for files and folders, and turn off the computer. If this is a computer assigned to you for log-on, your Start menu may contain items that differ from those of another user assigned to the same computer. To open and learn about the Start menu, first click the Start button on the Windows taskbar. The Start menu appears.

Figure 2
Start menu

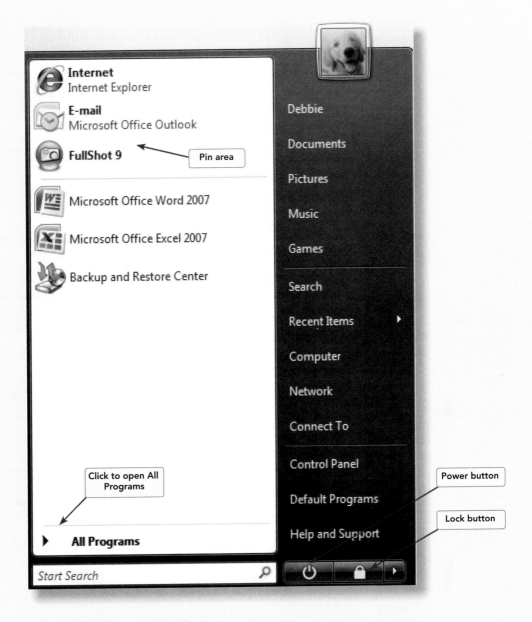

The left pane consists of three sections divided by separator lines. The top section, called the *pin area*, lists programs that are always available for you to click. These can include your Internet browser, e-mail program, your word processor, and so forth. You can remove programs you do not want listed, rearrange them, and add those you prefer.

Below the separator line are shortcuts to programs you use most often, placed there automatically by Windows. You can remove programs you do not want listed, rearrange them, but not add any manually.

All Programs displays a list of programs on your computer and is used to launch programs not listed on the Start menu.

Below the left pane is the *Search box* which is used to locate programs and files on your computer.

The right pane is also divided into three sections. It is used to select folders, files, and commands and to change settings. Use the icons at the bottom of the right pane to save your session, lock the computer, restart, switch users, and shut down.

Table 3 describes the typical components of the Start menu.

TABLE 3 Typical Components of the Start Menu

COMMAND	USE
Left Pane	
Pin area	Lists programs that are always available. You can add and delete items to the pin area.
Internet	Connects to the default browser.
E-mail	Connects to the chosen e-mail service.
Below the First Separator Line	
Programs	Lists programs that you use most often. You can add to and rearrange the programs listed.
Below the Second Separator Line	
All Programs	Click to display a list of programs in alphabetical order and a list of folders. Click to open a program.
Start Search	Use to search programs and folders. Key text and results appear.
Right Pane	
Personal folder	Opens the User folder.
Documents	Opens the Documents folder.
Pictures	Opens the Pictures folder.
Music	Opens the Music folder.
Games	Opens the Games folder.
Search	Opens the Search Results window. Advanced Search options are available.
Recent Items	Opens a list of the most recent documents you have opened and saved.
Computer	Opens a window where you can access disk drives and other hardware devices.
Network	Opens the Network window where you can access computers and other devices on your network.
Connect To	Opens a window where you can connect to a different network.
Control Panel	Opens the Control Panel.
Default Programs	Opens the Default Programs window where you can define default programs and settings.
Help and Support	Opens the Windows Help and Support window. Help offers instructions on how to perform tasks in the Windows environment.
Power button	Turns off the computer.
Lock button	Locks the computer, or click the arrow beside the Lock button to display a menu for switching users, logging off, restarting, or shutting down the computer.

Using the All Programs Command

Most programs on your computer can be started from the All Programs command on the Start menu. This is the easiest way to open a program not listed directly on the Start menu.

1. To open the All Programs menu, click the Start button. The Start menu appears.

2. Click **All Programs** or the triangle to the left near the bottom of the left pane. The All Programs menu appears, listing the programs installed on your computer. Every computer has a different list of programs. Notice that some menu entries have an icon to the left of the name and others display a folder. Click a folder, and a list of programs stored in that folder appears. Click a program to open it. Point to a program to see a short description of the program.

Figure 3
All Programs
window

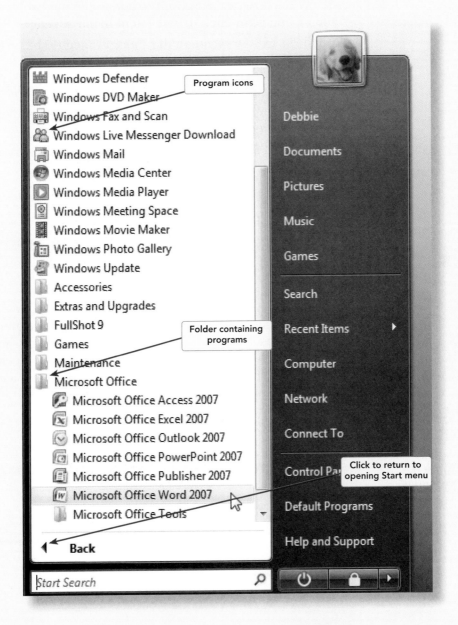

3. Click **Microsoft Office** to open a list of programs in the Microsoft Office folder. Click **Microsoft Office Word 2007**. (See Figure 3.) In a few seconds, the program you selected loads and the Word window appears. Notice that a button for the program appears on the taskbar. Leave Word open for the present.

Customizing the Start Menu

Both the Start menu and the desktop can be customized. You can add shortcuts to the desktop if you prefer, and you can add and delete items from the Start menu. However, if your computer is used by others, the administrator may limit some customization functions.

To add a program to the pin area of the Start menu:

1. Select the program you want to add to the pin list from the All Programs menu, and right-click it. A shortcut menu appears.
2. Click **Pin To Start Menu** on the shortcut menu. The program will be added to the pin list in the left pane above the first separator line.

To remove a program from the pin area of the Start menu:

1. Select the program you want to remove from the pin list, and right-click. A shortcut menu appears.
2. Click **Unpin From Start Menu**. The program will be removed from the pin list.

To change the order in which programs are listed in the pin area:

1. Point to the program icon.
2. Drag the icon to the desired position.

Using the Taskbar

The taskbar at the bottom of your screen is one of the most important features in Windows Vista. The taskbar is divided into several segments, each dedicated to a different use. It shows programs that are running, and you can use the taskbar to switch between open programs and between open documents within a program. If your computer has the Aero interface, a thumbnail preview appears when you move the mouse over a button on the taskbar.

Figure 4
The Desktop with the taskbar and the Word window

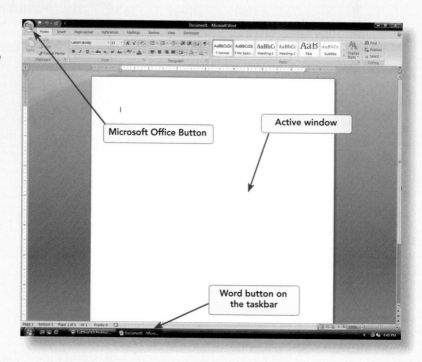

Microsoft Office Button

Active window

Word button on the taskbar

Windows displays a button on the taskbar for each opened program and document. Notice that there is a button for Word, showing the Word icon and the name of the program. Point to the Word button to view a thumbnail of the document window. Since the taskbar can become crowded, Windows combines access to documents or programs under single buttons. The button shows the name of the program (Microsoft Office Word) and the number of items in the group (9). The shape of the arrow varies, depending on what the button contains. Clicking the button opens the menu of available items.

Figure 5
Button contents for
Word documents

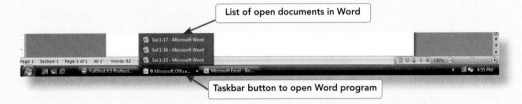

List of open documents in Word

Taskbar button to open Word program

Taskbar Notification Area

The *notification area* is on the right side of the taskbar, where the current time is usually displayed. Along with displaying the time, tiny icons notify you as to the status of your browser connection, virus protection, and so forth. It is also known as the *system tray*. In the interest of removing clutter, the notification area hides most of the icons. Clicking the Show Hidden Icons button "hides" or "unhides" the icons in the notification area. Click the left-pointing arrow next to the icons to expand the notification area. Click the right-pointing arrow to hide the notification area.

TIP

If you are not sure of what an item is or does, pointing to it without clicking displays a ScreenTip with a short description.

The Active Window

The window in which you are working is called the *active window*. The title bar for the active window is highlighted, and its taskbar button is also highlighted. The program window for Microsoft Word that you opened earlier should still be open. To examine additional features of the taskbar, open a second program, Microsoft Excel, a spreadsheet program in Microsoft Office.

1. If Word is not open, click the **Start** button and then click **All Programs, Microsoft Office, Microsoft Office Word 2007** from the Start menu. The Word window displays.

2. Click the **Start** button and then click **All Programs, Microsoft Office, Microsoft Office Excel 2007** from the Start menu. The Excel window displays. Notice how the Excel window covers the Word window, indicating that the window containing Excel is now active. Notice, too, that a new button for Excel has been added to the taskbar.

Figure 6
Excel (the active
window) covering
the Word window

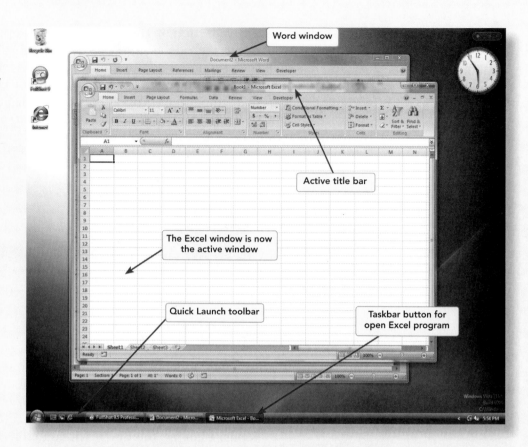

3. Click the button on the taskbar for Word, the first program you opened. Word reappears in front of Excel. Notice the change in the appearance of the title bar for each program.

4. Click the button on the taskbar for Excel. Notice that you switch back to Excel.

5. Click the button on the taskbar to return to Word.

6. Locate the Quick Launch toolbar to the right of the Start button, and point to the Switch between windows button .

7. Click the Switch between windows button, and notice the desktop view.

8. Click the Excel window.

Changing the Size of the Taskbar

You can change the size of the taskbar using your mouse if your toolbar is crowded. It is usually not necessary, because of the multiple document style buttons and other hide/unhide arrows on the taskbar. Before you can change the size of the taskbar, it may be necessary for you to unlock it. To unlock the taskbar, right-click an open area of the taskbar and click **Lock the Taskbar** to remove the checkmark. A checkmark is a toggle command. Click to turn it off, and click a second time to turn it on.

1. Move the pointer to the top edge of the taskbar until it changes from a pointer to a two-pointed arrow . Using the two-pointed arrow, you can change the size of the taskbar.

2. With the pointer displayed as a two-pointed arrow, hold down the left mouse button and move the arrow up until the taskbar enlarges upward.

3. Move the pointer to the top edge of the taskbar once again until the two-pointed arrow displays. Hold down the left mouse button, and move the arrow down to the bottom of the screen. The taskbar is restored to its original size.

Using Menus

Windows uses a system of menus that contain a choice of options for working with programs and documents. Most Windows programs use a similar menu structure. These operations are either mouse or keyboard driven. They are called commands because they "command" the computer to perform functions needed to complete the task you, the user, initiate at the menu level.

Executing a Command from a Menu

In Windows, a program may display a *menu bar*, a row of descriptive menu names at the top, just below the title bar. You open a menu by clicking the menu name listed in the menu bar. When a menu is opened, a list of command options appears. To execute a particular command from an open menu, press the left mouse button and then drag down and release the chosen option (click and drag). You can also click the command once the menu is open.

Keyboard Menu Commands

For people who prefer to use the keyboard to a mouse, Windows has provided keyboard commands for many menu items. You can use the keyboard to open menus and choose menu options.

Some menu items include not only the name of the command but a combination of keyboard keys. For example, under the File menu in WordPad, the Save command contains the notation Ctrl+S to its right. This means that you can also execute the command by pressing the Ctrl key together with the S key to save a document.

Figure 7
Title and menu bars
with the File menu
Open

Command name

Command with three
dots opens a dialog box.

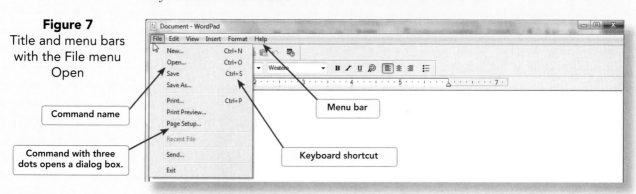

Other Menu Symbols

Three dots following a menu option indicate that a dialog box is displayed when that menu option is chosen. (Dialog boxes, discussed later, are small windows requesting and receiving input from a user.) Some commands also display a check box. Click an empty check box to select the option. A checkmark will appear in the square and indicates the option is selected. To turn off the option, click the check box to remove the checkmark. Commands that appear gray or dimmed are currently not available.

Perform the following steps for keyboard command practice:

1. Open the **Start menu**, click **All Programs**, and click the **Accessories** folder. Click **WordPad**. The WordPad program opens, and a button appears on the Windows taskbar.

2. Click **File** in the menu bar. The File menu displays. Click **File** to close the menu.

3. Press [Alt], and notice that the items in the menu bar display underlined letters (<u>F</u>ile, <u>E</u>dit). The underlined letters are a shortcut to open a menu. Press the letter "f" to open the File menu. Release [Alt], and click outside the menu in a blank area to close the menu.

4. Press [Alt]+[V], the keyboard shortcut for the View menu. The View menu displays.

5. Notice the four check boxes. All are selected. Click the **Options** command. The Options dialog box opens.

6. Click **Cancel** to close the dialog box.

7. Click **File** in the menu bar. Click **Exit**. Click **Don't Save** if prompted to save the document.

Displaying a Shortcut Menu

When the mouse pointer is on an object or an area of the Windows desktop and you right-click, a shortcut menu appears. A shortcut menu typically contains commands that are useful in working with the object or area of the desktop to which you are currently pointing.

1. Position the mouse pointer on a blank area of the desktop, and right-click. A shortcut menu appears with commands that relate to the desktop, including view and sort options.

2. Click outside the shortcut menu to close it.

3. Right-click the time in the bottom right corner of the taskbar. A shortcut menu appears.

4. Click Adjust Date/Time on the shortcut menu. The Date/Time Properties dialog box appears. You can use this dialog box to adjust your computer's date and time.

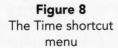

Figure 8
The Time shortcut menu

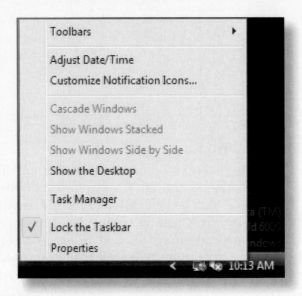

5. Click **Cancel**.

6. Right-click an icon on the desktop to display its shortcut menu, and then close the shortcut menu.

Using the Ribbon

Microsoft Office 2007 applications include a Microsoft Office Button, a Quick Access Toolbar, and a Ribbon. The *Microsoft Office Button* displays the Office menu which lists the commands to create, open, save, and print a document. The *Quick Access Toolbar* contains frequently used commands and is positioned to the right of the Microsoft Office Button. The *Ribbon* consists of seven tabs by default, and each tab contains a group of related commands. The number of commands for each tab varies. A command can be one of several formats. The most popular formats include buttons and drop-down lists.

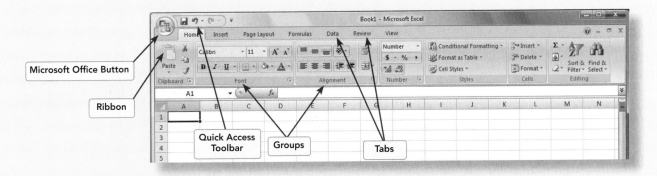

1. Activate the Excel program.

2. Point to and click the **Microsoft Office Button**. Notice the commands and icons in the menu.

3. Click a blank area of the window to close the menu.

4. Locate the Quick Access Toolbar beside the Microsoft Office Button. Point to each button in the Quick Access Toolbar to identify it. Notice that a keyboard shortcut displays beside each button.

5. Click the **Page Layout** tab. Notice the change in the groups and commands.

6. Click the **Home** tab.

Using Dialog Boxes

Windows programs make frequent use of dialog boxes. A *dialog box* is a window that requests input from you related to a command you have chosen. All Windows programs use a common dialog box structure.

1. Click the Excel program button on the taskbar to make Excel the active window if necessary.

2. Click the **Microsoft Office Button**. The File menu displays.

3. Click **Print** to display the Print dialog box.

4. The Print dialog box contains several types of dialog box options.

NOTE

A keyboard shortcut is available for the print dialog box: Press Ctrl+P to open the Print dialog box.

Figure 10
Print dialog box in
Excel

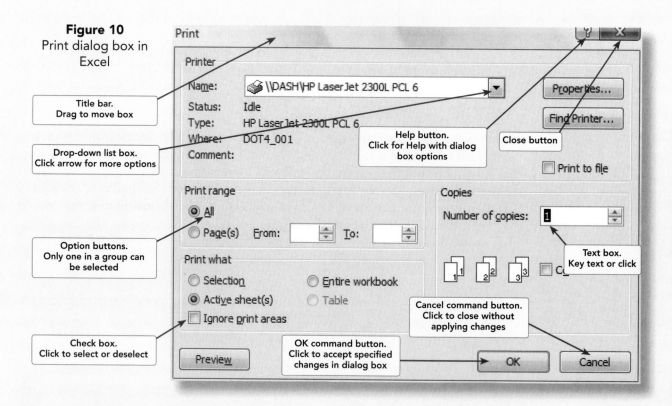

5. To close the Print dialog box, click **Cancel**, located in the lower right corner of the dialog box. The Print dialog box closes without applying any changes.

Another type of dialog box uses tabs to display related options. Only one tab can display at a time. The Word Font dialog box offers many options for choosing character formatting.

1. Make Word the active window.
2. Click the **Home** tab, and click the small arrow that appears on the right of the Font group ⬚⬚⬚⬚⬚⬚⬚⬚. The Font dialog box displays.

Figure 11
Font dialog box

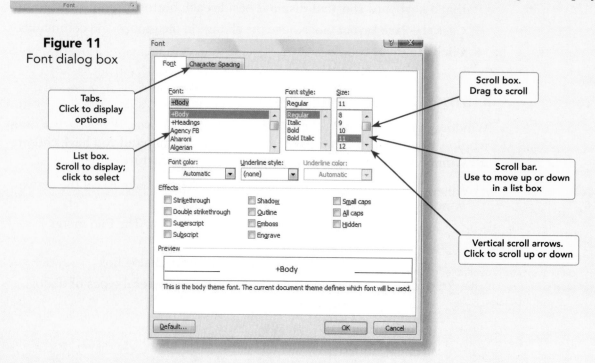

The scroll boxes are used to specify a font by name, its style, and its size. When you select a paragraph in a Word document, you can select its typographic features using this dialog box. The Font list box at the top left displays a list of all the typefaces installed on your computer. By clicking the name of the font, you select it for your paragraph.

The vertical scroll bar on the right side of a list box or a window indicates that there is more content to view. To view the hidden content, click the downward-pointing arrow or the upward-pointing vertical scroll arrow. You can also drag the scroll box on the scroll bar up or down to view all the content. The Character Spacing tab at the top of the Font dialog box displays additional character formatting options. Click the Character Spacing tab to view its contents, and then return to the Font tab.

Use the Font dialog box to style a paragraph as follows:

1. Type a very short paragraph in your Word document.
2. Position the I-beam at the beginning of the text, and hold down the left mouse button.
3. Drag the mouse to the end of the paragraph. The paragraph will change color, showing that it has been selected.
4. Open the Font dialog box by pressing Ctrl+D.
5. In the Font list box, click **Verdana**. You may need to scroll down to locate it.
6. In the Font style box, click **Bold**.
7. In the Size box, click **12**.
8. If you wish to change the color of your paragraph, move your pointer to the Font color drop-down list box and click the down-facing arrow. A color pallet appears. Point to the color you wish to use, and click.
9. When you have completed your selections, click **OK** at the bottom of the Font dialog box and look at the paragraph you have styled. If you wish, you can try other font formats, while your paragraph is selected.

Changing the Size of a Window

You can change the size of any window using either the mouse or the sizing buttons. Sizing buttons are the small buttons on the right side of the title bar that allow you to minimize or maximize the window (see Figure 12). This can be especially useful when you would like to display several open windows on your desktop and see them simultaneously.

NOTE

Notice that the window occupies the entire desktop, and the Maximize button has changed to a Restore Down button. This type of function is known as a toggle: When a button representing one state (Maximize) is clicked, an action is performed, the button toggles to the alternate state, and the other button (Restore Down) appears. A number of actions in Windows operate this way.

1. Make Excel the active window, if it is not already. Click the Maximize button on the Excel title bar if the Excel window does not fill the entire desktop.

Figure 12
Sizing buttons

Table 4 describes these buttons. To practice changing the size of a window, follow these steps:

TABLE 4 Sizing Buttons

BUTTON	USE
Minimize	Reduces the window to a button on the taskbar.
Maximize	Enlarges the window to fill the entire desktop (appears only when a window is reduced).
Restore Down	Returns the window to its previous size and desktop position (appears only when a window is maximized).

NOTE

You can double-click a window title bar to maximize or restore the window or right-click the program button on the taskbar and choose minimize, maximize, restore, or close.

2. Click the **Restore Down** button on the Excel title bar. The Excel window reduces in size, and the Word window appears behind it. The Restore Down button has now changed to a Maximize button. Notice that the highlighted title bar of the Excel window indicates it is the active window.

3. Click the **Minimize** button. The Excel window disappears, and its button appears on the taskbar.

How to Display Two Program Windows Simultaneously

1. Open the **Start** menu, and click **All Programs** to open Excel and Word if they are not already open from an earlier section of the tutorial.

TIP

Sometimes the borders of a window can move off the computer screen. If you are having trouble with one border of a window, try another border or drag the entire window onto the screen by using the title bar.

2. Click the **Excel** button on the taskbar to move its window to the front of the screen.

3. Click the **Restore Down** button if the Excel window is maximized.

4. Move the pointer to the right border of the Excel window. The pointer changes to a horizontal two-pointed arrow.

5. With the two-pointed arrow displayed ↔|, drag the border to the left to make the window narrower.

Figure 13
Sizing a window

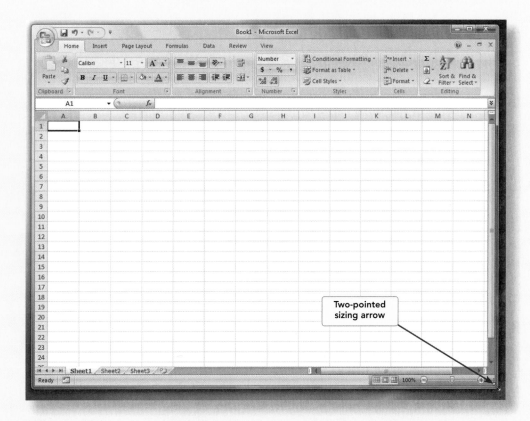

Two-pointed
sizing arrow

NOTE

You can place the pointer on any part of
the window border to change its size. To
change both the height and width of the
window, move the pointer to the bottom
right corner of the window. The double-
pointed arrow changes its orientation
to a 45-degree angle (see Figure 13).
Dragging this arrow resizes a window
vertically and horizontally.

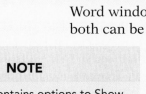

NOTE

The taskbar contains options to Show
Windows Stacked, Cascade Windows, and
Show the Desktop.

6. Click the title bar or any part of the Word window
   behind the Excel window. The Word window becomes
   the active window. The Excel window is still open, but
   it is now behind the Word window.

7. Click the **Maximize** button if the Word window does
   not fill the entire desktop.

8. Click the **Minimize** button on the title bar of the
   Word window. The Excel window becomes the active
   window.

9. Make the Word window the active window by clicking
   the **Word** button on the taskbar.

10. Click the **Restore Down** button on the Word window. The Word window
    reduces in size. The Excel window might be partially visible behind the
    Word window. You can drag the two reduced windows so that parts of
    both can be seen simultaneously.

11. Right-click the taskbar, and click **Show Windows Side
    by Side**. The windows display vertically.

12. Press the ⌊Alt⌋ key, and hold it down while pressing ⌊Tab⌋.
    You can switch to the previous window by pressing this
    shortcut, or you can continue to press ⌊Tab⌋ to switch to
    an open window on the desktop.

13. Click the **Show Desktop** button 🖳 located on the Quick Launch toolbar
    to see the desktop. The Word and Excel programs are minimized.

14. Click the **Show Desktop** button again to restore the programs.

15. Click the **Close** buttons on the title bars of each of the two program
    windows to close them and to show the desktop.

Using the Documents Command

Windows lets you open a recently used document by using the Recent Items command on the Start menu. This command allows you to open one of up to fifteen documents previously saved on your computer.

1. Click the Start button on the taskbar to display the Start menu.
2. Click Recent Items. The Recent Items submenu appears, showing you up to the last fifteen documents that were saved.
3. Click a document. The program in which the document was created opens, and the document displays. For example, if the document you chose is a Word document, Word opens and the document appears in a Word program window.
4. Click the program window's Close button. The program window closes, and the desktop is clear once again.

Changing the Desktop

The Control Panel lets you change the way Windows looks and works. Because your computer in school is used by other students, you should be very careful when changing settings. Others might expect Windows to look and work the standard way. Having Windows look or work in a nonstandard way could easily confuse other users. (Table 5 describes how to access other settings.)

To change the appearance of your computer, follow these steps. Talk to your instructor first, however, before changing any settings on your computer.

1. Click the Start button on the taskbar.
2. Click Control Panel on the right pane. The Control Panel window displays.
3. Click the Appearance and Personalization link. The Appearance and Personalization window displays.
4. Click Personalization and click Window Color and Appearance.
5. Click Default and click OK.
6. Close the Appearance and Personalization window.

TABLE 5 Setting Options

OPTION	USE
Control Panel	Displays the Control Panel window, which lets you change background color, add or remove programs, change the date and time, and change other settings for your hardware and software. The items listed below are accessed from the Control Panel.
Network and Internet	Includes options to view the network status, connect to a network, set up file sharing, change Internet options, and so on.
Hardware and Sound	Includes options to add a printer, change default settings for AutoPlay, sound, mouse settings, keyboard, and so on.
Appearance and Personalization	Includes options to change the desktop background, adjust screen resolution, customize the Start menu and icons on the taskbar, and change sidebar properties.

Using the Search Command

If you do not know where a file or folder is located, you can use the Search command on the Start menu to help you find and open it.

1. Click the Start button on the taskbar. Notice the blinking insertion point in the Start Search box. You can start typing the name of a program, folder, or file immediately.
2. Click Search in the right pane of the Start menu. The Search Results dialog box appears.
3. Click Document in the Show Only section.

Figure 14
Search Results
dialog box

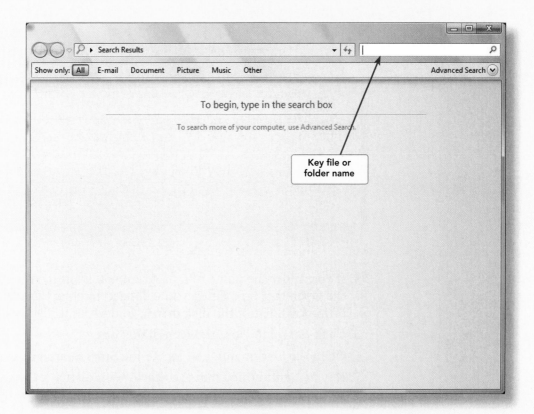

4. Type the name of the file or folder you want to find in the Search box. View the search results.

To search for files by date, size, type, or other attributes, click Advanced Search.

1. Click the arrow to the left of the Search Results text box to specify where you want Windows to search. The default location is the C drive.
2. Click Search to start the search. Any matches for the file are shown in the right pane of the dialog box.
3. Double-click any found item to open the program and view the file or folder Windows has located.
4. When you are finished with your search, close all open windows and clear your desktop.

Using the Run Command

Windows allows you to start a program by using the Run command and typing the program name. This command is often employed to run a "setup" or "install" program that installs a new program on your computer. It is best to use this command after you have become more familiar with Windows Vista.

1. Click the Start button on the taskbar.
2. Click All Programs, and click the Accessories folder.
3. Click Run.

Figure 15
Run dialog box

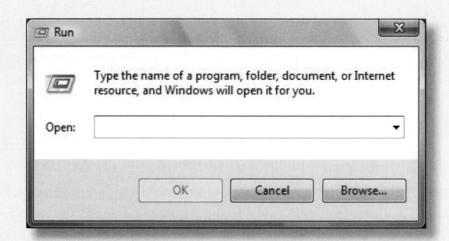

4. If you know the name of a program you want to run, type the name in the Open text box. Often you will need to click Browse to open a drop-down list of the disk drives, folders, and files available to you.
5. Click Cancel to close the Run dialog box.
6. Open the Start menu, and locate the Start Search box.
7. Key run, and notice that the Start menu displays the Run program.
8. Click the program name, and the Run dialog box displays.
9. Close the Run dialog box.

Deleting Files Using the Recycle Bin

The *Recycle Bin* is the trash can icon on your desktop. To delete a file:

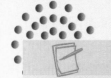

NOTE

As a protection against deleting a file unintentionally, any file you have placed in the Recycle Bin can be undeleted and used again.

1. Click its icon, and drag it to the Recycle Bin.
2. Double-click the Recycle Bin icon. A window opens listing files you have deleted.
3. To undelete a file, merely drag it out of the Recycle Bin window and place it on the desktop or right-click the file and click Restore.
4. To empty the Recycle Bin and permanently delete files, click Empty Recycle Bin in the Recycle Bin dialog box, or right-click the Recycle Bin icon. The shortcut menu appears.
5. Click Empty Recycle Bin.

Exiting Windows

You should always exit any open programs and Windows before turning off the computer. This is the best way to be sure your work is saved. Windows also performs other "housekeeping" routines that ensure everything is ready for you when you next turn on your computer. Failure to shut down properly will often force Windows to perform time-consuming system checks the next time it is loaded. You can either log off the computer to make it available for another user, or shut it down entirely.

To Log Off

1. Click the **Start** button on the taskbar.
2. Click the arrow to the right of the Lock this computer button , and click **Log Off**.

To Shut Down

To exit Windows, use the Lock this computer command on the Start menu. This command has several shut-down options.

- *Restart:* Restarts the computer without shutting off the power. This is sometimes necessary when you add new software.
- *Shut down:* Closes all open programs and makes it safe to turn off the computer. Some computers will turn off the power automatically.
- *Sleep:* Puts the computer in a low-activity state. It appears to be turned off but will restart when the mouse is moved. Press the computer power button to resume work.

1. Click the **Start** button on the taskbar.
2. Click the arrow beside the Lock this computer button.
3. Click the **Shut Down** option.
4. Windows prompts you to save changes in any open documents. It then prepares the computer to be shut down.

There is more to learning a word processing program like Microsoft Word than simply pressing keys. You need to know how to use Word in a real-world situation. That is why all the lessons in this book relate to everyday business tasks.

As you work through the lessons, imagine yourself working as an intern for Campbell's Confections, a fictional candy store and chocolate factory located in Grove City, Pennsylvania.

Campbell's Confections

It was 1950. Harry Truman was president. Shopping malls and supermarkets were appearing in suburban areas. And Campbell's Confections began doing business.

Based in Grove City, Pennsylvania, Campbell's Confections started as a small family-owned business. Originally, Campbell's Confections was a candy store, with a few display cases in the front of the building and a kitchen in the back to create chocolates and to try new recipes. The store was an immediate success, and word traveled quickly about the rich, smooth, creamy chocolates made by Campbell's Confections. Today, the store includes several display cases for chocolates and hard candies and special displays for greeting cards and gifts. The factory is located in a separate building on Monroe Street and offers tours for visitors.

Within a few years of opening the first store, the company expanded, and Campbell's Confections opened candy stores in Mercer, New Castle, and

Meadville. Today there are 24 stores in three states—Pennsylvania, Ohio, and West Virginia.

The goal of Campbell's Confections is to offer "quality chocolate," and the company has grown from selling chocolate in retail stores exclusively to adding wholesale and fund-raising divisions. E-commerce has been the latest venture with Internet sales increasing monthly.

Currently, Thomas Campbell is the president-owner, and Lynn Tanguay is the vice president.

To understand the organization of Campbell's Confections, take a look at Figure CS-1. Notice each of the specialty areas and management divisions.

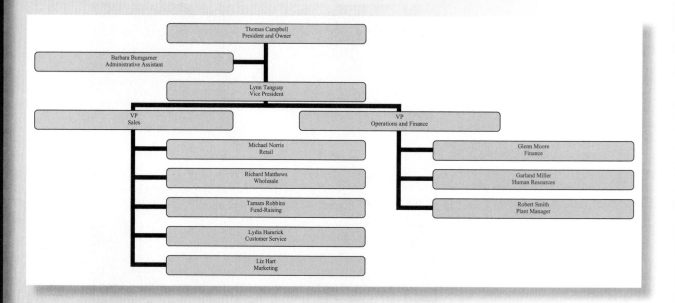

All the documents you will use in this text relate to Campbell's Confections. As you work through the documents in the text, take the time to notice the following:

- How the employees interact and how they respond to customers' queries.
- The format and tone of the business correspondence (if you are unfamiliar with the standard formats for business documents, refer to Appendix B).
- References to The Gregg Reference Manual, a standard reference manual for business writing and correspondence.
- The content of the correspondence (and its relation to Campbell's Confections).

As you use this text and become experienced with Microsoft Word, you will also gain experience in creating, editing, and formatting the type of documents that are generated in a real-life business environment.

unit 1

BASIC SKILLS

Lesson 1

Creating a Document

OBJECTIVES

MCAS OBJECTIVES

In this lesson:
WW 07 6.1.1

After completing this lesson, you will be able to:

1. Start Word.
2. Identify parts of the Word Screen.
3. Key text into a document.
4. Edit text.
5. Name and save a document.
6. Print a document.
7. Close a document and exit Word.

Estimated Time: 1 hour

Microsoft Word is a versatile, easy-to-use word processing program that helps you create letters, memos, reports, and other types of documents. This lesson begins with an overview of the Word screen. Then you learn how to create, edit, name, save, print, and close a document.

Starting Word

There are several ways to start Word, depending on your system setup and personal preferences. For example, you can use the Start button on the Windows taskbar or double-click a Word shortcut icon that might be on your desktop.

NOTE

Windows provides many ways to start applications. If you have problems, ask your instructor for help.

Figure 1-1
Starting Word from
the Windows taskbar

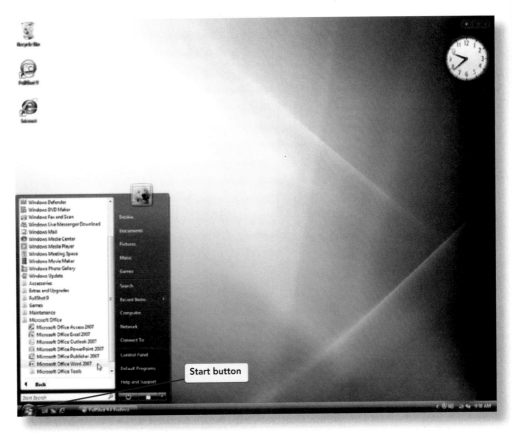

Start button

NOTE

Your screen will differ from the screen shown in Figure 1-1 depending on the programs installed on your computer.

Exercise 1-1 START WORD

1. Turn on your computer. Windows loads.

2. Click the Start button on the Windows taskbar and point to **All Programs**.

3. On the All Programs menu, click **Microsoft Office**, and then click **Microsoft Office Word 2007**. In a few seconds, the program is loaded and the Word screen appears.

NOTE

The document displays in Print Layout view. The Print Layout button appears in the lower right corner of your screen.

Figure 1-2
Word screen

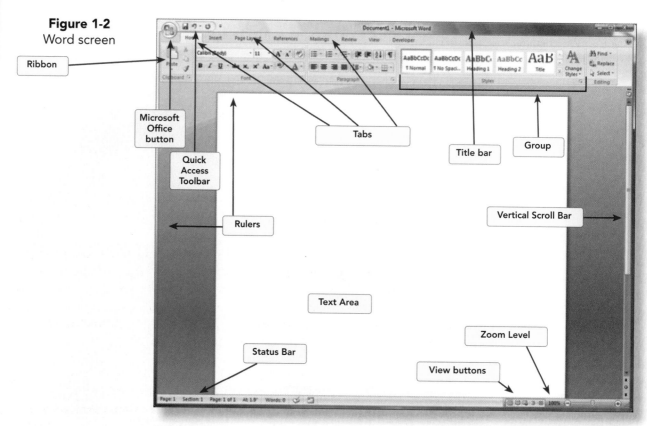

TABLE 1-1 Parts of the Word Screen

Part of Screen	Purpose
Microsoft Office Button	Displays the File menu, recently opened documents, and a command button to access Word Options.
Quick Access Toolbar	Displays icons for save, undo, and repeat. The Quick Access Toolbar can be customized, and the Quick Access Toolbar commands are available for all tabs on the Ribbon.
Title bar	Displays the name of the current document. The opening Word screen is always named "Document1."
Ribbon	Displays contextual tabs. Tabs contain groups of related commands. Commands can be buttons, menus, or drop-down list boxes.
Ruler	Shows placement of margins, indents, and tabs. The horizontal and vertical rulers display in Print Layout view.
Text area	Displays the text and graphics in the document.
Scroll bars	Used with the mouse to move right or left and up or down within a document.
Status bar	Displays the page number and page count of the document, the document view buttons, and the zoom control. It also displays the current mode of operation. The Status bar can be customized.

Identifying Parts of the Word Screen

To become familiar with Word, start by identifying the parts of the screen you will work with extensively, such as the Microsoft Office Button, the Quick Access Toolbar, and the Ribbon. As you practice using Word commands, you will see *ScreenTips* to help you identify screen elements such as buttons and commands.

Exercise 1-2 IDENTIFY THE MICROSOFT OFFICE BUTTON AND THE QUICK ACCESS TOOLBAR

The *Microsoft Office Button* displays the File menu which lists the commands to create, open, save, and print a document. Recently opened documents also appear when the File menu displays. The *Quick Access Toolbar* contains frequently used commands and is positioned to the right of the Microsoft Office Button and above the Ribbon by default. The commands on the Quick Access Toolbar are available for all tabs in the Ribbon.

1. Move the mouse pointer to the Microsoft Office Button . Notice a ScreenTip displays when you point to the button. Click the left mouse button to open the File menu. Word displays the File menu and a list of documents recently opened. The Word default setting is to show up to 17 documents in Recent Documents.

2. Click the text area to close the File menu.

3. Move the mouse pointer to the right of the Microsoft Office Button and point to the **Save** button . A ScreenTip and a keyboard shortcut to save a document display.

4. Point to the commands to the right of the Save command. Notice each command includes descriptive text and a keyboard shortcut. The Save, Undo, and Repeat commands are located in the Quick Access Toolbar by default. The Quick Access Toolbar contains commands you will use frequently and displays for each tab on the Ribbon.

NOTE

You can also close the File menu by pressing Esc or click the Microsoft Office Button.

TIP

Commands may appear in more than one location. For example, you can save a document by choosing **Save** from the File menu, by clicking the **Save** command on the Quick Access Toolbar, or by pressing Ctrl+S.

Figure 1-3
Displaying Microsoft
Office button
commands

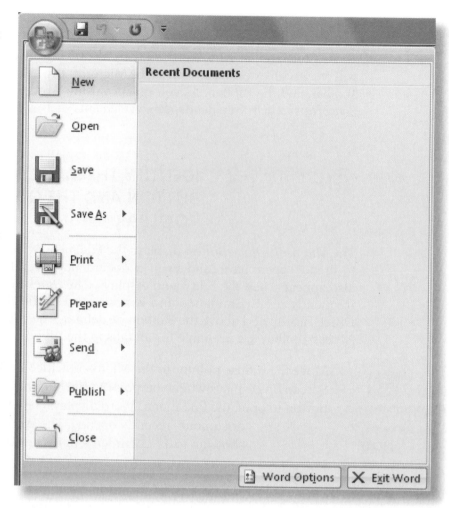

Exercise 1-3   IDENTIFY RIBBON COMMANDS

When you start Word, the Ribbon appears with the Home tab selected. The Ribbon consists of seven tabs by default. Each tab contains a group of related commands, and the number of commands for each tab varies. A command can be one of several formats. The most popular formats include buttons and drop-down lists. You can access Ribbon commands by using the mouse or Access Keys. Access Keys display badges or Key Tips. *Key Tips* are lettered or numbered squares that access or execute commands.

Figure 1-4
Ribbon

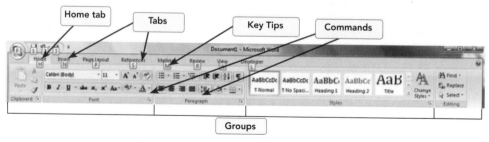

1. Move the mouse pointer to the **Insert** tab on the Ribbon and click **Insert**. Notice the change in the number and types of groups displayed. When you point to a Ribbon tab, the name of the tab is highlighted but not active. Click the Ribbon tab to display the commands.

2. Click the **Page Layout** tab. There are five groups of commands on the Page Layout tab.

Figure 1-5
Displaying the Page Layout tab

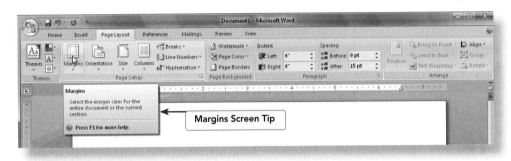

Margins Screen Tip

NOTE

Any Ribbon command with a light gray icon is currently not available. However, you can still identify the button by pointing to it with the mouse.

TIP

The keyboard shortcut to minimize the Ribbon is Ctrl+F1. To restore the Ribbon, press Ctrl+F1.

NOTE

The Quick Access Toolbar Key Tips are executed immediately.

3. Click the **Page Layout** tab if necessary, and point to the **Margins** command. Read the ScreenTip.

4. Click the **Home** tab. Notice the groups and buttons available for formatting and editing.

5. Double-click the **Home** tab. The Ribbon is minimized.

6. Click the **Home** tab to restore the Ribbon.

7. Press the Alt key. Small lettered or numbered squares, called badges, appear on the Microsoft Office Button, Quick Access Toolbar, and Ribbon. The letters and numbers represent Key Tips and are used to execute a command.

8. Press the letter P on the keyboard to select the **Page Layout** tab.

9. Press the letter M on the keyboard to display the **Margins** gallery. Press Esc to close the gallery.

TABLE 1-2 Ribbon Access Keys

Keystroke	Purpose
[Alt]	Select the active tab of the Ribbon and display badges for Key Tips. Press [Alt] a second time to cancel the access keys.
[Alt], [←] or [→]	Select the active tab of the Ribbon and move to the next or previous tab.
[Alt], [↓] or [↑]	Select the active tab of the Ribbon and move to the next or previous item on the Ribbon.
[Alt], [Tab]	Select the active tab of the Ribbon and move to the first command of the first group. Each time you press [Tab] you move to the next command of the group. When you reach the last command of the group, press [Tab] to move to the next group of commands.
[Alt], [Shift]+[Tab]	Rotate through Ribbon commands in the reverse direction.
[Alt], [Alt]	Display Key Tips if they disappear.

Exercise 1-4   IDENTIFY COMMANDS

Use the Ribbon to locate and execute commands to format and edit your document. Commands also control the appearance of the Word screen.

1. Activate the **Home** tab.

2. Locate the Paragraph group and click the Show/Hide ¶ button ¶. This button is used to show or hide formatting marks on the screen. You can see special formatting for spaces, paragraph marks, and tab characters. The command toggles between show and hide.

> **NOTE**
>
> Drag the slider to the right to zoom in, and drag the slider to the left to zoom out. You can also use [Ctrl]+the wheel on your mouse to zoom in and zoom out. The View tab on the Ribbon contains Zoom commands.

3. Locate the vertical scroll bar and click the View Ruler button. Notice the rulers disappear from the Word screen. Click the View Ruler button again to display the rulers.

4. Locate the Zoom button on the status bar.

5. Click the Zoom button and click **200%**. Click **OK**. The text area is magnified, and you see a portion of the page.

6. Point to and drag the Zoom slider to 100%. The document returns to normal display.

Keying Text

When keying text, you will notice various shapes and symbols in the text area. For example:

- The *insertion point* is the vertical blinking line that marks the position of the next character to be entered.

- The mouse pointer takes the shape of an *I-beam* when it is in the text area. It changes into an arrow when you point to a command on the Quick Access Toolbar or the Ribbon.

- The *paragraph mark* ¶ indicates the end of a paragraph. The paragraph mark displays when Show/Hide ¶ is selected.

Exercise 1-5 KEY TEXT AND MOVE THE INSERTION POINT

1. Before you begin, make sure the Show/Hide ¶ button on the Home tab Paragraph group is selected. When this feature is "turned on," you can see paragraph marks and spacing between words and sentences more easily.

2. Key the words **Campbell's Confections** (don't worry about keying mistakes now—you can correct them later). Notice how the insertion point and paragraph mark move as you key text. Notice also how a space between words is indicated by a dot.

Figure 1-6
The insertion point marks the place where you begin keying.

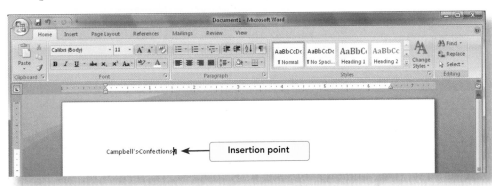

NOTE

The documents you create in this course relate to the case study about Campbell's Confections, a fictional candy store and chocolate factory (see the Case Study in the frontmatter).

3. Move the insertion point to the left of the word "Campbell's" by positioning the I-beam and clicking the left mouse button.

4. Move the insertion point back to the right of "Confections" to continue keying.

Exercise 1-6 WRAP TEXT AND CORRECT SPELLING

As you key more text, you will notice Word performs several tasks automatically. For example, Word does the following by default:

- Wraps text from the end of one line to the beginning of the next line.

- Alerts you to spelling and grammatical errors.

- Corrects common misspellings, such as "teh" for "the" and "adn" for "and."

- Suggests the completed word when you key the current date, day, or month.

> **TIP**
>
> The Proofing Errors icon at the left side of the Status bar displays an "x" instead of a checkmark when it detects an error. When the error is corrected, the "x" is replaced with a checkmark.

1. Continue the sentence you started in Exercise 1-5, this time keying a misspelled word. Press Spacebar, and then key **is western Pennsylvania's leeding candy maker** (don't key a period). Word recognizes that "leeding" is misspelled and applies a red, wavy underline to the word.

2. To correct the misspelling, use the mouse to position the I-beam anywhere in the underlined word and click the *right* mouse button. A shortcut menu appears with suggested spellings. Click "leading" with the *left* mouse button, and Word makes the correction. Notice the change in the Proofing Errors icon on the status bar.

Figure 1-7
Choose the correct spelling from the shortcut menu.

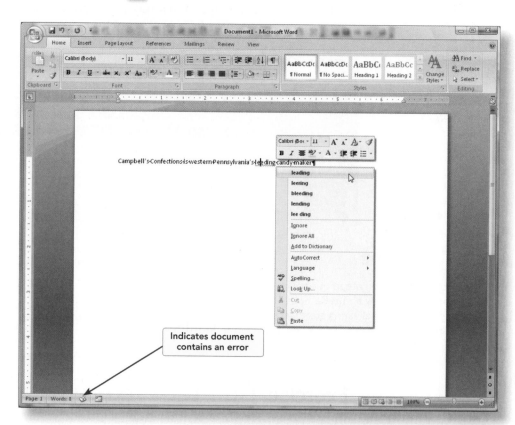

3. Move the insertion point to the right of "maker," and press Spacebar. Continue the sentence with another misspelled word by keying **adn**, and press Spacebar. Notice that "adn" is automatically corrected to "and" when you press Spacebar.

4. Complete the sentence by keying **is located in Grove City on Main Street.**

5. Verify that the insertion point is to the immediate right of the period following Street, and then press the Spacebar once. Key the following text:

> **It is a family-owned business with several stores located in western Pennsylvania, eastern Ohio, and northern West Virginia.**

Notice how the text automatically wraps from the end of the line to the beginning of the next line.

6. Press Enter once to start a new paragraph.

7. Key the second paragraph shown in Figure 1-8. When you key the first four letters of "Monday" in the first sentence, Word suggests the completed word in a small box. Press Enter to insert the suggested word, and then press Spacebar before you key the next word. Follow the same procedure for "Saturday."

NOTE

Throughout this text, one space is used after a period to separate sentences. This is the standard format for word processing and desktop publishing.

NOTE

When Word suggests a completed word as you key text, you can ignore the suggested word and continue keying or insert it by pressing Enter.

Figure 1-8

```
For more information about Campbell's Confections, visit one
of our stores Monday through Saturday, or visit our Web site
anytime. Our sales associates will be happy to help you.
```

Basic Text Editing

The keyboard offers many options for basic text editing. For example, you can press Backspace to delete a single character or Ctrl+Delete to delete an entire word.

TABLE 1-3 Basic Text Editing

Key	Result
Backspace	Deletes the character to the left of the insertion point.
Ctrl + Backspace	Deletes the word to the left of the insertion point.
Delete	Deletes the character to the right of the insertion point.
Ctrl + Delete	Deletes the word to the right of the insertion point.

Exercise 1-7   DELETE TEXT

1. Move the insertion point to the right of the word "It" in the second sentence of the first paragraph. (Use the mouse to position the I-beam, and click the left mouse button.)

2. Press [Backspace] twice to delete both characters and key Campbell's Confections.

3. Move the insertion point to the left of "one" in the second paragraph.

4. Press [Delete] three times and key any.

5. Move the insertion point to the left of the word "information" in the second paragraph.

6. Hold down [Ctrl] and press [Backspace]. The word "more" is deleted.

7. Move the insertion point to the right of "Grove City" in the first sentence of the first paragraph.

8. Hold down [Ctrl] and press [Delete] to delete the word "on." Press [Ctrl]+[Delete] two more times to delete the words "Main Street."

NOTE

When keyboard combinations (such as [Ctrl]+[Backspace]) are shown in this text, hold down the first key as you press the second key. Release the second key, and then release the first key. An example of the entire sequence is this: Hold down [Ctrl], press [Backspace], release [Backspace], and release [Ctrl]. With practice, this sequence becomes easy.

Exercise 1-8   INSERT TEXT

When editing a document, you can insert text or key over existing text. When you insert text, Word is in regular *Insert mode*, and you simply click to position the insertion point and key the text to be inserted. To key over existing text, you switch to *Overtype mode*. The Overtype feature is turned off by default.

1. In the first sentence of the first paragraph, move the insertion point to the left of the "G" in "Grove City." Key downtown, and press [Spacebar] once to leave a space between the two words.

2. Move the insertion point to the beginning of the document, to the left of "Campbell's."

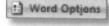

3. Click the **Microsoft Office Button**, and click the Word Options button 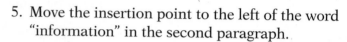 .

4. Click **Advanced**. Locate **Editing options**, and click to select **Use overtype mode**. Click **OK**.

5. Press [Caps Lock]. When you key text in Caps Lock mode, the keyed text appears in all uppercase letters.

TIP

Always remember to turn off Overtype mode as soon as you are done editing to avoid accidentally keying over text.

6. Key **campbell's confections** over the old text. Repeat the process for "Campbell's Confections" in the second sentence.

7. Press Caps Lock to turn off Caps Lock mode. Click the **Microsoft Office Button**, and click the Word Options button 🔲 Word Options . Click **Advanced**, locate **Editing options**, and click to deselect **Use overtype mode**. Click **OK**.

Figure 1-9
Edited document

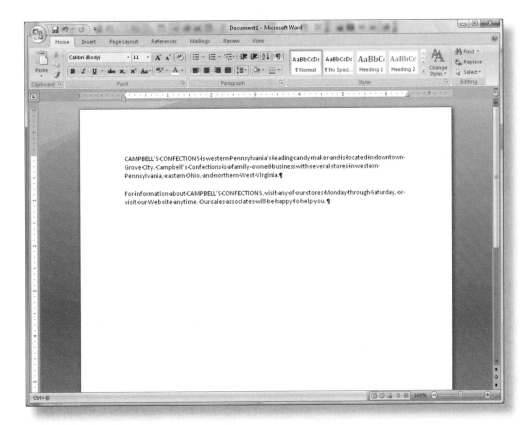

Exercise 1-9   COMBINE AND SPLIT PARAGRAPHS

1. At the end of the first paragraph, position the insertion point to the left of the paragraph mark (after the period following "West Virginia").

2. Press Delete. The two paragraphs are now combined, or merged, into one.

3. Press Spacebar once to insert a space between the sentences.

4. With the insertion point to the left of "For" in the combined paragraph, press Enter to split the paragraph.

Naming and Saving a Document

Your document, called "Document1," is stored in your computer's temporary memory. Until you name and save the document, the data can be lost if you have a power failure or a computer hardware problem. It is always good practice to save your work frequently.

The first step in saving a document for future use is to assign a *file name*. Study the following rules about naming documents:

- File names can be up to 255 characters long, including the drive letter and the folder name. The following characters cannot be used in a file name: **/ \ > < * ? ": |**

- File names can include uppercase letters, lowercase letters, or a combination of both. They can also include spaces. For example, a file can be named "Business Plan."

- Throughout this course, document file names will consist of *[your initials]* (which might be your initials or the identifier your instructor asks you to use, such as **rst**), followed by the number of the exercise, such as **4-1**. The file name would, therefore, be **rst4-1**.

You can use either the Save command or the Save As command to save a document. Here are some guidelines about saving documents:

- Use Save As when you name and save a document the first time.

- Use Save As when you save an existing document under a new name. Save As creates an entirely new file and leaves the original document unchanged.

- Use Save to update an existing document.

NOTE

Your instructor will advise you on the proper drive and folder to use for this course.

- Before you save a new document, decide where you want to save it. Word saves documents in the current drive and folder unless you specify otherwise. For example, to save a document to a floppy disk or a jump drive, you need to change the drive to A: or E:, whichever is appropriate for your computer.

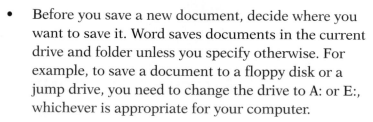

Exercise 1-10   NAME AND SAVE A DOCUMENT

1. Click the **Microsoft Office Button** to open the **File** menu and click **Save As**. The Save As dialog box appears.

2. In the File name text box, a suggested filename is highlighted. Replace this file name by keying *[your initials]*1-10.

NOTE

The default document type is Word Document (.docx). You can specify other file types such as RTF (Rich Text Format, which is a format used to exchange text documents between applications and operating systems) and TXT (Plain Text, which contains no formatting). To change the file type, simply click the down arrow beside the Save as type text box.

3. Drag the scroll box in the navigation pane, and choose the appropriate drive for your data disk—Removable Disk (F:), for example. Make sure you have a formatted disk in the drive.

4. Click [Save]. Your document is named and saved for future use.

Figure 1-10
Save As dialog box

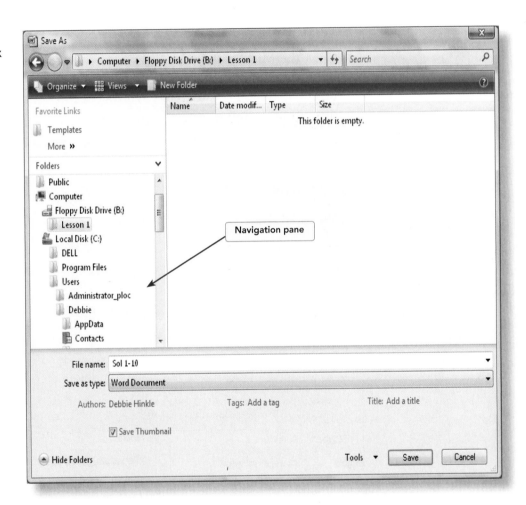

Printing a Document

After you create a document, printing it is easy. You can use any of the following methods:

- Choose Print from the File menu.

- Press Ctrl + P.

The Print option and the keyboard shortcut open the Print dialog box, where you can select printing options. Clicking Quick Print sends the document directly to the printer, using Word's default settings.

Exercise 1-11   PRINT A DOCUMENT

1. Click the Microsoft Office Button 🗐 to open the File menu. Click **Print**, then click **Print** from the submenu to open the Print dialog box. The dialog box displays Word's default settings and shows your designated printer.

Figure 1-11
Print dialog box

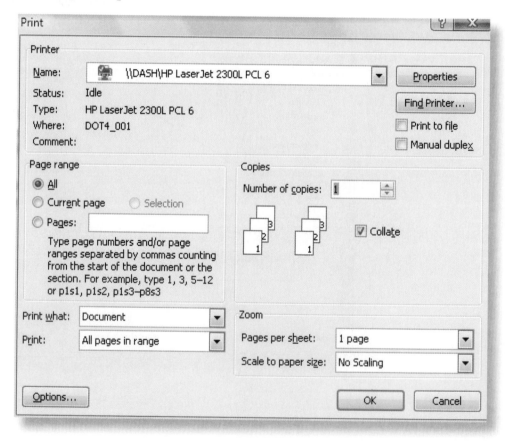

2. Click **OK** or press Enter to accept the settings.

Closing a Document and Exiting Word

When you finish working on a document and save it, you can close it and open another document or you can exit Word.

The easiest ways to close a document and exit Word include using the following:

- The Close button in the upper right corner of the window.

- The Close command from the File menu.

- Keyboard shortcuts: Ctrl+W closes a document and Alt+F4 exits Word.

> **NOTE**
>
> When no document is open, the document window is blue. If you want to create a new document, choose New from the File menu, and click Blank Document. Click the Create button Create. The keyboard shortcut to create a new document is Ctrl+N.

Exercise 1-12   CLOSE A DOCUMENT AND EXIT WORD

1. Click the **Microsoft Office Button**, and choose **Close** from the File menu to close the document.

2. Click the Close button in the upper right corner of the screen to exit Word and display the Windows desktop.

Using Online Help

Online Help is available to you as you work in Word. Click the Help button or press F1 to open the Word Help window. You can click a Word Help link or key a word or phrase in the Search box.

FIND OUT MORE ABOUT USING HELP:

1. Start Word.

2. Locate the Help button in the upper right corner of the screen. Click the button to open the Word Help window.

Figure 1-12
Using the Word Help
window

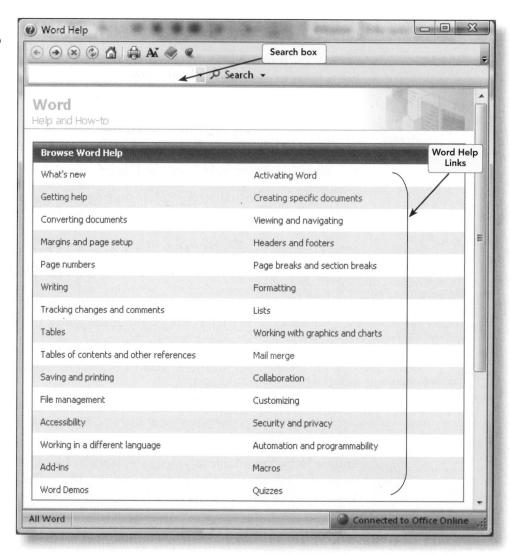

3. Locate and click the link **<u>Getting help</u>**.

4. Review the list of topics.

5. Click a topic and review the information.

 6. Click the Back button ⊙ to return to the list of categories.

7. Close Help by clicking the Word Help window's Close
button ⊠ .

Lesson 1 Summary

- To start Microsoft Word, click the Start button on the Windows taskbar, point to All Programs, click Microsoft Office, and click Microsoft Office Word 2007.

- The Microsoft Office Button is located in the upper left corner of the Word screen. Click the button to open the File menu.

- The title bar is at the top of the Word screen and displays the current document name.

- The Quick Access Toolbar displays icons for Save, Undo, and Repeat.

- The Ribbon contains tabs which include groups of related commands. Commands can be buttons, menus, or drop-down list boxes.

- Click a tab name to display related groups of commands. The number of groups and commands varies for each tab.

- Identify a command by name by pointing to it with the mouse. Word displays a ScreenTip with the button name.

- The horizontal ruler appears below the Ribbon.

- Scroll bars appear as blue shaded bars to the right and bottom of the text area. They are used to view different portions of a document.

- The status bar is a blue shaded bar below the horizontal scroll bar. It displays the page number and page count of the document, the document view buttons, and the zoom control. It also displays the current mode of operation. Right-click the status bar to customize it.

- The blinking vertical line is called the insertion point. It marks the position of the next character to be keyed.

- The mouse pointer displays on the screen as an I-beam ⌶ when it is in the text area and as an arrow ⬉ when you point to a command outside the text area.

- When the Show/Hide ¶ button ¶ is turned on, a paragraph mark symbol appears at the end of every paragraph. A dot between words represents a space.

- Word automatically wraps text to the next line as you key text. Press Enter to start a new paragraph or to insert a blank line.

- Word flags spelling errors as you key text by inserting a red, wavy line under the misspelled word. To correct the spelling, point to the underlined word, click the right mouse button, and choose the correct spelling.

- Word automatically corrects commonly misspelled words for you as you key text. Word can automatically complete a word for you, such as the name of a month or day. Word suggests the completed word, and you press Enter to insert it.

- Delete a single character by using Backspace or Delete. Ctrl+Backspace deletes the word to the left of the insertion point. Ctrl+Delete deletes the word to the right of the insertion point.

- To insert text, click to position the insertion point and key the text.
- To enter text over existing text, turn on Overtype mode by clicking the Microsoft Office Button. Click **Word Options**, and click **Advanced**. Click to select **Use overtype mode**. Click **OK**.
- Insert one space between words and between sentences.
- Document names, or file names, can contain 255 characters, including the drive letter and folder name, and can contain spaces. The following characters cannot be used in a file name: **/ \ > <* ? " : |**
- Save a new document by using the Save As command and giving the document a file name. Use the Save command to update an existing document.
- To start a new blank document, click the Microsoft Office Button. Click **New**, click **Blank document**, and click **Create**.
- To use Word Help, click the Microsoft Office Word Help button 🕮 or press F1.

LESSON 1		Command Summary	
Feature	**Button**	**Command**	**Keyboard**
Save As		**File** menu, **Save As**	F12
Print		**File** menu, **Print**	Ctrl + P
Close a document		**File** menu, **Close**	Ctrl + W or Ctrl + F14
Exit Word	X	**File** menu, **Exit Word**	Alt + F4

NOTE

Word provides many ways to accomplish a particular task. As you become more familiar with Word, you will find the methods you prefer.

Concepts Review

True/False Questions

Each of the following statements is either true or false. Indicate your choice by circling T or F.

T (F) 1. You can use the Ribbon to start or exit Word.

T (F) 2. Overtype mode appears on the Status bar by default.

(T) F 3. You can view more than one Ribbon tab at a time.

(T) F 4. The mouse pointer takes the shape of an arrow when it appears in the Ribbon.

(T) F 5. A red, wavy line appears under words that are misspelled in a document.

T (F) 6. Pressing [Delete] deletes characters to the left of the insertion point.

(T) F 7. [Ctrl]+[Delete] deletes the word to the right of the insertion point.

T (F) 8. You can save a document by choosing Save from the File menu.

Short Answer Questions

Write the correct answer in the space provided.

1. Which menu and menu option open the Print dialog box?

   The Microsoft Office button

2. Which tab contains the Show/Hide ¶ button ¶ ?

   Home Tab.

3. If you begin keying a word such as "January" or "Thursday," how can you have Word complete the word for you automatically?

   by Pressing Enter.

4. Which area of the Word screen shows the number of pages in the document and displays indicators that show the current mode of operation?

   Status bar.

5. Which toolbar contains the Save button?

   Quick Access Toolbar.

6. What shape is the mouse pointer when it appears in the text area of the screen?

_____I - beam_____

7. Which command is used to save a document under a different file name?

_____Save As_____

8. What is the keyboard shortcut for Help?

_____F1_____

Critical Thinking

Answer these questions on a separate page. There are no right or wrong answers. Support your answers with examples from your own experience, if possible.

1. You can use the Show/Hide ¶ button 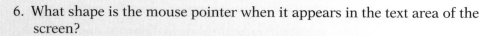 to hide paragraph marks and space characters. When might it be useful to show these characters? When would you want to hide them?

2. Word allows great flexibility when naming files. Many businesses and individuals establish their own rules for naming files. What kinds of rules would you recommend for naming files in a business? For personal use?

Skills Review

Exercise 1-13

Identify parts of the Word screen.

1. Start Word, if necessary, by following these steps:
   a. Click the Start button ⊚ on the Windows taskbar.
   b. Point to **All Programs**, point to **Microsoft Office**, point to **Microsoft Office Word 2007**, and click.

2. Move the pointer to the Save button 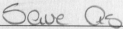 on the Quick Access Toolbar to identify it.

3. Click the **Page Layout** tab. Click the **Home** tab. Point to the Bullets button to identify it.

4. Point to, and then click the Microsoft Office Button ⊚. The File menu opens.

5. With the File menu still open, move the pointer up and down the menu list without clicking the mouse button. Notice the submenus for the Print and Save As commands.

6. Close the menu by clicking the Microsoft Office Button or clicking in the blank text area.

7. Close the document by clicking the Close button in the upper right corner of the window located on the title bar.

Exercise 1-14

Key text, correct the spelling of a word, and save a document.

1. Start Word if necessary.

2. Open a new document window by clicking the Microsoft Office Button . Click **New**, and click **Blank document**. Click **Create**.

3. Click the **Home** tab if necessary.

4. Locate the **Paragraph** group, and make sure the Show/Hide ¶ button is selected.

5. Key the text shown in Figure 1-13, including the intentional misspelling of "sponsored."

Figure 1-13

Become a retail candy store owner and develop skills in
business management! Come to the Small Business Fair and
learn how to operate a business. The fair is sponsord by the
Grove City Chamber of Commerce.

6. Correct the spelling of "sponsored" by following these steps:

    a. Move the I-beam anywhere within the word and click the right mouse button.

    b. Choose the correct spelling from the shortcut menu by clicking the word with left mouse button.

7. Save the document as *[your initials]***1-14** by following these steps:

    a. Open the **File** menu, and click **Save As** to open the Save As dialog box.

    b. Key the file name *[your initials]***1-14** in the **File name** text box.

    c. Choose the appropriate drive for your data disk—for example, Removable Drive (F:) or another drive specified by your instructor.

    d. Click **Save**.

8. Close the document by pressing Ctrl+W.

Exercise 1-15

Key, edit, and save a document.

1. Press Ctrl+N to create a new document.

2. Key the text shown in Figure 1-14. (Use default line spacing in all your documents, unless you are told otherwise.)

Figure 1-14

```
Campbell's Confections has just celebrated another
anniversary in the candy business. The company has proudly
created over 75,000 assorted chocolates including creams,
nuts, and bark. Campbell's Confections has been at its
current location for all of its 57 years.
```

3. Correct any spelling mistakes Word locates.

4. Delete the text "all of its" in the last sentence by following these steps:

   a. Move the insertion point to the right of the word "for" by positioning the I-beam and clicking the left mouse button.

   b. Hold down Ctrl and press Delete three times to delete the words "all of its."

5. Insert text after the word "creams" in the second sentence by following these steps:

   a. Move the insertion point to the immediate left of the the word "nuts."

   b. Key melt-a-ways followed by a comma and a space.

6. Split the paragraph by following these steps:

   a. Move the insertion point to the immediate left of the word "Campbell's" in the last sentence.

   b. Press Enter.

7. Save the document as *[your initials]*1-15 on your student data disk.

8. Close the document.

Exercise 1-16

Key, edit, save, and print a document.

1. Start a new blank document.

2. Key the text shown in Figure 1-15. Correct spelling mistakes as you key.

Figure 1-15

```
When you visit our inaugural store, take advantage of our
factory tour where you can see each of the steps in candy
making. All of our chocolates are hand decorated, and you
will receive a free sample. You will follow the chocolate
manufacturing line beginning with melting the chocolate,
preparing the rich cream centers, and dipping.
```

3. Move the insertion point to the left of the word "inaugural" in the first line of the paragraph.

4. Press ⟨Alt⟩+⟨F⟩ to open the File menu. Click Word Options, and click Advanced in the left pane. Under Editing options, click Use overtype mode to turn on Overtype mode. Click OK.

5. Key flagship over the word "inaugural." Be sure to delete the extra character.

6. Turn off Overtype mode by clicking the Microsoft Office Button, and clicking Word Options. Click Advanced in the left pane, and click Use overtype mode to turn off Overtype mode. Click OK.

7. Use ⟨Delete⟩ to delete the word "manufacturing" and key production to replace it.

8. Check the spacing before and after the replacement text.

9. Save the document as *[your initials]*1-16 on your data disk.

10. Press ⟨Ctrl⟩+⟨P⟩ to open the Print dialog box. Click OK to print the document.

11. Close the document.

Lesson Applications

Exercise 1-17

Key, edit, and print a document.

1. Start a new document. Turn on Caps Lock mode and key TO SALES ASSOCIATES:

2. Turn off Caps Lock and press Enter to start a new paragraph.

3. Key the text shown in Figure 1-16, including the corrections. Refer to Appendix A, "Proofreaders' Marks," if necessary. *Proofreaders' marks* are handwritten corrections to text, often using specialized symbols.

Figure 1-16

> September   May
> Chocolate can be shipped between June 1 and August 15 only. Chocolates
> shipped to warm climates will be surrounded with ice packs. It is
> recommended that you select a personal or businessaddress where someone
> will be available to handle the package as soon as it arrives. Remember:
>   is
> Fine chocolates are perishable.

4. Key **anywhere** to the left of the word "between" in the first sentence." Delete the word "only."

5. Key the following sentence after the last sentence in the first paragraph. **During the hottest months of the year, shipments may be postponed.**

6. In the second paragraph, delete "Fine" after "Remember" and key **Quality** before "chocolate."

7. Save the document as *[your initials]*1-17 on your data disk.

8. Print the document, and then close it.

TIP

When Word suggests the completed word for "September," you can press Enter to insert the word. Remember to press Spacebar after the completed word.

Exercise 1-18

Key, edit, and print a document.

1. Start a new document and key the two paragraphs shown in Figure 1-17.

Figure 1-17

```
Campbell's Confections has gained national recognition for
its delectable chocolates. It is highly recognized for its
unique, hand-molded chocolates in the mid-Atlantic area.

The staff of all stores are considered experts in the
history and manufacture of fine chocolate.
```

2. In the first paragraph, delete "area," and key region after "mid-Atlantic."

3. Switch to Overtype mode, and key sales associates over the text "staff of all stores." Delete the extra characters.

4. Turn off Overtype mode and move the insertion point to the beginning of the second sentence in the first paragraph.

5. Use Ctrl + Delete to delete "It" and key Each of the 24 stores affiliated with Campbell's Confections in the mid-Atlantic region in its place.

6. Delete "in the mid-Atlantic region" at the end of the first paragraph. Delete "its" before the word "unique."

7. Save the document as *[your initials]*1-18 on your data disk.

8. Print and then close the document.

Exercise 1-19

Key, edit, and print a document.

1. Start a new document. Key the text shown in Figure 1-18. Key each sentence on a new line.

Figure 1-18

```
Reminder

Will the first one to arrive at the store:

Turn on the lights.

Adjust the thermostat.

Turn on the music.

Turn on the computer.

Thank you!
```

2. In the sixth line, change "computer" to computer equipment.

3. In the third line, change "the lights" to all lighting fixtures.

4. Click at the beginning of the third line, and insert another line by keying Turn off the alarm and unlock the front door.

5. Press [Caps Lock] and use Overtype mode to change "Reminder" and "Thank you!" to uppercase letters.

6. Insert an extra line after every line of text by pressing [Enter] once.

7. Save the document as *[your initials]*1-19 on your data disk.

8. Print and then close the document.

Exercise 1-20 ◆ Challenge Yourself

Key, edit, and print a document.

1. Start a new document and key the two paragraphs shown in Figure 1-19, including the corrections. Refer to Appendix A, "Proofreaders' Marks," if necessary.

Figure 1-19

Group tours are an imprtant part of campbell's. Tours include watching a video on the history of Campbell's Confections as well as the history of chocolate. After the video, a tour thru the factory is conducted by the plant manager.
Group tours arranged are for families visiting the area, school, or any group with an interest in ~~learning about~~ chocolate.

2. Correct the spelling of "thru" in the third sentence to through.

3. In the last sentence, key type of after "or any." Delete "families visiting the area" and key tourists in its place.

4. Add the following sentence to the end of the second paragraph. Reservations are required two weeks in advance with a minimum of ten members in the tour.

5. Save the document as *[your initials]*1-20 on your data disk.

6. Print, and then close the document

7. Exit Word.

On Your Own

In these exercises you work on your own, as you would in a real-life business environment. Use the skills you've learned to accomplish the task—and be creative.

Exercise 1-21

Write a short paragraph about yourself that includes your first and last name. Include information about your family, school, or employment. Switch to Overtype mode, turn on Caps Lock, and then key over your name in uppercase letters. Save the document as *[your initials]*1-21 and print it.

Exercise 1-22

Browse the various tabs on the Ribbon until you find a command that looks intriguing; then find out more about it by using the Help feature. In a new blank document, write a brief paragraph about your findings. Save the document as *[your initials]*1-22 and print it.

Exercise 1-23

Log onto the Internet and search for Web sites that relate to a particular interest of yours. Record a few Web addresses, and then key the addresses into a blank document, under an appropriate heading. Save the document as *[your initials]*1-23 and print it.

Selecting and Editing

OBJECTIVES

MCAS OBJECTIVES

In this lesson:
WW 07 1.3.3
WW 07 6.1.1
WW 07 6.1.2

After completing this lesson, you will be able to:

1. Open an existing document.

2. Enter formatting characters.

3. Move within a document.

4. Undo and Redo actions.

5. Repeat actions.

6. Select text.

7. Save a revised document.

8. Work with document properties.

Estimated Time: 1¼ hours

To edit documents efficiently, you need to learn to select text and move quickly within a document. In this lesson you learn those skills, as well as how to open and save an existing document.

Opening an Existing Document

Instead of creating a new document, you start this lesson by opening an existing document. There are several ways to open a document:

- Choose **Open** from the File menu.

- Press Ctrl + O.

- Use the document links in the **Recent Documents** file listing.

TIP

The keyboard shortcut to open the File menu is [Alt]+[F].

NOTE

Click Folders to open and close the Folders list.

Exercise 2-1   OPEN AN EXISTING FILE

1. Click the Microsoft Office Button to open the File menu. The file names listed under Recent Documents are the files opened from this computer. If the file you want is listed, you can click its name to open it from this list. The Recent Documents section displays up to 17 documents.

2. Click Open to display the Open dialog box. You are going to open a student file named **Campbell-1**.

3. Locate the appropriate drive and folder according to your instructor's directions.

Figure 2-1
Files listed in the
Open dialog box

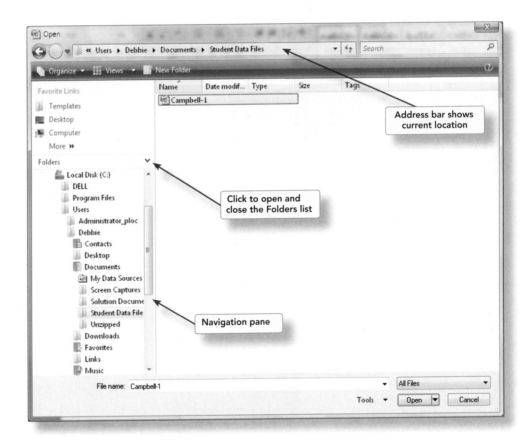

4. After you locate the student files, click the arrow next to the Views button in the Open dialog box to display a menu of view options.

5. Choose List to list all files by file name.

Figure 2-2
Views menu in the
Open dialog box

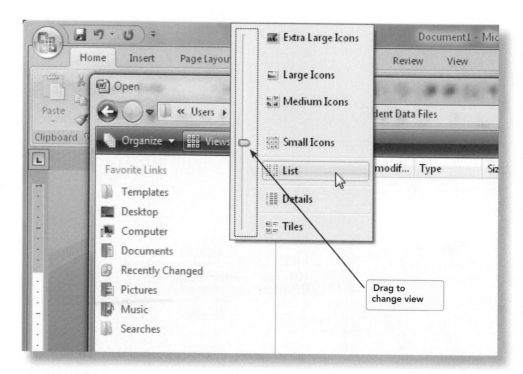

6. From the list of file names, locate **Campbell-1** and click it once to select it.

7. Click Open.

You can also double-click a file name to open a file.

NOTE

Documents created in earlier versions of Word display Compatibility Mode in the Title bar when opened. Compatibility Mode enables you to open, edit, and save documents that were created using earlier versions of Word. New features in Office Word 2007 are not available in Compatibility Mode. To check for features not supported by earlier versions of the Word program, click the Microsoft Office Button, and click the arrow beside Prepare. Click Run Compatibility Checker. To convert a document created in an earlier version of Word to Office Word 2007, click the Microsoft Office Button, and click Convert. Click OK.

TABLE 2-1 Open Dialog Box Buttons

Button	Name	Purpose
▶ Debbie ▶ Documents ▶ ▼ ↻	Address bar	Navigates to a different folder.
←	Back button	Works with the Address bar, and returns to most recent previous location.
→	Forward button	Works with the Address bar, and returns to location already opened.
Search 🔍	Search box	Looks for a file or subfolder.
Organize ▼	Organize	Opens a menu of file functions, such as cutting a file, copying a file, pasting a file, deleting a file, or renaming a file. Includes the Layout option to display the Navigation Pane, Details Pane, and the Preview Pane.
Views ▼	Views	Opens a menu of view options for displaying drives, folders, files, and their icons.
New Folder	New Folder	Creates a new folder to organize your files.

Exercise 2-2   CREATE A NEW FOLDER

Document files are typically stored in folders that are part of a hierarchal structure similar to a family tree. At the top of the tree is a disk drive letter (such as C: or A:) that represents your computer, network, floppy drive, jump drive, or CD-ROM drive. Under the disk drive letter, you can create folders to organize your files. These folders can also contain additional folders.

Here is a scenario: You store your files on the C: drive of your office computer. You create a folder on this drive named "Word Documents." Within this folder you create folders named "Letters," "Memos," and "Reports," each containing different types of documents.

For this course, you will create a new folder for each lesson and store your completed exercise documents in these folders.

1. Click the **Microsoft Office Button** and choose **Save As**. You are going to save **Campbell-1** under a new file name, in a new folder that will contain all the files you save in this lesson.

2. Choose the appropriate drive and folder location from the **Navigation pane**. (For example, to save your files to a jump drive, insert a jump

drive in the USB port, and make sure the **Address bar** indicates the appropriate drive).

3. Click the Create New Folder button New Folder. A New Folder icon appears in the File list section.

4. Key the folder name *[your initials]***Lesson2** and press Enter. The folder name appears in the Address bar and in the Navigation pane. Word is ready to save the file in the new folder.

5. Locate the **File name** box, and make sure the file's original name (**Campbell-1**) is selected. If not, double-click it.

6. Key the file name *[your initials]***2-2** and click **Save**.

> **NOTE**
>
> To rename a folder, locate the folder to rename and right-click the folder. Click Rename on the shortcut menu, key the new name, and press Enter.

Formatting Characters

The Show/Hide ¶ button ¶ on the Home tab shows or hides paragraph marks and other *formatting marks*. These characters appear on the screen, but not in the printed document. Formatting marks are included as part of words, sentences, and paragraphs in a document. Here are some examples:

* A word includes the space character that follows it.

* A sentence includes the end-of-sentence punctuation and at least one space.

* A paragraph is any amount of text followed by a paragraph mark.

The document you opened contains two additional formatting characters: *tab characters*, which you use to indent text, and *line-break characters*, which you use to start a new line within the same paragraph. Line-break characters are useful when you want to create a paragraph of short lines, such as an address, and keep the lines together as a single paragraph.

Another formatting character is a *nonbreaking space*, which you use to prevent two words from being divided between two lines. For example, you can insert a nonbreaking space between "Mr." and "Smith" to keep the name "Mr. Smith" undivided on one line.

TABLE 2-2 Formatting Characters

Character	To Insert, Press
Tab (→)	`Tab`
Space (·)	`Spacebar`
Nonbreaking space (°)	`Ctrl` + `Shift` + `Spacebar`
Paragraph mark (¶)	`Enter`
Line-break character (↵)	`Shift` + `Enter`

Exercise 2-3   ENTER FORMATTING CHARACTERS

1. Click the Show/Hide ¶ button ¶ if the formatting characters in the document are hidden.

2. Move the insertion point to the end of the document (after "family recipes.").

3. Press `Enter` to begin a new paragraph, and key **Campbell's Confections has been a member in good standing of the NCA for over 50** (do not press `Spacebar`).

4. Insert a nonbreaking space after "50" by pressing `Ctrl` + `Shift` + `Spacebar`. Then key **years.** (including the period). Word now treats "50 years" as a single unit.

Figure 2-3
Formatting characters

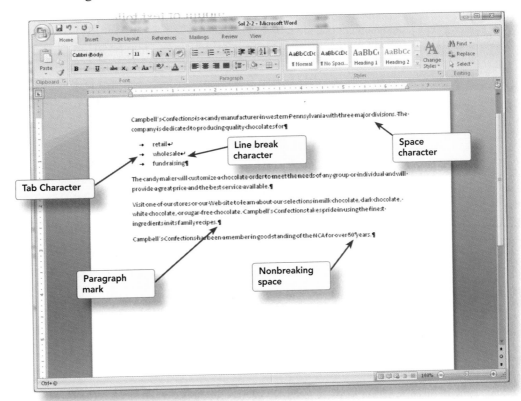

NOTE

A smart tag may appear in the address. Word applies *smart tags* (nonprinting, purple dotted underlines) to address text.

5. Press ⌈Enter⌋ and key the following text as one paragraph at the end of the document, pressing ⌈Shift⌋+⌈Enter⌋ at the end of the first and second lines instead of ⌈Enter⌋.

Campbell's Confections
25 Main Street
Grove City, PA 16127

6. Click the Show/Hide ¶ button ¶ to hide the formatting characters, and click it again to redisplay them.

Moving within a Document

You already know how to move around a short document by positioning the I-beam pointer with the mouse and clicking. This is the easiest way to move around a document that displays in the document window. If a document is too long or wide to view in the window, you need to use different methods to navigate within a document.

Word offers two additional methods for moving within a document:

NOTE

Scrolling through a document does not move the insertion point. It moves only the portion of the document you are viewing in the document window. When you use the keyboard to move within a document, the insertion point always moves to the new location.

- *Using the keyboard:* You can press certain keys on the keyboard to move the insertion point. The arrow keys, for example, move the insertion point up or down one line or to the left or right one character. Key combinations quickly move the insertion point to specified locations in the document.

- *Using the scroll bars:* Use the vertical scroll bar at the right edge of the document window to move through a document. The position of the scroll box indicates your approximate location in the document, which is particularly helpful in long documents. To view and move through a document that is wider than the document window, use the horizontal scroll bar at the bottom of the document window.

Exercise 2-4   **USE THE KEYBOARD TO MOVE THE INSERTION POINT**

1. Press ⌈Ctrl⌋+⌈Home⌋ to move to the beginning of the document. Press ⌈End⌋ to move to the end of the first line.

2. Press Ctrl+↓ several times to move the insertion point down one paragraph at a time. Notice how the text with the line-break characters is treated as a single paragraph.

3. When you reach the end of the document, press PageUp until you return to the beginning of the document.

TIP

Word remembers the last three locations in the document where you edited or keyed text. You can press Shift+F5 to return the insertion point to these locations. For example, when you open a document you worked on earlier, press Shift+F5 to return to the place where you were last working before you saved and closed the document.

TABLE 2-3 Keys to Move the Insertion Point

To Move	Press
One word to the left	Ctrl+←
One word to the right	Ctrl+→
Beginning of the line	Home
End of the line	End
One paragraph up	Ctrl+↑
One paragraph down	Ctrl+↓
Previous page	Ctrl+PageUp
Next page	Ctrl+PageDown
Up one window	PageUp
Down one window	PageDown
Top of the window	Alt+Ctrl+PageUp
Bottom of the window	Alt+Ctrl+PageDown
Beginning of the document	Ctrl+Home
End of the document	Ctrl+End

Exercise 2-5 SCROLL THROUGH A DOCUMENT

Using the mouse and the scroll bars, you can scroll up, down, left, and right. You can also set the Previous and Next buttons on the vertical scroll bar to scroll through a document by a specific object, such as tables or headings. For example, these buttons let you jump from one heading to the next, going forward or backward.

1. Locate the vertical scroll bar, and click below the scroll box to move down one window.

Figure 2-4
Using the Scroll bars

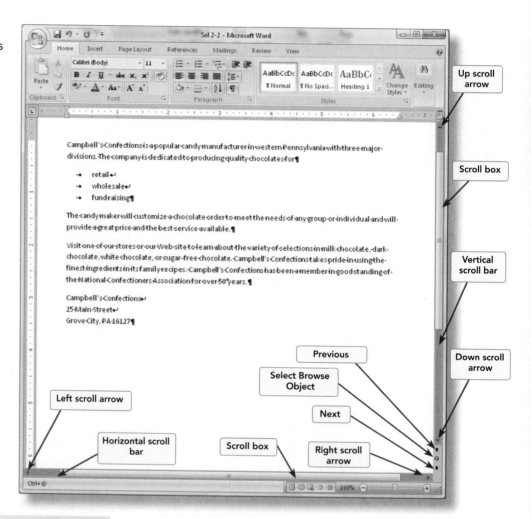

NOTE

The horizontal scroll bar does not display if the document window is wide enough to display the document text. To display the horizontal bar, size the window by dragging the resize handle (located in the lower right corner) to the left. When you resize the document window, the appearance of the Ribbon changes.

TIP

The keyboard shortcut to display the Select Browse Object menu is Ctrl + Alt + Home .

2. Drag the scroll box to the top of the scroll bar.

3. Click the down scroll arrow ⬇ on the scroll bar three times. The document moves three lines.

4. Click the right scroll arrow ▶ on the horizontal scroll bar once, and then click the left scroll arrow ◀ once to return to the correct horizontal position.

5. Click the up scroll arrow ⬆ on the vertical scroll bar three times to bring the document back into full view.
   Notice that as you scroll through the document, the insertion point remains at the top of the document.

6. Click the Select Browse Object button ⊙, located toward the bottom of the vertical scroll bar. A menu of icons appears.

7. Move the pointer over each icon to identify it. These browse options become significant as your documents become more complex. Click the Browse by Page icon ▯.

TABLE 2-4 Scrolling through a Document

To Move	Do This
Up one line	Click the up scroll arrow ▲.
Down one line	Click the down scroll arrow ▼.
Up one window	Click the scroll bar above the scroll box.
Down one window	Click the scroll bar below the scroll box.
To any relative position	Drag the scroll box up or down.
To the right	Click the right scroll arrow ▶.
To the left	Click the left scroll arrow ◀.
Into the left margin	Hold down Shift and click the left scroll arrow ◀.
Up or down one page	Click Select Browse Object ○, click Browse by Page ▯, and then click next ▼ or previous ▲.

> **TIP**
>
> If you are using a mouse with a wheel, additional navigating options are available. For example, you can roll the wheel forward or backward instead of using the vertical scroll bars, hold down the wheel and drag in any direction to pan the document, or hold down Ctrl as you roll the wheel to change the magnification.

Undo and Redo Commands

Word remembers the changes you make in a document and lets you undo or redo these changes. For example, if you accidentally delete text, you can use the Undo command to reverse the action and restore the text. If you change your mind and decide to keep the deletion, you can use the Redo command to reverse the canceled action.

There are two ways to undo or redo an action:

- Click the Undo button ↺ or the Redo button ↻ on the Quick Access Toolbar.

- Press Ctrl+Z to undo or Ctrl+Y to redo.

Exercise 2-6   UNDO AND REDO ACTIONS

1. Delete the first word in the document, "Campbell's," by moving the insertion point to the right of the space after the word and pressing Ctrl + Backspace. (Remember that a word includes the space that follows it.)

2. Click the Undo button to restore the word.

3. Move the insertion point to the left of the word "candy" in the first paragraph.

4. Key **mid-size** and press Spacebar once. The text now reads "mid-size candy manufacturer."

5. Press Ctrl + Z. The word "mid-size" is deleted.

6. Click the Redo button to restore the word "mid-size."

7. Click the down arrow to the right of the Undo button. Word displays a drop-down list of the last few actions, with the most recent action at the top. You can use this feature to choose several actions to undo rather than just the last action. Click the down arrow again to close the list.

8. Click the Undo button.

Figure 2-5
Undo Drop-Down list

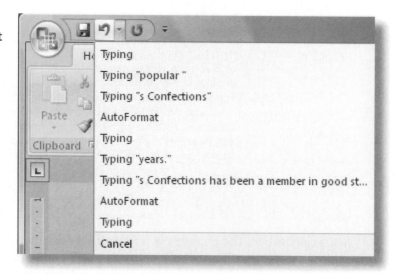

Repeat Command

Suppose you key text you want to add to other areas of a document. Instead of rekeying the same text, you can use the Repeat command to duplicate the text.
    To use the Repeat command:

- Press Ctrl + Y or

- Press F4.

Exercise 2-7 REPEAT ACTIONS

1. In the first paragraph position the insertion point to the left of the word "candy."

2. Key **popular** and press Spacebar once. The sentence now begins "Campbell's Confections is a popular candy."

3. Move the insertion point to the left of the word "selections" in the paragraph that begins "Visit one of our."

4. Press F4 and the word "popular" is repeated.

NOTE

If you want to undo, redo, or repeat your last action, do so before you press another key.

Selecting Text

Selecting text is a basic technique that makes revising documents easy. When you select text, that area of the document is called the *selection,* and it appears as a highlighted block of text. A selection can be a character, group of characters, word, sentence, or paragraph or the whole document. In this lesson, you delete and replace selected text. Future lessons show you how to format, move, copy, delete, and print selected text.

You can select text several ways, depending on the size of the area you want to select.

TABLE 2-5 Mouse Selection

To	Use the Mouse to Select
A series of characters	Click and drag, or click one end of the text block, and then hold down Shift and click the other end.
A word	Double-click the word.
A sentence	Press Ctrl and click anywhere in the sentence.
A line of text	Move the pointer to the left of the line until it changes to a right-pointing arrow, and then click. To select multiple lines, drag up or down.
A paragraph	Move the pointer to the left of the paragraph and double-click. To select multiple paragraphs, drag up or down.
The entire document	Move the pointer to the left of any document text until it changes to a right-pointing arrow, and then triple-click (or hold down Ctrl and click).

Exercise 2-8   SELECT TEXT WITH THE MOUSE

1. Select the first word of the document by double-clicking it. Notice that the space following the word is also selected.

Figure 2-6
Selecting a word

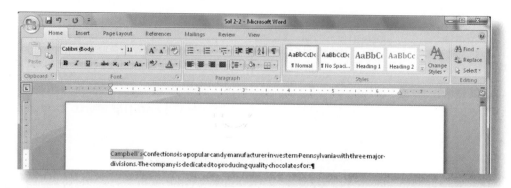

NOTE

When text is selected, a Mini toolbar appears with formatting options.

TIP

When selecting more than one word, you can click anywhere within the first word, and then drag to select additional text. Word will "smart-select" the entire first word.

TIP

You can also triple-click within a paragraph to select it.

2. Cancel the selection by clicking anywhere in the document. Selected text remains highlighted until you cancel the selection.

3. Select the first sentence by holding down Ctrl and clicking anywhere within the sentence. Notice that the period and space following the sentence are part of the selection. Cancel the selection.

4. Locate the paragraph that begins "Visit one of our."

5. To select the text "milk chocolate," click to the left of "milk." Hold down the left mouse button and slowly drag through the text, including the comma and space after "chocolate." Release the mouse button. Cancel the selection.

6. To select the entire paragraph by dragging the mouse, click to position the insertion point to the left of "Visit." Hold down the mouse button, and then drag across and down until all the text and the paragraph mark are selected. Cancel the selection.

7. Select the same paragraph by moving the pointer into the blank area to the left of the text "Visit." (This is the margin area.) When the I-beam pointer changes to a right-pointing arrow ⊿, double-click. Notice that the first click selects the first line and the second click selects the paragraph, including the paragraph mark. Cancel the selection.

Figure 2-7
Selecting text

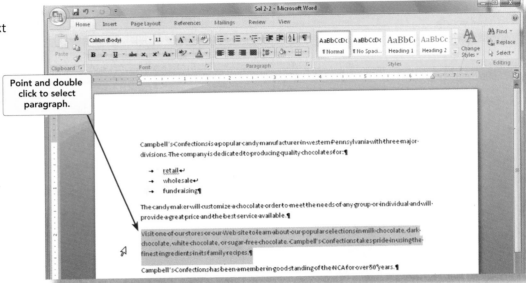

Point and double click to select paragraph.

Exercise 2-9   SELECT NONCONTIGUOUS TEXT

In the previous exercise, you learned how to select *contiguous text*, where the selected characters, words, sentences, or paragraphs follow one another. But sometimes you would like to select *noncontiguous text*, such as the first and last items in a list or the third and fifth word in a paragraph. In Word, you can select noncontiguous text by using Ctrl and the mouse.

1. Select the first line of the list ("retail").

2. Press Ctrl and select the third line of the list ("fundraising"). With these two separate lines selected, you can delete, format, or move them without affecting the rest of the list.

3. Cancel the selection and go to the paragraph that begins "Visit one of our."

4. In the paragraph that begins "Visit one of our," double-click the word "our" before "Web site." With the word now selected, hold down Ctrl as you double-click the word "popular" in the same sentence and "finest" in the next sentence. (See Figure 2-8.) All three words are highlighted.

Figure 2-8
Selecting
noncontiguous
words

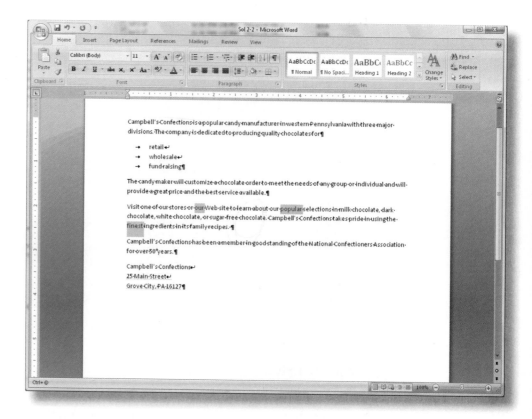

5. Cancel the selection.

Exercise 2-10 ADJUST A SELECTION USING THE MOUSE AND THE KEYBOARD

1. Select the paragraph beginning "Visit one of our."

2. Hold down Shift and press ← until the last sentence is no longer highlighted. Release Shift.

3. Increase the selection to include the last sentence by holding down Shift and pressing End and then pressing ↓. Release Shift.

4. Increase the selection to include all the text below it by holding down Shift and clicking at the end of the document (after the Zip Code).

5. Select the entire document by pressing Ctrl+A. Cancel the selection.

TABLE 2-6 Keyboard Selection

To Select	Press
One character to the right	Shift + →
One character to the left	Shift + ←
One word to the right	Ctrl + Shift + →
One word to the left	Ctrl + Shift + ←
To the end of a line	Shift + End
To the beginning of a line	Shift + Home
One line up	Shift + ↑
One line down	Shift + ↓
One window down	Shift + Page Down
One window up	Shift + Page Up
To the end of a document	Ctrl + Shift + End
To the beginning of a document	Ctrl + Shift + Home
An entire document	Ctrl + A

Exercise 2-11 EDIT TEXT BY REPLACING A SELECTION

You can edit a document by selecting text and deleting or replacing the selection.

NOTE

Although keying over selected text is an excellent editing feature, it sometimes leads to accidental deletions. Remember, when text is selected in a document (or even in a dialog box) and you begin keying text, Word deletes all the selected text with your first keystroke. If you key text without realizing a portion of the document is selected, use the Undo command to restore the text.

1. Locate the paragraph that begins "Visit one of our," select the words "our popular" using the Shift+click method: Click to the left of the word "our," hold down Shift, and click to the right of the word "popular."

2. Key the variety of to replace the selected text.

3. Locate the paragraph that begins "Campbell's Confections has been," select "NCA" and key National Confectioners Association. Notice that, unlike using Overtype mode, when you key over selected text, the new text can be longer or shorter than the selection.

Saving a Revised Document

You have already used the Save As command to rename the document you loaded at the beginning of this lesson. Now that you have made additional revisions, you can save a final version of the document by using the Save command. The document is saved with all the changes, replacing the old file with the revised file.

NOTE

If you wanted to save the current document with a different file name, you would use the Save As command.

Exercise 2-12 SAVE A REVISED DOCUMENT

1. Click the Save button 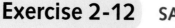 on the Quick Access Toolbar. This action does not open the Save As dialog box.

2. Open the File menu and point to the arrow beside Print. Click Quick Print to print the document.

Exercise 2-13 CHECK WORD'S AUTORECOVER SETTINGS

Word's *AutoRecover* feature can automatically save open documents at an interval you specify. However, this is not the same as saving a file yourself, as you did in the preceding exercise. AutoRecover's purpose is to save open documents "in the background," so a recently saved version is always on disk. Then if the power fails or your system crashes, the AutoRecover version of the document opens automatically the next time you launch Word. In other words, AutoRecover ensures you always have a recently saved version of your document.

Even with AutoRecover working, you need to manually save a document (by using the Save command) before closing it. AutoRecover documents are not always available; if you save and close your file normally, the AutoRecover version is deleted when you exit Word. Still, it is a good idea to make sure AutoRecover is working on your system and to set it to save recovery files frequently.

1. Open the File menu and click Word Options to open the Word Options dialog box.

2. Click Save in the left pane.

3. Make sure the Save AutoRecover information every box is checked. If it is not checked, click the box.

4. Click the up or down arrow buttons to set the minutes to 5. Click OK.

Figure 2-9
Setting AutoRecover
options

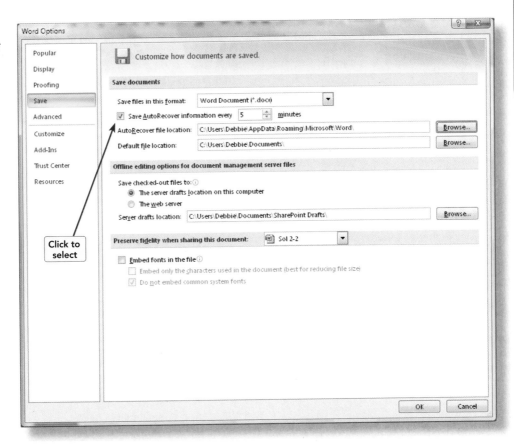

Working with Document Properties

Information that describes your document is called a *property*. Word automatically saves your document with certain properties, such as the file name, the date created, and the file size. You can add other properties to a document, such as the title, subject, author's name, and keywords. This information can help you organize and identify documents.

> **NOTE**
>
> You can also search for documents based on document properties by using the Search feature.

Exercise 2-14   REVIEW AND EDIT DOCUMENT PROPERTIES

1. With the file *[your initials]2-2* still open, open the **File** menu and click **Prepare**. Click **Properties**. The Document Information Panel opens above your document.

Figure 2-10
Opening the
Properties dialog
box

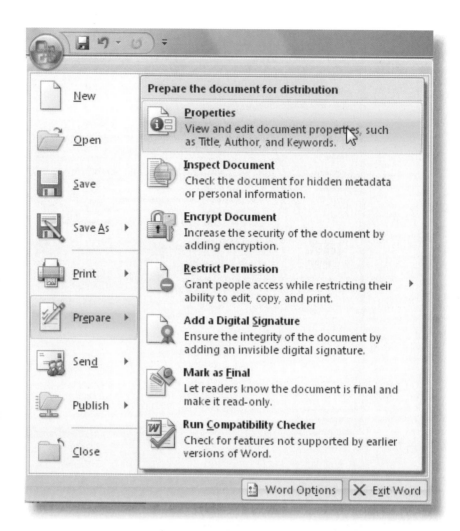

2. Notice the document properties displayed in the Document
   Information Panel.

Figure 2-11
Document
Information Panel

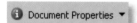

3. Click the Property Views and Options button . Click
   Advanced Properties. Click the **General** tab. This tab displays basic
   information about the file, such as file name, file type, location, size,
   and creation date.

4. Click the **Statistics** tab. This tab shows the exact breakdown of the
   document in number of paragraphs, lines, words, and characters.

5. Click the **Summary** tab. Here you can enter specific document property information or change existing information.

6. Edit the title to read **Campbell's Confections** and key *[your name]* as the author. Click **OK**.

 7. Click the Document Information Panel Close button to close the Document Information Panel.

Figure 2-12
Entering Summary
information

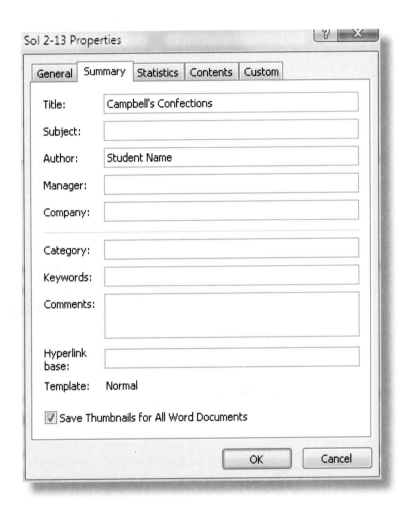

8. Save the document, and submit your work.

Lesson 2 Summary

- Use the Open dialog box to open an existing file. Use the Views button ⊞ Views ▾ in the dialog box to change the way files are listed.

- Create folders to organize your files. You can do this in the Save As dialog box, using the New Folder button 📁 New Folder . Rename folders by locating and selecting the folder. Right-click the folder name and choose Rename from the shortcut menu.

- Formatting characters—such as blank spaces or paragraph marks—appear on-screen, but not in the printed document. Insert a line-break character to start a new line within the same paragraph. Insert a nonbreaking space between two words to make sure they appear on the same line.

- Use the Show/Hide ¶ button ¶ to turn the display of formatting characters on and off.

- When a document is larger than the document window, use the keyboard or the vertical scroll bar to view different parts of the document. Keyboard methods for moving within a document also move the insertion point.

- Keyboard techniques for moving within a document include single keys (such as PageUp and Home)and keyboard combinations (such as Ctrl + ↑). See Table 2-3.

- Scrolling techniques for moving within a document include clicking the up or down scroll arrows on the vertical scroll bar or dragging the scroll box. Scrolling does not move the insertion point. See Table 2-4.

- If you make a change in a document that you want to reverse, use the Undo command. Use the Redo command to reverse the results of an Undo command.

- If you perform an action, such as keying text in a document, and you want to repeat that action elsewhere in the document, use the Repeat command.

- Selecting text is a basic technique for revising documents. A selection is a highlighted block of text you can format, move, copy, delete, or print.

- There are many different techniques for selecting text, using the mouse, the keyboard, or a combination of both. Mouse techniques involve dragging or clicking. See Table 2-5. Keyboard techniques are listed in Table 2-6.

- You can select any amount of contiguous text (characters, words, sentences, or paragraphs that follow one another) or noncontiguous text (such as words that appear in different parts of a document). Use Ctrl along with the mouse to select noncontiguous blocks of text.

- When text is selected, Word replaces it with any new text you key, or it deletes the selection if you press Delete .

- Use the Save command to save any revisions you make to a document.

- Word's AutoRecover feature periodically saves open documents in the background so you can recover a file in the event of a power failure or system crash.

- Document properties are details about a file that help identify it. Properties include the file name, file size, and date created, which Word updates automatically. Other properties you can add or change include title, subject, author's name, and keywords. View or add properties for an open document by using the **Properties** command (File menu, Prepare).

LESSON 2		Command Summary	
Feature	**Button**	**Command**	**Keyboard**
Open		File menu, Open	Ctrl + O or Ctrl + F12
Undo		Quick Access Toolbar	Ctrl + Z or Alt + Backspace
Redo		Quick Access Toolbar	Ctrl + Y or Alt + Shift + Backspace
Repeat			Ctrl + Y or F4
Select entire document			Ctrl + A
Save		File menu, Save	Ctrl + S or Shift + F12

Concepts Review

True/False Questions

Each of the following statements is either true or false. Indicate your choice by circling T or F.

(T) F   1. You can view Document Properties in the Open dialog box.

(T) (F)   2. A line-break character is used to begin a new paragraph.

(T) F   3. A tab mark is a formatting character.

(T) F   4. The Save As dialog box can be used to create a new folder.

T (F)   5. Noncontiguous text is text that does not appear consecutively in a Word document.

T (F)   6. You can undo only the last change made to a document.

(T) F   7. To select a sentence, you can double-click anywhere within the sentence.

(T) F   8. You can increase a selection by using [Shift]+[End].

Short Answer Questions

Write the correct answer in the space provided.

1. How do you display a list of the files recently opened?

   by click Microsoft Office button

2. Which formatting character would you insert between two words to keep them together in a sentence?

   line-break character

3. What is the keyboard shortcut to move the insertion point to the beginning of a document?

   Ctrl + Home

4. Where does [Home] move the insertion point?

   To the beginning of the sentence

5. What portion of the vertical scroll bar can you drag up or down?

   Scroll box

6. Which keyboard shortcut repeats the text you just keyed?

   _F4_

7. How do you open the Properties dialog box?

by clicking Microsoft Office button and selecting Prepare then click properties.

8. Which feature automatically saves an open document at regular intervals?

Word's AutoRecover.

Critical Thinking

Answer these questions on a separate page. There are no right or wrong answers. Support your answers with examples from your own experience, if possible.

1. You can use a nonbreaking space to prevent a line break between two words. Give some examples of word combinations and word-and-number combinations in which you would use a nonbreaking space.

2. Word provides many ways to select text by using the mouse. For example, you can use just the mouse, the mouse in combination with the keyboard, or just the keyboard. When would each of these methods be preferable? Which method do you prefer, and why?

Skills Review

Exercise 2-16

Open a document and enter formatting characters.

1. Open the file **Pitt** by following these steps:
   a. Click the Microsoft Office Button and click Open.
   b. Click the arrow to the right of the Views button  and choose List.
   c. Click the appropriate drive and folder.
   d. Scroll to the file name **Pitt** and double-click.

2. Position the insertion point at the end of the document by pressing Ctrl + End.

3. Key the text shown in Figure 2-13 as one paragraph, using line-break characters, by following these steps:
   a. Press Enter at the end of the document.
   b. Key the first three lines of text, pressing Shift + Enter at the end of each line.
   c. Key the last line (the phone number) and press Enter.

Figure 2-13

```
Campbell's Confections
40 Station Square
Pittsburgh, PA 15219
412-555-2025
```

4. Add new text and a nonbreaking space by following these steps:

  a. Move the insertion point to the immediate left of the word "area" in the first paragraph.

  b. Key **Station** and then press Ctrl + Shift + Spacebar.

  c. Key **Square** after the nonbreaking space and press Spacebar.

5. Save the document as *[your initials]*2-16 in your Lesson 2 folder.

6. Submit and close the document.

Exercise 2-17

Move within a document.

1. Open the file **Order**.

2. Move the insertion point to the immediate left of "We will" in the second line, and press Enter to split the paragraph.

3. Move the insertion point to the immediate left of the third sentence in the new paragraph (beginning with "If you"), and press Enter to split the paragraph.

4. With the insertion point to the left of "If," press ← once to move the insertion point to the end of the previous paragraph and key **We are confident you will want to return to try all of our flavors!**

5. Press Ctrl + End to move to the end of the document. Press Spacebar and key **Our unique hand-molded chocolates are delightful.**

6. Press Ctrl + Home to move to the beginning of the document. Press Caps Lock and key **thinking of chocolate?** Press Enter to split the paragraph.

7. Save the document as *[your initials]*2-17 in your Lesson 2 folder.

8. Submit and close the document.

Exercise 2-18

Undo, redo, and repeat editing actions.

1. Open the file **Meeting Favors**.

2. Position the insertion point after the heading "Meeting Favors" and press Enter. Click the Undo button ↺ to undo the insertion.

3. Move the insertion point to the left of "flavors" in the first sentence of the second paragraph. Key **chocolate** to create the phrase "chocolate flavors."

4. In the same paragraph, move the insertion point to the left of "favor shapes." Press F4 to create the phrase "chocolate favor shapes."

5. In the first sentence of the first paragraph, move the insertion point to the left of "for." Key **favors** and press Spacebar.

6. Locate "premier chocolate" in the last paragraph, and use the **Repeat** command to insert "favors" to the left of "for your."

7. Click the Undo button ↺ to undo the text. Then click the Redo button ↻ to redo the text.

8. In the last sentence of the last paragraph, replace the sentence by following these steps:

   a. Select the last sentence by pressing Ctrl and clicking anywhere in the sentence.

   b. Key **Visit www.campbellsconfections.biz** for additional information.

9. Save the document as *[your initials]*2-18 in your Lesson 2 folder.

10. Submit your work.

Exercise 2-19

Select text, save a revised document, and enter summary information.

1. Start a new document. Key the text shown in Figure 2-14.

Figure 2-14

Campbell's Confections chocolate factory tour and candy store is one of Butler County's major attractions. The factory tour enables visitors to watch the entire cycle of candy making from melting the bulk chocolate to packing the individual pieces in air-tight containers. The information provided by the tour guide is informative and educational.

If you are planning a family trip to Mercer County, be sure to research the other attractions in the area. You are miles away from museums, antique stores, a forge that makes aluminum, bronze, and other metal gifts, and many outdoor activities. There are opportunities for camping, hiking, biking, boating, and fishing. Winter activities include sledding, ice fishing, ice skating, snowmobile trails, and cross-country skiing. Contact us for brochures and other information on area attractions.

2. Save the document as *[your initials]*2-19 in your Lesson 2 folder.

3. Select and replace a word by following these steps:

   a. Place the insertion point in the word "Butler" in the first sentence of the first paragraph.

   b. Double-click the word to select it and key **Mercer** to replace it.

4. Select and replace the text in the second paragraph by following these steps:

   a. Double click "us" in the last line of the second paragraph.

   b. Key the Chamber of Commerce in place of the selected text.

5. Select "miles" in the second paragraph and key minutes to replace the text.

6. Select a sentence by following these steps:

   a. Position the I-beam pointer over any sentence.

   b. Hold down Ctrl and click the mouse button. Release Ctrl.

   c. Deselect the sentence.

7. Select the first paragraph by following these steps:

   a. Move the pointer to the left of the paragraph until it changes to a right-pointing arrow ⬈.

   b. Double-click the mouse button.

8. Extend the current selection by following these steps:

   a. Hold down Shift and press ↓ twice to extend the selection two lines.

   b. Continue holding down Shift and press End to select the entire line.

   c. Continue holding down Shift and press ↓ to select the rest of the document. Release Shift.

9. Click anywhere to cancel the selection.

10. Select noncontiguous text by following these steps:

    a. Double-click the document's first word ("Campbell's").

    b. Move the pointer to the left of the paragraph's third line until the pointer changes to a right-pointing arrow. Hold down Ctrl and click to select the line.

    c. Hold down Ctrl and select the second paragraph by dragging the pointer from the beginning of the paragraph to the end.

11. Click anywhere to cancel the selection.

12. Review the document properties and enter summary information by following these steps:

    a. Open the File menu and click Prepare. Click Properties.

    b. Click the down arrow beside Standard, and click Advanced.

    b. Review the data on the General tab and the Statistics tab, and click the Summary tab.

    c. Click in the Title box and press Home to move the insertion point to the beginning of the title. Press Shift + End to select the current title. With the title selected, key Mercer County as the new title, replacing the existing text.

    d. Click OK.

13. Click the Save button ⊟ to save the revised document.

14. Submit your work, and close the document.

Lesson Applications

Exercise 2-20

Select and edit text, and enter a nonbreaking space.

1. Open the file **Pitt**. Make the corrections shown in Figure 2-15 by selecting and then keying over the selected text.

Figure 2-15

Both tourists and local residents frequent the Pittsburgh candy store of
Campbell's Confections. The store is in a bustling downtown location and
is well known for its chocolate covered nuts, creams, and melt-a-ways. Be sure to
Drop in when you're visiting the area.

2. Press Ctrl+End to move to the end of the document. Press Enter to start a new paragraph. Then key:

   For information about monthly chocolate specials, or for directions to the store, call Rebecca Steigerwald at Campbell's Confections. You can also visit us on the Web at www.campbellsconfections.biz.

3. Insert a nonbreaking space between "Rebecca" and "Steigerwald" in the second paragraph. (Replace the regular space with a nonbreaking space.)

4. Save the document as *[your initials]*2-20 in your Lesson 2 folder.

5. Submit and close the document.

Exercise 2-21

Select and repeat text, and create a paragraph using line breaks.

1. Open the file **Video**.

2. In the first sentence, replace "our company" with Campbell's Confections.

3. Use the Repeat command to repeat the keyed text to the left of the word "Customers" in the last sentence. Enter a space after "Confections and change the "C" in "Customers" to lowercase.

4. In the second sentence, replace "the factory on Monroe Street" with **any of our 24 retail stores**.

5. Move to the end of the document and press Enter.

6. Key the text shown in Figure 2-16 as a single paragraph, using a line break for each new line.

Figure 2-16

```
Our newest stores are located in the following cities:
Fairmont, West Virginia
Edinboro, Pennsylvania
Massillon, Ohio
```

7. Save the document as *[your initials]***2-21** in your Lesson 2 folder.

8. Submit and close the document.

Exercise 2-22

Select and edit text, and insert a nonbreaking space.

1. Open the file **Factory - 2**.

2. Split the first paragraph at the sentence that begins "The chocolate factory."

3. Merge the second paragraph with the third paragraph. Be sure to insert a space between sentences.

4. Spell out "sq." and "ft." Replace "all of its" with **the**.

5. At the end of the last paragraph, key this sentence:

    Educational materials are available for elementary and middle school teachers.

6. Add a nonbreaking space between "June" and "30."

7. Insert the following sentence at the end of the first paragraph.

    The factory hosts special events throughout the year such as Candy Making 101 and Secrets of Dipping Strawberries. Each year it sponsors an expert chocolatier to demonstrate the art of making chocolate.

8. Save the document as *[your initials]***2-22** in your Lesson 2 folder.

9. Submit and close the document.

Exercise 2-23 ◆ Challenge Yourself

Select and edit text, use formatting characters, and enter summary information.

1. Open the file **Summer**.
2. Revise the document as shown in Figure 2-17.

Figure 2-17

```
                                                              in June
Summer is a great time to visit Grove City. In June, the Grove City Area
                                                              ‸
Chamber of Commerce hosts the annual Strawberry Days Art & Music Festival.
Visitors can                                                             ‸
‸Enjoy free working exhibitions, live entertainment, and wonderful ethnic food.
      fourth of                                                   fantastic
The July 4 patriotic celebration and fireworks are a special treat. Dozens of aerial
    ‸                                                                      ‸
displays and fantastic ground displays are all part of the Fireworks Spectacular at

Memorial Park.

In August, the Chamber of Commerce hosts Art in the Park. This annual event

features more than 100 artisans with a wide variety of fine art and handcrafted

treasures.
```

3. Add the following sentence after "Music Festival in June" in the first paragraph. The festival features more than 75 craftspeople and artists.
4. In the last sentence of the first paragraph, replace "wonderful" with a wide variety of
5. Change the last paragraph so it becomes three lines of text, as follows (use line breaks to start new lines):
   Coming in August:
   Art in the Park
   Fine art and handcrafted treasures
6. Select the three-line paragraph you just created.
7. Press [Delete], and then undo the deletion.
8. At the end of the first paragraph, change "food" to foods
9. Save the document named *[your initials]*2-23 in your Lesson 2 folder.
10. Open the Properties dialog box. Key Summer in Grove City as the Title, key your name as the Author, and key Summer tourist attractions in the Comments box.
11. Save the document and submit your work.

On Your Own

In these exercises you work on your own, as you would in a real-life business environment. Use the skills you've learned to accomplish the task—and be creative.

Exercise 2-24

Write a short paragraph about a nearby town or city. Print the document. Edit the document, using the skills you learned in this lesson and changing the information to reflect the town or city where you live. Use nonbreaking spaces, if needed. Key your name as the author in the Document Property dialog box. Save the document as *[your initials]*2-24 and submit it.

Exercise 2-25

Open the file **Meeting Favors**. Use your editing skills to change each paragraph, making the document more concise and changing the subject to school favors. Save the document as *[your initials]*2-25. Submit your work.

Exercise 2-26

Key a short portion of a historical text or novel (written before the twentieth century)—approximately one-half page of document text. Edit the text to make the language more contemporary. On the Summary tab of the Document Properties dialog box, show the original author under Author. Under Comments, key Modified by [your name]. Save the document as *[your initials]*2-26. Submit your work.

Formatting Characters

OBJECTIVES

After completing this lesson, you will be able to:

1. Work with fonts.

2. Apply basic character formatting.

3. Work with the Font dialog box.

4. Repeat and copy character formats.

5. Change case and highlight text.

6. Create a drop cap.

7. Automatically format text and numbers.

Estimated Time: 1 hour

Every document is based on a theme. A *theme* is a set of formatting instructions for the entire document. Themes include fonts, colors, and effects.

Character formatting is used to emphasize text. You can change character formatting by making text bold or italic, for example, or by changing the style of the type. Word also provides special features to copy formats, highlight text, and automatically format text and numbers.

Working with Fonts

A *font* is a type design applied to an entire set of characters, including all letters of the alphabet, numerals, punctuation marks, and other keyboard symbols. Every theme defines two fonts—one for headings and one for body text.

Figure 3-1
Examples of fonts

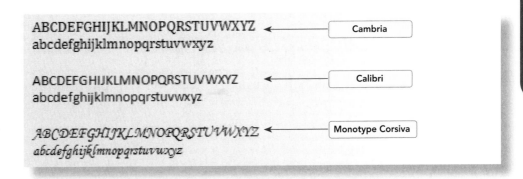

Calibri is an example of a plain font; Cambria is more ornate; and Monotype Corsiva is an example of a more stylized font. Calibri is a *sans serif* font because it has no decorative lines, or serifs, projecting from its characters. Cambria is a *serif* font because it has decorative lines. Fonts are available in a variety of sizes, measured in *points*. There are 72 points to an inch. Like other character formatting, you can use different fonts and font sizes in the same document.

NOTE

The default theme fonts are Calibri, a sans serif font, and Cambria, a serif font. The default font size is 11.

Figure 3-2
Examples of different point sizes

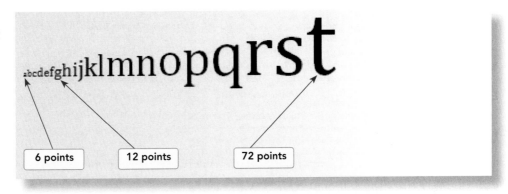

Exercise 3-1   CHANGE FONTS AND FONT SIZES USING THE RIBBON

The easiest way to choose fonts and font sizes is to use the Ribbon. The Home tab includes the Font group that contains frequently used formatting commands.

TIP

Press Ctrl + Shift + * to display formatting characters. (Do not use the asterisk on the numeric keypad.)

1. Open the file **Music**.

2. Click the Show/Hide ¶ button ¶ to display paragraph marks and space characters if they are not already showing.

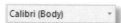

3. Move to the beginning of the document and select the first line, which begins "Attention." (Remember, you can press Ctrl + Home to move to the beginning of a document.)

4. Click the down arrow next to the Font box Calibri (Body) on the Ribbon to open the Font drop-down list. Fonts are listed alphabetically by name and are displayed graphically.

Figure 3-3
Choosing a font

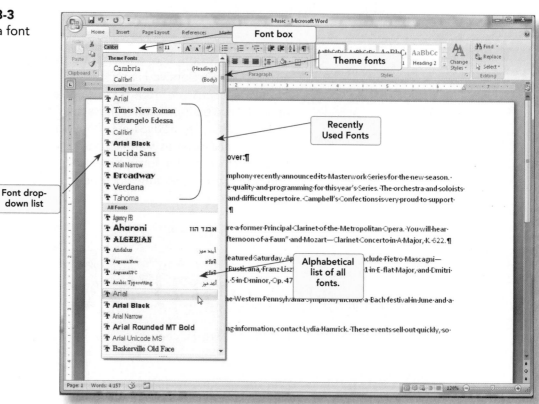

NOTE

The fonts you used most recently appear below the Theme Fonts. Shaded divider lines separate the Theme Fonts, Recently Used Fonts, and the list of All Fonts.

5. Using ↓ or the scroll box on the font list's scroll bar, choose Arial.

6. Click the down arrow to open the Font Size drop-down list 11 · and choose 16 points. Now the first line stands out as a headline.

Figure 3-4
Choosing a font size

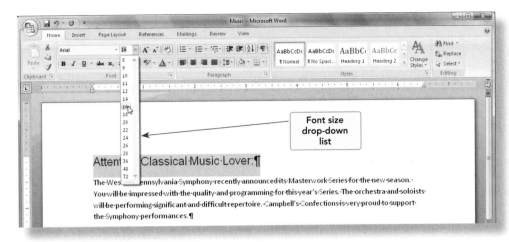

Exercise 3-2 CHANGE FONT SIZE USING KEYBOARD SHORTCUTS

If you prefer keyboard shortcuts, you can press Ctrl+Shift+> to increase the font size or Ctrl+Shift+< to decrease the font size.

TIP

Sometimes text might appear bold on your screen when it is simply a larger font size.

1. Move the insertion point to the end of the paragraph that begins "For reservations," and press Enter to start a new paragraph.

2. Press Ctrl+Shift+> and key **Call Lydia at 555-2025.** The new sentence appears in 12-point type.

3. Press Enter to begin another paragraph. Press Ctrl+Shift+< to reduce the font size to 11 points and key **Credit card payments are accepted.**

Basic Character Formatting

The basic font styles or character formats are bold, italic, and underline. Text can have one or more character formats.

TABLE 3-1 Character Formatting

Attribute	Example
Normal	This is a sample.
Bold	**This is a sample.**
Italic	*This is a sample.*
Underline	<u>This is a sample.</u>
Bold and italic	***This is a sample.***

The simplest ways to apply basic character formatting are to use:

- Commands on the Ribbon
- Keyboard shortcuts
- Commands on the Mini toolbar

You can apply character formatting to existing text, including existing text that is noncontiguous. You can also turn on a character format before you key new text and turn it off after you enter the text. For example, you can click the Bold button **B**, key a few words in bold, click the button again to turn off the format, and continue keying regular text.

Exercise 3-3　APPLY BASIC CHARACTER FORMATTING USING THE RIBBON

1. Select "Mozart—Clarinet Concerto in A Major, K. 622" (not including the period).

2. Click the Bold button **B** on the Ribbon to format the text bold. (The Bold command is located in the Font group.)

NOTE

The Home tab on the Ribbon displays by default. If the Home tab is not the active tab, click the Home tab to make it active and to display the Font group commands.

3. With the text still selected, click the Italic button **I** on the Ribbon to format the text bold and italic.

4. Click the Bold button **B** again to turn off the bold format and to leave the text as italic only. Click the Bold button **B** again to restore the bold-italic formatting.

Figure 3-5
Using the Ribbon to apply character formatting

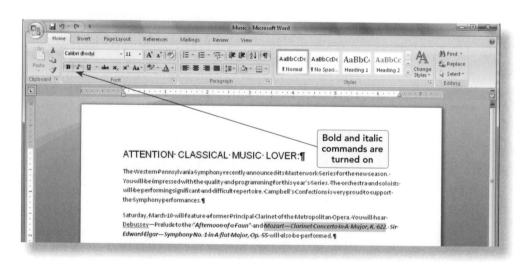

5. Move the insertion point to the end of the same paragraph and press Spacebar once.

6. Click the Bold button and the Italic button, and key Sir Edward Elgar—Symphony No. 1 in A-flat Major, Op. 55 in bold italic.

7. Click both buttons to turn off the formatting, press [Spacebar], and complete the sentence by keying will also be performed.

8. Select the bold italic text "Mozart—Clarinet Concerto in A Major, K. 622" again.

9. Press [Ctrl] and select the bold italic text "Sir Edward Elgar—Symphony No. 1 in A-flat Major, Op. 55" as well.

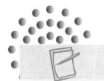

NOTE

When text is selected, a Mini toolbar appears with character and paragraph formatting commands.

10. Click the Underline button on the Ribbon to underline the noncontiguous selections.

11. Click the Undo button to remove the underlines.

12. Select the first line in the document.

13. Click the Change Case button and click UPPERCASE.

Exercise 3-4 — APPLY AND REMOVE BASIC CHARACTER FORMATTING USING KEYBOARD SHORTCUTS

If you prefer to keep your hands on the keyboard instead of using the mouse, you can use keyboard shortcuts to turn basic character formatting on and off. You can press [Ctrl]+[B] for bold, [Ctrl]+[I] for italic, and [Ctrl]+[U] for underline. To remove character formatting from selected text, press [Ctrl]+[Spacebar].

1. Select the text "Afternoon of a Faun."

2. Press [Ctrl]+[B] to format the selected text bold and press [Ctrl]+[I] to add italic.

3. Move the insertion point to the end of the document, and press [Enter] to start a new paragraph.

4. Press [Caps Lock], press [Ctrl]+[B] to turn on the bold option, and key jazz fans note: in bold capital letters.

5. Press [Caps Lock] to turn it off, press [Spacebar], and continue keying in bold:

   The first annual Jazz Festival, featuring some of the world's greatest musicians, will be held next May.

6. Select the bold-italic text "Afternoon of a Faun" again and press [Ctrl]+[Spacebar] to remove the formatting.

7. Click the Undo button to restore the bold-italic formatting.

Exercise 3-5 APPLY AND REMOVE BASIC CHARACTER FORMATTING USING THE MINI TOOLBAR

The Mini toolbar appears when you select text in a document. You can click any of the buttons to apply or remove character formatting from the selected text.

1. Select the first line of text. Notice the Mini toolbar displays.

Figure 3-6
Mini toolbar

2. Click the drop-down arrow beside the Font Color button and click **Blue**.

3. Click the Grow Font button , and notice the change in the font size. Click the Shrink Font button .

Using the Font Dialog Box

The Font dialog box offers a wider variety of options than those available on the Ribbon. You can conveniently choose several options at one time.

There are several ways to open the Font dialog box:

- Click the Font Dialog Box Launcher.

- Right-click (use the right mouse button) selected text to display a *shortcut menu,* and then choose **Font**. A shortcut menu shows a list of commands relevant to a particular item you click.

- Keyboard shortcuts.

Figure 3-7
Shortcut menu

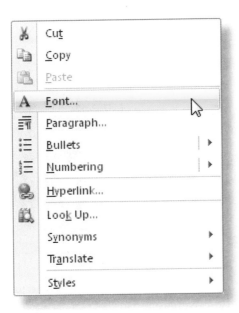

Exercise 3-6   CHOOSE FONTS AND FONT STYLES USING THE FONT DIALOG BOX

1. Select the first line of text, which is currently 16-point Arial and blue.

2. Click the arrow in the lower right corner of the Font group on the Ribbon. The Font dialog box displays.

Figure 3-8
Font Dialog Box
Launcher

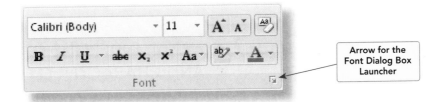

Arrow for the
Font Dialog Box
Launcher

NOTE

Font availability varies, depending on the type of printer you are using and the installed software. Ask your instructor to recommend a substitute font if the specified one is unavailable.

3. Choose **Monotype Corsiva** from the **Font** list, **Bold Italic** from the **Font style** list, and **18** from the **Size** list. Look at your choices in the **Preview** box and click **OK**.

Figure 3-9
Using the Font
dialog box

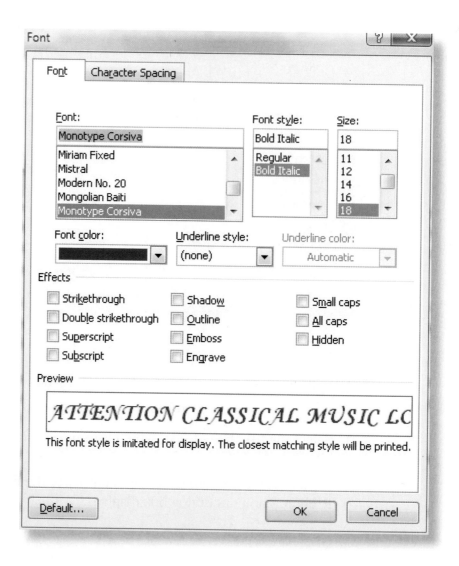

Exercise 3-7   APPLY UNDERLINE OPTIONS AND CHARACTER EFFECTS

In addition to choosing font, font size, and font style, you can choose font color, a variety of underlining options, and special character effects from the Font dialog box.

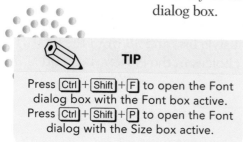

TIP

Press Ctrl + Shift + F to open the Font dialog box with the Font box active. Press Ctrl + Shift + P to open the Font dialog with the Size box active.

1. Select the text "JAZZ FANS NOTE" in the last paragraph (do not select the colon).

2. Press Ctrl + D to open the Font dialog box.

3. Click the down arrow to open the **Underline style** drop-down list. Drag the scroll box down to see all the available underline styles. Choose one of the dotted line styles.

4. Click the down arrow next to the Font color box and choose "Green". (Each color is identified by name when you point to it.) Both the text and the underline are now green in the **Preview** box.

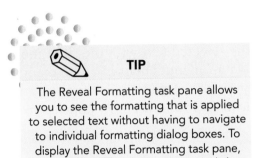

TIP

The Reveal Formatting task pane allows you to see the formatting that is applied to selected text without having to navigate to individual formatting dialog boxes. To display the Reveal Formatting task pane, press Shift + F1. To open the Font dialog box, move the mouse pointer over Font under the Font section. When the mouse pointer becomes a hand pointer ↚, click to open the Font dialog box.

Figure 3-10
Font color options in the Font dialog box

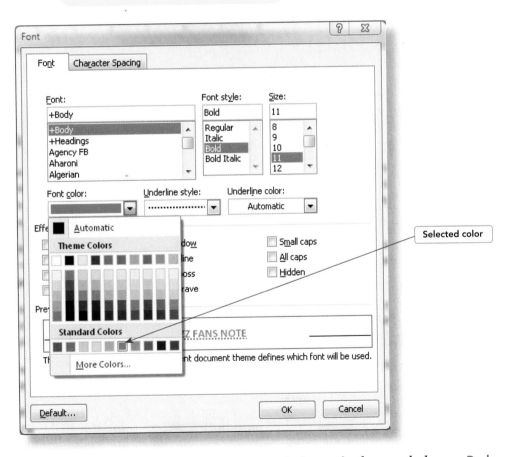

5. Click the down arrow next to the **Underline color** box and choose **Red**.

TIP

As a rule, punctuation such as colons and periods should not be underlined.

6. Click **OK**. The text is green with a red dotted underline.

7. Select the sentence after the green, dotted-underlined text "JAZZ FANS NOTE:"

8. Move the mouse pointer to the Ribbon and click the Clear Formatting button.

9. In the same sentence, select the text "Jazz Festival."

10. Click the selected text with the right mouse button, and from the shortcut menu, choose **Font** to open the Font dialog box. Under **Effects**, click the **Small caps** check box and click **OK**. The text that was formerly lowercase now appears in small capital letters.

11. Select the sentence that begins "Call Lydia."

12. Click the Strikethrough button on the Ribbon. The text appears with a horizontal line running through it.

TABLE 3-2 Font Effects in the Font Dialog Box

Effect	Description and Example
Strikethrough	Applies ~~a horizontal line~~.
Double strikethrough	Applies a ~~double horizontal line~~.
Superscript	Raises text ^{above} other characters on the same line.
Subscript	Places text $_{below}$ other characters on the same line.
Shadow	Applies a **shadow**.
Outline	Displays the inner and outer border of text.
Emboss	Makes text appear raised off the page.
Engrave	Makes text appear imprinted on the page.
Small Caps	Makes lowercase text SMALL CAPS.
All Caps	Makes all text UPPERCASE.
Hidden	Hidden text does not print and appears on-screen only if Word's Display options are set to display hidden text. See File menu, Word Options.

13. Click the Undo button to undo the strikethrough effect.

Exercise 3-8 USE KEYBOARD SHORTCUTS FOR UNDERLINE OPTIONS AND FONT EFFECTS

Word provides keyboard shortcuts for some underlining options and font effects as an alternative to using the Ribbon or opening the Font dialog box.

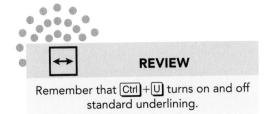

REVIEW

Remember that Ctrl + U turns on and off standard underlining.

1. Start a new sentence at the end of the last paragraph by keying To beat the heat, bring plenty of H2O.

2. Select the "2" in H2O.

3. Press Ctrl + = to make it subscript.

4. Select the green, dotted-underlined text "JAZZ FANS NOTE." Press Ctrl + Shift + W to change the dotted underlining to words-only underlining.

TABLE 3-3 Keyboard Shortcuts for Underlining and Character Effects

Keyboard Shortcut	Action
Ctrl + Shift + W	Turn on or off words-only underlining.
Ctrl + Shift + D	Turn on or off double underlining.
Ctrl + Shift + =	Turn on or off superscript.
Ctrl + =	Turn on or off subscript.
Ctrl + Shift + K	Turn on or off small capitals.
Ctrl + Shift + A	Turn on or off all capitals.
Ctrl + Shift + H	Turn on or off hidden text.

Exercise 3-9 CHANGE CHARACTER SPACING

The Character Spacing tab in the Font dialog box offers options for changing the space between characters or the position of text in relation to the baseline. Character spacing can be expanded or condensed horizontally, as well as raised or lowered vertically.

1. Select the first line of text, which begins "Attention."

2. Open the Font dialog box and click the Character Spacing tab.

3. Click the down arrow to open the Scale drop-down list. Click 150% and notice the change in the Preview box. Change the scale back to 100%.

Figure 3-11
Character Spacing
tab

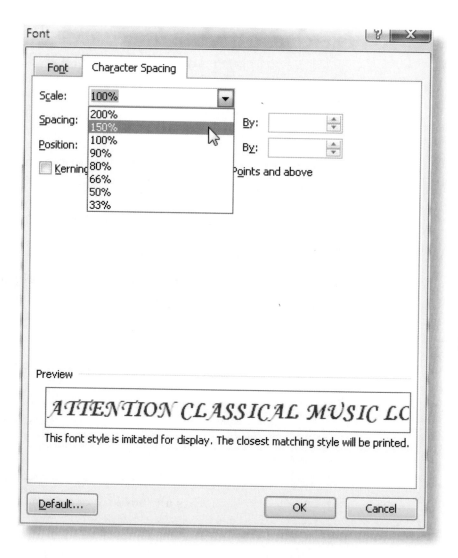

TIP

You can increase the space between characters even more by increasing the number in the **By** box (click the arrows or key a specific number). Experiment with the **Spacing** and **Scale** options on your own to see how they change the appearance of text.

4. Click the down arrow to display the **Spacing** options. Click **Expanded**, and then click **OK**. The text appears with more space between each character.

5. In the Save As dialog box, create a new folder for your Lesson 3 files and save the document as *[your initials]*3-9.

NOTE

Remember to use this folder for all the exercise documents you create in this lesson.

Repeating and Copying Formatting

You can use F4 or Ctrl+Y to repeat character formatting. You can also copy character formatting with a special tool on the Ribbon—the Format Painter button.

Exercise 3-10 REPEAT CHARACTER FORMATTING

Before trying to repeat character formatting, keep in mind that you must use the Repeat command immediately after applying the format. In addition, the Repeat command repeats only the last character format applied. (If you apply multiple character formats from the Font dialog box, the Repeat command applies all formatting.)

1. Select "Intermezzo" and click the Italic button *I* to italicize the text.

2. Select "Piano Concerto No. 1 in E-flat Major" and press F4 to repeat your last action (turning on Italic format).

3. Select the sentence that begins "Call Lydia."

4. Open the **Font** dialog box. Click the **Font** tab, if it is not already displayed, and choose another font, such as Impact. Select the font size **12 points**, and change the font color to **red**. Click **OK**. The text appears with the new formatting.

5. Select the text "JAZZ FANS NOTE:" (including the colon) and press F4. Word repeats all the formatting you chose in the Font dialog box. If you apply each character format separately, using the Ribbon, the Repeat command applies only the last format you chose.

Figure 3-12
Repeating character formatting

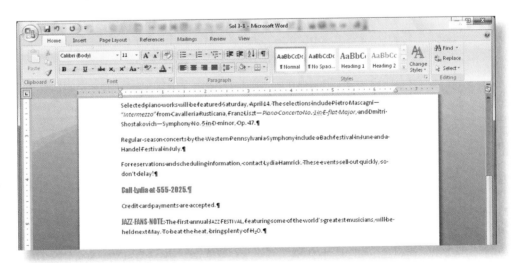

Exercise 3-11   COPY CHARACTER FORMATTING

The Format Painter button makes it easy to copy a character format. This is particularly helpful when you copy text with multiple formats, such as bold-italic small caps.

To use Format Painter to copy character formatting, first select the text with the formatting you want to copy, and then click the Format Painter button. The mouse pointer changes to a paintbrush with an I-beam pointer. Use this pointer to select the text to which you want to apply the copied formatting.

1. In the paragraph that begins "The Western," select "Masterwork Series" and click the Underline button.

2. With the text still selected, click the Format Painter button on the Ribbon. When you move the pointer back into the text area, notice the new shape of the pointer.

3. Use the paintbrush pointer to select "Series" in the next sentence. This copies the underlining to the selected text, and the pointer returns to its normal shape.

4. Select the small caps words "JAZZ FESTIVAL" in the last paragraph.

5. Double-click the Format Painter button. Double-clicking lets you copy formatting repeatedly.

6. Scroll to the top of the document. Notice that the paintbrush pointer becomes an arrow when you move out of the text area to use the scroll bars.

7. Select the sentence that begins "The Western." The small caps formatting is applied to the sentence, and the pointer remains the paintbrush pointer.

8. Scroll down to the line that begins "Call Lydia" and select the sentence. The paintbrush pointer copies the new formatting over the old formatting.

9. Press Esc or click the Format Painter button to stop copying and to restore the normal pointer.

Changing Case and Highlighting Text

You have used Caps Lock to change case, and you have seen the **Small Caps** and **All Caps** options in the Font dialog box. You can also change the case of characters by using keyboard shortcuts and the Change Case command on the Ribbon.

Exercise 3-12   CHANGE CASE

1. Select the sentence that begins "Credit card payments."
   Press [Shift]+[F3]. This keyboard shortcut changes case. Now the text
   appears in all uppercase letters.

2. With the sentence still selected, press [Shift]+[F3] again. Now the
   sentence appears in all lowercase letters.

3. Press [Shift]+[F3] again and the original case (sentence case) is
   restored.

4. Select the first line of the document, and click the Change Case
   button on the Ribbon.

5. Click **Capitalize Each Word**. This option changes the first letter of
   each word to uppercase, the common format for titles.

6. Click anywhere in the document to deselect the text.

Exercise 3-13   HIGHLIGHT TEXT

To emphasize parts of a document, you can mark text with a color highlighter
by using the Highlight button on the Ribbon, Font group. As with the
Format Painter button, when you click the Highlight button, the pointer
changes shape. You then use the highlight pointer to select the text you
want to highlight. In addition, you can choose from several highlighting
colors.

1. Make sure no text is selected. On the Ribbon, click the down
   arrow next to the Highlight button to display the color choices.
   Click **Yellow** to choose it as the highlight color. This turns on the
   Highlight button, and the color indicator box on the button is now
   yellow.

Figure 3-13
Choosing a highlight
color

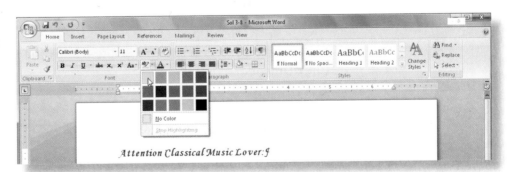

2. Move the highlight pointer into the text area.

3. Drag the pointer over the phone number in the paragraph that begins "Call Lydia."

4. Press Esc to turn off the highlighter and restore the normal pointer.

5. Select the first line of text, which begins "Attention."

6. Click the Highlight button to highlight the selection. This is another way to use the highlighter—by selecting the text and then clicking the Highlight button.

7. Select the first line of text again. Remove the highlight by clicking the down arrow to display the highlight color choices and choosing **No Color**.

8. Select the remaining highlighted text and click the Highlight button ⬥. Because "None" was last chosen (as shown in the color indicator box on the button), this action removes the highlight from the selected text.

> **NOTE**
>
> You can use highlighting to mark text as you work on a document or to point out text for others opening the same document later. It might not work as well for printed documents because the colors might print too dark. You can use the shading feature to emphasize text in a printed document.

Creating a Drop Cap

One way to call attention to a paragraph is to use a dropped capital letter, or a *drop cap*. A drop cap is a large letter that appears below the text baseline. It is usually applied to the first letter in the first word of a paragraph.

Exercise 3-14   CREATE A DROP CAP

1. Place the insertion point at the beginning of the paragraph that begins "The Western."

2. Click the **Insert** tab on the Ribbon, and click the Drop Cap button . Click **Dropped**.

3. Undo the drop cap.

4. Click the Drop Cap down arrow and click **Drop Cap Options**. The Drop Cap dialog box opens.

Figure 3-14
Drop Cap dialog box

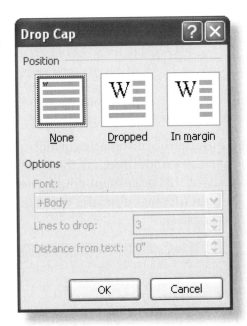

5. Under **Position**, click **Dropped**. This option is used to wrap the paragraph around the letter.

6. Click **OK**. Click within the document to deselect the "T" of "The," which is the height of three lines.

Word's AutoFormat Features

Word has several features that automatically change formatting as you key text or numbers. One of these *AutoFormat* features converts ordinal numbers and fractions into a more readable format, as shown in Table 3-4.

Another AutoFormat feature changes an Internet address into a hyperlink as you key the text. Clicking on the hyperlink takes you to another location, such as an HTML page on the Internet (assuming you are logged onto the Internet).

NOTE

Style manuals in general do not recommend superscript ordinals. To turn off the Ordinals and Fractions AutoFormat, open the Word Options dialog box, click Proofing, and click AutoCorrect Options to open the AutoCorrect dialog box. Click the AutoFormat tab, and click to deselect **Ordinals** and **Fractions** in the Replace section.

TABLE 3-4 Automatic Formatting of Ordinal Numbers and Fractions

Keyed Text	Format Change
1st	1st
2nd	2nd
1/2	$\frac{1}{2}$
1/4	$\frac{1}{4}$

Exercise 3-15   FORMAT ORDINAL NUMBERS AND FRACTIONS AUTOMATICALLY

1. In the paragraph that begins "Call Lydia," move the pointer to the immediate right of "2025" and key or send an e-mail message to lydiahamrick@campbellsconfections.biz.

2. Press Spacebar to initiate the automatic formatting. The e-mail address is now blue and underlined. If this were a real e-mail address, any reader of this document could press Ctrl and click the text to send an e-mail message to Lydia (providing the reader had an e-mail program installed).

Figure 3-15
Formatting Hyperlink text

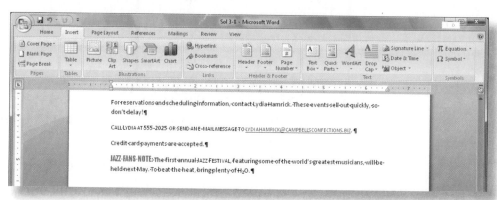

3. Move to the end of the paragraph that begins "Credit card payments." Add a new sentence by keying Matinee performances are 1/2 price. Notice that Word automatically converts the numbers and the slash into a fraction.

4. Save the document as *[your initials]*3-15 in your Lesson 3 folder.

5. Submit your work and close the document.

Lesson 3 Summary

- A font is a type design applied to an entire set of characters, including all the letters of the alphabet, numerals, punctuation marks, and other keyboard symbols.

- A font can be serif (with decorative lines) or sans serif (with no decorative lines).

- Fonts are available in a variety of sizes, which are measured in points. There are 72 points to an inch.

- You can use the Ribbon to change fonts and font sizes.

- Keyboard shortcuts can also be used to change font sizes: Ctrl+Shift+> increases the text size and Ctrl+Shift+< decreases the text size.

- Use the Ribbon, Home tab, Font group to apply basic character formatting (for example, bold, italic, and/or underline) to selected contiguous (text that is together) or noncontiguous text (text that is not together).

- Use keyboard shortcuts to apply and remove basic character formatting.

- Use the Mini toolbar to apply character formatting to selected text.

- The Font dialog box can be used to change fonts, font sizes, and font styles. The Font dialog box also has settings for underline styles, font and underline colors, effects such as small caps and shadow (see Table 3-2), and character spacing.

- A hyperlink often appears as blue underlined text you click to open a software feature (such as a dialog box or a Help topic) or to go to an e-mail or a Web address.

- Keyboard shortcuts are available for some underline styles and font effects (see Table 3-3).

- A shortcut menu shows a list of commands relevant to a particular item. To display a shortcut menu, point to the item and right-click the mouse.

- Use F4 or Ctrl+Y to repeat character formatting.

- Use the Format Painter command to copy character formatting. Double-click the button to apply formatting to more than one selection.

- To change the case of selected characters, use the keyboard shortcut Shift+F3 or the Change Case command on the Ribbon, Home tab.

- Use the Highlight command to apply a color highlight to selected text you want to emphasize on-screen.

- Use **Drop Cap** from the Insert tab to create a dropped cap. A drop cap is a large letter that appears below the text baseline. It is usually applied to the first letter in the first word of a paragraph.

- Take advantage of Word's automatic formatting of ordinal numbers and fractions as you key text. An ordinal number is a number that indicates an order (for example, 1st, 3rd, or 107th).

LESSON 3	Command Summary		
Feature	**Button**	**Command**	**Keyboard**
Bold	B	Home tab, Font group	Ctrl+B
Italic	I	Home tab, Font group	Ctrl+I
Underline	U ▾	Home tab, Font group	Ctrl+U
Remove character formatting		Home tab, Font group	Ctrl+Spacebar
Increase font size	A˄	Home tab, Font group	Ctrl+Shift+>
Decrease font size	A˅	Home tab, Font group	Ctrl+Shift+<
Change case	Aa ▾	Home tab, Font group	Shift+F3
Font color	A ▾	Home tab, Font group	
Text Highlight Color	ab/ ▾	Home tab, Font group	

Concepts Review

True/False Questions

Each of the following statements is either true or false. Indicate your choice by circling T or F.

(T) F   1. You can apply single underlining from the Ribbon.

T (F)   2. To remove character formatting, press Ctrl + Delete .

T (F)   3. The Home tab on the Ribbon is used to insert a Drop Cap.

T (F)   4. Times New Roman is an example of a sans serif font.

(T) F   5. You can use F4 to repeat text or to repeat character formatting.

(T) F   6. After clicking the Format Painter button ✐, you can press Esc to restore the normal pointer.

(T) F   7. You can use the Font dialog box to change character spacing.

(T) F   8. You must use the Font tab in the Font dialog box to apply the shadow effect.

Short Answer Questions

Write the correct answer in the space provided.

1. Which Ribbon tab contains a command to highlight text?

   _____ Home _____

2. Which dialog box do you use to choose bold-italic style?

   _____ font dialogo box. _____

3. What unit of measurement is used to measure fonts?

   _____ Points _____

4. What keyboard shortcut increases the font size of selected text?

   _____ Ctrl + > _____

5. What character effect places a horizontal line through text?

   _____ Strikethroug _____

6. Which command do you use to copy character formatting?

   _____ Format Painter. _____

7. What keyboard shortcut do you use to change the case of selected text?

Shift + F3

8. What character spacing setting inserts more space between characters?

Line break.

Critical Thinking

Answer these questions on a separate page. There are no right or wrong answers. Support your answers with examples from your own experience, if possible.

1. Select three examples of effective character formatting in magazine advertisements, articles, or other publications. Describe why you think the character formatting was particularly effective.

2. Using a large font size, key Fonts & styles 10 times on 10 separate lines (you can use the Repeat Typing command). Use a different font for each line. Describe the differences you see among the fonts.

Skills Review

Exercise 3-16

Apply basic character formatting. Change font and font size.

1. Open the file **Candy - 1**.
2. At the top of the document, press Enter. Move to the paragraph mark and key Fine Chocolates.
3. Change the font for the entire document by following these steps:
   a. Select the entire document by pressing Ctrl+A.
   b. Open the Font drop-down list on the Ribbon by clicking the down arrow.
   c. Locate and click Arial.
4. Change the first line you keyed to 16-point bold by following these steps:
   a. Select the text by moving the pointer to the left of the text. When the arrow points to the text, click the left mouse button.
   b. Choose 16 from the Font Size drop-down list on the Ribbon.
   c. Click the Bold button **B** on the Ribbon.
5. Apply italic formatting to noncontiguous text by following these steps:
   a. Move to the end of the document and press Enter.
   b. Key Call our toll-free number: 800-555-2025.
   c. Select the sentence you just keyed.

d. Press and hold ⌃Ctrl and select the text "Campbell's Confections" in the previous paragraph.

    e. Click the Italic button 🔳.

6. Key new bold text by following these steps:

    a. Move to the end of the document and place the insertion point to the immediate left of the period.

    b. Click the Italic button 🔳 to turn off italic.

    c. Click the Bold button 🔳 to turn on bold. Press the ⎵Spacebar and key **or visit our Web site at www.campbellsconfections.biz.**

    d. Turn off bold.

7. Save the document as *[your initials]*3-16 in your Lesson 3 folder.

8. Submit and close the document.

Exercise 3-17

Apply formatting options using the Font dialog box and using repeat character formatting.

1. Open the file **Easter Eggs**.

2. Apply character formatting to the first line. Use the Font dialog box and follow these steps:

    a. Select the first line. Click the selected text with the right mouse button, and choose Font from the shortcut menu.

    b. Click the Font tab, if it is not already displayed. For font, font style, and size, choose Arial, Bold, and 14 points.

    c. Apply the effect Small caps by clicking the check box.

    d. View your options in the Preview box and click OK.

3. Apply and repeat character formatting by following these steps:

    a. Select the text "Fruit and Nut:" and press ⌃Ctrl+D to open the Font dialog box.

    b. Choose the font style Bold Italic.

    c. Open the Font color drop-down list and choose Blue. Click OK.

    d. Select the text "Chocolate Nut:" and press F4. Repeat the formatting through "Chocolate Nut Fudge:"

4. Apply the strikethrough and hidden text effects from the Font dialog box by following these steps:

    a. Select the last line of text (beginning "Marshmallow:").

    b. Locate and click the Font Dialog Box Launcher icon on the Ribbon.

    c. Click the Strikethrough check box.

d. Click **OK**. Notice the strikethrough effect.

e. Open the Font dialog box by pressing Ctrl+D, and click the **Hidden** check box.

f. Click **OK**. The text appears with a dotted underline.

g. Click the Show/Hide button to hide the text and formatting characters.

5. Save the document as *[your initials]*3-17 in your Lesson 3 folder.

6. Submit your work.

Exercise 3-18

Copy character formatting and change case.

1. Open the file **WV Stores**.

2. Change the first line to read Campbell's Confections—West Virginia Retail Stores

3. At the end of the first line, press Enter and key premiere chocolates and specialty items

4. Select the first two lines of text and format them 14-point bold.

5. Use a keyboard shortcut to change the case of the first line to all uppercase by following these steps:

   a. Select the first line of text.

   b. Press Shift+F3.

6. Change the case of the second line using the Change Case dialog box by following these steps:

   a. Select the second line of text.

   b. Click the Change Case button on the Ribbon.

   c. Click Capitalize Each Word.

7. Use the Font dialog box to format the first store name, "Campbell's Confections," as bold-italic small caps.

8. Copy the character formatting to the other store names by following these steps:

   a. With the formatted text selected, double-click the Format Painter button .

   b. Drag the pointer over the next store name, "Campbell's Confections."

   c. Continue copying the formatting to the other store names. Use the scroll bar as needed. When you finish copying, click the Format Painter button to restore the normal pointer.

9. In the second line, change "and" to lowercase.

10. Save the document as *[your initials]*3-18 in your Lesson 3 folder.

11. Submit your work, and close the document.

Exercise 3-19

Highlight text, automatically format numbers, and create a dropped capital letter.

1. Start a new document by keying the text shown in Figure 3-16. Use 12-point Arial type.

Figure 3-16

> Bittersweet chocolate also known as semisweet chocolate is the darkest eating chocolate. It also has the highest percentage of chocolate liquor (unsweetened chocolate). Bittersweet chocolate usually consists of 50 percent chocolate liquor, and semi-sweet chocolate typically consists of 35 to 45 percent chocolate liquor. Both have a rich, smooth taste and are used for chocolate chips and baking.

2. Highlight part of the document by following these steps:

    a. Click the down arrow next to the Highlight button , and click the yellow highlight.

    b. Use the highlight pointer to select the text "50 percent."

    c. Press Esc to restore the normal pointer.

3. Create a dropped capital letter by following these steps:

    a. Position the insertion point at the beginning of the document.

    b. Click the **Insert** tab, and click **Drop Cap**.

    c. Click **Dropped**.

4. Remove the highlight by following these steps:

    a. Select the highlighted text "50 percent."

    b. Click the down arrow next to the Highlight button and choose **No Color**.

5. Format the first two words (beginning with "i") as 14-point bold.

6. Save the document as *[your initials]*3-19 in your Lesson 3 folder.

7. Submit and close the document.

Lesson Applications

Exercise 3-20

Apply and copy character formatting. Change font size.

1. Open the file **Milk Chocolate**.

2. Format the first line ("Milk Chocolate") to 14 points, and change the font to Impact. (If Impact is not available, choose another bold-looking font from the Font drop-down list.)

3. Select the text "10 percent" and format the text as italic. Change the font color to blue.

4. Use the Format Painter button 🖌 to apply the formatting of the text "10 percent" to "12 percent."

5. Apply the shadow and small caps effects to the first line.

6. Select "Milk chocolate" at the beginning of the descriptive paragraph under the heading. Use the Ribbon to bold the text and apply italic formatting.

7. Position the insertion point before the word "best." Press F4 to repeat the last selected character formatting (italic), key **very**, and press Spacebar.

8. Press Ctrl+End to go to the end of the document. Press Enter and key **Enjoy!**

9. Select the last line, and change the text to 12-point Times New Roman. Add red double underlining to the line, except the exclamation point.

10. Save the document as *[your initials]***3-20** in your Lesson 3 folder.

11. Submit your work, and close the document.

Exercise 3-21

Apply and copy basic character formatting. Change font size, case, and character spacing.

1. Start a new document by keying the text shown in Figure 3-17, including the corrections. Use 12-point Arial type.

Figure 3-17

A chocolate glossary is helpful to understand the differences and similarities among chocolate ingredients. Chocolate liquor is the ground up center of the roasted cocoa bean. It is the basic ingredient of chocolate cocoa products. Cocoa butter is the vegetable fat extracted during the refining process. It is the base of white chocolate. Cocoa powder is made by removing most of the cocoa butter from the chocolate liquor. The remaining solids are ground to produce unsweetened cocoa powder. There are two types of cocoa powder: Dutch-processed and natural unsweetened cocoa powder.

(editing marks: (unsweetened chocolate) inserted after "liquor"; (nibs) inserted after "center"; "and" inserted before "cocoa products"; "It is the base of white chocolate." struck out with (stet))

2. In the first line, change the case of the text "chocolate glossary" to all capitals.

3. Copy or repeat the all-capitals formatting to the following words in the paragraph: "Chocolate liquor," "Cocoa butter," and "Cocoa powder."

4. Create a new paragraph for each term, beginning with "CHOCOLATE LIQUOR." (You should have four paragraphs in the document.)

5. At the beginning of the document, insert one blank line (press Enter once). Key the title Guide to Chocolate Terminology at the paragraph mark.

6. Change the text you just keyed to bold, dark blue, and small caps in 16-point type.

7. Format the text "nibs" as italic. Repeat the italic formatting to "Dutch-processed" and "natural unsweetened cocoa powder."

8. Select all the paragraphs below the heading, and change the font size to 11 points.

9. Use the Ctrl key to select noncontiguous text, and select "CHOCOLATE GLOSSARY," "CHOCOLATE LIQUOR," "COCOA BUTTER," AND "COCOA POWDER." Change the font color to light blue.

10. Save the document named *[your initials]*3-21 in your Lesson 3 folder.

11. Submit your work, and close the document.

Exercise 3-22

Apply and copy character formatting, highlight text, and create a dropped capital letter.

1. Open the file **Favors - 2**.

2. Key the text shown in Figure 3-18 at the end of the document. The text should be the last sentence of the last paragraph.

Figure 3-18

```
For more information, call our toll-free number 800-555-2025
or visit our Web site www.campbellsconfections.biz.
```

3. Format the "C" of "Campbell's" in the first paragraph as a dropped capital letter.

4. Highlight the second paragraph (which begins "Our chocolate") in yellow.

5. Format the list of items from "wedding bells" through "other assorted shapes" as 11-point Arial italic small caps.

6. Repeat the formatting for the second list (from "solid milk chocolate" to "dark chocolate with mint filling").

7. Split the last paragraph so "For more information" starts a new paragraph.

8. Copy the formatting from one of the lists to the new last paragraph.

9. Format the phone number in the last paragraph as red, bold, and a dotted underline.

10. Remove the highlight from the second paragraph.

11. Select the first line of the document and format the text with bold, 14 points, and shadow effects.

REVIEW

You need select only one, or a portion of, the formatted words, click the Format Painter button , and then select the new paragraph.

12. Save the document as *[your initials]*3-22 in your Lesson 3 folder.

13. Submit your work, and close the document.

Exercise 3-23 ◆ Challenge Yourself

Apply character formatting, change case, and format numbers automatically.

1. Open the file **Club**.

2. Locate "CC" in the second paragraph. Select the text and apply the strikethrough format.

3. Repeat the strikethrough effect for "CC" in the next paragraph and in the last paragraph.

4. Select "Chocolate Club" in the second paragraph. Format the selected text as blue and small caps.

5. Move to the beginning of the document, and key Chocolate Club. Press Enter. Select the title and use the Ribbon to format the title as 14 points, bold, dark blue, and uppercase.

6. Select "$36." Use the Ribbon to format the text with a blue, dotted underline.

7. Copy the format applied to "$36" to "$400."

8. Select "Chocolate Club" in the second paragraph, and click the Clear Formatting button [AI] on the Ribbon.

9. Save the document as *[your initials]*3-23 in your Lesson 3 folder.

10. Submit your work, and close the document.

On Your Own

In these exercises you work on your own, as you would in a real-life business environment. Use the skills you've learned to accomplish the task—and be creative.

Exercise 3-24

Create a list of 10 companies in which you are interested. (They could be potential employers, local companies, companies that make products in which you are interested—any companies you want.) Include the companies' addresses. Apply interesting font effects to the company name. Copy and repeat the formatting to the other companies in the list. Save the document as *[your initials]*3-24 and submit it.

Exercise 3-25

Create an itinerary for a trip to visit Hershey, Pennsylvania. (Be imaginative! This could be a real trip or a fantasy trip!) To make the itinerary interesting, use as many as possible of the character formatting features you learned in this lesson. Remember, though, the itinerary must be readable. Save the document as *[your initials]*3-25 and submit it.

Exercise 3-26

Log onto the Internet and find an interesting Web site about chocolate. Summarize the information from the site in a Word document at least a half page long. Add a title to the document. Format the first paragraph with a drop cap. Format the document using the character formats presented in the lesson. Save the document as *[your initials]*3-26 and submit it.

Lesson 4

Writing tools

OBJECTIVES

MCAS OBJECTIVES

In this lesson:
WW 07 1.4.1
WW 07 1.4.2
WW 07 4.1.1
WW 07 4.1.2

After completing this lesson, you will be able to:

1. Use AutoComplete, AutoCorrect, and Smart Tags.

2. Work with Building Blocks.

3. Insert the date and time as a field.

4. Check spelling and grammar.

5. Use the Thesaurus and Research task pane.

Estimated Time: 1 hour

Word provides several automated features that save you time when keying frequently used text and correcting common keying errors. Word also provides important writing and research tools: a spelling and grammar checker, a thesaurus, and access to research services. These tools help you create professional-looking documents.

Using AutoComplete, AutoCorrect, and Smart Tags

By now, you might be familiar with three of Word's automatic features, though you might not know their formal names:

- *AutoComplete* suggests the completed word when you key the first four or more letters of a day, month, or date. If you key "Janu," for example, Word displays a ScreenTip suggesting the word "January," which you can insert by pressing Enter. Continue keying if you do not want the word inserted.

- *AutoCorrect* corrects commonly misspelled words as you key text. If you key "teh" instead of "the," for example, Word automatically changes the spelling to "the." You can create AutoCorrect entries for text you frequently use, and you can control AutoCorrect options.

- *Smart tags* help you save time by performing actions in Word for which you would normally open other programs (such as Outlook). Word recognizes names, dates, addresses, and telephone numbers, as well as user-defined data types through the use of smart tags, which appear as purple dotted lines.

Exercise 4-1 PRACTICE AUTOCOMPLETE AND AUTOCORRECT

1. Open a new document. Open the **File** menu, and click **Word Options**. Click **Proofing**, and click **AutoCorrect Options** to open the AutoCorrect dialog box. Notice the available AutoCorrect options.

2. Scroll down the list of entries and notice the words that Word corrects automatically (assuming the **Replace text as you type** option is checked).

Figure 4-1
AutoCorrect dialog box

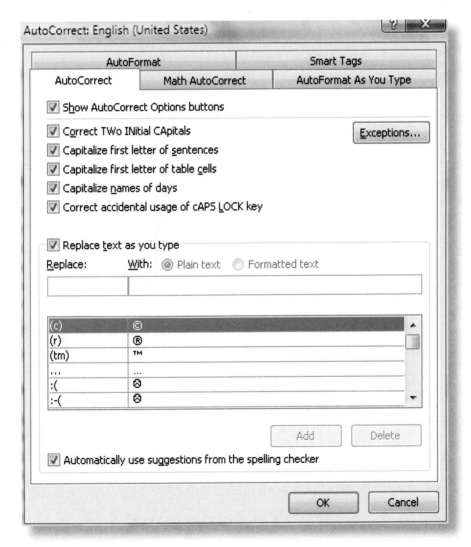

3. Click **Cancel** to close the dialog box. Click **Cancel** to close the Word Options dialog box.

4. Key **i am testing teh AutoCorrect feature.** Press [Spacebar]. Word corrects the "i" and "teh" automatically.

5. Try keying another incorrect sentence. Using the exact spelling and case as shown, key **TOdya is.** AutoCorrect corrects the spelling and capitalization of "Today."

6. Key today's date, beginning with the month, and then press [Spacebar]. When you see the AutoComplete ScreenTip that suggests the current date, press [Enter].

7. Key a period at the end of the sentence.

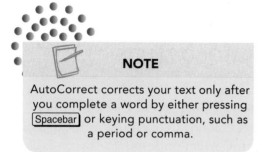

NOTE

AutoCorrect corrects your text only after you complete a word by either pressing [Spacebar] or keying punctuation, such as a period or comma.

TABLE 4-1 AutoCorrect Options

Options	Description
Correct TWo INitial Capitals	Corrects words keyed accidentally with two initial capital letters, such as "WOrd" or "THis."
Capitalize first letter of sentences	Corrects any word at the beginning of a sentence that is not keyed with a capital letter.
Capitalize first letter of table cells	Corrects any word at the beginning of a table cell that is not keyed with a capital letter.
Capitalize names of days	Corrects a day spelled without an initial capital letter.
Correct accidental usage of cAPS LOCK key	If you press [Caps Lock] accidentally and then key "tODAY," AutoCorrect changes the word to "Today" and turns off [Caps Lock].
Replace text as you type	Makes all corrections automatically.

Exercise 4-2   CREATE AN AUTOCORRECT ENTRY

You can create AutoCorrect entries for words you often misspell. You can also use AutoCorrect to create shortcuts for text you use repeatedly, such as names or phrases. Here are some examples of these types of AutoCorrect entries:

- "asap" for "as soon as possible"

- Your initials to be replaced with your full name, such as **"jh"** for **"Janet Holcomb"**

- "cc" for "Campbell's Confections"

Word 2007

1. Click the Microsoft Office Button ⊕ , and click **Word Options**. Click **Proofing**.

2. Open the AutoCorrect dialog box by clicking **AutoCorrect Options**. In the **Replace** box, key *fyi*.

3. In the **With** box, key *For your information*.

4. Click the **Add** button to move the entry into the alphabetized list. Click **OK** to close the AutoCorrect dialog box. Click **OK** to close the Word Options dialog box.

5. Start a new paragraph in the current document, and key *fyi, this really works*. Word spells out the entry, just as you specified in the AutoCorrect dialog box.

Exercise 4-3   CONTROL AUTOCORRECT OPTIONS

Sometimes you might not want text to be corrected. You can undo a correction or turn AutoCorrect options on or off by clicking the AutoCorrect Options button ⌐· and making a selection.

1. Move the I-beam over the word "For" until a small blue box appears beneath it.

Figure 4-2
Controlling
AutoCorrect options

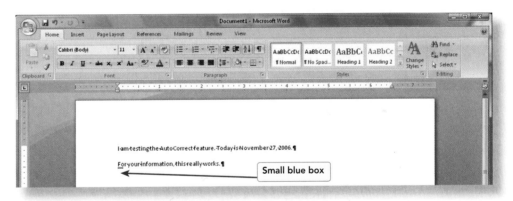

2. Drag the I-beam down over the small blue box until your mouse becomes a pointer and the box turns into the AutoCorrect Options button ⌐· .

3. Click the button and choose **Change back to "fyi"** from the menu list.

Word 2007

Figure 4-3
Undoing automatic
corrections

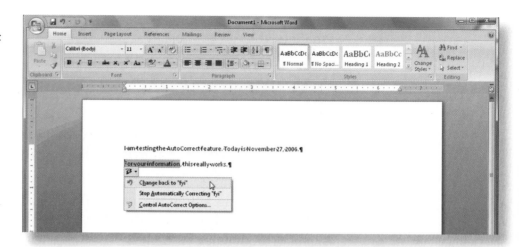

4. Click the AutoCorrect Options button 🕭▾ again, and choose **Redo AutoCorrect** from the menu list. The words "For your information" are restored.

5. Click the button again and choose **Control AutoCorrect Options**. The AutoCorrect dialog box opens.

6. Position the insertion point in the Replace text box, and key **fyi**. The AutoCorrect entry displays and is highlighted. Click **Delete**, and then click **OK**.

Exercise 4-4   CREATE AN AUTOCORRECT EXCEPTION

Another way to keep Word from correcting text you do not want corrected is to create an AutoCorrect exception. For example, you might have a company name that uses nonstandard capitalization such as "tuesday's child." In such a case, you can use the AutoCorrect Exceptions dialog box to prevent Word from making automatic changes.

1. In a new paragraph, key the following on two separate lines:
   The ABCs of chocolate:
   ABsolute is a must.

   Notice that AutoCorrect automatically makes the "B" in "ABsolute" lowercase.

2. Open the AutoCorrect dialog box and click **Exceptions**. The AutoCorrect Exceptions dialog box displays.

3. Click the **INitial CAps** tab.

4. Key the exception **ABsolute** in the **Don't Correct** text box. Click **Add.** The entry is now in the list of exceptions.

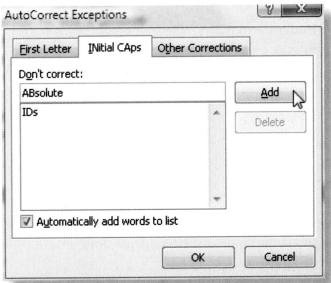

Figure 4-4
AutoCorrect
Exceptions dialog
box

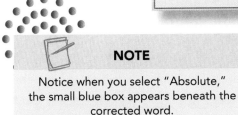

NOTE

Notice when you select "Absolute," the small blue box appears beneath the corrected word.

TIP

Another good example of an AutoCorrect exception is the use of lowercase initials, which are sometimes entered at the bottom of a business letter as reference initials (see Appendix B, "Standard Forms for Business Documents"). In this case, you would not want Word to capitalize the first letter.

5. Click **OK,** to close the AutoCorrect Exceptions dialog box, and then click **OK** again to close the AutoCorrect dialog box. Click **OK** to close the Word Options dialog box if necessary.

6. Select "Absolute" and then key **ABsolute Comfort**

7. Delete the exception: Open the AutoCorrect dialog box, click **Exceptions,** select "ABsolute" from the list, and click **Delete.** Click **OK** to close the AutoCorrect Exceptions dialog box, click **OK** to close the AutoCorrect dialog box, and then click **OK** again to close the Word Options dialog box if necessary.

Exercise 4-5 USE SMART TAGS

Just as Word recognizes an e-mail or Web address and automatically creates a hyperlink, it also recognizes names, dates, addresses, and telephone numbers, as well as user-defined data types through the use of smart tags. You can use this feature to perform actions in Word for which you would normally open other programs, such as Microsoft Outlook. Purple dotted lines beneath text in your document indicate smart tags.

1. Open the **File** menu, and click **Word Options**. Click **Proofing**, and click **AutoCorrect Options**.

2. Click the **Smart Tags** tab, and click the **Label text with smart tags** check box if it is not selected.

3. Under **Recognizers**, select **Address (English)** and **Date (Smart tag lists)**. Deselect all other **Recognizers**.

4. Click **OK** to close the AutoCorrect dialog box. Click **OK** to close the Word Options dialog box.

5. Position the insertion point at the end of the document, and press ⎆Enter twice and key:

   Campbells Confections
   25 Main Street
   Grove City, PA 16127

6. Notice that Word recognizes the text as an address and applies a smart tag indicator (the purple dotted underline).

7. Move the I-beam over the street address, and then move your pointer over the Smart Tag Actions button 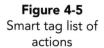.

8. Click the button to see the list of actions.

Figure 4-5
Smart tag list of actions

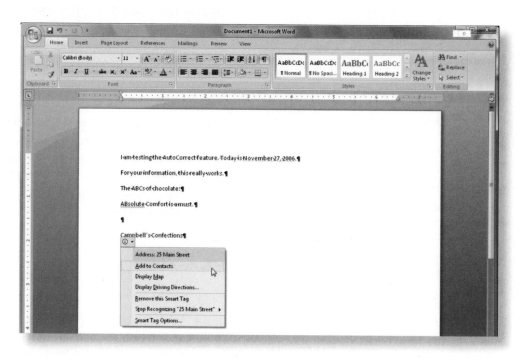

9. Choose **Add to Contacts**. Microsoft Outlook launches, and an Untitled-Contact dialog box opens. You can add the name and address as well as telephone numbers to the listing.

10. Look over the dialog box contents, and close the dialog box. Click **No** when you are asked if you want to save the changes.

11. Close the document without saving.

NOTE

Microsoft Outlook is a program included in the Microsoft Office suite. If it is not set up on your machine, just close the dialog box when it asks you to configure it, or ask your instructor for help. If Outlook does launch, the **Add to Contacts** option lets you record information about individuals and businesses. All this is done from within Word through the use of the smart tag.

Working with AutoText and Building Blocks

NOTE

You can also create AutoText entries for nontext items such as graphics and tables.

AutoText is another feature you can use to insert text automatically. This feature is extremely versatile. You can use it to create AutoText entries for text you use repeatedly (the AutoText entry can even include the text formatting). The text for which you create an AutoText entry can be a phrase, a sentence, paragraphs, logos, and so on.

After you create an entry, you can insert it with just a few keystrokes.

Exercise 4-6   **CREATE AN AUTOTEXT ENTRY**

To create an AutoText entry, you key the text that you want to save and select it, or you select text that already exists in a document. When you select the text to be used for an AutoText entry, be sure to include the appropriate spaces, blank lines, and paragraph marks.

1. Open the file **Letter - 1**.

2. Press Ctrl+A to select the document.

3. Click the **Insert tab** on the Ribbon.

4. Locate the **Text** group, and click **Quick Parts**. Click **Save Selection to Quick Part Gallery**. The Create New Building Block dialog box displays.

Figure 4-6
Quick Parts menu

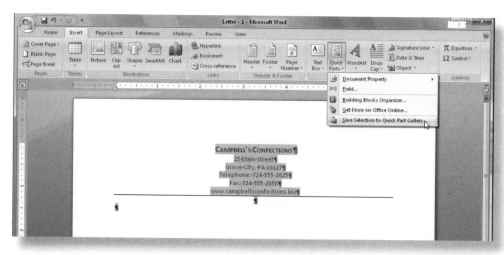

5. Key [your initials]Letterhead in the **Name** box. Each AutoText entry must have a unique name.

6. Select **AutoText** from the **Gallery** drop-down list box.

7. Select **General** from the **Category** drop-down list box.

8. Key Grove City in the **Description** text box.

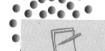

NOTE

You can choose to insert AutoText entries as a separate paragraph by choosing Insert content in its own paragraph. Choose Insert content in its own page if you want the AutoText entry to appear on a new page.

9. Select **Building Blocks** from the **Save in** drop-down list.

10. Select **Insert content only** from the Options drop-down list. Click **OK**.

11. Press Ctrl+End to move to the end of the document. Key the text in Figure 4-7.

Figure 4-7

```
Sincerely,

Thomas Campbell

President

[your initials]
```

12. Select the text you just keyed, and press Alt+F3 to open the Create New Building Block dialog box.

13. Key or select the following information in the Create New Building Block dialog box.

Name:	[your initials]Closing
Gallery:	**AutoText**
Category:	**General**
Description:	Closing
Save in:	**Building Blocks**
Options:	**Insert content only**

14. Click **OK** to close the Create New Building Block dialog box.

15. Close the document, and do not save the changes.

Exercise 4-7   INSERT AUTOTEXT ENTRIES

To insert an AutoText entry, position the insertion point and open the Building Blocks Organizer. When the Building Blocks Organizer dialog box opens, click one of the column headings to sort the lists. Click the **Name** heading to sort the text alphabetically by name. Click the **Gallery** heading to display the lists by gallery type. AutoText entries will appear at the top of the Gallery listing. If you have an AutoText entry that is unique or short, you can key the first three letters of the entry name and press F3 to insert the entry.

1. Create a new document.

2. Click the **Insert** tab and locate the **Text** group. Click **Quick Parts** and click **Building Blocks Organizer**. The Building Blocks Organizer dialog box displays.

Figure 4-8
Building Blocks
Organizer dialog box

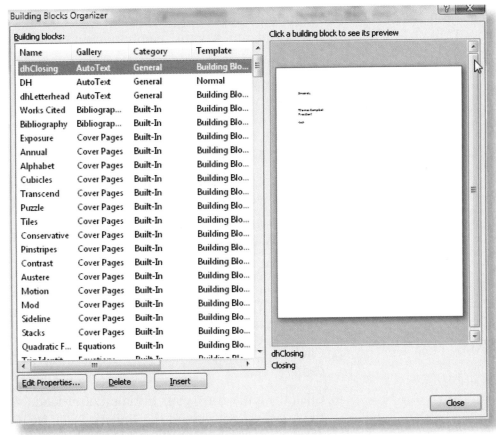

3. Click the **Gallery** heading, and the list sorts by gallery type.

4. Click the **Name** heading, and the list is sorted alphabetically by name.

5. Click the **Gallery** heading, and locate "[your initials]Letterhead" AutoText entry.

6. Click the *[your initials]***Letterhead** entry, and click **Insert**. The letterhead information is automatically inserted.

7. Click 🔄 to remove the AutoText entry.

8. Key **[your initials]Letterhead** and press [F3] to insert the Autotext entry using the keyboard shortcut.

9. Key **[your initials]Closing** and press [F3] to insert the Closing AutoText entry.

TIP

Check Appendix B, "Standard Forms for Business Documents," to double-check that your letter has the correct number of blank lines between items.

Exercise 4-8   EDIT AND DELETE AUTOTEXT ENTRIES

After you create an AutoText entry, it may need to be edited. If you no longer use an entry, you can delete it.

1. Position the insertion point to the right of "Telephone:" in the letterhead, and key the telephone number **724-555-2025**.

2. Select the letterhead text beginning with "Campbell's Confections" and ending with the left aligned paragraph mark.

3. Press [Alt]+[F3] to open the Create New Building Block dialog box.

4. Key **[your initials]Letterhead** in the **Name** box, and select **AutoText** from the **Gallery** drop-down list. Click **OK**.

5. Click **Yes** to redefine the AutoText entry. The entry now includes the telephone number.

6. To test the change, delete all the document text. Key **[your initials]Letterhead** and press [F3] to insert the letterhead AutoText.

7. Click the **Insert** tab on the Ribbon, and click the **Quick Parts** command. Click **Building Blocks Organizer** to open the Building Blocks Organizer dialog box.

8. Click the **Gallery** column heading to sort the entries in the list by Gallery type.

9. Click the entry for "[your initials]Letterhead." Click **Delete** to remove the AutoText entry from the Gallery. Click **No**. Click **Close** to return to your document.

Inserting the Date and Time

You have seen that when you begin keying a month, AutoComplete displays the suggested date, and you press [Enter] to insert the date as regular text. You can also insert the date or time in a document as a field. A *field* is a hidden code that tells Word to insert specific text that might need to be updated automatically, such as a date or page number. If you insert the date or time in a document as a field, Word automatically updates it each time you print the document.

There are two ways to insert the date or time as a field:

- Click the **Insert** tab on the Ribbon, and click the **Date and Time** command. Select the desired format from the Date and Time dialog box.

- Press [Alt]+[Shift]+[D] to insert the date, and [Alt]+[Shift]+[T] to insert the time.

Exercise 4-9   INSERT THE DATE AND TIME

You can enter date and time fields that can be updated automatically. You can also choose not to update these fields automatically.

1. Move the insertion point to the end of the current document.

2. Press [Alt]+[Shift]+[D] to enter the default date field.

3. Click the Undo button 🔄.

4. Click the **Insert** tab on the Ribbon, and click the **Date and Time** command to open the Date and Time dialog box.

Figure 4-9
Date and Time
dialog box

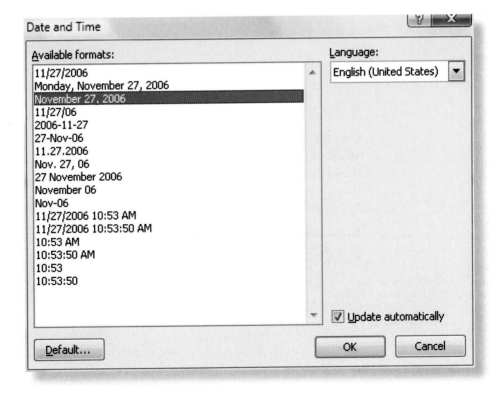

NOTE

You can also use this dialog box to insert the date and time in a particular text format without inserting it as an updatable field.

TIP

Although printing updates a field, you can also update a field on-screen by clicking the field and pressing F9.

5. Scroll the list of available time and date formats, and choose the third format in the list (the standard date format for business documents).

6. Check the **Update automatically** check box so the date is automatically updated each time you print the document. Click **OK**.

7. Move the insertion point after the date field, and press Spacebar twice.

8. Press Alt + Shift + T to insert the time as a field.

9. Save the document as *[your initials]*4-9 in your Lesson 4 folder.

10. Submit your work, and close the document.

TIP

Remember that the Update automatically option will change the date in your document. If you are sending correspondence, do not choose this option because the date in the letter will then always reflect the current date, not the date on which you wrote the letter.

Checking Spelling and Grammar

Correct spelling and grammar are essential to good writing. As you have seen, Word checks your spelling and grammar as you key text and flags errors with these on-screen indicators:

- A red, wavy line appears under misspelled words.
- A green, wavy line appears under possible grammatical errors.
- A blue, wavy line appears under possible formatting inconsistencies.
- The Proofing Errors icon on the status bar contains an "X."

TABLE 4-2 Spelling and Grammar Status

Icon	Indicates
	Word is checking for errors as you key text.
	The document has errors.
	The document has no errors.

Exercise 4-10   SPELL- AND GRAMMAR-CHECK ERRORS INDIVIDUALLY

You can right-click text marked as either a spelling or a grammar error and choose a suggested correction from a shortcut menu.

NOTE

If no green, wavy lines appear in your document, open the File menu, and click Word Options. Click Proofing in the left pane. Click the Check grammar with spelling check box, and click OK.

1. Open the file **Milk Chocolate - 2**. This document has several errors, indicated by the red and green wavy lines.

2. At the top of the document, press [Enter] and move the insertion point to the first paragraph mark. Notice that the Proofing Errors indicator on the status bar now contains an "X."

3. Using 14-point bold type, key a misspelled word by keying the title Mlk Chocolate. When you finish, "Mlk" is marked as misspelled.

TIP

Word's spelling and grammar tools are not foolproof. For example, it cannot correct a word that is correctly spelled but incorrectly keyed, such as "sue" instead of "use." It might also apply a green wavy line to a type of grammatical usage, such as the passive voice, which might not be preferred, but is not incorrect.

4. Right-click the misspelled word, and choose "Milk" from the spelling shortcut menu.

5. Right-click the grammatical error "It contain" in the second sentence. Choose "contains" from the shortcut menu.

Exercise 4-11   SPELL- AND GRAMMAR-CHECK AN ENTIRE DOCUMENT

Instead of checking words or sentences individually, you can check an entire document. This is the best way to correct spelling and grammar errors in a long document. Use one of these methods:

- Click the Spelling and Grammar button on the Review tab of the Ribbon.

- Press F7.

1. Position the insertion point at the beginning of the document and click the **Review** tab of the Ribbon. Click the Spelling and Grammar button. Word locates the first misspelling, "choclate."

Figure 4-10
Checking spelling

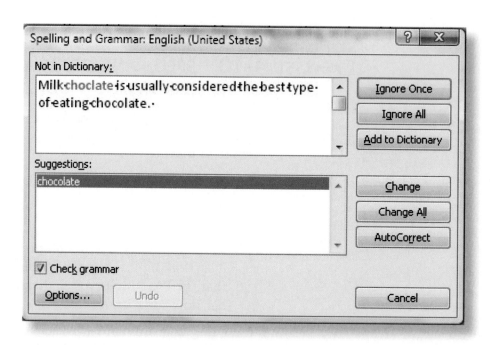

TIP

To check spelling without also checking grammar, click the **Check grammar** check box to clear it.

2. Click **Change** to correct the spelling to the first suggested spelling, "chocolate." Next, Word finds a word choice error, "hole."

3. Click **Change** to correct the word choice. Next, Word finds two words that should be separated by a space.

4. Click **Change** to correct the spacing. Next word finds a repeated word, "of."

5. Click **Delete** to delete the repeated word. Next Word finds a grammatical error—"it" is not capitalized.

6. Click **Change** to correct the capitalization in the document.

7. Click **OK** when the check is complete. Notice there are no more wavy lines in the document, and the Proofing Errors indicator shows a check mark.

8. Read the paragraph, and check for errors that were not found by the Spelling & Grammar checker.

9. Locate "10 per cent" in the second sentence. Delete the space between "per" and "cent."

10. Locate the sentence that begins "It is mild," and change "type" to "**types.**"

11. Locate the sentence that begins "It used," and change it to read "**It is used.**"

TABLE 4-3 Dialog Box Options When Checking Spelling and Grammar

Option	Description
Ignore Once	Skips the word.
Ignore All	Skips all occurrences of the word in the document.
Add to Dictionary	Adds the word to the default dictionary file in Word. You can also create your own dictionary and add words to it.
Change	Changes the word to the entry in the **Change To** box or to the word you chose from the **Suggestions** list.
Change All	Same as **Change**, but changes the word throughout the document.
AutoCorrect	Adds the word to the list of corrections Word makes automatically.
Options	Lets you change the Spelling and Grammar options in Word.
Undo	Changes back the most recent correction made.
Cancel	Discontinues the checking operation.

NOTE

You can create or add a custom dictionary for technical and specialized vocabulary. Open the **File** menu, click **Word Options**, and click **Proofing**. Click **Custom Dictionaries**, click **New**, and key a name for the custom dictionary. To add a custom dictionary that you purchased, follow the steps listed above, except choose Add instead of New. Locate the folder and double-click the dictionary file.

Using the Thesaurus and Research Task Pane

The *thesaurus* is a tool that can improve your writing. Use the thesaurus to look up a *synonym* (a word with a similar meaning) for a selected word to add variety or interest to a document. You can look up synonyms for any of these words to get additional word choices. The thesaurus sometimes displays *antonyms* (words with the opposite meaning) and related words.

After selecting a word to change, you can start the thesaurus in one of three ways:

- Click the **Review** tab, and click **Thesaurus**.
- Press 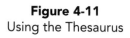 Shift + F7 .
- Right-click the word and choose **Synonyms** from the shortcut menu.

Exercise 4-12   USE THE THESAURUS

1. Select the word "best" in the first paragraph, or place the insertion point in the word.

2. Press Shift + F7 . The Research task pane appears with a list of synonyms for "best."

Figure 4-11
Using the Thesaurus

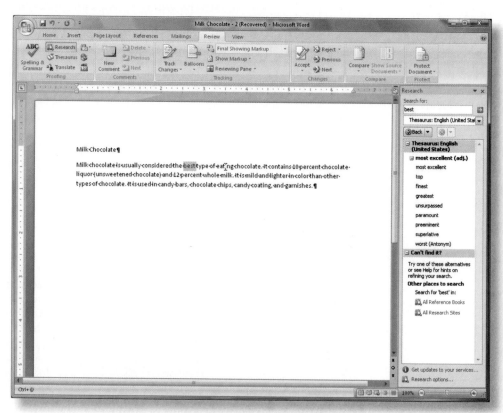

3. Point to the word "finest" and click the drop-down arrow. Click **Look Up**. A list of additional synonyms appears for "finest" in the task pane.

4. Go back to the word "finest" by clicking the Previous Search button 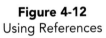 .

5. Point to "finest," click the down arrow, and choose **Insert**. Word replaces "best" with "finest" and returns to the document.

6. Save the document as *[your initials]*4-12 in your Lesson 4 folder.

7. Submit the document, but do not close it.

Exercise 4-13   USE REFERENCES

If you are connected to the Internet, you can access several research sources, such as a dictionary, an encyclopedia, and research sites such as MSN. From the Review tab on the Ribbon, you can click the Research button 📖 Research ; right-click a word and click **Look Up** in the shortcut menu; or press Alt and click a word to open the Research task pane.

1. Press Alt and click the word "chocolate" in the first sentence.

Figure 4-12
Using References

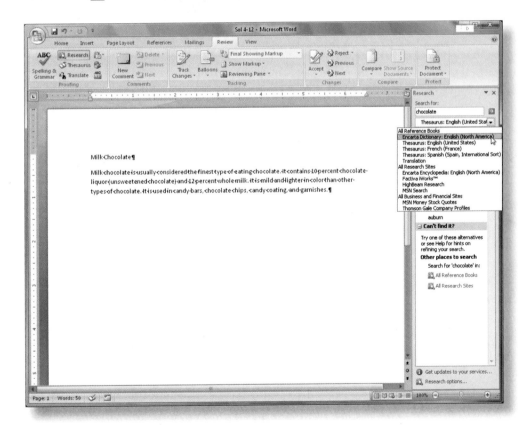

NOTE

Click Research options at the bottom of the Research task pane to open the Research Options dialog box.

TIP

Click the Translation Tool Tip button on the Ribbon to turn on or turn off a translation ScreenTip. Select a language to turn on the Translation ScreenTip. Click **Turn Off Translation ScreenTip** to turn off the ScreenTip.

2. Click the drop-down arrow beside the All Reference Books box and choose *Encarta Dictionary*. The task pane indicates the part of speech, syllabication, and several definitions for "chocolate."

3. Click the drop-down arrow beside the All Reference Books box, and choose Translation.

4. Choose **English** in the From box and **French (France)** in the To box. The bilingual dictionary displays the French word for chocolate—chocolat.

5. Close the document.

Lesson 4 Summary

- The AutoComplete feature suggests the completed word when you key the first four or more letters of a day, month, or date.

- The AutoCorrect feature corrects some misspelled words and capitalization errors for you automatically as you key text.

- Use the AutoCorrect dialog box to create entries for words you often misspell and the AutoCorrect Options button to control AutoCorrect options.

- Use the AutoCorrect Exceptions dialog box to create an AutoCorrect exception so Word will not correct it.

- Use smart tags to perform Microsoft Outlook functions, such as creating entries in Outlook's contact list.

- AutoText is another versatile feature you can use to insert text automatically. You create AutoText entries for text you use repeatedly, including text formatting.

- Use the Building Blocks Organizer to edit and delete AutoText entries.

- Insert the date and time in a document as an automatically updated field, which is a hidden code that tells Word to insert specific information—in this case, the date and/or time. Use the Date and Time dialog box to choose different date and time formats.

- Use the spelling and grammar checker to correct misspelled words in your document as well as poor grammar usage. Check errors individually or throughout your entire document.

- Use the thesaurus to look up synonyms (words with similar meaning) or sometimes antonyms (words with the opposite meaning) for a selected word to add variety and interest to your document.
- Use the Research task pane to look up words or phrases in a dictionary, to research topics in an encyclopedia, or to access bilingual dictionaries for translations. You can also access research sites such as MSN.

LESSON 4		Command Summary	
Feature	Button	Command	Keyboard
Create AutoText entry	Quick Parts	Insert tab, Text group, Quick Parts, Save Selection to Quick Part Gallery	Alt + F3
Insert Date	Date & Time	Insert tab, Text group, Date & Time	Alt + Shift + D
Insert Time	Date & Time	Insert tab, Text group, Date & Time	Alt + Shift + T
Check spelling and grammar	ABC Spelling & Grammar	Review tab, Proofing group, Spelling & Grammar	F7
Thesaurus	Thesaurus	Review tab, Proofing group, Thesaurus	Shift + F7
Research	Research	Review tab, Proofing group, Research	Alt + Click

Concepts Review

True/False Questions

Each of the following statements is either true or false. Indicate your choice by circling T or F.

(T) F   1. AutoCorrect automatically changes "THis" to "This" and "monday" to "Monday."

(T) F   2. You can edit an AutoText entry by redefining an existing AutoText entry.

T (F)   3. You can start a grammar check from the Home tab.

T (F)   4. To start the thesaurus, press [F7].

(T) F   5. The thesaurus finds synonyms for words.

(T) F   6. AutoComplete suggests a complete word or phrase for a date or an AutoText entry.

T (F)   7. You can choose to check only the spelling of a document, without checking the grammar.

T (F)   8. You can insert a date automatically by pressing [Ctrl]+[D].

Short Answer Questions

Write the correct answer in the space provided.

1. Which function key starts a spell check?

   _____ F7 _____

2. Which option in the Spelling and Grammar dialog box lets you skip over an incorrectly spelled word?

   _____ Ignore Once _____

3. Which dialog box is used to display and delete AutoText entries?

   _____ Building blocks Organizer _____

4. When you click **Quick Parts** on the Ribbon, which option do you click to create an AutoText entry?

   _____ Save Selection to Quick Part Gallery _____

5. Which tab on the Ribbon lists the Date and Time command?

   _____ Insert _____

6. Which Word feature corrects accidental usage of Caps Lock?

Autocorrect

7. Which task pane is used to access references such as dictionaries and encyclopedias?

research

8. What must you do to a word before using the thesaurus?

Select it.

Critical Thinking

Answer these questions on a separate page. There are no right or wrong answers. Support your answers with examples from your own experience, if possible.

1. Some educators believe the spell-checking feature in word processing programs will lead to decreased spelling skills in future generations. Do you think students' spelling skills will deteriorate? Explain your answer.

2. Key a sample of your writing that is at least one full page. Grammar-check the text. Did you find the analysis helpful? What are the advantages and disadvantages of using this tool?

Skills Review

Exercise 4-14

Use AutoCorrect and AutoComplete.

1. Start a new document.
2. Key the following sentence (including the errors in the first word):

   PEopel visiting western Pennsylvania enjoy its low humidity, blue skies, and rolling hills.
3. Press Caps Lock and key these sentences as shown. Be sure to press Shift to capitalize the first word in each sentence.

   The average high temperature is 60 degrees. The average low temperature is 35 degrees.
4. Continue the paragraph by keying the following sentence in all lowercase letters, letting AutoCorrect capitalize the first letter of each sentence. When you see the AutoComplete tip for the months, press Enter and continue keying.

   from january through december, you can find a wide variety of indoor and outdoor events and activities.

5. Start a new paragraph. Key the following sentence (including the errors in the first two words)

   thisyear, consider western Pennsylvania as a vacation destination.

6. Save the document as *[your initials]*4-14 in your Lesson 4 folder.

7. Submit your work, and close the document.

Exercise 4-15

Use AutoText and work with smart tags.

1. Open the file **Letter - 2**. Replace [Date] with the current date.

2. Select only the words "Campbell's Confections" in the letterhead of the document. (Do not select the space character or the paragraph mark.)

3. Using the text you just selected, create an AutoText entry by following these steps:

   a. Click the **Insert** tab on the Ribbon, and click **Quick Parts**.

   b. Click **Save Selection to Quick Part Gallery**.

   c. Key the AutoText entry name [your initials].

   d. Select AutoText in the Gallery drop-down list.

   e. Click **OK**.

4. Change the formatting for the entire letterhead to small caps, dark blue, and regular text (no italic). Select the first line and change the font size to 14.

5. At the second blank paragraph mark below "Dear Mr. Matthews," key the following sentence, substituting your AutoText entry "[your initials]" where indicated in the paragraph. After you key "[your initials]," press F3 to insert the AutoText entry.

   Thank you for your interest in *[your initials]*, western Pennsylvania's most popular chocolate factory and candy store.

6. Press Enter twice to start a new paragraph.

7. Click the **Insert** tab on the Ribbon. Click **Quick Parts**, and click **Building Blocks Organizer**.

8. Click the **Gallery** column heading to sort the list. Locate and click [your initials] to select the AutoText entry. Click **Insert**.

9. Complete the sentence by keying the following text:

   is your full-service candy store, offering the greatest selections of milk, dark, white, and sugar-free chocolates. We also create specialty chocolates with logos, monograms, or custom artwork.

10. Start a new paragraph and key the following text. Use either of the previous two methods to insert your AutoText entry in place of "[your initials]."

    The enclosed brochures will provide more information about [your initials]. We look forward to helping you place your next order.

11. Press Enter twice and key **Sincerely yours,**.

12. Press Enter four times and key the following information:

    Lydia Hamrick

    Customer Service

13. Press Enter twice, key **[your initials]** in lowercase, and press Enter.

14. Control the AutoCorrect function with the AutoCorrect Options button by following these steps:

    a. Move the I-beam over your first initial until you see the small blue box.

    b. Move the pointer to the small blue box until the AutoCorrect Options button appears.

    c. Click the button icon and choose **Undo Automatic Capitalization**.

15. On the line below your initials, key **Enclosures (2)**

16. Delete the AutoText entry by following these steps:

    a. Click the **Insert** tab on the Ribbon, and click **Quick Parts**. Click **Building Blocks Organizer**.

    b. Select your AutoText entry, *[your initials],* from the list.

    c. Click **Delete** and click **Yes**. Click **Close**.

17. Work with smart tags by following these steps:

    a. Move the I-beam over the street address "Main Street," and then move your pointer over the Smart Tag Actions button.

    b. Click the button to see the list of actions.

    c. Click **Add to Contacts**.

    d. Review the content of the Contact tab and close the window.

    e. Click **No** when you are asked if you want to save the changes.

18. Format all occurrences of Campbell's Confections in the body of the letter using italic, small caps, and dark blue font color.

19. Save the document as *[your initials]***4-15** in your Lesson 4 folder.

20. Submit and close the document.

Exercise 4-16

Spell-check and grammar-check a document.

1. Open the file **Favors - 3**.

2. Spell-check and grammar-check the document by following these steps:

   a. Click the **Review** tab on the Ribbon.

   b. Click the Spelling and Grammar button.

   c. When Word locates the first misspelled word, choose **Campbell's** from the **Suggestions** list and click **Change**. Next Word finds a misspelling, "ocasions." Click **Change**.

   d. When Word locates "sugarfree" as an error, click in the **Not in Dictionary** section of the Spelling & Grammar dialog box. Key a hyphen after the "r" and click **Change**.

   e. Correct the spelling of "wraped," "ribbon," and "minature." When Word locates "ment" as an error, click in the **Not in Dictionary** section, and press [Backspace] to delete the extra space and to form the word "assortment." Click **Change**.

   f. When Word locates "carmel" as an error, edit the text to read "caramel." Click **Change**.

   g. Continue checking the document, changing spelling, deleting words, or correcting grammar as appropriate.

3. Select the title, and change the font size to 14 and the font color to dark blue.

4. Save the document as *[your initials]*4-16 in your Lesson 4 folder.

5. Print and close the document.

Exercise 4-17

Use the thesaurus.

1. Open the file **Summer**.

2. Use the thesaurus to find another word for "wonderful" by following these steps:

   a. Select "wonderful" in the last sentence of the first paragraph.

   b. Press [Shift]+[F7].

   c. Point to a synonym, and click the drop-down arrow to the right of the word.

   d. Choose **Insert** from the drop-down list.

   e. Close the Research task pane by clicking the Research task pane Close button.

3. Start a new paragraph at the end of the document and key Come and enjoy the fun!

4. Select the word "fun."

5. Click the Review tab on the Ribbon. Click the Thesaurus button 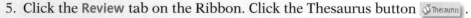 .

6. Replace "fun" with a noun listed in the Research task pane. Remember to click the down arrow and choose Insert.

7. Save the document as *[your initials]***4-17** in your Lesson 4 folder.

8. Use the Research task pane to define a word by following these steps:

   a. Press Alt and click "ethnic" in the first paragraph.

   b. Choose the *Encarta Dictionary* from the All Reference Books drop-down list.

   c. Read the definition.

   d. Close the task pane.

9. Submit your work, and close the document.

Lesson Applications

Exercise 4-18

Create an AutoText entry and check grammar and spelling.

1. Create a new document, and key the text Campbell's Confections and press Enter.

2. Select the text and the paragraph marks and format them as 12-point Arial.

3. Select the text "Campbell's Confections" (excluding the paragraph marks), and create an AutoText entry named *[your initials]*.

4. Go to the end of the document, and key the text shown in Figure 4-13. Include the corrections. Wherever "[your initials]" appears, key the name of the AutoText entry you just created, pressing F3 to expand the entry.

Figure 4-13

The best hand made chocolate candy in Western Pennsylvania is made by
<your initials>cc. The family owned business opened its first store in
1957. The ~~retail~~ *chocolate* store is located on Main ST grove city Pennsylvania, and *east*
the factory is two blocks away on Monroe Street.

<your initials>cc specialize *s* in assorted chocolate covered nuts, creams,
melt-a-ways, and truffles. You can also buy several varieties of hard *candies* and
soft candies. <your initials>cc takes pride in using the finest ingredients in *family*
its recipes.

<your initials>cc is open 6 days a week. In addition to buying your candy
at the store, you can call our toll free number at 800-555-2025, or visit our
Web site at www.campbellsconfections.biz.

5. Spell-check and grammar-check the document.

6. Format the title as 16-point bold, small caps with a text shadow.

REVIEW

Use the Repeat command F4 to format the name.

7. Format Campbell's Confections in small caps throughout the document.

8. Delete the AutoText entry you created.

9. Save the document as *[your initials]*4-18 in your Lesson 4 folder.

10. Submit your work, and close the document.

Exercise 4-19

Spell-check and grammar-check a document and use the Research task pane.

1. Open the file **Fountain - 2**.

2. Spell-check and grammar-check the document, making the appropriate corrections.

3. Proofread the document to ensure the document does not contain errors.

4. Use the thesaurus to look up the word "finest" in the second sentence of the paragraph that begins "Campbell's Confections."

5. Change the first line of the document to title case.

6. Format the title as 14-point bold, small caps with expanded character spacing.

7. Save the document as *[your initials]***4-19** in your Lesson 4 folder.

8. Submit and close the document.

Exercise 4-20

Format a document as a letter, check spelling and grammar, and use the thesaurus.

1. Open the document **Letter - 3**.

2. Position the insertion point on the second blank paragraph mark after the letterhead text.

3. Click the Insert tab, and click the Date and Time command. Click the third format in the Date and Time dialog box.

4. Press Enter four times, and key the text in Figure 4-14. Include one blank line after the address and the salutation. (Refer to Appendix B, "Standard Forms for Business Documents," for correct letter format.)

Figure 4-14

```
Mr. George Henderson

3850 Fifth Avenue

Altoona, PA 16602

Dear Mr. Henderson:
```

5. At the end of the document, press [Enter] twice. Key the closing Sincerely, and press [Enter] four times. Key Lydia Hamrick, and press [Enter]. On the next line, key Customer Service. Press [Enter] twice, and key your initials in lowercase. Press [Enter] and key Enclosure.

6. Use the AutoCorrect Options button 🔳 to undo the capitalization of your first initial.

7. Check the spelling and grammar of the document, making the appropriate corrections.

8. Use the thesaurus to find a synonym for "delighted" in the first sentence of the document.

9. Save the document as *[your initials]*4-20 in your Lesson 4 folder.

10. Submit and close the document.

Exercise 4-21 ◆ Challenge Yourself

Create an AutoText entry and check the grammar and spelling of a document.

1. Open the file **WV Stores**.

2. Select the complete address and contact information for the Clarksburg store, and create an AutoText entry named *[your initials]*clark.

3. Close the document and open the file **Refer**.

4. Place the insertion point on the second paragraph mark after the letterhead text, and insert the date using the Ribbon. Use appropriate format for a business letter.

5. Press [Enter] four times and key the inside address listed in Figure 4-15.

Figure 4-15

```
Ms. Jill Gresh

360 Lincoln Street

Grafton, WV 26354
```

6. Press [Enter] twice, and key Dear Ms. Gresh:.

7. Verify that there is one blank line between the inside address and the salutation and one blank line between the salutation and the first paragraph.

8. Position the insertion point at the beginning of the paragraph that begins "Please let."

9. Key [your initials]clark, and press [F3] to expand the Autotext entry. Press [Enter] if necessary to insert a blank line.

10. Spell- and grammar-check from the beginning of the document.

11. Delete the AutoText entry "*[your initials]*clark."

12. Save the document as *[your initials]*4-21 in your Lesson 4 folder.

13. Submit your work, and close the document.

On Your Own

In these exercises you work on your own, as you would in a real-life business environment. Use the skills you've learned to accomplish the task—and be creative.

Exercise 4-22

Write a summary about a book you have recently read, but before you start the summary, create an AutoCorrect entry for a word you know you often misspell. Use this word in the summary as often as you can. Delete the entry when you have finished. Spell- and grammar-check your document. Format the document, save it as *[your initials]*4-22, and submit it.

Exercise 4-23

Create a blank document, and create an AutoText to be used as a salutation in a letter. Create an AutoText entry to include a complimentary closing and signature line. Delete the text from the document, and write a letter to a friend. Insert the date using the Date and Time feature on the Insert tab of the Ribbon. Key your friend's inside address, and insert the AutoText entry you created for the salutation. Key the body of the letter, and insert the AutoText entry you created for the closing. Delete the AutoText entry when you have finished. Spell- and grammar-check your document. Format the document using correct business letter format. Save the document as *[your initials]*4-23, and submit your work.

Exercise 4-24

Log onto the Internet, and find a Web site about one of your hobbies or interests. Summarize the information from the site in a Word document. Add a title to the document and apply basic character formatting. Use the thesaurus to insert synonyms. Spell- and grammar-check the document. Proofread and apply additional formatting to create an attractive document. Save the document as *[your initials]*4-24, and submit your work.

Unit 1 Applications

Unit Application 1-1

Edit, spell-check, use the thesaurus, and apply formatting to a document.

1. Open the file **Chocolate**.

2. Format the entire document as 12-point Times New Roman.

3. Merge the first and second paragraphs.

4. Move to the top of the document, and key Types of Chocolate. Press Enter.

5. Format the title as 14-point bold, small caps, and brown font color.

6. Format the first paragraph with a dropped capital letter that drops three lines and is .1 inch from the text.

7. Spell-check and grammar-check the document. Ignore proper names.

8. In the first paragraph, use the thesaurus to choose a synonym for the word "type" in the last sentence.

9. Use noncontiguous text selection to format the names "Milk chocolate" in the second paragraph and "white chocolate" in the fifth paragraph as follows:

   - Small caps

   - Bold

   - Italic

   - Expanded character spacing

10. Copy the formatting to the remaining chocolate names: "Bittersweet chocolate" in the second paragraph, "semi-sweet chocolate" in the third paragraph, "Sweet or dark chocolate" in the fourth paragraph, and "Baking chocolate" in the last paragraph.

11. Save the document as *[your initials]***u1-1** in a new Unit 1 Applications folder.

12. Submit and close the document.

Unit Application 1-2

Create AutoText entries, use AutoComplete format, spell-check, and grammar-check a document.

1. Open the file **Form Letter Paragraphs**.

2. Select the letterhead information and one blank line below it, and create an AutoText entry named [your initials]gcletterhead.

3. Select the first paragraph, and create an AutoText entry named **[your initials]factorytour**. Remember to select the blank line following the paragraph.

4. Select each of the remaining paragraphs and create an AutoText entry using the naming pattern listed below.

Second paragraph beginning "Factory tours"	**[your initials]tourinfo**
Third paragraph beginning "We welcome"	**[your initials]size**
Fourth paragraph beginning "Call us"	**[your initials]call**
Fifth paragraph beginning "Enclosed"	**[your initials]brochure**
Sixth paragraph ending with "summer"	**[your initials]summer**
Seventh paragraph ending with "fall"	**[your initials]fall**
Eighth paragraph ending with "spring"	**[your initials]spring**
Ninth paragraph ending with "winter"	**[your initials]winter**
Remainder of document (closing)	**[your initials]closing**

5. Close the document without saving.

6. Start a new document. Insert the AutoText entry "**[your initials]gcletterhead.**"

7. Insert the date using the Date and Time dialog box and selecting the third format. Press Enter two times.

8. Address the letter as shown in Figure U1-1.

Figure U1-1

```
Ms. Margo Taylor

1660 North 13 Street

Reading, PA 19604

Dear Ms. Taylor:
```

9. For the body of the letter, insert the following AutoText entries. Insert in the order listed.

- *[your initials]***Factorytour**
- *[your initials]***Tourinfo**
- *[your initials]***Brochure**
- *[your initials]***Spring**
- *[your initials]***Closing**

10. Key your reference initials at the end of the document. Press Enter and key **Enclosure**. Control the capitalization of the first initial of your reference initials by using AutoCorrect Options.

11. Refer to Appendix B, "Standard Forms for Business Documents," to check your line spacing.

12. Insert nonbreaking spaces wherever a number appears at the end of a line.

13. Spell-check and grammar-check the document.

14. Delete the AutoText entries you created.

15. Save the document as *[your initials]***u1-2** in your Unit 1 Applications folder.

16. Submit and close the document.

Unit Application 1-3

Compose a document, apply formatting, and check grammar and spelling.

1. Start a new document.

2. Refer to Figure U1-2 to create a document describing the items listed in the table.

3. Format the title attractively using the Font dialog box.

4. Format the paragraph text attractively selecting an appropriate font, font size, and font effects.

Figure U1-2

Campbell's Confections—Product Listing			
Description	Choices	Weight	Price
Chocolate-covered nuts	Almond, Brazil, cashew, filbert, pecan	1 lb. Box 2 lb. Box	$12.95 $25.90
Chocolate-covered creams	Vanilla, chocolate, strawberry, butter, cherry, coconut, coffee, maple, orange, pineapple, raspberry, strawberry	1 lb. 2 lb.	$10.50 $21.00
Turtles	Pecan, cashew, peanut	1 lb. 2 lb.	$12.95 $25.90
Assortment—Chocolate-covered nuts and creams	See choices listed above.	1 lb. 2 lb.	$11.75 $23.50

5. Change the case of the title to all capitals.

6. Insert nonbreaking spaces in the document, if they are needed.

7. Spell-check and grammar-check the document.

8. Save the document as *[your initials]*u1-3 in your Unit 1 Applications folder.

9. Submit and close the document.

Unit Application 1-4 ◆ Using the Internet

Apply character formatting, use AutoFormat features, and check grammar and spelling.

1. Using the Internet, create a list of five organizations. Be creative. The organizations could be:

   • Companies where you would like to work

   • Schools you would be interested in attending

   • Associations related to your hobbies or interests

2. Include the organization's name and its Web site address.

3. Include any e-mail address, the physical address, and the telephone and fax numbers.

4. Allow AutoFormat to format the Web addresses and e-mail addresses as hyperlinks.

5. Create a title for the document, followed by a descriptive paragraph that describes the content of the list.

6. Apply appropriate formatting.

7. Check spelling and grammar, watching carefully as Word's spelling and grammar checker moves through the addresses.

8. Save the document named *[your initials]*u1-4 in your Unit 1 Applications folder.

9. Submit the document.

unit 2

PARAGRAPH FORMATTING, TABS, AND ADVANCED EDITING

Formatting Paragraphs

OBJECTIVES

After completing this lesson, you will be able to:

1. Align paragraphs.

2. Change line spacing.

3. Change paragraph spacing.

4. Set paragraph indents.

5. Apply borders and shading.

6. Repeat and copy paragraph formats.

7. Create bulleted and numbered lists.

8. Insert symbols and special characters.

MCAS OBJECTIVES

In this lesson:
WW 07 1.1.5
WW 07 2.1.4
WW 07 4.2.2
WW 07 4.2.3
WW 07 4.2.1

Estimated Time: 1¹/₂ hours

In Microsoft Word, a *paragraph* is a unique block of information. Paragraph formatting controls the appearance of individual paragraphs within a document. For example, you can change the space between paragraphs or change the space between lines. For emphasis, you can indent paragraphs, number them, or add borders and shading.

A paragraph is always followed by a *paragraph mark*. All the formatting for a paragraph is stored in the paragraph mark. Each time you press Enter, you copy the formatting instructions in the current paragraph to a new paragraph. You can copy paragraph formats to existing paragraphs and view formats in the Reveal Formatting task pane.

Paragraph Alignment

Paragraph alignment determines how the edges of a paragraph appear horizontally. There are four ways to align text in a paragraph, as shown in Figure 5-1.

Figure 5-1
Paragraph alignment
options

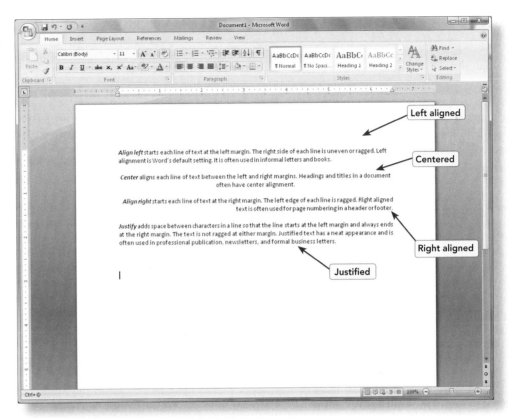

Exercise 5-1   CHANGE PARAGRAPH ALIGNMENT

The easiest way to change paragraph alignment is to use the alignment buttons on the Ribbon, Home tab, Paragraph group. You can also use keyboard shortcuts: Ctrl+L left align; Ctrl+E center; Ctrl+R right align; Ctrl+J justify.

Figure 5-2
Alignment buttons
on the Ribbon

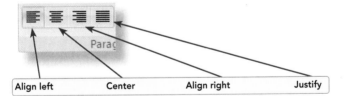

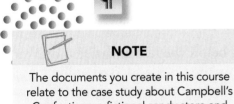

NOTE

The documents you create in this course relate to the case study about Campbell's Confections, a fictional candy store and chocolate factory (see Case Study in the frontmatter of the book).

1. Open the file **Corporate Gifts**. Click the Show/Hide ¶ button ¶ to display paragraph marks if they are turned off.

2. Position the insertion point anywhere in the first paragraph.

3. Click the Center button on the Ribbon (Home tab, Paragraph group) to center the paragraph.

4. Continue to change the paragraph's formatting by clicking the Align Right button ▤, the Justify button ▤, and the Align Left button ▤. Notice how the lines of text are repositioned with each change.

5. Position the insertion point in the second paragraph and press Ctrl+E to center the paragraph.

6. Use the keyboard shortcut Ctrl+R to right-align the third paragraph.

7. Press Ctrl+J to justify the fourth paragraph.

NOTE

When applying paragraph formatting, you do not have to select the paragraph—you just need to have the insertion point within the paragraph or just before the paragraph mark.

REVIEW

If you do not see one of the alignment buttons, check the Ribbon to verify that the Home tab is active.

TIP

To change the alignment of multiple paragraphs, select them, and then apply the alignment.

Exercise 5-2   USE CLICK AND TYPE TO INSERT TEXT

You can use *Click and Type* to insert text or graphics in any blank area of a document. This feature enables you to position the insertion point anywhere in the document without pressing Enter repeatedly. Word automatically inserts the paragraph marks before that point and also inserts a tab.

1. Open the file **Factory**, and leave the Corporate Gifts document open.

2. Click the **Microsoft Office Button** and click **Word Options**. Click **Advanced** in the left pane, and click **Enable click and type** if it is not already selected. Click **OK**.

3. Press Ctrl+End to move to the end of the document.

4. Position the I-beam about five lines below the last line of text, in the center of the page. The I-beam is now the Click and Type pointer ⌶, which includes tiny lines that show right or center alignment.

Figure 5-3
Using Click and Type

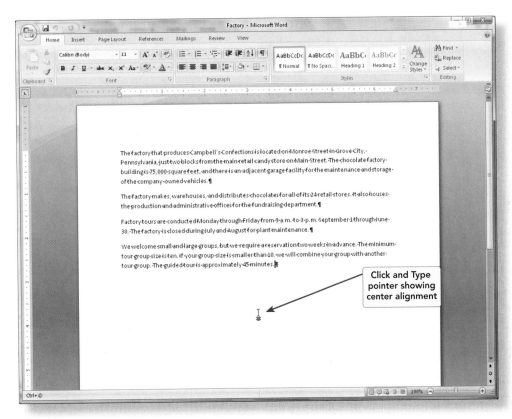

5. Move the I-beam back and forth until it shows center alignment. Double-click, and key **Visit us at www.campbellsconfections.biz**. The text is centered, and paragraph marks are inserted before it.

6. Save the document as ***[your initials]*5-2** in your Lesson 5 folder.

7. Submit your work, and close the document.

Line Spacing

Line space is the amount of vertical space between lines of text in a paragraph. Line spacing is typically based on the height of the characters, but you can change it to a specific value. For example, some paragraphs might be single-spaced and some double-spaced. The default line spacing is Multiple 1.15.

Exercise 5-3 CHANGE LINE SPACING

You can apply the most common types of line spacing by using keyboard shortcuts: single space, Ctrl+1; 1.5-line space, Ctrl+5; double space, Ctrl+2. Additional spacing options, as well as other paragraph formatting options, are available in the Paragraph dialog box or from the Line Spacing button .

1. Position the insertion point in the first paragraph of the Corporate Gifts document.

2. Press ⌈Ctrl⌋+⌈2⌋ to double-space the paragraph.

3. With the insertion point in the same paragraph, press ⌈Ctrl⌋+⌈5⌋ to change the spacing to 1.5 lines. Press ⌈Ctrl⌋+⌈1⌋ to restore the paragraph to single spacing.

4. With the insertion point in the same paragraph, click the down arrow to the right of the Line Spacing button 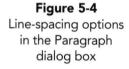 on the Ribbon, Home tab, Paragraph group, and choose **2.0** to change the line spacing to double. Choose **1.0** to restore the paragraph to single spacing.

5. Right-click the first paragraph and choose **Paragraph** from the shortcut menu. (You can also open the Paragraph dialog box by clicking the **Dialog Box Launcher** in the right corner of the Paragraph group.)

6. Click the down arrow to open the **Line spacing** drop-down list, and choose **Double**. The change is reflected in the **Preview** box.

Figure 5-4
Line-spacing options
in the Paragraph
dialog box

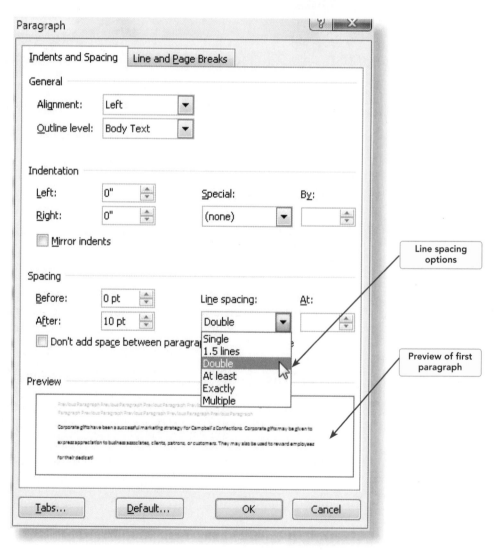

7. With the dialog box still open, choose **Single** from the **Line spacing** drop-down list. The **Preview** box shows the change.

8. Choose **Multiple** from the **Line spacing** drop-down list. In the **At** box, key **1.25**. (Select the text that appears in the box and key over it.) Press Tab to see the change displayed in the **Preview** box.

9. Click **OK**. Word adds an extra quarter-line space between lines in the paragraph.

Figure 5-5
Examples of line spacing

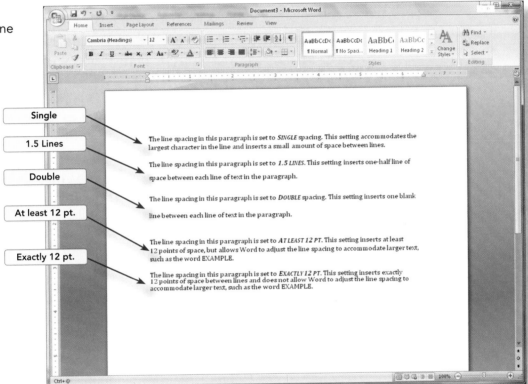

NOTE

The **At Least** option applies minimum line spacing that Word can adjust to accommodate larger font sizes. The **Exactly** option applies fixed line spacing that Word does not adjust. This option makes all lines evenly spaced. The **Multiple** option increases or decreases line spacing by the percentage you specify. For example, setting line spacing to a multiple of 1.25 increases the space by 25 percent, and setting line spacing to a multiple of 0.8 decreases the space by 20 percent.

Paragraph Spacing

In addition to changing spacing between lines of text, you can change *paragraph space*. Paragraph space is the amount of space above or below a paragraph. Instead of pressing Enter multiple times to increase space between paragraphs, you can use the Paragraph dialog box to set a specific amount of space before or after paragraphs.

Paragraph spacing is set in points. If a document has 12-point text, one line space equals 12 points. Likewise, one-half line space equals 6 points, and two line spaces equal 24 points. By default, **Paragraph Spacing** is **Before**: 0 points and **After**: 10 points.

Exercise 5-4 CHANGE THE SPACE BETWEEN PARAGRAPHS

1. Press Ctrl+Home to move the insertion point to the beginning of the document. Select the whole document by pressing Ctrl+A. Press Ctrl+L to left-align all paragraphs.

2. Use the keyboard shortcut Ctrl+1 to change the entire document to single spacing.

3. Deselect the text and position the insertion point at the beginning of the document.

4. Click the Bold button to turn on bold, key **CORPORATE GIFTS** in all capitals, and press Enter.

5. Move the insertion point into the heading you just keyed. Although this heading includes only two words, it is also a paragraph. Any text followed by a paragraph mark is considered a paragraph.

6. Open the Paragraph dialog box. You use the text boxes labeled **Before** and **After** to choose an amount of space for Word to insert before or after a paragraph.

7. Set the **Before** text box to 72 points (select the "0" and key **72**). Because 72 points equal 1 inch, this adds to the existing 1-inch top margin and places the title 2 inches from the top of the page.

NOTE

Most business documents start 2 inches from the top of the page. You can set this standard by using paragraph formatting, as done here, or by changing margin settings.

TIP

Word provides these keyboard shortcuts for paragraph spacing: Ctrl+0 adds 12 points of space before a paragraph; Ctrl+Shift+0 removes space before a paragraph; Ctrl+Shift+N removes all paragraph and character formatting, restoring the text to default formatting.

8. Press Tab, set the **After** text box to **24** points, and click **OK**. The heading now starts at 2 inches and is followed by two line spaces.

9. Right-click the **Status bar** and click **Vertical Page Position**. Deselect the shortcut menu. The Status bar displays **At 2″** on the left side.

10. Click the Center button to center the heading.

Paragraph Indents

An *indent* increases the distance between the sides of a paragraph and the two side margins (left and right). Indented paragraphs appear to have different margin settings. Word provides a variety of indents to emphasize paragraphs in a document, as shown in Figure 5-6.

Figure 5-6
Types of paragraph indents

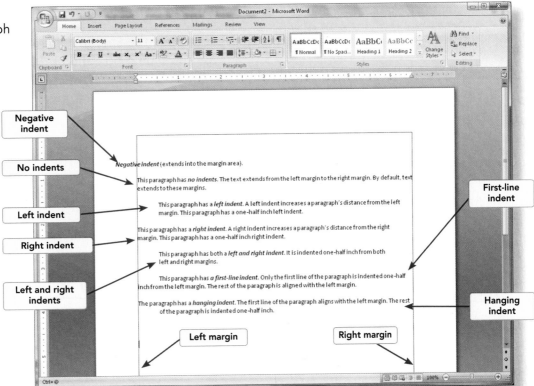

To set paragraph indents, you can use one of these methods:

- Indent buttons on the Ribbon, Home tab, Paragraph group

- Paragraph dialog box

- Keyboard

- Ruler

Exercise 5-5   SET INDENTS BY USING INDENT BUTTONS AND THE PARAGRAPH DIALOG BOX

1. Select the paragraph that begins "Our line" through the end of the document.

2. Click the Increase Indent button ⊞ on the Ribbon. The selected text is indented 0.5 inch from the left side.

3. Click the Increase Indent button ⊞ again. Now the text is indented 1 inch.

4. Click the Decrease Indent button ⊞ twice to return the text to the left margin.

NOTE

To set a *negative indent*, which extends a paragraph into the left or right margin areas, enter a negative number in the **Left** or **Right** text boxes. Any indent that occurs between the left and right margins is known as a *positive indent*.

5. With the text still selected, open the Paragraph dialog box by clicking the Paragraph Dialog Box Launcher arrow ▣.

6. Under **Indentation**, change the **Left** setting to **0.75** inch and the **Right** setting to **0.75** inch.

7. Click to open the **Special** drop-down list in the Paragraph dialog box and choose **First line**. Word sets the **By** box to 0.5″ by default. Notice the change in the Preview box.

Figure 5-7
Setting indents

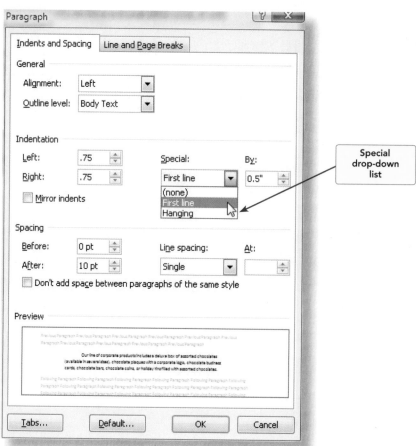

TIP

Word provides these keyboard shortcuts to set indents: Ctrl+M increases an indent; Ctrl+Shift+M decreases an indent; Ctrl+T creates a hanging indent; Ctrl+Shift+T removes a hanging indent.

8. Click **OK**. Now each paragraph is indented from the left and right margins by 0.75 inch, and the first line of each paragraph is indented another 0.5 inch.

Exercise 5-6 SET INDENTS BY USING THE RULER

You can set indents by dragging the *indent markers* that appear at the left and right of the horizontal ruler. There are four indent markers:

- The *first-line indent marker* is the top triangle on the left side of the ruler. Drag it to the right to indent the first line of a paragraph.

- The *hanging indent marker* is the bottom triangle. Drag it to the right to indent the remaining lines in a paragraph.

- The *left indent marker* is the small rectangle. Drag it to move the first-line indent marker and hanging indent marker at the same time.

- The *right indent marker* is the triangle at the right side of the ruler, at the right margin. Drag it to the left to create a right indent.

Figure 5-8
Indent markers on the ruler

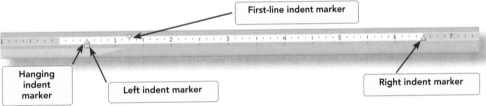

1. Make sure the horizontal ruler is displayed. If it is not, click the **View Ruler button** or open the **Word Options** dialog box and click **Advanced** in the left pane and scroll to **Display**.

2. Position the insertion point in the first paragraph below the title.

3. Point to the first-line indent marker on the ruler. A ScreenTip appears when you are pointing to the correct marker.

4. Drag the first-line indent marker 0.5 inch to the right. The first line of the paragraph is indented by 0.5 inch.

5. Press Shift+F1 to display the **Reveal Formatting** task pane. Locate the Paragraph section, and notice the settings under **Indentation**.

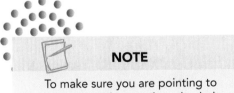

NOTE

To make sure you are pointing to the correct indent marker, check the ScreenTip identifier before you drag the marker.

6. Drag the first-line indent marker back to the zero position. Point to the hanging indent marker, and drag it 0.5 inch to the right. The lines below the first line are indented 0.5 inch, creating a hanging indent.

7. Drag the hanging indent marker back to the zero position. Drag the left indent marker (the small rectangle) 1 inch to the right. The entire paragraph is indented by 1 inch. ¶

8. Select the first two paragraphs below the title, and press Ctrl+Shift+N to remove all formatting from the paragraphs. Notice that the line spacing and spacing after return to the default settings.

9. Position the insertion point in the second paragraph, which begins "Our line," and re-create the indents by using the ruler:

   • Drag the left indent marker 0.75 inch to the right to indent the entire paragraph.

   • Drag the first-line indent marker to the 1.25-inch mark on the ruler.

   • Drag the right indent marker 0.75 to the left (to the 5.75-inch mark on the ruler). Now the paragraph is indented like the paragraphs below it.

10. Select all the indented paragraphs, and drag the first-line indent marker to the 1-inch mark on the ruler. Now the opening line of each paragraph is indented only 0.25 inch.

Figure 5-9
Document with indented text

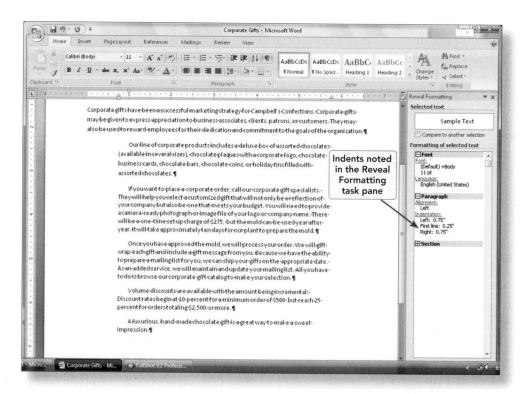

11. Save the document as *[your initials]*5-6 in a new folder for Lesson 5.

12. Submit the document, but do not close it.

Borders and Shading

To add visual interest to paragraphs or to an entire page, you can add a *border*—a line, box, or pattern—around text, a graphic, or a page. In addition, you can use *shading* to fill in the background behind the text of a paragraph. Shading can appear as a shade of gray, as a pattern, or as a color. Borders can appear in a variety of line styles and colors.

This lesson explains how to use the Borders and Shading dialog box to set border and shading options, and how to use the Borders command on the Ribbon (which applies the most recently selected border style). The Borders button ScreenTip will change to display the most recently selected border style.

Exercise 5-7 ADD BORDERS TO PARAGRAPHS

1. With the file *[your initials]*5-6 open, go to the end of the document. Press Enter to start a new paragraph, and press Ctrl+Q to remove the paragraph formatting carried over from the previous paragraph.

2. Key the text shown in Figure 5-10.

Figure 5-10

> Let Campbell's Confections help you with your marketing strategy and your employees' recognition plan! We can provide you with a unique and personalized gift that will create a lasting impression. Call us today at 724-555-2025 for more information.

3. Make sure the insertion point is to the left of the current paragraph mark or within the paragraph.

4. Click the down arrow beside the Borders button ▦ and click **Borders and Shading** at the bottom of the drop-down list. The Borders and Shading dialog box appears. Click the **Borders** tab if it is not displayed.

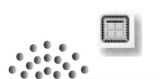

NOTE

The appearance of the Borders button and the Screen Tip change according to the most recently selected border style.

5. Under Setting, click the **Box** option. The **Preview** box shows the Box setting. Each button around the **Preview** box indicates a selected border.

6. Scroll to view the options in the **Style** box. Choose the first border style (the solid line).

7. Open the **Color** drop-down list and choose Green. (ScreenTips identify colors by name.)

8. Open the **Width** drop-down list and choose 2¹/4 **pt.**

9. Click the top line of the box border in the **Preview** box. The top line is deleted, and the corresponding button is no longer selected. Click the Top Border button or the top border area in the diagram to restore the top line border.

Figure 5-11
Borders and Shading
dialog box

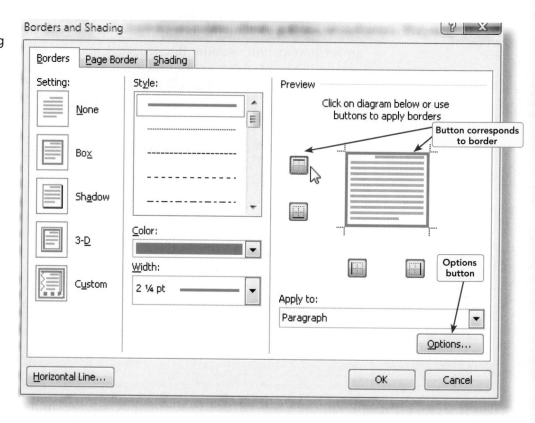

10. Click the **Options** button. In the Border and Shading Options dialog box, change the **Top**, **Bottom**, **Left**, and **Right** settings to **5 pt** to increase the space between the text and the border. Click **OK**.

11. Change the **Setting** from **Box** to **Shadow**. This setting applies a black shadow to the green border. Notice that the **Apply to** box is set to **Paragraph**. Click **OK**. The shadow border is applied to the paragraph.

12. Click anywhere within the title "CORPORATE GIFTS."

13. Click the down arrow next to the Borders button on the Ribbon. A drop-down menu of border options appears.

Figure 5-12
Border options on
the Ribbon

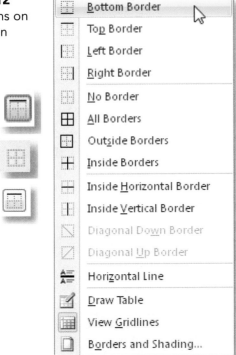

14. Click **Bottom Border**. A bottom border with the options previously set in the Borders and Shading dialog box is applied to the title.

15. Click the down arrow next to the Borders button . Click the **No Border** button to delete the border.

16. Reapply the bottom border, and click the Top Border button to add a top border as well.

17. Open the Paragraph dialog box, and change the left and right indents to *.5"*. Notice the border is indented from the left and right margins.

NOTE

Borders and shading, when applied to a paragraph, extend from the left margin to the right margin or if indents are set, from the left indent to the right indent.

Exercise 5-8   APPLY BORDERS TO SELECTED TEXT AND A PAGE

In addition to paragraphs, you can apply borders to selected text or to an entire page. When you apply a border to a page, you can choose whether to place the border on every page, the current page, the first page, or all but the first page in a document.

NOTE

When the **Apply to** box indicates **Text**, the borders are applied only to the selected text and not to the paragraph. If you include a paragraph mark in your selection, the borders are applied to all lines of the paragraph unless you change the **Apply to** setting to **Text**. It is important to notice the **Apply to** setting when applying borders and shading, or you might not get the results you intended.

---

1. In the third paragraph below the title (which begins "If you"), select the text "$275." Open the Borders and Shading dialog box.

2. From the **Style** box, scroll to the fifth line style from the bottom. Word automatically applies this style as the **Box** setting.

3. Change the **Color** to **Blue**. Notice that the **Apply to** box indicates **Text**.

Figure 5-13
Applying borders to
selected text

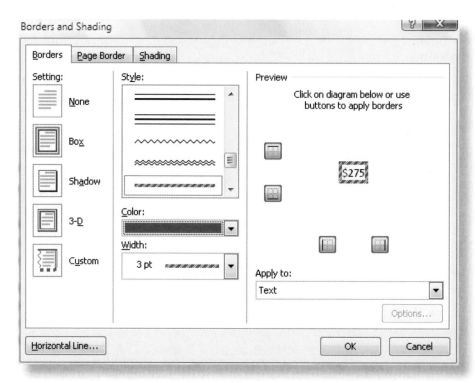

4. Click the **Page Border** tab. Choose the third-to-last line style (a band of three shades of gray), and click the **3-D** setting. The width should be **3 pt**.

5. Click **OK**. Notice the text border added to "$275" and the page border. Deselect the text so you can see the border color.

Figure 5-14
Document with
border formatting

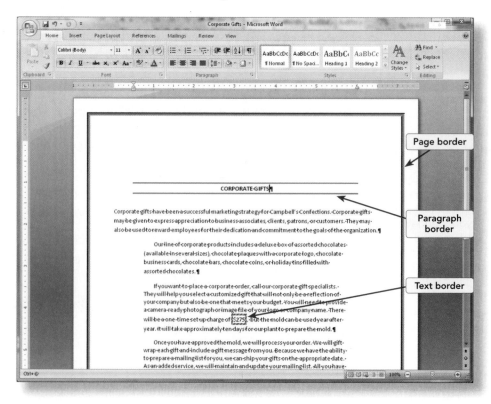

6. Save the document as *[your initials]*5-8 in your Lesson 5 folder. Print the document. Leave it open.

Exercise 5-9 ADD A HORIZONTAL LINE

Word provides special horizontal lines to divide or decorate a page. These lines are actually picture files (or "clips") in the shape of horizontal lines that are normally used when creating Web pages.

1. Position the insertion point anywhere in the last paragraph and open the Borders and Shading dialog box. Click the **Borders** tab.

2. Click **None** to remove the shadowed border. Click **OK**.

3. Position the insertion point at the beginning of the last paragraph.

4. Open the Borders and Shading dialog box. Click **Horizontal Line** at the bottom of the dialog box.

5. In the Horizontal Line dialog box, click the second box in the second row. Click **OK**. The line is inserted in the document.

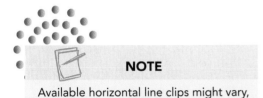

NOTE

Available horizontal line clips might vary, depending on which files are installed on your computer. Check with your instructor if the specified line is not available.

Figure 5-15
Inserting a horizontal line

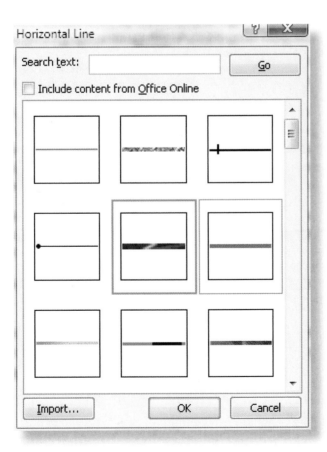

Exercise 5-10   APPLY SHADING TO A PARAGRAPH

1. Click anywhere in the last paragraph, and open the **Borders and Shading** dialog box.

2. Click the **Shading** tab.

3. Click the down arrow in the **Fill** box. Notice that you can apply Theme colors or Standard colors. Click the second gray color in the first column.

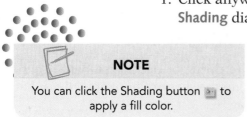

NOTE

You can click the Shading button to apply a fill color.

Figure 5-16
Shading options in the Borders and Shading dialog box

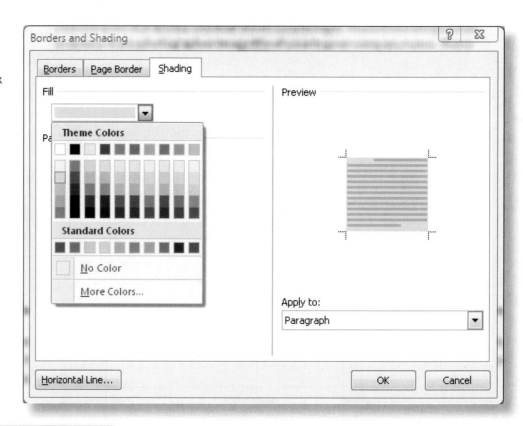

NOTE

Shading can affect the readability of text, especially when you use dark colors or patterns. It's a good idea to choose a larger type size and bold text when you use shading.

TIP

To remove all formatting from a paragraph (including borders, indents, and character formatting), click the Clear Formatting button in the Font group.

4. Open the **Style** drop-down list to view other shading options. Close the **Style** drop-down list without choosing a style.

5. Click **OK** to apply the gray shading to the paragraph.

6. With the insertion point still in the last paragraph, remove the gray shading by clicking the Shading button on the Ribbon. Click **No Color**.

7. Click the Undo button to restore the shading.

Exercise 5-11 APPLY BORDERS AUTOMATICALLY

Word provides an AutoFormat feature to apply bottom borders. Instead of using the Borders command or the Borders and Shading dialog box, you can key a series of characters and Word automatically applies a border.

1. Press Ctrl+N to create a new document and leave the current document open.

2. Key --- (three consecutive hyphens) and press Enter. Word applies a bottom border. Press Enter two times.

3. Key === (three consecutive equal signs) and press Enter. Word applies a double-line bottom border. Press Enter two times.

4. Key —— (three consecutive underscores) and press Enter. Word applies a thick bottom border.

5. Close the document without saving.

> **TIP**
>
> If you do not want to format borders automatically, click the AutoCorrect Options button 🗲 displayed after you key a series of characters and choose **Stop Automatically Creating Border Lines**.

TABLE 5-1 AutoFormatting Borders

You Key	Word Applies
Three or more hyphens (-) and press Enter	A thin bottom border
Three or more underscores (_) and press Enter	A thick bottom border
Three or more equal signs (=) and press Enter	A double-line bottom border

Repeating and Copying Formats

You can quickly repeat, copy, or remove paragraph formatting. For example, use F4 or Ctrl+Y to repeat paragraph formatting and the Format Painter button 🖌 to copy paragraph formatting.

Exercise 5-12 REPEAT, COPY, AND REMOVE PARAGRAPH FORMATS

> **NOTE**
>
> You can click in a paragraph when repeating, copying, or removing formatting. You do not have to select the entire paragraph.

1. Click anywhere in the first paragraph under the title (which begins "Corporate Gifts"), and change the paragraph alignment to justified.

2. Select the rest of the indented paragraphs, starting with the paragraph that begins "Our line" through the paragraph that begins "A luxurious." Press F4 to repeat the formatting.

3. Click anywhere in the last paragraph (with the shading).

4. Click the Format Painter button ; then click within the paragraph above the shaded paragraph to copy the formatting.

5. Click the Undo button to undo the paragraph formatting.

6. Click anywhere in the shaded paragraph. Click the Clear Formatting button  on the Ribbon to remove the formatting.

7. Click the Undo button to restore the formatting.

8. Click just before the paragraph mark for the horizontal line you inserted above the last paragraph. Open the **Paragraph** dialog box, add 24 points of spacing before the paragraph, and click **OK**.

9. Save the document as *[your initials]*5-12 in your Lesson 5 folder.

10. Submit and close the document.

Bulleted and Numbered Lists

Bulleted lists and *numbered lists* are types of hanging indents you can use to organize important details in a document. In a bulleted list, a bullet (•) precedes each paragraph. In a numbered list, a sequential number or letter precedes each paragraph. When you add or delete an item in a numbered list, Word automatically renumbers the list.

To create bulleted lists or numbered lists, use the Bullets command or the Numbering command on the Ribbon (which apply the most recently selected bullet or numbering style).

Exercise 5-13   CREATE A BULLETED LIST

1. Open the file **Memo - 1**. This document is a one-page memo. Key the current date in the memo date line.

2. Locate and select the four lines of text beginning with "Monday" and ending with "Thursday."

3. Click the Bullets button on the Ribbon, Home tab, Paragraph group. Word applies the bullet style that was most recently chosen in the Bullets list.

Figure 5-17
Bulleted list

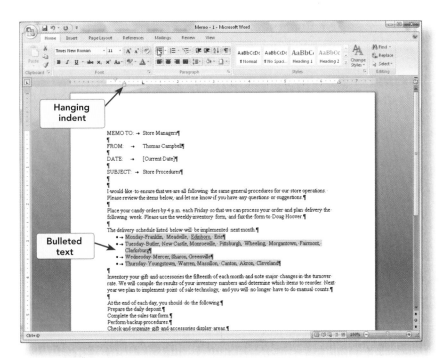

NOTE

When you create bulleted or numbered lists, Word automatically sets a 0.25-inch hanging indent.

4. With the list still selected, click the down arrow beside the **Bullets** button, and click one of the bullet shapes listed in the **Bullet Library**. The list is formatted with a different bullet shape. Deselect the list.

Figure 5-18
Bullet options

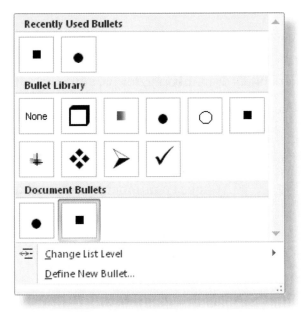

5. Click the first bullet in the bulleted list you just created to select all bullets.

6. Right-click the selected bullets, and click **Adjust List Indents** from the shortcut menu.

7. Change the **Bullet position** text box value to **.4**. Change the **Text indent** to **.65**. Click **OK**.

Exercise 5-14 CREATE A NUMBERED LIST

1. Select the last four paragraphs in the document, from "First Quarter" to "Fourth Quarter."

2. Click the Numbering button to format the list with the style that was most recently chosen from the Numbering list.

3. With the list still selected, click the down arrow beside the Numbering button. Click the roman numeral format. Word reformats the list with roman numerals.

Exercise 5-15 CHANGE A BULLETED OR NUMBERED LIST

Word's bulleting and numbering feature is very flexible. When a list is bulleted or numbered, you can change it in several ways. You can:

- Convert bullets to numbers or numbers to bullets in a list.

- Add or remove items in a bulleted or numbered list, and Word renumbers the list automatically.

- Interrupt a bulleted or numbered list to create several shorter lists.

- Customize the list formatting by changing the symbol used for bullets or changing the alignment and spacing of the bullets and numbers.

- Turn off bullets or numbering for part of a list or the entire list.

NOTE

When you select a bulleted or numbered list by dragging over the text, the list is highlighted but the bullets or numbers are not. You can select a list by clicking a bullet or number.

1. Select the bulleted list that starts with "Monday."

2. Click the down arrow beside the Numbering button.

3. Choose a numbered format that starts with "1" to convert the bullets to numbers.

4. Select and delete the line that begins "Wednesday." Word renumbers the list automatically.

5. Press Ctrl+Z to undo.

6. Place the insertion point at the end of the last item in the numbered list, after "Cleveland."

7. Press Enter and key **Friday-Emergency deliveries**. The formatting is carried to the new line.

8. Place the insertion point at the end of the fourth item (after "Cleveland.") and press Enter.

9. Key in italic *When absolutely necessary:*

TIP

To change the shape, size, and color of a bullet, click the down arrow on the Bullets button  and click **Define New Bullet**. Click the **Symbol** button to choose a new shape. Click the **Font** button to change size and color. Click the drop-down arrow of the **Alignment** box to change the bullet alignment. If you click the **Picture** button, you can insert a picture bullet—a decorative bullet often used in Web pages. You can format numbers or bullets of a list in a format different from the text of the list.

NOTE

After you format a list with bullets or numbering, each time you press Enter the format carries forward to the next paragraph. Pressing Enter twice turns off the format.

10. Click within the italic text, and click the Numbering button ⊞▾ on the Ribbon to turn off numbering for this item. The list continues with the following paragraph.

11. Select and right-click the numbered text below the italic text (the numbered item that begins "Friday").

12. Click the **Set Numbering Value** option to open the Set Numbering Value dialog box. Select, if necessary, **Start new list** so the list does not continue the numbering. Change the **Set value to** box to **1**. Click **OK**. The new list starts with "1."

13. Insert a blank line above the italic text (click to the left of "*When*" and press Enter).

14. Select the list beginning with "At the" through "Check and organize."

15. Click the down arrow beside the Bullets button ⊞▾ and click **Define New Bullet**.

16. Click **Symbol**, and change the **Font** to **Wingdings**. Scroll to locate and select the small, solid black square (▪). Click **OK** to close the Symbol dialog box, and click **OK** to close the Define New Bullet dialog box.

Exercise 5-16   CREATE LISTS AUTOMATICALLY

Word provides an AutoFormat feature to create bulleted and numbered lists as you type. When this feature is selected, you can enter a few keystrokes, key your list, and Word inserts the numbers and bullets automatically.

1. Press Ctrl+End to move to the end of the document.

2. Key the following: **Create a list of all equipment and fixtures in the store. Provide the following:**

3. Press Enter. Key * and press Spacebar.

4. Key **Description/Model number** and press Enter. Word automatically formats your text as a bulleted list.

5. Key the following text to complete the list, pressing Enter at the end of each line except the last line:

   Serial number
   Date acquired
   Purchase price
   Location
   Inventory number

TABLE 5-2 AutoFormatting Numbered and Bulleted Lists

You Key	Word Creates
A number; a period, closing parenthesis, or hyphen; a space or tab; and text. Example, **1.**, **1**), or **1**-Press Enter.	A numbered list
An asterisk (*) or hyphen (-); a space or tab; and text. Press Enter.	A bulleted list

Exercise 5-17 CREATE A MULTILEVEL LIST

A *multilevel list* has indented subparagraphs. For example, your list can start with item number "1)," followed by another level of indented items numbered "a)," "b)," and "c)." An outline numbered list can have up to nine levels and is often used for technical or legal documents. The Multilevel List command is located on the Ribbon, Home tab, Paragraph group.

1. Go to the end of the document and press Enter four times.

2. Click the arrow beside the Multilevel List button. Notice the outline numbering styles available in the List Library.

Figure 5-19
Multilevel List Library

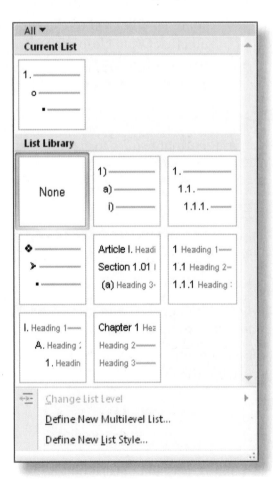

3. Click the outline numbering style that begins with "I." Notice the uppercase roman numeral in the text.

4. Key January and press Enter.

5. Click the Increase Indent button (or press Tab), and key A. Spacebar **Prepare memo to employees regarding changes to W-4 forms.**

6. Press Enter and key B. Spacebar **Prepare and mail W-2 forms to employees.** The numbered list now has two indented subparagraphs. Press Enter. Key C. Spacebar **Prepare and mail 1099 forms.** Press Enter.

7. With the insertion point at the beginning of a new line, click the Decrease Indent button (or press Shift + Tab) to position the insertion point at the left margin. You can now add a second first-level paragraph to your list.

8. Key II. **February.**

NOTE

You can create and define a multilevel list style and add it to the List Gallery. Click the arrow beside the Multilevel List button and click **Define New Multilevel List.** Enter the text and format for each level. Click **OK.**

Symbols and Special Characters

The fonts you use with Word include *special characters* that do not appear on your keyboard, such as those used in foreign languages (for example, ç, Ö, and Ω). There are additional fonts, such as *Wingdings* and *Symbol* that consist entirely of special characters.

To insert symbols and special characters in your documents, click the Insert tab on the Ribbon, locate the **Symbols** group, and click the **Symbol** command.

Exercise 5-18 INSERT SYMBOLS

1. Scroll toward the beginning of the document. Position the insertion point to the immediate left of the paragraph that begins "*When absolutely.*"

2. Click the Insert tab. Locate the **Symbols** group, and click the arrow beside the Symbol button. Click **More Symbols.** The Symbol dialog box appears.

3. Make sure the **Symbols** tab is displayed and choose **(normal text)** from the **Font** drop-down list box.

4. Scroll through the grid of available symbol characters for normal text, and notice that the grid contains diacritical marks that you can use for foreign languages. You will also see the symbol for cents (¢) and degrees (°).

5. Click the arrow to open the **Font** drop-down list box and choose **Symbol.** Review the available symbol characters.

6. Change the font to **Wingdings**. The characters included in the Wingdings font appear in the grid.

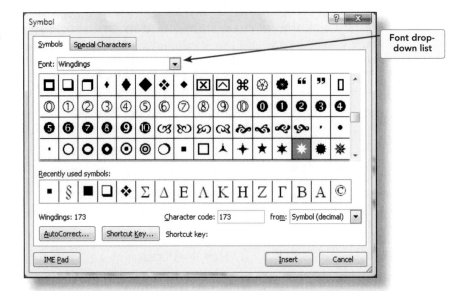

TIP

Notice the recently used symbols shown at the bottom of the Symbol dialog box. Word displays the 16 most recently used symbols.

7. Scroll down several rows until you see symbols similar to an asterisk (∗). Click one of the symbols.

8. Click **Insert,** and then click **Close.** The symbol appears in the document.

9. Select the list with roman numerals beginning with "I. First Quarter" through "IV. Fourth Quarter."

 10. Click the Home tab and click the arrow beside the Bullets button.

11. Click **Define New Bullet** and click **Picture.** Click one of the picture bullets, and click **OK,** and then click **OK** again. The roman numerals are replaced with your chosen picture bullet.

TIP

You can assign shortcut keys or AutoCorrect to a symbol by clicking **Shortcut Key** or **AutoCorrect** in the Symbol dialog box. You can also press Alt and key the numeric code (using the numeric keypad, if you have one) for a character. For example, if you change the font of the document to Wingdings and press Alt+0040, you will insert the character for a Wingdings telephone. Remember to change the Wingdings font back to your normal font after inserting a special character.

Exercise 5-19 INSERT SPECIAL CHARACTERS

You can use the Symbol dialog box and shortcut keys to insert characters such as an en dash, an em dash, or SmartQuotes. An *en dash* is a dash slightly wider than a hyphen. An *em dash,* which is twice as wide as an en dash, is used in sentences where you would normally insert two hyphens. *Smart quotes* are quotation marks that open a quote curled in one direction (") and close a quote curled in the opposite direction (").

NOTE

By default, Word inserts smart quotes automatically.

1. Make sure nonprinting characters are displayed in the document. If they are not, click the Show/Hide ¶ button ¶.

2. On page 1, locate the paragraph that begins "1. Monday." Position the insertion point to the immediate right of "Monday." Press Delete to remove the hyphen.

3. Click the Insert tab, and click the arrow beside the Symbol button Ω. Click More Symbols, and click the Special Characters tab.

4. Choose Em Dash from the list of characters. (Notice the keyboard shortcut listed for the character.) Click Insert, and then click Close. The em dash replaces the hyphen.

5. Select the hyphen immediately following "Tuesday." Press Alt+Ctrl+− (the minus sign on the numeric keypad). An em dash is inserted. (If you don't have a numeric keypad, press F4 to repeat the character.)

6. Insert em dashes after "Wednesday," "Thursday," and "Friday."

Exercise 5-20 CREATE SYMBOLS AUTOMATICALLY

You can use Word's AutoCorrect feature to create symbols as you type. Just enter a few keystrokes, and Word converts them into a symbol.

NOTE

To review the symbols AutoCorrect can enter automatically, open the Word Options dialog box, and click Proofing. Click AutoCorrect Options, and click the AutoCorrect tab.

1. Scroll to the "SUBJECT" line, and click to the left of "Store."

2. Key < = = and notice that Word automatically creates an arrow (←).

3. Position the insertion point to the right of "Procedures." Key = = >. Word creates another pointing to the right.

4. Format the first line of the memo with 72 points of paragraph spacing before it. This starts the first line two inches from the top of the page. (See Appendix B, "Standard Forms for Business Documents.")

5. Save the document as *[your initials]*5-20 in your Lesson 5 folder.

6. Submit and close the document.

Lesson 5 Summary

- A paragraph is any amount of text followed by a paragraph mark.

- Paragraph alignment determines how the edges of a paragraph appear horizontally. Paragraphs can be left-aligned, centered, right-aligned, or justified.

- The Click and Type feature enables you to insert text in any blank area of a document by simply positioning the insertion point and double-clicking.

- Line space is the amount of vertical space between lines of text in a paragraph. Lines can be single-spaced, 1.5-line spaced, double-spaced, or set to a specific value.

- Paragraph space is the amount of space above or below a paragraph. Paragraph space is set in points—12 points of space equals one line space for 12-point text. Change the space between paragraphs by using the Before and After options in the Paragraph dialog box or by using the Ctrl+0, Ctrl+Shift+0 keyboard shortcuts to add or remove 12 points before a paragraph.

- A left indent or right indent increases a paragraph's distance from the left or right margin. A first-line indent indents only the first line of a paragraph. A hanging indent indents the second and subsequent lines of a paragraph.

- To set indents by using the horizontal ruler, drag the left indent marker (small rectangle), the first-line indent marker (top triangle), or the hanging indent marker (bottom triangle), which are all on the left end of the ruler, or drag the right indent marker (triangle) on the right end of the ruler.

- A border is a line or box added to selected text, a paragraph, or a page. Shading fills in the background of selected text or paragraphs. Borders and shading can appear in a variety of styles and colors.

- In addition to regular borders, Word provides special decorative horizontal lines that are available from the Borders and Shading dialog box.

- The AutoFormat feature enables you to create a border automatically. Key three or more hyphens -, underscores _, or equal signs =, and press Enter. See Table 5-1.

- Repeat paragraph formats by pressing F4 or Ctrl+Y. Copy paragraph formats by using the Format Painter command. Remove paragraph formats by pressing Ctrl+Q or choosing the **Clear Formatting** command from the Ribbon, Home tab, Font group.

- Format a list of items as a bulleted or numbered list. In a bulleted list, each item is indented and preceded by a bullet character or other symbol. In a numbered list, each item is indented and preceded by a sequential number or letter.

- Remove a bullet or number from an item in a list by clicking the Bullets command or the Numbering command on the Ribbon. Press Enter in the middle of the list to add another bulleted or numbered item automatically. Press Enter twice in a list to turn off bullets or numbering.

Change the bullet symbol or the numbering type by clicking the arrow beside the Bullets command to display the Bullet Library or the arrow beside the Numbering command to open the Numbering Library.

- The AutoFormat feature enables you to create a bulleted or numbered list automatically. See Table 5-2.

- Create a multilevel list by clicking the Multilevel List command. A multilevel list has indented subparagraphs, such as paragraph "1)" followed by indented paragraph "a)" followed by indented paragraph "i)." To increase the level of numbering for each line item, click the Increase Indent command or press Tab. To decrease the level of numbering, click the Decrease Indent command or press Shift+Tab.

- Insert symbols, such as foreign characters, by clicking the Insert tab and clicking the Symbol command. Wingdings is an example of a font that contains all symbols.

- Insert special characters, such as an em dash (—), by using the Special Characters tab in the Symbol dialog box.

- Create symbols automatically as you type by keying AutoCorrect shortcuts, such as keying (c) to produce the ©.

LESSON 5		Command Summary	
Feature	**Button**	**Command**	**Keyboard**
Left-align text		Home tab, Paragraph group	Ctrl+L
Center text		Home tab, Paragraph group	Ctrl+E
Right-align text		Home tab, Paragraph group	Ctrl+R
Justify text		Home tab, Paragraph group	Ctrl+J
Single space		Home tab, Paragraph group	Ctrl+1
Double space		Home tab, Paragraph group	Ctrl+2
1.5-line space		Home tab, Paragraph group	Ctrl+5
Borders and Shading		Home tab, Paragraph group	
Remove paragraph formatting		Home tab, Paragraph group	Ctrl+Q
Restore text to Normal formatting		Home tab, Font group	Ctrl+Shift+N
Increase indent		Home tab, Paragraph group	Ctrl+M
Decrease indent		Home tab, Paragraph group	Ctrl+Shift+M
Hanging indent		Home tab, Paragraph group	Ctrl+T
Bulleted list		Home tab, Paragraph group	
Numbered list		Home tab, Paragraph group	
Symbols and special characters		Insert tab, Symbols group	

Concepts Review

True/False Questions

Each of the following statements is either true or false. Indicate your choice by circling T or F.

T (F)   1. You can use the Ribbon, Home tab, Font group to right-align paragraphs.

T   F   2. Text that is left-aligned has a ragged left edge.

(T) F   3. You can open the Paragraph dialog box from the shortcut menu.

(T) F   4. The keyboard shortcut Ctrl+5 changes line spacing to 1.5 lines.

T   F   5. You can use Word's AutoCorrect feature to create symbols as you type by using certain keyboard combinations.

(T) F   6. To apply a page border to a document, click the Borders tab in the Borders and Shading dialog box.

T (F)   7. Ctrl+Q removes paragraph formatting.

T   F   8. A hanging indent indents all lines in a paragraph except the first line.

Short Answer Questions

Write the correct answer in the space provided.

1. Which type of paragraph alignment adjusts spacing between words?

   _____

2. What is the keyboard shortcut for centering text?

   Ctrl + C
   _____

3. Single, 1.5, and double are examples of what type of spacing?

   _____

4. If you click 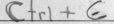 once, what happens to selected text?

   _____

5. With an outline numbered list, instead of clicking 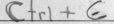, what key can you press to achieve the same result?

   _____

6. Which keystrokes apply a double-line border automatically?

_____

7. What is the procedure to display the Reveal Formatting task pane?

_____

8. Which indent marker is the top triangle on the left side of the ruler?

_____

Critical Thinking

Answer these questions on a separate page. There are no right or wrong answers. Support your answers with examples from your own experience, if possible.

1. You can use keyboard shortcuts to change paragraph alignment, or you can use the alignment buttons on the Ribbon. Which method do you prefer? Why? When might you use the other method?

2. Many people use bulleted lists and numbered lists interchangeably. Are there times when it would be more appropriate to use a bulleted list than a numbered list and vice versa? Explain your answer.

Skills Review

Exercise 5-21

Change paragraph alignment and line spacing.

1. Start a new document.
2. Change the character formatting and paragraph alignment for the first paragraph by following these steps:
   a. Select the paragraph mark and set the font to 14-point Cambria.
   b. Click the Center button ≣ on the Ribbon, Home tab, Paragraph group, to center the text you are about to key.
   c. Key the first two lines shown in Figure 5-21 in all capitals. Use a line break (press ⟦Shift⟧+⟦Enter⟧) after the first line to make the two lines one paragraph.

Figure 5-21

```
CAMPBELL'S CONFECTIONS
OHIO STORE MANAGERS

Sarah Dunlap
Patrick Rhodes
Paul Kellogg
Scott Edwards
Nancy Epperson
Leigh Brittain
```

3. At the end of this paragraph, press [Enter] twice, turn off [Caps Lock], and key the six names shown in Figure 5-21. Again, use a line break after each name to make the names all one paragraph.

4. Change the alignment of each paragraph by following these steps:

   a. Move the insertion point into the first paragraph and click the Align Right button ▤ on the Ribbon, Home tab, to right-align the first two lines.

   b. Move the insertion point into the paragraph containing the six names and press [Ctrl]+[L] to left-align the names.

   c. Select the entire document and click the Center button ▤ to center all the text.

5. Change line spacing by following these steps:

   a. Click within the second paragraph.

   b. Press [Ctrl]+[5] to change the line spacing to 1.5 lines.

6. Save the document as *[your initials]*5-21 in your Lesson 5 folder.

7. Submit and close the document.

Exercise 5-22

Change paragraph spacing and set indents.

1. Open the file **Club**. (Make sure the Show/Hide ¶ button ¶ is turned on.)

2. Change spacing between paragraphs by following these steps:

   a. Select the entire document, click the right mouse button, and choose Paragraph from the shortcut menu.

   b. Click the Indents and Spacing tab if it is not displayed.

   c. Click the up arrow to the right of After to set the spacing after paragraphs to 12 points. Click OK.

3. Press [Ctrl]+[Home] to move to the top of the document. Key in bold uppercase letters CAMPBELL'S CONFECTIONS' CHOCOLATE CLUB.

4. Press [Enter] once. Click within the new title and open the Paragraph dialog box. Change Spacing to 72 points Before and 24 points After. Change the Alignment to Centered and click OK.

5. Apply a first-line indent to the paragraphs by following these steps:

   a. Select all the paragraphs below the title.

   b. Make sure the horizontal ruler is displayed. Point to the first-line indent marker on the ruler. When a ScreenTip identifies it, drag it 0.5 inch to the right.

6. Change the indentation of the last paragraph by following these steps:

   a. Left-click to deselect the paragraphs.

   b. Right-click the last paragraph and open the Paragraph dialog box.

   c. Set the Left and Right indentation text boxes to 1 inch.

   d. Remove the first-line indent by choosing (none) from the Special drop-down list. Click OK.

7. Key Note: at the beginning of the newly indented paragraph. Format "Note" in bold, small caps.

8. Justify the four paragraphs below the title.

9. Save the document as *[your initials]*5-22 in your Lesson 5 folder.

10. Submit and close the document.

Exercise 5-23

Apply borders and shading; repeat and copy formatting.

1. Open the file **Retail Stores**.

2. At the end of the document, key the following text as a separate paragraph. Use bold text and be sure to insert a blank line before the new paragraph.

   To learn more about our stores and products, call Campbell's Confections at 800-555-2025 or visit our web site at www.campbellsconfections.biz.

3. Apply borders and shading to the new paragraph by following these steps:

   a. Place the insertion point in the paragraph.

    b. Click the arrow beside the Borders button on the Ribbon, Paragraph group. Click Borders and Shading, and click the Borders tab if it is not displayed.

   c. Use the first line style, and change the line Color to Blue.

   d. Change the Width to 1½ pt.

    e. In the Preview box, click the Top Border button and the Bottom Border button.

   f. Click the Shading tab. Click the down arrow beside the Fill box. From the Theme Colors palette, click the third box in the first column (White, Background 1, Darker 15%). Click OK.

4. Repeat the formatting by clicking within the first paragraph and pressing F4.

 5. Click the Undo button to undo the formatting in the first paragraph.

6. Apply a border to text automatically by following these steps:

   a. Key the following title at the top of the document: Campbell's Confections.

   b. Press Enter two times.

   c. Click in front of the blank paragraph mark. Key = = = and press Enter to automatically insert a double-line border under the first paragraph. Delete the blank paragraph mark.

7. Copy formatting from one paragraph to another by following these steps:

   a. Click in the last paragraph.

   b. Click the Format Painter button 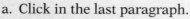.

   c. Click in the title paragraph.

8. Change the title paragraph to bold and all capitals. Add 72 points of spacing before and 24 points after the paragraph and center the title.

9. Save the document as *[your initials]*5-23 in your Lesson 5 folder.

10. Submit and close the document.

Exercise 5-24

Align paragraphs, change paragraph spacing, create bulleted lists, and insert symbols and special characters.

1. Open the file **Designs**.

2. Format the title as bold, all caps, centered. Set the paragraph spacing to 72 points before and 24 points after.

3. Create a bulleted list by following these steps:

   a. Select the text beginning with "Milk chocolate" and ending with "White chocolate."

   b. Click the arrow beside the Bullets button .

   c. Choose a bullet option.

4. Insert symbols by following these steps:

   a. Position the insertion point to the right of "Computer."

   b. Click the Insert tab on the Ribbon. Click the Symbol button . Click More Symbols.

   c. Change the Font to Wingdings. Double-click the computer symbol in the second row.

   d. Click Close.

5. Click to the right of "Camera," and open the Symbol dialog box. Change the Font to Webdings, and scroll to the tenth row to locate the camera symbol. Click Insert. Click Close.

6. Click to the right of "Cell phone," and open the Symbol dialog box. Change the Font to Webdings, and scroll to the eleventh row to locate the cell phone symbol. Click Insert. Click Close.

7. Insert an em dash by following these steps:

   a. Position the insertion point in front of the computer symbol.

   b. Press Alt+Ctrl+− (the minus key on the numeric keypad). Or click the Insert tab on the Ribbon, click the arrow beside Symbol, click More Symbols, and click the Special Characters tab to select the em dash.

8. Insert an em dash before the camera symbol and the cell phone symbol. Select each symbol, and change the font size to 14.

9. Save the document as *[your initials]*5-24 in your Lesson 5 folder.

10. Submit and close the document.

Lesson Applications

Exercise 5-25

Change alignment, line spacing, and paragraph spacing and apply shading.

1. Start a new document.

2. Key the text shown in Figure 5-22, including the corrections. Use Times New Roman, single spacing, and 0 points spacing before and 0 points spacing after. Use line breaks (Shift+Enter) to format the text as two paragraphs.

Figure 5-22

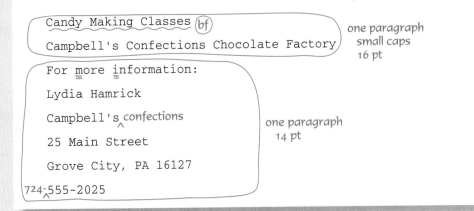

3. Center all text in the document.

4. Change the line spacing in only the second paragraph to 1.5 lines.

5. Change the paragraph spacing for only the first paragraph to 72 points before and 36 points after.

6. Add 10 percent gray shading to the first paragraph.

7. Add a page border, using the box setting and the double wavy line style.

8. Save the document as *[your initials]*5-25 in your Lesson 5 folder.

9. Submit and close the document.

Exercise 5-26

Change alignment, line spacing, and paragraph spacing; add a border; repeat formatting; and add symbols.

1. Open the file **WV Stores**.

2. Change the title to "Campbell's Confections—West Virginia Stores." There should be one blank line below the title and a blank line after each of the remaining office locations.

3. Format all lines of the first office location with 1.5-line spacing.

4. Repeat the formatting for the remaining locations.

5. Change the title to 20-point bold with paragraph spacing of 72 points before and 24 points after. Delete the blank paragraph mark after the title.

6. Add a $3/4$-point double-line bottom border to the title.

7. Center the second and third office location text, and right-align the last office location text.

8. Replace the text "Telephone:" throughout the document with the telephone symbol from the Wingdings font (first row, eighth symbol). Leave the space between the symbol and the telephone number.

9. Replace the text "Fax:" throughout the document with a fax symbol from the Webdings font (eleventh row, tenth symbol).

10. Save the document as *[your initials]*5-26 in your Lesson 5 folder.

11. Submit and close the document.

Exercise 5-27

Indent paragraphs, create bulleted and numbered lists, and change paragraph spacing.

1. Open the file **Favors - 2**.

2. Select the title and apply bold, 14 point, and shadow formatting. Change the spacing before to 72 points and the spacing after to 24 points. Center the title.

3. Select the text from "wedding bells" to "other assorted shapes." Format the selected text as a bullet list using the standard round bullet.

4. Select the text from "solid milk chocolate" to "dark chocolate with mint filling." Format the selected text as a bullet list using a picture bullet.

5. Set 0.25-inch first-line indents for all paragraphs except the title, the bulleted lists, and the final paragraph.

6. Format the final paragraph with 0.75-inch left and right indents.

7. Add gray shading to the final paragraph.

8. Save the document as *[your initials]*5-27 in your Lesson 5 folder.

9. Submit and close the document.

Exercise 5-28 ◆ Challenge Yourself

Indent and align paragraphs, change paragraph spacing, apply a border, copy formatting, create bulleted lists, and insert a special character.

1. Open the file **Fundraising**.

2. Key the heading Fundraising at the top of the document. Format the heading in bold, uppercase letters with a negative left indent of −0.25 inch and 12 points of spacing before the paragraph and 24 points of spacing after the paragraph.

3. Format the paragraphs from "Solid milk chocolate" to "Milk chocolate with double chocolate filling" as a bulleted list, using the bullet of your choice, with 6 points of spacing after paragraphs.

4. Format the paragraphs from "Sales Department" to "555-2025" with a.75-inch left indent and with 6 points of spacing after paragraphs.

5. Add one blank paragraph mark above "Specialty fundraising." Position the insertion point at the blank paragraph mark. Open the Borders and Shading dialog box, and click Horizontal Line. Add a horizontal line of your choice.

6. Justify all paragraphs in the document except the title and bulleted lists.

7. Add a page border to the document, using the third-to-last line style, 3-point width, and the 3-D setting.

8. Save the document as *[your initials]*5-28 in your Lesson 5 folder.

9. Submit and close the document.

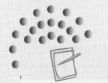

NOTE

If horizontal line clips are not available, use a border.

On Your Own

In these exercises you work on your own, as you would in a real-life business environment. Use the skills you've learned to accomplish the task—and be creative.

Exercise 5-29

Create a flyer for an event, such as a meeting or concert. Use a variety of paragraph alignment settings, line spacing, and paragraph spacing. Add shading to one or more paragraphs and a page border. Include a bulleted list. Save the document as *[your initials]*5-29. Submit the document.

Exercise 5-30

Create a set of instructions for how to make something. Use a bulleted list for the materials needed. Use a numbered list to describe the step-by-step instructions. Use borders or shading for emphasis or for paragraphs containing special notes or tips. Save the document as *[your initials]*5-30 and submit it.

Exercise 5-31

Review the foreign-language characters in the Symbols dialog box (normal text). Use a foreign-language dictionary (such as an online dictionary on the Internet) to find a few foreign words you can key in a document by inserting the appropriate foreign-language characters. Include the English translations. Display the Research task pane to help you define and translate vocabulary. Save the document as *[your initials]*5-31 and submit it.

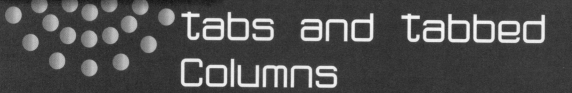

tabs and tabbed Columns

OBJECTIVES

After completing this lesson, you will be able to:

1. Set tabs.

2. Set leader tabs.

3. Clear tabs.

4. Adjust tab settings.

5. Create tabbed columns.

6. Sort paragraphs and tabbed columns.

MCAS OBJECTIVES

In this lesson:
WW 07 2.1.5
WW 07 4.2.2

Estimated Time: 1 hour

A *tab* is a paragraph-formatting feature used to align text. When you press Tab, Word inserts a tab character and moves the insertion point to the position of the tab setting, called the *tab stop*. You can set custom tabs or use Word's default tab settings.

As with other paragraph-formatting features, tab settings are stored in the paragraph mark at the end of a paragraph. Each time you press Enter, the tab settings are copied to the next paragraph. You can set tabs before you key text or for existing text.

Setting Tabs

Word's default tabs are left-aligned and set every half inch from the left margin. These tabs are indicated at the bottom of the horizontal ruler by tiny tick marks.

Word 2007

Figure 6-1
Default tabs

Default tabs every half inch

If you don't want to use the half-inch default tab settings, you have two choices:

- Change the distance between the default tab stops.

- Create custom tabs.

The four most common types of custom tabs are left-aligned, centered, right-aligned, and decimal-aligned. Custom tab settings are indicated by *tab markers* on the horizontal ruler. Additional custom tab options, such as leader tabs and bar tabs, are discussed in the section "Setting Leader Tabs" and in the exercise "Insert Bar Tabs."

Figure 6-2
Types of tabs

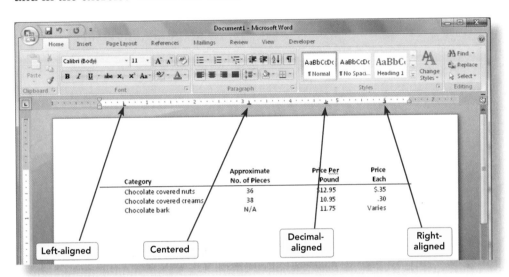

TABLE 6-1 Types of Tabs

Ruler Symbol	Type of Tab	Description
	Left-aligned	The left edge of the text aligns with the tab stop.
	Centered	The text is centered at the tab stop.
	Right-aligned	The right edge of the text aligns with the tab stop.
	Decimal-aligned	The decimal point aligns with the tab stop. Use this option for columns of numbers.
	Bar	Inserts a vertical line at the tab stop. Use to create a divider line between columns.

There are two ways to set tabs:

- Use the Tabs dialog box.

- Use the ruler.

Exercise 6-1   SET TABS BY USING THE TABS DIALOG BOX

1. Open the file **Memo - 2**.

2. Click the View Ruler button to display the horizontal ruler, if necessary.

3. Select the text near the end of the document that begins "Item New Price" through the end of the document.

4. Click the **Home** tab, and locate the **Paragraph** group. Click the **Paragraph Dialog Box Launcher**. Click **Tabs**. The Tabs dialog box appears. Notice that the **Default tab stops** text box is set to 0.5 inch.

> **TIP**
>
> Instead of selecting a paragraph, you can place the insertion point within a paragraph when setting tabs or applying other paragraph formatting.

Figure 6-3
Tabs dialog box

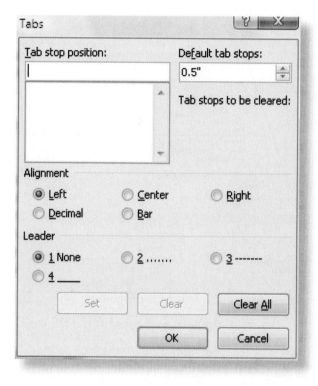

5. Key **.25** in the **Tab stop position** text box. The alignment is already set to **Left**, by default.

6. Click **OK**. The ruler displays a left tab marker ⌐, the symbol used to indicate the type and location of a tab stop on the ruler.

7. Move the insertion point to the left of the first word on the first line of the selected text, "Item".

8. Press Tab. The first line of the group is now indented 0.25 inch. This produces the same effect as creating a first-line indent.

REVIEW

Tabs are nonprinting characters that can be displayed or hidden. Remember, to display or hide nonprinting characters, click the Show/Hide ¶ button 🔳.

NOTE

When you set a custom tab, Word clears all default tabs to the left of the new tab marker.

NOTE

The column heading "New Price" does not contain a decimal, but is aligned at the decimal point. You will adjust the tab for this heading later in this lesson.

9. Press ⎆Tab at the beginning of each of the lines that you formatted with the .25-inch left tab ("1.25 oz.," "1 lb.," "1 lb.," "4 oz.," and "4 oz.").

10. Select the same six lines of text ("Item" through "2.25") at the end of the document. Notice that there are tab characters between some of the words and that the text is crowded and difficult to read. The text is aligned at the default tab settings (every .5").

11. Open the Tabs dialog box by double clicking the tab marker at .25 on the ruler. Key **3.0** in the **Tab stop position** text box.

12. Under **Alignment**, choose **Decimal**. Click **Set**. Notice that the tab setting appears below the **Tab stop position** text box. The setting is automatically selected so that another tab setting can be keyed.

13. Click **OK**. The column headings "Item" and "New Price," along with the text below the headings, are now aligned at the tab stops.

Exercise 6-2   SET TABS BY USING THE RULER

Setting tabs by using the ruler is an easy two-step process: Click the Tab Alignment button on the left of the ruler to choose the type of tab alignment, and then click the position on the ruler to set the tab.

1. Go to the end of the document, and press ⎆Enter if necessary to begin a new paragraph.

2. Key **Category** at the left margin.

3. Click the **Tab Alignment** button on the horizontal ruler until it shows center alignment 🔳. Each time you click the button, the alignment changes.

Figure 6-4
Tab alignment button on the ruler

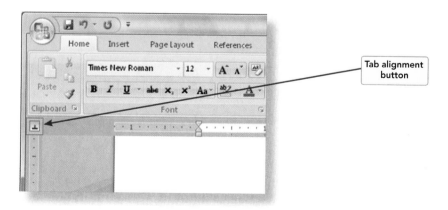

Word 2007

TIP

When choosing tab settings for information in a document, keep in mind that left-aligned text and right- or decimal-aligned numbers are easier to read.

TIP

As you toggle through the Tab Alignment button symbols, notice the appearance of the first-line indent symbol and the hanging indent symbol. You can display one of these symbols, and then just click the ruler to the desired indent position instead of using the point and drag method.

4. Click the ruler at 3.25, and a center tab marker displays.

5. Press Tab, and key **No. of Pieces**.

6. Click the **Tab Alignment** button on the horizontal ruler until it shows right alignment , and then click the ruler at 5.5.

7. Press Tab, and key **Price/Pound**.

8. Press Enter to start a new line. The tab settings will carry forward to the new line.

9. Key **Chocolate-covered nuts**, press Tab, key **36**, press Tab, and key **$12.95**.

10. Press Enter and key **Chocolate-covered creams**, press Tab, key **38**, press Tab, and key **10.95**. Press Enter.

Figure 6-5
Document with tabbed text

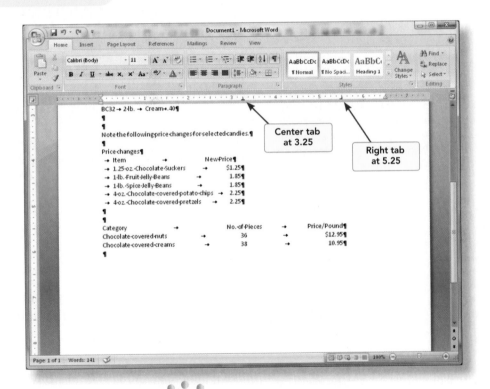

TIP

You can copy tab settings from one paragraph to another. Click in the paragraph whose tab settings you want to copy. Click the Format Painter button . Click in the paragraph to which you are copying the tab settings.

Setting Leader Tabs

You can set tabs with *leader characters,* patterns of dots or dashes that lead the reader's eye from one tabbed column to the next. Leaders may be found in a table of contents, in which dotted lines fill the space between the headings on the left and the page numbers on the right.

Word offers three leader patterns: dotted line, dashed line, and solid line.

Figure 6-6
Leader patterns

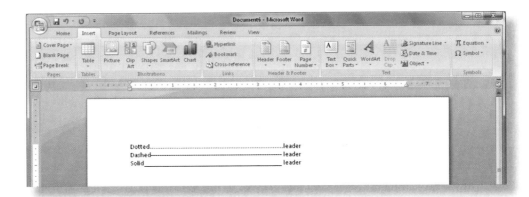

Exercise 6-3   SET LEADER TABS

1. Select the two columns of text under the headings "Item" and "New Price." The prices are aligned at a 3-inch decimal tab.

2. Open the **Tabs** dialog box. The tab settings for the selected text are displayed in the **Tab stop position** box with the **.25**-inch tab highlighted.

3. Click to select **3″** and under **Leader**, click the second leader pattern (the dotted line).

NOTE

Leader patterns always fill the space to the left of a leader tab setting.

4. Click **Set** and click **OK**. A dotted-line leader fills the space to the left of the 3-inch tab setting.

5. Select the heading "Price Changes" and apply bold, small caps formatting. Select the headings "Item" and "New Price" and apply bold and italic.

Clearing Tabs

You can clear custom tabs all at once or individually. When you clear custom tabs, Word restores the default tab stops to the left of the custom tab stop.

There are three ways to clear a tab:

- Use the Tabs dialog box.

- Use the ruler.

- Press Ctrl+Q.

Word 2007

Exercise 6-4 CLEAR A TAB BY USING THE TABS DIALOG BOX AND THE KEYBOARD

1. Select the six lines of text under the heading "Price Changes."

2. Open the Tabs dialog box. The 0.25-inch tab is highlighted in the **Tab stop position** box.

3. Click **Clear** and click **OK**. Word clears the 0.25-inch custom tab, and the text moves to the right to align at the tab at 3.0. (The text moves because each line is preceded by a tab character (→).

NOTE

Remember, to remove tabs from text, you must delete the tab characters.

4. Delete the tab character (→) at the beginning of each line. The text in the first column moves to the left margin, and the second column is aligned at the tab setting.

5. Select the six lines of text under the heading "Price Changes" once again.

6. Press [Ctrl]+[Q]. The remaining tab setting is deleted, and the text is no longer aligned.

7. Click the Undo button to restore the 3-inch custom tab.

8. Save the document as *[your initials]*6-4 in your Lesson 6 folder.

Exercise 6-5 CLEAR A TAB BY USING THE RULER

1. Position the insertion point at the beginning of the line of text with the heading "Category."

2. Position the pointer on the 5.5-inch right-aligned tab marker on the ruler.

NOTE

When clearing or adjusting tabs by using the ruler, watch for the ScreenTip to correctly identify the item to which you are pointing. If no ScreenTip appears, you might inadvertently add another tab marker.

3. When the ScreenTip "Right Tab" appears, drag the tab marker down and off the ruler. The custom tab is cleared, and the heading "Price/Pound" moves to a default tab stop.

4. Undo the last action to restore the tab setting.

5. Select the headings "Category," "No. of Pieces," and "Price/Pound," and apply bold, small caps formatting.

Adjusting Tab Settings

You can adjust tabs inserted in a document by using either the Tabs dialog box or the ruler. Tabs can be adjusted only after you select the text to which they have been applied.

Exercise 6-6   ADJUST TAB SETTINGS

1. Select the line with the headings "Item" and "New Price." The second heading is not aligned with the text below.

2. Point to the tab marker at 3 inches on the ruler.

3. Drag the tab marker to the right until the heading aligns with the text below.

4. Select the last three lines of text in the document ("Category" through "10.95").

5. Open the Tabs dialog box.

6. Click to select the tab setting **5.5** in the **Tab stop position** box.

7. Change the tab alignment setting by clicking **Left**. Click **OK**. Notice the change in the alignment of the heading and the text below.

8. Click the Undo button .

Figure 6-7
Using the ruler to adjust a tab setting

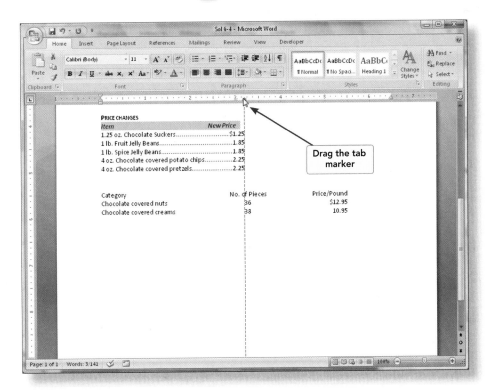

NOTE

When you change tab settings with the ruler, be careful to drag the tab marker only to the right or to the left. If you drag the tab marker up or down, you might clear it from the ruler. If you inadvertently clear a tab marker, undo your action to restore the tab.

9. With the text still selected, drag the 5.5-inch tab marker to 6.5 inches on the ruler. The text is now aligned at the right margin.

Creating Tabbed Columns

As you have seen in these practice documents, you can use tabs to present information in columns.

When you format a table using tabbed columns, follow these general rules based on *The Gregg Reference Manual*. Follow these rules for existing text or text to be keyed.

- The table should be centered horizontally within the margins.

- Columns within the table should be between six and ten spaces apart.

- The width of the table should not exceed the width of the document's body text.

- At least one blank line should separate the top and bottom of the table from the body text of the document.

Exercise 6-7   SET TABBED COLUMNS

1. Position the insertion point at the end of the document and press Enter twice.

2. Press Ctrl+Q to remove the tab settings from the paragraph mark; then key the text shown in Figure 6-8. Use single spacing.

Figure 6-8

```
The following stores offer a complete line of gifts and
accessories in addition to our fine chocolates. Other
stores offer a limited selection of gifts and accessories
due to space limitations.
```

3. Press Enter twice.

4. Study Figure 6-9 to determine the longest item in each column. (Pennsylvania is the longest item in the first column. Youngstown is the longest item in the second column, and West Virginia is the longest item in the third column.)

Figure 6-9

```
Pennsylvania          Ohio               West Virginia

Grove City            Akron              Clarksburg

Pittsburgh            Canton             Fairmont

Erie                  Cleveland          Morgantown

Monroeville           Youngstown         Wheeling
```

5. Create a guide line that contains the longest item in each column by keying the following with 10 spaces between each group of words:

Pennsylvania   Youngstown   West Virginia

6. Click the Center button on the Ribbon to center the line.

7. Scroll down until the guide line is below the ruler.

8. Change the Tab Alignment button to left alignment . Using the I-beam as a guide, click the ruler to set a left-aligned tab at the beginning of each group of words.

Figure 6-10
Guide line for centering tabbed columns

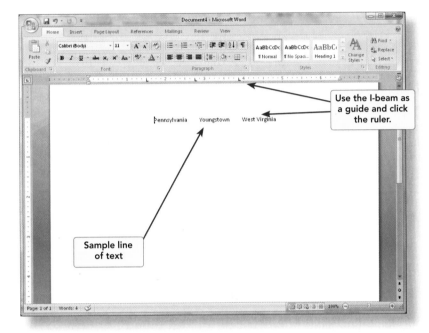

9. Delete the text in the guide line up to the paragraph mark. Do not delete the paragraph mark, which is now storing your left-aligned tab settings.

10. Click the Align Left button to left-align the insertion point.

11. Key the table text as shown in Figure 6-9, pressing Tab before each item and single-spacing each line. Underline each column heading.

12. Select the text near the top of the document beginning with "Item No." and ending with the line that begins "BC32."

13. Change the tab alignment button to left alignment and click the ruler at 2.5.

14. Change the tab alignment button to right alignment and click the ruler at 5.5.

15. Select the text if necessary, and click the Increase Indent button two times to move the text away from the left margin.

16. Drag the left tab marker (right or left) to position the middle column an equal distance from the first and third columns.

17. Bold and center the heading "Standard-Size Boxes." Format the title with all caps and 12 points spacing after. Apply bold and italic formatting to the column headings.

Exercise 6-8   SELECT A TABBED COLUMN

After text is formatted in tabbed columns, you can select columns individually by selecting a vertical block of text. Selecting tabbed text can be helpful for formatting or deleting text. You use Alt to select a vertical block of text.

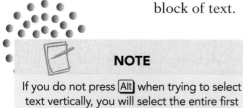

NOTE

If you do not press Alt when trying to select text vertically, you will select the entire first line of text, rather than just the column header for the column you are selecting.

1. Hold down Alt and position the I-beam to the immediate left of "Ohio."

2. Drag across the heading, and then down until the heading and all four cities are selected. Do not select the tab characters to the right of the column.

Figure 6-11
Selecting text vertically

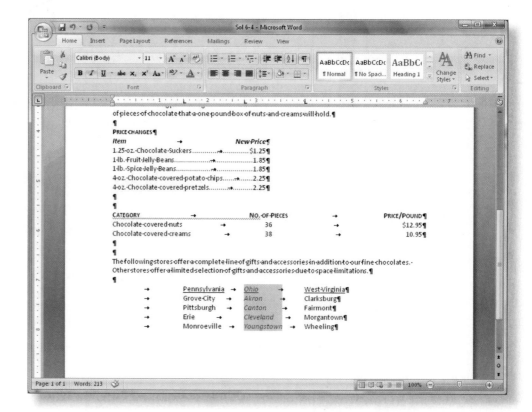

3. Press Delete to delete the column.

4. Undo the deletion.

5. Select the column again, this time selecting only the names under the column head "Ohio."

6. Click the Italic button 𝐼 to format the text.

Exercise 6-9 INSERT BAR TABS

Bar tabs are used to make tabbed columns look more like a table with gridlines. A bar tab inserts a vertical line at a fixed position, creating a border between columns. You can set bar tabs by using the ruler or the Tabs dialog box.

1. At the bottom of the document, select the four lines of tabbed text below the headings "Pennsylvania," "Ohio," and "West Virginia."

2. Open the **Tabs** dialog box. Key **2.5** in the text box, click **Bar**, and click **OK**. The vertical bar is placed between the first and second columns. Do not deselect the tabbed text.

3. To set bar tabs by using the ruler, click the Tab Alignment button until it changes to a bar tab . Click the ruler at 3.75 inches. The bar tab markers appear as short vertical lines on the ruler.

4. Adjust the bar tab markers on the ruler to make them more evenly spaced, as needed.

5. Deselect the tabbed text. Click the Show/Hide ¶ button to view the document without nonprinting characters. The bar tabs act as dividing borders between the columns.

Figure 6-12
Tabbed text with bar tabs

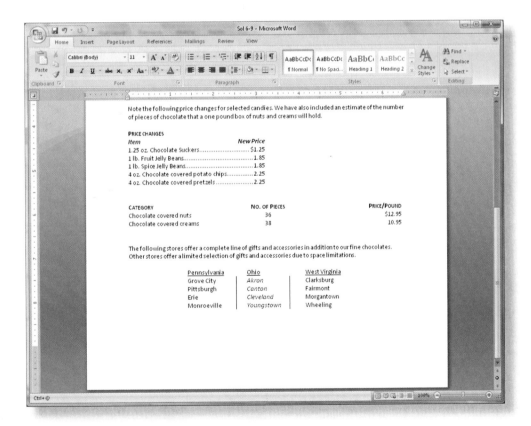

6. Position the insertion point in the line that contains "Grove City."

7. Point to the 3.75-inch bar tab on the ruler, and drag it off the ruler. The vertical line in the table disappears.

8. Undo the deletion to restore the bar tab.

9. Save the document as *[your initials]*6-9 in your Lesson 6 folder.

10. Submit the document.

Sorting Paragraphs and Tabbed Columns

Sorting is the process of reordering text alphabetically or numerically. You can sort to rearrange text in ascending order (from lowest to highest, such as 0–9 or A–Z) or descending order (from highest to lowest, such as 9–0 or Z–A).

You can sort any group of paragraphs, from a single-column list to a multiple-column table, such as one created by tabbed columns. When sorting a tabbed table, you can sort by any of the columns.

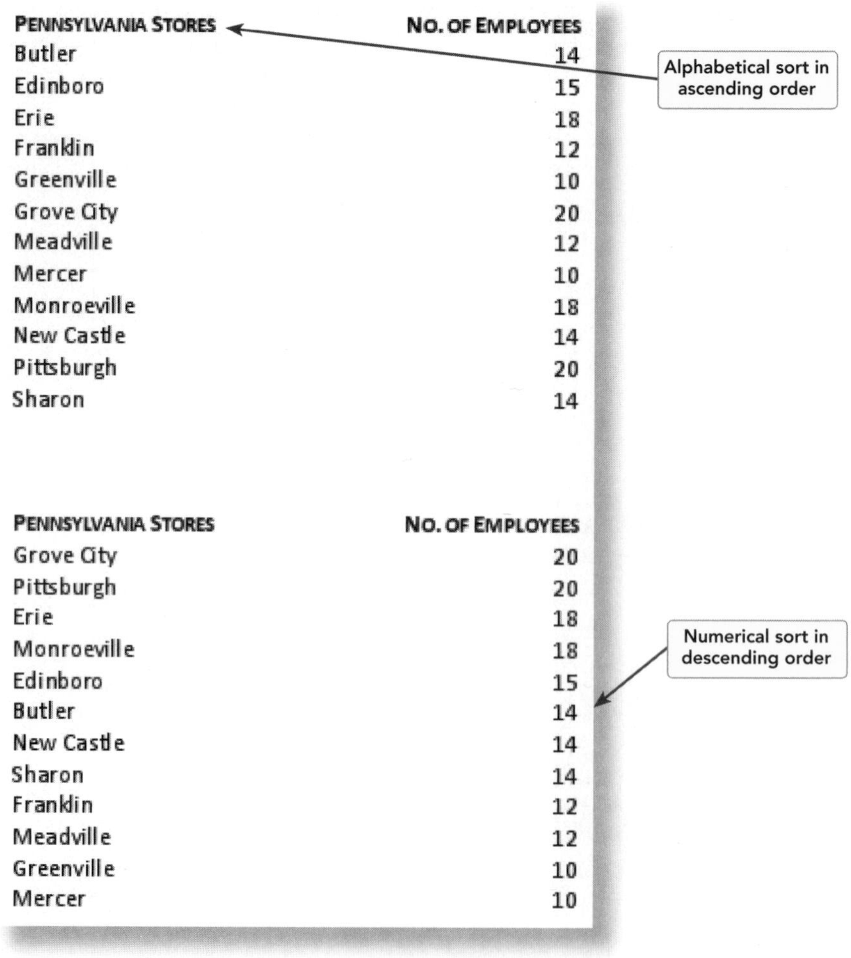

Figure 6-13
Sorting paragraphs and tables

PENNSYLVANIA STORES	NO. OF EMPLOYEES
Butler	14
Edinboro	15
Erie	18
Franklin	12
Greenville	10
Grove City	20
Meadville	12
Mercer	10
Monroeville	18
New Castle	14
Pittsburgh	20
Sharon	14

Alphabetical sort in ascending order

PENNSYLVANIA STORES	NO. OF EMPLOYEES
Grove City	20
Pittsburgh	20
Erie	18
Monroeville	18
Edinboro	15
Butler	14
New Castle	14
Sharon	14
Franklin	12
Meadville	12
Greenville	10
Mercer	10

Numerical sort in descending order

Exercise 6-10   SORT TABBED TABLES

1. Select the headings "Pennsylvania," "Ohio," and "West Virginia" and the four lines of text below the headings.

2. Click the Sort button 🔽 on the Ribbon, Paragraph group.

3. Open the **Sort by** drop-down list to view the other sort options. Field numbers represent each of the columns. Open the **Type** drop-down list. Notice that the type options include **Text**, **Number**, and **Date**.

4. Click **Descending** to change the sort order and click the **Header row** option to select it. Click **OK**. The text in the first column is sorted alphabetically in descending order.

5. Press Ctrl+Z to undo the sort. Do not deselect the text.

6. Click the Sort button 🔽 to open the Sort Text dialog box.

7. Click **Header row** at the bottom of the dialog box. This option indicates that the selection includes column headings, which should not be sorted with the text.

8. Open the **Sort by** drop-down list. Now you can sort by the table's column headings instead of by field numbers.

9. Choose **Ohio** from the drop-down list. Click **Descending** and click **OK**.

Figure 6-14
Sorting options
in the Sort Text
dialog box

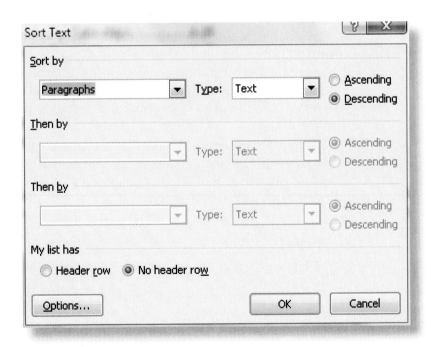

10. Save the document as *[your initials]*6-10 in your Lesson 6 folder.

11. Submit and close the document.

Lesson 6 Summary

- Tabs are a paragraph-formatting feature used to align text. When you press Tab, Word inserts a tab character and moves the insertion position to the tab setting, called the tab stop.

- Word's default tabs are left-aligned and set every half-inch from the left margin, as indicated at the bottom of the horizontal ruler.

- The four most common types of custom tabs are left-aligned, centered, right-aligned, and decimal-aligned. Custom tab settings are indicated on the horizontal ruler by tab markers.

- Set tabs by using the Tabs dialog box or the ruler. To use the ruler, click the Tab Alignment button on the left of the ruler to choose the type of tab alignment, and then click the position on the ruler to set the tab. See Table 6-1.

- A leader tab uses a series of dots, dashes, or solid underlines to fill the empty space to the left of a tab stop. Use the Tabs dialog box to set a leader tab.

- Clear custom tabs all at once or individually. To clear a tab, use the Tabs dialog box, or the ruler, or press Ctrl+Q.

- To adjust tab settings, position the insertion point in the tabbed text (or select the text), and then either open the Tabs dialog box or drag the tab markers on the ruler.

- Use tabs to present information in columns. Tabbed columns are a side-by-side vertical list of information.

- To select a tabbed column (for formatting or deleting the text), hold down Alt and drag the I-beam over the text.

- Use bar tabs to format tabbed columns similar to a table with gridlines. A bar tab inserts a vertical line at a fixed position, creating a border between columns. You can set bar tabs by using the ruler or the Tabs dialog box.

- Sorting is the process of reordering text alphabetically or numerically. You can sort to rearrange text in ascending order (from lowest to highest, such as 0–9 or A–Z) or descending order (from highest to lowest, such as 9–0 or Z–A).

LESSON 6		Command Summary	
Feature	**Button**	**Command**	**Keyboard**
Left tab		**Home** tab, **Paragraph** group	
Center tab		**Home** tab, **Paragraph** group	
Right tab		**Home** tab, **Paragraph** group	
Decimal tab		**Home** tab, **Paragraph** group	
Bar tab		**Home** tab, **Paragraph** group	
Leader tabs		**Home** tab, **Paragraph** group	
Clear tabs		**Home** tab, **Paragraph** group	Ctrl + Q
Sort text		**Home** tab, **Paragraph** group	

Concepts Review

True/False Questions

Each of the following statements is either true or false. Indicate your choice by circling T or F.

T F   1. In Word, you can use [Spacebar] to precisely align text.

T F   2. When you set a custom tab, Word clears all default tabs to the left of the tab stop.

T F   3. You cannot set tabs for existing text.

T F   4. You can either select a paragraph or place the insertion point within the paragraph when setting tabs for the paragraph.

T F   5. When custom tabs are cleared, you must reestablish default tabs or you will have no tabs at all.

T F   6. Tabs inserted in a document cannot be adjusted after they are set.

T F   7. The symbol for a bar tab marker is a short vertical line.

T F   8. You can use the ruler to set a leader tab.

Short Answer Questions

Write the correct answer in the space provided.

1. What are the two ways to set tabs?

_____

2. What are the five types of tabs you can set when using the Tab Alignment button?

_____

3. Which dialog box is used to set a leader tab?

_____

4. What type of tab do you use 🔲 to create?

_____

5. What interval does Word use for default tabs?

_____

6. How do you clear a tab by using the ruler?

_____

7. Which key is used to select a tabbed column?

_____

8. Which Ribbon tab and group contains the Sort feature?

_____

Critical Thinking

Answer these questions on a separate page. There are no right or wrong answers. Support your answers with examples from your own experience, if possible.

1. Books and magazines may use leader tabs in the table of contents and index. Based on representative books and magazines, create a few general guidelines on when to use leader tabs. Support your view with examples.

2. Do you find it easier to read text that is centered in a column or text that is left-aligned? What about numbers that are centered or right-aligned? Create samples to support your position.

Skills Review

Exercise 6-11

Set tabs and create a business memo.

1. Start a new document, and set a 1-inch left-aligned tab by following these steps:
   a. Make sure the Tab Alignment button on the horizontal ruler shows left alignment ⌊.
   b. Click the ruler at the 1-inch mark.

2. Select the paragraph mark and open the Paragraph dialog box. Change the **Spacing After** to **0** and change the **Line spacing** to **Single**.

3. Key the text in Figure 6-15, using the spacing shown. Press `Tab` after each colon. Refer to Appendix B, "Standard Forms for Business Documents."

Figure 6-15

```
        MEMO TO:        Store Managers
one    │FROM:           Thomas Campbell
blank  ├
line   │DATE:           <Current Date>
        SUBJECT:        Monroeville Store
two  →                                      tele                    412
blank  The Monroeville store has added a second phone line. The number is 814-555-8228.
lines                                            ^
        Please record the number and update the company directory.
```

4. In the date line, key today's date.

5. Select the first line of the memo heading and open the **Paragraph** dialog box. Change the **Spacing Before** to **72** points.

6. Add your reference initials at the end of the document.

7 Spell-check the document.

8. Save the document as *[your initials]***6-11** in your Lesson 6 folder.

9. Submit and close the document.

Exercise 6-12

Set leader tabs.

1. Start a new document. Format the paragraph mark as 14 points Arial Narrow. Change the **Spacing After** to **24 pt** and change the **Line spacing** to **Single**.

2. Key the first line in Figure 6-16.

3. Before keying the remaining text, set a solid leader tab that extends to the right margin by following these steps:

   a. Click the **Paragraph Dialog Box Launcher** to open the Paragraph dialog box. Click **Tabs**.

   b. In the **Tab stop position** box, key **6.5**. (The right margin setting.)

   c. Under **Alignment**, click **Right**.

   d. Choose the fourth leader option, click **Set**, and click **OK**.

Figure 6-16

```
Enter a drawing for a free pound of chocolate-covered nuts.
Complete the form below.

Name _____

Address _____

City/State/ZIP _____

Telephone _____
```

4. Key the remaining information, beginning with "Name." Press Tab to move to the 6.5-inch right-aligned tab setting, and then press Enter. Continue keying the text in the figure.

5. Format the text with the solid-line leaders as small caps.

6. Save the document as *[your initials]***6-12** in your Lesson 6 folder.

7. Submit and close the document.

Exercise 6-13

Adjust and clear tab settings.

1. Open the file **Campbell - 1**.
2. Position the insertion point in the first line of the tabbed text that begins "retail." (The tabbed text is a single paragraph.)
3. Set a 1-inch left-aligned tab by using the ruler.
4. Use the ruler to adjust the tab setting by following these steps:
   a. Point to the 1-inch left tab marker.
   b. When you see the ScreenTip identifying the tab marker, drag the marker to 2.5 inches on the ruler.

5. Click the Tab Alignment button until it shows center alignment . Click the ruler at 2 inches to set a tab.
6. Use the Tabs dialog box to clear both tabs by following these steps:
   a. Open the Tabs dialog box.
   b. Click Clear All and click OK.

7. Click the Tab Alignment button until it shows right alignment . Click the ruler at 1.5 inches.
8. Drag the 1.5-inch tab marker on the ruler to adjust it to 2 inches.
9. Save the document as *[your initials]*6-13 in your Lesson 6 folder.
10. Submit and close the document.

Exercise 6-14

Create tabbed columns and sort text.

1. Start a new document. Key MOST POPULAR HOLIDAY CHOCOLATES in uppercase bold. Center the text and press Enter.
2. Left-align the paragraph mark and turn off bold and uppercase. Change the Spacing After to 12 pt and change the Line spacing to Single.
3. Create a table with single-spaced, tabbed columns that are horizontally centered between the left and right margins by following these steps:
   a. Key a guide line containing the longest text from each column in Figure 6-17, with 10 spaces between columns. (Include the column headings when determining the longest item in each column.)
   b. Center the text.
   c. Scroll until the guide line is directly under the ruler.
   d. Using the I-beam for guidance, set a left-aligned tab for each of the columns.

   e. Delete the guide line up to the paragraph mark. Left-align the paragraph mark.

   f. Key the text shown in Figure 6-17, pressing ⎡Tab⎤ before each item in each column.

Figure 6-17

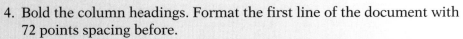

Holiday	Pennsylvania	Ohio	West Virginia
Valentine's Day	1 lb. chocolate nuts	1 lb. assorted	1 lb. turtles
Easter	1 lb. chocolate basket	8 oz. solid rabbit	8 oz. chocolate nut egg
Halloween	chocolate suckers	chocolate suckers	chocolate suckers

4. Bold the column headings. Format the first line of the document with 72 points spacing before.

5. Sort the table alphabetically by holiday by following these steps:

   a. Select the entire table, including the column headings.

   b. Click the Sort button ⧩ in the Paragraph group.

   c. Click **Header row** to display the column headings in the Sort by drop-down list.

   d. Choose **Holiday** from the **Sort by** drop-down list.

   e. Choose **Text** from the **Type** list and choose **Ascending**. Click **OK**.

6. Save the document as *[your initials]***6-14** in your Lesson 6 folder.

7. Submit and close the document.

Lesson Applications

Exercise 6-15

Set tabs for a memo, and then adjust the tab settings.

1. Start a new document. Open the Paragraph dialog box, and change the line spacing to single, and change the spacing after to 0 points.

2. Set a 1-inch left tab and key the text for a memo heading.

3. The memo is to Lydia Hamrick from Thomas Campbell. The subject is Renovation. Remember to include today's date, and insert a blank line between lines in the memo heading.

4. Press Enter three times after the subject line, and key the text shown in Figure 6-18, including the corrections. Use single spacing and insert a blank line between paragraphs.

Figure 6-18

```
                                                          , Pennsylvania
Renovation work is almost complete at Campbell's Confections in Erie. The Erie store is
our
the newest acquisition, and its modern up to date interior provides a spacious area for retail
        a              -controlled
sales, large temperature storage area, and a private office for the store manager.
                                                    tourists is
The Erie store is close enough to the Peninsula to attract visitors, two-blocks from the
           and is                                   from
hospital, conveniently located in a plaza with easy access to and the parking lot for local

residents.
                            d
The store renovation will be features in the Erie Times this weekend.
```

5. Change the font for the entire document to Arial.

6. Change the font for the memo-heading guidewords ("MEMO to:," "FROM:," "DATE:," and "SUBJECT:") to Arial Black.

7. Move to the beginning of the document, and change the spacing before to 72 points for the first line of the memo.

8. Spell-check the document.

9. Add your reference initials to the document.

10. Save the document as *[your initials]*6-15 in your Lesson 6 folder.

11. Submit and close the document.

Exercise 6-16

Set leader tabs and sort paragraphs.

1. Open the file **Chocolate Glossary**.

2. Select the title and change the spacing before to 72 points and the spacing after to 24 points.

3. Format the title size to 14 points, small caps, and center the text.

4. Position the insertion point at the beginning of the first line under the title, and key the paragraph shown in Figure 6-19. Use single spacing. Include one blank line below the paragraph.

Figure 6-19

```
The following list represents popular and commonly used
phrases in chocolate making. Refer to the list to help you
become familiar with the terms.
```

5. Select the list of terms and definitions. Drag the left tab marker off the ruler.

6. Set a dotted leader tab that right-aligns the glossary definitions at the right margin. (The right margin for this document is 6.5 inches as shown on the ruler.)

7. Sort each paragraph in the glossary alphabetically, from A to Z.

8. Change the spacing for each glossary definition to 6 points after paragraphs.

9. Apply a page border, using the box setting and the double wavy line style.

10. Spell-check the document.

11. Save the document as *[your initials]*6-16 in your Lesson 6 folder.

12. Submit and close the document.

Exercise 6-17

Set and adjust tab settings.

1. Start a new document.

2. Key the title in Figure 6-20. Format the title as 12-point Arial bold, uppercase, and centered.

3. Insert two blank lines below the title, and key the paragraph that begins "Even." Use left alignment, single spacing, 11 points, and Arial.

Figure 6-20

```
Chocolate Consumption

Even though Americans consume over 3 billion pounds of
chocolate a year, the United States is not ranked in the
top ten countries for worldwide consumption of chocolate.
Americans consume an average of 12 pounds of chocolate
per person per year. The following countries are listed
as the top five chocolate-consuming nations according to
the World Atlas of Chocolate.

                 Country              Pounds/Year

                 Switzerland              22.36

                 Austria                  20.13

                 Ireland                  19.47

                 Germany                  18.04

                 Norway                   17.93
```

4. Key the remaining text in the figure, beginning with "Country," using a 1.5-inch left indent and an appropriate right tab setting for the second column. The text should be evenly spaced between the left and right margins, as shown in the figure.

5. Format the paragraph that begins with "Even" with justified alignment and a dropped capital letter (use the default drop cap settings). There should be one blank line between this paragraph and the table below it.

6. Adjust the tab setting for the table, so it includes a dotted leader.

7. Change the line spacing for the table text to 1.5 lines.

8. Increase the font size of the title to 14 points and change the Spacing Before to 72 points. Apply bold and small caps to "Country" and "Pounds/Year."

9. Spell-check the document.

10. Save the document as *[your initials]*6-17 in your Lesson 6 folder.

11. Submit and close the document.

Exercise 6-18 ◆ Challenge Yourself

Create a memo with tabbed columns, sort the text, and add bar tabs.

1. Start a new document. Using the proper line spacing, margin settings, and a 1-inch left tab setting, create a memo to Thomas Campbell from Lydia Hamrick. The subject is Weekend Hours for the Ohio Stores.

2. For the body of the memo, key the text in Figure 6-21. Use single spacing. For the tabbed columns, create a guide line to set the tabs. Align the tabbed columns as indicated. Insert a blank line above and below the tabbed columns.

Figure 6-21

```
As you requested, the following is a list of the hours of
operation for the Ohio stores.

Store            Weekdays         Saturday         Sunday

Akron            9 to 5           9 to 3           Closed

Cleveland        10 to 6          9 to 4           1 to 6

Massillon        9 to 5           9 to 4           Closed

Warren           9 to 6           9 to 5           Closed

Youngstown       9 to 6           9 to 5           Closed

Canton           9 to 6           9 to 4           Closed

Let me know if you need additional information.
```

3. Apply a ³/₄-point box border around the entire memo heading (excluding the blank lines below "SUBJECT:"). Add 10 percent gray shading to the memo heading. Click in the first line and apply 72 points spacing before.

4. Adjust the tab setting for the memo heading to 1.25 inches, and set a 1-inch bar tab to create a vertical dividing line.

5. Select the first column of the memo heading (which begins "MEMO TO:") and apply bold formatting.

6. Sort the tabbed table by store in ascending order.

7. Add your reference initials to the bottom of the memo.

8. Spell-check the document.

9. Save the document as *[your initials]*6-18 in your Lesson 6 folder.

10. Submit, and close the document.

On Your Own

In these exercises, you work on your own, as you would in a real-life business environment. Use the skills you've learned to accomplish the task—and be creative.

Exercise 6-19

Write a short business memo. The memo is from you, to a person you work with or a friend and about a subject related to work or a subject of your choosing. Use the correct spacing and tab settings for the memo heading. Save the document as *[your initials]*6-19 and submit it.

Exercise 6-20

Create a monthly budget in the form of a tabbed table. Set and adjust the tabs, using the ruler. Sort the table. Save the document as *[your initials]*6-20 and submit it.

Exercise 6-21

Log onto the Internet, and find a chocolate store you would like to visit. Create a tabbed table containing the names of your favorite chocolates, a brief description, and the price. Use leaders and sort the information. Save the document as *[your initials]*6-21 and submit it.

Move and Copy

OBJECTIVES

After completing this lesson, you will be able to:

1. Use the Office Clipboard.
2. Move text by using cut and paste.
3. Move text by dragging.
4. Copy text by using copy and paste.
5. Copy text by dragging.
6. Work with multiple document windows.
7. Move and copy text among windows.

Estimated Time: 1 hour

MCAS OBJECTIVES
In this lesson:
WW 07 2.2.1
WW 07 5.1.2

One of the most useful features of word processing is the capability to move or copy a block of text from one part of a document to another or from one document window to another, without rekeying the text. In Word, you can move and copy text quickly by using the Cut, Copy, and Paste commands or the drag-and-drop editing feature.

Using the Office Clipboard

Perhaps the most important tool for moving and copying text is the *Clipboard*, which is a temporary storage area. Here's how it works: Cut or copy text from your document and store it on the Clipboard. Then move to a different location in your document and insert the Clipboard's contents using the Paste command.

There are two types of clipboards:

- The system Clipboard stores one item at a time. Each time you store a new item on this Clipboard, it replaces the previous item. This Clipboard is available to many software applications on your system.

- The Office Clipboard can store 24 items, which are displayed on the Clipboard task pane. The Office Clipboard lets you collect multiple items without erasing previous items. You can store items from all Office applications.

Exercise 7-1   DISPLAY THE CLIPBOARD TASK PANE

1. Click the **Home** tab. The **Clipboard** group contains a Dialog Box Launcher arrow to open the Clipboard task pane.

2. Click the **Clipboard Dialog Box Launcher** arrow. The Clipboard task pane opens. At the top of the task pane, notice the Paste All [Paste All] and Clear All [Clear All] buttons. At the bottom of the screen, at the right end of the Taskbar, notice the Clipboard icon , indicating that the Office Clipboard is in use.

Figure 7-1
Clipboard task pane

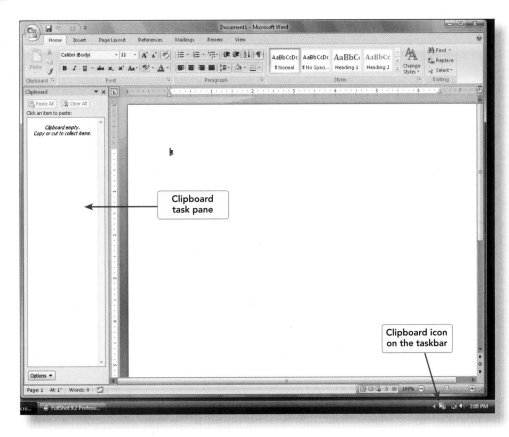

NOTE

You can also press Ctrl+C twice to open the Office Clipboard task pane if the option is turned on. Click the **Options** button at the bottom of the Clipboard task pane, and select the **Show Office Clipboard When** Ctrl+C **Pressed Twice** option.

Options ▼

3. If the Office Clipboard contains items from previous use, click the Clear All button to empty the Clipboard.

4. Click the **Options** button at the bottom of the task pane. Notice the options available for using the Office Clipboard.

5. Click outside the task pane, making sure not to choose any of the options in the list.

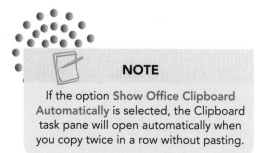

NOTE

If the option **Show Office Clipboard Automatically** is selected, the Clipboard task pane will open automatically when you copy twice in a row without pasting.

Moving Text by Using Cut and Paste

To move text by using the *cut-and-paste* method, start by highlighting the text you want to move and using the Cut command. Then move to the location where you want to place the text and use the Paste command. When you use cut and paste to move paragraphs, you can preserve the correct spacing between paragraphs by following these rules:

- Include the blank line below the paragraph you are moving as part of the selection.

- When you paste the selection, click to the left of the first line of text following the place where your paragraph will go—not on the blank line above it.

There are multiple ways to cut and paste text. The most commonly used methods are:

- Use the Cut and Paste buttons on the Ribbon, Home tab.

- Use the shortcut menu.

- Use the keyboard shortcuts Ctrl+X to cut and Ctrl+V to paste.

- Use the Clipboard task pane.

Exercise 7-2 USE THE RIBBON TO CUT AND PASTE

1. Open the file **Festival Memo**. Display the Clipboard task pane if necessary.

2. Key the current year in the date line of the memo heading.

3. Select the text "Strawberry Days" in the subject line of the memo.

4. Click the **Home** tab, and click the Cut button to remove the text from the document and place it on the Clipboard. Notice the Clipboard item in the task pane.

5. Position the insertion point to the left of "Art" in the Subject line to indicate where you want to insert the text.

6. Click the Paste button to insert "Strawberry Days" in its new location. The Paste Options button appears below the pasted text, and the Clipboard item remains in the task pane.

NOTE

When you point to the Paste button, the button displays two colors and a divider line. Click the upper part of the button to paste text, or click the lower part of the button to display a list of options.

7. Move the I-beam over the Paste Options button. (The I-beam will change to an arrow when it passes over the Paste Options button.) When you see the button's drop-down arrow, click to view the list of options. Click in the document window to close the list of options.

8. Delete the em dash at the end of the subject line.

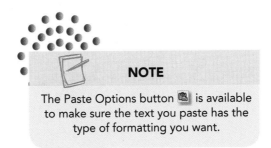

NOTE

The Paste Options button is available to make sure the text you paste has the type of formatting you want.

Exercise 7-3 USE THE SHORTCUT MENU TO CUT AND PASTE

1. Select the paragraph near the bottom of the document that begins "All hotels are." Include the paragraph mark on the blank line following the paragraph.

Figure 7-2
Using the shortcut
menu to cut

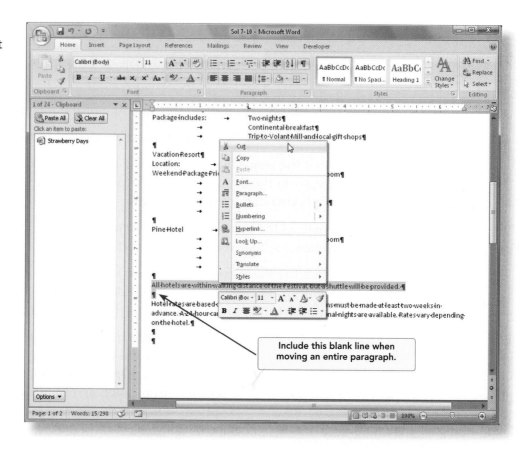

2. Point to the selected text and right-click to display the shortcut menu.

3. Click **Cut**. The item is added to the Clipboard task pane.

NOTE

Each new item you cut (or copy) is added to the top of the Clipboard task pane.

4. Position the I-beam to the left of the paragraph that begins "Several special." Right-click and choose **Paste** from the shortcut menu. The paragraph moves to its new location, and the Paste Options button appears below the pasted text.

Figure 7-3
Using the shortcut
menu to paste

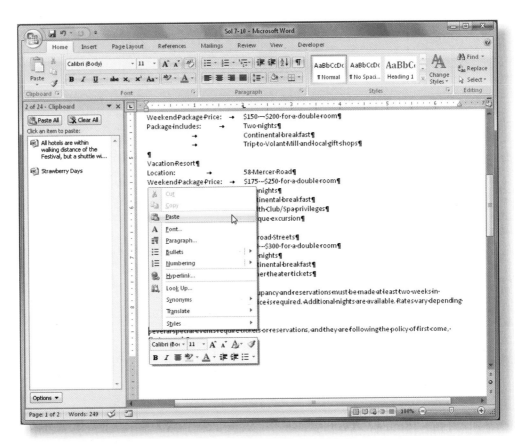

Exercise 7-4   USE KEYBOARD SHORTCUTS
TO CUT AND PASTE

If you prefer using the keyboard, you can press Ctrl+X to cut text and Ctrl+V
to paste text. You can also use Ctrl+Z to undo an action. The location of these
shortcut keys is designed to make it easy for you to move your mouse with your
right hand while you press command keys with your left hand.

1. Select the paragraph that begins "Several special." Press Ctrl+X to
   cut the text. A new item appears in the task pane.

2. Position the insertion point just before the paragraph that begins
   "Please refer." Press Ctrl+V to paste the text.

3. Press Ctrl+Z to undo the paste. Press Ctrl+Y. (Remember, you can
   also click the Undo button 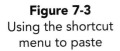 to undo actions.) Notice that the
   Clipboard item remains in the task pane.

Exercise 7-5   USE THE OFFICE CLIPBOARD
TO PASTE

Each time you cut text in the previous exercises, a new item was added to the
Office Clipboard. You can paste that item directly from the task pane.

Word 2007

1. Select all the information that goes with the "Pine Hotel," including the title "Pine Hotel" and the blank line that follows the hotel information.

2. Cut this text, using the Cut button on the Ribbon. The text is stored as a new item at the top of the Clipboard task pane.

3. Position the insertion point to the left of the paragraph that begins "Wolf Creek Hotel."

4. Click the task pane item for the Pine Hotel text that you just cut. (Do not click the drop-down arrow.) This pastes the text at the location of the insertion point.

5. Press Ctrl+Z to undo the paste. Press Ctrl+Z again to undo the cut. The Clipboard item remains in the task pane.

6. Point to this Clipboard item in the task pane, and click the drop-down arrow that appears to its right.

7. Choose **Delete** from the list to delete the item from the Clipboard.

NOTE

Choosing the Paste option from the drop-down list pastes that item, just like clicking directly on the item. The Paste All button on the Clipboard task pane is used to copy all Office Clipboard items to the location of the insertion point.

Moving Text by Dragging

You can also move selected text to a new location by using the *drag-and-drop* method. Text is not transferred to the Clipboard when you use drag and drop.

Exercise 7-6 USE DRAG AND DROP TO MOVE TEXT

1. Select all the information related to "Vacation Resort," including the title "Vacation Resort' and the blank line below the information.

2. Point to the selected text. Notice that the I-beam changes to a left-pointing arrow.

3. Click and hold down the left mouse button. The pointer changes to the drag-and-drop pointer . Notice the dotted insertion point near the tip of the arrow and the dotted box at the base of the arrow.

4. Drag the pointer until the dotted insertion point is positioned to the left of the line beginning "Wolf Creek Hotel." Release the mouse button. The paragraph moves to its new location and the Paste Options button appears.

TIP

Use cut and paste to move text over long distances—for example, onto another page. Use drag and drop to move text short distances where you can see both the selected text and the destination on the screen at the same time.

Figure 7-4
Drag-and-drop
pointer

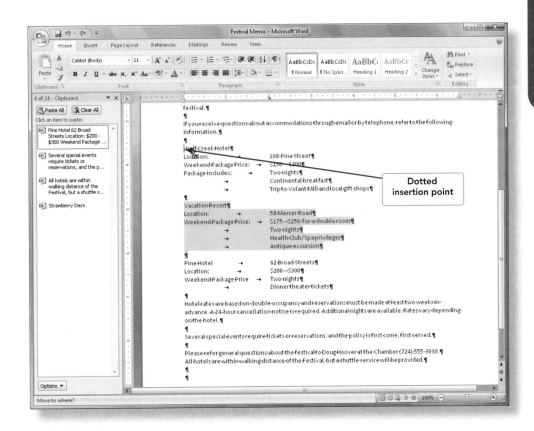

Copying Text by Using Copy and Paste

Copying and pasting text is similar to cutting and pasting text. Instead of removing the text from the document and storing it on the Clipboard, you place a copy of the text on the Clipboard.

There are several ways to copy and paste text. The most common methods are:

- Use the Copy and Paste buttons on the Ribbon, Home tab.

- Use the shortcut menu.

- Use keyboard shortcuts [Ctrl]+[C] to copy and [Ctrl]+[V] to paste.

- Use the Clipboard task pane.

Exercise 7-7   USE COPY AND PASTE

1. Under "Wolf Creek Hotel," select the entire line that contains the text "Continental breakfast." Include the tab character to the left of the text and the paragraph mark to the right of the text. Click the Show/Hide button to display formatting characters. (The selected text should begin at the left margin and end with the paragraph mark.)

Copy

2. Click the Copy button on the Ribbon to transfer a copy of the text to the Clipboard. Notice that the selected text remains in its original position in the document.

3. Position the insertion point to the left of the paragraph that begins with a tab character and includes "Health Club/Spa privileges" in the text under "Vacation Resort."

4. Right-click and choose **Paste** from the shortcut menu. A copy of the paragraph is added to the "Vacation Resort" package description, and the Paste Options button appears.

5. Point to the Paste Options button. When you see the down arrow, click the button. Notice that the same options are available when you copy and paste text. Click in the document window to close the list of options and keep the source formatting.

6. Position the insertion point to the left of the paragraph that begins "Dinner theater tickets." Press Ctrl+V to paste the text into the "Pine Hotel" package description.

Exercise 7-8   USE THE OFFICE CLIPBOARD TO PASTE COPIED TEXT

A new item is added to the Office Clipboard each time you copy text. You can click this item to paste the text into the document.

1. Under "Vacation Resort," select the text "for a double room." Include the space character to the left of the text and the paragraph mark to the right of the text.

NOTE

You can store up to 24 cut or copied items on the Office Clipboard. When the Clipboard is full and you cut or copy text, the bottom Clipboard item is deleted and the new item is added to the top of the task pane.

2. Press Ctrl+C to copy this text.

3. Position the insertion point to the right of the text that begins "$150–$200."

4. Click the Clipboard that contains the text "for a double room." The Clipboard content is pasted into the document at the location of the insertion point.

Copying Text by Dragging

To copy text by using the drag-and-drop method, press Ctrl while dragging the text. Remember, drag and drop does not store text on a Clipboard.

Exercise 7-9   USE DRAG AND DROP TO COPY TEXT

1. Scroll until you can see the text under "Wolf Creek Hotel" and "Pine Hotel."

NOTE

You may already have noticed that when you delete, cut, move, or paste text, Word automatically adjusts the spacing between words. For example, if you cut a word at the end of a sentence, Word automatically deletes the leftover space. If you paste a word between two other words, Word automatically adds the needed space as part of its Smart Cut-and-Paste feature. The Smart Cut-and-Paste feature is turned on by default.

2. Select the text under the Wolf Creek Hotel beginning with "for a double room." Include the paragraph mark.

3. While pressing Ctrl, drag the selected text to the immediate right of the text "$200–$300" in the "Pine Hotel" section. The plus (+) sign attached to the drag-and-drop pointer indicates the text is being copied rather than moved.

4. The text is copied, and a space is automatically inserted between "$300" and "for."

Figure 7-5
Copying with the drag-and-drop pointer

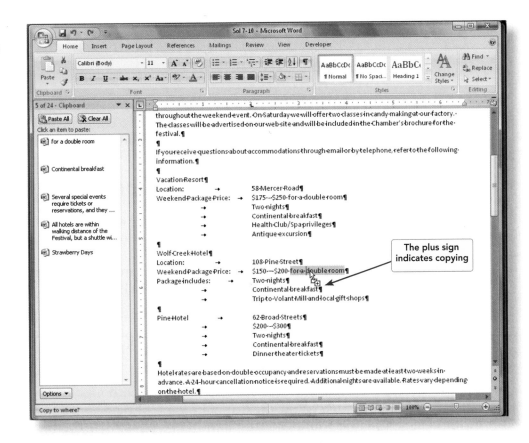

5. Move to the top of the document, and change the spacing before to 72 points, and insert your reference initials at the end of the document.

Word 2007

TIP

Dragging is not effective over long distances within a document. Try these alternative methods: To cut, select the text, hold down Ctrl, scroll as needed, and right-click where you want to paste the text. To copy, select the text, hold down Ctrl and Shift, scroll as needed, and right-click where you want to paste the text.

6. Open the **File** menu, and click the arrow beside **Print**. Click **Print Preview** to switch to Print Preview. Display both pages of the document by clicking **Two Pages**.

7. Locate and click the Shrink One Page button . The document is reduced to a one-page document.

8. Close Print Preview.

9. Save the document as *[your initials]*7-9 in a new folder for Lesson 7.

10. Click the Clear All button ✂ Clear All on the Office Clipboard to clear all items. Click the Close button ✕ on the task pane to close the Office Clipboard.

11. Submit and close the document.

Working with Multiple Document Windows

In Word, you can work with several open document windows. Working with multiple windows makes it easy to compare different parts of the same document or to move or copy text from one document to another.

Exercise 7-10 SPLIT A DOCUMENT INTO PANES

Splitting a document divides it into two areas separated by a horizontal line called the *split bar*. Each of the resulting two areas, called *panes*, has its own scroll bar.

To split a screen, click the View tab and click the Split button or use the split box at the top of the vertical scroll bar.

1. Open the file **Fund2**.

2. Click the **View** tab and click the Split button . A gray bar appears along with the split pointer .

3. Move your mouse up or down (without clicking) until the gray bar is just below the last paragraph of the list of candy bars.

Figure 7-6
Splitting a document
into two panes

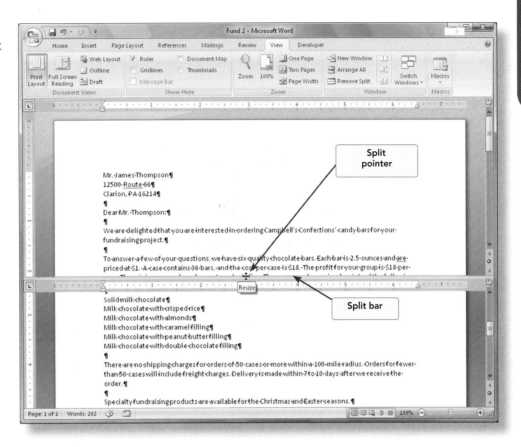

4. Click the left mouse button to set the split. The document divides into two panes, each with its own ruler and scroll bar.

5. To change the split position, move the mouse pointer over the split bar (between the top and bottom panes) until you see the split pointer ÷ and a ScreenTip that says "Resize." Then drag the bar above the list.

6. To remove the split bar, move the mouse pointer over it. When you see the split pointer, double-click. The split bar is removed.

7. Position the pointer over the *split box*—the thin gray rectangle at the top of the vertical scroll bar. (Refer to Figure 7–7 on the next page.)

8. When you see the split pointer ÷, double-click. Once again the document is split into two panes. (You can also remove the split bar by choosing Remove Split ⬚ from the View tab.)

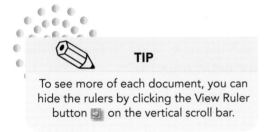

TIP

To see more of each document, you can hide the rulers by clicking the View Ruler button ⬚ on the vertical scroll bar.

Figure 7-7
Double-click the split
box to create two
window panes.

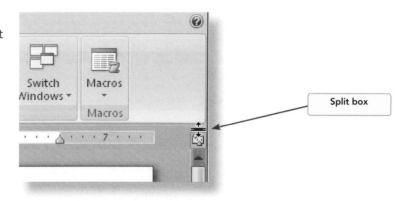

Split box

Exercise 7-11   MOVE BETWEEN PANES TO EDIT TEXT

After you split a document, you can scroll each pane separately and easily move from pane to pane to edit separate areas of the document. To switch panes, click the insertion point in the pane you want to edit.

1. Click in the top pane.

2. With the insertion point in the top pane, click the insertion point in the bottom pane.

3. Use the scroll bar in the bottom pane to scroll to the top of the document. Both panes should now show the inside address.

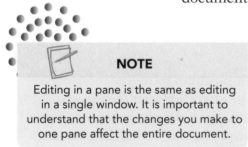

NOTE

Editing in a pane is the same as editing in a single window. It is important to understand that the changes you make to one pane affect the entire document.

4. In the bottom pane, change the street address to **12575 Route 66"** and the state to **PA**. Notice that the changes also appear in the top pane.

5. In the bottom pane, scroll until the paragraph beginning "Specialty fundraising" is displayed. Click within the top pane, and scroll until the paragraphs beginning "Specialty fundraising" and "There are no" are both displayed.

 Cut

6. Go back to the bottom pane. Select the paragraph beginning "Specialty fundraising," and click the Cut button ⅄ Cut . (Remember to include the blank line after the paragraph when selecting it.)

Paste

7. Move to the top pane, position the insertion point to the left of "There are no," and click the Paste button 📋. The paragraph is moved from one part of the document to another.

8. Drag the split bar to the top of the screen. This is another way to remove the split bar. The document is again displayed in one pane.

9. Apply the correct letter formatting to the document by adding the date and your reference initials. Use the correct spacing between all letter elements, and place 72 points spacing before the date.

10. Save the document as *[your initials]***7-11** in your Lesson 7 folder.

11. Submit and close the document.

Exercise 7-12 OPEN MULTIPLE DOCUMENTS

In addition to working with window panes, you can work with more than one document file at the same time. This is useful if you keyed text in one document that you want to use in a second document.

1. Display the Open dialog box. Simultaneously open the noncontiguous files **Bittersweet** and **Milk Chocolate**. To do this, click **Bittersweet** once, press Ctrl, and click **Milk Chocolate** once. With both files selected, click **Open**.

2. Click the **View** tab. Click the Switch Windows button , and notice that the two open files are listed at the bottom of this menu. The active file has a check next to it. Switch documents by clicking the file that is not active.

3. Press Ctrl+F6 to switch back.

4. Look at the taskbar at the bottom of your screen. Notice the two buttons that contain the names of your open documents. The highlighted button shows that it is the active document. Click the **Bittersweet** button to activate that document.

Figure 7-8
Window menu

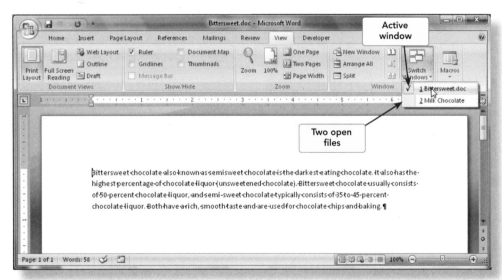

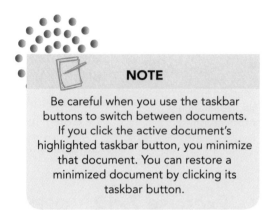

NOTE

Be careful when you use the taskbar buttons to switch between documents. If you click the active document's highlighted taskbar button, you minimize that document. You can restore a minimized document by clicking its taskbar button.

5. Click the **View** tab, if necessary. Click the Arrange All button to view both documents at the same time. The two documents appear one below the other.

Figure 7-9
Two documents displayed on one screen

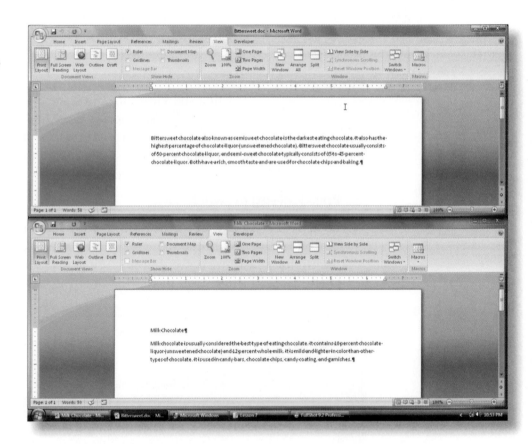

6. Press Ctrl+F6 to switch between documents. Press Ctrl+F6 again. Notice that the active window—the one containing the insertion point—has a highlighted title bar.

7. Close the **Bittersweet** and **Milk Chocolate** documents.

8. Click the Maximize button to maximize the Word window.

9. Simultaneously open three files, **Bittersweet**, **Chocolate - 2**, and **Milk Chocolate**, by accessing the Open dialog box. Select the first file, Bittersweet, and then press Ctrl and select the other two files. Click Open.

10. Choose Arrange All from the Window menu to display all three documents simultaneously.

Exercise 7-13 REARRANGE AND RESIZE DOCUMENT WINDOWS

You can rearrange the open documents in Word by using basic Windows techniques for minimizing, maximizing, restoring, and sizing windows.

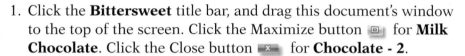

1. Click the **Bittersweet** title bar, and drag this document's window to the top of the screen. Click the Maximize button for **Milk Chocolate**. Click the Close button for **Chocolate - 2**.

2. Minimize the **Milk Chocolate** window by clicking its Minimize button . The document disappears from view. The **Milk Chocolate** button is on the taskbar, indicating that Word is still running.

3. Restore the **Milk Chocolate** document for viewing by clicking its taskbar button.

4. Drag a corner of the window's border diagonally down and to the right a few inches to make the window a different size.

5. Click the Maximize button in the **Milk Chocolate** window to return the window to full screen.

6. Click the Close button for **Milk Chocolate**.

Moving and Copying Text among Windows

When you want to copy or move text from one document to another, you can work with either multiple (smaller) document windows or full-size document windows. Either way, you can use cut and paste or copy and paste. If you work with multiple windows, you can also use drag and drop. To use this technique, you must display both documents at the same time.

Exercise 7-14 COPY TEXT FROM ONE DOCUMENT TO ANOTHER BY USING COPY AND PASTE

When moving or copying text from one document into another, the Paste command pastes text in the format of the document from which it was cut or copied. To control the formatting of pasted text, you can use the Paste Options button 🗎 or the Paste Special function. In this exercise, you will use the Paste Special function to paste text without formatting.

1. Open the files **Bittersweet**, **Chocolate - 2**, and **Milk Chocolate**. Click the **Bittersweet** button on the taskbar to make it the active document.

2. In **Bittersweet**, select the entire document and change the font to 12-point Arial. Click the Copy button .

3. Switch to the **Chocolate - 2** document.

4. Click the insertion point at the beginning of the paragraph that begins "Sweet or." Click the Paste button to insert the text copied from **Bittersweet**. Notice the format of the new text does not match the format of the current document.

5. Click the Undo button 🔄 to remove the new text.

6. Click the **Home** tab, and click the lower part of the Paste button 🗎. Click **Paste Special** and select **Unformatted Text**. Click **OK**. Now the format of the new text matches the format of the current document. Press Enter if necessary.

7. Click the **View** tab, and click the Switch Windows button 🗎 to activate **Bittersweet** again. Close this document without saving it.

> **TIP**
>
> You can insert an entire file into the current document by using the Insert tab. Move the insertion point to the place in the document where you want to insert the file. Then from the Insert tab, click the Object button 🗎 Object ▾. Click Text from File and double-click the filename. The text from the entire file is inserted at the insertion point.

Exercise 7-15 MOVE TEXT FROM ONE DOCUMENT TO ANOTHER BY USING DRAG AND DROP

1. Arrange the two open documents (**Milk Chocolate** and **Chocolate - 2**), so they are both displayed.

2. Switch to the **Milk Chocolate** document, and select the paragraph below the title.

3. Drag the selected paragraph to the **Chocolate - 2** document, and position the insertion point in front of the paragraph that begins "Sweet or."

Figure 7-10
Dragging a
paragraph between
document windows

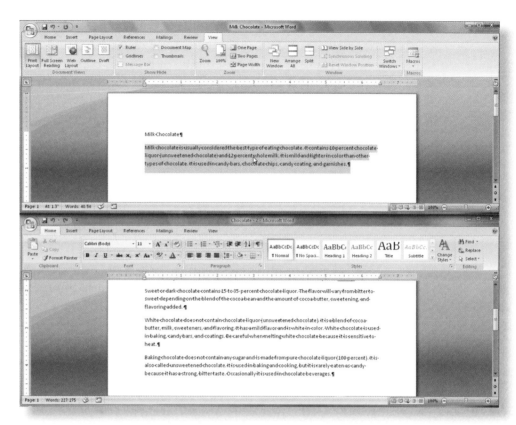

4. Close the **Milk Chocolate** document without saving.

5. Maximize the **Chocolate - 2** document. Correct the spacing between paragraphs (if you have extra paragraph marks, for example).

6. At the top of the document, add the title TYPES OF CHOCOLATE, formatted as 14-point bold and centered. Add 72 points spacing before and 24 points spacing after the title.

7. Save the document as *[your initials]*7-15 in your Lesson 7 folder; then print and close it.

Lesson 7 Summary

- The most important tool for moving and copying text is the Clipboard, which is a temporary storage space.

- When you display the Clipboard task pane, you are activating the Office Clipboard, which can store up to 24 cut or copied items. With the Clipboard task pane open, cut or copied text appears as a new item in the task pane.

- You move text by cutting and pasting—cut the text from one location and paste it to another.

- Copy and paste is similar to cut and paste, but instead of removing the text from the document, you place a copy of it on the Clipboard.

- There are many methods for cutting, copying, and pasting text. Use commands on the Ribbon, keyboard shortcuts, or the shortcut menu. Use the Clipboard task pane to paste stored text items.

- Use the Paste Options button 📋 to control the formatting of pasted text.

- You can use the drag-and-drop method to copy or move text from one location to another in a document or between documents.

- Split a document into panes to compare different parts of the document or to cut or copy text from one part of the document to another. Use the View tab or the split box above the vertical scroll bar to split a document.

- Open multiple documents and arrange them to fit on one screen to move or copy text from one document to another.

LESSON 7		Command Summary	
Feature	**Button**	**Command**	**Keyboard**
Open Office Clipboard	Clipboard ⤢	**Home** tab, **Clipboard** group	Ctrl + C twice
Cut	✂ Cut	**Home** tab, **Clipboard** group	Ctrl + X
Copy	📋 Copy	**Home** tab, **Clipboard** group	Ctrl + C
Paste	📋 Paste	**Home** tab, **Clipboard** group	Ctrl + V
Split a document	⬚ Split	**View** tab, **Window** group	
Arrange multiple windows	⬚ Arrange All	**View** tab, **Window** group	
Next window		**View** tab, **Switch Windows**, *[filename]*	Ctrl + F6
Previous window		**View** tab, **Switch Windows**, *[filename]*	Ctrl + Shift + F6

Concepts Review

True/False Questions

Each of the following statements is either true or false. Indicate your choice by circling T or F.

T F   1. Drag and drop stores text on the clipboard.

T F   2. The content of the Office Clipboard is replaced each time you copy or cut text.

T F   3. The keyboard shortcut for cut is Ctrl+C.

T F   4. You can drag text between two documents when they are maximized.

T F   5. The Cut, Copy, and Paste commands are all available from the shortcut menu.

T F   6. The only difference between cut and copy is that selected text remains in the document after copying.

T F   7. When you move a paragraph, you should select the blank line following it to preserve proper line spacing.

T F   8. When a document is split into panes, you can remove the split by double-clicking the split bar.

Short Answer Questions

Write the correct answer in the space provided.

1. How can you copy text without using the Clipboard?

_____

2. Which commands on the Ribbon, Home tab, do you use to move text?

_____

3. What is the keyboard shortcut for moving between two documents?

_____

4. For which command is Ctrl+V the keyboard shortcut?

_____

5. Which command displays all open documents at the same time?

_____

6. What is the keyboard shortcut to Undo?

_____

7. What is different about the drag-and-drop pointer when you are copying, as opposed to moving, text?

_____

8. Where is the split box located?

_____

Critical Thinking

Answer these questions on a separate page. There are no right or wrong answers. Support your answers with examples from your own experience, if possible.

1. Many people once wrote first-draft documents by hand or by using a typewriter. In either case, people would then literally cut and paste pieces of their document together and type a final draft. Some people say that word processing—specifically moving and copying text—has caused a basic change in the way people write. What do you think? Explain your answer.

2. You learned different methods for moving text by using cut and paste. You also learned the drag-and-drop method of moving text. Which method do you prefer? Why?

Skills Review

Exercise 7-16

Move text to a new location by using cut and paste and by dragging.

1. Open the file **Property**.
2. Display the Office Clipboard by following these steps:
   a. Click the **Home** tab, and click the **Clipboard Dialog Box Launcher**.
   b. Click Clear All ![Clear All] if there are any items in the task pane.
3. Use keyboard shortcuts to move text by following these steps:
   a. Click the insertion point at the beginning of the line that starts "Equipment – Office." Press and hold [Shift]. Click at the end of the line beginning "Key employees."
   b. Press [Ctrl]+[X] to cut the text.
   c Position the insertion point to the left of the line that begins "Types of coverage."
   d. Press [Ctrl]+[V] to paste the text. Press [Enter] to add a line space between the paragraphs.

4. Drag text by following these steps:

   a. Select the text "All employees" through "Customers."

   b. Point to the selected text. Press and hold down the left mouse button to display the drag-and-drop pointer and the dotted insertion point.

   c. Drag the dotted insertion point to the left of the word "Research" and release the mouse button.

   d. Press Enter after "Customers."

5. Use the Ribbon to cut and paste text by following these steps:

   a. Select the text "Fire" through "Loss of income."

   b. Click the Cut button ✂ Cut .

   c. Position the insertion point at the beginning of the line that starts "Who to cover."

   d. Click the Paste button 📋 .

   e. Press Enter after "Loss of income."

6. Select "Types of insurance." Press Ctrl and select "Types of Coverage," "Who to cover," and "Research."

7. Apply bold, small caps, and 12 points format to the selected text. A blank line should precede each heading.

8. Clear and close the Office Clipboard by following these steps:

   a. Click Clear All ✖ Clear All to remove all Clipboard items.

   b. Click the task pane's Close button ✖ .

9. Select the title of the document, and change it to bold, 14 points, uppercase, and apply 72 points spacing before and 24 points spacing after.

10. Save the document as *[your initials]*7-16 in your Lesson 7 folder.

11. Submit and close the document.

Exercise 7-17

Copy text by using copy and paste and by dragging.

1. Open the file **Stores - 2**.

2. Display the Office Clipboard, and clear the Office Clipboard if it contains any items.

3. Select all text in the document beginning with "Pennsylvania" through the end of the document.

4. Set a left tab at 2 inches on the ruler.

5. Position the insertion point to the right of "Grove City," and press Tab. Key Carole Walters.

6. Use the Office Clipboard to copy text by following these steps:

   a. Select the tab character (→) and "Carole Walters."

   b. Click the Copy button 📋 Copy to copy the text to a Clipboard.

   c. Position the insertion point to the right of "Meadville:"

   d. Paste the text by clicking the Clipboard.

7. Position the insertion point to the right of "Clarksburg" and press [Tab]. Key Rebecca Surrena.

8. Select the tab character and "Rebecca Surrena," and press [Ctrl]+[C] to place the selected text on a clipboard.

9. Position the insertion point to the right of "Fairmont," and press [Ctrl]+[V].

10. Use the drag-and-drop method to copy "Carole Walters" by following these steps:

    a. Select the tab character, the text "Carole Walters," and the paragraph mark.

    b. Point to the text. Press and hold down [Ctrl]; then click and hold down the left mouse button.

    c. Drag the dotted insertion point to the right of the word "Mercer:" and release both the mouse button and [Ctrl].

11. Click to the right of "Butler," press [Tab], and key Cynthia Rhodes. Select the tab character and the text you just keyed and copy it to the clipboard.

12. Click to the right of "Akron," press [Tab], and key Jane Daniels. Select the tab character and the text you just keyed and copy it to the clipboard. The clipboard should contain four names. Paste the text "Jane Daniels" to all cities listed under Ohio.

13. Use the Clipboard task pane to paste the text "Carole Walters" to the following cities: Edinboro, Erie, Sharon, Greenville, and Franklin.

14. Use the Clipboard task pane to paste the text "Rebecca Surrena" to Morgantown and Wheeling.

15. Use the Clipboard task pane to paste the text "Cynthia Rhodes" to New Castle, Pittsburgh, and Monroeville.

16. Bold and center the two lines at the top of the document. Format the first line in all caps and 16 points and 72 points spacing before. Format the second line in small caps and 14 points.

17. Format each of the state names as bold, italic, and small caps.

18. Select the text from "Pennsylvania" through the end of the document, and format the selected text with a 1-inch left indent. Drag the left tab marker on the ruler to 4 inches.

19. Clear and close the Office Clipboard.

20. Save the document as *[your initials]*7-17 in your Lesson 7 folder.

21. Submit and close the document.

Exercise 7-18

Split a document into panes.

1. Open the file **Favors - 2**.

2. Split the document into two panes by double-clicking the split box above the vertical scroll bar.

3. In the top pane, use the scroll bar to display the list beginning with "wedding bells" through "other assorted shapes." Format the selected text as a bulleted list.

4. In the bottom pane, scroll to the list that begins with "solid milk chocolate." Sort the list alphabetically.

REVIEW

Click the Sort button in the Paragraph group.

5. In the bottom pane, format the list of chocolate squares as a bulleted list.

6. Remove the split by double-clicking the split bar.

7. Scroll through the document to view the changes.

8. Apply bold formatting to the title and change the spacing before to 72 points and the spacing after to 24 points.

9. Place the insertion point in the title line and apply a bottom border.

10. Save the document as *[your initials]*7-18 in your Lesson 7 folder.

11. Submit and close the document.

Exercise 7-19

Arrange windows to move and copy text.

1. Start a new document. Key the text shown in Figure 7-11, and format it as a standard business memo. Use single spacing for the body of the memo and include today's date.

Figure 7-11

```
Memo to Robert Smith from Pete Barnes
Subject is Vehicle Reports
Please review the following information, and let me know if
the information provided is compatible with the new fleet
management software.
Mileage numbers will be provided the first of each month.
```

2. Save the document as *[your initials]*7-19 in your Lesson 7 folder.

3. Simultaneously open the files **Vehicle** and **Maintenance**.

4. Arrange the documents by following these steps:

   a. Switch to **Maintenance** if necessary, and minimize it by clicking the Minimize button ⬜.

   b. Display the other two documents at the same time by clicking the View tab and clicking Arrange All.

5. Drag a paragraph between documents by following these steps:

   a. In the *[your initials]*7-19 window, scroll to display the sentence beginning "Mileage numbers."

   b. In the **Vehicle** window, select the entire document by pressing Ctrl + A.

   c. Holding down Ctrl to copy, drag the paragraph to the *[your initials]*7-19 window until it precedes the paragraph beginning "Mileage."

6. Close the **Vehicle** document and restore the **Maintenance** document by clicking its taskbar button.

7. Use **View tab**, **Arrange All** to display *[your initials]***7-19** and **Maintenance** at the same time, if necessary.

8. In **Maintenance**, select the text beginning "Scheduled Maintenance Guide" through the blank line preceding "10,000 miles." Copy and paste this text to the end of *[your initials]***7-19**.

9. Close the **Maintenance** document without saving it. Maximize *[your initials]***7-19**. Format the entire document in 12-point Times New Roman. Insert your reference initials at the bottom of the memo.

10. Select "Vehicle Listing" and "Scheduled Maintenance Guide," and format each heading with 14 point, bold and small caps. Format the column headings of the tabbed text to bold, small caps, and underlined.

11. Save the document again.

12. Submit and close the document.

13. If the Word window is not maximized, click the Maximize button .

Lesson Applications

Exercise 7-20

Move and copy text.

1. Open the file **OH Stores - 2**.

2. Move the address text for the Cleveland store to follow the address text for the Canton store.

3. Click on the blank line following the Akron address, and key the following text on two lines. Press Enter after each line.
   Telephone:
   Fax:

4. Select "Telephone:" and "Fax:" and copy the text to the Clipboard.

5. Paste the copied text at the end of each address.

6. Format the document heading as uppercase, bold, and 14 points with 72 points of spacing before and 24 points of spacing after. Delete the blank paragraph mark below the heading.

7. Apply bold, italic, and small caps formatting to each store name.

8. Save the document as *[your initials]*7-20 in your Lesson 7 folder.

9. Submit and close the document.

Exercise 7-21

Copy and move text in a memo.

1. Open the file **Walk**.

2. At the top of the document, insert a memo heading to the staff from you, using today's date.

3. Move the first line in the document (which begins "Getting ready") to the subject line and apply italic formatting. In the subject line, replace "walk" with a copy of the words "Chamber of Commerce Walk-a-Thon" found in the paragraph that begins "Here is." Match the destination formatting, and apply the appropriate capitalization to the subject line.

4. Delete the punctuation at the end of the subject line and extra blank lines below the subject line.

5. Use copy and paste to replace "walk-a-thon" in the last sentence of the document with the words "Chamber of Commerce Walk-a-Thon." Match destination formatting.

6. In the paragraph that begins "Once again," move the last two sentences (beginning with "We are") to the end of the document, combining them with the paragraph that begins "As I'm sure you all know."

7. At the top of the document, combine the paragraphs that begin "Once again" and "Here is."

8. In the paragraph that begins "We need," delete the words "We need a volunteer to" and capitalize the next word "check."

9. Format the three action paragraphs, beginning "Arrange," "Go through," and "Contact," as a numbered list.

10. Format the two uppercase and blue headings as uppercase, bold (no color), and with 6 points of spacing after them.

11. Save the document as *[your initials]7-21* in your Lesson 7 folder.

12. Submit and close the document.

REVIEW

Remember to add your reference initials to the memo.

Exercise 7-22

Copy text from multiple documents into an existing document.

1. Open the file **Holtz**. Copy the inside address and salutation. Close the document without saving.

2. Create a new document, and insert the date using the Insert tab on the Ribbon. (Use appropriate format for a business letter.) Press Enter, and paste the copied text.

3. Format the date with 72 points spacing before and 36 points spacing after.

4. For the first paragraph of the new letter, key the text shown in Figure 7-12.

Figure 7-12

```
I am looking forward to your visit to Grove City in June.
You will be staying at the Wolf Creek Hotel as our guest.
```

5. From the file **Wolf Creek**, copy the second paragraph, beginning "The hotel has 200 rooms," and paste it at the end of the paragraph you keyed in step 4. Delete the last sentence in the paragraph.

6. Start a new paragraph by keying When you arrive, the Strawberry Days Arts and Music Festival will be in full swing.

7. From the file **Summer**, copy the last sentence of the first paragraph, and paste it at the end of the sentence you just keyed. Edit the beginning of the sentence to "You can enjoy."

8. Key the text shown in Figure 7-13 as a closing paragraph.

Figure 7-13

```
Jack, I am delighted that you are coming to Grove City! I
know you are going to have a great time at the Festival and
touring our facilities.
```

9. Add an appropriate closing. The letter is from Thomas Campbell, President.

10. Check for correct spacing, and spell-check the document.

11. Save the document as *[your initials]7-22* in your Lesson 7 folder. Submit and close the document.

12. Close all other open documents without saving them. Maximize the Word window if needed.

Exercise 7-23 ◆ Challenge Yourself

Copy text from multiple documents to create a new document.

1. Start a new document. Key the title west virginia contact information in 12-point Arial small caps. Center the title and make it bold.

2. Insert two blank lines after the title.

3. Save the document as *[your initials]7-23* in your Lesson 7 folder. Keep the document open.

4. Open the files **Stores - 3**, **WV Managers**, and **WV Stores**.

5. Refer to the three open documents to create a new document that includes the name and complete address for each store, the telephone and fax numbers for each store, the name of the store manager, and the name of the account executive.

6. Use tabs to arrange the text attractively.

7. Format document headings to include character and paragraph formatting.

8. Add 72 points of spacing before the first line in the document (the title). Increase the size of the title to 14 points.

9. Save the document again.

10. Submit and close the document.

On Your Own

In these exercises, you work on your own, as you would in a real-life business environment. Use the skills you've learned to accomplish the task—and be creative.

Exercise 7-24

Write a short proposal for changing something in your city, neighborhood, or school. Make the proposal at least three paragraphs long. At the end of the document, create a bulleted summary of the proposal, copying and pasting text from the proposal for the bulleted items. Save the document as *[your initials]*7-24 and submit it.

Exercise 7-25

Copy text from the Internet about a person (present day or historical) you admire. Use Paste Special to paste the text, without formatting, into a new document. Apply your own character and paragraph formatting. Save the document as *[your initials]*7-25 and submit it.

Exercise 7-26

Write a summary about a TV show you have recently seen. Save it as *[your initials]*7-26a. Keep this document open, and start a new document. Begin a letter to a friend, telling him or her about the TV show. Copy and paste or drag and drop text from the summary document into the letter. Save the document as *[your initials]*7-26b and submit both documents.

Lesson 8

Find and Replace

OBJECTIVES

MCAS OBJECTIVES

In this lesson:
WW 07 2.2.2
WW 07 5.1.1

After completing this lesson, you will be able to:

1. Find text.

2. Find and replace text.

3. Find and replace special characters.

4. Find and replace formatting.

Estimated Time: 1¹/₄ hours

When you create documents, especially long documents, you often need to review or change text. In Word, you can do this quickly by using the Find and Replace commands.

The *Find* command locates specified text and formatting in a document. The *Replace* command finds the text and formatting and replaces it automatically with a specified alternative.

Finding Text

Instead of scrolling through a document, you can use the Find command to locate text or to move quickly to a specific document location.

Two ways to use Find are:

- Ribbon, Home tab, Editing group, Find command.

- Press Ctrl+F.

You can use the Find command to locate whole words, words that sound alike, font and paragraph formatting, and special characters. You can search an entire document or only selected text and specify the direction of the search. In the following exercise, you use Find to locate all occurrences of the word "Campbell."

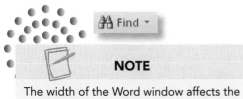

Exercise 8-1 FIND TEXT

1. Open the file **Stevenson - 1**.

2. Click the **Home** tab, and locate the **Editing** group. Click the Find button to open the Find and Replace dialog box. The **Find** tab is selected by default.

3. Delete any text in the **Find what** text box and key **Campbell**.

> **NOTE**
>
> The width of the Word window affects the appearance of the Ribbon buttons. The Editing group may or may not display the Find and Replace buttons. If the buttons do not appear, click the Editing button.

More >>

4. Click the **More** button More >> , if it is displayed, to expand the dialog box.

Figure 8-1
Expanded Find and
Replace dialog box

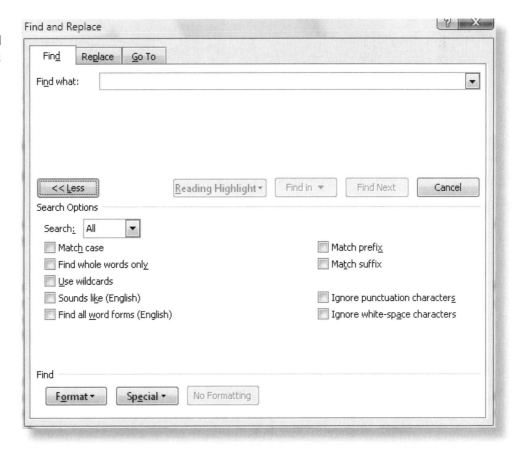

5. Click the **No Formatting** button No Formatting (if it is active) to remove any formatting from previous searches. Then click the **Less** button << Less . The dialog box should look like the one in Figure 8-2.

Figure 8-2
Using the Find
feature

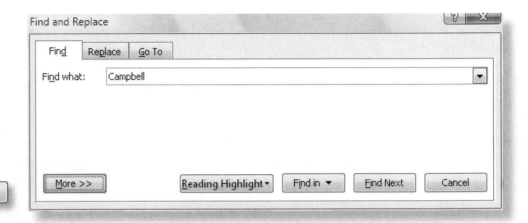

NOTE

To see more of the document text during a search, drag the Find and Replace dialog box by its title bar to the bottom right corner of the screen.

6. Click the Find Next button [Find Next]. Notice that the first occurrence of "Campbell" found in the document is capitalized and italicized.

7. Continue clicking **Find Next** until you reach the end of the document. Notice that Word locates "Campbell" as a word and as text embedded in "Campbell's."

8. Click **OK** in the dialog box that says Word finished searching the document.

9. Click **Cancel** to close the Find and Replace dialog box.

10. Place the insertion point at the beginning of the paragraph that begins "Thank you." Press Ctrl+F to open the Find and Replace dialog box.

11. Key **Campbell's Confections** in the **Find what** text box. Click the Reading Highlight button [Reading Highlight ▾] and click **Highlight All**. The document highlights every occurrence of the text.

12. Click the Reading Highlight button [Reading Highlight ▾] and click **Clear Highlighting**. Close the dialog box.

Exercise 8-2　FIND TEXT BY USING THE MATCH CASE OPTION

The Find command includes options for locating words or phrases that meet certain criteria. One of these options is Match case, which locates text that matches the case of text keyed in the Find what text box. The next exercise demonstrates how the Match case option narrows the search when using the Find command.

1. Move to the end of the document by pressing Ctrl+End. Position the insertion point to the right of "Hamrick" in the closing.

2. Locate the **Editing** group, and click the Find button [🔍 Find ▾]. Click the More button [More >>] to display an expanded dialog box that contains search options.

3. Key confections in the **Find what** text box.

4. Click the **Match case** check box to select this option. Choose **Up** from the **Search:** drop-down list to reverse the search direction. Notice the **Options** that appear below the **Find what** text box.

Figure 8-3
Choosing search options

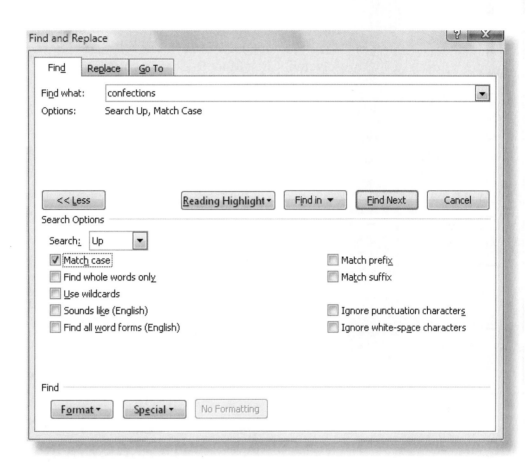

5. Click the Less button to collapse the dialog box. Click the Find Next button ⬚End Next⬚ to begin the search. (If the dialog box is in your way, drag it to a preferred location.) Word ignores all occurrences of the word that do not match the search criteria ("confections").

6. Click **Find Next**. Word reaches the beginning of the document with no other matches found. Notice how the **Match case** option narrows the search.

7. Click **No** in the dialog box that asks if you want to continue searching.

8. Click **Cancel** to close the Find and Replace dialog box.

NOTE

The dialog box that appears when you end the search process is determined by the search direction and the position of the insertion point when you begin the search. When Word searches through the entire document, the dialog box tells you Word is finished searching, and the insertion point returns to its original position. When you search from a point other than the top or bottom of the document and choose Up or Down as your search direction, Word asks if you want to continue the search. If you choose not to continue, the insertion point remains at the last occurrence found.

Exercise 8-3 FIND TEXT BY USING THE FIND WHOLE WORDS ONLY OPTION

The **Find whole words only** option is another way to narrow the search criteria. Word locates separate words, but not characters embedded in other words.

1. Move the insertion point to the beginning of the document. Press Ctrl+F to open the Find and Replace dialog box with the **Find** tab selected. Click **More** to expand the dialog box. Click **Match case** to clear the option.

2. Key **or** in the Find what text box. Click the down arrow next to the **Find what** text box, and notice that the previous entries are listed. The last seven entries of the **Find what** text box are displayed in this list. Click the arrow to close the list. Change the **Search:** drop-down list to **Down**.

3. Click the Find Next button [Find Next] and notice that "for" is highlighted. Click the Find Next button [Find Next]. "Factory" is highlighted because it contains the characters "or."

4. Click **Find whole words only** to select it. Click and choose **Down** from the **Search:** drop-down list.

5. Click **Less**, and then click **Find Next** to begin the search. Word locates the word "or," but not other word forms, such as "factory."

6. Click **Find Next** two times. Click **No** to end the search.

7. Click **Cancel** to close the Find and Replace dialog box.

Exercise 8-4 FIND TEXT BY USING THE WILDCARD OPTION

You can use the Use wildcards option to search for text strings using special search operators. A *wildcard* is a symbol that stands for missing or unknown text. For example, the Any Character wildcard "^?" finds any character. Using the "^?" wildcard, a search for "b^?te" would find both "bite" and "byte." The question mark is replaced by a character that follows "b" and precedes "te."

TIP

Press Esc to cancel a search. You can also interrupt a search by clicking outside the Find and Replace dialog box, editing the document text, and then clicking the dialog box to reactivate it.

1. Position the insertion point at the beginning of the document. Open the Find and Replace dialog box with the **Find** tab displayed.

2. Display the expanded dialog box and click **Use wildcards** to select this option.

3. Select the text in the **Find what** text box and key **ca**.

4. Click the **Special** button [Special ▼] and choose **Any Character** from the list. The "?" is inserted.

Figure 8-4
Choosing a Special
search operator

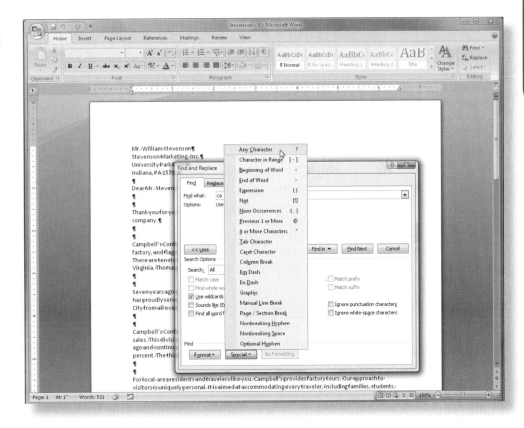

5. Choose **All** from the **Search:** drop-down list, if it is not already selected. Then click **Less**.

6. Click **Find Next**. The first occurrence appears in the word "candy."

7. Continue clicking **Find Next** and notice all the occurrences of "ca?" in the document.

8. Click **OK** in the dialog box that says Word finished searching the document.

9. Click **Cancel** to close the Find and Replace dialog box.

TIP

After you initiate a Find by using the Find and Replace dialog box, you can close the dialog box and use the Next Find/Go To button ⬇ and Previous Find/Go To button ⬆ located at the bottom of the vertical scroll bar to continue the search without having the dialog box in your way. (See Figure 8-5.)

Figure 8-5
Finding text without
the Find and Replace
dialog box

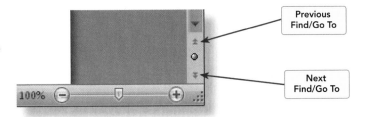

Previous
Find/Go To

Next
Find/Go To

Exercise 8-5 FIND FORMATTED TEXT

In addition to locating words and phrases, the Find command can search for text that is formatted. The formatting can include character formatting, such as bold and italic, and paragraph formatting, such as alignment and line spacing.

1. Position the insertion point at the beginning of the document. Press [Ctrl]+[F].

2. Key **Campbell's Confections** in the **Find what** text box. Expand the dialog box and choose **All** from the **Search:** drop-down list. Click any checked search options to clear them.

3. Click the **Format** button [Format ▾] and choose **Font**.

Figure 8-6
Format options

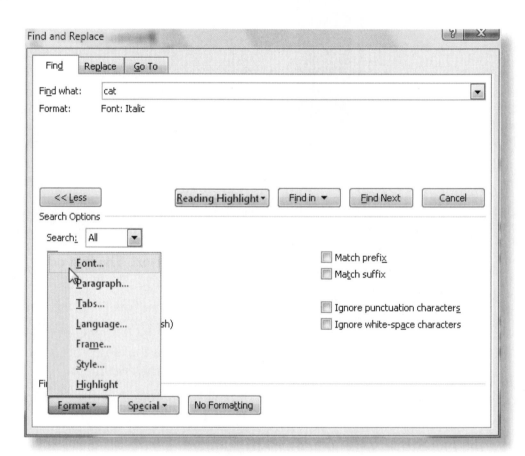

4. In the Find Font dialog box, choose **Italic** from the Font style list and click **OK**. Italic now appears below the Find what text box.

5. Click **Less**, and then click **Find Next**. Word locates *"Campbell's Confections."*

6. Click **Cancel** to close the Find and Replace dialog box.

Finding and Replacing Text

The Replace command searches for specified text or formatting and replaces it with your specified alternative. You can replace all instances of text or formatting at once, or you can find and confirm each replacement.

Two ways to replace text are:

- Ribbon, Home tab, Editing group, Replace command.
- Press Ctrl + H.

Exercise 8-6   REPLACE TEXT BY USING FIND NEXT

1. Position the insertion point at the beginning of the document, locate the **Editing** group, and click the Replace button . The **Replace** tab is now selected in the dialog box.

2. Key traveler in the **Find what** text box. Expand the dialog box and click the **No Formatting** button to remove formatting from previous searches. Make sure no options under **Search:** are selected.

3. Press Tab to move to the **Replace with** text box, and key visitor. Click the **No Formatting** button if it is active.

Figure 8-7
Replacing text

Find and Replace

| Find | Replace | Go To |

Find what: traveler

Replace with: visitor

<< Less

Search Options

Search: All

- Match case
- Find whole words only
- Use wildcards
- Sounds like (English)
- Find all word forms (English)

- Match prefix
- Match suffix

- Ignore punctuation characters
- Ignore white-space characters

Replace

Format ▾   Special ▾   No Formatting

Replace   Replace All   Find Next   Cancel

NOTE

Remember, pressing Tab in a dialog box moves the insertion point from one text box to another and highlights existing text. Pressing Enter executes the dialog box command.

4. Adjust the position and size (click **Less**) of the dialog box so you can see the document text. Click **Find Next**. Click **Replace** to replace the first occurrence of "traveler" with "visitor."

5. Continue to click **Replace** until Word reaches the end of the document.

6. Click **OK** when Word finishes searching the document.

7. Close the Find and Replace dialog box.

Exercise 8-7 REPLACE TEXT BY USING REPLACE ALL

The **Replace All** option replaces all occurrences of text or formatting in a document without confirmation.

1. Move the insertion point to the beginning of the document and press Ctrl+H to open the Find and Replace dialog box with the **Replace** tab selected.

NOTE

After replacing text or formatting, you can always undo the action. If you used **Replace All**, all changes are reversed at once. If you used **Replace**, only the last change is reversed, but you can undo the last several changes individually by selecting them from the Undo drop-down list.

2. Key **Campbell's Confections** in the **Find what** text box. Press Tab and key **CAMPBELL'S CONFECTIONS** in the **Replace with** text box.

3. Expand the dialog box, clear the **Match case** check box if necessary, and click **Replace All**. Word will indicate the number of replacements made.

4. Click **OK** and close the Find and Replace dialog box. "Campbell's Confections" now appears as "CAMPBELL'S CONFECTIONS" throughout the document.

 5. Click the Undo button to undo the Replace All command.

Exercise 8-8 DELETE TEXT WITH REPLACE

You can also use the Replace command to delete text automatically. Key the text to be deleted in the **Find what** text box and leave the **Replace with** text box blank. You can find and delete text with confirmation by using the **Find Next** option or without confirmation by using the **Replace All** option.

1. Position the insertion point at the beginning of the document, and open the Find and Replace dialog box with the **Replace** tab selected.

2. Key **Campbell's** in the **Find what** text box and press Spacebar once. The space character is not visible in the text box.

3. Press [Tab] to move to the **Replace with** text box and press [Delete] to remove the previous entry.

4. Click the Replace All button [Replace All].

5. Click **OK** and close the dialog box. The word "Campbell's" followed by a space is deleted from the company name throughout the document. If the word "Campbell's" was followed by a punctuation mark, the word would not be deleted.

6. Click the Undo button [icon].

7. Save the document as *[your initials]*8-8 in a new folder for Lesson 8. Leave the document open for the next exercise.

TIP

The last option in the Find and Replace dialog box is **Find all word forms**. Use this option to find different forms of words and replace the various word forms with comparable forms. For example, if you key "walk" in the **Find what** text box and key "jump" in the **Replace with** text box, Word replaces "walk" with "jump" and "walked" with "jumped." Use **Replace**, rather than **Replace All**, when you choose this option to verify each replacement and ensure that correct word forms are used.

Finding and Replacing Special Characters

The Find and Replace features can search for characters other than ordinary text. Special characters include paragraph marks and tab characters. Special characters are represented by codes that you can key or choose from the Special drop-down list.

Exercise 8-9   FIND AND REPLACE SPECIAL CHARACTERS

1. Click the Show/Hide ¶ button [¶] to display special characters in the document if they are not showing.

2. Position the insertion point at the top of the document. Open the Find and Replace dialog box with the **Replace** tab selected. Expand the dialog box, if it is not already. Delete the text that appears in the **Find what** text box.

3. Click the **Special** button and choose **Paragraph Mark**. A code (^p) is inserted in the **Find what** text box. Add two additional paragraph mark codes in the **Find what** text box to search for three consecutive paragraph marks in the document. (Use the **Special** drop-down list or key ^p^p.)

4. Move to the **Replace with** text box and insert two paragraph mark codes.

5. Clear any **Search Options** check boxes and click **Less**.

6. Click **Find Next**. Word locates the extra paragraph mark after the salutation of the letter.

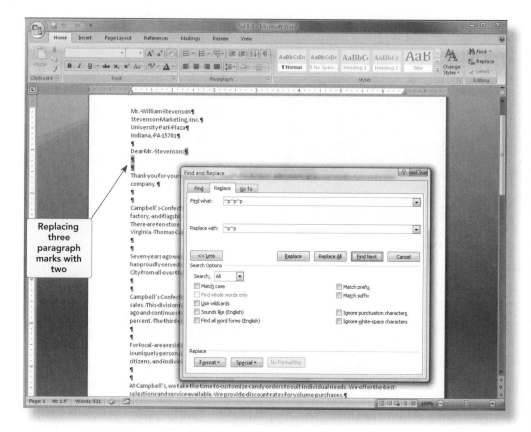

7. Click **Replace**. Notice the elimination of the extra paragraph mark. Continue to click **Replace** for each paragraph mark until you reach the paragraph marks just after "Sincerely."

8. Close the Find and Replace dialog box. The document paragraphs are now correctly spaced.

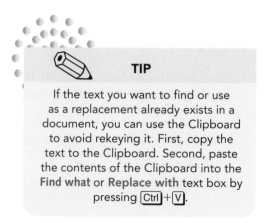

TIP

If the text you want to find or use as a replacement already exists in a document, you can use the Clipboard to avoid rekeying it. First, copy the text to the Clipboard. Second, paste the contents of the Clipboard into the **Find what** or **Replace with** text box by pressing Ctrl + V.

TABLE 8-1 Find and Replace Special Characters

Find or Replace	Special Character Code to Key
Paragraph mark (¶)	^p (must be lowercase)
Tab character →	^t (must be lowercase)
Any character (Find only)	^?
Any digit (Find only)	^#
Any letter (Find only)	^$
Column break	^n
Clipboard contents (Replace only)	^c
Em dash	^+
En dash	^=
Field (Find only)	^d
Footnote mark (Find only)	^f
Graphic (Find only)	^g
Manual line break	^l
Manual page break	^m
Nonbreaking hyphen	^~
Nonbreaking space	^s
Section break (Find only)	^b
White space (Find only)	^w

Finding and Replacing Formatting

Word can search for and replace both character and paragraph formatting. You can specify character or paragraph formatting by clicking the Format button [Format ▾] in the Find and Replace dialog box or using keyboard shortcuts.

[Format ▾]

Exercise 8-10 FIND AND REPLACE CHARACTER FORMATTING

1. Position the insertion point at the top of the document and open the Find and Replace dialog box with the **Replace** tab selected. Expand the dialog box.

2. Key **Campbell's Confections** in the **Find what** text box. Press ⎋Tab⎊ and delete the text in the **Replace with** text box.

3. Click the **Format** button and choose **Font**. Choose **Bold** for **Font style** and click **Small caps**. Click **OK**.

4. Click **Replace All**.

5. Click **OK** when Word finishes searching the document, and close the dialog box. "Campbell's Confections" appears bold and in small caps throughout the document.

6. Reopen the Find and Replace dialog box with the **Replace** tab selected.

7. Highlight the text in the **Find what** text box, if it is not already. Click the **Format** button and choose **Font**. Choose **Bold** and **Small caps** and click **OK**.

8. Press ⎋Tab⎊ to move the insertion point to the **Replace with** text box. Click the No Formatting button [No Formatting] to clear existing formatting.

9. Click the **Format** button [Format▾] and choose **Font**. Choose the **Not Bold** style, deselect **Small caps**, and click **OK**.

10. Press ⎋Ctrl⎊+⎋I⎊ (the keyboard shortcut for italic text). Now the format for the **Replace with** text box is "**Not Bold, Not Small caps, Not All caps, Italic.**"

11. Click **Replace All**.

12. Click **OK** and close the Find and Replace dialog box. "Campbell's Confections" is now italic, and not bold, throughout the document.

Exercise 8-11   FIND AND REPLACE PARAGRAPH FORMATTING

1. Position the insertion point at the end of the first paragraph that begins "Thank you." Open the Find and Replace dialog box with the **Replace** tab selected.

2. In the **Find what** text box, insert two paragraph mark special characters (use the **Special** list or key ^p^p). Clear existing formatting.

3. Move to the **Replace with** text box, enter two paragraph mark special characters, and clear existing formatting.

4. Click the **Format** button and choose **Paragraph**. Click the **Indents and Spacing** tab if it is not active. Deselect **Mirror indents** if necessary.

5. Choose **First Line** from the **Special** drop-down list. If "0.5" is not the measurement displayed in the **By** text box, select the text in the **By** box and key **0.5**. Click **OK**.

6. Click **Find Next** and Word highlights the paragraph marks after "company." Click **Replace** to format that paragraph.

7. Click **Replace** seven more times (through the paragraph ending "enclosed brochure").

8. Close the Find and Replace dialog box. Scroll through the document to view the paragraph formatting changes. All these paragraphs should now have a 0.5-inch first-line indent.

9. Position the insertion point at the top of the document. Open the Find and Replace dialog box with the **Replace** tab selected.

10. Delete the text in the **Find what** text box, and set the text box to look for a 0.5-inch first-line indent. Deselect **Mirror indents** if necessary.

Figure 8-9
Defining paragraph formatting

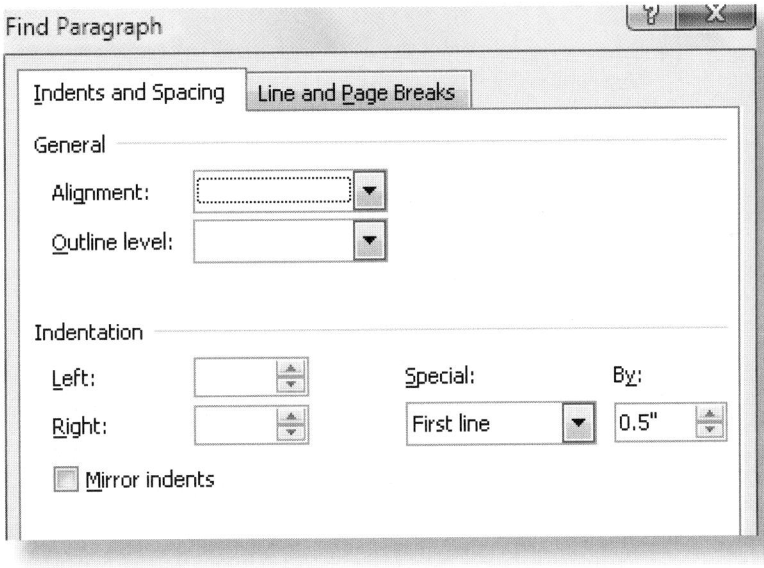

11. Delete the text in the **Replace with** text box, clear the formatting, and replace with 0.25-inch left and right indents and no first-line indent (choose **(none)** from the **Special** drop-down list in the Replace Paragraph dialog box).

Figure 8-10
Replacing paragraph
formatting

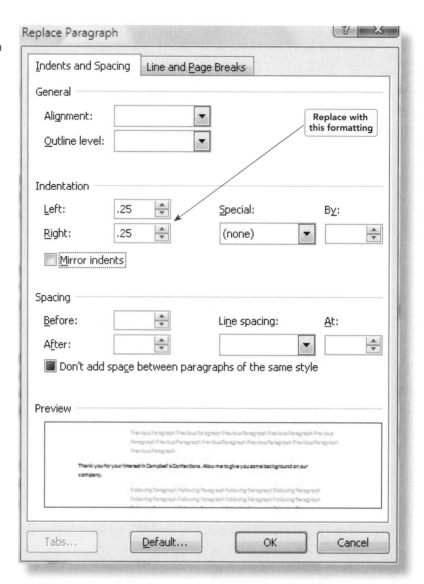

12. Click **Replace All** and click **OK**. Close the dialog box.

13. Scroll through the document to observe the replacement of first-line indented paragraphs with 0.25-inch left- and right-indented paragraphs.

14. Enter the date at the top of the document, with 72 points spacing before and three blank lines after it. Replace "xx" with your reference initials.

15. Save the document as *[your initials]*8-11 in your Lesson 8 folder.

16. Submit and close the document.

TABLE 8-2 Find and Replace Formatting Guidelines

Guideline	Procedure
Find specific text with specific formatting.	Key the text in the **Find what** text box and specify its formatting (choose **Font** or **Paragraph** from the **Format** drop-down list or use a keyboard shortcut).
Find specific formatting.	Delete text in the **Find what** text box, and specify formatting.
Replace specific text but not its formatting.	Key the text in the **Find what** text box. Click the **No Formatting** button to clear existing formatting. Key the replacement text in the **Replace with** text box, and clear existing formatting.
Replace specific text and its formatting.	Key the text in the **Find what** text box and specify its formatting. Delete any text in the **Replace with** text box, and specify the replacement formatting.
Replace only formatting for specific text.	Key the text in the **Find what** text box, and specify its formatting. Delete any text in the **Replace with** text box and specify the replacement formatting.
Replace only formatting.	Delete any text in the **Find what** text box, and specify formatting. Delete any text in the **Replace with** text box, and specify the replacement formatting.

Lesson 8 Summary

- The Find command locates specified text and formatting in a document. The Replace command finds text and formatting and replaces it automatically with specified alternatives.

- Use the Find command to locate whole words, words that sound alike, font and paragraph formatting, and special characters. Using the Find command, you can search an entire document or selected text. You can also specify the direction of the search.

- Use the Match case option to locate text that matches the case of document text. Example: When searching for "Confections," Word would not find "confections."

- When you want to locate whole words and not parts of a word, use the Find whole words only option. Example: When searching for the whole word "can," Word would find only "can," but not "candy" or "candidate."

- Use the Use wildcards option to search for text strings by using special search operators. A wildcard is a symbol that stands for missing or unknown text. Example: A search for "b^?yte" would find "bite" and "byte." See Table 8-1.

- Use the Sounds like option to find a word that sounds similar to the search text but is spelled differently or to find a word you do not know how to spell. When you find the word, you can stop the search process and edit your document.

- Use the Find command to search for formatted text. The formatting can include character formatting, such as bold and italic, and paragraph formatting, such as alignment and line spacing. Use the Replace command to replace the formatting. See Table 8-2.

- Use the Replace command to search for all instances of text or formatting at once or to find and confirm each replacement.

- Use the Replace command to delete text automatically. Key the text to be deleted in the Find what text box and leave the Replace with text box blank.

LESSON 8		Command Summary	
Feature	**Button**	**Command**	**Keyboard**
Find	🔍 Find ▾	**Home** tab, **Editing** group	Ctrl + F
Replace	ᵃᵇᵪ Replace	**Home** tab, **Editing** group	Ctrl + H

Concepts Review

True/False Questions

Each of the following statements is either true or false. Indicate your choice by circling T or F.

T F   1. You can use keyboard shortcuts to specify formatting in the Find and Replace dialog box.

T F   2. To find text or formatting, you must have the insertion point at the beginning of the document.

T F   3. Line spacing and indents are two examples of paragraph formatting that you can specify in the Replace with text box.

T F   4. The question mark represents a special character code used to search for any character.

T F   5. You use the Match case option to specify only uppercase when finding or replacing text.

T F   6. The keyboard command to find text is Ctrl+H.

T F   7. The Undo command undoes all replacements made if you used the Replace All option.

T F   8. You can use the Find command to search either selected text or an entire document.

Short Answer Questions

Write the correct answer in the space provided.

1. What is the special character code for a paragraph mark?

_____

2. Which button can you use to continue a Find operation when the Find and Replace dialog box is closed?

_____

3. With the insertion point in the Find what text box, how do you move to, and automatically highlight the contents of, the Replace with text box?

_____

4. Which Find option do you use to locate a specific word rather than all occurrences of the text?

_____

5. If the insertion point is in the Find what text box, what is the shortcut to insert text for which you previously searched?

6. How do you clear previous formatting when it appears below the text boxes in the Find and Replace dialog box?

7. Which button expands the Find and Replace dialog box to show more options, and which button reduces the dialog box to make it smaller?

8. Which option, Replace or Replace All, allows for selective replacement of text?

Critical Thinking

Answer these questions on a separate page. There are no right or wrong answers. Support your answers with examples from your own experience, if possible.

1. Click the **Start** button, and click the link for Windows **Help and Support**. In the **Search Help** text box, key find files and press Enter. Read the information about finding files and folders. Create a document to summarize the facts. Be sure to include the instructions for finding a file that contains specific text as well as files created on a particular date.

2. The Replace All option can be very useful. It can also lead to occasional problems if you have not thought through a specific Replace All operation. After you experiment with the feature, describe some precautions you would suggest for the use of Replace All.

Skills Review

Exercise 8-12

Find and Replace text.

1. Open the file **Walk - 2**.
2. Use the Find command to locate the text "8 a.m." by following these steps:

   a. Position the insertion point at the beginning of the document and click the **Home** tab. Click the Find button.

   b. Key 8 a.m. in the **Find what** text box. Click **More**, if the dialog box is not already expanded.

　　c. Click **No Formatting** to clear previous formats. Make sure no search options are selected. Click **Find Next**.

　　d. Click **Cancel** to close the dialog box, and edit the found text to 8:30 a.m.

3. Change the text "walk-a-thon" to "Walk-a-Thon," using the Replace command, by following these steps:

　　a. Move the insertion point to the beginning of the document. Click the **Home** tab, and click the Replace button .

　　b. Key walk-a-thon in the **Find what** text box, press Tab, and key Walk-a-Thon in the **Replace with** text box.

　　c. Click **No Formatting** if any formatting remains.

　　d. Click **Less** to reduce the size of the dialog box, and drag the dialog box to the bottom of the screen.

　　e. Click **Find Next,** and then click **Replace**. Click **Replace** until Word reaches the end of the document. Click **OK**, and close the dialog box.

4. Change the date, using the Replace command, by following these steps:

　　a. Position the insertion point at the beginning of the document and press Ctrl+H.

　　b. Key May 1 in the **Find what** text box.

　　c. Press Tab and key April 25 in the **Replace with** text box.

　　d. Click **More** to expand the dialog box, and click any checked search options to deselect them.

　　e. Click **Replace All**. Click **OK** and close the dialog box.

5. Replace the text "Education Fund" with "Outreach Program."

6. Move to the top of the document, and format the first line with 72 points spacing before. Edit the text to read "Put on your walking shoes—Become a Friend of the Library Outreach Program."

7. Format the first line of text as 14-point bold.

REVIEW

Format "Campbell's Confections," select the formatted text, click the Format Painter button 🖌, and then select "Chamber of Commerce."

8. Move to the end of the document and format "Campbell's Confections" as bold italic. Copy the formatting to the text "Chamber of Commerce" located below the address.

9. Spell-check the document.

10. Save the document as *[your initials]*8-12 in your Lesson 8 folder.

11. Submit, and close the document.

Exercise 8-13

Use Replace to replace special characters and delete text.

1. Start a new document.

2. Key the text shown in Figure 8-11, using single spacing. When keying the hyphens, do not insert space characters before or after the hyphen.

Figure 8-11

```
Campbell's Confections
Chocolate Factory Hours
September 1 through June 30
Monday-Saturday
9 a.m.-4 p.m.
Summer Schedule
July 1 through August 31
Monday-Friday
9 a.m.-5 p.m.
For more information, call 724-555-2025
```

3. Center the entire document horizontally, and change the font to Arial.

4. Change the first line to 16-point bold and the last line to bold italic. Apply bold and small caps format to the second line.

5. Replace special characters by following these steps:

   a. Position the insertion point at the end of the document and click the **Home** tab, and click the Replace button ![Replace]. Click **More** to expand the dialog box, if it is not already expanded.

   b. Key a hyphen in the **Find what** text box.

   c. Press [Tab] to move to the **Replace** with text box.

   d. Click the **Special** button and choose **En Dash**.

   e. Choose **Up** from the **Search:** drop-down list, and clear any search options that are selected.

   f. Click **Less**, and then click **Find Next**. Do not replace the hyphens in the telephone number.

   g. Click **Find Next** and click **Replace** to replace the hyphen in the time.

   h. Continue replacing hyphens until you reach the beginning of the document.

   i. Click **OK** and close the dialog box when the search is complete.

6. Use the Replace feature to delete text by following these steps:

   a. Position the insertion point at the top of the document and press [Ctrl]+[H].

   b. Key **Summer Schedule** in the **Find** what dialog box.

   c. Expand the dialog box and clear any formatting.

   d. Delete any text or formatting in the **Replace with** text box.

   e. Select **All** for the **Search:** direction.

   f. Click **Replace All** to delete the text. Click **OK** and close the dialog box.

7. Undo the replacement by clicking the Undo button ▾ on the Quick Access Toolbar.

8. Change the spacing after to 12 points for the entire document. Change the spacing before for the first line to 72 points.

9 Spell-check the document.

10. Save the document as *[your initials]*8-13 in your Lesson 8 folder.

11. Submit and close the document.

Exercise 8-14

Use Replace to delete special characters, replace text, and replace formatting.

1. Open the file **OH Hours**.

2. Use the Replace command to delete all tabs by following these steps:

    a. Position the insertion point at the beginning of the document, and click the Replace button ⟨Replace⟩.

    b. Key ^t (the code for a tab character) in the Find what text box, and clear existing formatting.

    c. Delete any text in the Replace with text box, and clear existing formatting and search options.

    d. Click Replace All, click OK, and click Close.

3. Undo the replacement.

4. Replace the em dash (—) with the word "to," by following these steps:

    a. Press [Ctrl]+[H].

    b. Delete text or formatting that appears in the Find what text box. Click More to expand the dialog box. Click the Special button ⟨Special ▾⟩, and click Em Dash.

    c. In the Replace with text box, press [Spacebar], key to, and press [Spacebar].

    d. Click Replace All. Click OK and click Close.

5. Replace the underline format with bold small caps format by following these steps:

    a. Press [Ctrl]+[H].

    b. Delete text or formatting that appears in the Find what text box. Click More to expand the dialog box. Press [Ctrl]+[U]. "Underline" should display under the Find what text box.

    c. In the Replace with text box, click the Format button ⟨Format ▾⟩, and click Font. Click the arrow in the Underline Style box, and click (none). Select Bold and Small caps formatting. Click OK.

    d. Click Replace All. Click OK and click Close.

⟨ Sp**e**cial ▾ ⟩

6. Change the heading of the document to 14 point with 72 points spacing before. Change the line spacing for all the tabbed text, including the tabbed heading, to double spacing.

7. Save the document as *[your initials]*8-14 in your Lesson 8 folder.

8. Submit and close the document.

Exercise 8-15

Replace character and paragraph formatting.

1. Open the file **Homecoming**.

2. Format the first page of the document as a memo. Key the memo heading information as shown in Figure 8-12. Add your reference initials and an enclosure notation (use the word "Attachment" instead of "Enclosure").

Figure 8-12

```
MEMO TO: Robert Smith

FROM: Thomas Campbell

DATE: May 30, 20—

SUBJECT: Homecoming Dates
```

3. Find and replace special characters by following these steps:

   a. Position the insertion point at the top of page 2, and open the Find and Replace dialog box with the **Replace** tab selected.

   b. Delete existing text in the **Find what** text box, and clear all search options and formatting. Click the Special button [Special▼] and click **Manual Line Break**.

   c. Tab to the **Replace with** text box, and delete all text. Click the **Special** button [Special▼] and click **Paragraph Mark**. (Notice that "^p" should appear in the Replace with text box.)

   d. Change the search direction to **Down** and click **Replace All**. When Word reaches the end of the document, click **No** to end the task and close the Find and Replace dialog box.

4. Find and replace character formatting by following these steps:

   a. Position the insertion point at the top of page 2, and open the Find and Replace dialog box with the **Replace** tab selected.

   b. Delete existing text in the **Find what** text box, and clear all search options and formatting. Press [Ctrl]+[U] to specify underline formatting.

    c. Tab to the **Replace with** text box, and delete all text. Click the **Format** button and choose **Font**.

    d. In the Replace Font dialog box, choose **Bold Italic** and set the **Underline style** to **(none)**. Click **OK**.

    e. Change the search direction to **Down** and click **Replace All**. When Word reaches the end of the document, click **No** to end the task and close the Find and Replace dialog box.

5. Find and replace paragraph formats by following these steps:

    a. Place the insertion point before the text *"Allegheny College"* on page 2, and open the Find and Replace dialog box with the **Replace** tab selected.

    b. In the **Find what** text box, enter two paragraph mark codes by keying ^p^p or by using the **Special** button. Clear all search options and formatting.

    c. In the **Replace with** text box, clear any text, formatting, and search options. Enter one paragraph mark code.

    d. Click the **Format** button and choose **Paragraph**. Set **Spacing After** to 6 points (**6 pt**) and click **OK**.

    e. Click **Less**, and then click **Find Next**. Replace the formatting on page 2 only. Close the dialog box.

6. Format the title on page 2 ("Homecoming Events") as 14-point bold, uppercase, and centered. Format all the text below the title with a 2.25-inch left indent.

7. Spell-check the memo portion of the document.

8. Save the document as *[your initials]*8-15 in your Lesson 8 folder.

9. Submit and close the document.

Lesson Applications

Exercise 8-16

Replace text and character formatting.

1. Open the file **Chocolate - 3**.

2. Format the document as a memo to "Store Managers" from Thomas Campbell. Use today's date. The subject is "Chocolate Terms."

3. Replace the text "cocoa bean" with cacao bean throughout the document.

4. Replace the italic formatting of the chocolate terms with bold, small caps formatting. Check the format options under the Replace with text box. (It should read "Bold, Not Italic, Small caps, Not All caps." Press Ctrl + I to turn off italic format if necessary.) Make sure no search options are checked before you begin replacing.

5. Add your reference initials to the document.

6. Save the document as *[your initials]*8-16 in your Lesson 8 folder.

7. Submit and close the document.

Exercise 8-17

Find and replace text, special characters, and formatting.

1. Open the file **Holiday**. Format the document as a memo to "Store Managers" from Thomas Campbell. Use the current date, and the subject is holiday sales.

2. Revise the first paragraph as shown in Figure 8-13.

Figure 8-13

> The table below lists the most ^popular^ items sold for our busiest holidays by state.
> We compiled the ~~numbers~~ results using sales from the ③-week period preceding
> each holiday. ¶ If you would like a breakdown by individual stores, let me
> know. We will use these figures to determine our production schedules ^for next year^. If
> you have any comments regarding this information, please call me.

3. Replace the text "chocolate suckers" with Halloween favors.

4. Replace the 3 points spacing after paragraph formatting with double spacing.

5. Replace all bold formatting with blue underline, small caps, and blue font color formatting.

6. Format the first line of text in the document with 72 points of spacing before the paragraph.

7. Add your reference initials, and spell-check the document.

8. Save the document as *[your initials]*8-17 in your Lesson 8 folder.

9. Submit and close the document.

Exercise 8-18

Find and replace text and formatting.

1. Open the file **Club - 2**.

2. Alphabetize the list that begins "milk chocolate–covered nuts" through "three-tier."

3. Copy the text "CC Chocolate Club" and paste the text at the beginning of the document. Press Enter.

4. Replace the text "CC Chocolate Club" with "Campbell's Confections' Chocolate Club."

5. Replace the single-spaced paragraph format with 12 points spacing after (**12 pt**) and **.25** first-line indent.

6. Replace all hyphens with an en dash.

7. Format the list beginning with "caramel" through "truffles" as a bulleted list.

8. Format the first line as a title—uppercase, bold, 14 points, shadow, center alignment, and no indent. Apply 72 points spacing before and 24 points spacing after.

9. Add a page border to the document. (Open the Borders and Shading dialog box, and click the **Page Border** tab. Click **Box** under setting, and choose a geometric pattern located near the bottom of the Art drop-down list. Select an appropriate width and color.)

10. Spell-check the document.

11. Save the document as *[your initials]*8-18 in your Lesson 8 folder.

12. Submit and close the document.

Exercise 8-19 ◆ Challenge Yourself

Find and replace text, special characters, and formatting.

1. Open the file **Agenda**.

2. Replace each single paragraph mark with 12 points spacing after (**12 pt**).

3. Find the text "PM" and replace it with **p.m.** Include the **Match case** option.

TIP

Click in the Find what text box. Key "Session" and press [Spacebar] then click Special and choose Any Character; that is, Session ^?.

4. Find the text "AM" and replace it with **a.m.**

5. Replace italic formatting with 12-point bold and small caps formatting.

6. Replace each hyphen (-) with an em dash.

7. Use the **Replace** command to format all session numbers (Session 1, Session 2, etc.) with italic format by using the wildcard "?".

8. Center the three-line title and apply 16-point bold and small caps formatting. Add 48 points of spacing before the first line and 24 points of spacing after the third line. Apply a bottom border to the third line of the title.

9. Format "Agenda" with center alignment, 14 points, bold, and small caps.

10. Save the document as *[your initials]*8-19 in your Lesson 8 folder.

11. Submit and close the document.

On Your Own

In these exercises, you work on your own, as you would in a real-life business environment. Use the skills you've learned to accomplish the task—and be creative.

Exercise 8-20

Key a song lyric you know, preferably one with a repetitive chorus. Copy the lyric, and paste it below the original. In the copy of the lyric, find an important word that is used repeatedly in the lyric and replace it with its opposite. Save the document as *[your initials]*8-20 and submit it.

Exercise 8-21

Write a summary about a book you recently read. Replace paragraph returns that begin new paragraphs with 6 points of spacing after paragraphs. Replace any occurrence of two spaces with one space. Save the document as *[your initials]*8-21. Submit the document.

Exercise 8-22

Log onto the Internet, and find a Web site about one of your favorite hobbies or interests. Copy-and-paste information from the Web site to a new document. Find and replace any formatting you do not want in the document. Give the document a title. Save the document as *[your initials]*8-22 and submit it.

Unit 2 Applications

Unit Application 2-1

Apply paragraph spacing, indent text, set tabs, add borders and shading, replace text.

1. Open the file **Customer Service**.

2. Format the document as a memo to "Customer Service Account Executives" from Thomas Campbell. Use today's date, and the subject is brochure information.

3. Select the first line of the memo heading ("MEMO TO") and apply 72 points spacing before.

4. Below the memo heading, key the text shown in Figure U2-1. Include the corrections. Use single spacing.

Figure U2-1

> The   department   company
> ^marketing ^is revising our ^brochre and updating the information on our web
>
> site. Please review the following paragraphs, and let me know your
>
> suggestions or recommendations. If you would like to^meet to discuss your
> proposed
> ^changes, let me know.

5. Format the paragraph heading ("Customer Service") as 14-point bold and small caps.

6. Format the "Customer Service" paragraph and the paragraph that follows the heading using a .5-inch left and right indent and Times New Roman.

7. Select the "SUBJECT" line, and apply a bottom border.

8. Apply a box border and light gray shading to the "Customer Service" paragraphs.

9. Replace each hyphen with an en dash.

10. Save the document as *[your initials]*u2-1 in a new folder for Unit 2 Applications.

11. Submit and close the document.

Unit Application 2-2

Apply paragraph spacing and change alignment; create a bulleted list; create tabbed text; find and replace text; copy and paste text.

1. Open the file **Ordering**. Change the font size of the document to 11 points.

2. Format the title in the first line of the document as 14-point uppercase, centered, with 72 points spacing before and 24 points spacing after.

3. Insert the following tabbed text near the end of the document so that it follows the paragraph that begins "Orders shipped." A blank line should precede and follow the tabbed text. Right-align the numbers in the second and third columns.

Figure U2-2

Amount	Standard	Rush
$0 to $20.00	$5.95	$18.95
20.01 to 40.00	8.95	21.95
40.01 to 60.00	11.95	24.95
60.01 to 80.00	14.95	27.95
80.01 to 100.00	17.95	30.95
100.01 to 125.00	20.95	33.95
125.01 to 150.00	23.95	36.95
150.01 to 200.00	26.95	39.95
Over $200.00	10% of Total	18% of Total

4. Key the text Delivery Chart as a heading above the tabbed text.

5. Format "Delivery Chart" as 14-point bold, centered, and small caps. Format the column headings for the tabbed text to be bold and underlined.

6. Select the paragraph headings ("Online," "Telephone," etc.), and format the headings as a bulleted list, using the small square-shaped bullet (▪).

7. Indent the text below the bulleted paragraphs so the paragraph text aligns with the text that follows the bullet.

8. Remove the bullet format from the paragraphs that begin "Note." Indent the "Note" paragraphs to match the other paragraphs (.5).

9. Use the Find and Replace commands to format the text "Note:" as bold, italic, and small caps.

10. Find the text "April through September" and key the following sentence after "September" but before the period: or when temperatures reach 72. Add the degree symbol to follow "72" (°).

11. Spell-check the document.

12. Save the document as *[your initials]*u2-2 in your Unit 2 Applications folder.

13. Submit and close the document.

Unit Application 2-3

Apply and change bulleted lists, create tabbed columns, apply indents, and sort text.

1. Start a new document and change the left and right indents to .5 inch.

2. Key the text shown in Figure U2-3, using 12-point Arial. Use leader tabs to create the lines under "Task completed." The leaders should extend to the right margin.

Figure U2-3

```
Before you go on vacation, use this handy checklist to make
sure you have not forgotten any details.


                                               Task completed

Change your voice mail recording            _____

Create an out-of-office message             _____

Meet with supervisor                        _____

Backup important files                      _____

Create a checklist for the temp             _____

Check calendar                              _____

File/archive papers and data files          _____
```

TIP

You need to set two tabs—one for the leader and one to begin the second column.

3. Center the text "Task completed" above the leader characters, and insert two blank lines above it. Apply bold and small caps format to "Task completed."

4. Format the list with 18-point spacing before paragraphs. Apply bullets to the list, using the checkmark bullet.

5. Format the opening paragraph as bold italic.

6. Select the list with the checkmark bullets, and customize the bullet as the 3-D box (❑) Wingding character.

7. Customize the 3-D box bullet format by increasing the bullet size to 14 points and changing the bullet color to blue.

8. Apply a 3-D page border, using the fourth-to-last line style.

9. Select the bulleted list, and sort the text in ascending order.

10. Save the document as *[your initials]***u2-3** in your Unit 2 Applications folder.

11. Submit and close the document.

Unit Application 2-4 ◆ Using the Internet

Work with a variety of paragraph formatting features, move and copy text, and find and replace text.

1. Locate three or more Web sites that contain information on your favorite hobby or on a topic that interests you.

2. Copy text from each site (make sure you select text only, no images, and press Ctrl + C to copy), and paste it into a new Word document.

3. Use the Keep Text Only option from the Paste Options button to remove Web formatting.

4. Create a formatted title for the document.

5. Use paragraph and character formatting features to format the document attractively.

6. Use the Find and Replace features to locate selected text, and apply formatting for emphasis.

7. Check spelling and grammar (Web sites may contain misspelled words or poor grammar).

8. Save the document as *[your initials]***u2-4** in your Unit 2 Applications folder.

9. Submit and close the document.

unit 3

PAGE FORMATTING

Margins and Print Options

OBJECTIVES

After completing this lesson, you will be able to:

1. Change margins.

2. Preview a document.

3. Change paper size and orientation.

4. Print envelopes and labels.

5. Choose print options.

MCAS OBJECTIVES

In this lesson:
WW 07 1.2.1
WW 07 4.5.3

Estimated Time: 1¹/₂ hours

In a Word document, text is keyed and printed within the boundaries of the document's margins. *Margins* are the spaces between the edges of the text and the edges of the paper. Adjusting the margins can significantly change the appearance of a document.

Word offers many useful printing features: changing the orientation (the direction, either horizontal or vertical, in which a document is printed), selecting paper size, and printing envelopes and labels.

Changing Margins

By default, a document's margin settings are:

- Top margin: 1 inch

- Bottom margin: 1 inch

- Left margin: 1 inch

- Right margin: 1 inch

Figure 9-1
Default margin
settings

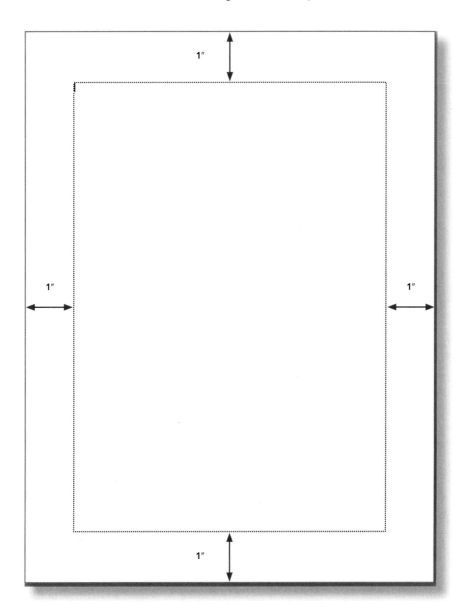

Using standard-size paper (8.5 by 11 inches) and Word's default margin
settings, you have 6^1/$_2$ by 9 inches on the page for your text. To increase or
decrease this workspace, you can change margins by using the Page Setup
dialog box or the rulers or Print Preview.

To set margins, you can use one of these methods:

- Change settings in the Page Setup dialog box.

- Drag margins using the horizontal and vertical rulers.

- Drag margins in Print Preview.

Word 2007

Figure 9-2
Actual workspace
using default
margin settings and
standard-size paper

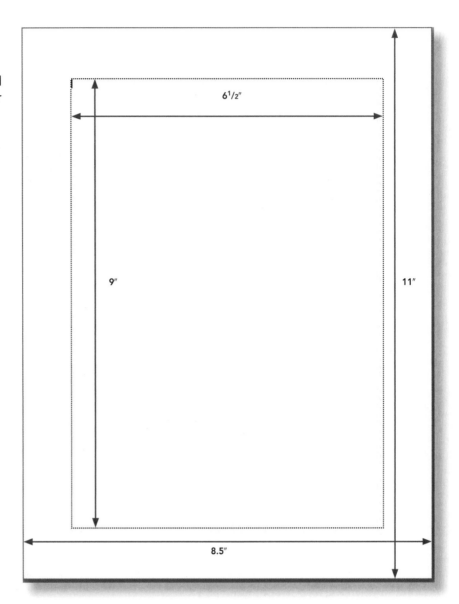

6¹/₂″

9″

11″

8.5″

Exercise 9-1 CHANGE MARGINS FOR A
DOCUMENT USING THE PAGE
SETUP DIALOG BOX

One way to change margins for a document is to use the
Page Setup dialog box. You can change margins for an
entire document or selected text. You can open the Page
Setup dialog by clicking the Margins command or clicking
the Page Setup Dialog Box Launcher.

1. Open the file **Corporate Gifts**. (Make sure no text is selected.)

2. Click the Page Layout tab and click the Margins button . Notice that
the first option is Normal which displays the default margin settings.

3. Click Custom Margins and click the Margins tab, if it is not active.
The dialog box shows the default margin settings.

TIP

You can view page margins by opening the Word Options dialog box. Click **Advanced** and scroll to **Show document content**, and click **Show text boundaries**.

4. Edit the margin text box settings so they have the following values (or click the arrow boxes to change the settings). As you do so, notice the changes in the **Preview** box.

Top	1.5
Bottom	1.5
Left	2
Right	2

Figure 9-3
Changing margins in the Page Setup dialog box

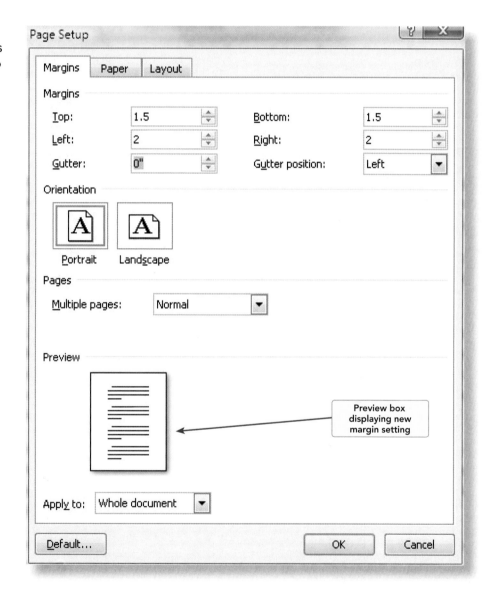

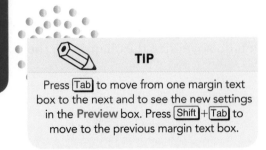

TIP

Press Tab to move from one margin text box to the next and to see the new settings in the **Preview** box. Press Shift + Tab to move to the previous margin text box.

5. Click the down arrow to open the **Apply to** drop-down list. Notice that you can choose either **Whole document** or **This point forward** (from the insertion point forward). Choose **Whole document** and click **OK** to change the margins of the entire document.

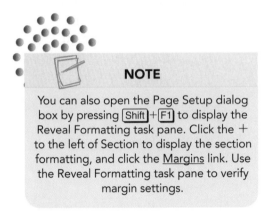

NOTE

You can also open the Page Setup dialog box by pressing Shift + F1 to display the Reveal Formatting task pane. Click the + to the left of Section to display the section formatting, and click the Margins link. Use the Reveal Formatting task pane to verify margin settings.

Exercise 9-2   CHANGE MARGINS FOR SELECTED TEXT BY USING THE PAGE SETUP DIALOG BOX

When you change margins for selected text, you create a new section. A *section* is a portion of a document that has its own formatting. When a document contains more than one section, *section breaks* indicate the beginning and end of a section. Section breaks in Draft view are represented by double-dotted lines.

1. Select the text from the second paragraph to the end of the document.

2. Click the **Page Layout** tab. Click the **Page Setup Dialog Box Launcher** to display the Page Setup dialog box.

Figure 9-4
Page Setup Dialog
Box Launcher

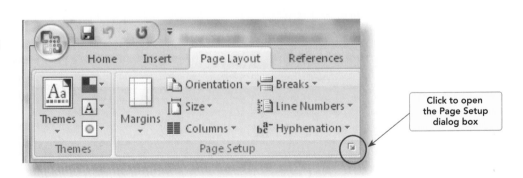

Click to open the Page Setup dialog box

3. Change the margins to the following settings:

Top	2
Bottom	2
Left	1.5
Right	1.5

4. Choose **Selected text** from the **Apply to** box. Click **OK**.

5. Deselect the text, and scroll to the beginning of the selection. Word applied the margin changes to the selected text and created a new section. The section appears on a new page. The status bar displays section numbers and page numbers.

TIP

Display nonprinting characters if necessary, and switch to Draft view to see the section break double-dotted line in the document. Remember that Draft view does not show documents as they will appear when printed.

Figure 9-5
Changing margins for selected text creates a new section

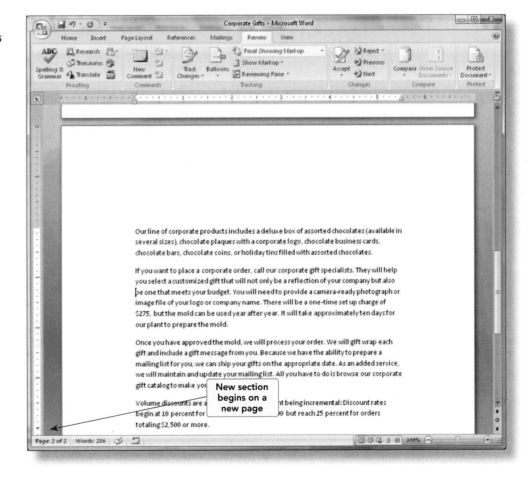

Exercise 9-3   CHANGE MARGINS FOR A SECTION BY USING THE PAGE SETUP DIALOG BOX

After a section is created, you can change the margins for just the section (not the entire document) by using the Page Setup dialog box. To help you know which section you are formatting, customize the status bar to display sections.

1. Move the insertion point anywhere in the new section (section 2), and right-click the status bar. Click **Section** and click in the document to close the shortcut menu. Open the **Page Setup** dialog box.

2. Change the left and right margin settings to **1.25** inches.

3. Open the **Apply to** drop-down list to view the options. Notice that you can apply the new margin settings to the current section, to the whole document, or from the insertion point forward.

4. Choose **This section** and click **OK** to apply the settings to the new section.

Exercise 9-4   CHANGE MARGINS USING THE RULERS

To change margins using the rulers, use Print Layout view. The status bar includes five buttons for changing document views: The default view for Word documents is Print Layout, which displays text as it will appear on the printed page. Print Layout view displays headers, footers, and other page elements.

There are two ways to switch document views:

- Click a view button on the right side of the status bar.

- Click the View tab, and click a view button.

Figure 9-6
View buttons

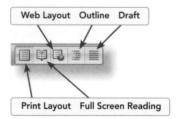

1. Place the insertion point at the beginning of the document ([Ctrl]+[Home]). In bold uppercase letters, key **CORPORATE GIFTS** and then press [Enter]. Center the title and add a blank line below it.

2. Click the **View Ruler** button at the top of the vertical scroll bar if the rulers are not displayed.

3. Click in the new section (page 2). The status bar shows that the document contains two pages and two sections. Notice the extra space at the top of the page. The new section has a larger top margin (2 inches).

4. To see more of the page, including the margin areas, click the Zoom button and then choose **Page width**. Click **OK**.

5. Move the insertion point to the top of the document (the first section). The blue area on the vertical ruler shows the 1.5-inch top margin. The blue areas on the horizontal ruler show the 2-inch left and right margins. The white area in the horizontal ruler shows the text area, which is a line length of 4.5 inches. (See Figure 9-7.)

Figure 9-7
Rulers in Print
Layout view

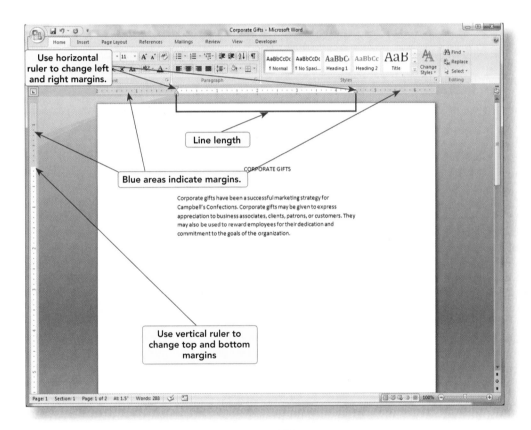

6. To change the top margin, position the pointer over the top margin boundary on the vertical ruler. The top margin boundary is between the blue area and the white area on the ruler. The pointer changes to a two-pointed vertical arrow ↕ and a ScreenTip displays the words "Top Margin."

7. Press and hold down the left mouse button. The margin boundary appears as a dotted horizontal line.

8. Drag the margin boundary slightly up, and release the mouse button. The text at the top of the document moves up to align with the new top margin.

9. Click the Undo button 🔽 to restore the 1.5-inch top margin.

10. Hold down the Alt key, and drag the top margin boundary down until it is at 2 inches on the ruler. Release Alt and the mouse button. Holding down the Alt key as you drag shows the exact margin and text area measurements.

11. To change the left margin, position the pointer over the left margin boundary on the horizontal ruler. The left margin boundary is between the blue area and the white area on the ruler. The pointer changes to a two-pointed horizontal arrow, and a ScreenTip displays the words "Left Margin."

Figure 9-8
Adjusting the left margin

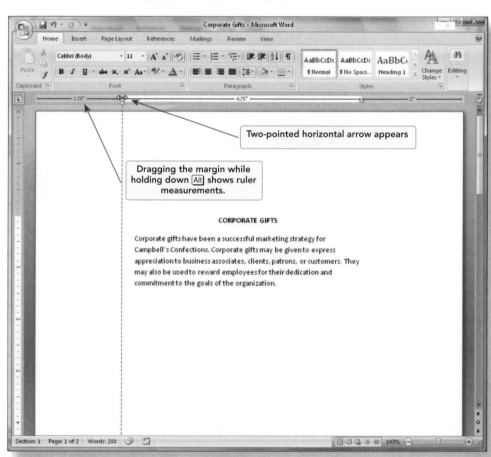

NOTE

You might have to fine-tune the pointer position to place it directly on the left margin boundary. Move the pointer slowly until you see the two-pointed arrow and the "Left Margin" ScreenTip.

12. Hold down the Alt key, and drag the margin boundary to the left to create a 1.75-inch left margin. (See Figure 9-8.)

13. Using the same procedure, drag the right margin boundary until it is located 1.75 inches from the right. Be sure to watch for the two-pointed arrow

before dragging. The first section now has 1.75-inch left and right margins and a 2-inch top margin.

14. Scroll to the next page (section 2). Click within the text to activate this section's ruler. Change the top margin to 1.75 inches.

15. Click the Microsoft Office Button ⬢, and click the Word Options button ⬛ Word Options . Click **Advanced** in the left pane and scroll to **Show document content**. Click **Show text boundaries**, and click **OK**. The page margins are displayed as dotted lines.

16. Remove the page margins from view by clicking the Microsoft Office Button, clicking the Word Options button ⬛ Word Options , clicking **Advanced**, scrolling to **Show document content**, and deselecting **Show text boundaries**. Click **OK**.

17. Save the document as *[your initials]*9-4 in a new Lesson 9 folder, and leave the document open for the next exercise.

NOTE

If you move the pointer to the top of the page in Print Layout view, you will see the Hide White Space button ⊬. Double click the button to hide the white space (the margin area) at the top and bottom of each page and the gray space between pages so you can see more document text. Point to the top of the page, and double-click the Show White Space button ⊬ to restore the space.

Exercise 9-5 SET FACING PAGES WITH GUTTER MARGINS

If your document is going to be bound—put together like a book, with printing on both sides of the paper—you will want to use mirror margins and gutter margins. *Mirror margins* are inside and outside margins on facing pages that mirror one another. *Gutter margins* add extra space to the left or top margins to allow for binding.

Figure 9-9
Mirror margins

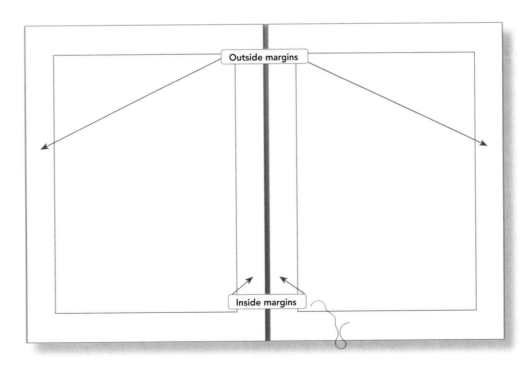

Figure 9-10
Gutter margins

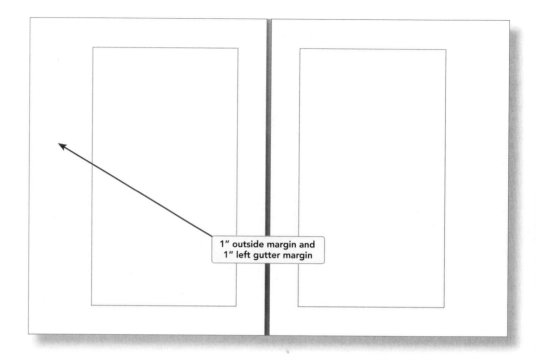

1" outside margin and
1" left gutter margin

1. Open the Page Setup dialog box, and open the **Multiple pages** drop-down list. Choose **Mirror margins**. Notice that the **Preview** box now displays two pages. The left and right margins are called the inside and outside margins.

2. Change the **Inside** margins to **1.25** inches and the **Outside** margins to **1** inch.

3. Set the **Gutter** margin to **1** inch, and press Tab to reflect the change in the Preview box. Click **OK**. A 1-inch gutter margin is added to the document. (Make sure you use at least 1-inch gutter margins to allow room for binding.)

TIP

Visualize the document as double-sided, facing pages in a book by placing the back of page 2 against the back of page 1 and placing page 3 beside page 2. The gutter margin of page 1 is on the left. The gutter margin on the right of page 2 and on the left of page 3 allows space for the binding and represents facing pages.
Facing pages appear as a two-page spread with odd-numbered right pages and even-numbered left pages.

4. Open the Page Setup dialog box, and open the **Multiple pages** drop-down list. Choose **Normal**. Change the **Gutter** setting to **.75** and change the **Gutter** position to **Top**. Click **OK**. The document is ready for top binding.

5. Open the Page Setup dialog box. Change the **Left** and **Right** margins to **1.5** inches, change the **Gutter** setting to **0"**, and change the **Gutter position** to **Left**. Click **OK**.

6. Save the document as *[your initials]*9-5 in your Lesson 9 folder.

7. Print the document, and keep it open for the next exercise.

Using Print Preview

Viewing a document in Print Preview is the best way to check how a document will look when you print it. You can view multiple pages at a time, adjust margins and tabs, and edit text.

To display a document in Print Preview, click the Microsoft Office Button, click the arrow beside **Print**, and click **Print Preview**. The keyboard shortcut for Print Preview is [Alt]+[Ctrl]+[I].

Exercise 9-6 VIEW A MULTIPLE-PAGE DOCUMENT IN PRINT PREVIEW

Print Preview displays entire pages of a document in reduced size. You can view one page at a time or two pages at a time.

1. Move the insertion point to the beginning of the document.

2. Click the Microsoft Office Button, click the arrow beside Print, and click **Print Preview**. Click the One Page button [One Page] on the Print Preview tab to display the first page of the document.

3. Click the Two Pages button [Two Pages] to see both pages.

Figure 9-11
Viewing multiple pages in Print Preview

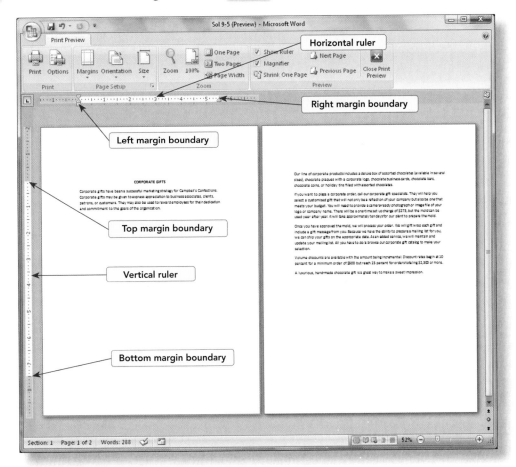

TIP

You use the Zoom box to view multiple pages of your document. Click the Zoom Level button on the status bar. Click Many Pages, and a grid appears to choose the number of pages you want to view and how they are configured in the window. If you drag the pointer as you move across the grid, you can expand the grid to display additional rows and pages, which is useful in a long document. Drag the Zoom Slider to 100% to return to a one-page view.

4. To zoom into page 2, click once on the page with the arrow pointer to make page 2 active and then click again with the magnifier pointer ⚲.

5. Click again to zoom out. Notice that the horizontal ruler shows the settings for page 2.

6. Click the Close Print Preview button 🔲 to close the Print Preview window and to return to Print Layout view.

TABLE 9-1 Print Preview Toolbar

Button	Description	Function
	Print	Print the document in the Print Preview window.
	Options	List printing options.
	Margins	Change margin settings.
	Orientation	Switch between portrait and landscape orientation.
	Size	Select paper size.
	Zoom	Choose a magnification to reduce or enlarge the page or pages displayed.
	100%	Zoom document to 100 percent.
One Page	One Page	Display one page at a time.
Two Pages	Two Pages	Display two pages at a time.
Page Width	Page Width	Zoom the document to the width of the window.
Show Ruler	Show Ruler	Display or hide the Print Preview ruler, which you can use to change margins, tabs, and indents.
⚲	Magnifier	Change the I-beam pointer to a magnifying glass and vice versa. With the magnifying glass pointer, click in the document to zoom in and out. With the I-beam pointer, edit document text.
Shrink One Page	Shrink One Page	Shrink a document to fit on one less page when the last page contains only a few lines of text.
Next Page	Next Page	Move to the next page of the document.
Previous Page	Previous Page	Move to the previous page of the document.
	Close Print Preview	Close the Print Preview window and return to the previous view

Exercise 9-7 CHANGE MARGINS IN PRINT PREVIEW

When you view a page in Print Preview, you can see all four margins and adjust margin settings using the horizontal and vertical rulers or by opening the Page Setup dialog box within the Print Preview window.

1. Move the insertion point to the beginning of the document (page 1, section 1).

2. Click the **Microsoft Office Button** and click the arrow beside **Print**. Click **Print Preview**.

3. Click the One Page button 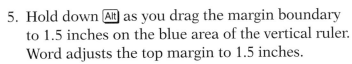 on the Print Preview tab to display only page 1. Click the Show Ruler button if it is not checked.

4. Move the pointer to the top margin boundary on the vertical ruler. The pointer changes to the two-pointed arrow, and the top margin is identified in a ScreenTip.

5. Hold down Alt as you drag the margin boundary to 1.5 inches on the blue area of the vertical ruler. Word adjusts the top margin to 1.5 inches.

6. Click the **Page Setup Dialog Box Launcher**.

7. Change the top margin to 2 inches and click **OK**.

8. Use the horizontal ruler to change the left and right margins to 1.25 inches.

NOTE

Changing margins in Print Preview is similar to changing margins in Print Layout view. You use the vertical and horizontal rulers to drag the margins to the desired positions.

TIP

You can check the exact measurement of a margin in Print Preview or Print Layout view by moving the pointer over the margin boundary, holding down the left mouse button without dragging it, and holding down Alt.

Exercise 9-8 EDIT A DOCUMENT IN PRINT PREVIEW

To edit text in Print Preview, you magnify a page to the desired size and then switch to edit mode. You would not, however, want to make extensive changes in Print Preview.

1. Click on page 1 to zoom in. The view of the document is enlarged to 100 percent.

2. Click the Magnifier button to deselect the option and change the pointer to the I-beam.

3. Select "Campbell's Confections" in the first paragraph, and press Ctrl+I to apply italic formatting.

4. Click the Magnifier button 🔍 to cancel edit mode.

5. Click **Close Print Preview** to close the Print Preview window.

6. Save the document as *[your initials]*9-8.

7. Submit the document, and leave it open for the next exercise.

Paper Size and Orientation

When you open a new document, the default paper size is 8.5 by 11 inches. Using the Page Setup dialog box, you can change the paper size to print a document on legal paper or define a custom-size paper.

The Page Setup dialog box also gives you a choice between two page orientation settings: portrait and landscape. A *portrait* page is taller than it is wide. This orientation is the default in new Word documents. A *landscape* page is wider than it is tall. You can apply page-orientation changes to sections of a document or to the entire document.

Exercise 9-9   **CHANGE PAPER SIZE AND PAGE ORIENTATION**

Figure 9-12
Changing page orientation

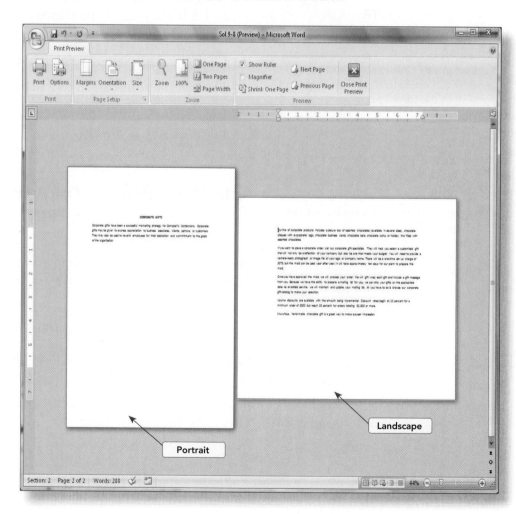

1. Open the **Page Setup** dialog box.

2. On the **Margins** tab, click **Landscape**.

3. Click the **Paper** tab. Notice the default paper size for letter paper.

4. Open the **Paper size** drop-down list and choose **Legal**. Click **OK**. Notice how the orientation and paper size changed.

5. Press ⌨Ctrl+⌨Z to undo the changes to paper size and orientation.

6. Switch to Print Preview, and click the Two Pages button .

7. Click page 2, and click the Orientation button. Click **Landscape**. Section 2 on page 2 is formatted with landscape orientation and page 1 is formatted with portrait orientation. Click **Close Print Preview** to close the Print Preview window.

8. Save the document as *[your initials]*9-9.

9. Submit and close the document.

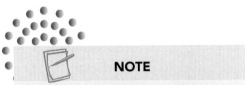

NOTE

You can change orientation for an entire document or from the insertion point forward by choosing an option from the **Apply to** drop-down list. When you choose **This point forward**, a new section is created with the orientation you choose. When selected text is formatted with a different orientation, a section break is automatically inserted before and after the selected text.

Printing Envelopes and Labels

Word provides a tool to print different-size envelopes and labels. Using the Envelopes and Labels command, you can:

- Print a single envelope without saving it or attach an envelope to a document for future printing. The attached envelope is added to the beginning of the document as a separate section.

- Print labels without saving them, or create a new document that contains the labels. You can print a single label or a full page of the same label.

Exercise 9-10   PRINT AN ENVELOPE

Printing envelopes often requires that you manually feed the envelope to your printer. If you print labels that are on other than 8½ by 11 inch sheets, you might need to feed the labels manually. Your printer will display a code and not print until you feed an envelope or label sheet manually.

1. Open the file **Matthews**. This document is a one-page letter.

2. Click the **Mailings** tab, and locate the **Create** group. Click the Envelopes button.

3. Click the **Envelopes** tab if it is not active. Notice that Word detected the address in the document and placed this text in the **Delivery address** text box. You can edit this text as needed.

Figure 9-13
Envelopes and
Labels dialog box

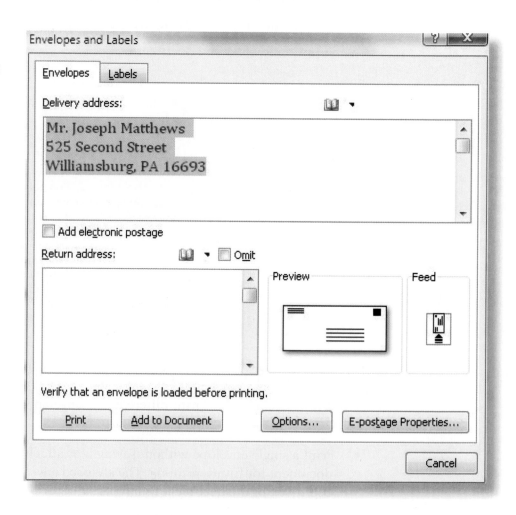

4. In the **Delivery address** text box, enter the full ZIP+4 Code by keying **-1129** after "16693."

5. Make sure the **Omit** box is not checked. Select and delete any text in the **Return address** text box, and then key the following return address, starting with your name:

   [your name]
   Campbell's Confections
   25 Main Street
   Grove City, PA 16127-0025

6. Place a standard business-size envelope in your printer. The **Feed** box illustrates the feeding method accepted by your printer.

7. Click **Print**. When Word asks if you want to save the return address as the default return address, click **No**. Word prints the envelope with the default font and text placement settings.

NOTE

If you don't have an envelope, you can use a blank sheet of paper to test the placement of the addresses. Ask your instructor how to proceed. You might have to feed the envelope or blank sheet manually.

NOTE

Check your printer to see what you need to do to complete a manual envelope feed. If the printer is flashing or displaying a message, you might have to press a button.

Exercise 9-11 CHOOSE ENVELOPE OPTIONS

Before printing an envelope, you can choose additional envelope options. For example, you can add the envelope content to the document for future use. You can also click the **Options** button in the Envelopes and Labels dialog box to:

- Change the envelope size. The default size is size 10, which is a standard business envelope.

- Change the font and other character formatting of the delivery address or return address.

- Verify printing options.

1. Open the **Envelopes and Labels** dialog box again.

2. Type your name and address in the **Return address** box.

3. Click the **Options** button in the Envelopes and Labels dialog box to open the Envelope Options dialog box. Click the **Envelope Options** tab if it is not active.

4. Under **Envelope size**, click the down arrow to look at the different-size options. Click the arrow again to close the list.

Figure 9-14
Envelope Options
dialog box

5. Click the **Font** button  for the **Delivery address**. The Envelope Address dialog box for the delivery address opens.

6. Format the text as bold and all caps and change the font size to **10**. Click **OK** to close the Envelope Address dialog box. Click **OK** to close the Envelope Options dialog box.

7. Delete the punctuation from the delivery address and add **-1129** to the ZIP Code.

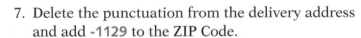

NOTE

The delivery address format preferred by the U.S. Postal Service is all caps with no punctuation.

8. Click **Add to Document** to add the envelope information to the top of the document as a separate section. Don't save the return address as the default address.

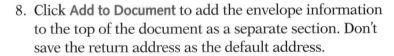

NOTE

Once the envelope is added to the document, you can also format or edit the envelope text just as you would any document text. The default font for envelope addresses is Cambria.

9. Replace [Today's date] with the current date. Correct any spacing between the elements of the letter. Add your reference initials followed by Enclosures (2). To make sure the letter follows the correct format, see Appendix B, "Standard Forms for Business Documents."

10. View the letter and envelope in Print Preview.

11. Close the Print Preview window, and save the document as *[your initials]*9-11 in your Lesson 9 folder.

12. Print the document.

13. Leave the document open for use in the next exercise.

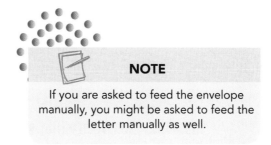

NOTE

If you are asked to feed the envelope manually, you might be asked to feed the letter manually as well.

Exercise 9-12 PRINT LABELS

The Labels tab in the Envelopes and Labels dialog box makes it easy to print different-size labels for either a return address or a delivery address.

1. Position the insertion point in the envelope section of the document. Click the Mailings tab. Click the Labels button 🏷️.

2. Click the Use return address check box to create labels for the letter sender.

3. Select the address text, and press Ctrl+Shift+A to turn on all caps. Delete the comma after the city.

4. Click the option Full page of the same label, if it is not active, to create an entire page of return address labels.

5. Click the Options button 📋 to choose a label size.

Word 2007

Figure 9-15
Label Options dialog
box

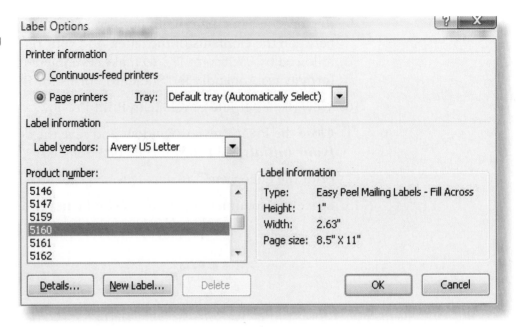

NOTE

Be sure to verify the options selected in the **Printer information** and **Label information** sections.

6. Verify that **Page printers** is selected under **Printer information** and that **Avery US Letter** is listed in the **Label vendors** box.

7. Scroll the **Product number** list to see the various label options, and choose **5160**, the product number for a standard Avery address label.

8. Click **OK**, and then click **New Document** to save the labels as a separate document. (If you click **Print**, you can print the labels without saving them.) Do not save the return address.

9. Select all text in the new document and reduce the font size to 11 points.

10. Save the document as *[your initials]*9-12 in your Lesson 9 folder.

11. Switch to Print Preview to view the labels on the page.

12. Prepare the printer for a sheet of 5160-size labels or feed a blank sheet of paper into the printer, and then print the labels.

13. Close the document containing the full sheet of labels.

Setting Print Options

When you click the Quick Print option, Word prints the entire document. If you open the Print dialog box, however, you can choose to print only part of a document. You can also select other print options from the dialog box, including collating copies of a multipage document, printing selected text, or printing multiple document pages on one sheet of paper.

Exercise 9-13 CHOOSE PRINT OPTIONS FROM THE PRINT DIALOG BOX

1. Position the insertion point to the left of the date in the letter to Mr. Joseph Matthews (*[your initials]*9-11). Click the Microsoft Office Button, and click the arrow beside Print to view the print options. Click Print to open the Print dialog box. (You can also click Print to open the Print dialog box.)

2. Click Current Page and click OK. Word prints page 1 of the document.

3. Open the Print dialog box again. Key 1-2 in the Pages text box. You can also enter specific page numbers or page ranges.

4. In the Number of copies text box, use the up arrow to change the number of copies to 2.

5. If the Collate check box is not active, click it to select it. Notice the change in the preview of the number of copies. Click the Collate check box to uncheck it (make sure it is unchecked). With this box not checked, Word will print two copies of page 1 and then two copies of page 2.

6. Change the number of copies back to 1.

7. Click the down arrow to open the Print what drop-down list. It shows the various elements you can print in addition to the entire document. Click again to close the list.

8. Click the down arrow to open the Print drop-down list, which gives you the option to print even or odd pages. Click again to close the list.

9. Click the down arrow to open the Pages per sheet drop-down list, which gives you the option to print your selection over a specified number of sheets. Choose the 2 pages setting. This option prints two pages on one sheet of $8^{1}/_{2}$- by 11-inch paper, with each page reduced to fit on the sheet.

Figure 9-16
Print dialog box

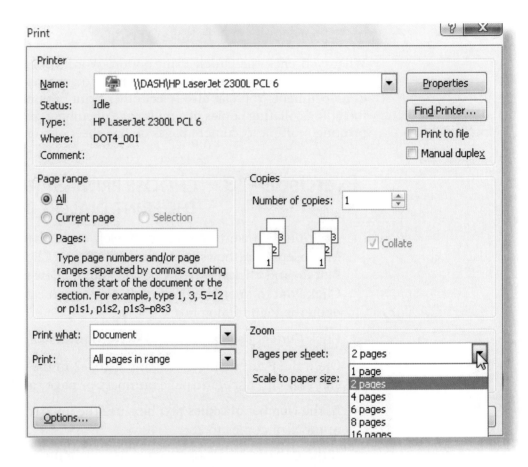

10. Open the **Scale to paper size** drop-down list, which gives you the option to print on a different paper or envelope size (Word adjusts the scaling of the fonts, tables, and other elements to fit the new size). Close the drop-down list.

11. Click **OK**. Word prints reduced versions of pages 1 and 2 on one sheet of paper.

12. Close the document without saving.

Lesson 9 Summary

- In a Word document, text is keyed and printed within the boundaries of the document's margins. Margins are the spaces between the edges of the text and the edges of the paper.

- Change the actual space for text on a page by changing margins (left, right, top, and bottom). You can key new margin settings in the Page Setup dialog box.

- Changing margins for selected text results in a new section for the selected text. A section is a portion of a document that has its own formatting. When a document contains more than one section, you see double-dotted lines, or section breaks, between sections to indicate the beginning and end of a section.

- Print Layout view shows how text is positioned on the printed page. Use the View buttons on the right of the status bar to switch between Print Layout view and Draft view.

- Print Preview shows how an entire document looks before printing. Use the One Page command, the Two Pages command, and the scroll bar to view all or part of the document. Change the Zoom as needed.

- Change margins in Print Layout view or in Print Preview by positioning the pointer over a margin boundary on a ruler and dragging. Press [Alt] to see the exact ruler measurement as you drag.

- Edit a document in Print Preview by clicking the Magnifier command to change the magnifier pointer to the I-beam pointer.

- For bound documents, use mirror margins and gutter margins. Mirror margins are inside and outside margins on facing pages that mirror one another. Gutter margins add extra space to the left and top margins to allow for binding

- A document can print in either portrait ($8\frac{1}{2}$- by 11-inch) or landscape (11- by $8\frac{1}{2}$-inch) orientation. Choose an orientation in the Page Setup dialog box, Margins tab.

- A document can be scaled to fit a particular paper size. Choose paper size options in the Page Setup dialog box, Paper tab.

- Use Word to print different-size envelopes. You can change address formatting and make the envelope part of the document for future printing. Use Word to print different-size address labels—either a single label or a sheet of the same label.

- Choose print options such as printing only the current page, specified pages, selected text, collated copies of pages, and reduced pages by opening the Print dialog box.

LESSON 9		Command Summary	
Feature	**Button**	**Command**	**Keyboard**
Print Preview		Microsoft Office Button, Print, Print Preview	Ctrl + F2 or Alt + Ctrl + I
Print Layout view	▤	View tab, Print Layout command	Alt + Ctrl + P
Choose print options		Microsoft Office Button, Print	Ctrl + P
Print envelopes or lables		Mailings tab, Envelopes or Mailings tab, Labels command	

Concepts Review

True/False Questions

Each of the following statements is either true or false. Indicate your choice by circling T or F.

T   F   1. Word has default settings for margins that are automatically set for each new document.

T   F   2. You can change margins in Print Layout view by using the ruler.

T   F   3. You can edit a document in Print Preview.

T   F   4. Both Print Preview and the Page Setup dialog box use horizontal and vertical rulers to drag margins to desired positions.

T   F   5. You can change margins for an entire document only by using the Page Setup dialog box.

T   F   6. Gutter margins are outside margins on a bound document.

T   F   7. The Shrink One Page feature reduces the size of the document by one page.

T   F   8. Landscape is the default page orientation.

Short Answer Questions

Write the correct answer in the space provided.

1. What is the default document view?

   _____

2. What does the pointer look like when it is located over the margin boundary on the ruler in Print Layout view?

   _____

3. What is created when you change margins for selected text?

   _____

4. Which kind of document needs gutter margins?

   _____

5. Which tab, in which dialog box, do you use to change page orientation?

   _____

6. How do you switch to edit mode in Print Preview?

_____

7. Which key to you press to show the exact margin and text area measurements when using the ruler to change margins?

_____

8. What is the term for pages that appear as a two-page spread with odd-numbered right pages and even-numbered left pages?

_____

Critical Thinking

Answer these questions on a separate page. There are no right or wrong answers. Support your answers with examples from your own experience, if possible.

1. Collect samples of printed documents with interesting treatments of margins (such as books, advertisements, or reports). Pay particular attention to mirror margins and gutter margins. How does the margin treatment contribute to the overall feeling of the document?

2. Use Microsoft Office Word Help (F1) or practice on your own to explore the Book fold feature that is located in the Page Setup dialog box, Multiple Pages section. What type of document would you create to use this feature? Is the feature helpful?

Skills Review

Exercise 9-14

Set margins for an entire document and for selected text by using the Page Setup dialog box.

1. Open the file **Gresh**.
2. Change the margins for the entire document by following these steps:

   a. Click the Page Layout tab, and click the Margins button.
   b. Click Custom Margins, and set the Top margin to 2 inches, the Bottom margin to .75 inch, and the Left and Right margins to 1.25 inches. Click OK.
3. Change the margins, and create a new section for selected text by following these steps:
   a. Select the text that begins "Campbell's Confections." through "Fax: 304-555-6660."

   b. Open the Page Setup dialog box.

   c. Set the left and right margins to 2 inches.

   d. Choose Selected text from the Apply to drop-down list, and click OK. The address appears by itself on a new page.

4. Click the Undo button to undo the new section.

5. Key the text Matthew Garrett, Manager as a separate line before "Campbell's Confections" in the body of the letter.

6. Save the document as *[your initials]*9-14 in your Lesson 9 folder.

7. Submit and close the document.

Exercise 9-15

Set margins in Print Layout view and Print Preview and change orientation.

1. Open the file **Chocolate**.

2. Change the left and right margins in Print Layout view by following these steps:

   a. Click the Print Layout View button located on the right of the status bar.

   b. If the rulers are not displayed, click the View Ruler button .

   c. Using the horizontal ruler, position the pointer on the left margin boundary until it becomes a two-pointed horizontal arrow (and the ScreenTip "Left Margin" appears).

   d. Hold down [Alt] and drag the margin boundary until the left margin measures 1.5 inches.

   e. Position the pointer on the right margin boundary and use the same method to drag it to 1.5 inches.

3. Change the top margin in Print Preview by following these steps:

   a. Click the Microsoft Office Button. Click the arrow beside Print, and click Print Preview.

   b. If the rulers are not displayed, click to select the Show Ruler command.

   c. Using the vertical ruler, position the pointer on the top margin boundary until it becomes a two-pointed arrow.

   d. Hold down [Alt] and drag the top margin boundary to 2 inches.

   e. Click the Close Print Preview button to return to Print Layout view. Drag the Zoom control to 100% if necessary.

4. Add a bold, centered, and uppercase title TYPES OF CHOCOLATE to the top of the document, with 24 points spacing after.

5. Change the orientation to landscape by following these steps:

   a. Open the Page Setup dialog box.

   b. Click the Margins tab and choose Landscape.

   c. Change the top margin to 2 inches, change the bottom margin to 1 inch, and change the left and right margins to 1.25 inches.

   d. Click OK to close the Page Setup dialog box.

6. Save the document as *[your initials]*9-15 in your Lesson 9 folder.

7. Submit and close the document.

Exercise 9-16

Set mirror and gutter margins.

1. Open the file **Corporate Gifts - 2**.

2. Use the Page Setup dialog box to set mirror and gutter margins by following these steps:

   a. Open the Page Setup dialog box.

   b. Choose Mirror margins from the Multiple pages drop-down list.

   c. Change the inside and outside margins to 1.5 inches.

   d. Set the Gutter margin to .5 inch.

   e. Click OK.

3. Scroll through the document in Print Layout view to see the new margin settings.

4. Switch to Print Preview.

5. Click the Two Pages button , to see both pages display with the new margin settings. Click the Close Print Preview button.

6. Save the document as *[your initials]*9-16 in your Lesson 9 folder.

7. Print the document two pages per sheet, by following these steps:

   a. Click the Microsoft Office Button.

   b. Click Print to open the Print dialog box.

   c. Click the drop-down arrow beside the Pages per sheet option and choose 2 pages.

   d. Click OK.

8. Submit and close the document.

Exercise 9-17

Set print options, print an envelope, and print labels.

1. Open the file **WV Stores**.

2. Print a portion of the document by following these steps:

   a. Select the text for the "Wheeling, WV" store—from "Campbell's Confections" through the fax number.

   b. Press Ctrl+P to open the Print dialog box.

   c. Choose Selection and click OK.

3. Insert the date by following these steps:

   a. Go to the end of the document, and press Enter four times. Key the text **Updated** and press Spacebar.

   b. Click the **Insert** tab, and click **Date and Time**.

   c. Choose the fourth date format, make sure **Update automatically** is not checked, and click **OK**.

   d. Insert a blank line after the date.

4. Prepare an envelope addressed to the Morgantown store by following these steps:

   a. Select the name and address lines for the Morgantown store. Do not select the telephone and fax numbers.

   b. Click the **Mailings** tab. Click the **Envelopes** button. Click the **Envelopes** tab.

   c. In the **Delivery address** box, delete the comma in the address, and key **-3301** at the end of the ZIP Code.

   d. In the **Return address** box, key your name, followed by the office address:

   Campbell's Confections

   25 Main Street

   Grove City, PA 16127

TIP

Because this document contains many addresses, you need to select the text you want to appear in the **Delivery address** box of the Envelopes and Labels dialog box.

5. Choose additional envelope options, and add the envelope to the document by following these steps:

   a. Click the **Options** button and choose the **Envelope Options** tab, if it is not already displayed.

   b. Make sure the envelope size is **10**.

   c. Click the **Font** button for the Delivery Address. Change the format to bold and all caps and click **OK**.

   d. Click **OK** in the Envelope Options dialog box. Click **Add to Document** in the Envelopes and Labels dialog box. Do not save the return address as the default.

6. Prepare the printer for a standard business envelope (or feed a blank sheet of paper into the printer). Print the document (envelope included).

7. Save the document as *[your initials]*9-17a in your Lesson 9 folder.

8. Create and print a page of return address labels by following these steps:

   a. With the insertion point in section 1 (the envelope), open the Envelopes and Labels dialog box and click the **Labels** tab.

   b. Examine the **Use return address** box. (Word recognizes the return address you previously entered for the envelope.)

   c. Choose the option **Full page of the same label**.

   d. Click **Options**. Set the **Product number** to **5160** and verify that **Page Printer** and **Avery US Letter** are selected. Click **OK**.

   e. Click **New Document** to save the labels as a separate document. Do not save the return address as the default.

   f. Save the labels as *[your initials]*9-17b in your Lesson 9 folder.

   g. Print the labels on a blank sheet of paper.

9. Close both documents.

Lesson Applications

Exercise 9-18

Set margins for a document and for selected text.

1. Open the file **PA Stores**.

2. At the beginning of the document, key the text shown in Figure 9-17, including the corrections. Use single spacing, and insert one blank line between paragraphs.

Figure 9-17

Than^k you for cho^sing Campbell's Confect^ions to provide your company
with our boxed chocolates. We began as ^a small down‿town off^store ice over 50
yea^stores rs ago. Today we have off^ices in three states^, and we provide quality
chocolates to all our customers.

All of our stores work together ᵗᵒ meet ~~all of your~~ group or individual
needs. We offer our products in the following areas:

Retail
Wholesale   *create as one paragraph using line breaks.*
Fundraising

For your convenience, Campbell's Confections offers complete service
from any one of our Pennsylvania locations. Our store^#locations and ^tele phone
numbers are listed on the following page^s.

3. At the top of the document, key the title Pennsylvania Stores in 14-point bold small caps as a separate line. Center the title, and add 24 points spacing after. Copy the title, and paste it to the left of the first store.

4. Using the Page Setup dialog box, set the top margin to 2 inches and the left and right margins to 1.25 inches.

5. Select the text beginning with the second title "Pennsylvania Stores" through the end of the document. Use the Page Setup dialog box to change the left and right margins for *only* the selected text to 3 inches.

6. Change the top margin of the new section to 1.5 inches.

7. Use the Replace command to format all occurrences of "Campbell's Confections" in the second section as bold italic.

8. Save the document as *[your initials]*9-18 in your Lesson 9 folder.

9. Print the document using the 2 Pages per sheet option in the Print dialog box. Close the document.

Exercise 9-19

Set margins for a document and for selected text, change page orientation, and set print options.

1. Open the file **Memo - 3**.

2. Insert today's date in the date line.

3. In the opening paragraph of the memo, replace the text "items below" with following information.

4. Change the top margin to 2 inches and the left and right margins to 1.25 inches.

5. Select the text from "Beginning next quarter" through the end of the document. Change the orientation to landscape.

6. Format the new section as follows: change the top margin to 1.5 inches, change the bottom margin to 1 inch, and change the left and right margins to 1 inch.

7. Place a blank line above "Description/Model number." Delete the paragraph mark after "Model Number," and insert a tab character. Delete the paragraph mark after "Serial Number," and insert a tab character. Continue this procedure until the line includes all items. Adjust the tab settings to distribute the text evenly between the margins. Change the font of the headings to Arial Narrow, and apply bold and small caps formatting. Apply a bottom border to the headings.

8. Save the document as *[your initials]*9-19 in your Lesson 9 folder.

9. Print the document two pages per sheet. Close the document.

Exercise 9-20

Set margins, set mirror and gutter margins, and address an envelope.

1. Open the file **Orders**.

2. Change the left and right margins to 1.25 inches.

3. Set mirror margins and a .5-inch gutter margin.

4. Format the title as 14-point bold with a shadow effect. Add 72 points of paragraph spacing before the title.

5. Justify all text below the title except the tabbed information.

6. At the end of the document, format the address with 1.5-inch left and right indents (not margins), a 1-point box border, and gray shading. Key a colon after "at."

7. Add an envelope to the document, using the company address. Use your name and address as the return address. Do not save the return address.

8. Select the paragraph headings beginning with "Online" through "Customer Service," and change the font size to 12 points. Do not change the font size for the paragraphs beginning with "Note."

9. Save the document as *[your initials]*9-20 in your Lesson 9 folder.

10. Submit and close the document.

Exercise 9-21 ◆ Challenge Yourself

Create labels.

1. Open the file **Haas**.

2. Format the document as a standard business letter. (Refer to Appendix B, "Standard Forms for Business Documents," for margin and spacing requirements.) Enter the date as a field. The letter is from you with the title Sales Associate and to the following person:

   Mr. Mark Haas

   215 Lake Street

   Girard, PA 16417

3. Key the text shown in Figure 9-18 as the closing paragraphs.

Figure 9-18

```
Call our corporate gift specialists for assistance in
selecting your customized gifts, maintaining your mailing
list, and for information on volume discounts. The enclosed
brochure explains the procedure for ordering.

We look forward to doing business with you.
```

4. Add an enclosure notation to the letter.

5. Switch to Print Preview for a final view of the document.

6. Save the document as *[your initials]*9-21a in your Lesson 9 folder.

7. Create a sheet of labels (Avery Standard 5160) of Mr. Haas's address as a new document. Use all caps and no punctuation in the address.

8. Save the labels as *[your initials]*9-21b in your Lesson 9 folder.

9. Submit both documents and close them.

On Your Own

In these exercises you work on your own, as you would in a real-life business environment. Use the skills you've learned to accomplish the task—and be creative.

Exercise 9-22

Write a summary about a book you have recently read. Change the margins for the document, and change the margins of one of the sections of the summary that you want to highlight. Save the document as *[your initials]*9-22 and submit it.

Exercise 9-23

Create a document, and use the Page Layout tab to create a custom paper size. Change the width to 5 inches and the height to 3 inches. Change all margins to .4 inch, and change the orientation to landscape. Key a favorite recipe and format the text attractively. Save the document as *[your initials]*9-23 and submit it.

Exercise 9-24

Log onto the Internet, and find five Web sites about today's current political topic. Create a document summarizing the topic with a pro and con approach. Format the document using landscape orientation. Save the document as *[your initials]*9-24 and submit it.

Page and Section Breaks

OBJECTIVES

After completing this lesson, you will be able to:

1. Use soft and hard page breaks.

2. Control line and page breaks.

3. Control section breaks.

4. Format sections.

5. Use the Go To feature.

MCAS OBJECTIVES

In this lesson:
WW 07 1.1.6
WW 07 1.2.1
WW 07 2.3.1
WW 07 2.3.2
WW 07 5.1.1

Estimated Time: 1 hour

In Word, text flows automatically from the bottom of one page to the top of the next page. This is similar to how text wraps automatically from the end of one line to the beginning of the next line. You can control and customize how and when text flows from the bottom of one page to the top of the next. This process is called *pagination*.

Sections are a common feature of long documents and have a significant impact on pagination. This lesson describes how to use and manage sections.

Using Soft and Hard Page Breaks

As you work on a document, Word is constantly calculating the amount of space available on the page. Page length is determined by the size of the paper and the top and bottom margin settings. For example, using standard-size paper and default margins, page length is 9 inches. When a document exceeds this length, Word creates a *soft page break*. Word adjusts this automatic page break as you add or delete text. A soft page break appears as a horizontal dotted line on the screen in Draft view. In Print Layout view, you see the actual page break—the bottom of one page and the top of the next.

Draft view is frequently used to edit and format text. It does not show the page layout as it appears on a printed page, nor does it show special elements of a page such as columns, headers, or footers.

NOTE

When you format and edit a long documents, check the status bar settings to make sure Section and Page Numbers display. To verify the settings, right-click the status bar and click to select the options.

NOTE

The page breaks described in this lesson might appear in slightly different locations on your screen.

Exercise 10-1 ADJUST A SOFT PAGE BREAK AUTOMATICALLY

1. Open the file **History**. Switch to Draft view by clicking the Draft button ▤ on the status bar. Change the zoom level to **100%** if necessary.

2. Scroll to the bottom of page 3. Notice the soft page break separating the heading "Gourmet Chocolate" from the paragraph below it.

3. Locate the paragraph just above the heading "Gourmet Chocolate" (it begins "In 2001"). Move the insertion point to the left of "The Web site has proven" in the middle of the paragraph, and press Enter to split the paragraph. Notice the adjustment of the soft page break. Undo ⤺ the paragraph split.

Figure 10-1
Adjusting the position of a soft page break

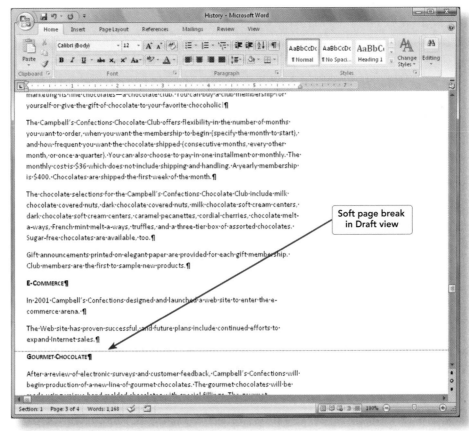

Exercise 10-2 INSERT A HARD PAGE BREAK

When you want a page break to occur at a specific point, you can insert a *hard page break*. In Draft view, a hard page break appears on the screen as a dotted line with the words "Page Break." In Print Layout view you see the actual page break.

There are two ways to insert a hard page break:

- Use the keyboard shortcut Ctrl+Enter.
- Click the **Insert** tab, and click the Page Break command.

1. Move the insertion point to the bottom of page 2, to the beginning of the paragraph that starts "The most popular."

2. Press Ctrl+Enter. Word inserts a hard page break so the paragraph and bulleted text are not divided between two pages.

3. Move to the middle of page 4, and place the insertion point to the left of the text that begins "Chronology."

4. Click the **Insert** tab, and click the Page Break button 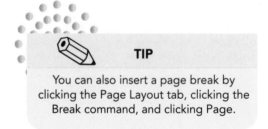 to insert a page break. Word inserts a hard page break and adjusts pagination in the document from this point forward.

Figure 10-2
Insert tab, Pages group

TIP

You can also insert a page break by clicking the Page Layout tab, clicking the Break command, and clicking Page.

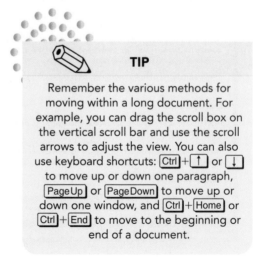

TIP

Remember the various methods for moving within a long document. For example, you can drag the scroll box on the vertical scroll bar and use the scroll arrows to adjust the view. You can also use keyboard shortcuts: Ctrl+↑ or ↓ to move up or down one paragraph, PageUp or PageDown to move up or down one window, and Ctrl+Home or Ctrl+End to move to the beginning or end of a document.

Figure 10-3
Inserting a hard page
break

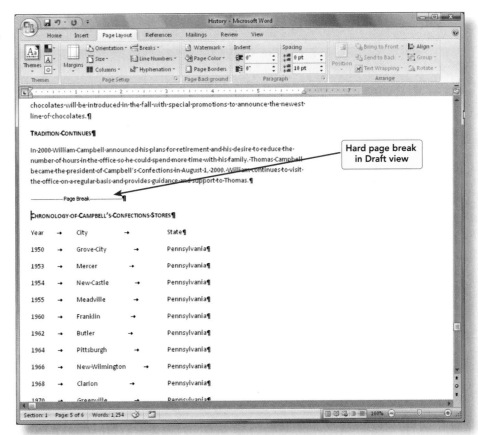

Exercise 10-3   DELETE A HARD PAGE BREAK

You cannot delete a soft page break, but you can delete a hard page break by
clicking the page break and pressing [Backspace] or [Delete].

1. Select the page break you just inserted by dragging the I-beam over
   the page break. Be sure to select the paragraph mark.

2. Press [Delete] to delete the page break.

3. Scroll back to the hard page break you inserted at the top of page 3.
   Position the insertion point to the left of "The most popular" and
   press [Backspace] two times (one time to delete the paragraph mark and
   one time to delete the page break). The page break is deleted, and
   Word adjusts the pagination.

Controlling Line and Page Breaks

To control the way Word breaks paragraphs, choose one of four line and page break options from the Paragraph dialog box:

- *Widow/Orphan control:* A *widow* is the last line of a paragraph and appears by itself at the top of a page. An *orphan* is the first line of a paragraph and appears at the bottom of a page. By default, this option is turned on to prevent widows and orphans. Word moves an orphan forward to the next page and moves a widow back to the previous page.

- *Keep lines together:* This option keeps all lines of a paragraph together on the same page rather than splitting the paragraphs between two pages.

- *Keep with next:* If two or more paragraphs need to appear on the same page no matter where page breaks occur, use this option. The option is most commonly applied to titles that should not be separated from the first paragraph following the title.

- *Page break before:* Use this option to place a paragraph at the top of a new page.

Exercise 10-4 APPLY LINE AND PAGE BREAK OPTIONS TO PARAGRAPHS

1. Close **History** without saving; then reopen the document. Switch to Draft view.

2. At the bottom of page 3, click within the heading "Gourmet Chocolate." You are going to format this heading so it will not be separated from its related paragraph.

3. Click the Home tab, and click the Paragraph Dialog Box Launcher to open the Paragraph dialog box. Click the Line and Page Breaks tab.

TIP

To reopen the file quickly, click the Microsoft Office Button and click the filename **History** under Recent Documents.

Figure 10-4
Line and Page
Breaks options in the
Paragraph dialog
box

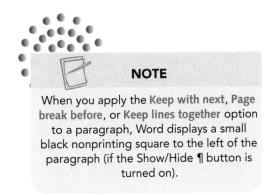

Paragraph

| Indents and Spacing | Line and Page Breaks |

Pagination

☑ Widow/Orphan control
☑ Keep with next
☐ Keep lines together
☐ Page break before

Formatting exceptions

☐ Suppress line numbers
☐ Don't hyphenate

Textbox options

Tight wrap:

None

Preview

Gourmet Chocolate

| Tabs... | Default... | OK | Cancel |

4. Click **Keep with next** to select it and click **OK**. Word moves the soft page break, keeping the two paragraphs together.

NOTE

When you apply the Keep with next, Page break before, or Keep lines together option to a paragraph, Word displays a small black nonprinting square to the left of the paragraph (if the Show/Hide ¶ button is turned on).

Figure 10-5
Applying the Keep with next option

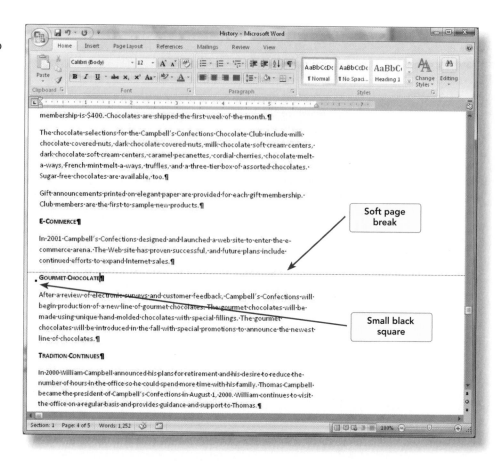

5. Press Ctrl+Home to go to the top of the document. Select the title, and apply 72 points spacing before.

6. Locate the text at the bottom of page 1 that begins "By 1980." The paragraph is divided by a soft page break.

7. Right-click the paragraph to open the shortcut menu. Click **Paragraph**. Click the **Line and Page Breaks** tab if necessary.

8. Choose **Keep lines together** and click **OK**. The soft page break moves above the paragraphs to keep the lines of text together.

9. Move to page 4, and place the insertion point in the paragraph that begins "Chronology." You will format this paragraph so it begins at the top of the page.

10. Open the **Paragraph** dialog box, click **Page break before**, and click **OK**. Word starts the paragraph at the top of page 5 with a soft page break.

11. Press Shift+F1 to open the **Reveal Formatting** task pane. Click the + to the left of Paragraph to display the paragraph formatting. Notice the link for **Line and Page Breaks**. Close the task pane.

12. Save the document as *[your initials]*10-4 in a new folder for Lesson 10. Leave it open for the next exercise.

Controlling Section Breaks

Section breaks separate parts of a document that have formatting different from the rest of the document. You may want to insert a section at the beginning of a document to include a title page with special formatting. A separate section is created when you change the left and right margins of selected text.

For better control in creating section breaks, you can insert a section break directly into a document at a specific location by using the Breaks command. You can also specify the type of section break you want to insert. Switch to Draft view to see the double-dotted section break lines.

TABLE 10-1 Types of Section Breaks

Type	Description
Next page	Section starts on a new page.
Continuous	Section follows the text before it without a page break.
Even page or Odd page	Section starts on the next even- or odd-numbered page. Useful for reports in which chapters must begin on either odd-numbered or even-numbered pages.

Exercise 10-5 INSERT SECTION BREAKS BY USING THE BREAKS COMMAND

1. Place the insertion point to the left of the paragraph at the top of page 5 that begins "Chronology."

2. Press Ctrl+Q. This clears the formatting for the paragraph, removing the soft page break you applied earlier.

3. Click the **Page Layout** tab, and click the Breaks button . Under **Section Breaks**, click **Continuous**. Word begins a new section on the same page, from the position of the insertion point.

4. Click above and below the section mark. Notice that the section number changes on the status bar but the page number stays the same.

Word 2007

Figure 10-6
Inserting a
continuous section
break

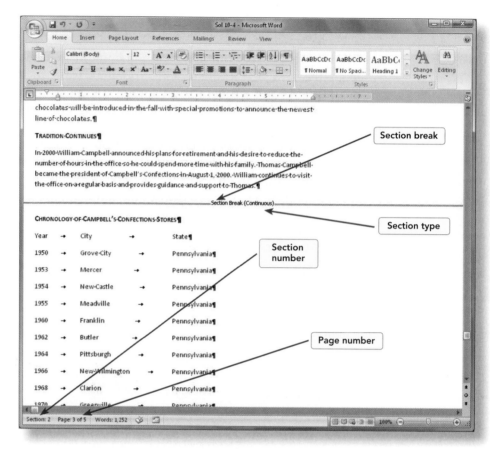

Formatting Sections

After you create a new section, you can change its formatting or specify a different type of section break. This is often useful for long documents, which sometimes contain many sections that require different page formatting, such as different margin settings or page orientation. For example, you can change a next page section break to a continuous section break, or you can change the page orientation of a section, without affecting the rest of the document.

NOTE

The formatting you apply to the section is stored in the section break. If you delete a section break, you also delete the formatting for the text above the section break. For example, if you have a two-section document and you delete the section break at the end of section 1, the document becomes one section with the formatting of section 2.

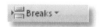

Exercise 10-6 APPLY FORMATTING TO SECTIONS

1. Position the insertion point before the text "Wholesale" on page 2. Use the **Page Layout** tab, Breaks button to insert a **Next page** section break.

2. With the insertion point in the new section (section 2), open the **Page Setup** dialog box by clicking the **Page Setup Dialog Box Launcher**.

3. Click the **Layout** tab, and click to open the **Section start** drop-down list. From this list you can change the section break from **Next page** to another type.

4. Choose **Continuous** so the section does not start on a new page.

Figure 10-7
Using the Page
Setup dialog box to
modify the section

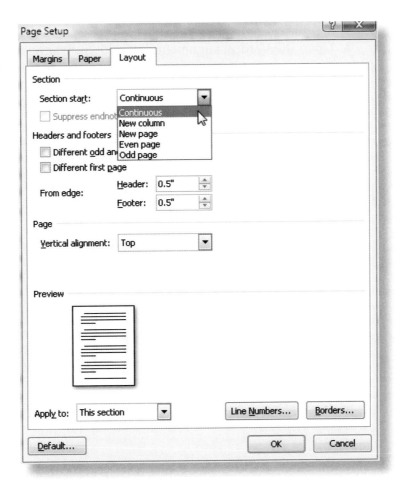

5. Click the **Margins** tab.

6. Set 1.5-inch left and right margins. Make sure **This section** appears in the **Apply to** box, and click **OK**. Section 2 of the document now has new margin settings.

Exercise 10-7   CHANGE THE VERTICAL ALIGNMENT OF A SECTION

Another way to format a section is to specify the vertical alignment of the section on the page. For example, you can align a title page so the text is centered between the top and bottom margins. Vertical alignment is a Layout option available in the Page Setup dialog box.

1. Move the insertion point to the last section of the document (which begins "Chronology"). Notice that, because this section does not start on a new page, a page break interrupts the list of stores.

2. Open the **Page Setup** dialog box and click the **Layout** tab.

3. Use the **Section start** drop-down list to change the section from **Continuous** to **New page**.

4. Open the **Vertical alignment** drop-down list and choose **Center**. Click **OK**.

TABLE 10-2 Vertical Alignment Options

Options	Description
Top	Aligns the top line of the page with the top margin (default setting).
Center	Centers the page between the top and bottom margins with equal space above and below the text.
Justified	Aligns the top line of the page with the top margin and the bottom line with the bottom margin, with equal spacing between the lines of text (similar in principle to the way Word justifies text between the left and right margins).
Bottom	Aligns the bottom line of a partial page along the bottom margin.

Figure 10-8
Vertical alignment options

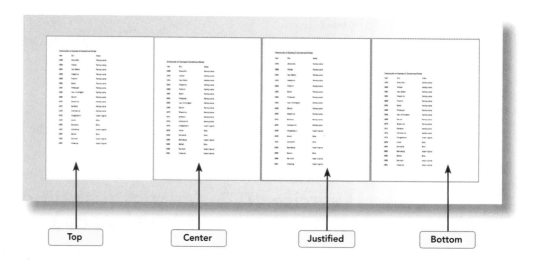

Top   Center   Justified   Bottom

Exercise 10-8 CHECK PAGINATION IN PRINT PREVIEW AND PAGE LAYOUT VIEW

After you apply page breaks, section breaks, or section formatting, use Print Preview or Print Layout view to check the document. Viewing the pages in relation to one another provides ideas for improvement before printing.

Remember, you can edit and change the formatting of a document in Print Layout view or Print Preview.

1. Click the **Microsoft Office Button** and click the arrow beside **Print**. Click **Print Preview** to preview the current section. Click the One Page button ⊞One Page if necessary. Notice that the text is centered between the top and bottom margins. Notice also that Print Preview does not show the dotted lines of the section breaks, but it does show how the page will look when you print it.

2. While still in Print Preview, open the **Page Setup** dialog box, and change the vertical alignment to **Justified**. Click **OK**. Word justifies the last page of the document so the text extends from the top margin to the bottom margin.

3. Click the Previous Page button ⊞Previous Page to scroll back, page by page, to page 2, section 1, of the document. (Check the status bar for location.)

4. Click the Zoom Level button 100%, choose **Page width** and click **OK**. You cannot see the continuous section break before "Wholesale. . ." but you can check the formatting and see how the document will look when printed.

5. Click the Print Layout View button to close Print Preview and to switch to Print Layout view.

6. Scroll to page 2, section 1. Notice that in Print Layout view, page breaks are indicated by the actual layout of each page as it will look when printed.

7. Click the Zoom Level button on the status bar to open the Zoom dialog box. Click **Many Pages** and click on the grid to display **1 × 2** (one row, two pages). Click **OK**. This reduces the document display so you can see two pages at the same time.

8. Scroll to the end of the document. Click the Draft View button ≡ to switch to Draft view. Drag the **Zoom Slider** to **100%** if necessary.

Using the Go To Feature

You use Go To to move through a document quickly. For example, you can go to a specific section, page number, comment, or bookmark. Go To is a convenient feature for long documents—it is faster than scrolling, and it moves the insertion point to the specified location.

There are three ways to initiate the Go To command:

- Click the Home tab, and click the Find or Replace commands to open the Find and Replace dialog box. Click the Go To tab.

- Double-click on the status bar (anywhere to the left of "Words").

- Press Ctrl+G or F5.

Exercise 10-9   GO TO A SPECIFIC PAGE OR SECTION

1. With the document in Draft view, press F5. Word displays the **Go To** tab, located in the Find and Replace dialog box.

Figure 10-9
Using the Go To feature

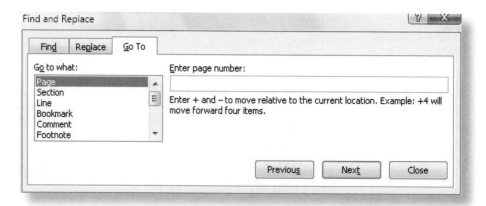

2. Scroll through the **Go to what** list to review the options. Choose **Section** from the list, and click **Previous** until you reach the beginning of the document.

3. Click **Next** until the insertion point is located at the beginning of the last section, which is section 3.

4. Choose **Page** from the **Go to what** list and click **Previous**. The insertion point moves to the top of the previous page.

5. Key **2** in the **Enter page number** text box and click **Go To**. The insertion point moves to the top of page 2.

6. **Close** the dialog box.

Exercise 10-10   GO TO A RELATIVE DESTINATION

You can use the Go To command to move to a location relative to the insertion point. For example, with **Page** selected in the **Go to what** list, you can enter "+2" in the text box to move forward two pages from the insertion point. You can move in increments of pages, lines, sections, and so on.

Another option is to move by a certain percentage within the document, such as 50 percent—the document's midpoint.

1. Double-click the word "Page" on the status bar to reopen the Find and Replace dialog box.

2. Choose **Line** from the **Go to what** list, and key **4** in the text box. Click **Go To**. The insertion point moves to the fourth line in the document.

3. Key **+35** in the text box, and click **Go To**. The insertion point moves forward 35 lines from the previous location.

4. Key **-35** in the text box, and click **Go To**. The insertion point moves back to the previous location.

5. Click **Page** in the **Go to what** list, key **50%** in the text box, and click **Go To**. The insertion point moves to the midpoint of the document.

6. Close the dialog box.

7. Save the document as *[your initials]*10-10 in a new Lesson 10 folder.

8. Open the Print dialog box, and choose **4 pages** in the **Pages per sheet** list box. Click **OK**.

9. Close the document.

NOTE

You must select Page in the Go to what list to use a percentage.

TIP

You can use the Go To feature to delete a single page of content. Position the insertion point, and open the Find and Replace dialog box. Click the Go To tab, and key \page in the text box. Click Go To. Click Close (the text will be highlighted), and press ⌑Delete⌑.

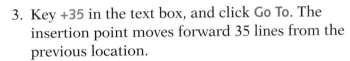

Lesson 10 Summary

- Pagination is the Word process of flowing text from line to line and from page to page. Word creates a soft page break at the end of each page. When you edit text, you adjust line and page breaks. You can adjust the way a page breaks by manually inserting a hard page break (⌑Ctrl⌑+⌑Enter⌑).

- Delete a hard page break by clicking it and pressing ⌑Delete⌑ or ⌑Backspace⌑.

- The Paragraph dialog box contains line and page break options to control pagination. To prevent lines of a paragraph from displaying on two pages, click in the paragraph and apply the **Keep lines together** option. To keep two paragraphs together on the same page, click in the first paragraph and apply the **Keep with next** option. To insert a page break before a paragraph, click in the paragraph and choose the **Page break before** option.

- Use section breaks to separate parts of a document that have different formatting. Apply a **Next page** section break to start a section on a new page or a **Continuous** section break to continue the new section on the same page. Apply an **Even page** or **Odd page** section break to start a section on the next even- or odd-numbered page.

- Change the vertical alignment of a section by clicking within the section and opening the Page Setup dialog box. On the **Layout** tab, under **Vertical alignment**, choose an alignment (Top, Center, Justified, or Bottom).

- Check pagination in Print Preview or Print Layout view. Scroll through the document or change the zoom level to display a different view.

- Use the Go To command to go to a specific page or section in a document. You can also go to a relative destination, such as the midpoint of the document or the 50th line.

LESSON 10		Command Summary	
Feature	**Button**	**Command**	**Keyboard**
Hard page break	Page Break	**Insert** tab, **Pages** group, **Page Break**	Ctrl + Enter
Line and page break options		**Home** tab, **Paragraph** group, **Paragraph** dialog box, **Line and Page Breaks** tab	
Section breaks	Breaks ▾	**Page Layout** tab, **Page Setup** group, **Breaks** command	
Formatting sections		**Page Layout** tab, **Page Setup** group, **Page Setup** dialog box	
Go To	Find ▾ / Replace	**Home** tab, **Editing** group, **Find** or **Replace** command, **Go To** tab	Ctrl + G or F5

Concepts Review

True/False Questions

Each of the following statements is either true or false. Indicate your choice by circling T or F.

T F   1. You can delete a hard or soft page break by pressing `Delete`.

T F   2. To insert a section break, press `Ctrl`+`Enter`.

T F   3. One way to insert a page break is to choose Break from the Insert tab.

T F   4. Page break before is a paragraph formatting option that starts a paragraph at the top of a new page.

T F   5. A nonprinting character appears to the left of any paragraph to which you apply the Keep with next option.

T F   6. Section breaks appear in the Print Preview window as double-dotted lines.

T F   7. Page breaks appear in Print Layout view as single-dotted lines.

T F   8. You can use the Go To feature to move the insertion point from one section to another.

Short Answer Questions

Write the correct answer in the space provided.

1. Which type of page break is automatically adjusted as you key text?

_____

2. Which type of section break does not start on a new page?

_____

3. What is the term for the last line of a paragraph that appears alone at the top of a page?

_____

4. Which option would you apply to a paragraph so it is not divided by a page break?

_____

5. Which dialog box and tab would you display to change the vertical alignment of a section?

_____

6. Which type of vertical alignment spaces text so the top line aligns with the top margin and the bottom line aligns with the bottom margin?

_____

7. In Print Layout view, which feature do you use to view two pages at the same time?

_____

8. Describe the appearance of the nonprinting character Word displays next to a paragraph when you apply certain line and page break options.

_____

Critical Thinking

Answer these questions on a separate page. There are no right or wrong answers. Support your answers with examples from your own experience, if possible.

1. In a long document that requires extensive editing, why would it be most efficient to perform all your edits before inserting hard page breaks?

2. Describe a situation where you would use a continuous section break.

Skills Review

Exercise 10-11

Adjust soft page breaks and insert hard page breaks.

1. Open the file **Terms**. Position the insertion point in the first line of the memo, and change the spacing before to 72 points.
2. Scroll to the bottom of page 1 to see where the soft page break occurs.
3. Change the font size for the entire document to 11 points. Notice how the change affects the soft page break.
4. Insert a page break before the text "Chocolate Terms" by following these steps:
   a. Place the insertion point to the left of the text.
   b. Press Ctrl + Enter.
5. Change the last line on page one to read: is listed on the next page. Change the font size of the title on page 2 to 14 points, and apply 24 points spacing after. Center the title.
6. Key today's date in the memo heading, and key your reference initials at the bottom of page 1.

7. View the document in Print Preview, one page at a time.

8. Click the Two Pages button to view two pages at once. Return to a one-page view, and zoom to view the "SUBJECT:" line.

9. Click the Magnifier check box to deselect it. Select the text for the subject line ("Chocolate Terms"), and apply italic formating using the keyboard shortcut Ctrl + I.

10. Save the document as *[your initials]*10-11 in your Lesson 10 folder.

11. Submit and close the document.

Exercise 10-12

Apply line and page break options to paragraphs.

1. Open the file **Directory**.

2. Change the left and right margins to 1.25 inches.

3. Format the first line of the title as 14-point bold, centered, and uppercase. Add 36 points of spacing before. Format the second line as 12-point bold, small caps, and centered.

4. Key the current date.

5. Apply paragraph formatting to the heading "Ohio Stores" so it begins on a new page by following these steps:

   a. Move the insertion point within the heading.

   b. Click the Home tab, and click the Paragraph Dialog Box Launcher.

   c. Click the Line and Page Breaks tab.

   d. Choose Page break before and click OK.

6. Click within the heading "West Virginia Stores," and press F4 to repeat the format. Repeat the formatting to the heading "Pennsylvania Stores" if necessary.

7. Scroll through the document to verify that the stores are listed by state on a new page. The document should be four pages.

8. Save the document as *[your initials]*10-12 in your Lesson 10 folder.

9 Submit and close the document.

Exercise 10-13

Specify section breaks by type and change the margin settings in sections.

1. Open the file **Homecoming - 2**.

2. Insert a next page section break on page 1 before the heading "Homecoming Events" by following these steps:

   a. Place the insertion point to the left of the heading.

   b. Click the Page Layout tab, and click the Breaks button . Click Next Page.

3. Move the insertion point to section 1. Change the top margin to 2 inches, and change the left and right margins to 1.25 inches. Be sure to apply the format to the section and not the whole document.

4. Use the Page Setup dialog box to format section 2 with 1.5-inch left and right margins. Make sure This section appears in the Apply to box.

5. Select the list of colleges, and change the left indent to 1.5 inches.

6. Change the vertical alignment for section 2 to centered by following these steps:

   a. Place the insertion point in the second section.

   b. Open the Page Setup dialog box, and click the Layout tab. Select Centered from the Vertical alignment drop-down list. Click OK.

7. Format page 2 (section 2) with a page border using the Box setting and a 3-point double line. Be sure to apply the border to "This Section."

8. Save the document as *[your initials]*10-13 in your Lesson 10 folder.

9. Submit and close the document.

Exercise 10-14

Vertically align a section and move around a document by using the Go To feature.

1. Open the file **Leadership**.

2. Insert Next page section breaks at *"Please join us for"* on page 1 and at "Possible Agenda Topics" at the bottom of the same page.

3. Vertically align the text in section 2 by following these steps:

   a. With the insertion point in section 2, click the Page Layout tab, and click the Page Setup Dialog Box Launcher. Click the Layout tab.

   b. Choose Center from the Vertical alignment drop-down list.

   c. Make sure This section appears in the Apply to box, and click OK.

4. Switch to Print Preview, and view only the second page (section 2).

5. From the Print Preview window, open the Page Setup dialog box again, and change the vertical alignment to Justified.

6. Close Print Preview.

7. Select all the text in section 2, and center the text horizontally.

8. Use the Go To feature to move within the document by following these steps:

   a. Press F5.

   b. Choose Section from the Go to what list, and enter 3 in the text box.

   c. Click Go To and close the dialog box.

9. Select the first line of section 3, and change the font to 14-point bold and small caps. Select the second line through the end of the document, and apply a bullet format.

10. Use the Zoom Level to view three pages at one time by following these steps:

    a. Click the Zoom Level button 100% on the status bar.

    b. Click the Many Pages button 📖 and drag across the first row to highlight three pages.

    c. Click **OK**.

11. Drag the Zoom Slider to **100%**. Add 72 points of spacing before the first line on page 1. Add your reference initials to the bottom of page 1.

12. Save the document as *[your initials]***10-14** in your Lesson 10 folder.

13. Submit and close the document.

Lesson Applications

Exercise 10-15

Insert page breaks, apply line and page break options, and format text as a new section.

1. Open the file **Staff - 2**.

2. Key the text in Figure 10-10 at the beginning of the document.

Figure 10-10

> ────────format 14 points-bold-small caps
>
> Corporate Staff—Brief Biographies
>
>   significant   financial
> Campbell's Confections has experienced growth and success since Wiliam
>   the
> Campbell started the company in 1905. One explanation for this success of
> this company is the continued commitment to people—both customers
> and employees. ⌐ merge
> Campbell's Confections has been able to attract and hold employees and is
>   15
> proud of the fact that the average length of service for employees is 51
> years. William Campbell believed in the importance of demonstrating care
>   es   Thomas
> for employee, and Tom Campbell continues this philosophy.

3. Use the Find feature or scroll to locate "Tamara Robbins." Use the Keep with next feature to place the heading "Tamara Robbins" with the descriptive paragraph.

4. Place the insertion point to the left of "Corporate Staff." And insert a next page section break.

5. Change the top margin for section 1 to 2 inches and the left and right margins to 1.5 inches.

6. Locate the text "Cynthia Parker," and insert a page break at the beginning of the line.

7. Increase the font size of the title in section 1 to 20 points, and apply the shadow text effect. Change the font size of the title in section 2 to 20 points, and apply bold, small caps, and the shadow text effect.

8. Add a 3-D page border to all pages of the document. Select a double-line style, dark blue color, and 3-point width.

9. In section 2, center the text vertically.

10. Preview the document.

11. Save the document as *[your initials]*10-15 in your Lesson 10 folder.

12. Print the document 4 sheets per page, and then close it.

Exercise 10-16

Add and format sections.

1. Open the file **Forman**.

2. Set a 2-inch top margin, and change the left and right margins to 1.25 inches. Key the current date at the top of the document, and include an enclosures notation.

3. Position the insertion point at the end of the document. Click the Insert tab, and click the arrow beside the Object button . Click Text from file. Locate the file **Retail Stores - 2**, and click Insert.

4. Position the insertion point at the end of the document, and follow the same procedure to insert the file **Store Directory**.

5. Locate the text "There are 24" and insert a next page section break. In the new section, key the title Campbell's Confections' Retail Stores using bold uppercase text. Center the title, and increase the font size to 14 points. Add 24 points of spacing after.

6. Insert a next page section break before the text "Pennsylvania Stores."

7. Format section 2 so it is vertically centered and in landscape orientation. Set 1.5 inch left and right margins. Change the top and bottom margins to 1 inch. Select all paragraphs below the title and change the spacing after to 12 points.

8. Go to section 3, and insert a page break before "Ohio Stores" and "West Virginia Stores."

9. Change the top margin for section 3 to 1.5 inches.

10. Save the document as *[your initials]*10-16 in your Lesson 10 folder.

11. Submit and close the document.

Exercise 10-17

Apply line and page break options, add and format sections, and use the Go To feature.

1. Open the file **Price Change**.

2. Add a continuous section break before the line "Standard-size" and another at the bottom of the list (before the paragraph that begins "Price changes").

3. Format section 2 with a 1.5-inch left margin and double spacing. Adjust the tab settings to space the columns evenly between the margins. The third column should be formatted with a right tab at 5 inches. Bold and underline the column headings. Center, bold, and apply 14-point small caps to the title. Change the spacing before to 24 points.

4. Go to section 1, and key a memo heading to "Store Managers" from Thomas Campbell. Use the current date, and the subject is "Price changes." Align memo heading information with a left tab. Add your

reference initials at the end of section 1 with an attachment reference. Change the top margin to 2 inches and the bottom margin to 0.5 inch.

5. Go to section 3, and copy the formatting from the title in section 2 to the title in section 3.

6. Change the double-spaced text in section 2 to 1.5-line spacing.

7. Change the section layout for section 3 from a continuous section break to a section break that starts on a new page using the Page Setup dialog box.

8. Change the left and right margins for section 3 to 1 inch. Select the tabbed text in section 3, and change the left indent to 1 inch. Set a right dotted-leader tab at 5.5 inches. Bold and underline the column headings, and format the tabbed text with 1.5-line spacing. Remove the dotted leaders from the column heading. Format the title with 24 points spacing before and 12 points spacing after.

9. Change the alignment in section 3 so it is centered vertically.

10. Preview the document, and save it as *[your initials]***10-17** in your Lesson 10 folder.

11. Submit and close the document.

Exercise 10-18 ◆ Challenge Yourself

Add and delete page breaks, and add and format a new section.

1. Create a standard business memo from you to store managers. Key September 1 for the date. The subject is "Candy Bar Wrapper Contest." Key the body text shown in Figure 10-11.

Figure 10-11

Thank you for sending your comments regarding our first candy bar wrapper contest. We want our first contest to be a success, and we hope to use one of the winning designs for one of our fundraising candy bar wrappers.

Please review the following list, and provide your comments no later than Wednesday. We want to send the rules and guidelines to the graphic artist for layout and printing. When we receive the flyer, we will e-mail it to you for printing and distribution to high schools in your service area.

Your comments regarding possible awards were enlightening. Because Campbell's Confections' stores are located in a tri-state area, we have taken great effort to work with three state treasurers to establish our scholarship awards program.

2. At the end of the memo, add an attachment reference. After the reference, create a new section that starts on a new page.

3. In the new section, insert the file **Wrapper**.

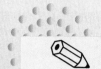

TIP

To insert a file, place the insertion point in the new section, click the Insert tab and click the arrow beside Object. Click Text from File. Locate the file and click Insert.

4. Format the two-line title as 14-point bold, all caps, and centered, with two blank lines below it.

5. Select all lines below the title and format with 12 points spacing after.

6. Select "Rules/Guidelines" and "Prizes" and apply bold, italic, and small caps formatting. Select the text below each side heading, and format it as a bulleted list.

7. Use the Replace feature to replace all occurrences of "contest" with competition.

8. Add a page border to section 2. Select a geometric-pattern border from the Art drop-down list. Select an appropriate width and color.

9. If you have not already done so, format section 1 with a 2-inch top margin. Make sure section 2 has the regular 1-inch top margin and is centered vertically.

10. Spell-check section 1 only.

11. Save the document as *[your initials]*10-18 in your Lesson 10 folder.

12. Submit and close the document.

On Your Own

In these exercises you work on your own, as you would in a real-life business environment. Use the skills you've learned to accomplish the task—and be creative.

Exercise 10-19

Write a short report about your 10 favorite television shows or movies. Include a document title. Each show or movie should be a separate paragraph with its own heading. Adjust page breaks as needed to keep headings with their related paragraphs. Save the document as *[your initials]*10-19 and submit it.

Exercise 10-20

Create a document that includes three poems by three different poets. Use headings to identify each poet and title. Use page breaks to start each poem on a separate page. Save the document as *[your initials]*10-20 and submit it.

Exercise 10-21

Create a document that lists three different categories of restaurants in your area. Include descriptions of two to three restaurants per category. Format each category as a separate section and apply a different, page, paragraph, and character format to each. Save the document as *[your initials]*10-21 and submit it.

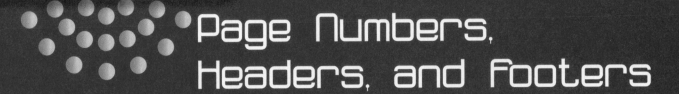

Lesson 11

Page Numbers, Headers, and Footers

OBJECTIVES

After completing this lesson, you will be able to:

1. Add page numbers.

2. Change the starting page number.

3. Add headers and footers.

4. Work with headers and footers within sections.

5. Link section headers and footers.

6. Change starting page numbers.

7. Create continuation page headers.

8. Create alternate headers and footers.

Estimated Time: 1¹/₂ hours

MCAS OBJECTIVES

In this lesson:
WW 07 1.2.1
WW 07 1.2.2
WW 07 4.1.1
WW 07 4.1.3
WW 07 4.1.4

Page numbers, headers, and footers are useful additions to multiple-page documents. Page numbers can appear in either the top or bottom margin of a page. The text in the top margin of a page is a *header;* text in the bottom margin of a page is a *footer*. Headers and footers can also contain descriptive information about a document, such as the date, title, and author's name.

Adding Page Numbers

Word automatically keeps track of page numbers and indicates on the left side of the status bar the current page and the total number of pages in a document. Each time you add, delete, or format text or sections, Word adjusts page breaks and page numbers. This process, called *background repagination,* occurs automatically when you pause while working on a document. Right-click the status bar to select **Formatted Page Numbers**, **Section**, and **Page Number** options when working with long documents.

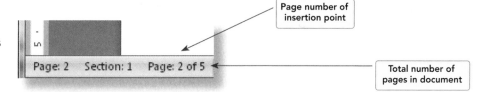

Figure 11-1
How Word paginates
when you open a
document

Exercise 11-1 ADD AND PREVIEW PAGE NUMBERS

Page numbers do not appear on a printed document unless you specify that they do. The simplest way to add page numbers is to click the Insert tab and click Page Number.

1. Open the file **History**.

2. With the insertion point at the top of the document, click the **Insert** tab and click the **Page Number** command. Word displays a list of options for placing your page number in the document. Notice that you can choose Top of Page, Bottom of Page, or Page Margins. Once you choose a position for the page number, you select a design from the gallery. A *gallery* is a list of design options for modifying elements of a page.

Figure 11-2
Page number
options

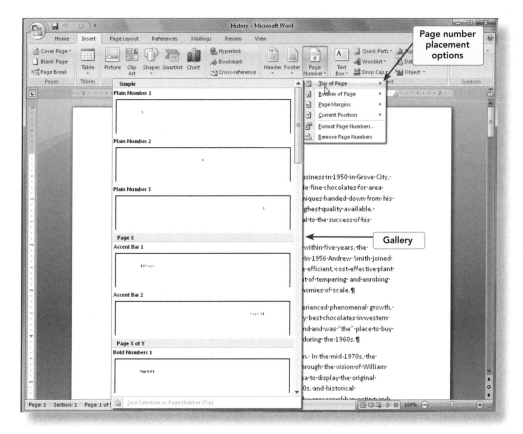

NOTE

You can see page numbers only in Print Preview, Print Layout view, or on the printed page.

3. Click **Top of Page** to display the gallery for placing numbers at the top of the page. Click **Plain Number 3** to place a page number in the upper right corner of the document.

4. Scroll through the document to view the page numbers. By default Word places page numbers on every page.

5. Notice that the **Ribbon** adds a new tab when page numbers have been added to a document. The **Header and Footer Tools Design** tab includes additional options for formatting the document.

6. Click the Close Header and Footer button 🔳.

7. Click the **Insert** tab and click the Page Number button 🔳. Click **Bottom of Page** and scroll to the bottom of the gallery. Click **Triangle 2**. A page number appears at the bottom right corner of each page.

8. Switch to Print Preview, and notice that page numbers appear in the header and footer of the page.

9. Use the magnifier pointer 🔍 to click the upper right corner of the first page. The page number appears within the 1-inch top margin. Specifically, the page number is positioned 0.5 inch from the top edge of the page at the right margin.

Figure 11-3
Viewing page numbers in Print Preview

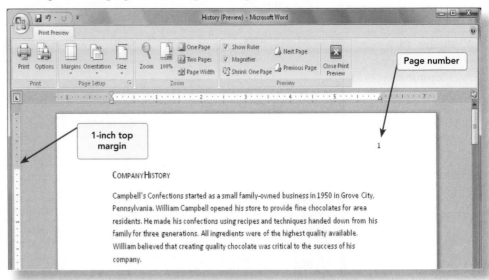

NOTE

The available print area varies according to the type of printer. If your footer is not completely visible, ask your instructor about changing the footer position from 0.5 inch to 0.6 inch from the bottom edge of the page.

10. Close Print Preview. Click the Undo button 🔄 to remove the page number in the footer.

Exercise 11-2 CHANGE THE POSITION AND FORMAT OF PAGE NUMBERS

Not only can you change the placement of page numbers and decide if you want to number the first page, but you can also change the format of page numbers. For example, instead of using traditional numerals such as 1, 2, and 3, you can use roman numerals (i, ii, iii) or letters (a, b, c). You can also start page numbering of a section with a different value. For instance, you could number the first page ii, B, or 2.

1. Double click the header of page 1. This activates the header pane (the area at the top of the page that contains the page number), displays the Headers and Footer Tools Design tab, and dims the document text.

2. Select the page number, and change the format of the number to italic using the Mini toolbar. Press Ctrl+E to center the number. Click the Undo button ↺ to undo the center alignment.

3. Locate the Header and Footer group on the Ribbon. Click the Page Number button ⊞ and click **Format Page Numbers**.

4. Open the **Number format** drop-down list, and choose uppercase roman numerals (I, II, III...). Click **OK**.

Figure 11-4
Page Number
Format dialog box

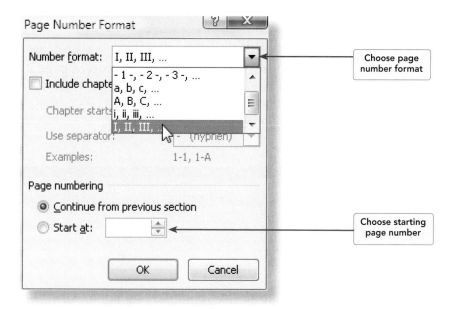

Choose page number format

Choose starting page number

5. Locate the **Options** group on the Ribbon, and click **Different First Page**. Selecting the Different First Page option removes the page number from page 1 of the document. Click the Close Header and Footer button ⊠.

6. View the document in Print Preview, and note that page 1 does not display a page number. The header page numbering is now italic, starting with roman numeral II on page 2.

7. Close Print Preview.

Changing the Starting Page Number

In addition to formatting page numbers and changing the page number placement, you can change the starting page numbering. You can format a document with a cover page to display no page number on page 1 and define the actual page 2 of the document to display page number 1.

To add a cover page, click the Insert tab and click the Cover Page command. Select a design from the gallery, and the cover page automatically appears at the beginning of the document. You can also insert a blank page by clicking the Blank Page command on the Insert tab.

Exercise 11-3   ADD A COVER PAGE

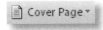

1. Position the insertion point at the beginning of the document. Click the **Insert** tab, and click the Cover Page button . Click the **Sideline** design from the gallery. Click the text "[Type the document title]" and key **History**.

2. Notice that the cover page is not numbered. The second page of the document is numbered page 2.

3. Position the insertion point at the top of page 2. Click the **Insert** tab, and click the Page Number button . Click **Format Page Numbers**. Change the **Number format** to **1, 2, 3**, and change the **Start at** number to **0**. Click **OK**.

Figure 11-5
Preview Page
Numbers

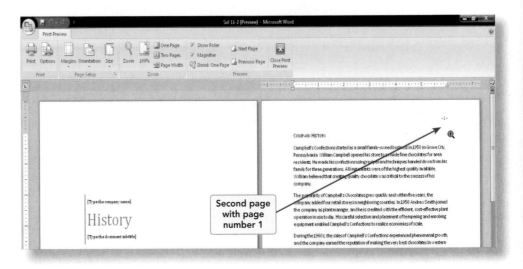

Word 2007

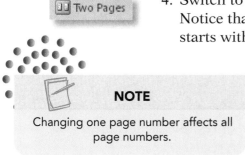

4. Switch to Print Preview, and click the Two Pages button . Notice that the cover page is not numbered and that page numbering starts with one on page 2. Close Print Preview.

5. Double-click the page number of page 2 of the document. Position the insertion point to the immediate left of the page number. Key **Page** and press Spacebar once.

6. Scroll to the header pane on page 3 to view the revised header text.

NOTE

Changing one page number affects all page numbers.

Figure 11-6
Formatted page number with "Page" added

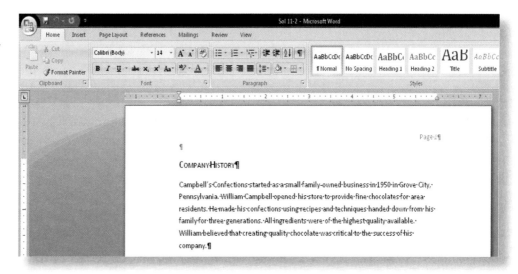

7. Save the document as *[your initials]***11-3** in your Lesson 11 folder.

Exercise 11-4 REMOVE PAGE NUMBERS

To remove page numbers, delete the text in the header or footer area or click the Remove Page Numbers command.

1. Click the **Insert** tab, and click the Page Number button . Click **Remove Page Numbers**.

2. Scroll the document and notice that the page numbers in the header and footer are deleted.

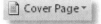

3. Click the Cover Page button , and click **Remove Current Cover Page**.

4. Close the document without saving it.

Adding Headers and Footers

Headers and footers are typically used in multiple-page documents to display descriptive information. In addition to page numbers, a header or footer can contain:

- The document name

- The date and/or the time you created or revised the document

- An author's name

- A graphic, such as a company logo

- A draft or revision number

This descriptive information can appear in many different combinations. For example, the second page of a business letter typically contains a header with the name of the addressee, the page number, and the date. A report can contain a footer with the report name and a header with the page number and chapter name. A newsletter might contain a header with a title and logo on the first page and a footer with the title and page number on the pages that follow.

Figure 11-7
Examples of headers and footers

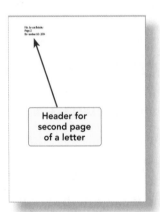 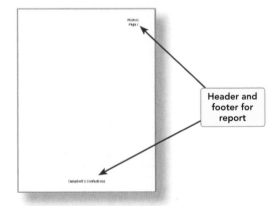

Exercise 11-5 ADD A HEADER TO A DOCUMENT

1. Open the file **History - 2**. This file is a six-page document with a title page. You will add a header and footer to pages 2 through 6.

2. Click the **Insert** tab, and click the Header button. Click the **Blank** design at the top of the Header gallery. Word displays the Header and Footer Tools Design tab, and the header pane is also visible.

 Different First Page

3. Click the Different First Page check box ☑ Different First Page. This enables you to give the document two different headers—a header for the title page, which you will leave blank, and a header for the rest of the document, which will contain identifying text. Notice that this header pane is labeled "**First Page Header.**"

⤵ Next Section

4. Click the Next Section button ⤵ Next Section. Notice that this header pane is labeled "**Header.**" The Previous Section button ⤵ Previous Section and the Next Section button ⤵ Next Section are useful when you move between different headers and footers within sections of a document, as you will see later in the lesson.

NOTE

These preset tab settings are default settings for a document with the default 1-inch left and right margins. In such a document, the 3.25-inch tab centers text and the 6.5-inch tab right-aligns text. This document, however, has 1.25-inch left and right margins, so it is best to adjust the tabs.

5. Key **Campbell's Confections History** in the page 2 header pane. This text now appears on every page of the document except the first page.

6. Press ⌨Tab once. Notice that the ruler has two preset tab settings: 3.25-inch centered and 6.5-inch right-aligned. Drag the center tab marker to 3 inches on the ruler and the right-aligned tab marker to the right margin (6 inches). Press ⌨Tab again to move to the right-aligned tab setting.

📋 Quick Parts ▾

7. Click the Quick Parts button 📋 Quick Parts ▾, and click **Building Blocks Organizer.** Click the **Gallery** heading to alphabetize the Building Blocks by Gallery.

8. Scroll through the Building blocks to locate the **Page Numbers** Gallery. Click to select **Bold Numbers 3** and to preview the page number Building block.

9. Click **Insert**, and notice that the page number displays on the right margin, but the text on the left margin of the header disappeared. Click the Undo button ↺▾.

10. Click the Quick Parts button 📋 Quick Parts ▾, and click **Field**. Scroll the list of **Field names** to locate the **Page** field and click it one time. Click the **1, 2, 3 Format**, and click **OK**. Word inserts the page number. Click to the immediate left of the page number, and key **Page**, and press ⌨Spacebar.

⤵ Previous Section

11. Click the Previous Section button ⤵ Previous Section and notice that the first-page header pane is still blank. Click the Next Section button ⤵ Next Section to return to the header you created.

TABLE 11-1 Header and Footer Tools Design Tab

Button	Name	Purpose
	Header	Edit the document header.
	Footer	Edit the document footer.
	Insert Page Number	Insert the page number.
	Date and Time	Insert the current date or time.
Quick Parts	Quick Parts	Insert common header or footer items, such as running total page numbers (for example, page 1 of 10).
Picture	Picture	Insert a picture from a file.
Clip Art	Clip Art	Insert clip art.
	Go to Header	Activates header for editing.
	Go to Footer	Activates footer for editing.
Previous Section	Previous Section	Show the header or footer of the previous section.
Next Section	Next Section	Show the header or footer of the next section.
Link to Previous	Link to Previous	Link or unlink the header or footer in one section to or from the header or footer in the previous section.
Different First Page	Different First Page	Create a header and footer for the first page of the document.
Different Odd & Even Pages	Different Odd and Even Pages	Specify a header or footer for odd-numbered pages and a different header or footer for even-numbered pages.
Show Document Text	Show Document Text	Display or hide the document text.
Header from Top: 0.5"	Header from Top	Specify height of header area.
Footer from Bottom: 0.5"	Footer from Bottom	Specify height of footer area.
Insert Alignment Tab	Insert Alignment Tab	Insert a tab stop.

Exercise 11-6 ADD A FOOTER TO A DOCUMENT

Go to
Footer

1. With the header on page 2 displayed, click the Go to Footer button to display the footer pane.

2. Key your name and press Tab.

3. Save the document as *[your initials]*11-6 in your Lesson 11 folder.

4. With the insertion point at the center of the footer, click the Quick Parts button Quick Parts ▾ on the Header and Footer Tools Design tab. Click **Field**. The Field dialog box displays.

5. Click **CreateDate** from the **Field names** list. Click the third item in the **Date formats** list. Click **OK**. A field is inserted that displays the date the document was created.

6. Press Tab and click Quick Parts Quick Parts ▾ . Click **Field** and scroll the list of **Field names** to locate **FileName**. Click **FileName** and notice that a list of **Field properties** appears. Click **First capital**. Click **OK**.

Figure 11-8
Inserting fields

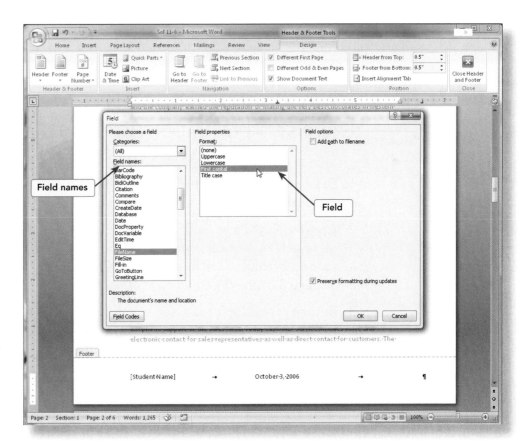

7. View the footer text. The document's filename is inserted. This footer information prints at the bottom of each page except the first.

8. Improve the tab positions by dragging the center tab marker to 3 inches and the right tab marker to 6 inches. (Remember, this document has 1.25-inch left and right margins, not the default 1-inch margins.)

9. Click the Close Header and Footer button to return to the document.

10. Switch to Print Preview. Check that no header or footer appears on the title page. Scroll through each page and view the header and footer.

11. Return to Page Layout view and save the document. Leave it open for the next exercise.

Adding Headers and Footers within Sections

Section breaks have an impact on page numbers, headers, and footers. For example, you can number each section differently or add different headers and footers.

When you add page numbers to a document, it is best to add the page numbers first and then add the section breaks.

Exercise 11-7   ADD SECTIONS TO A DOCUMENT WITH HEADERS AND FOOTERS

1. Delete the hard page break that follows the title page of the document, and insert a Next Page section break.

2. Insert a Next Page section break before the heading "Fundraising" on page 2 of section 2 (page 3 of the document) and a Next Page section break before the heading "Chronology" on page 2 of section 3 (page 5 of the document).

3. Return to the top of the document (by pressing Ctrl+Home), and click the **Insert** tab. Click the Header button . Click **Edit Header**. Notice that the blank header pane indicates the section number.

4. Click the Next Section button to move to the next header, in section 2, page 1. Notice that this header is also blank, because the Page Setup option **Different First Page** was selected for the entire document. This means the first page of each section can have a different header or footer than the rest of the pages in the section or it can have no header or footer.

5. Click the Next Section button 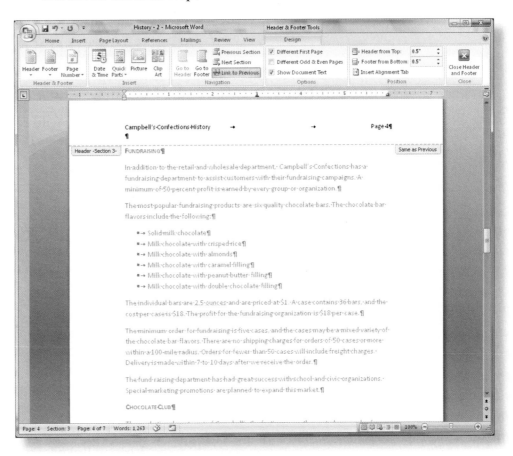 again to move to section 2, page 2. The header and footer begin on page 3.

6. Click the Next Section button to move to section 3, page 1. Because the **Different First Page** option applies to the document, the first page of this section also has no header or footer.

7. Turn off the **Different First Page** option for section 3 by clicking the Different First Page button on the Ribbon to clear the check box. Now page 1 of section 3 starts with the document header and footer. Turning off this option applies only to this section, as you will see in the next step.

Figure 11-9
The header on page 1, section 3, of the document

8. Click the Previous Section button twice to move to the header on page 1 of section 2. Notice that the header pane is still blank because the **Different First Page** option is still checked for this section.

9. Repeat step 7 to turn off the **Different First Page** option for this section. Now the header and footer start on page 1 of section 2. Repeat for section 4.

10. View each header in the document by dragging the scroll box (on the vertical scroll bar) down one page at a time. As you display each page's header, notice the page numbering. Also notice that the text "Same as Previous" appears on the header panes.

Linking Section Headers and Footers

By default, the Link to Previous command is "on" when you work in a header or footer pane. As a result, the text you originally enter in the header (and the footer) for the document is the same from section to section. Any change you make in one section header or footer is reflected in all other sections. You can use the Link to Previous command to break the link between header/footer text from one section to another section and enter different header or footer text for a section.

NOTE

Breaking the link for the header does not break the link for the footer. You must unlink them separately.

Exercise 11-8   LINK AND UNLINK SECTION HEADERS AND FOOTERS

1. Scroll to the header for section 3, page 1, select the text "Campbell's Confections History" and apply italic formatting.

2. Click the Previous Section button to move to the header in section 2. The header text is italic, demonstrating the link that exists between section headers and footers.

3. Click the Next Section button ⏭ to return to section 3, page 1. Click the Link to Previous button ⏮ to turn off this option. Now sections 2 and 3 are unlinked and you can create a different header or footer for section 3.

TIP

To select text in a header or footer, you can point and click from the area to the immediate left of the header or footer pane.

4. Delete all the text in the header for section 3, including the page number.

5. Press Tab to move to the center tab setting and key **Supplement**. Press Tab again and click the **Quick Parts** button. Click **Field**, and select **Page** in the **Field names** list box. Select the first number format, and click **OK**. Drag the center tab marker to 3 inches and the right tab marker to 6 inches, as needed.

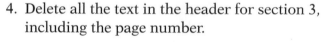

Go to Footer

6. Click the Go to Footer button 📄 to switch to the footer. The footer text between sections 2 and 3 is still linked, so click the Link to Previous button ⏮ to break the link.

Previous Section

Next Section

7. Delete all the footer text in section 3 except your name. Click the Previous Section button ⏮ to see that the original footer text is still in section 2. Click the Next Section button ⏭ to return to the section 3 footer.

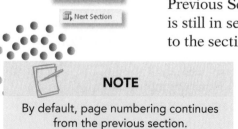

NOTE

By default, page numbering continues from the previous section.

8. Click the Link to Previous button ⏮ to restore the link between section footers. When Word asks if you want to delete the current text and connect to the text from the previous section, click **Yes**.

Figure 11-10
Restoring the link
between section
footers

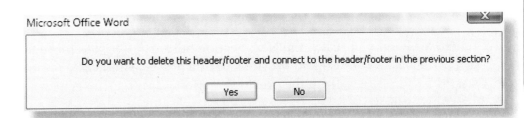

9. With the link and the original footer text restored, click the Close
   Header and Footer button [icon].

10. Format the title page attractively. Adjust page breaks throughout the
    document as needed.

11. Save the document as *[your initials]***11-8**. Print the document six
    pages per sheet.

Changing the Starting Page Number

So far, you have seen page numbering start either with 1 on page 1 or 2 on
page 2. When documents have multiple sections, you might need to change
the starting page number. For example, in the current document, section 1 is
the title page and the header on section 2 begins numbering with page 2. You
can change this format so numbering starts in section 2, page 1, with page 1.

Exercise 11-9 **CHANGE THE STARTING
PAGE NUMBER**

1. Double-click the page number on section 2, page 1 to display the
   header.

2. Click the Page Number button [icon], and click **Format Page Numbers** to
   open the Page Number Format dialog box.

3. Change the **Start at** number to **1**.

Figure 11-11
Changing the
starting page
number for any part
of a document

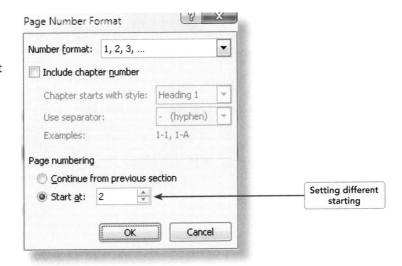

Link to Previous

4. Click **OK**. Section 2 now starts with page 1.

5. Click the Next Section button [Next Section] to move to section 3. Click the Link to Previous button [Link to Previous] and click **Yes** to restore the header from the previous section.

6. Open the **Page Number Format** dialog box. Choose the option **Continue from previous section** if necessary. Click **OK**. Notice that the section header begins with page 4.

7. Save the document as ***[your initials]*11-9** in your Lesson 11 folder.

8. Submit and close the document.

> **NOTE**
>
> You can change the starting page number for any document, with or without multiple sections. For example, you might want to number the first page of a multiple-page document "Page 2" if you plan to print a cover page as a separate file.

Creating Continuation Page Headers

It is customary to use a header on the second page of a business letter or memo. A continuation page header for a letter or memo is typically a three-line block of text that includes the addressee's name, the page number, and the date.

There are three rules for letters and memos with continuation page headers:

- Page 1 must have a 2-inch top margin.

- Continuation pages must have a 1-inch top margin.

- Two blank lines must appear between the header and the continuation page text.

Exercise 11-10   ADD A CONTINUATION PAGE HEADER TO A LETTER

The easiest way to create a continuation page header using the proper business format is to apply these settings to your document:

- Top margin: 2 inches.

- Header position: 1 inch from edge of page.

- Page Setup Layout for Headers and Footers: Different First Page.

- Additional spacing: Add two blank lines to the end of the header.

By default, headers and footers are positioned 0.5 inch from the top or bottom edge of the page. When you change the position of a continuation page header to 1 inch, the continuation page appears to have a 1-inch top margin, beginning with the header text. The document text begins at the page's 2-inch margin, and the two additional blank lines in the continuation header ensure correct spacing between the header text and the document text.

1. Open the file **Mendez**.

2. Add the date to the top of the letter, followed by three blank lines.

3. Open the **Page Setup** dialog box, and display the **Layout** tab. Check **Different first page** under **Headers and Footers**. Set the **Header** to 1 inch **From edge**.

4. Click the **Margins** tab, and set a 2-inch top margin and 1.25-inch left and right margins. Click **OK**.

5. Click the **Insert** tab, and click the Header button ▤. Click **Edit Header** to display the header pane.

▤ Next Section

6. Click the Next Section button ▤ Next Section to move to the header pane on page 2.

7. Create the header in Figure 11-12, inserting the information as shown. Press [Enter] twice after the last line.

Figure 11-12

Ms. Isabel Mendez

Page [*Click* **Quick Parts**, **Field**, **Page** *for the page number.*]

[*Click* **Date and Time** *for the current date.*]

TIP

Letters and memos should use the spelled-out date format (for example, December 25, 2007), and the date should not be a field that updates each time you open the document. To insert the date as text, with the correct format, click the Date and Time command and clear the Update automatically check box.

Figure 11-13
Continuation page
header for a letter

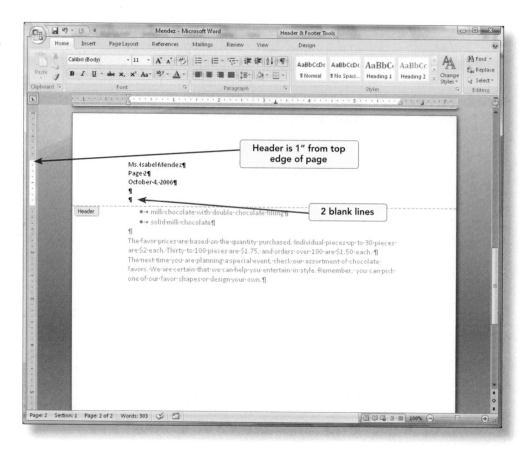

8. Close the header pane, and view both pages in Print Preview. Close Print Preview.

9. Add a complimentary closing, and key **Lydia Hamrick** and the title **Customer Service** at the end of the letter, followed by your reference initials.

10. Save the document as *[your initials]*11-10 in your Lesson 11 folder.

11. Submit, and close the document.

Creating Alternate Headers and Footers

In addition to customizing headers and footers for different sections of a document, you can also change them for odd and even pages throughout a section or document. For example, a textbook displays the unit name for even pages and displays the lesson name for odd pages.

Exercise 11-11 CREATE ALTERNATE FOOTERS IN A DOCUMENT

To create alternate headers or footers in a document, you use the **Different odd and even** check box and then create a header or footer for both even and odd pages.

1. Open the file **History - 2**. Delete the page break on page 1 and insert a next page section break.

2. Position the insertion point in section 1, click the **Insert** tab, and click the Footer button .

3. Click **Edit Footer**, and click the Different Odd and Even Pages button 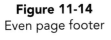 Different Odd & Even Pages. Click the Different First Page button so the first page does not display a footer.

4. Click the Next Section button Next Section, and verify that the insertion point is in the Even Page Footer pane.

5. Click the Footer button, and scroll through the gallery. Select **Transcend (Even Page)**. The footer displays on page 2.

Figure 11-14
Even page footer

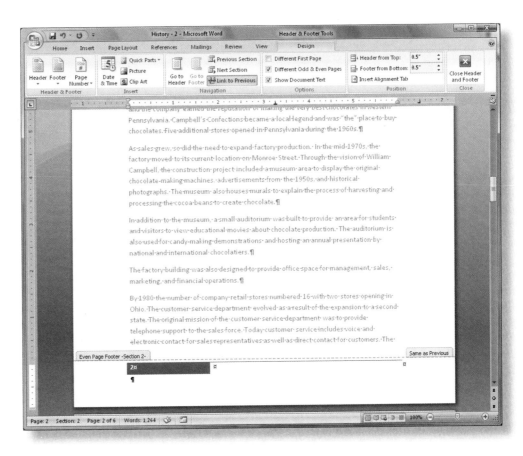

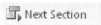

6. Click the Next Section button 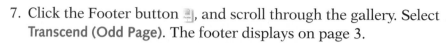 to move to the footer on page 3. The footer pane is labeled "**Odd Page Footer**" and is blank.

7. Click the Footer button , and scroll through the gallery. Select **Transcend (Odd Page)**. The footer displays on page 3.

8. Click the Close Header and Footer button , and switch to Print Preview.

9. Click the Zoom Level button 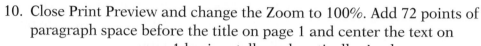, and click the Many Pages button . Drag over the grid to select six pages. Click **OK**. View each page of the document. Notice the position of the page number on the odd and even pages.

10. Close Print Preview and change the Zoom to 100%. Add 72 points of paragraph space before the title on page 1 and center the text on page 1 horizontally and vertically. Apply a page border to section 1. Adjust page breaks throughout the document as needed.

> **NOTE**
>
> To create different odd and even headers or footers within a section, you must first break the link between that section's header or footer and the previous section's header or footer.

11. Save the document as *[your initials]***11-11** in your Lesson 11 folder.

12. Print the document four pages per sheet, or submit the document, and then close it.

Lesson 11 Summary

- A header is text that appears in the top margin of the printed page; a footer is text that appears in the bottom margin. These text areas are used for page numbers, document titles, the date, and other information.

- Always add page numbers to long documents. You can choose the position of page numbers (examples: bottom centered or top right) and the format (examples: 1, 2, 3 or A, B, C). You can also choose to number the first page or begin numbering on the second page.

- Check page numbers in Print Preview or Print Layout view (they are not visible in Draft view). In Print Layout view, you can activate the header or footer pane that contains the page number by double-clicking the text and then modify the page number text (examples: apply bold format or add the word "Page" before the number).

- To remove page numbers, activate the header or footer pane that contains the numbering, select the text, and then delete it. You can also click the Page Number command and select Remove Page Numbers.

- To add header or footer text to a document, click the Insert tab, and click Header or Footer. Select a design from the gallery. Use the Header and Footer Tools Design tab buttons to insert the date and time or to insert Quick Parts for the filename, author, print date, or other information. See Table 11-1.

- Adjust the tab marker positions in the header or footer pane as needed to match the width of the text area.

- A document can have a header or footer on the first page different from the rest of the pages. Apply the Different first page option in the Page Setup dialog box (Layout tab), or use the Different First Page button on the Ribbon, Header & Footer Tools Design tab.

- Header and footer text is repeated from section to section because headers and footers are linked by default. To unlink section headers and footers, click the Link to Previous command. To relink the header or footer, click the button again.

- Sections can have different starting page numbers. Click the Page Number command to open the Page Number Format dialog box, and then set the starting page number.

- Memos or letters that are two pages or longer should have a continuation page header—a three-line block containing the addressee's name, page number, and date. Set the header to 1 inch from the edge, add two blank lines below the header, and use a 2-inch top margin. Apply the Different first page option, and leave the first-page header blank.

- Use the Ribbon, Header and Footer Tools Design Tab, or the Page Setup dialog box to change the position of the header or footer text from the edge of the page. The default position is 0.5 inch.

- A document can have different headers and footers on odd and even pages. Apply the Different odd and even option.

LESSON 11		Command Summary	
Feature	**Button**	**Command**	**Keyboard**
Add page numbers	Page Number	Insert tab, Page Number	
Change page number format		Insert tab, Page Number, Format Page Numbers	
Add or edit header	Header	Insert tab, Header	
Add or edit footer	Footer	Insert tab, Footer	
Change layout settings		Page Layout tab, Page Setup or Header and Footer Tools Design tab	

Concepts Review

True/False Questions

Each of the following statements is either true or false. Indicate your choice by circling T or F.

T F   1. The simplest way to add page numbers is to choose Page Numbers from the Page Layout tab.

T F   2. You can position a page number as a header or a footer.

T F   3. You can change the number format (for example, from numbers to roman numerals) by using the Page Number Format dialog box.

T F   4. You can apply character formatting to headers and footers in Draft view.

T F   5. A gallery displays designs for page numbers, headers, and footers.

T F   6. Deselect the Link to Previous command on the Header and Footer Tools Design tab to unlink a header in one section to the header in the previous section.

T F   7. Use Quick Parts to insert fields and document properties.

T F   8. The only way to create alternate page headers or footers is to use the Page Setup dialog box.

Short Answer Questions

Write the correct answer in the space provided.

1. What is the name of the process in which Word automatically adjusts page numbers and page breaks when you edit a document?

   _____

2. In addition to numbering such as 1, 2, 3 and roman numerals such as I, II, III, what other page number formatting can you use?

   _____

3. Which option do you use to leave the first page of a document blank and begin a header or footer on the second page?

   _____

4. Which Ribbon tab displays the Header and Footer buttons?

   _____

5.   🔲 Previous Section   is used for what purpose?

_____

6. What three items are included in a continuation page header for a letter?

_____

7. By default, how far from the edge of the page does Word print headers and footers?

_____

8. If you create different odd and even pages in a document, how is the header pane on page 1 labeled?

_____

Critical Thinking

Answer these questions on a separate page. There are no right or wrong answers. Support your answers with examples from your own experience, if possible.

1. What information do you think most businesses would include in the header or footer for a business report? Does the information included in a business report header or footer differ from the information found in a business letter header or footer?

2. Where do you prefer to place the page number in a business report? In a business letter? Explain your answer.

Skills Review

Exercise 11-12

Add and modify page numbers and add a header.

1. Open the file **Chronology - 2**.
2. Add page numbers to the bottom of each page by following these steps:
    a. Click the Insert tab, and click the Page Number button 📄.
    b. Click **Bottom of Page**, scroll through the gallery, and click to select **Two Bars 1**. Close the **Header and Footer Tools Design** tab.
3. Modify the page numbers in Print Layout view by following these steps:
    a. Scroll to the bottom of page 1 to see the page number.
    b. Double-click the page number to activate the footer pane.

c. Drag the I-beam over the page number, and click the Bold button 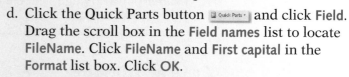 and the Italic button 𝐼 on the Mini toolbar. Change the **Font Size** to 14.

d. Close the Header and Footer Tools Design tab.

4. Add 72 points of spacing before the title on page 1.

5. View the document in Print Preview; then display it in Print Layout view.

6. Add a header to the document by following these steps:

a. Click the **Insert** tab, and click the Header button 📄. Click the **Blank** design at the top of the gallery.

b. Press [Tab] twice to position the insertion point at the right-aligned tab setting.

c. Key your name, followed by a comma and space.

d. Click the Quick Parts button ⬛ Quick Parts ▾ and click **Field**. Drag the scroll box in the **Field names** list to locate **FileName**. Click **FileName** and **First capital** in the **Format** list box. Click **OK**.

e. Close the Header and Footer Tools Design tab.

NOTE

The filename Chronology - 2 will change to the filename you assign the document after you close and reopen the document, print the document, or update the field.

7. Save the document as *[your initials]*11-12 in your Lesson 11 folder.

8. Submit and close the document.

Exercise 11-13

Add a footer to a document with sections, unlink the header, and change the starting page number.

1. Open the file **Wrapper - 2**.

2. Insert a **Next page** section break at "CAMPBELL'S CONFECTIONS."

3. On page 2, section 2, justify the text vertically on the page.

4. Create a footer for section 2 that is not linked to section 1 by following these steps:

a. Move the insertion point to section 2, and click the **Insert** tab. Click the Footer button 📄 and select the **Blank design**.

b. Click the Link to Previous button ⬛ Link to Previous to unlink the section 2 footer from section 1 (to keep the section 1 footer blank) and key *Instructions for the design of the wrapper are on the application form.

c. Press [Tab] and key Page. Insert a space, click the Quick Parts button 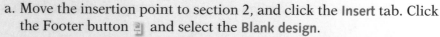, click **Field**, click **Page** in the **Field names** list, and **1, 2, 3** in the **Format** list.

d. Click the Previous Section button ⬛ Previous Section to show the footer for section 1, which should be blank.

5. Change the starting page number of section 2 to page 1 by following these steps:

   a. Click the Next Section button to go back to section 2.

   b. Click the Page Number button , and click **Format Page Numbers**.

   c. Click **Start at** and make sure the number 1 appears in the text box. Click **OK** and then close the Header and Footer Tools Design tab.

6. Change the top margin in section 1 to 2 inches.

7. Save the document as *[your initials]***11-13** in your Lesson 11 folder.

8. Print the document two pages per sheet, or submit the document, and then close it.

Exercise 11-14

Create a continuation page header for a memo.

1. Open the file **Bio Memo**. Delete the page break and insert a Next Page section break.

2. Key the current date in the memo heading.

3. Open the **Page Setup** dialog box, and change the top margin to 2 inches. Change the left and right margins to 1.25 inches. Click the Layout tab and click to select **Different first page**. Click **OK**.

4. Add a continuation page header to page 2 of the memo by following these steps:

   a. Click the **Insert** tab, and click the Header button . Click **Blank**.

   b. Click the Next Section button to move to the header on page 2.

   c. Change the **Header from Top** setting to 1 inch. (**Header & Footer Tools Design** tab, **Position** group.)

   d. Key the text in Figure 11-15, inserting the information as shown.

Figure 11-15

```
Staff

Page [Click Quick Parts, Field, Page, and Format.]

[Key current date or insert as text.]
```

   e. To insert the current date in the correct format, click the Date and Time button and select the correct format. Be sure to clear the Update automatically box so the memo date does not change.

   f. Press Enter twice after the date and verify that there are two blank lines following the date.

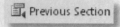

5. Click the Previous Section button to check that no header appears on page 1, and close the Header and Footer Tools Design tab.

6. Adjust line and page breaks if necessary.

7. Save the document as *[your initials]*11-14 in your Lesson 11 folder.

8. Submit and close the document.

Exercise 11-15

Add alternate footers to a document, and add a different first page footer.

1. Open the file **Guidelines - 2**.

2. Add a page break before the bold heading "Identification Numbers."

3. Move the insertion point to the top of the document (page 1).

4. Create a footer that appears only on even pages by following these steps:

   a. Click the **Insert** tab, and click the Footer button. Click Blank at the top of the gallery.

   b. Click the Different First Page button and the Different Odd and Even Pages button.

   c. Click the Next Section button to move to the Even Page Footer.

   d. Key **Guidelines—New Store Owners**. Press Tab twice.

   e. Key **Page** and press Spacebar. Click the Quick Parts button, click **Field**, click **Page**, and click the **1, 2, 3** format. Click **OK**.

   f. Select the footer text, and use the Mini toolbar to apply italic formatting.

5. Create and format a footer that appears only on odd pages by following these steps:

   a. Click the Next Section button to move to the odd page footer pane on page 3.

   b. Click the Date and Time button. Click the third format.

6. Close the Header and Footer Tools Design tab.

7. On page 1, format the two-line title in bold, 14 points, and all caps. Apply bold and small caps formatting to "Campbell's Confections." Apply italic formatting to "Preliminary Draft." Vertically center the text on the first page, and apply a page border to section 1.

8. View the document in Print Preview. Check the odd and even footers, and make sure the first page footer is blank.

9. Save the document as *[your initials]*11-15 in your Lesson 11 folder.

10. Submit and close the document.

Lesson Applications

Exercise 11-16

Add page numbers, change the page number font, and adjust the starting page number.

1. Open the file **Directory - 2**.

2. Position the insertion point at the beginning of the document, and click the Insert tab. Click Blank Page.

3. Format page 1 as a memo. The memo is to the staff from Barbara Bumgarner. Use today's date, and the subject is "Updated Directory." Key the text in Figure 11-16.

Figure 11-16

Attached is an updated directory for the corporate office and Campbell's Confections'
stores in (PA), (OH), and (WV). A few of the area codes have changed so you may
need to update your files.

Our goal is to have toll free numbers for all stores by ~~the end of the year~~ December.
We will update the directory on an on going basis, and changes will be
emailed to you.

If information pertaining to your department changes, please notify me
~~immediately~~.

4. Replace the page break after page 1 with a Next Page section break. Go to page 2, and insert a Next Page section break immediately preceding the bold heading "Pennsylvania." Insert a page break preceding the bold headings "Ohio" and "West Virginia."

5. Add page numbering to section 2 only. (Be sure to place the insertion point in section 2 first.) Position the page numbers at the bottom center of the section and select the Thick Line design from the gallery. Change the start number to 1.

6. In the footer of section 3, select the page number and change the format to 11-point Arial.

7. View the page numbers in Print Preview.

8. Format the memo on page 1 with a 2-inch top margin. Format the first three lines of section 2, and key today's date.

9. Spell-check the document.

10. Save the document as *[your initials]*11-16 in your Lesson 11 folder.

11. Print the document as four pages per sheet, or submit the document, and then close it.

Exercise 11-17

Create and unlink headers and footers within sections.

1. Open the file **Orders - 2**.

2. Insert a Next Page section break at the bold heading "How to Place an Order." Select the text on page 1, and format the text with a paragraph box border, using a double-line style, dark blue color, and width of 2¼ points. On the title page, center the boxed title vertically and horizontally on the page, and reduce the width of the border by formatting the text in the box with 1-inch left and right indents.

3. Position the insertion point in section 1, and deselect any text that may be highlighted. Open the Borders and Shading dialog box, and click the Page Border tab. For the box setting, select the double-line style used in the previous step, with dark blue color and 1½ points wide. Apply the border to this section.

4. Format the tabbed text on page 2 (which starts with the text "Delivery Chart") as a separate section by placing a Next Page section break before it. Format this new section (section 3) with a 2-inch top margin.

5. Create a footer that starts on the first page of section 2 and is not linked to section 1. Key Campbell's Confections at the left margin. Move to the right margin, and key Page followed by a space and include the page number. Press Spacebar after the page number, and key of followed by a space. Open the Field dialog box, and click the NumPages field name and the 1, 2, 3 format. Click OK.

6. Italicize the footer text, and format the footer with a single-line, 1½-point top border.

7. Change the top margin for section to 2 to 1.5 inches.

8. View the document in Print Preview.

9. Save the document as *[your initials]*11-17 in your Lesson 11 folder.

10. Submit and close the document.

Exercise 11-18

Create a continuation page header for a business letter.

1. Open the file **Yang**.

2. Format the document as a business letter. Use the address shown in Figure 11-17. The letter will be from Tamara Robbins, Fundraising Coordinator.

Figure 11-17

```
Ms. Emiko Yang

7 South Diamond Street

Greenville, PA 16125
```

3. Adjust page setup options for a continuation page header by choosing the Different first page option, changing the header to 1 inch from the edge, and setting a 2-inch top margin and 1.25-inch left and right margins.

4. Insert a page break at the beginning of the paragraph that begins "Specialty."

5. Create a three-line continuation page header that prints on page 2. (Use the correct date format.)

6. Switch to Print Preview to view the document.

7. Add your reference initials, and spell-check the document.

8. Save the document as *[your initials]***11-18** in your Lesson 11 folder.

9. Submit and close the document.

Exercise 11-19 ◆ Challenge Yourself

Create alternate footers, unlink and format section footers, change starting page numbers, and change page formats.

1. Open the file **Company**.

2. Replace the page break after page 1 with a Next Page section break. On page 2, insert a Next Page section break at the bold heading "Pennsylvania." Insert Next Page Section breaks at the bold heading "Services" and one at the bold heading "Customer Service."

3. Insert page breaks at the bold headings "Ohio Stores," "West Virginia Stores," "Chocolate Club," "Corporate Gifts," "Favors," "Chocolate Fountains," "Fundraising," "Wholesale," and "Customer Service Account Executives."

4. Go to section 5 (Customer Service heading on page 13), and insert a blank footer. Deselect the Different First Page option and select the Different Odd and Even Pages options. Break the link for the even page footer for section 5 and the odd page footer for section 5. Key Customer Service in the odd page footer for section 5, and apply italic formatting. Center the footer text. Copy the text to the even page footer for section 5. Change the bottom margin for section 5 to 0.5 inch,

and change the font size for text beginning with "Pennsylvania" through the end of the document to 11 points. Verify that only section 5 has footer text.

5. Go to section 4 and unlink the first page footer from the previous section. Key Campbell's Confections at the left margin in the first page footer for section 4. Go to the odd page footer for section 4, and key Page followed by a space. Insert the Page field to add page numbering to the section. Change the start number to 1. Go to the even page footer for section 4, and tab to the right margin. Key Page followed by a space. Insert the Page field to add numbering to the section.

6. Go to section 3, and unlink the first page footer from the previous section. Unlink the even page and odd page footers for section 3.

7. Key Store Directory at the left margin in the first page footer pane of section 3. Press Tab to move to the right margin, and key Page followed by a page number. Change the start the number for this section to 1.

8. Go to section 2, and break the link from the previous section. Delete any text in the footer pane.

9. Go to section 1, and verify that the footer is blank. Add a page border to this section.

10. Go to section 5, and insert a blank header. Starting at section 5 and moving to the beginning of the document, break the link for all headers in the document. Go to the section 2 header, and click the header button to open the header gallery. Select the Annual design. Click the Company placeholder, and key Campbell's Confections. Key the current year.

10. Preview the document; then save it as *[your initials]*11-19 in your Lesson 11 folder.

11. Print the document four pages per sheet, or submit the document, and then close it.

On Your Own

In these exercises you work on your own, as you would in a real-life business environment. Use the skills you've learned to accomplish the task—and be creative.

Exercise 11-20

Write a two-page letter. Create your letterhead in the first-page header pane, and create a continuation header in the second-page header pane. Use correct business letter format. Save the document as *[your initials]*11-20 and submit it.

Exercise 11-21

Write a two-page report on a current event. Check pagination. Add appropriate headers and footers, and include page numbering. Create a title page as a separate section without a header or footer. Save the document as *[your initials]*11-21 and submit it.

Exercise 11-22

Write a short report about 10 places you would like to visit. Each place should be a separate paragraph with its own heading. Include a title page. Adjust page breaks as needed. Format the document for odd and even headers and footers, and then insert different identifying information in the headers or footers. Save the document as *[your initials]*11-22 and submit it.

Lesson 12

Styles and Themes

OBJECTIVES

MCAS OBJECTIVES

In this lesson:
WW 07 1.1.2
WW 07 1.1.3
WW 07 1.1.4
WW 07 2.1.1
WW 07 2.1.2

After completing this lesson, you will be able to:

1. Apply styles.

2. Create new styles.

3. Redefine, modify, and rename styles.

4. Use style options.

5. Apply and customize a theme.

Estimated Time: 1¹/₄ hours

A *style* is a set of formatting instructions you can apply to text. Styles make it easier to apply formatting and ensure consistency throughout a document.

In every document, Word maintains *style sets*—a list of style names and their formatting specifications. A style set, which is stored with a document, includes standard styles for body text and headings that appear in the Quick Style Gallery. You can apply styles, modify them, or create your own. A *theme* is a set of formatting instructions for the entire document. A theme includes style sets, theme colors, theme fonts, and theme effects. Themes can be customized and are shared across Office programs.

Applying Styles

The default style for text is called *Normal* style. Unless you change your system's default style, Normal is a paragraph style with the following formatting specifications: 11-point Calibri, English language, left-aligned, 1.15-line spacing, 10 points spacing after, and widow/orphan control.

To change the appearance of text in a document, you can apply five types of styles:

- A *character style* is formatting applied to selected text, such as font, font size, and font style.

- A *paragraph style* is formatting applied to an entire paragraph, such as alignment, line and paragraph spacing, indents, tab settings, borders and shading, and character formatting.

- A *linked style* formats a single paragraph with two styles. It is typically used to assign a heading style to the first few words of a paragraph.

- A *table style* is formatting applied to a table, such as borders, shading, alignment, and fonts.

- A *list style* is formatting applied to a list, such as numbers or bullet characters, alignment, and fonts.

Exercise 12-1 APPLY STYLES

There are two ways to apply styles:

NOTE

The keyboard shortcut to open the Styles task pane is Ctrl+Alt+Shift+S.

- Open the Styles task pane and select a style to apply. To open the Styles task pane, click the Styles Dialog Box Launcher.

- Click the Home tab; click a Quick Style.

1. Open the file **Volume 1**.

2. Click the Home tab, and click the Styles Dialog Box Launcher to open the Styles task pane. The task pane lists formatting currently used in the document and includes some of Word's built-in heading styles.

NOTE

Define a style set before you apply formatting to ensure you are using the appropriate styles.

3. Click the Change Styles button. Click Style Set, and click Default.

4. Click in the line "Choc Talk," and place the mouse pointer (without clicking) over the Heading 1 style in the task pane. A ScreenTip displays the style's attributes.

NOTE

To apply a style to a paragraph, you can simply click anywhere in the paragraph without selecting the text. Remember, this is also true for applying a paragraph format (such as line spacing or alignment) to a paragraph.

5. Click the Heading 1 style in the Styles task pane. The text is formatted with 14-point bold Cambria, blue, 24 points spacing before, and 1.15-line spacing.

Figure 12-1
Using the Styles task
pane to apply a style

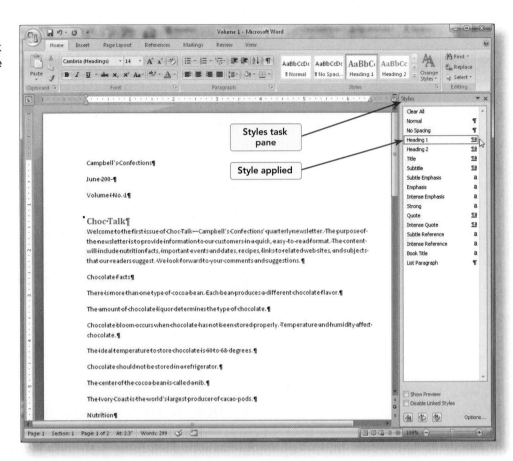

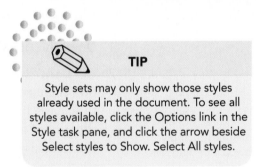

TIP

Style sets may only show those styles
already used in the document. To see all
styles available, click the Options link in the
Style task pane, and click the arrow beside
Select styles to Show. Select All styles.

6. Close the Styles task pane by clicking the Styles task pane Close
   button .

7. Position the insertion point in the text "Chocolate Facts."

8. Click the **Home** tab, and locate the **Styles** group. Click the More
   arrow to display all the styles in the Quick Style Gallery. Move
   the mouse pointer over each of the quick styles to preview the
   format.

9. Choose **Heading 2**. Notice the applied formatting.

Figure 12-2
Using the Quick
Style Gallery

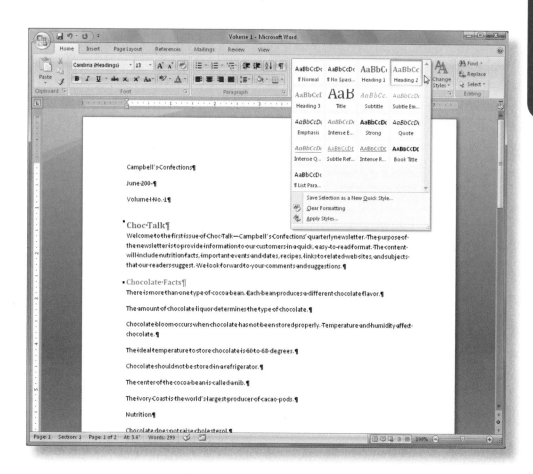

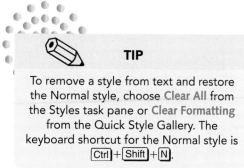

TIP

To remove a style from text and restore the Normal style, choose **Clear All** from the Styles task pane or **Clear Formatting** from the Quick Style Gallery. The keyboard shortcut for the Normal style is Ctrl + Shift + N.

10. Position the insertion point in the heading "Nutrition." Press F4 to repeat the Heading 2 style.

Creating New Styles

Creating styles is as easy as formatting text and then giving the set of formatting instructions a style name. Each new style name must be different from the other style names already in the document.

Word saves the styles you create for a document when you save the document.

Exercise 12-2 CREATE A PARAGRAPH STYLE

There are two ways to create a new paragraph style:

- Use the Quick Style Gallery.
- Click the **New Style** button in the Styles task pane.

1. Reopen the Styles task pane by clicking the **Styles Dialog Box Launcher**.

2. Select the heading "Chocolate Facts."

3. Increase the font size to 14 points, and press Ctrl + Shift + K to apply small caps.

4. Click the New Style button at the bottom of the Styles task pane. The Create New Style from Formatting dialog box opens.

5. Key **Side Heading** in the **Name** box. Verify that **Paragraph** is the **Style type**.

TIP

Click to the left of the text to select the entire paragraph. (Be sure your mouse is in the margin area and the mouse pointer changes into a white arrow.)

NOTE

Click to select the **Show Preview** check box in the Style task pane to display style names with formatting.

Figure 12-3
Create New Style from Formatting dialog box

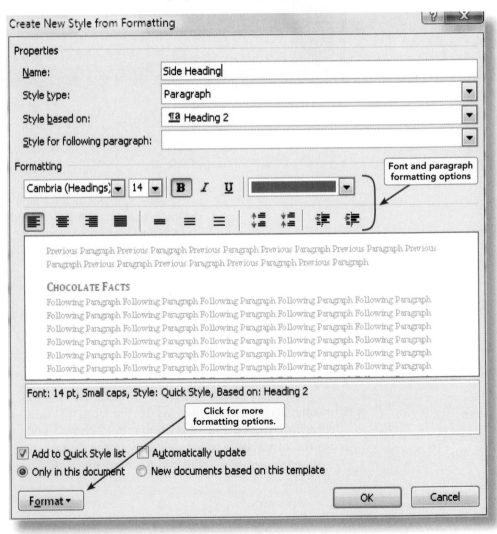

NOTE

If you key a style name that already exists in the Style box, you apply the existing style; you do not create a new one.

TIP

Use the Formatting buttons in the New Style dialog box to apply basic font and paragraph formatting. For more formatting options, click the Format button, and choose Font, Paragraph, Tabs, Border, or Numbering to open the corresponding dialog boxes.

6. Notice the two rows of buttons under **Formatting**. The first row is for font formatting, and the second row is for paragraph formatting. Point to the buttons, and notice a ScreenTip appears to identify each button.

7. Click **OK**.

8. Locate the heading "Nutrition." Click in the paragraph, and click the **Side Heading** style in the task pane. The new style is applied.

9. Repeat the formatting to the side headings "Pets and Chocolate" and "Important Chocolate Dates."

10. Select the text "June 200-" and change the font size to 12.

11. Right-click the selected text, and click **Styles** in the shortcut menu. Click **Save Selection as a New Quick Style**.

Figure 12-4
Creating a new style

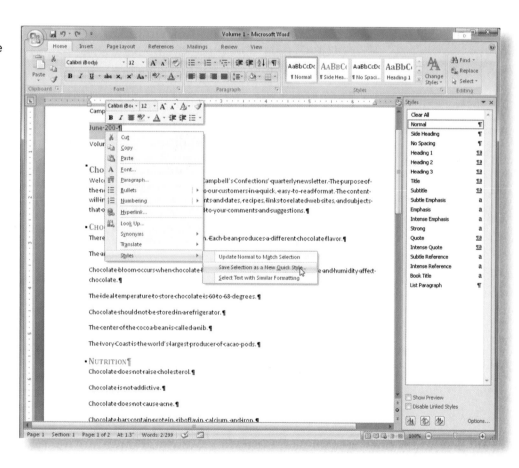

12. Key Issue Date in the **Name** box, and click **OK**.

13. Notice that the Side Heading style and the Issue Date style appear in the Style task pane and the Quick Style Gallery.

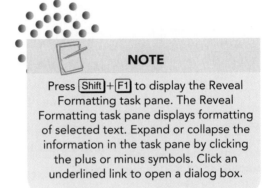

NOTE

Press [Shift]+[F1] to display the Reveal Formatting task pane. The Reveal Formatting task pane displays formatting of selected text. Expand or collapse the information in the task pane by clicking the plus or minus symbols. Click an underlined link to open a dialog box.

Exercise 12-3 CREATE A CHARACTER STYLE

A character style is applied to selected text and only contains character formatting.

1. Select the text "Choc Talk" in the first paragraph under the heading "Choc Talk." Open the Create New Style from Formatting dialog box and key Accent in the **Name** box.

2. Choose **Character** from the **Style type** drop-down list box.

3. Click the **Format** button, choose **Font**, and set the formatting to 11-point Calibri and italic.

4. Click **OK** to close the Font dialog box. Click **OK** to close the Create New Style from Formatting dialog box. The selected text is formatted, and the Accent style appears in the task pane.

5. Note that a character style is applied to selected text, not the entire paragraph.

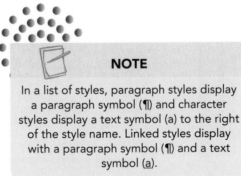

NOTE

In a list of styles, paragraph styles display a paragraph symbol (¶) and character styles display a text symbol (a) to the right of the style name. Linked styles display with a paragraph symbol (¶) and a text symbol (a).

Figure 12-5
Applying the
character style

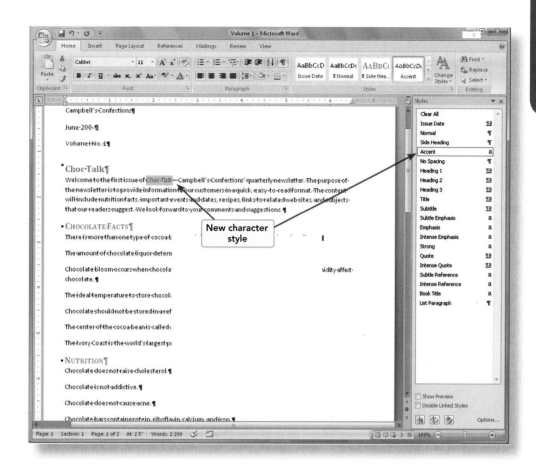

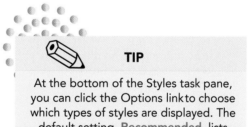

6. Save the document as *[your initials]***12-3** in a new folder for Lesson 12. Do not print the document; leave it open for the next exercise.

TIP

At the bottom of the Styles task pane, you can click the Options link to choose which types of styles are displayed. The default setting, Recommended, lists styles and unnamed formats available to the current document. "In use" lists styles and unnamed formats applied in the current document. "In current document" lists styles and unnamed formats available in the current document. "All styles" lists styles in the current document and all of Word's built-in styles. You can also specify how the styles are sorted: Alphabetical, As Recommended, Font, Based on, and By type.

Word 2007

Modifying and Renaming Styles

After creating a style, you can modify it by changing the formatting specifications or renaming the style. When you modify a style, the changes you make affect each instance of that style. You can quickly replace one style with another by using the Replace dialog box.

Exercise 12-4 MODIFY AND RENAME STYLES

To modify a style, right-click the style in the Styles task pane and then choose Modify. Or select the styled text, modify the formatting, right-click the style name in the Styles task pane, and choose Update to Match Selection.

1. In the Styles task pane, right-click the style name **Heading 1**. Choose **Modify** from the drop-down list.

2. In the **Modify Style** dialog box, change the point size to 18, and click **OK** to update the style.

3. Select the text "June 200-" and open the **Paragraph** dialog box. Change the spacing after to 0 points and click **OK**. Right-click the style name **Issue Date** in the task pane. Choose **Update Issue Date to Match Selection**. The style is updated to match the selected text formatting.

Figure 12-6
Modifying a style by
updating it

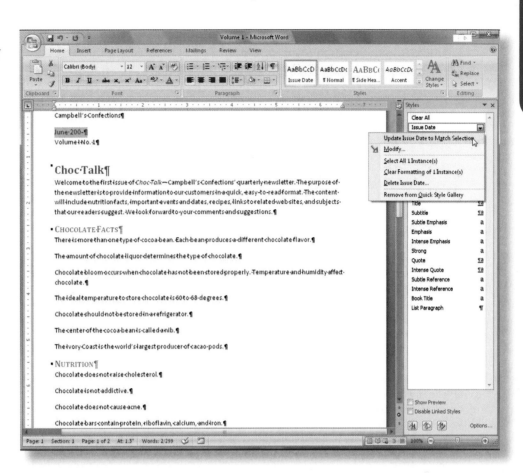

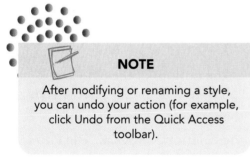

NOTE

After modifying or renaming a style,
you can undo your action (for example,
click Undo from the Quick Access
toolbar).

4. Position the insertion point in the text "June 200-."
Right-click the Issue Date style in the task pane and
choose Modify.

5. Rename the Issue Date style by keying **Pub Date** in
the **Name** text box. Click **OK**. The style Pub Date
appears in the task pane, replacing the style name
Issue Date.

Exercise 12-5 REPLACE A STYLE

1. Click the Home tab, and locate the **Editing** group. Click the Replace
button. Click the **More** button, if needed, to expand the
dialog box. Clear any text or formatting from a previous search.

2. Click the **Format** button and choose **Style**. The Find Style dialog box
displays.

3. Click **Side Heading** from the **Find what style** list, and click **OK**.

Figure 12-7
Find Style dialog box

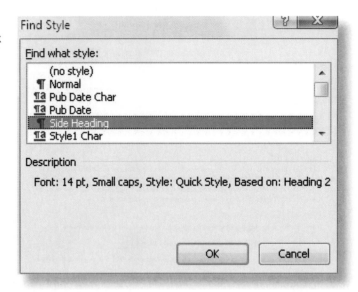

TIP

You can also use the Styles task pane to replace one style with another style: Right-click a style name in the task pane, choose **Select All Instances**, and then click another style name in the task pane.

4. Click in the **Replace with** text box, click **Format**, and choose **Style**.

5. Choose **Heading 3** from the **Replace With Style** list, and click **OK**.

6. Click **Replace All**. Word replaces all occurrences of the Side Heading style with the Heading 3 style. Notice the change in the format. Click the Undo button .

Exercise 12-6 DELETE A STYLE

1. Click the Manage Styles button 🗐 at the bottom of the Styles task pane. Click the **Edit** tab. Select the **Pub Date** style in the **Select a style to edit** list box. Click **Delete**.

2. Click **Yes** when prompted to verify the deletion. Click **OK**. The Pub Date style is deleted, and the paragraph returns to Normal, the default style.

NOTE

When you delete a style from the style sheet, any paragraph that contained the formatting for the style returns to the Normal style. You cannot delete the standard styles (Word's built-in styles) from the style sheet.

NOTE

A style deleted from the Quick Style Gallery is not deleted from the Style task pane.

Using Style Options

Word offers two options in the Style dialog box to make formatting with styles easier:

- *Style based on:* This option helps you format a document consistently by creating different styles in a document based on the same underlying style. For example, in a long document, you can create several different heading styles that are based on one heading style and several different body text styles that are based on one body text style. Then if you decide to change the formatting, you can do so quickly and easily by changing just the base styles.

NOTE

The standard styles available with each new Word document are all based on the Normal style.

- *Style for following paragraph:* This option helps you automate the formatting of your document by applying a style to a paragraph and specifying the style that should follow immediately after the paragraph. For example, you can create a style for a heading and specify a body text style for the next paragraph.

Exercise 12-7 USE THE STYLE FOR FOLLOWING PARAGRAPH OPTION

1. Go to the end of the document, and position the insertion point in the blank paragraph above "Copyright."

 2. Click the **New Style** button in the Styles task pane.

3. Key StaffName in the **Name** text box.

4. Click **Format** and choose **Font**. Set the font to 11-point Cambria and click **OK** to close the Font dialog box. Click **OK** to close the Create New Style from Formatting dialog box.

5. Click the **New Style** button in the Styles task pane. Key StaffTitle in the name box. The **Style type** is **Paragraph**, and change the **Style based on** to **Normal**. Click **Format** and choose **Font**. Set the font to 12-point Calibri, with bold and small caps, and click **OK**.

6. Check that the Align Left button is selected. Change the spacing after to 0 points and the line spacing to single. Click the arrow for **Style for following paragraph**, and select **StaffName**. Click **OK**.

Figure 12-8
Choosing a style
for the following
paragraph

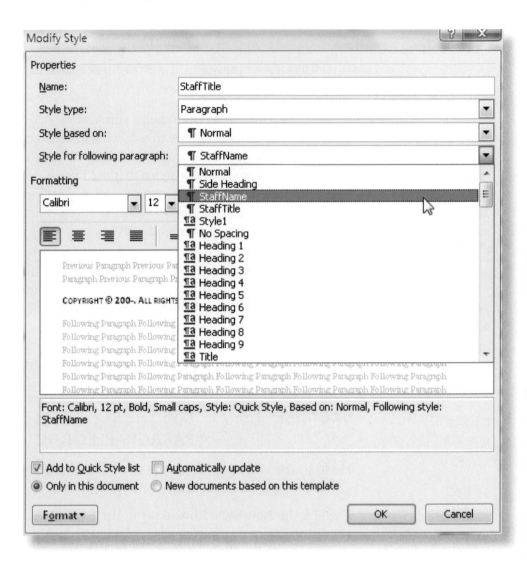

7. Key **President** and apply the **StaffTitle** style. Notice the format of the text. Press [Enter]. Key **Thomas Campbell**. Notice the change in the style name.

8. Press [Enter]. Note that the style automatically changes from StaffTitle to StaffName, which was the style indicated as the style for the following paragraph.

9. Key the text shown in Figure 12-9. Apply the appropriate styles.

Figure 12-9

Vice President ◄——— StaffTitle, [Enter] StaffName
Lynn Tanguay

Editor ◄——— StaffTitle, [Enter] StaffName
Margo Razzano

Exercise 12-8 USE THE BASED ON OPTION

1. Select the text near the bottom of page 2, from "Choc Talk" to "16127." Click the New Style button on the Style task pane. Key **BaseBody** in the **Name** box. Verify that **Paragraph** is selected for the **Style type**, and **Normal** is selected for **Style based on**.

2. Change the font to Times New Roman, 12 points. Change the paragraph formatting to 0 points spacing after and single spacing. Click **OK** to close the Create New Style from Formatting dialog box.

3. Click the **New Style** button in the task pane.

4. Key **Body2** as the name of the new style. Click the Italic button in the Create New Style from Formatting dialog box to change the font to italic. Check that Basebody appears in the **Style based on** box. Click **OK**.

TIP

When you want to use an existing style as the based-on style, select the text with that style before opening the New Style dialog box. The style will automatically appear in the **Style based on** box.

5. Notice that the selected paragraph(s) are formatted with the Body2 style. Apply the BaseBody text to the text that was formatted by the new style. Deselect the text and press Enter after the ZIP Code.

6. Place the mouse pointer over (without clicking) the Body2 style in the task pane. The ScreenTip indicates that the Body2 style is based on the Basebody style.

7. Click the **New Style** button in the task pane to create another style.

8. Key **Body3** as the name of the new style. Choose **Basebody** from the **Style based on** list, if it is not already selected. Change the font size to 10 points. Click **OK**. Apply the BaseBody text to any text that was formatted by the new style.

9. Select the text from "June 200-" to "Volume 1 No. 1." Apply the Body2 style. Deselect the text.

10. Right-click the style **Basebody** in the task pane and choose **Modify**.

11. Change the font to Calibri. Click **OK**. All the text using or based on the Basebody style changes to Calibri.

Exercise 12-9 DISPLAY AND PRINT STYLES

To make working with styles easier, you can display a document's styles on the screen and print the style sheet. To see the styles, switch to Draft view.

1. Switch to Draft view. Open the **Word Options** dialog box, and click **Advanced** in the left pane. Scroll to the **Display** group of options.

Word 2007

NOTE

The style area is intended for on-screen purposes in Draft view only (it is not available in Print Layout view). If you switch to Print Preview, this area does not display or appear on the printed document. Additionally, when you display the style area, it will be displayed for any document you open unless you reduce the view to 0 inches. The default Style area width is 0 inches.

2. Set the **Style area width** box to **0.5"** and click **OK**. The style area appears in the left margin.

3. Right-click the Normal style in the Styles task pane. Click **Select All Instance(s)**. Click the Basebody style in the Styles task pane.

4. Select the text under "Chocolate Facts" beginning with "There is" through "cacao pods." Format the list as a bulleted list using a small square bullet.

5. Select the bulleted list you just formatted if necessary. Right-click the selected bulleted list, and select **Styles** from the shortcut menu. Select **Save Selection as a New Quick Style**. Name the style **Basebullet** that is based on Basebody.

6. Apply the Basebullet style to the text under the headings "Nutrition," "Pets and Chocolate," and "Important Chocolate Dates."

7. Change the Heading 2 style so it is based on Basebody. Apply the Heading 2 style to the first line of the document "Campbell's Confections." Move to the last page of the document, and repeat the Heading 2 format for the "Choc Talk" line.

Figure 12-10
Styles shown in style area

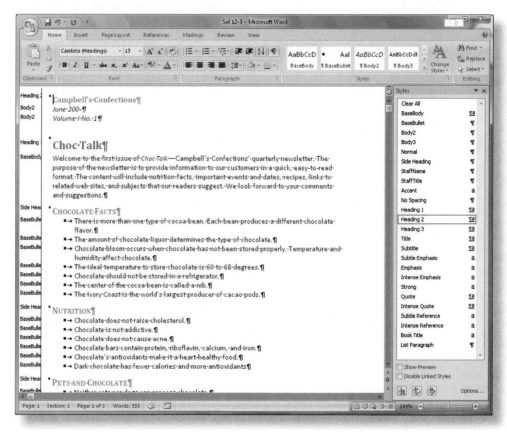

> **NOTE**
>
> You can assign a shortcut key to a style you use frequently. In the Styles task pane, right-click the style to which you want to assign a shortcut key. Choose Modify. Click Format and then click Shortcut key. In the Customize Keyboard dialog box, press an unassigned keyboard combination, such as Alt+B for a body text style. The shortcut key is saved with the document.

8. Open the **Word Options** dialog box, and click **Advanced**. Scroll to the **Display** section, and set the **Style area width** box to **0"** and click **OK**. Switch to Print Layout view.

9. Save the document as *[your initials]*12-9 in your Lesson 12 folder.

10. Open the **Print** dialog box. Choose **Styles** from the **Print what** drop-down list and click **OK**. Word prints the styles for your active document.

11. Submit the document.

Exercise 12-10   CHANGE STYLE SET

Word provides several style sets to format your document. The number and types of styles available varies for each style set.

1. Position the insertion point at the top of the document. Click the Change Styles button and click **Style Set**. The default style set is currently selected. Click **Distinctive**, and scroll through the document to notice the changes in format.

2. Change the style set to the default style.

3. Save and close the document.

Apply and Customize a Document Theme

You can use document themes to format an entire document quickly. A gallery of theme designs is available to format your document, or you can go to Microsoft Online for additional theme selections. Themes can also be customized and saved. Themes define the fonts used for body text and the fonts used for headings. For example, the default theme is Office, and Calibri is the default font for body text, and Cambri is the default font for headings. Themes affect the styles of a document.

Exercise 12-11   APPLY A THEME

1. Reopen the file **Volume 1**. Make sure the Styles task pane is open.

2. Click the **Page Layout** tab and click the Themes button. The design gallery for themes displays.

Figure 12-11
Theme gallery

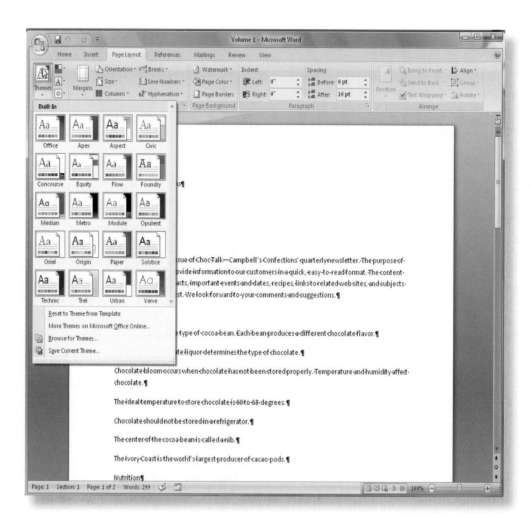

NOTE

The design gallery includes a link for additional themes on Microsoft Office Online.

3. Move your mouse over each of the theme designs and preview the changes in your document. Click the **Technic** theme.

4. Scroll through the document, and notice the changes made. The default body text font is 11-point Arial, and the default heading font is Franklin Gothic Book.

5. View the style names in the Styles task pane. When you change a document theme, styles are updated to match the new theme.

6. Using the new styles, change the text "Campbell's Confections" at the beginning of the document to the Heading 2 style, and change "Choc Talk" to the Heading 1 style.

Exercise 12-12   CUSTOMIZE A THEME

Theme colors include text and background colors, accent colors, and hyperlink colors. The Theme Colors command displays the text and background colors for the selected theme.

1. Click the **Page Layout** tab, and locate the **Theme** group. Click the Theme Colors button . The design gallery for theme colors displays with the current theme colors selected.

Figure 12-12
Theme colors

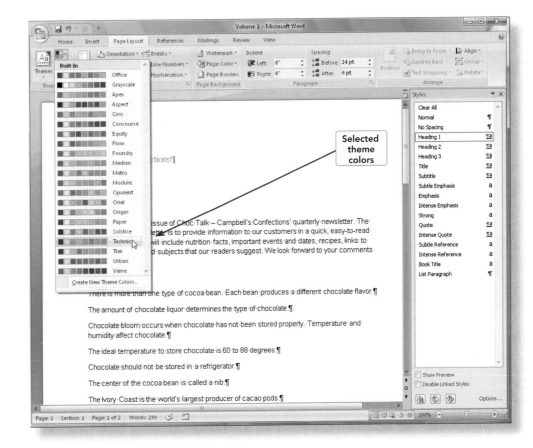

2. Click **Create New Theme Colors**. Notice that there is a button for each element of the theme. Click the down arrow beside the Accent 1 button , and notice that the first color in the fifth row of Theme Colors is selected. Click the last color in the fifth row, **Aqua, Accent 1, Darker 50%**. Key **Custom Accent 1** in the **Name** box. Click **Save**. The accent color for the heading text in the document changes.

Figure 12-13
Create New Theme
Colors dialog box

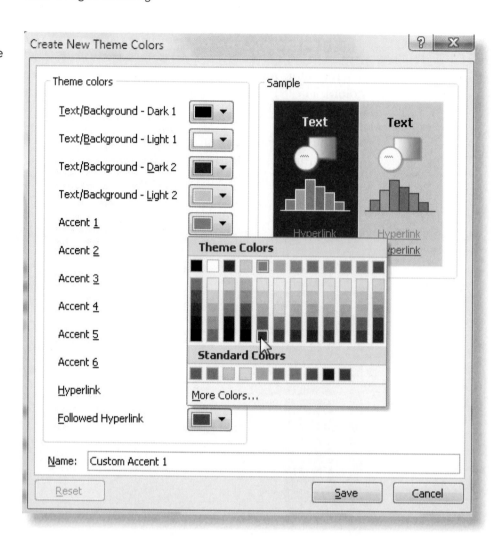

NOTE

The Sample area of the Create New
Theme Colors dialog box displays
the color changes for each element
you change.

3. Click the Theme Colors button and notice that the Custom Accent 1 theme color appears at the top of the list. Right-click the Custom Accent 1 color, and click **Delete**. Click **No**.

4. Click the **Page Layout** tab, and click the Theme Fonts button . The heading and body text font for each theme displays.

5. Click the option to **Create New Theme Fonts**. The current Heading font and Body font are selected in the Create New Theme Fonts dialog box.

Figure 12-14
Create New Theme
Fonts

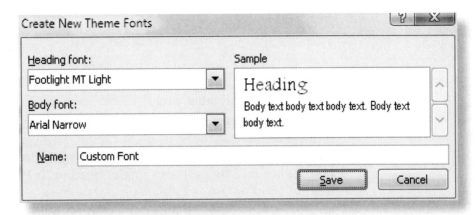

6. Change the **Heading font** to **Footlight MT Light**, and change the **Body font** to **Arial Narrow**. Key Custom Font in the **Name** box. Click **Save**.

7. Click the Theme Fonts button , and notice that "Custom Font" appears at the top of the list. Right-click **Custom Font**, and click **Edit**. Change the **Heading font** to **Eras Medium ITC**, and change the **Body font** to **Footlight MT Light**. Click **Save**.

8. Apply the Heading 5 style to the second line "June 200-." Apply the Heading 4 style to the line that begins "Volume."

9. Select the headings "Chocolate Facts," "Nutrition," "Pets and Chocolate," and "Important Chocolate Dates," and apply the Heading 3 style.

10. Select the lines of text under each of the headings formatted with the Heading 3 style, and format the lines as a bulleted list.

11. At the end of the document, delete the text that begins "Choc Talk" through the end of the document.

12. Click the **Page Layout** tab, and click the Themes button . Click **Save Current Theme**. Key Custom Theme in the **File name** box. Click **Save**.

13. Click the Themes button, and notice that the design gallery displays Built In designs and Custom designs. Right-click the **Custom Theme** at the top of the gallery, and click **Delete**. Click **Yes** to delete the theme.

14. Save the document as *[your initials]*12-12 in your Lesson 12 folder.

15. Submit and close the document.

Lesson 12 Summary

- A style is a set of formatting instructions you can apply to text to give your document a unified look. The five types of styles are character, paragraph, linked, table, and list.

- Word's default style for text is called the Normal style. The default settings for body text are 11-point Calibri, left-aligned, 1.15-line spacing, 10 points spacing after, with widow-orphan control. Word provides built-in heading styles (for example, Heading 1, Heading 2). The default font for heading text is Cambria.

- To apply a style, select the text you want to style (or click in a paragraph to apply a paragraph style). Then choose the style from the Styles task pane or the Quick Styles gallery.

- View the attributes of a style by placing the mouse pointer over the style name in the Styles task pane and reading the text in the ScreenTip.

- Select all instances of a style by clicking the arrow for the style name in the Styles task pane or by right-clicking a style name in the task pane and choosing Select All Instance(s).

- To create a new paragraph style: Select text, modify the text, right-click the text, select Styles, select Save Selection as a New Quick Style, key a new style name, and click OK. Or click the New Style button in the Styles task pane, and set the style's attributes in the Create New Style from Formatting dialog box. You must use the Create New Style from Formatting dialog box to create a character style and specify Character as the style type.

- To modify or rename a style, right-click the style name in the Styles task pane (or point to the style name and click the down arrow), choose Modify, and then change the attributes. Or select text that uses the style, change the format, right-click the style name in the task pane, and choose Update to Match Selection.

- After applying a style throughout a document, you can replace it with another style. Click Replace on the Home tab (in the dialog box, click Format, choose Style, and select the style name in both the Find what and Replace with boxes).

- You can also replace styles by using the Styles task pane (select all instances of a style and then choose another style).

- To delete a style, click the Manage Styles button in the Styles task pane, select the style, and click Delete. Click Yes to delete the style, and click OK.

- When creating new styles, you can specify that they be based on an existing style. You can also specify that one style follows another style automatically. Both these options are offered in the Create New Style from Formatting dialog box.

- Display styles along the left margin of a document in Draft view by opening the Word Options dialog box, clicking Advanced, and scrolling to the Display group. Change the Style area width box to 0.5 inch. Do the reverse to stop displaying styles.

- Print a style sheet by choosing Print from the File menu and choosing Styles from the Print what drop-down list.
- The Theme feature formats an entire document using design elements. Themes include theme colors, theme fonts, and theme effects.

LESSON 12		Command Summary	
Feature	**Button**	**Command**	**Keyboard**
Styles task pane		Home tab, Styles group, Styles Dialog Box Launcher	Shift + Ctrl + Alt + S
Apply styles		Home tab, Styles group	
View style area		Word Options, Advanced, Display	
Themes		Page Layout tab, Themes group	

Concepts Review

True/False Questions

Each of the following statements is either true or false. Indicate your choice by circling T or F.

T F   1. Paragraph styles can include both paragraph- and character-formatting instructions.

T F   2. You can apply character styles to selected text within a paragraph.

T F   3. You can use either the Styles task pane or the Quick Styles Gallery to apply a paragraph style.

T F   4. If you select only part of a paragraph to change the paragraph style, only the selected portion is reformatted.

T F   5. You can create a character style by changing the formatting of selected text, right-click the selection, and select Styles.

T F   6. A style named and created for a specific document cannot be modified for that document.

T F   7. When you delete a style from the style sheet, any paragraph or text containing that style returns to the Normal style.

T F   8. You save the styles created for a document by saving the document.

Short Answer Questions

Write the correct answer in the space provided.

1. In the list of styles, what symbol designates a paragraph style?

_____

2. In the list of styles, what symbol designates a character style?

_____

3. How do you print a list of a document's styles?

_____

4. What is the purpose of a theme?

_____

5. How do you display style names in the left margin of a document?

_____

6. How do you open the New Style dialog box?

_____

7. What are the five types of styles?

_____

8. On what style are all standard styles based?

_____

Critical Thinking

Answer these questions on a separate page. There are no right or wrong answers. Support your answers with examples from your own experience, if possible.

1. The Based On option is often used to create a group of heading styles based on one style and a group of body text styles based on another style. Why aren't heading styles and body text styles typically based on the same style?

2. Create complementary styles for a heading and for body text, using two different fonts. Describe the formatting for each style, and provide a sample of the styles used together. Describe the type of document for which this combination would be suited.

Skills Review

Exercise 12-13

Apply styles and create new styles.

1. Open the file **Agenda - 1**.
2. Use the Quick Styles Gallery to apply a style to the document title by following these steps:
   a. Position the insertion point in the title (the first line).
   b. Click the More Arrow button to open the Quick Styles Gallery.
   c. Click **Title**.
3. Use the Styles task pane to apply a style by following these steps:
   a. Click the **Home** tab, and click the **Styles Dialog Box Launcher** to display the **Styles** task pane.
   b. Position the insertion point in the next heading, "Sponsored by."
   c. Click **Subtitle** in the task pane.
4. Apply the Heading 1 style to the heading "Agenda."

5. Create a new paragraph style for a heading by following these steps:

   a. Select the heading "Thursday, February 10."

   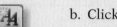 b. Click the New Style button , and key **Day** in the **Name** text box.

   c. Change the font formatting to 14-point bold and small caps.

   d. Change the paragraph formatting to 12 points spacing before and 6 points spacing after. Click **OK**.

   e. Apply the Day style to the line beginning "Friday."

6. Use the New Style dialog box to create a new style for the agenda text by following these steps:

   a. Position the insertion point at the beginning of the line that begins "12 Noon." Click **New Style** in the task pane.

   b. Key **Agenda Items** in the **Name** text box.

   c. Change the font size to 12.

   d. Click **Format** and choose **Paragraph**.

   e. Change the left indent to 0.25" and change the spacing after to 3 points. Click **OK**.

   f. Click **OK** in the Create New Style from Formatting dialog box.

7. Select all the agenda text under the headings "Thursday" and "Friday." Choose the **Agenda Items** style from the Styles task pane.

8. Apply the Heading 2 style to the line that begins "Grove City College."

9. Change the document title to small caps and 72 points of spacing before paragraphs. Replace the hyphens following each session number with em dashes.

10. Save the document as *[your initials]*12-13 in your Lesson 12 folder.

11. Submit and close the document.

Exercise 12-14

Create, redefine, modify, and rename styles.

1. Open the file **OH Stores**. Display the Styles task pane.

2. For the document title, create and apply a paragraph style named **Office Heading** with the formatting 14-point Times New Roman, bold and italic.

3. For the text "Campbell's Confections," create and apply a paragraph style named **Subhead** with the formatting 12-point Arial, with bold and italic and with 12 points spacing before and 3 points spacing after paragraphs.

4. Position the insertion point in each line of text that contains a Campbell's Confections' store name, and apply the Subhead style (press F4 to repeat the style).

5. Redefine the Subhead style by following these steps:

   a. Select the first occurrence of "Campbell's Confections," and remove the italics by clicking the italic button 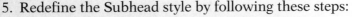.

   b. Right-click the **Subhead** style in the task pane. Choose **Update Subhead to Match Selection**.

6. Create a new character style for the word "Fax" by following these steps:

   a. Position the insertion point at the beginning of the second telephone number for the Akron Office. Click the **New Style** button 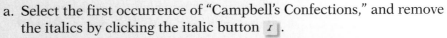 in the Styles task pane.

   b. Key **Fax Num** in the **Name** text box.

   c. Choose **Character** from the **Style type** drop-down list.

   d. Click the Font Color button 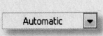 in the dialog box, and change the color to dark blue.

   e. Click **Format**, choose **Font**, and choose **Small caps**. Click **OK**. Click **OK** again.

7. Key the word **Fax:** followed by a space at the beginning of the second telephone number for the Akron office. Repeat for the other five offices.

8. Select the word "Fax" the first time it occurs, and apply the **Fax Num** style from the task pane. Apply the same style to each occurrence of "Fax" by selecting the word and pressing F4.

9. Rename the **Fax Num** style by following these steps:

   a. Right-click the Fax Num style in the task pane and choose **Modify**.

   b. In the Name text box, edit the text to "Fax" and click **OK**.

10. Delete the Office Heading style by following these steps:

    a. Right-click the **Office Heading** style in the task pane.

    b. Choose **Delete**. Click **Yes**.

11. Apply the Title style to the document title. Modify the style to include small caps. Delete the blank paragraph after the title.

12. Change the top margin to 1.5 inches and the bottom margin to 0.5.

13. Key **Telephone:** followed by a space to the left of each telephone number for all offices. (The telephone number is the first number listed.)

14. Save the document as *[your initials]*12-14 in your Lesson 12 folder.

15. Submit and close the document.

Exercise 12-15

Create styles, use style options, and display and print styles.

1. Open the file **Health Fair**. Display the Styles task pane. Change the date in the memo heading to today's date. Change the date in the third paragraph below the memo heading to a date two weeks from today's date. Delete the instruction text.

2. Select the text "Board Room No. 1," and create and apply a new paragraph style named **Room** with the formatting 12-point Arial, with bold and italic and with 3 points spacing after.

3. Apply the new style to "Board Room No. 2" and "Board Room No. 3."

4. Create a new paragraph style named "Session" that is based on the Room style by following these steps:

   a. Position the insertion point after "Board Room No. 1" and press Enter. Key **30-Minute Sessions**. Click the **New Style** button on the task pane.

   b. Key **Session** in the **Name** text box.

   c. Check that **Style based on** is set to the **Room** style.

   d. Using the Formatting buttons in the Create New Style from Formatting dialog box, change the font formatting to 11 points and turn off bold and italic.

   e. Click **OK**.

5. Click at the beginning of the paragraph that starts with the word "Topics." Create a new paragraph style named **Info** that is based on the Normal style. Use the formatting 11-point Arial, with 3 points of spacing after paragraphs.

6. Assign Session as the following paragraph style for Room and assign Info as the following paragraph style for Session by following these steps:

   a. Right-click the **Room** style in the task pane.

   b. Choose **Modify**.

   c. Choose **Session** from the **Style for following paragraph** drop-down list.

   d. Click **OK**. Repeat the procedure to assign Info as the following paragraph style for Session.

7. Position the insertion point at the end of the heading "Board Room No. 2," press Enter to apply the Session style, and key **45-Minute Sessions**.

8. Press Enter to apply the Info style and key **Topics:**.

9. At the end of "Board Room No. 3," press Enter, and key the following two lines of text:

   30-Minute Sessions
   Topics:

10. Select the text from "CPR" through "First Aid," and format the text as a bulleted list using a small square bullet (■). Right-click the selected text, and choose **Styles** from the shortcut menu. Click **Save Selection as a New Quick Style**. Name the style **Content**, and click **OK**.

11. Select the two lines of text that follow "Topics for Board Room No. 2," and apply the Content style. Repeat the style for the three lines of text under "Topics for Board Room No. 3."

12. Modify the Normal style to be Arial, with single spacing.

13. Display the style area for the document by following these steps:

    a. Open the **Word Options** dialog box, and click **Advanced**. Scroll to the **Display** group.

    b. Set the **Style area width** to 0.5 inch and click **OK**. Switch to Draft view.

14. Format the memo with the correct spacing at the top of the page, and remember to include your reference initials at the end of the document. Change the bottom margin to 0.5 inch.

15. Restore the style area width to zero. Switch to Print Layout view.

16. Print the document style sheet by following these steps:

    a. Open the **Print** dialog box.

    b. Choose **Styles** from the **Print what** drop-down list and click **OK**.

17. Spell-check the document, and save it as *[your initials]***12-15** in your Lesson 12 folder.

18. Submit and close the document.

Exercise 12-16

Apply and customize document themes.

1. Open the file **Health Fair - 2**. Display the Styles task pane.

2. Change the document theme by following these steps:

    a. Click the **Page Layout** tab, and click the Themes button .

    b. Click the **Median** design from the Themes gallery.

3. Change the theme font by following these steps:

    a. Click the Theme Fonts button .

    b. Click **Create New Theme Fonts**.

    c. Change the heading font to Tahoma, and change the body font to Tahoma.

    d. Key **Custom Font** in the **Name** text box. Click **Save**.

4. Modify the Normal style by changing the font size to 12.

5. Apply the style Heading 1 to the first line of the document. Apply the Heading 2 style to the text that begins "Saturday."

6. Apply the Heading 3 style to the headings "Employee's Full Name," "Store Location," and "Preferred Sessions." Modify the Heading 3 style to 24 points spacing before.

7. Format the document with a 1.5-inch top margin.

8. Spell-check the document.

9. Save the document as *[your initials]***12-16** in your Lesson 12 folder.

10. Submit and close the document.

Lesson Applications

Exercise 12-17

Create, apply, and modify styles; print styles.

1. Start a new document. Key the text shown in Figure 12-15. Create the styles as indicated for the first two lines.

Figure 12-15

```
Health Screening Day ———— New style: Headline 1
                            24-pt Arial bold, centered
For More Information:
                            New style: Headline 2
Garland Miller              18 pt Arial Italic, centered

Campbell's Confections

250 Monroe Street

Grove City, PA 16127

800-555-2025

Campbell's Confections-Makers of Fine Chocolate
```

2. Apply the Headline 2 style to the last line of text. Modify the style to include 18 points of paragraph spacing before and after.

3. Create a style called **Body 1** (based on the Normal style) for the remainder of the text; the style should be 12-point Arial, centered, with 1.5-line spacing.

4. Center the document vertically on the page.

5. Spell-check the document.

6. Save the document as *[your initials]*12-17 in your Lesson 12 folder.

7. Submit the document and the style sheet, and close the document.

Exercise 12-18

Create, modify, and rename styles; print styles.

1. Open the file **Screening**.

2. Create a character style named **Memo Heading** using Arial Black, 12 points.

3. Select "Memo To" and apply the Memo Heading style. Repeat the style formatting for "From," "Date," and "Subject."

4. Select the four lines in the memo heading, and adjust the tab setting to 1.25 inches.

5. Modify the Normal style to include 12-point Times New Roman and 12 points spacing after.

6. Select the text beginning "Height and weight" through "Asthma screening," and format the text using a picture bullet.

7. Rename the style Memo Heading with the name Memo Head.

8. Position the insertion point in the subject line of the memo heading, and change the spacing after to 24 points. Add a bottom border to the subject line.

9. Change the top margin to 2 inches and the bottom margin to 0.5 inch.

10. Add your reference initials to the document.

11. Save the document as *[your initials]*12-18 in your Lesson 12 folder.

12. Submit and close the document.

Exercise 12-19

Modify styles, use style options, and print styles.

1. Open the file **Property - 2**.

2. Format the document as a letter to the name and address shown below, from Lynn Tanguay, vice president. Remember to use the correct top margin and spacing and to include your reference initials. Change the bottom margin to 0.5 inch.

   Dr. James Wenner
   West College
   PO Box 1000
   New Wilmington, PA 16172

3. Edit the first line of the letter to read:

   Thank you for agreeing to present a seminar on property insurance for Campbell's Confections' store owners/managers. Please discuss the following topics.

4. Select the text "Types of insurance," and create a style named Topic with 12-point, bold, and small caps formatting.

5. Position the insertion point at the end of the document, and create a new style named Subjects with 12-point formatting.

6. Modify the Topic style by changing the style for following paragraph to Subjects.

7. Position the insertion point at the end of the line "Types of Insurance." Press [Enter] and key the text shown in Figure 12-16.

Figure 12-16

```
Equipment

Inventory

Buildings

Land

Liability

Business Interruption

Key Employees
```

8. Apply the Topic style to the text "Types of Coverage," press Enter, and key the following items. Place each on a separate line, and omit the commas.

   Fire, Theft, Catastrophes, Accidents, Loss of Income

9. Press Enter twice after keying "Loss of income," and apply the Normal style.

10. Key the following closing paragraph.

    If time permits, you may want to include comments on how to select an insurance agent. We look forward to your presentation next month.

11. Key the closing lines of the letter.

12. Modify the font size of the Normal style to 12 points.

13. Spell-check the document.

14. Save the document as *[your initials]*12-19 in your Lesson 12 folder.

15. Print the style sheet and the document, and close the document.

Exercise 12-20 ◆ Challenge Yourself

Create, apply, and modify styles; apply themes.

1. Open the file **Ordering**. Display the Styles task pane.

2. Apply the Opulent theme to the document.

3. Apply the Title style to the first line of the document.

4. Position the insertion point in the "Online" paragraph. Create a style called Side Heading using 14-point, bold, and small caps formatting.

5. Apply the Side Heading style to each of the document side headings. (There are seven side headings.)

6. Position the insertion point in the paragraph that begins "Note," and create a new style named Special Note using 11 points and 0.25-inch left indent.

7. Apply the Special Note style to each "Note" paragraph and the paragraph that follows "Note."

8. Modify the Normal style font to 11 points.

9. Modify the Title style to small caps.

10. Create a left-aligned header for page 2 to include the following text. Place two blank paragraphs after the second line of the header.

    Place an Order
    Page *[Number]*

11. Add a bottom border to the page number paragraph in the header.

12. Add your reference initials to the bottom of the document.

13. Save the document as *[your initials]***12-20** in your Lesson 12 folder.

14. Print the document and the style sheet, and close the document.

On Your Own

In these exercises you work on your own, as you would in a real-life business environment. Use the skills you've learned to accomplish the task—and be creative.

Exercise 12-21

Create your own one-page newsletter. Create and use styles for the different newsletter elements, such as the title, date line, body text, and publisher information. Save the document as *[your initials]***12-21**. Submit the document and the styles.

Exercise 12-22

Assume you have been on a job interview. Write a simple follow-up letter, and compare the document appearance by using three different themes. Apply the appropriate theme and styles to your letter. Save the document as *[your initials]***12-22**. Submit the document and the styles.

Exercise 12-23

Create a document that includes your five favorite songs. Each song should appear as a three-line description—song title, songwriter, and performer—with each line using a different style. The songwriter and performer styles should be based on the song title style. Specify the songwriter style as the style following the title style, and the performer style as the style following the songwriter style. Create the styles first; then key the text. Modify the styles as desired. Save the document as *[your initials]***12-23**. Submit the document and the styles.

templates

If you often create the same types of documents, such as memos or letters, you can save time by using templates. Word provides a variety of templates that contain built-in styles to help you produce professional-looking documents. You can also create your own templates and reuse them as often as you like.

Using Word's Templates

A *template* is a file that contains formatting information, styles, and sometimes text for a particular type of document. It provides a reusable model for all documents of the same type. Every Word document is based on a template. You can modify templates to include formatting and text that you use frequently.

The following features can be included in templates:

- Formatting features, such as margins, columns, and page orientation.

- Standard text that is repeated in all documents of the same type, such as a company name and address in a letter template.

- Character and paragraph formatting that is saved within styles.

- Macros (automated procedures).

Templates also include *placeholder text* that is formatted and replaced with your own information when you create a new document.

The default template file in Word is called **Normal**. New documents that you create in Word are based on the Normal template and contain all the formatting features assigned to this template, such as the default font, type size, paragraph alignment, margins, and page orientation. The Normal template differs from other templates because it stores settings that are available globally. In other words, you can use these settings in every new document even if they are based on a different template. The file extension for template files is .dotx or .dotm. (A .dotm file is used to enable macros in the file.)

TIP

Pressing Ctrl + N or clicking the New button opens a new document but does not open the New Document dialog box. You can customize the Quick Access Toolbar to include a New button.

Exercise 13-1   USE A WORD TEMPLATE TO CREATE A NEW DOCUMENT

Starting Word opens a new blank document that is based on the Normal template.

1. Click the Microsoft Office Button , and click New to open the New Document dialog box.

Figure 13-1
New Document dialog box

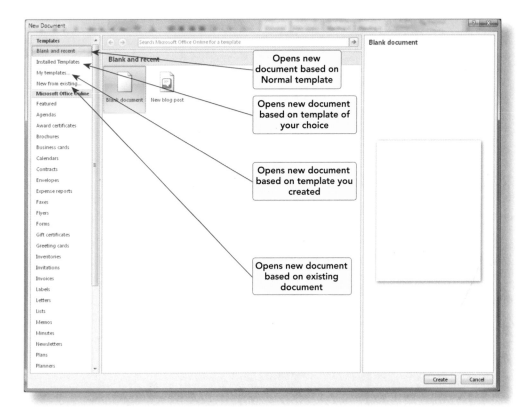

2. Under **Templates** in the New Document dialog box, click **Blank Document**, and click **Create**. Word opens a new document based on the default template Normal and closes the New Document dialog box. (You could also double-click **Blank Document**.)

NOTE

Some templates might not be installed on your computer. Check with your instructor for instructions on locating the template.

3. Close the document without saving it.

4. Reopen the New Document dialog box, and click **Installed Templates**.

5. Click the **Equity Fax** icon. Notice the design of the template in the **Preview** box.

Figure 13-2
Installed Templates

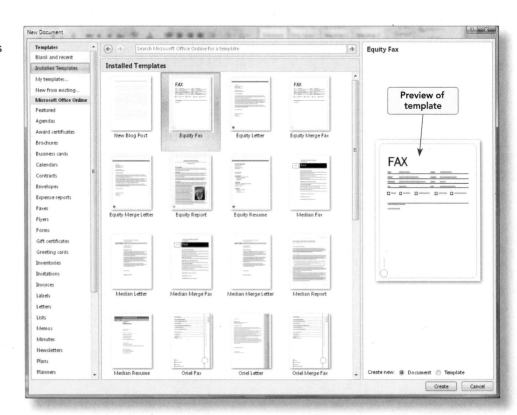

6. Use the **Preview** box to view other Word templates in the dialog box.

7. Click **Letters** under **Microsoft Office Online**. Click **Business**, and click **To Suppliers and vendors**. Click **Acceptance of bid** to preview the letter. Click the Download button [Download]. Click **Continue**. The document displays in a new window.

[Download]

Figure 13-3
Creating a document from the downloaded template

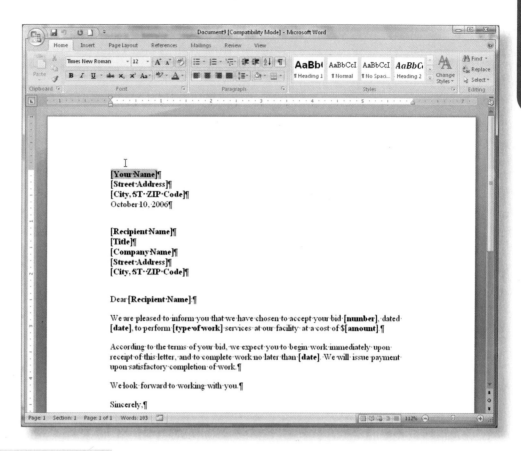

8. Select the first line of the return address, "[Your Name]," and key Campbell's Confections. Click to select the placeholder text that reads "[Street Address]." Key 25 Main Street. Click to select the placeholder that reads "[City, ST ZIP Code]," and key Grove City, PA 16127.

9. Click each of the placeholders for the inside address, and key the following replacement text.

    Mr. Paul Sakkal
    President
    Liberty Storage
    1000 Millington Court
    Cincinnati, OH 45242

10. Click the placeholder in the salutation, and key Mr. Sakkal.

11. Edit the first paragraph that begins "We are pleased" as shown in Figure 13-4.

Figure 13-4

We are pleased to inform you that we have chosen to accept your bid No. 876, dated February 1, to install chrome wire shelving at our Grove City factory at a cost of $1,500.

12. Change the date placeholder in the second paragraph to April 15. Key Robert Smith in the [Your Name] placeholder and Plant Manager in the [Title] placeholder. Key your initials at the end of the document.

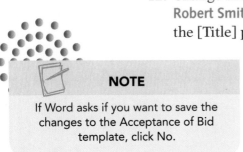

NOTE

If Word asks if you want to save the changes to the Acceptance of Bid template, click No.

13. Format the first line of the return address (Campbell's Confections) using 14-point bold and small caps.

14. Save the document as *[your initials]*13-1 in a new Lesson 13 folder. Click Yes, if a message box appears.

15. Submit and close the document.

Creating New Templates

You can create your own templates for different types of documents by using one of three methods:

- Create a blank template file by using the default template and define the formatting information, styles, and text according to your specifications.

- Open an existing template, modify it, and save it with a new name.

- Open an existing document, modify it, and save it as a new template.

Exercise 13-2   CREATE A NEW TEMPLATE

1. Open the New Document dialog box (by clicking the Microsoft Office Button and then New), and click My templates under Templates. Click the Blank Document icon.

Figure 13-5
New dialog box showing My Templates

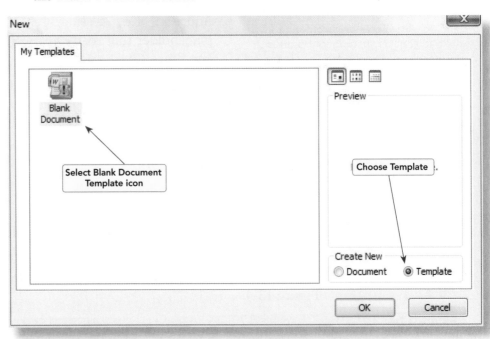

2. In the lower right corner of the dialog box, under **Create New**, click **Template** and then click **OK**. A new template file opens with the default name Template1.

3. Change the top margin to 0.5 inch.

4. Key the text shown in Figure 13-6.

NOTE

If you select **Blank and recent** under **Templates**, you open a document window which can be saved as a template. If you select **My templates** under **Templates**, you can choose to open a document or template window.

Figure 13-6

```
Campbell's Confections

25 Main Street

Grove City, PA 16127

Telephone: 724-555-2025

Fax: 724-555-2050

www.campbellsconfections.biz
```

5. Select the letterhead information, and center the text horizontally. Select the first line, and apply 14-point bold and small caps formatting.

6. Modify the Normal style to 0 points spacing after and single spacing. Press [Enter] three times to insert blank lines after the Web address, and change the paragraph alignment to left.

7. Insert the date as a field at the third blank paragraph mark after the letterhead by clicking the **Insert** tab, and clicking **Date and Time**. Use the third date format in the **Available formats** list in the Date and Time dialog box. Check **Update automatically** so the date field is updated each time the document is printed. Click **OK**.

8. Press [Enter] four times.

9. Click the last line of the letterhead text, and apply a bottom border.

10. Click the **Microsoft Office Button**, click the arrow beside **Save As** and click **Word Template**. A folder named "Templates" should appear in the **Save As** dialog box, and "**Word Template**" should appear in the **Save as type** box.

Figure 13-7
Save As dialog box

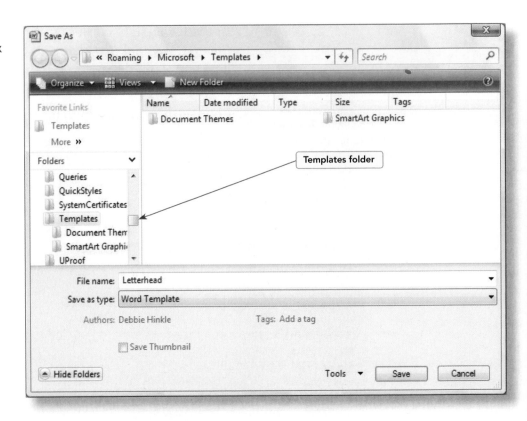

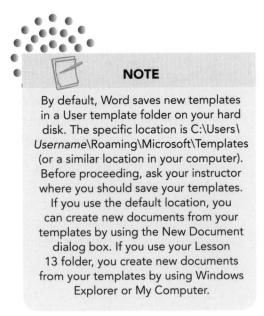

NOTE

By default, Word saves new templates
in a User template folder on your hard
disk. The specific location is C:\Users\
Username\Roaming\Microsoft\Templates
(or a similar location in your computer).
Before proceeding, ask your instructor
where you should save your templates.
If you use the default location, you
can create new documents from your
templates by using the New Document
dialog box. If you use your Lesson
13 folder, you create new documents
from your templates by using Windows
Explorer or My Computer.

11. Save the template with the filename *[your initials]*Letterhead in
    your Lesson 13 folder (unless your instructor advises you to save in
    the default Templates folder).

12. Close the template.

Exercise 13-3 CREATE A NEW TEMPLATE BY USING AN EXISTING DOCUMENT

1. Reopen the New Document dialog box by choosing New from the File menu. Under Templates, click New from existing.

2. Locate and click to select the student data file **Memo - 1**. Click the Create New button `Create New ▼`. Word opens a copy of the document.

3. Change the top margin to 2 inches. Select the document, and change the font size to 12.

4. Delete all text to the right of each tab character in the memo heading.

5. Insert the date as a field; use the third date format. Check Update automatically so the date field is updated each time the document is printed.

6. Delete all the document paragraphs, but include the blank paragraph marks after the subject line.

7. Open the File menu, click the arrow beside Save As, and click Word Template. Verify that Word Template displays in the Save as type drop-down list box.

8. Save the file as *[your initials]*Memo in your Lesson 13 folder (unless your instructor advises you to save in the default Templates folder).

9. Close the template.

Attaching Templates to Documents

All existing documents have an assigned template—either Normal or another template that you assigned when you created the document. You can change the template assigned to an existing document by *attaching* a different template to the document. When you attach a template, that template's formatting and elements are applied to the document, and all the template styles become available in the document.

Exercise 13-4 ATTACH A TEMPLATE TO A DOCUMENT

1. Open the New Document dialog box. Click the Memos link for the Microsoft Office Online templates.

2. Click Memo (Professional design), and click the Download button `Download`. Click Continue.

3. Save the professional memo as a template file named *[your initials]*ProMemo in your Lesson 13 folder (unless your instructor advises you to save in the default Templates folder). Click OK if necessary, and close the template.

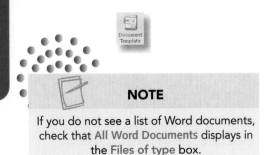

NOTE

If you do not see a list of Word documents, check that **All Word Documents** displays in the **Files of type** box.

4. Open the file **Memo - 4**.

5. Open the Word Options dialog box, and click **Popular** in the left pane. Click to select **Show Developer tab in the Ribbon**. Click **OK**.

6. Click the **Developer** tab in the Ribbon. Click the Document Template button ⬜. The Templates and Add-ins dialog box shows that the document is currently based on the Normal template.

Figure 13-8
Templates and
Add-ins dialog box

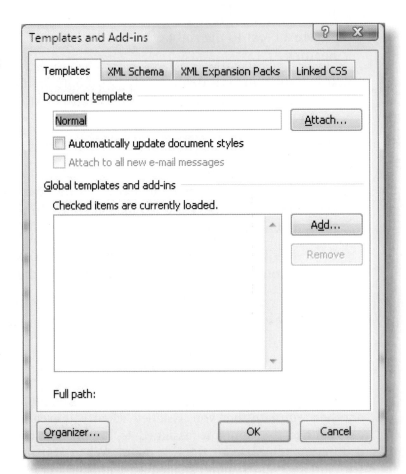

7. Click **Attach**. The Attach Template dialog box opens, displaying available templates and folders in the current folder.

8. Change to the folder that contains Word templates. The full default path of this folder is C:\Program Files\Microsoft Office\ Templates\1033. (The folder may not be on the C: drive of your computer. Check with your instructor.)

9. Locate your Lesson 13 folder, and display **All Word Templates** in the **Files of type** box.

Figure 13-9
Attach Template
dialog box

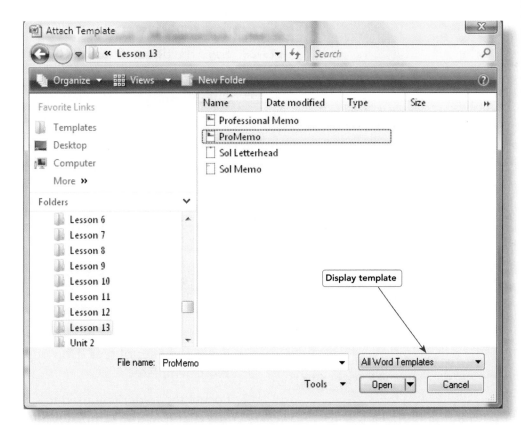

10. Double-click the template **ProMemo**.

11. Click the **Automatically update document styles** check box and click **OK**. Formatting from the Professional Memo template is applied to this document, and you can now apply any of the Professional Memo styles.

12. Display the Styles task pane.

13. Position the insertion point in the subject line of the memo heading, and apply the style **Message Header Last**.

14. Position the insertion point immediately to the left of "TO:" in the memo heading, and press Enter. Place the insertion point in the first line of text ("MEMO"), and apply the style **Document Label**.

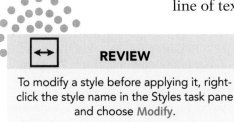

REVIEW

To modify a style before applying it, right-click the style name in the Styles task pane and choose **Modify**.

15. Apply the character style **Message Header Label** to the text "TO:," "FROM:," "DATE:," and "SUBJECT:" in the message header. (Remember, you must select text before applying a character style.) Select all four lines of the message header, and change the left tab setting to 1.5 inches to improve alignment.

16. Delete the text in the date line, and key today's date.

17. Set a 1-inch top margin and a 0.5 inch bottom margin.

18. Modify the Normal style to 12 points spacing after.

NOTE

Attaching a template replaces the template that is currently attached to the document.

19. Add your reference initials.

20. Save the document as *[your initials]*13-4 in your Lesson 13 folder.

21. Submit and close the document. If you are asked to save changes to the Professional Memo template, click **No**.

Modifying Templates

After you create a template, you can change its formatting and redefine its styles. You can also create new templates by modifying existing templates and saving them with a new name.

NOTE

Any changes you make to the formatting or text in a template affect future documents based on that template. The changes do not affect documents that were created from the template before you modified it.

Exercise 13-5 MODIFY TEMPLATE FORMATTING

1. Click the **Microsoft Office Button**, and click **Open**. From the **Files of type** drop-down list, choose **All Word Templates**.

2. Locate the folder you used to save your templates (for example, the Templates folder on your hard disk under either C:\Documents and Settings*<your name>*\ Application Data\Microsoft or your Lesson 13 folder).

3. Locate the file *[your initials]*Letterhead.

4. Double-click the file *[your initials]*Letterhead to open it. Display the Styles task pane.

5. Click the **Page Layout** tab, and click the Themes button . Change the document theme to **Flow**.

TIP

You can point to a file name to check its file type.

TIP

Opening a template through the Open dialog box opens the actual template. Double-clicking a template in Windows Explorer, My Computer, or the Templates dialog box opens a new document based on the template. Changes that you make to the new document do not affect the template.

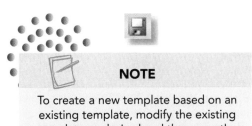

NOTE

To create a new template based on an existing template, modify the existing template as desired and then save the template with a new name.

6. Modify the Normal style font size to 12 points.

7. Click the Save button 🔲 to save the changes. The earlier version of the template is overwritten by the new version.

8. Close the template.

Using the Organizer

Instead of modifying template styles, you can copy individual styles from another document or template into the current document or template by using the Organizer. The copied styles are added to the style sheet of the current document or template. When you copy styles, remember these rules:

- Copied styles replace styles with the same style names.

- Style names are case sensitive—if you copy a style named "HEAD" into a template or document that contains a style named "head," the copied style is added to the style sheet and does not replace the existing style.

You can also copy macros by using the Organizer. To open the Organizer, display and activate the Developer tab if necessary. Click the Document Template command. Click the Organizer button ; then select the Styles tab.

Organizer...

Exercise 13-6   COPY STYLES TO ANOTHER TEMPLATE

1. Open the **New Document** dialog box, and click **Installed Templates**. Click to select the **Equity Lettter** icon, and click **Create**.

2. Save the document as a template named *[your initials]***EquityLetter** in your Lesson 13 folder. Display the Styles task panel, and notice the list of styles. Close the document.

3. Open the template *[your initials]***Letterhead** revised in Exercise 13-5.

4. Click the **Developer** tab, and click the Document Template button 🔲. Click the **Organizer** button .

5. Click the **Styles** tab in the Organizer dialog box. On the left side of the dialog box, the Organizer lists the template and styles currently in use. You use the right side of the dialog box to copy styles to or from another template.

6. Click the **Close File** button ⟨Close File⟩ on the right side of the dialog box. The Normal template closes, and the **Close File** button changes to **Open File**.

7. Click the **Open File** button ⟨Open File...⟩. In the Open dialog box, make sure **All Word Templates** appears in the **Files of type** box.

8. Locate the folder that contains the *[your initials]*EquityLetter template.

9. Double-click the *[your initials]*EquityLetter template. You can now choose styles from this template to copy into your letterhead template.

Figure 13-10
Organizer dialog box

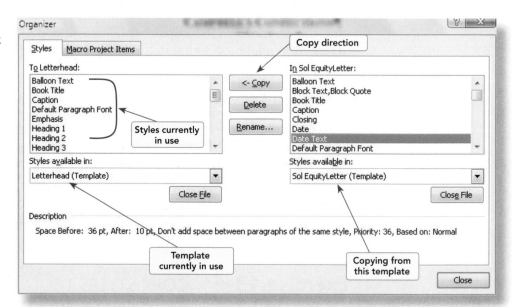

10. Scroll down the list of styles in the EquityLetter template. Click **Date Text** and click **Copy**.

11. Choose the **Normal** style from the EquityLetter style list. Notice the style description.

12. Click **Copy** and then click **Yes** to overwrite the existing style Normal.

13. Close the Organizer dialog box. The styles you chose from the EquityLetter template are copied to the current template. Notice that the Normal style from the EquityLetter template replaced the previous Normal style, so the text is formatted in Constantia 11 point with 8 points spacing after.

14. Click the Options link ⟨Options...⟩ at the bottom of the Styles task pane. Click the arrow for **Select styles to show** and select **All styles**. Click **OK**.

15. Apply the newly copied style Date Text to the date line.

16. Close the template without saving changes.

Lesson 13 Summary

- A template is a reusable model for a particular type of document. Templates can contain formatting, text, and other elements. By default, all new documents are based on the Normal template.

- Word provides a variety of templates upon which you can base a new document or a new template. You can modify any existing template and save it with a new name. You can also modify any existing document and save it as a new template.

- Every document is based on a template. You can change the template assigned to an existing document by attaching a different template to the document, thereby making the new template's styles available in the document.

- To modify a template you created, open it from the Open dialog box and choose All Word Templates from the Files of type drop-down list.

- Instead of modifying template styles, use the Organizer to copy individual styles from one document or template to another.

LESSON 13		Command Summary	
Feature	**Button**	**Command**	**Keyboard**
Use a template		Microsoft Office Button, New	
Attach template		Developer tab, Templates group, Document Template	
Copy styles		Developer tab, Templates group, Document Template, Organizer	

Concepts Review

True/False Questions

Each of the following statements is either true or false. Indicate your choice by circling T or F.

T F 1. The file extension for a Word template is .tmp.

T F 2. You can open the New Document dialog box by pressing Ctrl + N.

T F 3. After a template is assigned to a document, it cannot be changed.

T F 4. A Word template can contain placeholder text that you replace with your own information.

T F 5. When styles are copied to a template, if the style names do not match the existing styles, they are added to the style sheet.

T F 6. Existing templates cannot be modified.

T F 7. If you do not specify a template when you create a new document, the document is created without one.

T F 8. You can use the Organizer to copy styles between templates or documents.

Short Answer Questions

Write the correct answer in the space provided.

1. What is the file extension assigned to a template filename?

2. When you choose New from the Microsoft Office Button menu, what happens?

3. Which commands would you use to open the dialog box to attach a different template to a document?

4. How can you create a new template by using an existing document?

5. How can you change the styles in a template to match the styles in another template or document?

6. What is the procedure to download a template from Microsoft Office Online?

7. What is the procedure to save a template?

8. How do you change a template theme?

Critical Thinking

Answer these questions on a separate page. There are no right or wrong answers. Support your answers with examples from your own experience, if possible.

1. Review Word's templates for letters, memos, and reports. How do they compare with the standard business format for these documents as described in *The Gregg Reference Manual* (or a similar handbook)?

2. Many businesses create templates that are used by all employees for internal and external correspondence. Why would a business take this approach? What advantages does it offer to a business?

Skills Review

Exercise 13-7

Use an existing Word template to create a letter.

1. Create a letter based on a template from Microsoft Office Online by following these steps:
   a. Click the Microsoft Office Button and click New.
   b. Click Letters under Microsoft Office Online, and click Community. Locate and click the Congratulations on appointment to city council icon. Click Download. Click Continue.

2. At the top of the document, click the placeholder text for [Your Name] and key Campbell's Confections. Key the following address in the appropriate placeholders.

   25 Main Street
   Grove City, PA 16127

3. Modify the Sender Address style to 14-point bold and small caps.

4. Replace or edit the placeholder text in the document with the text shown in Figure 13-11. Click or select each placeholder before entering the appropriate text. You might want to increase the zoom when keying the last two lines.

Figure 13-11

```
Ms. Ann Foster

Vice President

Foster Travel

600 Broad Street

Grove City, PA 16127

Dear Ms. Foster:

Thank you for your willingness to participate in our local
government. This recent appointment will enable you to
continue your longstanding commitment to the community and
our civic projects.

Thomas Campbell

President
```

5. At the blank paragraph marks below the closing, add your reference initials.
6. Modify the Normal style to the font Cambria. (This changes all the styles used below the company name, which are based on the Normal style.)
7. Change the paragraph spacing for the Date style to 24 points before and 36 points after.
8. Save the document as *[your initials]*13-7 in your Lesson 13 folder.
9. Submit and close the document.

Exercise 13-8

Create a new template, attach it to another document, and modify a template.

1. Create a new template by following these steps:
   a. Open the File menu, and click New.
   b. Click My templates, and click the icon for the Blank Document template.
   c. Under Create New, click Template and click OK.
2. Modify the Normal style to be 11-point Arial.

3. Modify the Heading 1 style so the paragraph formatting is center-aligned and the font size is 18 points.

4. Modify the Heading 2 style so the paragraph formatting is center-aligned with bold and italic formatting.

5. Modify the Heading 3 style to include small caps format. (If necessary click **Options** at the bottom of the Styles task pane and click the arrow for **Select styles to show** and select **All styles**.)

6. Save the template as *[your initials]*Agenda in your Lesson 13 folder or in the default Templates folder on the hard disk, whichever your instructor told you to use. Close the template.

7. Start a new document based on the Normal template by clicking the **Microsoft Office Button** and clicking **New**. Click the Blank Document icon and click **Create**.

8. Key the text shown in Figure 13-12. Use single spacing. Apply the heading styles to the paragraphs indicated.

Figure 13-12

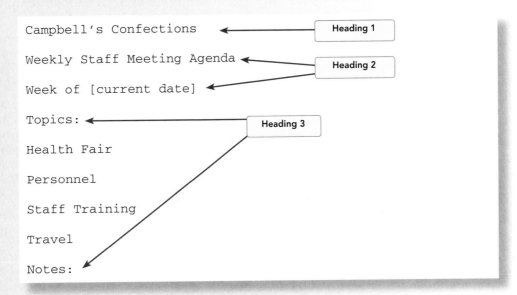

9. Attach the template you created, and automatically update the styles by following these steps:

a. Click the **Developer** tab, and click the Document Template button.

b. Click **Attach**.

c. Locate *[your initials]*Agenda and click **Open**.

d. Check the **Automatically update document styles** check box, and click **OK**.

10. Save the document as *[your initials]*13-8 in your Lesson 13 folder.

11. Submit and close the document.

Exercise 13-9

Use the Organizer to copy styles.

1. Open the New Document dialog box, and click Installed Templates. Locate and click the icon for Equity Report. Click Create.

2. Save the document template as *[your initials]*EquityReport in your Lesson 13 folder. Close the template.

3. Open the file **Company - 2**.

4. Apply the Heading 1 style to the first line (the company name). Apply the Heading 2 style to the bold side headings.

5. Display all styles by following these steps:

   a. Click Options in the Styles task pane.

   b. Click the arrow to display the drop-down list for Select styles to show.

   c. Click All styles. Click OK.

6. Use the Organizer to copy styles from another template by following these steps:

   a. Click the Developer tab and click the Document Template button ▣. Click Organizer.

   b. Click the Styles tab. Click the Close File button on the right side of the dialog box (under Normal.dot).

   c. Click the Open File button on the right side of the dialog box.

   d. Locate the folder that contains the *[your initials]*EquityReport template, and click Open.

   e. Click Normal in the list on the right side of the dialog box (under EquityReport), and then click Copy. Click Yes to overwrite the existing style entry.

   f. Repeat the previous step to copy the Footer, Heading 1, Heading 2, and Heading 3 styles from the EquityReport template on the right to the **Company - 2** document on the left. To copy the styles simultaneously, hold down Ctrl while selecting each of the styles to copy. When prompted, overwrite the existing style entries in the **Company - 2** document.

   g. Click the Close button to close the Organizer dialog box.

7. Insert page numbers at the bottom right of the document, starting with 2 on page 2.

8. Modify the paragraph spacing for the Heading 1 style to 72 points before and 24 points after.

9. Save the document as *[your initials]*13-9 in your Lesson 13 folder.

10. Submit and close the document.

Exercise 13-10

Use an online template to create a new template.

1. Open the New Document dialog box, and click Gift certificates under Microsoft Office Online.

2. Click Employee gift certificate, and download the template. Save the template as *[your initials]*Gift in your Lesson 13 folder or in the default Templates folder on the hard disk, whichever your instructor told you to use.

3. Key Campbell's Confections in the [Company Name or Logo] placeholder for each gift certificate.

4. Key $25 Gift Certificate in the [Gift Name] placeholder for the first gift certificate. Key $50 Gift Certificate for the second certificate and $75 Gift Certificate for the third certificate.

5. Modify the Heading 1 style by changing the font color to black and applying bold and small caps formatting.

6. Modify the giftname style by changing the font color to black and applying small caps.

7. Use the replace command to modify the gift certificates. Change Group to Store. Change Department/Account to Certificate Number.

8. Save the template.

9. Submit and close the template.

Lesson Applications

Exercise 13-11

Use a template to create a document.

1. Create a document based on the template you created: *[your initials]*Letterhead.

2. Key the following information for the inside address:

   Ms. Barbara Scott
   National Fitness Center
   1237 West Main Street
   Grove City, PA 16127

3. Key Dear Ms. Scott for the salutation.

4. Open the file **Fitness**. Copy all the text and paste it into the letter.

5. Add as a closing paragraph.

   Thank you for your assistance. I will call for an appointment to discuss a formal agreement.

6. Key an appropriate complimentary closing and the following signature name and title:

   Garland Miller
   Human Resources

7. On the next line, key your reference initials followed by an enclosure notation.

8. Modify the Normal style by changing the font to Cambria.

9. Spell-check the document, and save it as *[your initials]*13-11 in your Lesson 13 folder.

10. Submit the document. Close both open documents.

Exercise 13-12

Use a template and copy styles by using the Organizer.

1. Start a new document based on the template you created: *[your initials]*Memo.

2. The memo is to "All Employees" from Garland Miller. The subject is "Fitness Center Membership."

3. Two blank lines below the subject line, key the text from Figure 13-13

Figure 13-13

```
Campbell's Confections is contacting area fitness centers to
negotiate a contract to provide lower membership fees for
our employees.

Please complete the attached survey so that we can determine
which programs you prefer as well as your preferences for
hours of operation, types of membership, and payment plans.

Please return the completed survey by Friday.
```

4. Open the Organizer dialog box by displaying the Developer tab, and clicking Document Template. Click Organizer. On the right side of the dialog box, close the Normal template file and open *[your initials]*ProMemo template.

5. Copy the styles Company Name, Normal, Message Header First, Message Header Label, and Message Header Last to the current document, replacing the Normal style entry when prompted. Close the Organizer dialog box.

6. Insert a new paragraph mark above the "TO:" line. At the new paragraph mark, key Campbell's Confections and apply the Company Name style.

7. Modify the Company Name style by changing the font size to 24 points and adding 24 points spacing after. Change the line spacing to At least 12 pt. Change the top margin to 1 inch.

8. Key your reference initials at the end of the document.

9. Modify the Normal style by increasing the font size to 12 points.

10. Save the document as *[your initials]*13-12 in your Lesson 13 folder.

11. Submit and close the document.

Exercise 13-13

Modify a template and attach a template.

1. Open the template you created: *[your initials]*Letterhead. (Use the Open dialog box—do not create a document based on this template.)

2. Modify the Normal style to a 12-point font of your choice.

3. Save the template as *[your initials]*Letterhead2 in the folder where you saved the other templates. Close the template.

4. Open the file **Hernandez**.

5. Attach the template *[your initials]*letterhead2, updating document styles automatically.

6. Key the date at the top of the document followed by three blank lines.

7. Add your reference initials and an enclosure notation.

8. Set a 2-inch top margin. Add blank lines between paragraphs to format the document as a business letter.

9. Save the document as *[your initials]*13-13 in your Lesson 13 folder.

10. Submit and close the document.

Exercise 13-14 ◆ Challenge Yourself

Copy and apply styles.

1. Open the template file **Equity Fax** (Installed Templates).

2. Use the Organizer dialog box to copy all styles from the Origin Fax template (Installed Templates) to the Equity Fax template. (Remember: to select all styles, click the first file, scroll to the last file, press Shift and click.)

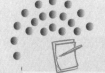

NOTE

To locate the Origin Fax template, change to the folder that contains the installed Word Templates (Program Files\Microsoft Office\Templates\1033\Fax).

3. Click **Yes** to overwrite the styles, and close the dialog box.

4. Open the Styles task pane.

5. Select "To:" in the heading, and apply the Message Header style.

6. Apply the Message Header style to all headings in the Equity Fax template.

7. Save the template as *[your initials]*13-14 in your Lesson 13 folder.

8. Submit and close the document.

On Your Own

In these exercises you work on your own, as you would in a real-life business environment. Use the skills you've learned to accomplish the task—and be creative.

Exercise 13-15

Use a résumé template to create your résumé. Include as much detail about yourself as possible. Modify the formatting as needed. Save the document as *[your initials]*13-15 and submit it.

Exercise 13-16

Create a cover letter for your résumé, using a matching template style. Address the cover letter to a prospective employer. Create an envelope for the letter. Save the document as *[your initials]*13-16 and submit it.

Exercise 13-17

Using the New Document dialog box, go to Microsoft Office Online and choose a template from any category. Preview and download the template, and then edit it in Word, using your own information. Save the document as *[your initials]*13-17 and submit it.

Unit 3 Applications

Unit Application 3-1

Create a cover letter for a document as a separate section; insert a page break and a continuation page header.

1. Open the file **Assortment**.

2. Add a blank page to the beginning of the document (use a section break to separate the cover letter from the **Assortment** document). To create the cover letter, key the text shown in Figure U3-1, including the corrections on page 1 of the document. Use the standard letter format. The letter should be from Richard Matthews, Wholesale Sales Division. Include your reference initials and an enclosure notation.

Figure U3-1

Mr. Patrick O'Reilly

Village Center

226 Pierce Avenue

Sharpsville, PA 16150

Dear Mr. O'Reilly:

As you requested, enclosed is the information about our wholesale division.

Campbell's Confections entered the wholesale market during the mid 1990s. A contract was negotiated with a large hotel chain to provide *boxed* chocolates for the *gift* stores. A second contract was approved ~~in 1997~~ with the Pittsburgh Airport.

Wholesale contracts are only negotiated with business*es* that can provide *multiple* locations for our chocolates. Wholesale prices are based on a minimum order of $570. *the* wholesale agreements also stipulate the proper conditions for storing and displaying Campbell's Chocolates.

Initial chocolate offerings for the wholesale market include as*s*orte*d* chocolate covered nuts (milk and dark chocolate), assorted chocolate covered creams (milk and dark chocolate), and assorted melt-a-ways (milk and dark chocolate). Sugar-free chocolates and chocolate bars are also available.

Let me know if you have any questions. I look forward to speaking with you soon.

3. Change the top margin for section 1 to 2 inches.

4. Create a right-aligned footer for section 2. The text should include the text Updated followed by today's date inserted as a field that is automatically updated.

5. In section 2, delete blank paragraphs, and center the text vertically.

6. Select the bulleted list for each category on the page, and sort the text alphabetically.

7. Spell-check the letter only.

8. Change the first heading in section 2 to all caps, and center the heading.

9. Save the document as *[your initials]*u3-1 in a new folder for Unit 3 Applications.

10. Submit and close the document.

Unit Application 3-2

Create a memo; change page orientation; apply section formatting.

1. Open the file **Emboss**. Format the document as a memo to "Store Managers" from Robert Smith. Use the current date, and the subject is "New Products."

2. Add a Next Page section break at the end of the document, and key the text shown in Figure U3-2. Set a left-aligned tab for the text in each column under "Sample Letters." Use the Symbol dialog box (Symbol font) to insert the Greek letters.

Figure U3-2

```
Campbell's Confections

announces

Chocolate Embossing:

Greek Alphabet

Mascots

Sample Letters:

Alpha        A

Beta         B

Gamma        Γ

Delta        Δ

Epsilon      E
```

3. Change the top margin for section 1 to 2 inches. Key your reference initials and an attachment notation at the end of section 1.

4. Format section 2 with landscape orientation and centered vertically. Center the first six lines.

5. Open the Styles task pane, and modify the Heading 1 style for center alignment, 18 points, and small caps. Modify Heading 2 style for center alignment, 16 points spacing after, and 14-point small caps.

6. Select "Chocolate Embossing" through "Sample Letters," and apply 14-point bold and italic formatting.

7. Apply the Heading 1 style to the first line of section 2, and apply the Heading 2 style to the second line of section 2.

8. Format "Sample Letters" to have 24 points spacing before and small caps formatting.

9. Select the text from "Sample Letters" through "E," and apply 1-inch left and right indents, 18-point font size, and a $2^1/_4$ pt box border with 10 percent gray shading.

10. Add a double-line page border to section 2.

11. Preview the document, and then save it as *[your initials]*u3-2 in your Unit 3 Applications folder.

12. Submit and close the document.

Unit Application 3-3

Create a new template, create and apply paragraph and character styles, modify styles, and use style options.

1. Create a new document based on the default template. Change the left and right margins to 1.25 inches.

2. Key the title Campbell's Confections, and press Enter. Center the title, and change the font size to 20 points and apply small caps.

3. Key Holiday Update and press Enter two times.

4. Create a paragraph style named Subhead that is 14-point Arial, all caps, and centered, and apply it to the second line of text.

5. At the last paragraph mark, key Chocolate Events. Create and apply a paragraph style for this text based on the Normal style and named UpdateHead. Use 12-point Arial bold with all caps.

6. Save the document as a template named *[your initials]*update in your Unit 3 Applications folder or in the default Templates folder on the hard disk, whichever your instructor tells you to use. Close the template.

7. Start a new document based on the template *[your initials]*update.

8. Replace the words "CHOCOLATE EVENTS" with the current year.

9. One line below "200-," key Akron, Ohio, and apply the Normal style.

10. To the right of "Akron, OH," insert a tab character and key January 3.

11. To this line of text, create and apply a paragraph style named CityName using 12-point Arial bold with a 3-inch left tab setting.

12. Create a paragraph style named IndentedPara based on the CityName style, using 12-point Arial regular, with 12 points spacing after paragraphs and a 3-inch hanging indent.

13. Assign Indentedpara as the style for the paragraph following CityName.

14. Assign CityName as the style for the paragraph following Indentedpara.

15. Create a character style named EventDate using 11-point Arial bold italic, and apply it to the text "January 3."

16. Press Enter after "3," press Tab, and key National Chocolate-Covered Cherry Day.

17. Press Enter and key the text shown in Figure U3-3. Press Tab before each date and before each description. Apply the EventDate style to all the date text.

Figure U3-3

```
Clarksburg, WV        February 19
                      Chocolate Mint Day

Grove City, PA        March—Third Week
                      American Chocolate Week

Canton, OH            April 21
                      National Chocolate-Covered Cashews Day

Morgantown, WV        May 15
                      National Chocolate Chip Day

Monroeville, PA       June
                      National Candy Month

Youngstown, OH        July 7
                      Chocolate Day

Fairmont, WV          September 22
                      National White Chocolate Day

Butler, PA            October 28
                      National Chocolate Day
```

18. Modify the CityName style to 11 points.

19. Align the entire document vertically on the page.

20. Spell-check the document, and save it as *[your initials]*u3-3 in your folder for Unit 3 Applications.

21. Submit and close the document.

Unit Application 3-4 ◆ Using the Internet

Work with sections, page numbers, and headers and footers.

1. Using the Internet, research the history of chocolate.

2. Create a 3- to 5-page report, and organize the document into sections.

3. Include the following topics and create sections for each topic:

   - A timeline of the history of chocolate—include a brief description of major events for each century.

   - Mention Columbus, Aztecs, Mayas, and European influence.

   - Major producers of cacao pods.

   - Create a title page for the document as a separate section.

   - Title each subsequent section of the document.

   - Check pagination, and apply line and page break options where needed.

   - Include appropriate headers/footers and page numbering on all pages except the title page.

4. Save the document as *[your initials]*u3-4 in your Unit 3 Applications folder, and submit it.

unit 4

TABLES AND COLUMNS

OBJECTIVES

After completing this lesson, you will be able to:

1. Insert a table.

2. Key and edit text in tables.

3. Select cells, rows, and columns.

4. Edit table structures.

5. Format tables and cell contents.

6. Convert tables and text.

MCAS OBJECTIVES

In this lesson:
WW 07 4.2.1
WW 07 4.2.2
WW 07 4.3.1
WW 07 4.3.2
WW 07 4.3.3
WW 07 4.3.5

Estimated Time: 1¹/₂ hours

A *table* is a grid of rows and columns that intersect to form *cells*. The lines that mark the cell boundaries are called *gridlines*. It is often easier to read or present information in table format than in paragraph format. Using Word's table feature, you can create a table and insert text, pictures, and other types of data into the table's cells.

Inserting a Table

There are three ways to insert a table:

- Insert a table by using the Insert Table menu.

- Insert a table by using the Insert Table command.

- Insert a table by using a table template.

You can also create a table by drawing cells and columns or converting text to tables. These methods are discussed later in the lesson.

Figure 14-1
Columns, rows, and
cells in a table

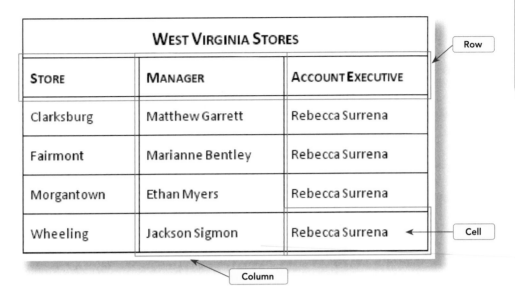

WEST VIRGINIA STORES		
STORE	MANAGER	ACCOUNT EXECUTIVE
Clarksburg	Matthew Garrett	Rebecca Surrena
Fairmont	Marianne Bentley	Rebecca Surrena
Morgantown	Ethan Myers	Rebecca Surrena
Wheeling	Jackson Sigmon	Rebecca Surrena

Row

Cell

Column

NOTE

You can apply formatting options, such as borders and shading, to tables. You can also display tables without gridlines.

Exercise 14-1 INSERT A TABLE

Use the Insert Table menu or the Insert Table command to create a table with the number of rows and columns you specify.

- Use the Table command on the Ribbon, Insert tab to display an adjustable grid.

- Use the Insert Table dialog box, which is accessed by clicking the Table button on the Ribbon, Insert group.

1. Open the file **Shipping**. Enter today's date in the memo date line.

2. Position the insertion point at the end of the document.

3. Click the Insert tab, and click the Table button . A grid containing columns and rows appears below the button.

4. Position the pointer in the upper left cell of the grid. Drag the pointer across to highlight four columns, and then drag the pointer down past the bottom of the grid to highlight five rows. The table dimensions are highlighted in the grid, and a table displays in the document.

NOTE

The documents you create in this course relate to the case study about Campbell's Confections, a fictional candy store and chocolate factory. (See Case Study in the frontmatter of the book).

Figure 14-2
Specifying table dimensions with the table grid

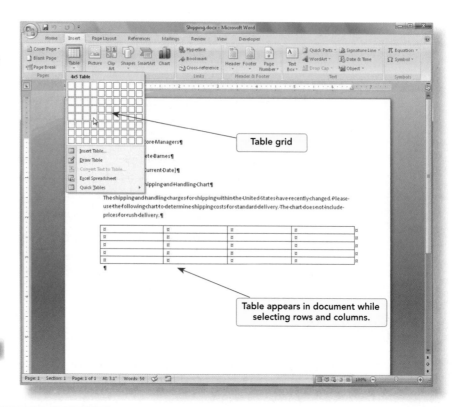

Table grid

Table appears in document while selecting rows and columns.

NOTE

When you create a table, each gridline automatically has a 0.5-point black border that is printed. You can remove borders by clicking the arrow beside the Borders command and choosing No Border. You can also open the Borders and Shading dialog box, display the Borders tab, and choose None under Setting. Gray table gridlines appear on-screen only and not in the printed document.

5. Release the mouse button. A 5-row by 4-column table appears with the insertion point in the first cell. Each column is the same width, and the table extends from the left to the right margin. Notice the markers on the ruler that indicate the column widths.

6. Click the Undo button 🔄 to undo the table. You will now try a second method for inserting a table.

7. Click the **Insert** tab, and then click **Table**. Click the **Insert Table** command that appears below the grid. The Insert Table dialog box appears.

Figure 14-3
Insert Table dialog box

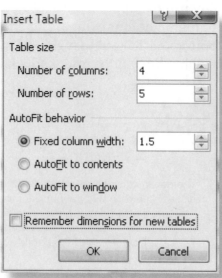

8. Key **4** in the **Number of columns** text box and **5** in the **Number of rows** text box. You can also click the up or down arrows to the right of these boxes.

9. In the **Fixed column width** text box, change the default (**Auto**) to **1.5″** and click **OK**. Word inserts a 4 × 5 table with 1.5-inch columns. The insertion point is positioned in the first cell, and the table is left-aligned.

Exercise 14-2 DRAW A TABLE

You can draw a table in your document by using the Draw Table command, which is located on the Table menu. When you create a table, the Ribbon displays **Table Tools** when the insertion point is located in a table. Table Tools includes two tabs: **Design** and **Layout**.

TABLE 14-1 Table Tools: Design Tab

Button	Purpose
	Table Style Options Group
☑ Header Row	Displays formatting for the first row of the table.
☐ Total Row	Displays formatting for the last row of the table.
☑ Banded Rows	Displays formatting for even and odd rows.
☑ First Column	Displays formatting for the first column of the table.
☐ Last Column	Displays formatting for the last column of the table.
☐ Banded Columns	Displays formatting for even and odd columns.
	Table Styles Group
	Displays built-in styles for tables.
Shading ▾	Displays shading colors for cell background.
Borders ▾	Displays border options.
	Draw Borders Group
─── ▾	Changes a border style.
½ pt ─── ▾	Changes the width of a border.
Pen Color ▾	Changes the pen color.
Draw Table	Draws a freehand table.
Eraser	Erases the borders of a table.

1. Click the **Insert** tab, and click the Table button . Click the **Draw Table** command in the Table menu, and the pointer changes to a pencil shape ✏.

2. Position the pencil pointer at the last paragraph mark below the current table. Drag diagonally down to draw a rectangle about the same size as the current table. As you drag, the pointer creates a dotted rectangle. Release the mouse button.

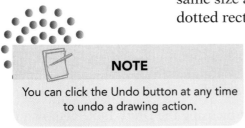

NOTE

You can click the Undo button at any time to undo a drawing action.

3. After drawing the outside border of the table, draw three vertical lines in the table to create four columns (just as in the other table).

Figure 14-4
Drawing a table

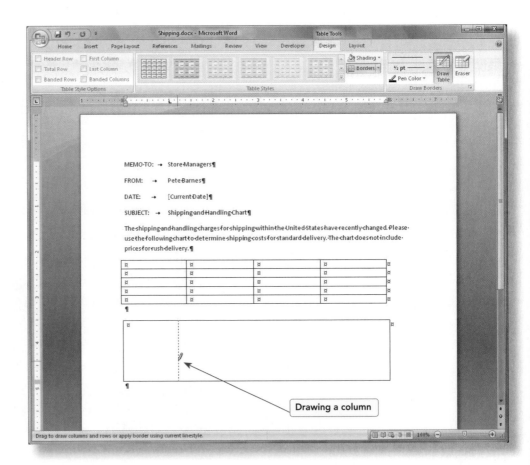

4. Draw four horizontal lines, creating five rows. Don't worry about creating perfectly spaced rows or columns—you will space them evenly later in the lesson.

Figure 14-5
Adding rows

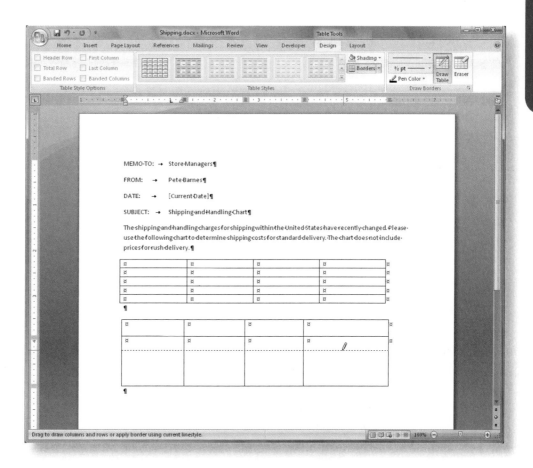

Eraser

5. Click the Eraser button 🖹 on the Ribbon, and drag the eraser pointer ⌀ across one of the row lines you drew. Release the mouse button.

6. Click the Undo button ↺ to restore the line.

7. Press Esc or click the Eraser button 🖹 to restore the normal pointer.

Exercise 14-3 INSERT A TABLE USING A TABLE TEMPLATE

You can insert a preformatted table by selecting a design from the Built-In table gallery. Each of the designs contains sample data that you replace with your own text.

1. Press Ctrl+N to start a new document. Leave the Shipping document open.

2. Click the **Insert** tab, and click the Table button 🖽. Click the **Quick Tables** command in the Table menu, to display the Built-In table designs.

3. Click the **Calendar 4** design.

Figure 14-6
Quick tables

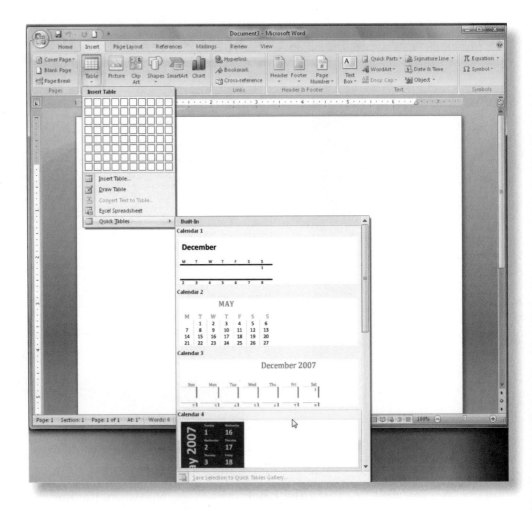

4. Notice the layout and format of the design. The font, font size, and other elements can be customized.

5. Close the document without saving it.

Keying and Editing Text in Tables

Keying and editing text in tables is similar to working with text in paragraphs. But if you key text in a cell and press Enter, a new paragraph is created within the same cell.

To move the insertion point to different cells in a table, use the mouse, the arrow keys, or the keyboard shortcuts in Table 14-2.

TABLE 14-2 Shortcuts for Moving between Cells.

Movement	Press
Next cell	[Tab]
Previous cell	[Shift]+[Tab]
First cell in the current row	[Alt]+[Home]
Last cell in the current row	[Alt]+[End]
Top cell in the current column	[Alt]+[PageUp]
Last cell in the current column	[Alt]+[PageDown]

Exercise 14-4 KEY AND EDIT TEXT IN A TABLE

1. In the first table of the Shipping document, position the insertion point in the first cell and key **Up to 1 pound**.

2. Press [Tab] and key **$7.25** in the next cell. Press [Tab] and key **Up to 1 pound**. Press [Tab] and key **$12.00**. A *header row* is the first row of a table (or the second row, if the table has a title row). Each cell contains a heading for the column of text beneath it and will be added in a later exercise.

3. Press [Tab] to go to the first cell of the second row, and key **2 pounds**.

4. Press [Tab] or [→] to go to the next cell, and key **7.90**. Go to the next cell, key **2 pounds**, press [Tab], and key **12.40**.

5. Key the text shown in Figure 14-7 in the remaining rows of the table, inserting each word or number into a different cell. Remember not to press [Enter].

Figure 14-7

3 pounds	8.25	3 pounds	12.75
4 pounds	8.75	4 pounds	12.75
5 pounds	9.00	5 pounds	13.75

6. Press [Alt]+[Home] to move to the first cell in the last row, and [Shift]+[Tab] to move to the fourth cell in the previous row. Change "12.75" to **13.25**.

Selecting Cells, Rows, and Columns

There are several ways to select the contents of cells, rows, and columns. You can delete, copy, or move the contents or change the format of selected cells, rows, or columns.

To help with selection, *end-of-cell markers* ¤ indicate the end of each cell. In addition, *end-of-row markers* ¤ to the right of the gridline of each row indicate the end of each row.

Exercise 14-5 SELECT CELLS

1. Click the Show/Hide ¶ button ⚟ to display the end-of-cell markers, if nonprinting characters are not visible.

2. To select the first cell in the first table, position the pointer just inside the left edge of the cell (between the cell's left border and the letter "U"). When the pointer becomes a solid black, right-pointing arrow ▸, click to select the cell.

Figure 14-8
Selecting a cell

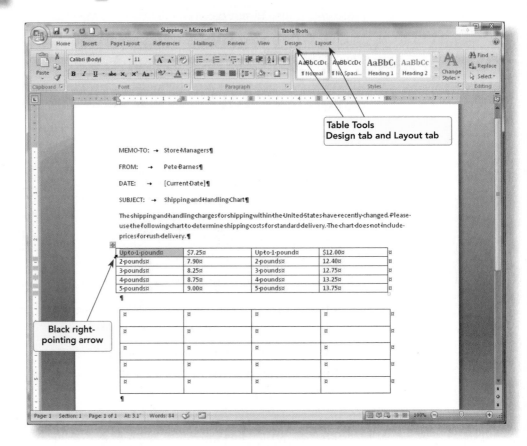

3. Next, using the I-beam pointer, drag over the text "12.75" in the third row. Notice that the text is highlighted, but the end-of-cell marker is not.

4. Press ⟨Tab⟩ to move to the next cell. Again, the text in the cell is highlighted, but the end-of-cell marker is not.

5. Using the I-beam pointer, triple-click within any cell to select the entire cell.

Exercise 14-6 SELECT ROWS, COLUMNS, AND TABLES

1. In the first table, point to the left of the fourth row. When you see the white right-pointing arrow ⟋, click to select the row.

Figure 14-9
Selecting a row

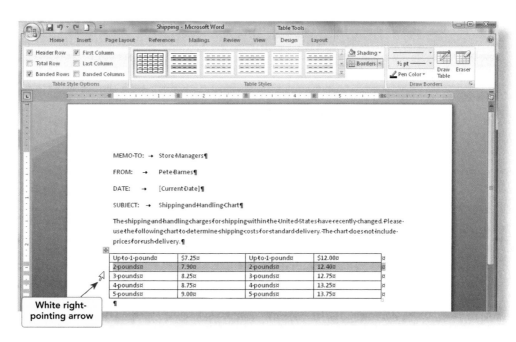

White right-
pointing arrow

2. Point just inside the left border of any cell in the previous row, and double-click. That row is selected.

3. Position the insertion point anywhere in "4 pounds" in the fourth row. Click the **Layout** tab of **Table Tools**, and click the arrow beside the Select button . Click **Select Row**. The fourth row is selected again.

4. Point to the left of the third row, and drag the pointer down one row to select both the third and fourth rows.

5. Point to the top border of the third column. When the pointer changes to a solid black down arrow ↓, click to select the column.

Figure 14-10
Selecting a column

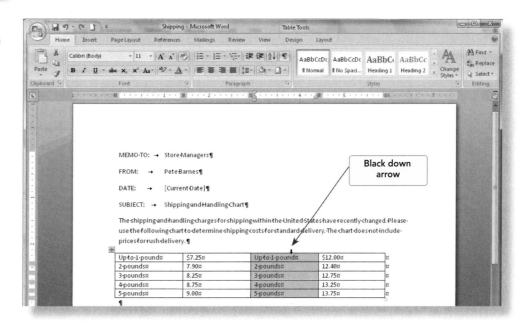

Black down
arrow

6. Position the insertion point to the immediate left of "$7.25" in the second column. Drag down through "9.00" to select column 2.

7. Point to the top of column 2, and drag the black arrow pointer across to select columns 2 and 3. Click anywhere in the table to deselect the columns.

8. With the insertion point anywhere in the table, click the **Layout** tab of **Table Tools**. Click the arrow beside the Select button 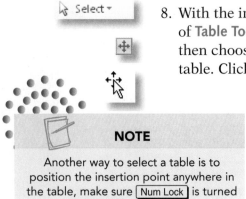 and then choose **Select Table** from the drop-down list to select the entire table. Click anywhere in the table to deselect it.

9. Move the I-beam over the table until the table move handle ⊞ appears at the top left of the table.

10. Move the I-beam over the handle. When the I-beam changes to a four-headed arrow pointer ⊹, click to select the table.

11. Click anywhere in the table to deselect it.

> **NOTE**
>
> Another way to select a table is to position the insertion point anywhere in the table, make sure Num Lock is turned off, and press Alt + 5 on the numeric keypad.

TABLE 14-3 Selecting Table Elements

Selecting	Mouse	Command	Keyboard
Cell	Click left inside edge of cell.	Table Tools, Layout tab, Select	Shift + End
Row	Click to the left of the row, *or* double-click left inside edge of a cell.	Table Tools, Layout tab, Select	
Column	Click column's top border.	Table Tools, Layout tab, Select	
Table	Click table move handle in Print Layout view.	Table Tools, Layout tab, Select	Alt + 5 (Numeric keypad)

Editing Table Structures

In addition to editing the contents of a table, you can edit a table's structure. You can add, delete, move, and copy cells, rows, and columns. You can also merge and split cells or change a table's position or dimensions.

To modify tables, you can use the Table Tools (Layout tab on the Ribbon) or the shortcut menu.

Exercise 14-7   INSERT CELLS, ROWS, AND COLUMNS

1. Display the Table Tools Layout tab on the Ribbon.

2. Select the first cell in the first row of the first table.

3. Click the Rows and Columns Dialog Box Launcher. The Insert Cells dialog box opens.

4. Click Shift cells right and click OK. Word inserts a new cell and shifts the other cells in row 1 to the right.

NOTE

To insert cells, position the insertion point in a cell that is to the right of or below where you want to insert a cell.

5. Click the Undo button .

6. Drag the insertion point from "Up to 1 pound" in the first cell through "7.90" in the second column. Click the Rows and Columns Dialog Box Launcher.

7. Click Shift cells down, if it is not already selected. Click OK. Four new cells appear above the selected cells. Deselect the text.

Figure 14-11
Insert Cells dialog box

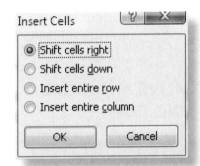

8. Select the first row. Click the Insert Above button on the Table Tools Layout tab. A new row appears at the top of the table.

9. Select the second row. Click the Insert Below button . A new row appears below the selected row.

10. Click the Undo button .

11. Select the second column of the first table. Click the Insert Left button on the Table Tools Layout tab. The new column appears to the left of the selected column.

TIP

When the insertion point is in the last cell of the last row, pressing Tab inserts a row below the current last row.

12. Select the third column. Click the Insert Right button on the Table Tools Layout tab. A new column appears to the right of the selected column.

13. Click the Undo button .

TIP

When just the end-of-row markers are selected, you can click the Insert Right command from the Table Tools Layout tab to extend the table to the right.

Exercise 14-8   DELETE CELLS, ROWS, AND COLUMNS

Deleting cells, rows, and columns is different from deleting text (selecting text and pressing Delete). You must first select the table structure you wish to delete and then choose Delete from the Table Tools Layout tab.

1. In the first table, select the blank cells in the third and fourth rows. Locate the **Rows and Columns** group, and click the Delete button . Click **Delete Cells**. The Delete Cells dialog box opens.

2. Click **Shift cells up**. Click **OK** and the blank cells disappear.

Figure 14-12
Delete Cells dialog box

3. Select the blank rows at the bottom of the first table. Click the Delete button and then choose **Rows**. The blank rows are deleted.

4. Select the second column (which is blank). Right-click the column, and choose **Delete Columns** from the shortcut menu. Only the top row of your table is now blank.

Exercise 14-9 MOVE AND COPY CELLS, ROWS, AND COLUMNS

In addition to using the Ribbon and the shortcut menu, you can also use keyboard shortcuts to cut, copy, and paste.

1. Select the row that begins "Up to 1 pound."

2. Point to the first selected cell in the row. When you see a left-pointing arrow, drag and drop the selection into the empty row above. The text now appears in the first row.

3. Select the row that begins "2 pounds," but not its end-of-row marker.

4. Click the **Home** tab, and click the Cut button . The text is deleted, but the empty row remains.

5. Position the insertion point in the first cell of the second row. Press Ctrl+V to paste the text.

6. Select the bottom three cells in the fourth column, and copy them to the Clipboard.

7. Click within the cell containing "8.25" and paste the text. The pasted cells overwrite the previous text.

NOTE

If you paste text somewhere on the table where there is not enough room for all the cells, Word adds additional columns or rows to accommodate the text.

8. Undo the Paste command.

9. Select the blank row and right-click. Click **Delete Rows**.

Exercise 14-10 MERGE AND SPLIT CELLS

1. Select the first two rows of the table. Click the Table Tools Layout tab, and click Insert Above 📋. Two rows are added to the table.

2. Select the first row of blank cells in the table. Click the Merge Cells button 📋 on the Table Tools Layout tab. The cells in the first row merge into a single cell.

3. Key the table title Shipping and Handling Weight Chart in the first row.

4. Select the second row of blank cells, and click the Merge Cells button 📋. The cells in the row merge into a single cell. Once you merge a row of cells, you can undo the merge or use the split cells command.

Figure 14-13
Split Cells dialog box

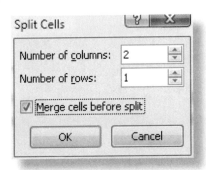

5. Select the second row which is now one cell, and click the Split Cells button 📋. The Split Cells dialog box displays.

6. Key 2 in the Number of columns text box, and verify that "1" appears in the Number of rows text box. Click OK. The row is split into two cells.

7. Key the title Without Ice Pack in the first cell, and key With Ice Pack in the second cell.

Exercise 14-11 CHANGE TABLE DIMENSIONS AND POSITION TABLES

You can adjust and position a table in the following ways:

- Change the width of columns, the space between columns, and the height of rows.

- Use AutoFit to change the width of a column to fit the longest text.

- Indent a table or center it horizontally on the page.

NOTE

You can also select a table by positioning the insertion point in any cell and clicking Select from the Table Tools Layout tab, or positioning the insertion point in any cell and pressing [Alt]+[5] on the numeric keypad with [Num Lock] turned off.

1. Select the second table by clicking the table move handle ⊞.

2. Click the Table Tools Layout tab if necessary, and click the Properties button . Click the Column tab in the Table Properties dialog box.

Figure 14-14
Table Properties
dialog box

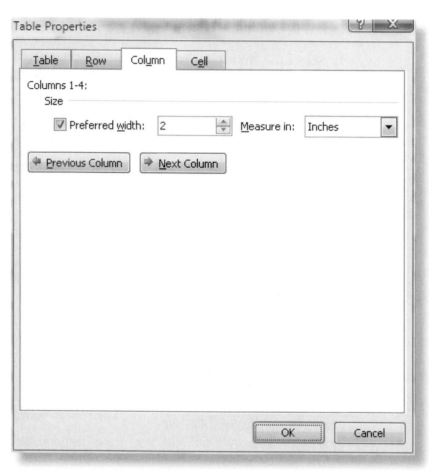

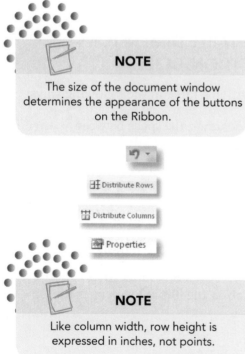

NOTE

The size of the document window determines the appearance of the buttons on the Ribbon.

NOTE

Like column width, row height is expressed in inches, not points.

3. Click **Preferred width** and key **2** in the text box. Click **OK**. The columns are now 2 inches wide.

4. Click the Undo button .

5. With the second table selected and using the **Table Tools Layout** tab, click the Distribute Rows button . Then click the Distribute Columns button . The hand-drawn rows and columns are now evenly spaced.

6. Select the first table. Click the **Table Tools Layout** tab if necessary, and click the Properties button . Click the **Row** tab.

7. Click **Specify height** and key **0.4** in the text box. Choose **At least** from the **Row height is** drop-down list, if it is not already selected.

8. Click the **Table** tab in the Table Properties dialog box. Under **Alignment**, choose **Center** and click **OK**. The table is centered horizontally on the page and the row heights are taller.

9. Deselect the table, and position the pointer on the right border of the last column until it changes to a vertical double bar for resizing .

TIP

When a table appears on a page by itself, center it vertically and horizontally. Use the Layout tab in the Page Setup dialog box to choose vertical alignment.

Figure 14-15
Dragging a table border

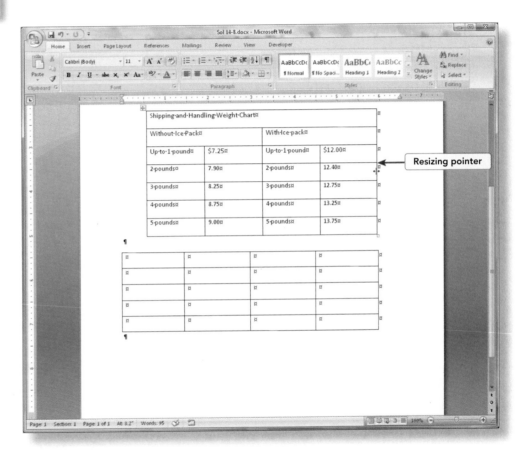

10. Drag the border 0.5 inch to the right to widen the column. (Hold down [Alt] as you drag to see the exact ruler measurements.)

11. Click the Undo button and position the pointer on the right border of the cell containing "8.25." Drag 0.5 inch to the right. The second column is wider, but the last column is now narrower.

12. Click the Undo button . Hold down [Shift] and drag the second column border 0.5 inch to the right again. The second column is now wider, and the last column remains the same width. Click the Undo button .

NOTE

As long as the cell is not selected, dragging the right border adjusts the entire column width, not just the cell width.

13. Double-click the right border of the second column. The column is adjusted to the width of the widest cell entry.

14. Click anywhere in rows 3 through 5 of the first table.

15. On the ruler, point to the right column marker for the second column. When you see the ScreenTip "Move Table Column," drag the marker a short distance to the right and then release the mouse button.

Figure 14-16
Dragging a column marker

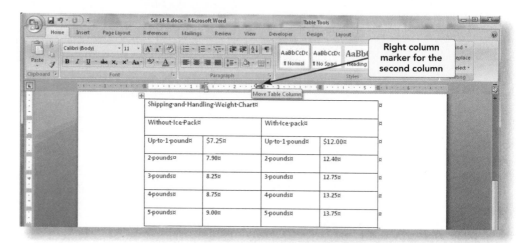

16. Hold down [Alt] and drag the marker until the ruler measurement for the second column is 1.2 inches.

17. Use the same technique to adjust the other column widths to 1.2 inches. Each table column is now 1.2 inches wide, and the merged row adjusts to the new table width.

Exercise 14-12   RESIZE A TABLE PROPORTIONATELY

The table resize handle in the lower right corner of a table provides a convenient way to resize a table proportionately. When you drag the handle to the left, each column becomes proportionately narrower. When you drag the handle to the right, each column becomes proportionately wider. If needed, word wrapping will occur to fit a cell's contents into a narrower column.

1. Click anywhere inside table 2, and let the mouse pointer rest on the table. The table resize handle appears below the lower right corner of the table.

2. Point to the table resize handle. The mouse pointer changes to a two-pointed diagonal arrow. Drag the table resize handle to the left until the dotted box's right border is even with the 4.5-inch marker on the horizontal ruler. Release the mouse button. The table columns are now narrower.

Figure 14-17
Resizing a table

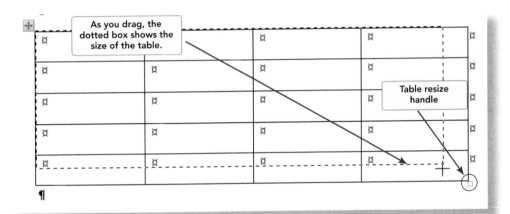

Formatting Tables and Cell Contents

There are many ways to make a table more attractive and easier to read. For example, you can:

- Format table text.

- Align text horizontally within columns.

- Align text vertically within cells or rows.

- Apply borders and shading.

- Use Table Styles to apply a predesigned table style.

- Rotate the direction of text from horizontal to vertical.

- Sort table text.

TIP

The default alignment for text in a table cell is top left. Text can be positioned vertically at the top, bottom, or center of the cell. Text can be positioned horizontally at the left, center, or right of the cell.

TIP

When a column contains all text, it should be left-aligned. When it contains all numbers, it should be right-aligned.

TIP

To change the vertical alignment of a large group of cells without affecting the horizontal alignments in each cell (left, right, or center), choose Properties from the Table Tools Layout tab. Click the Cell tab. Under Vertical alignment, click Center to vertically center the text in every cell.

Exercise 14-13   FORMAT TABLE TEXT

1. Select the table title in the first row of the first table, and format it as centered, bold, 14 points, and small caps.

2. Select row 2 and apply bold formatting. With the row selected, click the **Table Tools Layout** tab, and locate the **Alignment** group. Click the Align Center button ▤ to align the text horizontally and vertically in the cell.

3. Select "Up to 1 pound" in the first column and the cells below it. Click the Align Center Left button ▤ on the Ribbon to left-align the text horizontally and center the text vertically.

4. Select "Up to 1 pound" in the third column and the cells below it, and format the text using the Align Center Left button ▤.

5. Click within the title in the first row, and then click the Align Center button ▤ on the Ribbon to center the text vertically.

6. Select "$7.25" and the cells below it. Click the Align Center Right button ▤ to right-align the text and vertically center it within the selected cells.

7. Select "$12.00" and the cells below it. Click the Align Center Right button ▤ to right-align the text and vertically center it within the selected cells.

8. Format the second row as italic.

Exercise 14-14   SORT TABLE TEXT

You can sort a table by any of its columns. Sorting means arranging items in a particular order. When you sort items in a table, you select a sort order in either ascending (A to Z or 0 to 9) or descending order (Z to A or 9 to 0). When sorting a table, you do not need to select the entire table. The contents of an entire row always sort together unless you specifically choose to sort only one column. If the beginning row or rows of a table have been defined as header rows, they automatically stay at the top of the table after sorting.

1. Select rows 3 (the text below the header row) through 7 of the first table.

2. From the **Table Tools Layout** tab, click **Sort**. 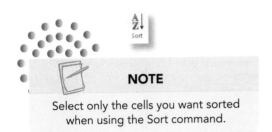 Choose **Column 1** from the **Sort by** drop-down list, choose **Text** from the **Type** drop-down list, and click **Descending**.

3. Click **OK** to sort the rows alphabetically in descending order.

4. Click Undo .

NOTE

Select only the cells you want sorted when using the Sort command.

NOTE

Selecting black shading creates reverse text. *Reverse text* displays white text on a black background, which is the opposite of black type on a white background.

Exercise 14-15 APPLY BORDERS AND SHADING

You can increase the attractiveness of your table by adding borders and shading. It is important to choose appropriate line color, line style, and shading options so that text is easy to read and to ensure an attractive document.

1. Select the first row (the title). Click the **Table Tools Design** tab, click the arrow next to the Shading button , and click **Black** on the palette (the first color in the second column).

2. Select the entire table.

3. Click the Line Style button 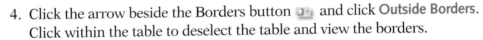 and select a double-line border. Click the Line Weight button 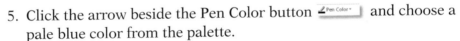 and click $\frac{1}{2}$-point weight.

4. Click the arrow beside the Borders button  and click **Outside Borders**. Click within the table to deselect the table and view the borders.

5. Click the arrow beside the Pen Color button and choose a pale blue color from the palette.

6. Click the Draw Table button to activate the pencil pointer, and drag the pencil over each outside border of the second table, one border at a time, and then over the bottom border of the first row.

NOTE

You can also apply formats to tables by using the Borders and Shading dialog box. (From the Home tab, Paragraph group, click the arrow beside the Borders and Shading button.) You can apply the changes to a cell or to the entire table.

Word 2007

Figure 14-18
Drawing a border

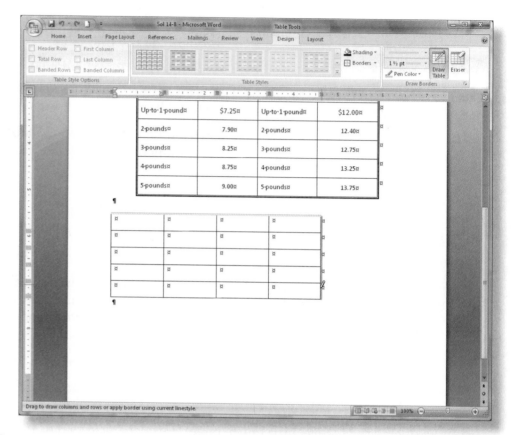

Draw
Table

7. Click the Draw Table button or press Esc to restore the normal pointer.

Exercise 14-16 USE TABLE STYLES TO FORMAT A TABLE

Word can format your table attractively when you use table styles.

1. Select the text in rows 3 through 7 (from "Up to 1 pound" to "13.75") but not the end-of-row markers. Copy the selected text to the Clipboard.

2. Click the first cell in the blank table, and paste the copied text.

3. Click the first cell of the second table. Click the Table Tools Design tab. Move the pointer over each table style in the Table Styles group to preview each table style.

4. Click the More arrow 🔽 to view additional styles.

Figure 14-19
Selecting a table
style

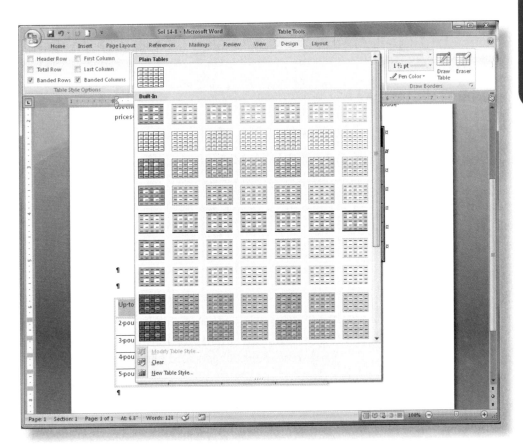

5. Click a style with gray shading.

6. Locate the **Table Style Options** group on the **Table Tools Design** tab, and clear the check box for **First Column**.

7. Click the More arrow and click **Clear**. The table style is removed.

8. Select the second table, and apply a table style of your choice.

9. Select the second table, including the blank paragraph marks above and below it, and press Delete.

10. Add an extra paragraph mark above the table, and add your reference initials below the table. Change the top margin to 2 inches.

11. Save the document as *[your initials]***14-16** in a new Lesson 14 folder.

12. Submit and close the document.

Exercise 14-17 ROTATE TEXT

1. Start a new document.

2. Click the **Insert** tab, and click the Table button. Click **Insert table** on the Table menu.

3. In the Insert Table dialog box, set the **Number of columns** to **2** and the **Number of rows** to **8**. Click **OK**.

4. In the first cell of the first row, key **Customary Units**. Press Tab and key **Metric Equivalent**. Format both headings as bold.

5. Key **1 ounce** in the first cell of the second row. Press [Tab] and key **23.3495 grams**. Key the data shown in Figure 14-20 for the remaining table cells.

Figure 14-20

```
1 pound    0.4536 kilogram

1 ton      0.907 metric ton

1 inch     2.54 centimeters

1 foot     30.48 centimeters

1 yard     0.9144 meter

1 mile     1.6093 kilometers
```

6. Select the first column, and click the **Table Tools Layout** tab on the Ribbon. Click the Insert Left button ▤.

7. Select the first row, and click the Insert Above button ▤ on the Ribbon.

8. Position the insertion point in the first cell of the second row. Key **Weight** in bold. Position the insertion point in the first cell of the sixth row. Key **Length** and format it as bold.

9. Select the table, and format all text as 14 points.

10. Select the cell containing "Weight" and the three blank cells below it. Click the **Table Tools Layout** tab, and click the Merge Cells button ▤.

11. With the insertion point in the merged cell, click the Text Direction button ▤ on the Table Tools Layout tab to rotate "Weight" until it reads from top to bottom. Click ▤ again so "Weight" reads from bottom to top.

12. Select the cell containing "Length" through the last cell of the first column. Click the Merge Cells button ▤ on the Table Tools Layout tab.

13. With the merged cell selected, click the Text Direction button ▤ on the Table Tools Layout tab twice to rotate "Length" until it reads from bottom to top.

14. Merge the cells in the first row, and key the title **Metric Conversion Table** in the merged row. Format the title as 16-point bold uppercase and centered.

15. Select the entire table. Click the **Table Tools Layout** tab, and click the Properties button ▤Properties ▤ to open the Table Properties dialog box. Click the **Row** tab. Set the row height to exactly **0.5"**.

16. Click the **Table** tab. Click **Center** to horizontally center the table on the document page. Click **OK**.

17. With the table still selected, click the **Table Tools Layout** tab, click the AutoFit button ▤ AutoFit▾ ▤, and then click **AutoFit Contents** to change all column widths to be as wide as the longest text in the column.

18. With the table still selected, click the Align Center Left button ▤ to vertically center all text.

NOTE

When a table has a title, AutoFit changes the title's column to fit the length of the title. This might make the column much wider than is required for the widest text in the remaining columns. You can insert a line break to create a two-line title.

19. Apply **Gray-15%** shading to the first row and to the cells that contain "Customary Units," "Metric Equivalent," "Weight," and "Length."

20. Select the table again. Using the Table Tools Design tab, change the **Line Style** to a **double line**, change the **Line Weight** to ³/₄ **point**, and change the **Pen Color** to **black**. Click **Borders** to select **Outside Borders** to apply the double-line border to the outside of the table.

21. Draw the same style border to separate the "Weight" and "Length" sections of the table.

22. Open the Page Setup dialog box. On the **Layout** tab, set the **Vertical alignment** to **Center** and click **OK**.

23. Save the document as *[your initials]***14-17** in your Lesson 14 folder. Submit and close the document.

Figure 14-21
Table with rotated text

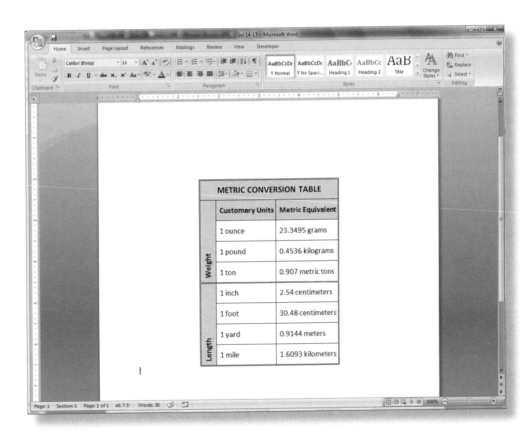

Converting Tables and Text

You can convert existing tabbed text to a table, which can be faster than keying text into an existing table. You can also convert an existing table to paragraphs of text, and you can choose to separate the converted text by paragraph marks, commas, or tabs. This might be useful when converting Word data for use in a database.

Exercise 14-18 CONVERT TEXT INTO TABLES

1. In a new document, key the text shown in Figure 14-22, with one tab character between each entry. Press [Enter] at the end of each line as usual. Use single spacing. (Your text might line up differently from the figure. You will correct the document in the following steps.)

Figure 14-22

Quarters	2006	2007	2008
Q1	42.8	40.8	41.3
Q2	34.6	38.2	37.9
Q3	33.5	39.0	39.1
Q4	41.6	39.2	40.4

2. Select all the text. Click the **Insert** tab, and click the Table button ▤. Click **Convert Text to Table**. The Convert Text to Table dialog box appears.

3. Make sure the **Number of columns** text entry is **4**. In addition, check that **Tabs** is chosen under the **Separate text at** section. Click **OK**. The selected text appears in a 5 × 4 table.

4. Click the **Table Tools Design** tab, and click the **Light Shading – Accent 1** table style. Locate the **Table Style Options** group on the **Table Tools Design** tab, and verify that the **Header Row**, **Banded Rows**, and **First Column** check boxes are selected.

5. Select the table, and copy it to the Clipboard. You will need this table for the next exercise.

6. With the table still selected, click the **Table Tools Layout** tab, and open the Table Properties dialog box. Click the **Row** tab, and set the row height to at least **0.3"**. Click **OK**.

7. With the table still selected, click the Align Center button ▤ on the Table Tools Layout tab to vertically and horizontally center the text.

8. Use the Page Setup dialog box to center the table vertically on the page.

9. Insert a new row at the top of the table, and merge the cells in the row. In the first row, key the title **CAMPBELL'S CONFECTIONS SALES** as 16-point bold type.

10. Save the document as *[your initials]***14-18** in your Lesson 14 folder.

11. Submit and close the document.

Exercise 14-19 CONVERT TABLES TO TEXT

1. Start a new document. Paste the Clipboard contents that contain the copied table from step 5 of the previous exercise.

2. Select the table.

3. Click the **Table Tools Layout** tab, and locate the **Data** group on the Ribbon. Click the Convert to Text button . The Convert Table to Text dialog box opens.

Figure 14-23
Convert Table to
Text dialog box

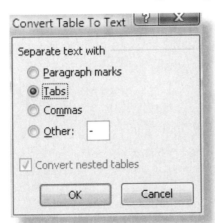

4. Choose **Tabs**, if it is not already selected, to separate the contents of each cell with tabs.

5. Click **OK**. The text appears outside the table, with a tab replacing each end-of-cell marker and a paragraph mark replacing each end-of-row marker.

6. Close the document without saving it.

Lesson 14 Summary

- A table is a grid of rows and columns that intersect to form cells. The lines that mark the cell boundaries are called gridlines.

- There are several ways to create a table: use the Insert Table menu, Insert Table command, use table templates, draw a table, or convert text to a table.

- Keying and editing text in tables is similar to working with text in paragraphs. But if you key text in a cell and press Enter, a new paragraph is created within the same cell.

- To move the insertion point to different cells in a table, use the mouse, the arrow keys, or keyboard shortcuts.

- Select cells by using the black right-pointing arrow ◢ or the shortcut keys or by dragging over text. With the cells selected, you can delete, copy, or move their contents or change the format.

- To help with selection, end-of-cell markers indicate the end of each cell. In addition, end-of-row markers to the right of the gridline of each row indicate the end of each row.

- Select rows by using the white right-pointing arrow ◪, select columns by using the black column selector arrow ◼, and select tables by using the table move handle ⊞. You can also use the Select command on the Table Tools Layout tab or drag to select.

- The header row is the first row of a table (or second row if the table has a title row), in which each cell contains a heading for the column of text beneath it.

- In addition to editing the contents of a table, you can edit a table's structure by adding, deleting, moving, and copying cells, rows, and columns. You can also merge and split cells or change a table's position or dimensions.

- In addition to using Ribbon commands and the shortcut menu, you can also use keyboard shortcuts to cut, copy, and paste.

- There are many ways to make a table more attractive and easier to read: Format table text, align text horizontally and vertically, apply borders and shading, use table styles, rotate the direction of text, and sort table text.
- You can convert existing tabbed text to a table, which can be faster than keying text into an existing table. You can also convert an existing table to paragraphs of text, and you can choose to separate the converted text by paragraph marks, commas, or tabs.

LESSON 14 — Command Summary

Feature	Button	Command	Keyboard
Insert table	Table	Insert tab, Tables group	
Draw table	Draw Table	Insert tab, Tables group	
Insert cells	Rows & Columns	Table Tools Layout tab, Rows & Columns group	
Insert rows above	Insert Above	Table Tools Layout tab, Rows & Columns group	
Insert rows below	Insert Below	Table Tools Layout tab, Rows & Columns group	
Insert columns to left	Insert Left	Table Tools Layout tab, Rows & Columns group	
Insert columns to right	Insert Right	Table Tools Layout tab, Rows & Columns group	
Select a row	Select	Table Tools Layout tab, Rows & Columns group	
Select a column	Select	Table Tools Layout tab, Rows & Columns group	
Select a table	Select	Table Tools Layout tab, Rows & Columns group	Alt + 5 (Numeric keypad)
Delete selected table	Delete	Table Tools Layout tab, Rows & Columns group	
Merge cells	Merge Cells	Table Tools Layout tab, Rows & Columns group	
Split cells	Split Cells	Table Tools Layout tab, Rows & Columns group	
Distribute rows evenly	Distribute Rows	Table Tools Layout tab, Rows & Columns group	
Distribute columns evenly	Distribute Columns	Table Tools Layout tab, Rows & Columns group	
Sort text	Sort	Table Tools Layout tab, Data group	
Table Styles		Table Tools Design tab, Rows & Columns group	
Change text direction	Text Direction	Table Tools Layout tab, Rows & Columns group	

Concepts Review

True/False Questions

Each of the following statements is either true or false. Indicate your choice by circling T or F.

T   F   1. You can insert a table by using the Ribbon, Page Layout tab.

T   F   2. To move to the top cell in the current column, you press [Alt]+[Page Down].

T   F   3. You can use the Table Properties dialog box to apply formats to existing tables.

T   F   4. You press [Alt]+[7] to select a table.

T   F   5. Table templates insert tables with sample data.

T   F   6. To split a merged cell, first delete all paragraph marks in the merged cell.

T   F   7. By default, when you insert a table, it has borders that will be printed.

T   F   8. You can apply shading by using the Table Tools Design tab.

Short Answer Questions

Write the correct answer in the space provided.

1. Which dialog box do you use to change column width?

2. Which keyboard shortcut moves the insertion point to the previous cell?

3. Which nonprinting character marks the end of a cell?

4. What are the nonprinting lines called that mark the boundaries of cells?

5. Which command is used to add a row above a selected row?

6. Which feature on the Table Tools Design tab do you use to delete a line you drew?

7. Which table element can you select when the pointer appears as ➴?

_____

8. What would the button ▤ do to selected cells in a table?

_____

Critical Thinking

Answer these questions on a separate page. There are no right or wrong answers. Support your answers with examples from your own experience, if possible.

1. You learned how to insert a table automatically and draw a table manually. What are the benefits of each method? Which do you prefer?

2. Review the table formats in the Table Styles gallery. Which table formats would you be most likely to use on a day-to-day basis? Can you think of any formats that are not particularly useful?

Skills Review

Exercise 14-20

Create a table. Key and edit text in the table.

1. Start a new document.

2. Key the following text on three separate lines.

   Gift Certificates and Store Credits

   Location: _____

   Month:_____

3. Press ⌷Enter⌷ two times after the last line.

4. Position the insertion point at the last paragraph mark, and insert a table by following these steps:

   a. Click the Insert tab, and click the Table button ▤.

   b. Click Insert Table to open the Insert Table dialog box.

   c. Key **4** in the **Number of columns** text box, and key **32** in the **Number of rows** text box.

   d. Click OK.

5. Key text in the first row of the table by following these steps:

   a. With the insertion point in the first cell, key Day.

   b. Press ⌷Tab⌷ and key Issued.

   c. Press ⌷Tab⌷ and key Redeemed.

   d. Press ⌷Tab⌷ and key Balance.

6. Create a numbered list by following these steps:

   a. Select all cells in column 1 beginning with the cell below "Day."

   b. Click the Home tab, and click the down arrow beside the Numbering button .

   c. Select **Define New Number Format**. Select **1, 2, 3** for the **Number style**. In the **Number format** text box, delete the comma, but do not delete the number. Click OK.

   d. Open the Paragraph dialog box, and change the **Left** indent to **0**, and change the **Special** indent to **(none)**. Click OK.

7. Move around and edit text in the table, using keyboard shortcuts, by following these steps:

   a. With the insertion point in the last cell of column one, press `Alt`+`PageUp`. Apply bold and small caps format to "Day."

   b. Press `Tab` and apply bold and small caps to "Issued."

   c. Select "Redeemed" and "Balance," and apply bold and small caps format.

   d. Center "Issued," "Redeemed," and "Balance."

8. Select the three lines in the heading, and press `Ctrl`+`E` to center the lines.

9. Format the first line of the heading using 14-point bold and small caps. Format the second and third lines using 12-point bold and small caps.

10. Change the top margin to 1.5 inches.

11. Save the document as *[your initials]***14-20** in your Lesson 14 folder.

12. Submit and close the document.

Exercise 14-21

Select, move, and copy cells, rows, and columns. Edit table structures.

1. Open the file **Rates**.

2. Cut the text in the table by following these steps:

   a. Make sure the Show/Hide ¶ button ⊞ is turned on.

   b. Drag to select all the text in the table—but not the end-of-row markers.

   c. Cut the text.

3. Modify the table structure by inserting three columns by following these steps:

   a. Point to the top border of the first column, and click to select the column. Drag to the right to select the three empty columns.

   b. Click the Table Tools Layout tab.

   c. Click the Insert Right button ⊟ to add three columns to the table.

4. Paste the text in the table by following these steps:

  a. Position the insertion point in the second cell of the first column.

  b. Paste the text.

5. Click in the second row of column 4, and key the text from Figure 14-24 in the new columns:

Figure 14-24

Column 4	Column 5
$25,000	$50,000
34.75	44.75
37.75	47.75
40.75	50.75
43.75	53.75
46.75	56.75
49.75	59.75
52.75	62.75
55.75	65.75

6. Delete column 6 by following these steps:

  a. Select the sixth column.

  b. Right-click and choose **Delete Columns** from the shortcut menu.

7. Change the column width and row height and center the table by following these steps:

  a. Select the entire table by clicking the table move handle ⊞.

  b. Click the **Table Tools Layout** tab, and click the Properties button .

  c. Click the **Column** tab and set the **Preferred width** text box to **1"**.

  d. Click the **Row** tab. Select **Specify height** and set the height to at least **0.3"**.

  e. Click the **Cell** tab. Select **Center** for the vertical alignment.

  f. Click the **Table** tab. Under Alignment, choose **Center**. Click **OK**.

8. Merge cells in the first row by following these steps:

  a. Select the second and third cells in the first row.

  b. Click the **Table Tools Layout** tab, and click the Merge Cells button ⊟. Key **Female—Nonsmoker** in the merged cell.

  c. Select the cells in the first row for columns 4 and 5, and merge the cells. Key **Male—Nonsmoker**.

9. Center the text in row 1, and format it as 14-point bold and small caps.

10. Select the text in rows 3 through 10, and press Ctrl+R to right-align the numbers. Center and bold the text in the second row.

11. Apply shading to the table by following these steps:

   a. Select the first row, and click the Table Tools Design tab. Click the arrow beside the Shading button 🔲▾ and click black.

   b. Select the second row, and apply a light shade of gray.

12. Format the document as a memo to "Store Managers" from Garland Miller. The subject is "Life Insurance." Use the current date.

13. Use the Page Setup dialog box to change the top margin to 2 inches. Change the spacing after for the subject line to 24 points.

14. Save the document as *[your initials]*14-21 in your Lesson 14 folder.

15. Submit and close the document.

Exercise 14-22

Convert text to a table and format the table.

1. Open the document **Nutrition - 1**.

2. Convert tabbed text to a table by following these steps:

   a. Select the tabbed text from "Nutritional Facts" to the end of the line beginning "Protein."

   b. Click the Insert tab, and click the Table button 🗔 .

   c. Click Convert Text to Table in the Table menu.

   d. Key 5 in the Number of columns text box, and 14 in the Number of rows. Verify that Tabs is selected under Separate text at. Click OK.

3. Click anywhere in the table, and click the Table Tools Design tab. Click the More arrow ▾ to display the Table Styles gallery. Select a style in the second row of the gallery.

4. Locate the Table Style Options group, and click the check box for Banded Columns.

5. Select the first row, click the Table Tools Layout tab, and click Insert Above to add a row to the top of the table. Merge the cells in the first row. Key DARK CHOCOLATE SQUARES in the new row. Center the text and apply 14-point formatting.

6. Use the Table Properties dialog box to increase the height of every row in the table to at least 0.3".

7. Use the Table Properties dialog box, Cell tab, to vertically center the text in every cell of the table.

8. Select the text in columns 2 through 4, and right-align the text. Click the Table Tools Layout tab, and click the AutoFit button . Choose AutoFit Contents.

9. Center the table horizontally and vertically on the page.

10. Save the document as *[your initials]*14-22 in your Lesson 14 folder.

11. Submit and close the document.

Exercise 14-23

Convert text to a table and format the table.

1. Open the file **Trip**.

2. Select the text from "NAME:" to the end of the document. Convert the text to an 18-row by 1-column table, and define the **Fixed column width** to **2** inches. Click **OK**.

3. Select the first column, and insert a column to the right.

4. Change row height for the entire table to exactly **0.4**", and center the table horizontally. Vertically center the text in the cells.

5. Select the cells containing the text "Name," "Outbound Pickups," "Outbound Deliveries," and "Mileage." Apply bold formatting and light blue shading.

6. Select the "Name" cell and the empty cell in row 1, column 2. Merge the cells. Select the cell "Outbound Pickups" and the cell beside it. Merge the cells. Repeat this procedure for the "Outbound Deliveries" cell and the "Mileage" cell.

7. Center the two heading lines at the top of the document. Apply 24 points spacing after to the "Trip Report" line.

8. Change the top margin to 1.5 inches.

9. Save the document as *[your initials]*14-23 in your Lesson 14 folder.

10. Submit and close the document.

Lesson Applications

Exercise 14-24

Create a table, enter text in the table, and edit and format the table.

1. Start a new document. Format the document as a memo to Robert Smith from Lynn Tanguay. Use today's date, and the subject is "Greek Alphabet."

2. Key the text in Figure 14-25 below the memo heading.

Figure 14-25

Listed below is a table containing the letters of the Greek alphabet. Please post and file this table so that everyone in production will have a reference for the correct mold to use when embossing Greek letters on our chocolate bars and chocolate squares.

Please let me know if you have any questions.

3. Press Enter two times. Create a table using the Table button ⬛ and selecting the Quick Table command. Select the Greek Alphabet table under the Double Table heading.

4. Select the title above the table and apply 18-point bold and small caps formatting. Center the title.

5. Select the table, and open the Table Properties dialog box. Center the table horizontally, change the row height to 0.3 inch, and center the text vertically within every cell.

6. Select the table, and click the Table Tools Design tab. Click the arrow beside the Borders button ⬛, and select Inside Horizontal Border.

7. Change the spacing after for the subject line to 24 points.

8. Select every other row beginning with "Beta," and apply light gray shading.

9. Select the first row of the table and apply small caps.

10. Save the document as *[your initials]*14-24 in your Lesson 14 folder.

11. Submit and close the document.

Exercise 14-25

Edit and format a table.

1. Open the file **WV Stores - 2**.

2. Select the table, and place a column to the left of the address information. Add a column to the right of the address information.

3. Select each of the rows containing an address, and change the row height to 1.5 inches.

4. Select the first column, and change the column width to 0.5 inch. Change the column width for the second and third columns to 2 inches.

5. Key Manager in the first cell of the third column. Key Matthew Garrett in the second cell of the third column. Key the following manager names in the appropriate cell of column 3: Fairmont store, Marianne Bentley; Morgantown store, Ethan Myers; and Wheeling store, Jackson Sigmon.

6. Key Contact Information in the first cell of the second column. Format the text in the first row using 16-point bold and small caps. Apply gray shading.

7. Click in the first cell of the second row, and key Clarksburg. Format the text using 16-point bold, small caps, and black shading. Center the text. Rotate the text so that it reads from the bottom of the cell to the top.

8. Key each city name in the first column, and apply the format used in Step 7.

9. Add a row to the top of the table. Merge the cells, and key WEST VIRGINIA STORES. Format the text in the first row using 18-point bold, all caps, and center alignment. Place 12 points spacing before and 12 points spacing after the title.

10. Select the cells in the blank row below the Clarksburg store. Merge the cells and apply gray shading. Merge the cells in the other three blank rows, and apply gray shading.

11. Select each of the cells containing the contact information, and center the text vertically within the cell. Select the text "Manager" and all the names below it, and center the text horizontally and vertically.

12. Center the table horizontally and vertically on the page.

13. Apply a 3-point double-line outside border to the table.

14. Save the document as *[your initials]*14-25 in your Lesson 14 folder.

15. Submit and close the document.

Exercise 14-26

Create a table, and edit and format the table.

1. Start a new document, and change the page to landscape orientation.

2. Insert a table with 5 rows and 6 columns, and key the text shown in Figure 14-26 in the table.

Figure 14-26

Monday	Tuesday	Wednesday	Thursday	Friday	sat./sun.
			1	2	3/4
5	6	7	8	9	10/11
12	13	14	15	16	17/18
19	20	21	22	23	24/25

REVIEW

You might need to use the AutoCorrect Options button to undo the fraction ³/₄ after you key "3/4."

3. Add a sixth row to the table and key 26, 27, 28, 29, and 30, beginning with the first cell.

4. Change each column width to 1.2 inches.

5. Change the weekday headings in the top row to 16-point bold, italic, and centered. Change the top row height to at least 0.4″, and vertically center the text.

6. In the cell for the day 6, key Chamber of Commerce meeting as a new paragraph below the date.

7. In the cell for the day 1, key Mail newsletter as a new paragraph below the date.

8. In the cell for the day 19, key Meet with store managers as a new paragraph below the date.

9. Key Staff meeting below the date in the cells for days 16 and 30.

10. Change the row height for rows 2 through 6 to exactly 0.9″.

11. Insert a new first column, merge the cells in the column, and key JUNE.

12. Rotate the text "JUNE" until it reads from the bottom to the top of the column. Change the font size to 72 points and the column width to 1 inch. The text should be bold but not italic.

13. Center the text in column 1 vertically and horizontally within the column.

14. Change the zoom to Page Width to view the entire table.

15. Apply a ¹/₂-point triple-line outside border to columns 2 through 7.

16. Apply a 3-point solid-line outside border and gray shading to the first column.

17. Draw a 2¹/₄-point solid-line border at the bottom of row 1.

18. Center the table vertically and horizontally on the page.

19. Save the document as *[your initials]***14-26** in your Lesson 14 folder.

20. Submit and close the document.

Exercise 14-27 ◆ Challenge Yourself

Convert text to a table, and then edit and format the table.

1. Open the file **Office Supplies**, and change the page orientation to landscape.

2. At the top of the document key the text in Figure 14-27.

Figure 14-27

```
Campbell's Confections
Internal Supply Requisition
Name:
Department:
```

3. Select the line that begins "Quantity," and convert the text to a table.

4. Insert 12 rows below the column headings.

5. Change the column width of the first column to 0.8 inch, the second column to 0.5 inch, and the Description column to 2 inches.

6. Select the header row, apply bold format, and center the text.

7. Apply a table style with header row and banded rows formatting.

8. Select the table, click the Borders button [Borders ▾], select **All Borders**, and apply a single-line ¹/₂-point format.

9. Format the first line of the document title as 20-point bold, small caps, and centered. Format the second line of the title as 12-point, bold, small caps, and centered.

10. Format the "Name" and "Department" lines using bold, small caps, and a right-aligned, solid-leader tab at 9 inches. Press [Tab] at the end of each line to insert the leader line.

11. Change the row height for the table to 0.3 inch, and vertically center the text within the cells.

12. Horizontally center the table.

13. Check the document in Print Preview. Save it as *[your initials]***14-27** in your Lesson 14 folder.

14. Submit and close the document.

On Your Own

In these exercises you work on your own, as you would in a real-life business environment. Use the skills you've learned to accomplish the task—and be creative.

Exercise 14-28

Create a table of monthly expenses. Include an expense name column, an average amount column, and a due date column. Adjust the row height and column width, and format the table so it is readable and attractive. Spell- and grammar-check your document, and save it as *[your initials]*14-28. Submit the document.

Exercise 14-29

Log onto the Internet, and find statistics on five stocks in which you are interested. Create a table showing the history of the stocks. (You might wish to copy and paste information into your document and then convert the text to a table). Give the document a title, and spell- and grammar-check the document. Save the document as *[your initials]*14-29 and submit it.

Exercise 14-30

Using the table feature, create a calendar for one of the months of the year, similar to the one you created in Exercise 14-26. Format the calendar attractively, and add information you want to remember for particular days. Save the document as *[your initials]*14-30 and submit it.

Lesson 15

Advanced Tables

OBJECTIVES

After completing this lesson, you will be able to:

1. Work with long tables.

2. Use advanced table-formatting options.

3. Work with multiple tables.

4. Perform calculations in a table.

5. Work with Excel worksheets within Word documents.

MCAS OBJECTIVES

In this lesson:
WW 07 2.1.2
WW 07 4.3.4
WW 07 4.3.5
WW 07 4.4.2

Estimated Time: 1³/₄ hours

Tables can be an important part of any document. To make your tables readable, you need to know how to control page breaks, create header rows, and even split very long tables. Because tables add a graphical element to a document, Word provides formatting features to enhance them with special styles, spacing, margins, and captions. You can also size tables in a variety of ways, to make sure they best fit their contents and the page. If a document includes multiple tables, you might even need to use more than one table on a single page. Word's capability to "nest" tables allows you to create tables within tables.

Word tables can do more than display text in rows and columns. You can use special sorting tools to arrange tabular information and perform calculations on the data in a table. But if your needs are more complex, you can create an Excel worksheet and import the worksheet into a Word document.

Working with Long Tables

When a table spans more than one page, it can be difficult to read unless the column headings appear at the top of each page. Another problem can occur when rows contain multiple lines of text and a page break occurs in the middle of a row. Word provides options for controlling page breaks in a table and for repeating column headings at the top of each page in a multipage table.

Exercise 15-1   CONTROL PAGE BREAKS IN A TABLE

1. Open the file **Order Form**. This document contains a long, unformatted table that spans three pages.

2. Select the entire table.

3. Click the Table Tools Layout tab, and click the Properties button 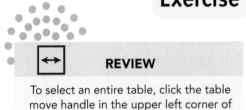. Click the Row tab.

REVIEW

To select an entire table, click the table move handle in the upper left corner of the table.

Figure 15-1
Table Properties dialog box with the Row tab displayed

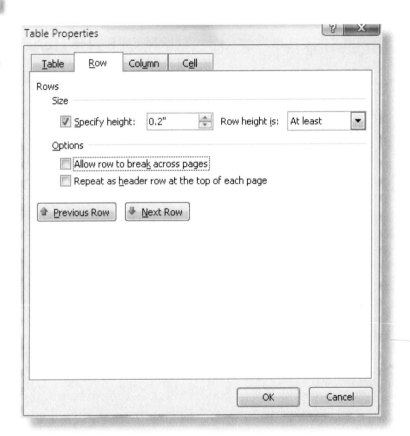

4. Under Options, clear the Allow row to break across pages check box. Click OK. When this option is not checked, page breaks can occur before or after a row, but not in the middle of a row.

5. Click any cell to deselect the table.

Exercise 15-2   DEFINE A HEADER ROW FOR A TABLE

To create table header rows, you must first select the row or rows you want to appear at the top of each page. You can select one or more rows to serve as the table's header rows, but they must be at the beginning of the table.

1. Scroll to the top of the table, and select the first two rows of the table.

2. Click the **Table Tools Layout** tab, and click the Repeat Header Rows button .

3. Scroll to the top of page 2. The column headings now appear at the top of the page. They are also repeated at the top of page 3.

> **REVIEW**
>
> To select a row, position the mouse pointer to the left of the row, and then click the white right-pointing arrow or drag the I-beam pointer across all the cells in the row.

🔲 Repeat Header Rows

Exercise 15-3   TURN OFF THE HEADER ROWS REPEAT OPTION

1. With the first two rows still selected, locate the Data group of the Table Tools Layout tab. Notice that **Repeat Header Rows** is "on." Click **Repeat Header Rows** to turn off the header rows.

2. Scroll to the top of page 2 to see that the header row no longer appears there. Click the Undo button 🔄 to reset the header rows.

3. With the first two rows still selected, click the Properties button 🔲 Properties. Click the **Row** tab. Notice that the **Repeat as header row at the top of each page** check box is selected. Click **Cancel** to close the dialog box. Click anywhere in the table to deselect the rows.

Exercise 15-4   SPLIT A TABLE TO CREATE TWO SEPARATE TABLES

1. Near the top of page 3, click in the row containing the text "Chocolate Suckers." Check that the Show/Hide ¶ button ¶ is selected.

2. Click the **Table Tools Layout** tab, and click the Split Table button . Word inserts a paragraph mark above the selected row, and all the rows below the paragraph mark become a separate table. Notice that the new table does not contain the header row you defined previously.

3. Click in the row containing the text "Foil-Wrapped Chocolates," on page 2.

4. Click the Split Table button 🔲 Split Table again to create another split.

Figure 15-2
Second and third
tables: created by
using the split table
command

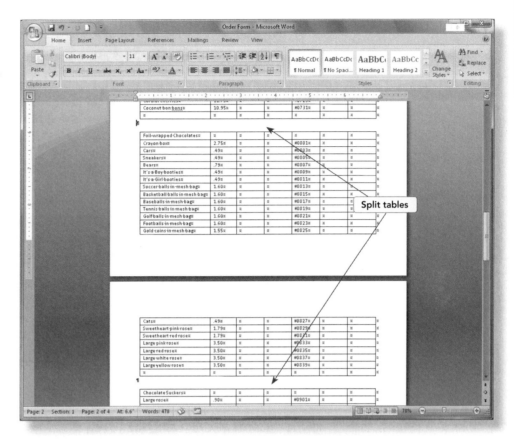

Exercise 15-5 INSERT TEXT ABOVE A TABLE

Sometimes a table is the very first object on a page. In this case, there is no paragraph mark before the table, indicating that there is no blank line above the table on which to key text. Use the Split Table command to insert a blank line above a table when needed.

1. Move to the top of the first page, and click in the table's first cell.

2. Click the Table Tools Layout tab, and click the Split Table button ⊞ Split Table. A paragraph mark appears above the table.

3. Key the following text to create a title above the table. Use character and paragraph formatting to create your own design.

   Campbell's Confections
   Store Order Form
   For internal use only

4. Create a header that appears on all pages except page 1 with the following information:

   Order Form   **Page** *<page number>*

5. Format the header text as 10-point Tahoma bold. "Order Form" should be left-aligned, and the page number should be right-aligned.

Exercise 15-6 PREVENT A TABLE FROM BREAKING ACROSS PAGES

In a previous exercise, you used the Row tab of the Table Properties dialog box to prevent page breaks from occurring in the middle of a row. To control page breaks between rows, use the Keep with next paragraph-formatting option.

1. Display nonprinting characters. Go to page 2, and scroll to see table 2 which begins with the row "Foil-Wrapped Chocolates." Notice that the table spans two pages.

Figure 15-3
Table 2, with a page break between rows

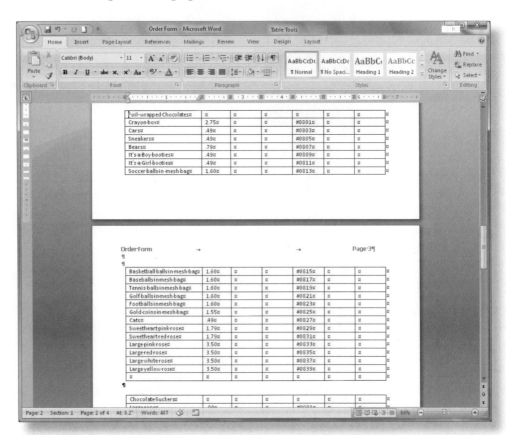

2. Select the first eight rows of the table (all rows on the bottom of page 2).

3. Open the **Paragraph** dialog box. On the **Line and Page Breaks** tab, select the **Keep with next** check box. Click **OK**. The entire table now appears on page 3.

4. Go to the bottom of page 1, and select the last three rows ("Almond bark" through "Coconut bark").

5. Apply the **Keep with next** paragraph-formatting option.

6. Go to page 3, and locate the table that begins with the text "Chocolate Suckers." Select all the lines of the table that appear on page 3 and apply the **Keep with next** option.

Using Advanced Table-Formatting Options

Advanced formatting features can enhance the appearance of a table. By changing cell margins, for example, you can add space between columns and rows. Or if needed, you can decrease cell margins to fit more text within a cell. The Table Styles gallery formats a table by using a *table style*—a predesigned table format that includes fonts, colors, borders, and other formatting options. AutoFit enables you to automatically resize elements of a table or resize an entire table.

Exercise 15-7   CHANGE CELL MARGINS

A few of the cells in the document appear crowded because the cell contents are too close to the cell border; a little extra white space between the text and borders will give the cells a cleaner appearance. You can control the amount of white space in cells by setting cell margins. You can set cell margins for an entire table, or you can adjust the margins of individual cells.

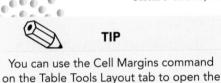

TIP

You can use the Cell Margins command on the Table Tools Layout tab to open the Table Options dialog box.

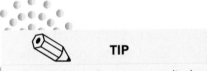

TIP

If nonprinting characters are displayed, your table's cells might look more crowded than they actually are. To get a better idea of the amount of space in your cells, click the Show/Hide ¶ button to hide these characters.

1. Go to the last table in the document, and select the entire table. Right-click the table, and choose **Table Properties** from the shortcut menu. Click the **Table** tab, and then click the Options button [Options...]. The Table Options dialog box opens.

2. Under **Default cell margins**, change the **Left** and **Right** margin settings to **0.1** inch. Click **OK** to close the Table Options dialog box; then click **OK** again to close the Table Properties dialog box. The slightly wider cell margins indent each cell's contents from the right and left borders, which makes the cells look less crowded. This change has no apparent effect in the table's top row or in the second column, where the text is already centered in the cells and surrounded by plenty of white space.

Figure 15-4
Changing Left and Right cell margins in the Table Options dialog box

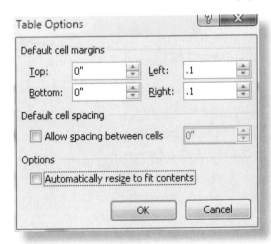

3. Select the first two rows of the first table (the header rows); then right-click to open the shortcut menu.

4. Choose **Table Properties** from the shortcut menu, and then click the **Cell** tab.

5. Click the Options button to open the Cell Options dialog box.

6. Under **Cell margins**, clear the **Same as the whole table** check box. The **Top**, **Bottom**, **Left**, and **Right** boxes become active.

7. Change the top and bottom margins to **0.08** inch. Click **OK**; then click **OK** again. The header row now has additional white space at the top and bottom.

Figure 15-5
Setting top and bottom margins in the Cell Options dialog box

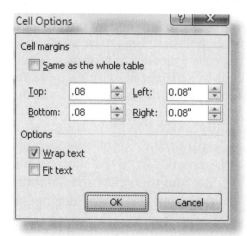

8. Go to the last table in the document, and select the first row of the table (the title row, containing the text "Chocolate Suckers"), and right-click to open the shortcut menu.

9. Choose **Table Properties** from the shortcut menu, and click the **Cell** tab. Click the Options button to open the Cell Options dialog box. Under **Cell margins**, clear the **Same as the whole table** check box.

10. Change the top and bottom margins to **0.08** inch. Click **OK**; then click **OK** again. The title row now has additional white space at the top and bottom.

Exercise 15-8 CHANGE VERTICAL ALIGNMENT

TIP

The alignment buttons on the Table Tools Layout tab offer nine options, specifying both vertical and horizontal alignment. (If you right-click a selected table to open the shortcut menu, its Cell Alignment submenu will have the same nine options.) If you want to change the vertical alignment for an entire table but keep the existing horizontal alignments for various columns, use the options offered on the Cell tab of the Table Properties dialog box.

In addition to adjusting cell margins, you can change the vertical alignment of text relative to a cell's top and bottom borders.

1. Select the document's last table, and reopen the **Table Properties** dialog box.

2. Click the **Row** tab, and change the row height to **0.3** inch.

3. Click the **Cell** tab.

4. Under **Vertical alignment**, choose **Top**. Click **OK** and then deselect the table. The cells' contents vertically align themselves at the top of each cell.

Figure 15-6
Table after changing
cell margins and
vertical alignment

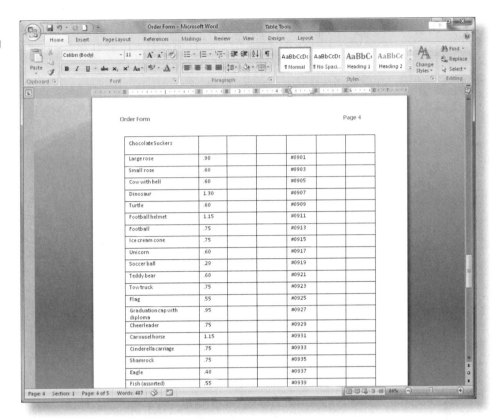

5. Save the file as *[your initials]*15-8 in a new folder for Lesson 15. Do not print the document, but leave it open for the next exercise.

Exercise 15-9   CREATE AND MODIFY CUSTOM TABLE STYLES

If you cannot find a table style in the gallery that suits your needs, you can create your own table style. You can even add the new style to Word's gallery for use at a later time. When you save a style this way, Word adds it to the template used by the active document; the style will be available in any other document based on the same template.

1. Go to the second table in the document (with the title "Foil-Wrapped Chocolates"), and click in the first row.

2. Click the Table Tools Design tab, and locate the Table Styles group. Click the More arrow to open the Table Styles gallery. Click New Table Style.

3. Key *[your initials]* Table Special 1 in the Name box.

4. Verify that the Style type is Table.

5. Click the Apply formatting to drop-down arrow, and choose Header row. The formatting options you select next will apply only to the table's header row.

6. Using the font-formatting tools in the dialog box, set the font to 10-point Tahoma bold. Set the line style to No Border. Set the shading color to a medium blue.

Figure 15-7
Creating a table style
for the Header row

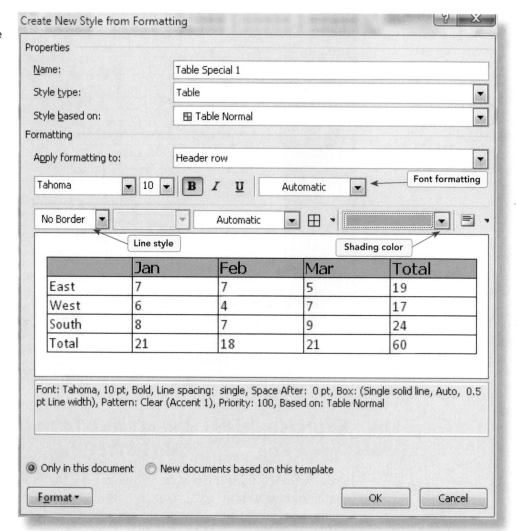

7. Reopen the **Apply formatting to** drop-down list, and choose **Even banded rows**.

8. Set the shading color to light blue.

9. Select the **New documents based on this template** option, then click **OK**. The new style is added to the list of styles in the **Table Styles** gallery.

10. Make sure that the insertion point is in the document's second table (with the title "Foil-Wrapped Chocolates"); then click the More arrow in the Table Styles group.

11. Locate the **Custom** heading in the Table Styles Gallery. Point to the table style in the Custom section, and read the ScreenTip. Click the **Table Special 1** style. The new table style is applied to the table.

12. Point to the first table style in the **Table Styles** group of the **Design** tab, and notice that the custom style appears on the Ribbon.

13. Click the More arrow, and click **Modify Table Style**. The Modify Style dialog box appears. It provides the same options as the New Style dialog box.

14. Open the **Apply formatting to** drop-down list, and choose **Whole table**. Change the Line Style from no border to the thin solid line. Set the Line Weight to $1/4$ pt. Click the Borders button arrow and choose **Outside Borders**. Click the Borders button arrow again, and choose **Inside Horizontal Border**.

> **NOTE**
>
> If vertical gridlines appear in your table, click the Table Tools Layout tab, and click the View Gridlines command. Gridlines do not print.

15. Select the **New document based on this template** option; then click **OK**. The table now has an outside border and horizontal borders between all the rows.

Figure 15-8
Table with a new custom style

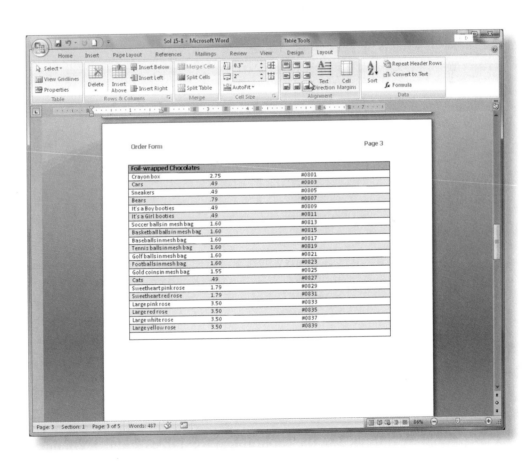

16. Save the document as *[your initials]***15-9** in your Lesson 15 folder. Select just the styled table and print it.

Exercise 15-10   ADD TABLE CAPTIONS

A *caption* is a label that identifies a part of a document, usually with a number. A table caption, for example, might include a number for the table, followed by a short description, such as "Table 1: Delivery Schedule." In this exercise, you will add captions to all the tables in your document.

1. Go to the top of the document, and click anywhere in the first table's header row.

2. Click the **Reference** tab, and click the Insert Caption button . The Caption dialog box opens with the text "Table 1" displayed in the **Caption** text box.

3. After "Table 1" in the text box, insert a colon (:) and a space. Then key **Signature Chocolates** and click **OK**. The dialog box closes, and the new caption appears above the table.

Figure 15-9
Inserting a table caption

4. Click anywhere in the document's second table. To make this table look more consistent with the third table, remove the table style you created earlier. Click the **Table Tools Design** tab, and locate the Table Styles buttons. Point to and click the **Table Grid** table style. The table returns to a simple format, with borders around all cells and no colors.

5. Insert a table caption, using the text **Table 2: Foil-Wrapped Chocolates.**

6. Move to the table with the title "Chocolate Suckers."

7. Insert a table caption, using the text **Table 3: Chocolate Suckers.**

8. For the caption text for Tables 2 and 3, change the font size to 9 points and the paragraph spacing to 6 points before and after.

9. Save the document as ***[your initials]*15-10** in your Lesson 15 folder.

10. Submit and close the document.

Working with Multiple Tables

When working with multiple tables on the same page, you can control the position of the tables in several ways. For example, you can do the following:

- Set a table's Text Wrapping property to Around and then drag the table to any position on the page. If there is already text on the page, it will "flow" around the table.

- Create nested tables by placing tables inside the cells of another table.

Nested tables offer great ease and flexibility for arranging tables and text on a page. You control the position of objects (tables, graphics, or text) by changing the size, position, and margins of the table cells that contain those objects. You can draw a table directly in a cell of another table, or you can move and copy existing tables into another table's cells. A table that contains nested tables is often referred to as a *parent table*.

Exercise 15-11 DRAW A PARENT TABLE

You begin by drawing the parent table, which will contain two nested tables.

1. Open the file **Order Form - 2**.

2. Go to the end of the document. Draw the table shown in Figure 15-10. Draw the table approximately the same size as shown in the figure, but it does not need to be exact. You will adjust it later.

Figure 15-10
Drawing the parent table

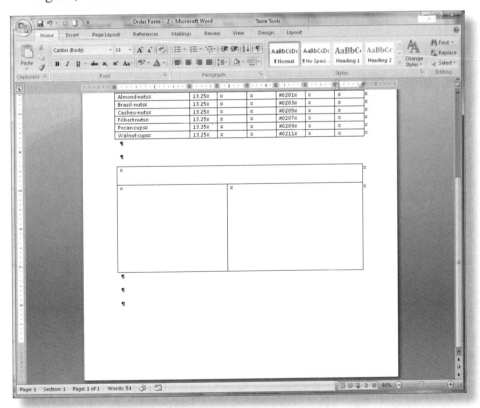

3. Select the drawn table. Click the **Table Tools Layout tab**, and click the AutoFit button. Click **AutoFit Window**. Word adjusts the table's width to fill the space between the page margins.

4. Key the following text in the first cell of the drawn table.

   Three times a year, Campbell's Confections schedules a special promotional sale for its chocolate-covered nuts and chocolate melt-a-ways. The chocolate nuts and melt-a-ways are available in milk or dark chocolate. Dates for the promotional sale are listed on the company Web site.

Exercise 15-12   CREATE NESTED SIDE-BY-SIDE TABLES

1. Select the first table.

2. Cut the selected cells, and paste them into the left cell in the second row of the table you drew in the previous exercise.

3. Click anywhere in the nested table, click to select the **Table Tools Layout** tab, and click **AutoFit** and **AutoFit to Contents**.

4. Select the table that begins "Almond nuts," cut, and then paste the table into the right cell of the new table's second row.

5. Position the insertion point above the table, and key **Chocolate Promotional Sale** as a title for the document. Select the title and apply 14-point bold and small caps formatting. Delete the extra paragraph marks above the title.

NOTE

Formatting a parent table does not affect settings within nested tables.

6. Select the parent table (which now contains the two nested tables). Set all the cell margins to **0.05** inch, and set the vertical alignment to Top.

Exercise 15-13   ADJUST THE HEIGHT OF A TABLE

You can adjust the height of a table by adjusting the height of individual rows or by dragging the table resize handle up or down. However, to use the table resize handle, you need to first clear the **Specify height** option on the **Row** tab of the **Table Properties** dialog box. Otherwise, the rows will automatically readjust to the specified height when you release the table resize handle.

1. Select the melt-a-way table on the left within the parent table, and then open the **Table Properties** dialog box.

2. Click the **Row** tab, deselect the **Specify height** check box, and click **OK**.

3. Using steps 1 and 2 as a guide, clear the **Specify height** check box for the table on the right within the parent table.

4. Select the table on the left, and apply the **AutoFit to Window** property. Then apply the **AutoFit to Window** property to the table on the right. Now both of the nested tables should fill the space of the parent table's cells.

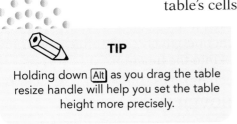

TIP

Holding down Alt as you drag the table resize handle will help you set the table height more precisely.

5. Click within the table on the left, and drag the resize handle downward to make the table the same height as the parent table cell height. Drag the resize handle for the table on the right downward to make the table equal the size of the table on the left.

6. Select the entire parent table, and apply a light gray shading. Click in the first column in the table on the left (melt-a-ways), and click the Sort button. Sort the Description column in ascending order. Click **OK**.

Figure 15-11
Nested tables

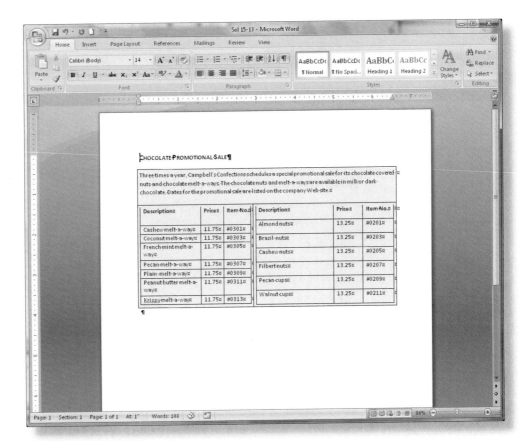

7. Save the document as *[your initials]***15-13** in your Lesson 15 folder. Submit and close the document.

Performing Calculations in a Table

You can insert fields in any table to perform basic calculations.

To perform a calculation in a Word table, you insert a formula field within the cell that will display the result. The formula includes a *function*, which is a predefined mathematical operation. The function must also include a reference to the cells containing the numbers to be calculated. A function can use special built-in bookmarks that tell it to calculate all the cells above it or to its left. You can also tell the function which cells to include in the calculation by keying their cell addresses into the function.

Here is an example of a formula field that you might use in a Word table:

{=SUM(ABOVE)}

In this formula, =SUM() is the function, and ABOVE (placed inside the function's parentheses) is the bookmark, telling Word to add the values in the cells directly above the formula. The equals sign (=) indicates that the field is a formula field. Curly braces always surround fields.

TABLE 15-1 Common Functions for Tables

Function	Result
AVERAGE()	The average of a list of values.
COUNT()	The number of items in a list.
PRODUCT()	The result from multiplying a list of numbers.
SUM()	The result from adding a list of numbers.

TABLE 15-2 Special Bookmarks for Tables

Bookmark	Result
ABOVE	All the cells in the formula's column above the formula, from the formula to the first cell that does not contain a number.
LEFT	All the cells in the formula's row to the left of the formula, from the formula to the first cell that does not contain a number.

Exercise 15-14 CREATE A TABLE THAT PERFORMS CALCULATIONS

1. Start a new document. Key the following text as a document heading. Format it attractively, using character and paragraph formatting.

Campbell's Confections
State Totals
Chocolate-Covered Nuts—2006 through 2008

TIP

Tables are made up of rows and columns. Each column is identified by a letter (A, B, C, and so on), and each row is identified by a number (1, 2, 3, and so on). Each cell has a unique address, which is determined by combining its column letter and its row number. The first cell in a table occurs where the first column (column A) intersects the first row (row 1), so the cell's address is A1. Likewise, the second cell in the first column is cell A2, the third cell in the fourth row is C4, and so on. Figure 15-12 includes headings to help you identify the columns, rows, and cell addresses.

2. Insert three blank lines after the heading.

3. With the insertion point on the third blank line, insert a new table with 5 columns and 5 rows. (Use the **Insert** tab and **Table** command.)

4. Key the data shown in Figure 15-12, but do not key the column headings (A, B, C, and so on) or the row headings (1, 2, 3, and so on). Remember to key the commas.

Figure 15-12

	A	B	C	D	E
1		2006	2007	2008	Average
2	Pennsylvania	4,129	4,560	4,401	
3	Ohio	1,206	1,117	1,040	
4	West Virginia	3,588	4,264	4,502	
5	Total				

5. Open the **Table Properties** dialog box, and click the **Table** tab. Set the table's preferred width to 5.5 inches, and center it horizontally on the page. Format the table text as 10-point Arial, and apply a light aqua shading. Select columns 2 through 5, and center the text. Apply bold text to the first row and the first column.

Exercise 15-15 FIND AVERAGE VALUES IN A TABLE

In the "Average" column of the table, you want to show the average number of sales of chocolate-covered nuts for each state during the past three years. You can do this by inserting a formula field into cells E2, E3, and E4. Each formula will calculate the average value of the three cells immediately to its left.

1. Click in cell E2 (the first cell below the "Average" column heading).

ƒx Formula

2. Click the **Table Tools Layout** tab, and click the Formula button *ƒx Formula* to open the Formula dialog box.

Figure 15-13
Formula dialog box

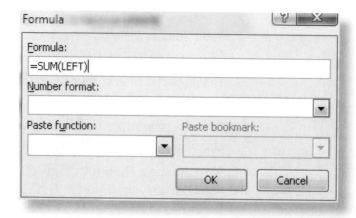

3. Select all the text in the **Formula** text box except the equals sign (=), and press [Delete]. Only the equals sign should remain in the box.

4. Open the **Paste function** drop-down list and choose **AVERAGE**. The function name AVERAGE appears in the **Formula** box, followed by a set of empty parentheses. A blinking insertion point appears between the parentheses.

5. Key **LEFT** between the parentheses. This bookmark tells the function to calculate the values in all the cells immediately to the left that contain numbers.

6. Open the **Number format** drop-down list, choose the **#,##0** option, and click **OK**. In cell E2, the number 4,363 appears; this is the average of the values in the three cells to the left of the formula.

7. Press [Alt]+[F9]. Word displays the field code in cell E2, which looks like this:

{ =AVERAGE(LEFT) \# "#,##0" }

8. Press [Alt]+[F9] again to hide the field code and display normal values in the table.

9. Click in cell E3, and then click the **Table Tools Layout** tab. Click the Formula button . Delete the contents of the **Formula** box and key **=AVERAGE(B3,C3,D3)**. Do not insert any blank spaces in the formula. Set the **Number format** to **#,##0** and click **OK**. The value 1,121 appears in the cell. This time, instead of using a bookmark to identify the cells to be calculated, you identified them individually by typing each cell's address, separated by commas.

NOTE

If you create a formula field in one cell and copy it into another cell, the copied formula will display the same results as the original. This is because Word's formulas are not relative; that is, they do not automatically adjust themselves when copied or moved to a new location. If you want to use the same formula in different cells, you should create a new formula each time to make sure it contains the correct cell references.

10. Click in cell E4, and open the Formula dialog box. Delete the contents of the **Formula** box and key =AVERAGE(B4:D4). Do not insert any blank spaces in the formula. Set the **Number format** to #,##0 and click **OK**. The value 4,118 appears in the cell. This time, you identified the range of cells to be calculated by typing the range's first cell (B4) and last cell (D4), separated by a colon.

Figure 15-14
Table with averages

CAMPBELL'S CONFECTIONS
STATE TOTALS
CHOCOLATE-COVERED NUTS –2006 THROUGH 2008

	2006	2007	2008	Average
Pennsylvania	4,129	4,560	4,401	4,363
Ohio	1,206	1,117	1,040	1,121
West Virginia	3,588	4,264	4,502	4,118
Total				

11. Save the file as *[your initials]*15-15 in your Lesson 15 folder. Leave it open for the next exercise.

Exercise 15-16   FIND TOTAL VALUES IN A TABLE

In the "Total" row of the table, you want to show the total number of sales of chocolate-covered nuts for each of the past three years. You can do this by inserting a formula field into cells B5, C5, and D5. Each formula will sum the values of the three cells immediately above it.

1. Click in cell B5 (the first cell to the right of the "Total" row heading), and open the Formula dialog box.

2. Look at the **Formula** box; it should already contain the formula =SUM(ABOVE). If so, go on to step 3. If not, select the **Formula** box contents and key =SUM(ABOVE).

3. Set the number format to #,##0 and click **OK**. In cell B5, the number 10,929 appears. This total is too high. That's because the ABOVE bookmark told Word to total the values in all four cells above the formula, including the date. You don't want to include the date in the total, so you need to make a change.

4. Click in cell B5, and open the **Formula** dialog box. Delete the contents of the **Formula** box and key =SUM(B2,B3,B4). Do not insert any blank spaces in the formula. Set the number format to #,##0 and click **OK**. The correct value (8,923) appears in the cell.

NOTE

The Paste function drop-down list in the Formula dialog box includes functions that range from simple (such as COUNT, which shows how many items are in a list) to complex (such as IF, which is a logical function that determines whether a criterion is true or false). By familiarizing yourself with these functions, you can add more power to your tables and avoid using Excel worksheets in your Word documents.

5. Click in cell C5, and open the **Formula** dialog box. Delete the contents of the **Formula** box and key **=SUM(C2:C4)**. Do not insert any blank spaces in the formula. Set the number format to **#,##0** and click **OK**. The correct value 9,941 appears in the cell.

6. Click in cell D5, open the Formula dialog box, and create a formula that totals the values in cells D2, D3, and D4. Choose the same number format used in the preceding steps.

Figure 15-15
Table with totals

CAMPBELL'S CONFECTIONS			
STATE TOTALS			
CHOCOLATE-COVERED NUTS –2006 THROUGH 2008			

	2006	**2007**	**2008**	**Average**
Pennsylvania	4,129	4,560	4,401	4,363
Ohio	1,206	1,117	1,040	1,121
West Virginia	3,588	4,264	4,502	4,118
Total	8,923	9,941	9,943	

7. Save the file as *[your initials]***15-16** in your Lesson 15 folder. Print and close the document.

Using Excel Worksheets in Word Documents

Word's advanced table features help you control many visual and structural effects in tables. Sometimes, however, you need the full strength of an Excel worksheet. You can insert an Excel worksheet into a Word document.

When you create a new Excel worksheet from within Word, it becomes an *embedded worksheet*. An embedded worksheet is completely contained in the Word document and does not have a corresponding Excel file. You can also create an embedded worksheet from an existing Excel file, but if you do this, changes you make in the embedded worksheet will be reflected only in the Word document and not in the original Excel file.

If you want an Excel file to be updated each time you make changes to its worksheet from within a Word document, you must *link* the worksheet rather than embed it. When you work with a linked worksheet, all the worksheet's information is stored within the Excel file, and the Word document contains only a reference or pointer to the Excel file. None of the actual information is saved with the Word file.

Exercise 15-17 EMBED A NEW EXCEL WORKSHEET IN A WORD DOCUMENT

1. Start a new document. Key the following text as a document heading. Format it attractively, using character and paragraph formatting, graphics, or other effects.

   Campbell's Confections
   Cost Analysis
   Chocolate-Covered Nuts—2006 through 2008

2. Press Enter twice after the heading.

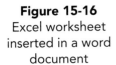

3. With the insertion point on the second blank line, click the **Insert** tab, click the Table button 🔳, and click **Excel Spreadsheet** in the table menu. An Excel worksheet is inserted into your document.

4. Notice that the Ribbon tabs contain Excel options, and the group commands have changed to Excel's options.

Figure 15-16
Excel worksheet inserted in a word document

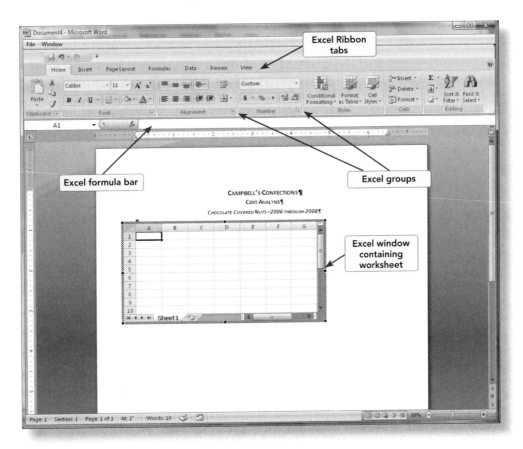

Exercise 15-18 ENTER AND FORMAT DATA

1. Key the data shown in Figure 15-17 into the cells of the Excel worksheet. Press the arrow keys to move between cells. In cell E2, key the formula as shown in the figure, including the punctuation.

Do not include spaces before or after the formula. Press Enter after keying the formula.

Figure 15-17

	A	B	C	D	E
1		2006	2007	2008	Average
2	Pennsylvania	2200	2500	2800	=AVERAGE (B2:D2)
3	Ohio	1800	2200	2600	
4	West Virginia	3000	3300	3600	

2. Click anywhere outside the Excel window to view your worksheet in Word.

3. Double-click the worksheet to reopen the Excel window.

4. Working in the Excel window, move your mouse pointer over cell A1. When you see the white cross pointer ⬦, drag diagonally down and across to select all the cells from A1 to E4 in the Excel window.

5. Click the Increase Indent button ⬥ on the **Home** tab, **Alignment** group. This button adds more space between the columns of text and numbers.

6. Right-click the selected cells, and choose **Format Cells** from the shortcut menu. The Format Cells dialog box opens.

7. Click the **Fill** tab, and choose a light aqua color under **Background Color**.

8. Click the **Font** tab. Change the font to **10-point Arial**. Click **OK**.

9. With the cells still selected, click the Format button ⬥ Format ⬥ on the **Home** tab, **Cells** group. Click **AutoFit Column Width** from the drop-down list. The cells are now wide enough for all the text and numbers.

10. Select cells B2 through E4, and click the Format button ⬥ Format ⬥. Click **Format Cells**. Choose the **Number** tab, click the **Number** category, set **Decimal places** to **0**, and click the **Use 1000 Separator (,)** box to use commas in values that are greater than 1,000. Click **OK**.

11. Click cell E2 to make it active. (You previously keyed a formula in this cell.)

12. Move the white cross pointer from within the cell to the bottom right corner of the cell until it becomes a black cross pointer + ⎤.

13. Drag down to cell E4, and then release the mouse button. The formula in cell E2 is automatically copied into cells E3 and E4. This is Excel's AutoFill feature.

Figure 15-18
Using Excel's AutoFill feature

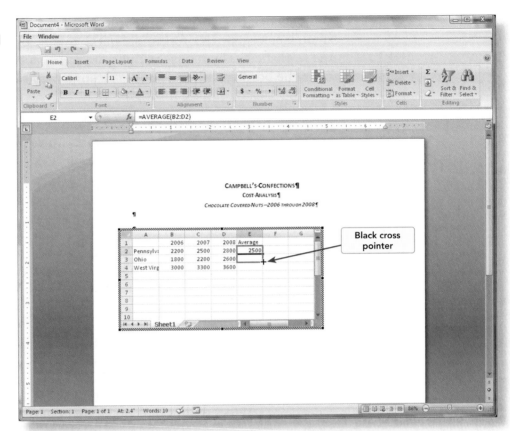

14. Click outside the worksheet to close Excel and return to the Word document.

NOTE

If you accidentally include too many or too few cells, just click the Undo command and try again.

Exercise 15-19 ADD A CAPTION TO AN EMBEDDED EXCEL WORKSHEET

1. Click the embedded worksheet once to select it as a Word object. When selected, a worksheet is surrounded by a border and sizing handles.

2. Click the References tab, and click the Insert Caption button ▤. In the Caption dialog box, check that the Label box is set to Table.

3. In the Caption text box, edit the caption to read Table 1: Cost of Chocolate-Covered Nuts. Click OK.

4. Select both the caption and the table; and press Ctrl + E. The table and its caption are now centered horizontally.

5. Select just the caption, and change it to 10-point Tahoma bold.

6. Double-click the worksheet to reopen the Excel window. Point to the small black square sizing handle in the middle of the right border of the worksheet. The mouse pointer changes to a two-pointed arrow ↔. Drag the border to the left until the empty columns no longer display and you see columns A through E.

7. Drag the sizing handle of the bottom border (black square in the middle of the border) up until the empty rows no longer display. You should see rows one through four. Deselect the worksheet.

8. Right-click the worksheet, and choose **Format Object** from the shortcut menu. The Format Object dialog box appears. Click the **Size** tab and change the **Width** to **4.0** inches. Click **OK**. Click outside the table to deselect it.

9. Save the document as *[your initials]***15-19** in your Lesson 15 folder. Keep the document open for the next exercise.

Exercise 15-20   CREATE A WORD TABLE FROM AN EXCEL WORKSHEET

You can easily copy information from an Excel worksheet and paste it into a Word document. When you do this, the pasted information becomes a Word table you can treat just as you would any other Word table.

1. Insert two blank lines below the embedded worksheet you created in the previous exercise. Place the insertion point on the second blank line.

2. While keeping the Word document open, start Excel. Open the Excel file **2008**.

3. Select cells A4 to D8, and copy them to the Clipboard.

Figure 15-19
Selecting cells in the excel worksheet

	A	B	C	D
1		Cost Breakdown		
2		2008		
3				
4		Pennsylvania	Ohio	West Virginia
5	Retail	800.00	800.00	800.00
6	Wholesale	1,000.00	900.00	1,500.00
7	Fundraising	1,000.00	900.00	1,300.00
8	Total	2,800.00	2,600.00	3,600.00

REVIEW

The simplest way to switch to an open document or application is to click its button on the Windows taskbar.

NOTE

When you paste the table into the Word document, the Paste Options button appears. This button's options let you keep the table's current formatting, format the table to match the document's formats, and create a link to the Excel worksheet. If you do not use this button to select any options, the pasted object maintains its original formatting by default.

4. Without closing the Excel worksheet, switch to *[your initials]*15-19 Word document.

5. With the insertion point on the second blank line below the table you created earlier, paste the Clipboard contents. The Excel worksheet cells appear in the Word document as a table.

6. Select the table and format it with the following attributes:

   • Using the Table Properties dialog box, **Table** tab, change the preferred width to **4.0** inches and center the table horizontally. Use the **Row** tab to format the row heights to at least **0.2** inch.

   • Text in the second, third, and fourth columns should be right-aligned. Text in the first column should be left-aligned.

   • Change the font in all cells to 10-point Arial, with no bold or italic.

   • Change the cell shading to match Table 1.

   • Insert a caption with the text Table 2: Cost Breakdown—2008.

   • Change the caption font to 10-point Tahoma bold, centered.

Figure 15-20
Formatted table in the word document

Table 1: Cost Breakdown--2008			
	Pennsylvania	Ohio	West Virginia
Retail	800	800	800
Wholesale	1,000	900	1,500
Fundraising	1,000	900	1,300
Total	2,800	2,600	3,600

NOTE

Because pasting Excel information into Word creates a Word table, you can edit the information just as you would any Word table. You can also create a nested table by pasting the Excel information into a cell of an existing Word table.

7. Save the document as *[your initials]*15-20 in your Lesson 15 folder. Keep the document open for the next exercise.

8. Switch to Excel, and close the file **2008** without saving it.

Exercise 15-21   EMBED AN EXISTING EXCEL WORKSHEET

After you copy Excel worksheet cells to the Clipboard, you can use the Paste command to insert the cells into a Word document, creating a Word table. If you use the Paste Special command, however, you can insert the table in one of several different formats.

1. With your Word document still open, switch to Excel and open the file **2007**.

2. Select cells A4 to D8, and copy them to the Clipboard.

3. Switch to your Word document. Insert two blank lines below Table 2, and position the insertion point on the second line.

4. Click the **Home** tab, and click the Paste button down arrow. Click **Paste Special**. The Paste Special dialog box opens.

5. Choose **Microsoft Office Excel Worksheet Object** from the list. Read the contents of the **Result** box at the bottom of the Paste Special dialog box.

Figure 15-21
Paste Special dialog box

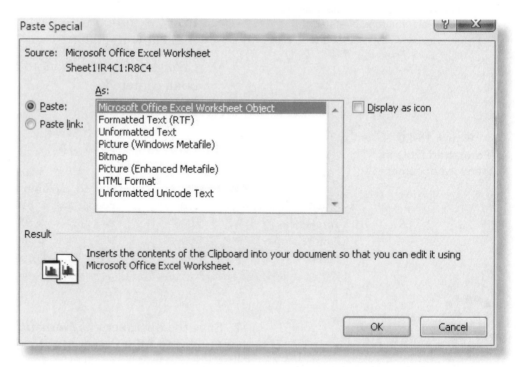

6. Make sure the **Paste** option is selected (not **Paste link**), and click **OK**. An embedded worksheet appears in the Word document. If you edit this worksheet, changes will be saved in Word. The original Excel worksheet will not be changed.

TIP

If an object's wrapping style is set to In line with text, you can use the alignment buttons on the Ribbon for horizontal positioning. When the in-line option is not set, use the Format Object dialog box or the Table Properties dialog box to control the horizontal position.

7. Right-click the embedded worksheet, and choose Format Object from the shortcut menu to open the Format Object dialog box.

8. Click the Layout tab, and set the wrapping style to In line with text, if it is not already selected. Click the Size tab and change the Width to 4.0 inches. Click OK. If the table is not already center-aligned, press Ctrl+E. The worksheet is now aligned with the table above it and surrounded by a border and sizing handles.

9. Insert a caption for the embedded worksheet, using the text Table 3: Cost Breakdown—2007. Format the caption to match the other captions in the document.

10. Double-click the worksheet to open the Excel window. Change the font, font size, and cell shading to match the other tables in the document.

11. Save the document as *[your initials]***15-21** in your Lesson 15 folder. Keep the document open for the next exercise.

12. Switch to Excel, and close **2007** without saving it.

Exercise 15-22   LINK AN EXCEL WORKSHEET

If you link cells from an Excel worksheet, all changes you make—whether in Excel or in Word—are saved in the Excel worksheet and reflected in the Word document. When you are working with a linked worksheet inside a Word document, the worksheet file is called the *source document,* and the Word document to which you link it is called the *destination document.*

1. Switch to your Word document. Insert two blank lines below Table 3 and position the insertion point on the second line.

2. Switch to Excel and open the file **2006**. Save the file as *[your initials]***15-22** in your Lesson 15 folder.

3. Select cells A4 to D8, and copy them to the Clipboard.

4. Switch to your Word document, and click the Paste button down arrow . Click Paste Special. The Paste Special dialog box opens.

5. Select the Paste link option, and choose Microsoft Excel Worksheet Object from the list box. Click OK.

6. Use the Format Object dialog box to change the linked worksheet's width to 4.0 inches. Center the object horizontally between the page margins, if it is not already centered.

7. Double-click the linked worksheet object to switch to Excel.

8. Press Esc to turn off the moving marquee border around cells A4: D8. (In Excel, this marquee border indicates that the selected cells have been copied to the Clipboard.) Click cell C6, which contains the number 999. Key **500** and press Enter. The number 500 appears in the cell.

NOTE

When you double-click a linked worksheet to make changes, the source document opens. After making the changes, you must save the source document. If you do not save it, the changes will not be reflected the next time you open the destination document (the Word document). This happens because when you open the Word document, it looks at the Excel worksheet to find the information that will be displayed.

9. Reselect cells A4 to D8, and change the cell shading, font size, and font effects to match the other tables in the Word document.

10. Resave the Excel worksheet; then close the worksheet and close Excel. Your Word document appears with the changes reflected in the last table. If the document does not reflect the changes, right click the table and click **Update Link**.

11. Create a caption for the last table, using the text **Table 4: Cost Breakdown—2006**. Format the caption to match the other captions in the document.

12. Save the document as *[your initials]***15-22**.

Exercise 15-23 EDIT A LINK TO MAKE A DOCUMENT PORTABLE

A linked worksheet in a Word document exists within Word as a Link field. A Link field is similar to a Ref field, but it references a worksheet instead of a bookmark. When you link a worksheet, the Link field includes the source document's entire path as part of the link (for example, "C:\\StudentData\\ Lesson15\\gl15-22.xlsx"). If you move the source and data file to a different folder or a removable disk, the link will be broken because the destination document (Word) will still look for the source document (Excel) in the C:\StudentData\Lesson15 folder.

You can edit the link to remove the path, leaving only the filename. Then Word will look for the source file in the same folder in which the Word document is saved. In this case, you can copy and move the source and destination files wherever you want, as long as you put them both in the same folder.

1. With Table 4 selected, press Alt+F9 to display field codes. Notice that all the tables except the Word table (Table 2) change to field codes. Notice also that the captions contain a Seq field.

2. Locate the Link field at the bottom of the document. This field starts with the text "LINK."

Figure 15-22
Editing a Link field

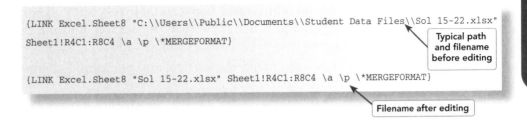

```
{LINK Excel.Sheet8 "C:\\Users\\Public\\Documents\\Student Data Files\\Sol 15-22.xlsx"
Sheet1!R4C1:R8C4 \a \p \*MERGEFORMAT}
```
Typical path and filename before editing

```
{LINK Excel.Sheet8 "Sol 15-22.xlsx" Sheet1!R4C1:R8C4 \a \p \*MERGEFORMAT}
```
Filename after editing

3. Within the Link field, locate the path and filename. It might be similar to "C:\\Lesson15*[your initials]*15-22.xls."

4. Edit the path and filename so it reads "*[your initials]*15-22.xls" but be careful not to change any other part of the Link code.

5. Press Alt+F9 to hide the field codes and redisplay all the tables. Save the document as *[your initials]*15-23 in your Lesson 15 folder, and then close it.

6. If possible, copy the two files *[your initials]*15-22 (the Excel file) and *[your initials]*15-23 (the Word file) to a different folder or a removable disk. Follow your instructor's directions.

7. Open the file *[your initials]*15-23 from the new folder or disk; then double-click Table 4. The linked Excel file appears. Close Excel.

8. Print the Word document with field codes displayed. Then print it again without the field codes. Close the document.

REVIEW

To print field codes, open the Print dialog box, click the Options button, and click the Advanced tab. Scroll to the Print group, and select Print field codes instead of their values check box. After printing, reopen the Print dialog box, click the Options button, click the Advanced tab, scroll to the Print group, and clear the Print field codes instead of their values check box.

Lesson 15 Summary

- You can prevent a page break from occurring in the middle of a table row. Open the Table Properties dialog box, click the Row tab, and clear the Allow row to break across pages check box. To prevent a page break from occurring between rows, use the Keep with next paragraph-formatting option.

- In tables that span multiple pages, you can define column headings to repeat at the top of each page by using the Repeat Header Rows option.

- You can split a long table into two shorter tables by using the Split Table command.

- To insert text above a table when there is no paragraph mark above the table, click in the table's first cell and choose Table, Split Table. Word inserts a blank paragraph mark above the table.

- To add white space between table text and cell borders, you can change cell margins in a table. You can set top, bottom, right, and left margins for individual cells or an entire table.

- You can change the vertical and horizontal alignment of text within table cells.

- Word's Table Styles gallery can quickly format a table by using one of many predefined styles. Word's AutoFit feature automatically adjusts the width of columns, based on the amount of text they contain.

- You can use the Create New Style dialog box to create your own table styles. A table style can contain formatting for the entire table or for different parts of a table (such as the header row, the last row, the right column, and so on).

- A caption is a numbered label, such as "Figure 1" or "Table 1: Year-End Revenue," that you can add to a table or other object.

- Use the mouse pointer to resize table rows and columns by dragging their borders. Press Alt as you drag, and Word displays the precise row or column measurement on its rulers.

- Use the Table Properties dialog box to set precise row heights or column widths.

- To resize a table proportionally, adjusting its height or width, drag the table resize handle.

- To make sure multiple tables stay in position on the same page, nest them in the cells of a larger, parent table. Draw the parent table; then select and drag each of the other tables into its own cell.

- You can sort a table by any of its columns, in either ascending or descending order. You can also sort selected paragraphs or items in a list.

- Insert formula fields in a table to perform calculations on the table's data. Word's formulas can perform operations such as adding, averaging, and counting. See Table 15-1.

- To find the average of a row or column of values, insert the =AVERAGE() formula field. Between the parentheses, use the ABOVE or LEFT bookmark, type individual cell addresses, or type the cell range.

- To sum a row or column of values, insert the =SUM() formula field. Between the parentheses, use the ABOVE or LEFT bookmark, type individual cell addresses, or type the cell range.

- If you have data in an Excel worksheet, you can use it in a Word document. You can embed the worksheet data in Word, making it a table. If you link the worksheet, you can update the data either in Excel or Word, and the changes will appear in both files.

- You can embed a new Excel worksheet in a Word document. To enter data in an embedded Excel worksheet, double-click the table to turn on Excel toolbars and menus in the Word window. Key data into cells, and format them as desired. Click outside the table to deactivate the Excel tools.

- To create a Word table from an Excel worksheet, select the data in Excel and use the Copy command. Switch to your Word document and use the Paste command.
- To embed an Excel worksheet into Word and keep it as an Excel object (rather than a Word table), copy the worksheet data, switch to Word, and use the Paste Special command (Microsoft Excel Worksheet Object option).
- To link an Excel Worksheet into Word, copy the worksheet data and use Word's Paste Special command (Paste link option).
- To maintain the connection between source and destination documents, even if you move them, edit the object's Link field in the destination document. Remove all path information from the field so it contains only the source document's name.

LESSON 15		Command Summary	
Feature	**Button**	**Command**	**Keyboard**
Table properties	Properties	Table Tools Layout tab, Properties group	
Repeat header row	Repeat Header Rows	Table Tools Layout tab, Data group	
Split table	Split Table	Table Tools Layout tab, Merge group	
Table styles		Table Tools Design tab, Table Styles group	
Fit table to contents	AutoFit	Table Tools Layout tab, Cell Size group	
Insert table caption	Insert Caption	References tab, Captions group	
Fit table to window	AutoFit	Table Tools Layout tab, Cell Size group	
Insert formula in table	f_x Formula	Table Tools Layout tab, Data group	
Insert Excel worksheet	Table	Insert tab, Tables group	
Embed/link copied worksheet	Paste	Home tab, Clipboard group	

Concepts Review

True/False Questions

Each of the following statements is either true or false. Indicate your choice by circling T or F.

T F   1. You prevent page breaks in the middle of a row by applying the Keep with next paragraph-formatting option.

T F   2. Custom table styles cannot be added to the Table Style gallery.

T F   3. You can use the Split Table command to insert a blank line above a table.

T F   4. You can define a table's column headings so they appear at the top of each page for a long table.

T F   5. When you embed an Excel worksheet, the changes you make to it are automatically saved in a new worksheet file.

T F   6. You can use the Table Properties dialog box or the Cell Margins button on the Table Tools Layout tab to open the Table Options dialog box.

T F   7. You cannot format an Excel worksheet that you create in Word.

T F   8. The Insert Caption command is located on the Insert tab.

Short Answer Questions

Write the correct answer in the space provided.

1. In the Table Properties dialog box, which tab contains the Options button you use to change the margins for all cells in the table?

_____

2. Which button do you click to insert a new Excel worksheet in a Word document?

_____

3. When an Excel worksheet is linked to a Word document, the workbook containing the worksheet is called the source document. What is the Word document called?

_____

4. Which option in the Table Properties dialog box determines if a page break will occur before or after a row?

_____

5. Which command is used to divide a table into two tables?

_____

6. Which command can you use to display column headings on each new page of a long table?

_____

7. What is a nested table?

_____

8. What do you call a table that contains another table?

_____

Critical Thinking

Answer these questions on a separate page. There are no right or wrong answers. Support your answers with examples from your own experience, if possible.

1. With side-by-side nested tables, you can create an attractive page layout. What are some examples of documents you can create by using these types of tables? What benefits and disadvantages do these types of tables offer?

2. Embedding and linking Excel worksheets makes Word a more powerful tool for developing tables. When would it be more appropriate to embed a worksheet versus linking it, and vice versa?

Skills Review

Exercise 15-24

Insert text above a table, define a table heading, use Table Styles and AutoFit, add a table caption, change cell margins and alignment, and control page breaks.

1. Open the file **Novelty**.
2. Insert a blank paragraph above the table by following these steps:
   a. Click in the first cell of the table.
   b. Click the Table Tools Layout tab, and click Split Table.
   c. With the insertion point in the blank line above the table, key CAMPBELL'S CONFECTIONS is pleased to announce the addition of the following novelty chocolates, starting in February.
   d. Change the spacing after to 24 points.
3. Style and AutoFit the table by following these steps:
   a. Select the table and click the Table Tools Design tab. Click the More arrow to display the Table Styles gallery.

b. Click a style in the third row of the **Built-In** styles. Locate the **Table Style Options** group on the Table Tools Design tab, and select the check boxes for **Header Row**, **Banded Rows**, and **First Column**.

    c. Select the table, and click the **Table Tools Layout** tab. Click the AutoFit button 🔲, and select **AutoFit Contents**.

4. Add a table caption by following these steps:

    a. Click anywhere in the table's header row.

    b. Click the **References** tab, and click the Insert Caption button 🔳.

    c. Edit the text in the **Caption** box to read Table 1: Novelty Chocolates. Click **OK**.

    d. Format the caption as 10-point Arial bold, left-aligned.

5. Change cell margins and alignments by following these steps:

    a. Select the entire table. Click the **Table Tools Layout** tab, and click the Properties button 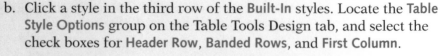.

    b. Click the **Table** tab and click **Options**.

    c. Change the **Top**, **Bottom**, **Left**, and **Right** cell margins to **0.15** inch. Click **OK** twice.

6. Define a header row for the table by following these steps:

    a. Select the table's first row. Format the header row's text as 12-point bold and small caps.

    b. Click the **Table Tools Layout** tab, and locate the **Data** group. Click **Repeat Header Rows**.

    c. Scroll to the second page to verify that the header row appears at the top of the page.

7. Prevent page breaks from occurring in the middle of a row by following these steps:

    a. Select the entire table.

    b. Open the **Table Properties** dialog box and click the **Row** tab. Clear the **Allow row to break across pages** check box and click **OK**.

8. Sort the table according to novelty name by following these steps:

    a. Select the entire table.

    b. Click the **Table Tools Layout** tab, and click the Sort button 🔳.

    c. Select **Name** in the **Sort by** box, **Text** in the **Type** box, and **Ascending** for the sort order. Verify that **Header Row** is selected. Click **OK**.

9. Add a right-aligned header to the second page only that contains Page followed by the page number.

10. Save the document as ***[your initials]*15-24** in your Lesson 15 folder. Submit and close the document.

Exercise 15-25

Split a table, create and modify a custom table style, and resize tables.

1. Open the file **Easter Candy**.

2. Use the Split Table command to insert a blank line above the table. Then use the following text to create an attractive title for the document, using character and paragraph formatting:

   Campbell's Confections
   Easter Candy Molds

3. Split this long table into five shorter ones by following these steps:

   a. Scroll down to the row containing the text "Peanut Butter Molds," and click the Table Tools Layout tab. Click Split Table.

   b. Scroll down to the row containing the text "Dark Chocolate Molds," and click at the beginning of the cell. Click Split Table.

   c. Scroll down to the row containing the text "Sugar-Free Molds," and click at the beginning of the cell. Click Split Table.

   d. Scroll down to the row containing the text "Pink Molds," and click at the beginning of the cell. Click Split Table.

4. Merge the cells in the first row of each table.

5. Click anywhere inside the first table, and create a new custom table style by following these steps:

   a. Click the Table Tools Design tab, and click the More arrow in the Table Styles group.

   b. Click New Table Style.

   c. In the Name box, key Table Special 2. Verify that the Style type drop-down list displays Table.

   d. Open the Apply formatting to drop-down list and choose Whole table. Use the font-formatting tools to set the table's font to 11-point Arial, with no effects.

   e. Click the Borders button arrow ⊞▾, and choose No Border. Click the arrow again, and choose Inside Horizontal Border.

   f. Open the Apply formatting to drop-down list, and choose Header row. Use the font-formatting tools to change the font to 11-point Calibri bold and italic. Set the shading color to a medium gray color (Darker 25%).

   g. From the Apply formatting to drop-down list, choose Even banded rows. Set the shading to a light gray color (Darker-5%).

   h. Select the New documents based on this template option, and click OK.

   i. Click the new style (Table Special 2) in the Table Styles group to apply the style to the table. Apply the Table Special 2 style to the other tables.

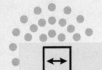

REVIEW

To merge cells, select the cells, right-click the selection, and choose Merge Cells from the shortcut menu.

6. Modify the new table style by following these steps:

a. Click anywhere in the first table, and right-click the Table Special 2 button in the Table Styles group.

b. Click **Modify Table Style**.

c. From the **Apply formatting to** list, choose **Whole Table**. Click the Align button ▦, and change the alignment to Align Center Left ▤.

d. From the **Apply formatting to** list, choose **Header Row**. Change the alignment to **Align Center** and remove the italic formatting.

e. Select the **New document based on this template** option and click **OK**.

f. Scroll through the document, and make sure the style has been updated for all three tables.

7. Change the column size for the first column of each table by following these steps:

a. In the first table, point to the border of the first column (in any row but the header row). When the pointer becomes a resizing pointer ╫, press [Alt] and drag the border to the right until the column's width is **2** inches.

b. Go to the second table. Click in any cell in the first column (in any row but the header row). Right-click and click **Table Properties**. Click the **Column** tab.

c. Click the **Preferred width** check box to activate it (so it is no longer dimmed). Then set the column width to **2** inches.

d. Resize the first column for each of the remaining tables.

8. Resize a table proportionally by following these steps:

a. Click the table resize handle of the last table, and drag the handle directly to the left. (Be careful not to drag downward.)

b. Release the handle when it is even with the 6.75-inch marker on the horizontal ruler. Resize column 1 to 2 inches if necessary.

c. Use the Table Properties dialog box, **Table** tab, to resize the other tables to 6.75 inches. Adjust the column width for column 1 to 2 inches if necessary.

9. Create header rows for the tables by following these steps:

a. Go to the top of the first table, and click in its first cell. Click the **Table Tools Layout** tab, and click **Repeat Header Rows**.

b. Go to the top of the second table, and click in its first cell. Click the **Table Tools Layout** tab, and click **Repeat Header Rows**.

c. Apply the **Repeat Header Rows** command for the other tables.

d. Scroll through the document to make sure the header rows are present where a table breaks across pages.

10. Select each table, and use the Table Properties dialog box, **Row** tab, to specify row height of at least **0.25** inch.

11. Add a right-aligned header to page 2 that contains **Page** followed by the page number. Format the header as 10-point Arial, and add two blank lines below the header text.

12. Save the document as *[your initials]*15-25 in your Lesson 15 folder. Submit and close the document.

Exercise 15-26

Create nested tables, use AutoFit and alignment features, change column sizes, and sort a table.

1. Open the file **Prices**.
2. Insert the current date in the "DATE" line of the memo heading.

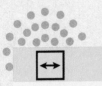
3. Select the seven lines of columnar tabbed text below the heading "Retail Prices" (do not select the heading). Convert the selected text to a table.
4. Select the columnar tabbed text under the heading "Wholesale Prices." Convert the selected text to a table.
5. Resize the table by following these steps:
   a. Click in the first table, and click the Table Tools Layout tab.
   b. Click AutoFit, AutoFit Contents, to resize the table.
6. Use the table resize handle to change the overall size of a table by following these steps:
   a. Click anywhere in the second table. Move your mouse pointer over the table to display the table resize handle in the lower right corner.
   b. Drag the table resize handle to the left, making the table the same width as the table above it.
7. Insert a blank paragraph mark below the memo's opening paragraph of text, and insert a 1-row by 2-column table.
8. Create nested side-by-side tables by following these steps:
   a. Select the paragraph "Retail Prices" and the table following it; then drag them into the first cell of the new blank table.
   b. Select the paragraph "Wholesale Prices" and the table following it; then drag them into the second cell of the new table.
9. Adjust the size and position of the parent table by following these steps:
   a. To select the parent table, click the table move handle for the parent table.
   b. Click the Table Tools Layout tab, AutoFit, AutoFit Contents.
   c. With the parent table still selected, open the Table Properties dialog box.
   d. Click the Table tab, and click Center.
   e. On the Table tab, click the Options button. Change all cell margins to 0.1 inch. Click OK twice.
10. Adjust properties for the nested tables by following these steps:
    a. Select the entire "Retail Prices" table, and open the Table Properties dialog box.
    b. On the Table tab, under Alignment, choose Center. Make sure the text-wrapping option None is selected.

c. Click the **Row** tab, and make sure the **Specify height** check box is not selected. Click **OK**.

d. Repeat steps *a*, *b*, and *c* for the "Wholesale Prices" table.

e. Use the resize handles of the nested tables to adjust the table heights to be equal.

11. Format the two nested tables by following these steps:

   a. Format both table titles ("Retail Prices" and "Wholesale Prices") as 10-point bold, small caps, and centered over the tables.

   b. In both tables, center and italicize the column headings.

   c. Select the entire "Wholesale Prices" table, and open the Table Properties dialog box. Click the **Cell** tab, click the **Center** option, and click **OK**.

   d. Select the entire "Retail Prices" table, and open the Table Properties dialog box. Click the **Cell** tab, click the **Center** option, and click **OK**.

12. Sort the "Retail Prices" table according to size, by following these steps:

   a. Select the "Retail Prices" table.

   b. Click the **Table Tools Layout** tab, and click **Sort**.

   c. In the Sort dialog box, select the **Header row** option.

   d. Under **Sort by**, click the drop-down arrow and choose **Size**.

   e. Click the **Type** drop-down arrow and choose **Text**.

   f. Click the **Descending** option to arrange the list from the lowest value to the highest. Click **OK**.

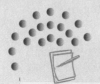

NOTE

You choose descending order because "8" is larger than "1." You could change 8 ounces to 0.5 pound for consistency in weight format.

13. Save the document as *[your initials]***15-26** in your Lesson 15 folder. Submit and close the document.

Exercise 15-27

Perform calculations in a Word table, insert a blank Excel worksheet, enter and format data in the worksheet, and copy and paste information from an Excel workbook.

1. Open the file **Novelty - 2**.

2. Insert a new, blank row at the bottom of the table. Then insert a new column to the right of the fourth column.

3. Click in the first cell of the new row (under "Greek letters") and key **Total**. Click in the first cell of the new column (to the right of "Q3") and key **Average**.

REVIEW

To add a new row to the bottom of a table, place the insertion point at the end of the table's last cell and then press Tab. To add a new column to the end of a table, select the end-of-row markers, then right-click, and choose Insert Columns.

4. Add formula fields to the bottom row by following these steps:

a. Click cell B4 and click the **Table Tools Layout** tab. Click **Formula**. In the **Formula** box, key =SUM(B2,B3). Open the Number format drop-down list, and select #,##0. Click **OK**.

b. Using the preceding step as a guide, add formula fields in cells C4 and D4.

5. Add formula fields to the last column to average the dollar amounts in the cells to the left of them, by following these steps:

a. Click cell E2 and open the **Formula** dialog box. In the **Formula** box, key =AVERAGE(LEFT). Choose #,##0 as the number format. Click **OK**.

b. Using the preceding step as a guide, add formula fields in cells E3 and E4 that average the sales amounts in the cells to their left.

6. Create a new Excel worksheet in the Word document by following these steps:

a. Position the insertion point on the last line of the document. Press Enter once.

b. Click the **Insert** tab and click **Table, Excel Spreadsheet**.

c. Point to the black square handle on the right side of the spreadsheet, and drag to the left to display four columns (A–D). Drag the bottom center black handle up to display four rows.

7. In the new worksheet, key the data shown in Figure 15-23.

Figure 15-23

	A	B	C	D
1		2007	2008	2009
2	Mascots	8,600	9,150	9,590
3	Greek letters	4,300	4,850	5,190
4	Total	=SUM(B2,B3)		

8. Use Excel's AutoFill feature to copy formulas by following these steps:

a. Select cell B4.

b. Move the white cross pointer to the bottom right of cell B5 until it becomes a black cross pointer ⁺⌐.

c. Drag the black cross pointer to the right to include cells C4 and D4.

d. Release the mouse button.

9. Format the new Excel worksheet to match the other table by following these steps:

a. Drag the white cross pointer from cell A1 to cell D4 to select all the cells.

b. Right-click the worksheet, and choose **Format Cells** from the shortcut menu.

c. Click the **Fill** tab and select a light blue color.

d. Click the **Font** tab and set the font to 11-point Arial.

e. Click the **Border** tab, click the **Outline** button , and then click the **Inside** button . Click **OK**.

f. Format the worksheet's first row and first column as bold.

g. Center the text in the first row.

h. In the worksheet, drag the column dividers for columns A, B, C, and D to the right until they are the same width as the table above them. Click the selection handle in the middle of the worksheet's right edge, and drag it back to the left to hide the blank columns that are displayed.

i. Click outside the worksheet window to return to the Word document.

10. Add a caption to the second table by following these steps:

a. Click the second table to select it.

b. Click the **References** tab, and click **Insert Caption**.

c. In the **Label** list, make sure **Table** is selected.

d. Edit the text in the **Caption** box to read **Table 2: Projected Sales: 2007—2009**.

e. Format the caption to match the first table's caption.

11. Delete the blank paragraphs between the tables. Then format each of the captions with 12 points spacing before and 6 points spacing after.

12. Save the document as *[your initials]***15-27** in your Lesson 15 folder. Submit and close the document.

Lesson Applications

Exercise 15-28

Split a long table into multiple tables, set up header rows, resize tables and columns, insert text above a table, and use table styles.

1. Open the file **Chronology - 3**.

2. Convert the text to a table.

3. Sort the text in the table in ascending order by state and city.

TIP

Sort by state and then by city. Be sure to select Header Row.

4. Use the Split Table command to insert a blank line above the table. Then key the following document title as 14-point bold and small caps.

Campbell's Confections
Chronology of Stores by State

5. Change the spacing after for the first line to 0, and change the spacing after for the second line to 24 points.

6. Center the first column text.

7. Change the second and third column width to 1.75 inches.

8. Insert a new first row at the top of the table.

9. Split the table at the row beginning "1962—the first row for Pennsylvania" so that this cell is in the first row of the new table.

10. Scroll down a few lines, and split the table at the text "1982" so that Clarksburg is the first cell in the new table.

11. Merge the cells in the first row of the first table, and key Ohio.

12. Format the text as 12-point bold and small caps, with 12 points of spacing before and 6 points of spacing after. Center-align the text (you will center the table later).

13. Delete the second row of the first table ("Year, City, State").

14. Add a blank row at the top of the other tables, and key the appropriate state name for each table. Format the row to match the formatting of the first row in the first table.

15. Define each table's first row as a repeating header row for the table.

16. Select all the rows in the first table except the header row, and change the row height to 0.25 inch. Center the text vertically in the rows.

17. Change the row height for the rows below the header row for the second and third tables. Use 0.25 inch for the row height, and center the text vertically.

18. Apply a table style from the first row in the Table Styles gallery.

19. Center the tables between the page's margins.

20. Insert a page break before the third table.

21. Add a header, starting on page 2. Key the left-aligned text Store Chronology, and insert a right-aligned page number. Format the header as 10-point bold and small caps. Make sure it does not appear on the document's first page.

22. Save the document as *[your initials]*15-28 in your Lesson 15 folder. Submit and close the document.

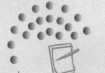

NOTE

After applying the table style, you might have to turn on the Repeat Header Rows option again.

Exercise 15-29

Create nested tables, sort tables, add formula fields to tables, and format tables.

1. Open the file **Trade**.

2. Change the letter's date to the current date.

3. On the second blank line below the paragraph beginning "The approximate cost of," insert a 1-row, 2-column table to be used as a parent table.

4. With your insertion point in the first cell, insert a blank table containing 2 columns and 6 rows.

5. Insert another 2-column by 6-row table in the second cell of the parent table.

6. Key the following information in the nested table on the left:

All Candy Expo
Registration	125.00
Lodging	550.00
Airfare	160.00
Car Rental	315.00

7. Key the following information in the nested table on the right:

Chocolate Show
Registration	200.00
Lodging	945.00
Airfare	180.00
Car Rental	320.00

In both tables, leave the last row blank.

8. Sort both tables in descending order according to the column that contains the dollar amounts.

9. In the bottom left cell of each nested table, key Total.

10. Insert table formulas in the appropriate places to total the cost of each trip.

11. Format both the parent table and the nested tables attractively, using all the following features:

- Merge cells.

- Align text in cells.

- Apply text formatting.

- Apply cell shading.

- Insert dollar signs in front of the amounts in the first and last cells in the column.

- Change cell margins to add space in the parent table surrounding the nested tables and to position aligned text and numbers within columns.

12. Adjust sizing and spacing of the tables as needed to fit the entire document on one page. You can also change the bottom margin to 0.5 inch.

13. Replace the text "xx" with your reference initials.

14. Save the document as *[your initials]*15-29 in your Lesson 15 folder. Submit and close the document.

Exercise 15-30

Create a table, add formula fields, and format the table.

1. Start a new document, and change the orientation to landscape. Format all cells in the table using right alignment.

2. Key Deposit Report at the top of the document, and format the text using 18-point bold and small caps, with center alignment and 18 points spacing after.

3. Insert a 12-column by 33-row table.

4. Key the text in Figure 15-24 across row 1.

TIP

In the Sort dialog box, be sure to select the Header row option. Sort by the second column, in descending order. Make sure the type is set to Number.

TIP

You can use the "ABOVE" bookmark with the formula's function, in both tables. Be sure to select the #,##0.00 number format.

Figure 15-24

Column 1	Day
Column 2	Cash
Column 3	Check
Column 4	Cash/Check Total
Column 5	Visa
Column 6	Mastercard
Column 7	Visa/MC Total
Column 8	Discover
Column 9	American Express
Column 10	Other Charge
Column 11	Total Charges
Column 12	Total Deposit

5. Format the first row using 10-point bold, Arial Narrow font. Vertically align the text in the row using the Bottom option. Center the text in row 1.

6. Key the numbers 1 through 31 in the first column starting in row 2. In the last row of column 1, key Total.

7. Key 100 in row 2 for columns 2 ("Cash"), 3 ("Check"), 5 ("Visa"), 6 ("Mastercard"), 8 ("Discover"), 9 ("AMEX"), and 10 ("Other Charge"). The amount 100.00 should appear in seven cells.

8. Click in the second row, fourth column ("Cash/Check Total"), and insert a formula to add the amounts in the second and third columns (columns B and C). Use appropriate number format.

9. Click in the second row, seventh column ("Visa/MC Total"), and insert a formula to add the amounts in the fifth and sixth columns (columns E and F). Use appropriate number format.

10. Click in the second row, eleventh column ("Total Charges"), and insert a formula to add the amounts in columns 5, 6, 8, 9, and 10 (columns E, F, H, I, and J). Use appropriate number format.

11. Click in the second row, last column ("Total Deposit"), and insert a formula to add the amounts in columns 4 and 11 (columns D and K). Use appropriate number format.

12. Click in the last row of column 1, and insert a formula to add the amounts in the first column. (Use the ABOVE function.)

13. Save the document as *[your initials]***15-30** in your Lesson 15 folder. Submit and close the document.

Exercise 15-31 ◆ Challenge Yourself

Create side-by-side and nested tables and embed Excel worksheets.

1. Open the file **Revenue**.

2. Draw a table below the last paragraph similar to the one shown in Figure 15-25.

Figure 15-25

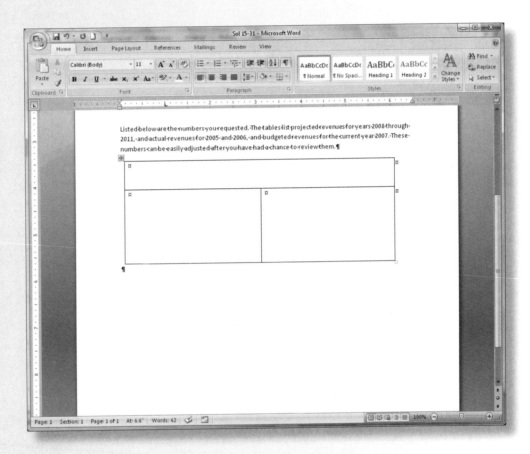

3. Open the Excel file **RevComp**.

4. Copy cells A1 to E8 to the Clipboard. Switch to Word, and paste the cells as an embedded worksheet into the first row of your Word table.

5. Switch to Excel. Press Esc to stop the copy/paste procedure (removing the marquee around the selected cells). Open the Excel file **Rev06**.

TIP

To embed an Excel worksheet in Word, use the Paste Special command and paste (not paste link) as a Microsoft Excel Worksheet object.

6. Copy cells A1 to C8 to the Clipboard, and then paste them as an embedded worksheet into the first cell in row 2 of the Word table.

7. Open the Excel file **Rev07**.

8. Copy cells A1 to B8 to the Clipboard, and then paste them as an embedded worksheet into the remaining cell of the Word table.

9. Click the worksheet in row 1 of your parent table; then drag the table sizing handle until its right border aligns with the right border of the second worksheet in row 2.

10. Select the entire parent table, and apply the AutoFit Contents setting. Remove all borders from the parent table.

11. Double-click the second worksheet in row 2 so you can edit it. Select cell A2 (which contains the text "2007"). Change the text to read 2007 Budgeted Revenue.

12. Return to the Word document, and insert today's date in the memo's date line. Center the table horizontally.

13. Save the Word document as *[your initials]*15-31 in your Lesson 15 folder. Submit and close the document.

14. Close the Excel worksheets without saving them; then close Excel.

On Your Own

In these exercises, you work on your own, as you would in a real-life business environment. Use the skills you've learned to accomplish the task—and be creative.

Exercise 15-32

Log on to the Internet and visit the home page of your favorite professional sports team. Research the team's win-loss record for the past four years, and use this information to create a set of four tables—one table for each year. Show each game's opponent, score, and whether the game was a win or a loss. Save the document as *[your initials]*15-32 and submit it.

Exercise 15-33

Create a table to include a daily sales breakdown by category. Include categories for various types of chocolate (creams, nuts, clusters, etc.). Format the tables using landscape orientation, and apply a table style. Format the table using the Table, Row, Column and Cell tabs in the Table Properties dialog box. Include formulas in the table. Save the document as *[your initials]*15-33 and submit it.

Exercise 15-34

Create a new document—a memo to your boss, listing clients with past-due accounts. Insert a formula field to total the past-due amounts. Add text describing the status of these accounts. Save the document as *[your initials]*15-34 and submit it.

Lesson 16

Columns

OBJECTIVES

After completing this lesson, you will be able to:

1. Create multiple-column layouts.

2. Key and edit text in columns.

3. Format columns and column text.

4. Control column breaks.

5. Use hyphenation.

MCAS OBJECTIVES

In this lesson:
WW 07 1.2.3
WW 07 2.3.2

Estimated Time: 1 hour

Word can arrange document text in multiple columns on a single page like those used in newspapers and magazines. The continuous flow of text from one column to another can make a document more attractive and easier to read.

Documents commonly have between one and three columns. A single document can also use different column layouts. For example, a document might use a standard one-column layout in one section and a three-column layout in another section.

Creating Multiple-Column Layouts

There are two ways to create multiple-column layouts:

- Use the Columns command on the Ribbon, Page Layout tab.

- Use the Columns dialog box.

You can change the column format for the whole document, for the section containing the insertion point, or for selected text.

Exercise 16-1 USE THE RIBBON TO CREATE COLUMNS

NOTE

Draft view displays columnar text in a single, continuous, narrow column. Use Print Layout view or Print Preview to see how columns are arranged on a page.

NOTE

The size of the document window determines the appearance of the Columns button. A maximized window displays the column button 🔲, and a window that is not maximized displays the column button 🔲.

1. Open the file **Company - 3**. If nonprinting characters are not displayed, click the Show/Hide ¶ button 🔳 to display them.

2. Position the insertion point at the beginning of the bold heading "Services" near the bottom of page 1 of the document.

3. Insert a continuous section break before the heading "Services" (Page Layout tab, Breaks).

4. Click the **Page Layout** tab, and locate the **Page Setup** group. Click the Columns button 🔲 on the Ribbon. A menu appears below the button with options for the number of columns that will appear in your document.

Figure 16-1
Choosing a column layout

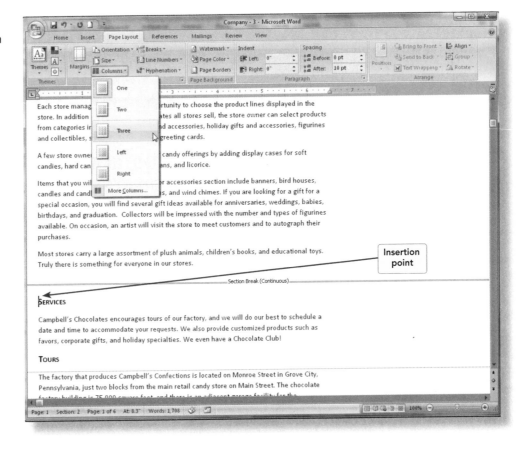

5. Point to the menu option for **Three**, and click to choose a three-column layout. The new section is now in three columns.

Figure 16-2
One- and three-column layouts in print layout view

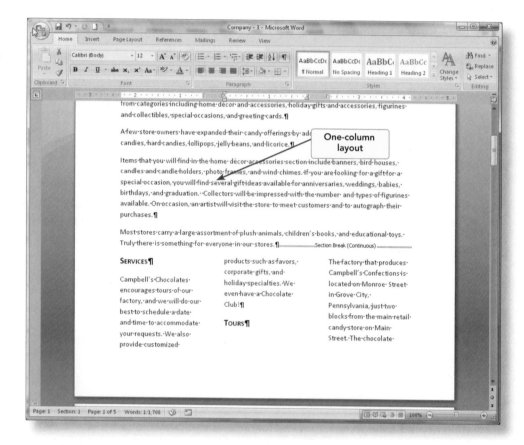

Exercise 16-2 USE THE COLUMNS DIALOG BOX TO CREATE COLUMNS

When you use the Columns command menu, Word applies default settings for column width and formats the section where the insertion point is located or formats the entire document if the document does not contain sections. You can change these settings in the Columns dialog box.

1. While still in Print Layout view, position the insertion point at the beginning of the paragraph that starts "Fundraising." (The paragraph is near the end of the document.)

2. Click the **Page Layout** tab, and click the Columns button to display the Columns menu. Click **More Columns** to open the Columns dialog box.

Figure 16-3
Columns dialog box

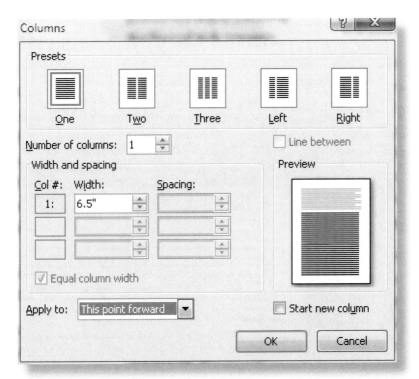

3. Key **1** in the **Number of columns** text box, or click **One** in the **Presets** section.

4. Choose **This point forward** from the **Apply to** drop-down list. The **Preview** box reflects the options you specify.

5. Click **OK**. A continuous section break is automatically inserted at the location of the insertion point, and the new section is formatted as one column. To see the section break, switch to Draft view 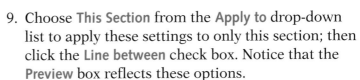. Remember Draft view does not display multicolumn layouts. Switch to Print Layout view.

6. Press [Enter] to insert an extra blank line between the sections.

7. Position the insertion point at the beginning of the heading "Services" on the first page, and open the Columns dialog box.

8. Set the **Spacing** text box for **Col #1** to **0.25"** to specify spacing between columns. Click the **Equal column width** check box to make all the columns equal in width.

NOTE

You can manually adjust the width and spacing settings for individual columns if you clear the Equal column width check box. Then you can key a number in the appropriate Width and Spacing box or click the up and down arrows.

9. Choose **This Section** from the **Apply to** drop-down list to apply these settings to only this section; then click the **Line between** check box. Notice that the **Preview** box reflects these options.

10. Click **OK**. The columns in this section are spaced 0.25 inch apart with a line between them.

11. Open the Word Options dialog box, and click Advanced. Scroll to the Show document content group, and click Show text boundaries to select the option. Click OK. A single dotted line displays column boundaries and page margins.

Figure 16-4
Display column boundaries

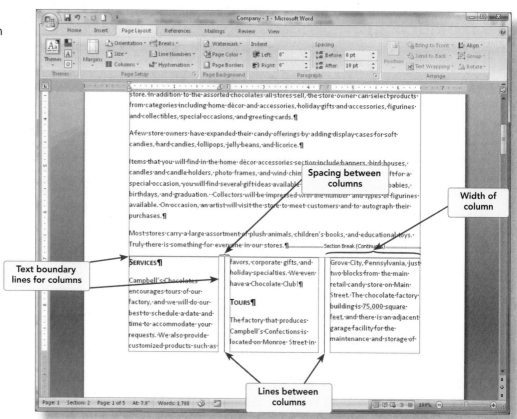

12. Scroll through the document and review all boundary lines.

13. Reopen the Word Options dialog box. Click Advanced, and scroll to Show document content. Click Show text boundaries to deselect this option.

14. Click OK. The boundary lines are hidden.

NOTE

Text boundary lines do not appear when a document is printed.

Keying and Editing Text in Columns

You can key and edit text in multiple-column layouts the same way you do in standard one-column layouts. Moving the insertion point around is a little different, however.

Exercise 16-3 KEY AND EDIT COLUMN TEXT

Keying and editing text in columns is very similar to keying and editing text in a standard document.

To move the insertion point from the bottom of a column to the top of the next column, you press →. You press ← to move from the top of a column to the bottom of the previous column. To move from the bottom line of a column to the first line of the same column on the next page, press ↓.

TIP

If a document has a page that contains blank lines between the end of the text in a column and the page break, press ↓ more than once to move to the top line of the column on the next page.

1. Scroll to the middle of page 3, to the paragraph that begins "Volume discounts" in the second column. Position the insertion point before the text "Volume."

2. Key the text shown in Figure 16-5. Notice that the text is inserted into the column paragraph just as it would be in a standard one-column document.

Figure 16-5

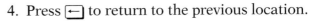

```
A luxurious, handmade chocolate gift is a great way to
make a sweet impression.
```

3. Position the insertion point at the end of the text in the third column on page 3, and press →. The insertion point moves to the first column at the top of the next page.

NOTE

When you use arrow keys to navigate in columns, you might need to press an arrow key twice to move past a space.

4. Press ← to return to the previous location.

5. Position the insertion point at the end of the first column on page 2, and press → again. The insertion point moves to the top of the second column.

6. Press ← to return to the end of the first column. Position the insertion point anywhere in the middle of the last line of the first column.

7. Press ↓, and the insertion point moves to the same position in the same column at the top of the next page. If the first line is a blank line, you might have to press ↓ again.

Formatting Columns and Column Text

You can create and change font and paragraph formats for text in columns the same way you create and change them for standard layouts.

There are two ways to change the width of a column and the amount of space between columns:

- Use the ruler.
- Use the Columns dialog box.

Exercise 16-4 FORMAT COLUMN TEXT

1. Just below the section break on the first page, select the text "Services."

2. Format the text as 16-point bold and italic, with 18 points of spacing after the paragraph.

3. Press Ctrl+A to select the document.

4. Click the Justify button ▤ on the Home tab to justify the text. Notice the additional white space between words as a result of the justified text.

5. Click the Undo button ↶.

TIP

When you justify column text, it looks like text in a newspaper. Left-align column text to create more of a newsletter effect. It is rarely appropriate to center column material.

Exercise 16-5 CHANGE COLUMN WIDTH AND SPACING

1. Display the ruler if it is not displayed.

2. On page 2, position the insertion point in the first column. Notice that the column has its own indent markers and margin settings on the ruler.

3. Point to the column's right margin on the ruler. When you see the ScreenTip "Right Margin" and the two-pointed arrow ↔, drag the right margin 0.5 inch to the left. Hold down Alt while dragging to see the exact measurement.

Figure 16-6
Using the ruler to adjust column width

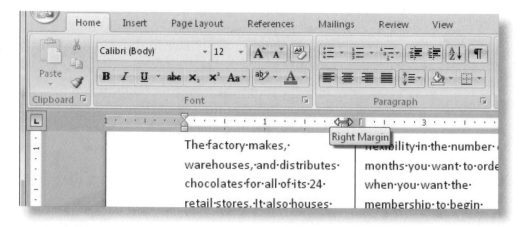

4. Release the mouse button. Because these columns were set to be of equal width, they all become narrower, and the spacing between them increases. Notice that the page breaks change because the text reflows.

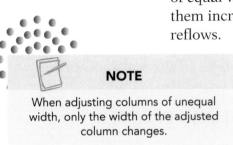

NOTE

When adjusting columns of unequal width, only the width of the adjusted column changes.

5. Open the Columns dialog box. Click Equal column width to deselect this option.

6. Click OK. The ruler now contains column markers in the blue shaded areas on the ruler. You can drag these markers to adjust the width of individual columns.

7. Position the pointer over the first column marker. A ScreenTip displays "Move Column."

Figure 16-7
Dragging a column marker

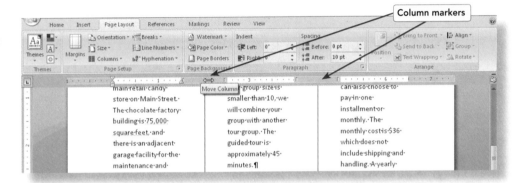

8. Drag the column marker 0.5 inch to the right. The width of the first column increases as it makes the second column narrower.

9. Move the pointer to the left margin area of the second column. The ScreenTip "Left Margin" appears.

Figure 16-8
Adjusting left margin of second column

10. Drag the two-pointed arrow pointer 0.5 inch to the left. This decreases the space between the first two columns.

11. Open the Columns dialog box. Notice the different settings for columns 1 and 2.

12. Set the spacing for column 1 to **0.4"** and check **Equal column width**.

13. Click OK. Word changes the width for all three columns to 1.9 inches and the space between columns to 0.4 inch.

Controlling Column Breaks

Word automatically breaks columns at the end of the page or section, so column lengths are often uneven. However, you can insert a column break manually so the columns end where you want them to end. You can also balance the columns by adjusting the column breaks to make them even.

Exercise 16-6   INSERT COLUMN BREAKS

There are three ways to insert column breaks:

*   Use the Breaks command.

*   Press Ctrl + Shift + Enter.

*   Use the Columns dialog box.

In this exercise you practice inserting column breaks by using each of the three methods.

1. On the fourth page of the document, position the insertion point before "Fundraising."

2. Click the **Page Layout** tab, and click **Breaks** to open the Breaks menu.

3. Click **Column**. A column break is inserted, and "Fundraising" appears at the top of the next page.

4. Press Backspace to delete the column break.

5. Press Ctrl + Shift + Enter to insert a column break again.

6. Press Backspace to remove it.

TIP

You can also use the Paragraph dialog box to control column breaks. For example, if a column break separates a paragraph from its heading, you can use the Keep with next pagination option.

7. Open the **Columns** dialog box.

8. Choose **This point forward** from the **Apply to** drop-down list, click **Start new column**, and click **OK**. A new section is inserted. Notice that the section break has the same effect as the previous column breaks.

9. Click the Undo button 🔄.

Exercise 16-7   BALANCE THE LENGTH OF COLUMNS

You can balance the length of your columns on a partial page to add a professional appearance to a document.

1. At the end of the three-column section on page 4, position the insertion point to the immediate right of the paragraph mark after "Confection's catalog."

2. Press Delete. Section 2 becomes one column. (The formatting in the last paragraph mark now applies to section 2.)

3. Click within section 2, open the **Columns** dialog box, and reapply the formatting for this section: three columns with equal column width, spacing between the columns of 0.25 inch, and a vertical line between the columns.

4. Open Print Preview, and notice that the columns on the last page are not balanced.

5. Close Print Preview, and position the insertion point at the end of the three-column section, after "fundraising packet."

6. Insert a **Continuous** section break. Word creates columns of equal length on the last page.

7. Switch to Print Preview to view the document.

Figure 16-9
Document with columns of equal length

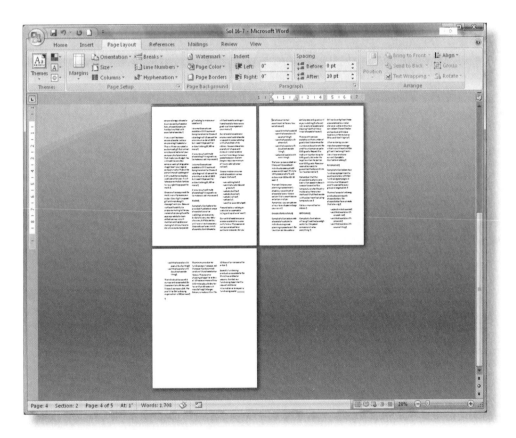

8. Return to Print Layout view.

9. At the end of page 1, change the continuous section break to a **Next page** section break using the Page Setup dialog box, Layout tab.

10. Scroll through section 2, and use the **Keep with next** option to prevent side headings from being separated from the paragraph that follows.

11. Apply page numbering, beginning in the second section, with numbers centered at the bottom of the page. Start numbering at 1, and make sure there is no page number in section 1.

12. Save the document as *[your initials]*16-7 in a new Lesson 16 folder.

Using Hyphenation

Hyphenation is used to divide words at the end of a line. You can hyphenate text manually, or Word can hyphenate text for you automatically. Word uses three types of hyphens:

• A normal hyphen is used for words that should always be hyphenated, such as "twenty-three" or "mother-in-law."

• A *nonbreaking hyphen* is used when a hyphenated word should not be divided at a line break. For example, you could use a nonbreaking hyphen in a hyphenated word, such as "self-employed." A nonbreaking hyphen is similar in purpose to a nonbreaking space.

• An *optional hyphen* indicates where a word should be divided if the word falls at the end of a line. If the word does not fall at the end of a line, the optional hyphen disappears from the screen and is not printed.

Exercise 16-8   INSERT NORMAL, NONBREAKING, AND OPTIONAL HYPHENS

It is a good idea to use hyphenation when a document contains lines that seem to break very irregularly. You can also use hyphenation to potentially shorten a document's length.

1. In the current document, scroll to the top of page 3 and locate the telephone number in the first column. Delete the hyphen after "1," and insert a nonbreaking hyphen by pressing Ctrl + Shift + - (the Hyphen key). The nonbreaking hyphen will prevent the telephone number from being divided between two lines.

2. Go to page 2, and locate the paragraph that begins "The factory makes." Place the insertion point between the "s" and "t" of "distributes."

3. Insert an optional hyphen by pressing Ctrl + -. The optional hyphen indicates where "distributes" should be divided.

4. Locate the phrase "melt-a-ways" in the bulleted list in the third column on page 2. The phrase contains a normal hyphen. Notice the difference in shape and size among the three types of hyphens. All hyphens, however, have the same appearance when printed.

Figure 16-10
Normal,
nonbreaking, and
optional hyphens

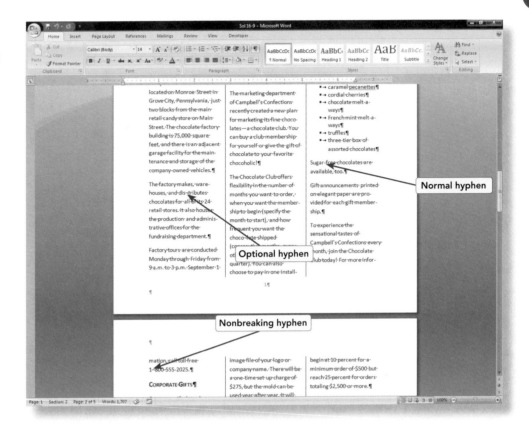

Exercise 16-9 HYPHENATE A DOCUMENT

Word offers automatic hyphenation to control ragged edges at the ends of paragraph lines and to reduce the amount of space Word inserts in justified text. In the Hyphenation dialog box you can:

- Hyphenate the document automatically as you key text.

- Hyphenate words written in all-capital letters.

- Set a hyphenation zone measurement to control the amount of raggedness in the right margin. The default setting is 0.25 inch. A lower number reduces the raggedness, and a higher number reduces the amount of hyphenation.

- Limit the number of consecutive hyphens in lines of text by a number you enter.

- Manually hyphenate a document, which lets you confirm each hyphen.

Figure 16-11
Hyphenation dialog
box

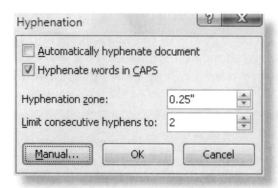

NOTE

You can also automatically hyphenate a document by clicking the Page Layout tab, clicking Hyphenation in the Page Setup group, and clicking Automatic. To remove automatic hyphenation, click the Page Layout tab, Page Setup group, Hyphenation, and click None.

TIP

You can move the hyphenation point for a word in the Hyphenate at box by clicking another point in the word or by using ← or →.

1. Move the insertion point to the beginning of the document. Click the **Page Layout** tab; click the arrow beside the Hyphenation button ; and then choose **Hyphenation Options**. The Hyphenation dialog box appears.

2. Set the **Limit consecutive hyphens** box to **2**, so no more than two consecutive lines end with hyphens.

3. Click **Manual**. Word begins the hyphenation process. The program asks for confirmation for each word to be hyphenated.

4. Click **Yes** to accept the hyphenation, but avoid hyphenating proper names or words containing fewer than six letters, such as "ha-ven."

5. When the dialog box appears to tell you hyphenation is complete, click **OK** to return to the document.

6. Save the document as ***[your initials]*16-9** in your Lesson 16 folder.

7. Submit and close the document.

NOTE

The Gregg Reference Manual contains several guidelines for preferred hyphenation practices. For example, you should not hyphenate abbreviations or contractions (such as "shouldn't"), or hyphenate a word to create a one-letter syllable (such as "a-ware"). For more information about hyphenation, see Section 9, "Word Division," in *The Gregg Reference Manual.*

Lesson 16 Summary

- Word can arrange document text in columns like those used in newspapers and magazines. There are two ways to create multiple-column layouts: by using the Columns menu and by using the Columns dialog box.

- You can key and edit text in multiple-column layouts the same way as in standard one-column layouts. Use the arrow keys to move between columns.

- You can create and change font and paragraph formats for text in columns the same way you create and change them for standard layouts.

- Adjust column width and spacing by dragging column markers and column margins on the ruler or by using the Columns dialog box. Create equal column widths by clicking the Equal column width check box in the Columns dialog box.

- Word automatically breaks columns at the end of the page or section. However, you can insert a column break manually so the columns end where you want them to end.

- Column lengths are often unequal at the ends of sections or pages. Insert a continuous section break after the unbalanced columns and Word will balance the columns.

- Hyphenation is the division of words that cannot fit at the end of a line. A normal hyphen is used for words that should always be hyphenated. A nonbreaking hyphen is used when a hyphenated word should not be divided at a line break. An optional hyphen indicates where a word should be divided if the word falls at the end of a line.

LESSON 16		Command Summary	
Feature	**Button**	**Command**	**Keyboard**
Insert columns	Columns	Page Layout tab, **Page Setup** group, **Columns**	
Insert columns break		Page Layout tab, **Page Setup** group, **Breaks**	Ctrl + Shift + Enter
Optional hyphen			Ctrl + -
Nonbreaking hyphen			Ctrl + Shift + -

Concepts Review

True/False Questions

Each of the following statements is either true or false. Indicate your choice by circling T or F.

T F   1. You can open the Columns dialog box by using the Insert tab on the Ribbon.

T F   2. A continuous section break is used to balance columns.

T F   3. Formatting text in multiple columns is very different from formatting text in a typical document.

T F   4. Pressing ⟶ at the end of any column moves the insertion point to the top of the next column.

T F   5. Words containing nonbreaking hyphens cannot be divided across two lines.

T F   6. You can use the ruler to change column width.

T F   7. A single document can use different column layouts.

T F   8. When working with columns, use Draft view to see the columns as they are arranged on the page.

Short Answer Questions

Write the correct answer in the space provided.

1. What is the keyboard shortcut to insert a column break?

_____

2. Which dialog box do you use to add a vertical line between columns?

_____

3. Which arrow do you press to move from the top of any column to the bottom of the previous column?

_____

4. Which tab on the Ribbon includes the Columns command?

_____

5. Which key do you press while adjusting column widths on the ruler to see an exact measurement display?

_____

6. What shape is the pointer when you use the ruler to adjust column widths?

_____

7. Which kind of hyphen do you use if you want to indicate where a word should be divided if the word falls at the end of a line?

_____

8. What option in the Columns dialog box do you select to make all columns the same width?

_____

Critical Thinking

Answer these questions on a separate page. There are no right or wrong answers. Support your answers with examples from your own experience, if possible.

1. Imagine a newspaper that doesn't use columns. Then imagine an $8\frac{1}{2}$-by 11-inch newsletter, also without columns. What problems would these publications present to readers?

2. Find examples in magazines, newspapers, and newsletters of columns of different widths. Which width do you feel is most readable?

Skills Review

Exercise 16-10

Create multiple-column layouts.

1. Open the file **Orders**.
2. Format the text from "Online" to the end of the paragraph that begins "Delivery" into two equal-width columns with a vertical rule between columns by following these steps:

   a. Position the insertion point at the beginning of the paragraph that begins "Online." Scroll to the paragraph that begins "Delivery." Press Shift and click at the end of the paragraph (after $25).

   b. Click the Page Layout tab, and click the Columns button . Click More Columns to open the Columns dialog box.

   c. Specify 2 for Number of columns and 0.25″ for the Spacing of column 1.

   d. Choose Equal column width.

  e. Choose Selected text from the Apply to drop-down list, and check the Line between box.

  f. Click OK.

3. Go to the top of the document, and format section 1 with a 2-inch top margin.

4. Locate the "Mail" paragraph, and apply the Keep with next paragraph option.

5. Insert page numbering at the bottom center of the second page only. The number "2" should display at the bottom of the second page.

6. Insert a page break at the beginning of the title "Delivery Chart."

7. Save the document as *[your initials]*16-10 in your Lesson 16 folder.

8. Submit and close the document.

Exercise 16-11

Key and edit text in columns.

1. Open the file **Newsletter**. Change the top and bottom margins to 0.75 inch.

2. Position the insertion point at the beginning of the paragraph that begins "Chocolate Facts." Format the document from "Chocolate Facts" through the end of the document as two columns with 0.25 inch distance between the columns.

3. Insert column text by following these steps:

  a. Position the insertion point at the end of the bullet paragraph that begins "Chocolate should not."

  b. Press Enter; then key the text shown in Figure 16-12.

Figure 16-12

- The center of the cocoa bean is called a nib.

- The Ivory Coast is the world's largest producer of cacao pods.

4. Edit document text by following these steps:

  a. Select "detrimental" at the top of the second column, and key harmful.

  b. Edit the first bullet paragraph under "Chocolate Facts" so that it is one sentence. Delete the period after "bean" and key , and. Change "Each" to lowercase.

5. Select the text at the end of the second column from "Choc Talk" to the end of the document, and apply a thin-line box border with light gray shading.

6. Add a box page border, using a thin, double-line style.

7. Save the document as *[your initials]*16-11 in your Lesson 16 folder.

8. Submit and close the document.

Exercise 16-12

Format columns. Adjust column width and spacing.

1. Open the file **Earth Day - 2**.
2. Create columns of unequal width by following these steps:
   a. Position the insertion point before the text "Earth Day will" in the first paragraph.
   b. Open the Columns dialog box.
   c. Choose the Left option in the Presets section, choose Line between, and choose This point forward from the Apply to list.
   d. Click OK.
3. Because this format is not appropriate for the document, use the ruler to change column width and spacing by following these steps:
   a. Place the insertion point in column 1, and point to the column marker (a ScreenTip displays "Move Column").
   b. Hold down Alt and drag the marker to the right to change column 1 to 2 inches wide.
   c. Point to the left margin area on the ruler for column 2 (a ScreenTip displays "Left Margin").
   d. Drag the margin 0.5 inch to the right, making the second column 3 inches wide and increasing the space between columns to 1 inch.
4. Open the Columns dialog box. Select Equal column width. Change columns 1 and 2 to 2.75 inches wide with 0.5-inch spacing.
5. Balance the columns by following these steps:
   a. Move the insertion point to the end of the document, after the Web site address.
   b. Click the Page Layout tab. Open the Breaks menu, click Continuous, and click OK.
6. Format the title of the document as 24-point bold, small caps, centered, and 72 points spacing before and 24 points spacing after.
7. Change the entire document font to Cambria.
8. Apply a double-line box page border to the document.
9. Save the document as *[your initials]*16-12 in your Lesson 16 folder.
10. Submit and close the document.

Exercise 16-13

Control column breaks and hyphenate a document.

1. Open the file **History - 3**.
2. Select the first line of the document, and apply 72 points spacing before.
3. Format the document from "Services" forward as three columns of equal width, with a line between columns.

4. Change the continuous section break to a next page section break.

5. Insert a column break before the paragraph that begins "We also make" at the bottom of page 3 by following these steps:

   a. Position the insertion point to the left of the text.

   b. Press Ctrl+Shift+Enter.

6. Balance the columns by following these steps:

   a. Move the insertion point to the end of the document, after "fundraising packet."

   b. Click the Page Layout tab. Open the Breaks menu, and choose Continuous.

7. Hyphenate the document by following these steps:

   a. Move the insertion point to the beginning of the document.

   b. Click the Page Layout tab, and click Hyphenation.

   c. Select Hyphenation Options.

   d. Change the value in the Limit consecutive hyphens to box to 2, and click Manual.

   e. Click Yes to confirm each hyphenation, but avoid hyphenating proper names.

   f. Click OK when hyphenation is complete.

8. Save the document as *[your initials]*16-13 in your Lesson 16 folder.

9. Submit and close the document.

Lesson Applications

Exercise 16-14

Create a two-column layout, format text, and balance the columns.

1. Open the file **Guidelines**.

2. Position the insertion point at the beginning of the paragraph that begins "Business Structure." Use the Columns dialog box to create a two-column layout from this point forward, with 1 inch between the columns and no vertical lines.

3. Format each side heading using 14-point bold and small caps.

4. Key the title **GUIDELINES** in bold, all caps, with 24 points spacing after at the top of the document. Center the heading, and change it to 16 points.

5. Balance the columns, and delete blank paragraph marks that may appear at the top of a column.

6. Change the top margin for section 1 to 2 inches. Add a page number to print at the top right of pages 2 and 3 only. Include Page in front of the number.

7. Spell-check the document, and save it as *[your initials]*16-14 in your Lesson 16 folder.

8. Submit and close the document.

Exercise 16-15

Create a three-column layout, change column spacing, and balance columns.

1. Open the files **Stores - 1** and **Intro**.

2. Select and copy the paragraphs in the Intro document.

3. Paste the selected text at the beginning of **Stores - 1**, and insert a blank line after the pasted text.

4. Insert a continuous section break before "Ohio Stores."

5. Create a three-column layout for the list of stores. Change the spacing between columns to 0.2 inch. Keep the columns equal width (with no line between columns).

6. Key Campbell's Confections as a title at the top of the document. Change the spacing after to 24 points, and format the title as all caps, 16-point bold, italic, and centered.

7. Change the top margin of section 1 to 2 inches.

8. Format the three state headings as 12-point bold, italic, and small caps.

9. Insert a column break at the start of the listing for the "Warren, Ohio" store at the bottom of the first column using `Ctrl`+`Shift`+`Enter`.

10. Insert a column break at the start of the listing for the "Morgantown, WV" store at the bottom of the second column, and the "Butler, PA" store at the bottom of page 1.

11. Balance the columns on page 2. Control column breaks if necessary.

12. Create a footer for page 2 only to include a centered Page followed by the page number.

13. Save the document as *[your initials]*16-15 in your Lesson 16 folder.

14. Submit the document. Close both documents.

Exercise 16-16

Create a two-column layout, key text in columns, and format and balance the columns.

1. Open the file **Staff**.

2. Change the page orientation to landscape.

3. Format the entire document as two columns.

4. At the top of the first column, key the heading Campbell's Confections: Corporate Staff.

5. Add 24 points spacing after to the heading.

6. Format the heading as 24-point italic.

7. At the end of the document, key the new paragraph shown in Figure 16-13. Use the Format Painter to copy the format from one of the side headings in the document to the new heading.

Figure 16-13

```
Liz Hart, Advertising/Marketing
Liz has been with the company for 15 years. She started
working as a part-time employee when she was in high school
to save money for college. She joined the company full-time
after she graduated from college. She is married with two
sons. Her hobby is cooking, collecting recipe books, and
spending time with her family.
```

8. Change the space between columns to 1 inch, and keep the columns equal width.

9. At the beginning of the text under the heading, insert a continuous section break.

10. Format the heading section as one column.

11. In the heading, delete the colon, and start the heading text beginning *"Corporate Staff"* on a new line.

12. Change the text in the new line to small caps, and center both lines of the heading. Change the spacing after for the first line of the heading to 0 points, and change the line spacing to single.

13. Delete the heading "Corporate Staff" in the middle of the first column.

14. Select all text below the document heading, and change the font size to 11 points.

15. Balance the length of the columns in section 2.

16. Insert a page number to print in the upper right corner of page 2 only.

17. Save the document as *[your initials]*16-16 in your Lesson 16 folder.

18. Submit and close the document.

Exercise 16-17 ◆ Challenge Yourself

Create a three-column layout, format columns and column text, balance columns, and hyphenate the document.

1. Open the file **Corporate Gifts**.

2. Key the title Corporate Gifts as 24-point bold and small caps. Center the title, and add 24 points spacing after.

3. Insert a continuous section break at the first paragraph below the title.

4. Format the second section as three equal columns.

5. Balance the columns.

6. Change the font in section 2 to Cambria.

7. Format all the paragraphs in section 2 with a 0.25-inch first-line indent.

8. Change the space between the columns to 0.4 inch, and insert a line between columns.

9. Change the document left and right margins to 1.25 inches. Center the whole document vertically on the page.

10. Hyphenate the document manually. Avoid hyphenating words that are six characters or less or any proper names.

11. Apply a triple-line 1½-point page border to the document.

12. Save the document as *[your initials]*16-17 in your Lesson 16 folder.

13. Submit and close the document.

On Your Own

In these exercises you work on your own, as you would in a real-life business environment. Use the skills you've learned to accomplish the task—and be creative.

Exercise 16-18

Create a newsletter about a neighborhood activity. Apply a three-column layout. Format the newsletter attractively, and balance the columns. Add a title to the newsletter, and spell- and grammar-check your document. Save the document as *[your initials]*16-18. Submit the document.

Exercise 16-19

Create a newspaper article about a topic you would enjoy reporting. Use landscape orientation, and format the article with four columns and justified alignment. Apply very simple formatting that might appear in a newspaper. Balance the columns. Give the article a title, and spell- and grammar-check the document. Save the document as *[your initials]*16-19 and submit it.

Exercise 16-20

Log onto the Internet. Find Web sites about a health issue that interests you. Using the information, create a magazine article that is two columns, left-justified, with attractive formatting. Balance the columns. Add a title to the article, and spell- and grammar-check the document. Save the document as *[your initials]*16-20 and submit it.

Unit 4 Applications

Unit Application 4-1

Create a memo that includes a table. Edit and format table structures and text.

1. Open the file **Fitness - 2**.

2. Insert a line above the table using the Split Table command.

3. Create a standard business memo format at the beginning of the document. The memo is to "Store Managers" from Garland Miller. Use the current date, and key **Fitness Centers** for the subject line. Format the subject line to 24 points spacing after.

4. As the body of the memo, key the text in Figure U4-1. Include your reference initials at the end of the memo.

NOTE

Refer to Appendix B, "Standard Forms for Business Documents," if you need help with the memo.

Figure U4-1

We have compiled the survey responses from the area fitness centers, and the results appear in the following table. Please review the table information before our next managers' meeting.

5. Insert a next page section break after the memo. Change the orientation for section 1 to portrait, and change the top margin to 2 inches.

6. Study the column headings above columns 2 and 3. Use the Split cells and Merge cells commands to apply similar formatting to the fourth and fifth columns and to the sixth and seventh columns. Edit the text for each column heading.

TIP

Try splitting the cells into one column two rows before merging the cells.

7. Adjust the row height for the heading rows, and center the text within the cells vertically and horizontally.

8. Select the seven rows below the heading rows, and change the row height to 0.4 inch, and center the text vertically.

9. Change the vertical alignment for section 2 to center. Center the table horizontally.

10. Right-align the dollar amounts, and change the right cell margin to 0.4 inch. (Use the Cell Margins command on the Table Tools Layout tab.)

11. Sort the seven rows below the heading rows in alphabetical order.

12. Apply gray shading to the heading rows.

13. Key the title Fitness Center Survey Results at the top of section 2. Format the title using 20-point bold and small caps, with 24 points spacing after and centered horizontally.

14. Key a $ in front of each of the numbers in the second row.

15. Select the table, and apply a double-line outside border.

16. Save the document as *[your initials]*u4-1 in a new Unit 4 Applications folder.

17. Submit and close the document.

Unit Application 4-2

Create column layouts, change column width and spacing, add a line between columns, and balance columns.

1. Open the file **Fundraising**.

2. Format the document as two columns.

3. Change the column spacing to 0.4 inch. Keep the column width equal, and add a vertical line between columns.

4. Key the title FUNDRAISING in 20-point bold and small caps at the top of the document.

5. Format the title as one column, center the text, and add 72 points of spacing before and 24 points of spacing after.

6. Select the six lines of text from "Solid milk chocolate" to "Milk chocolate with double chocolate filling," and format as a bulleted list.

7. Sort the list of candy bars alphabetically.

8. Balance the columns.

9. Select text in the second column beginning with "Sales Department" through the end of the document. Apply a double-line outside border and gray shading.

10. Add a footer that contains the date at the left margin and the page number (preceded by the word "Page") at the right margin.

11. Format the footer text as 10-point italic.

12. Save the document as *[your initials]*u4-2 in your Unit 4 Applications folder.

13. Submit and close the document.

Unit Application 4-3

Create a long table with nested tables.

1. Start a new document, and change the orientation to landscape.

2. Insert a parent table that is two columns wide by two rows.

3. In the first column, starting in the first row, key the following. Press Enter after each line.

   Repair Order No.
   Date:
   Notes:

4. In the second column, starting in the first row, key the following. Press Enter after each line.

   Vehicle No.
   License:
   VIN:
   Mileage:

5. Select the text in the first cell of the first column, and set a right-aligned solid leader tab at 4.25 inches. Position the insertion point after "Repair Order No.," and press Ctrl+Tab to insert the solid leader tab. Insert a solid leader tab for each line in the first cell of the first column.

6. Set a right-aligned solid leader tab for the text in the first cell of the second column. Insert the solid leader tab after each line of text.

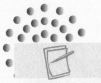

NOTE

Remember to press Ctrl+Tab to insert a tab character in a table.

7. Select the text in the first row of the table, and apply 14-point bold, small caps, and 15 points spacing after.

8. Center the document vertically. Adjust the column width for each column to 4.5 inches.

9. Save the new document as *[your initials]***u4-3** in your Unit 4 Applications folder.

10. Open the file **VM Form**.

11. Select the first table, and copy the table to the clipboard.

12. Switch to the file *[your initials]***u4-3**. Paste the Clipboard's contents in the first cell of the second row.

13. Switch to the file **VM Form**, and select the second table. Copy and paste the second table in the second row, second column.

14. Use the AutoFit Window feature for each of the nested tables.

15. Select the parent table, and change the cell margins for the top, bottom, left, and right to 0.1 inch. Apply a double-line outside border to the parent table.

16. Select each nested table, and change the row height to 0.25 inch.

17. Apply a 3-point, single-line border below the first row and between the columns of the first row of the parent table.

18. Use the Split Table command to insert a blank line above the parent table. Key Campbell's Confections Vehicle Maintenance Form. Format the title using character and paragraph formatting.

19. Apply a 1½-point, single-line outside border to each of the nested tables. Select the first row of the nested table on the left, and merge the cells. Merge the cells in the first row of the second nested table. Format the text in the first row of each nested table to 14-point bold, small caps, and centered. Apply gray shading to the first row in each nested table.

20. Select the text in the second row of the nested table on the left, and apply bold formatting. Repeat the format to the second row of the second nested table.

21. Select the nested table on the left, and center the text within the cells vertically. Repeat for the second nested table.

22. Resave, submit, and close the document.

Unit Application 4-4 ◆ Using the Internet

Create a newsletter with tables and columns.

1. Start a new document, which will be a simple newsletter that is one to two pages in length.

2. Write a newsletter title. Use appropriate spacing and character formatting.

3. Develop four articles, which can be about school, your town, your family, a hobby, or any topic that interests you. Research the content of the articles online. You can write the articles from information you obtain from various Web sites or copy and paste the content from the Web sites. (Paste the text without its formatting.) Make sure the information contained in the newsletter is based directly on information you find.

4. Each article should have a title.

5. All paragraphs within an article should be separated by the appropriate paragraph spacing.

6. One of the articles should contain a bulleted list, using any bullet style.

7. Use column breaks, continuous section breaks, and page breaks to arrange the columns in a visually suitable layout.

8. Include one or two formatted tables with rotated text and shading.

9. Determine if you need to horizontally center your table(s) within the boundaries of a column or the margins of the newsletter.

10. Each page should have a header or footer.

11. Include any other formatting to make the newsletter attractive.

12. On a new page in the document, create a bulleted list containing the references or Web sites you used. Save the document as *[your initials]*u4-4 in your Unit 4 Applications folder.

13. Submit and close the document.

unit 5

GRAPHICS AND CHARTS

Lesson 17

Graphics

After completing this lesson, you will be able to:

1. Insert clip art.

2. Move and format clip art.

3. Create WordArt.

4. Work with shapes.

5. Modify shapes.

6. Control order, group, and align shapes.

MCAS OBJECTIVES

In this lesson:
WW 07 1.1.4
WW 07 3.1
WW 07 3.2
WW 07 3.3

Estimated Time: 1¹/₂ hours

This is the first of three lessons that teaches graphics and desktop publishing using Word. This lesson focuses on clip art and shapes. You learn how to insert and modify clip art as well as create and format *drawing objects*— shapes such as squares, circles, stars, banners, arrows, and more.

Inserting Clip Art

Microsoft Office provides access to a wide variety of drawings, photographs, sound effects, music, videos, and other media files, called *clips*. This lesson focuses mainly on clip art, which are drawings.

When you want to insert clips in a document, you can use one of two search methods:

• Open the Clip Art task pane, and search for pictures by keyword.

• Open the Microsoft Clip Organizer window, and view collections of clips organized by category (such as business, people, and transportation).

Exercise 17-1 FIND CLIPS BY USING KEYWORDS

Each clip in the Microsoft Office collection has keywords associated with it. Using a keyword is an easy way to narrow your search for an appropriate clip.

NOTE

The documents you create in this course relate to the case study about Campbell's Confections, a fictional candy store and chocolate factory (see the Case Study in the frontmatter of the book).

Clip Art

NOTE

If the Search in text box is set for Everywhere, the search results will include clips from the Microsoft Web collection. These clips are identified by a tiny globe at the bottom left corner of the picture.

1. Open the file **Chocolate Terms**.

2. Position the insertion point at the beginning of the first paragraph below the title.

3. Click the Insert tab, and click the Clip Art button. The Clip Art task pane opens.

4. In the Search text box in the task pane, key chocolate. The task pane has two search option boxes, one for searching specific collections of clips and the other for searching for specific types of clip files. You would use these boxes to narrow your search.

5. Make sure the Search in text box is set for All collections. If it is not, click the down arrow and check the Everywhere box. A check should appear in My Collections, Office Collections, and Web Collections. Make sure the Results should be text box is set for All media file types. If it is not, click the down arrow and check the All media types box.

Figure 17-1
Using a keyword to find clips

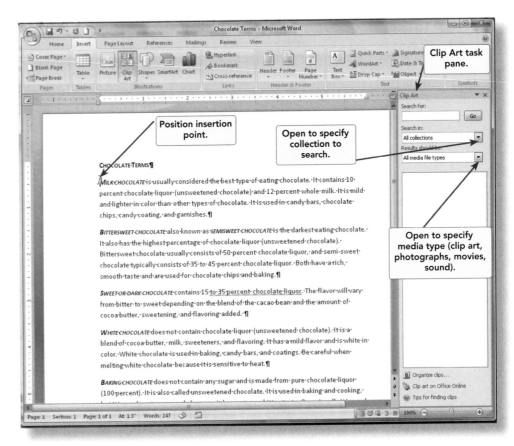

NOTE

To search for additional clips, enter another keyword in the Search for text box.

6. Click the **Go** button 🔲. The task pane displays chocolate-related clips.

7. Scroll to locate a picture of chocolate candies. A ScreenTip displays the image size, file format (WMF), and keywords associated with the clip.

8. Click the clip to insert it into the document.

Figure 17-2
Inserting a clip from the task pane

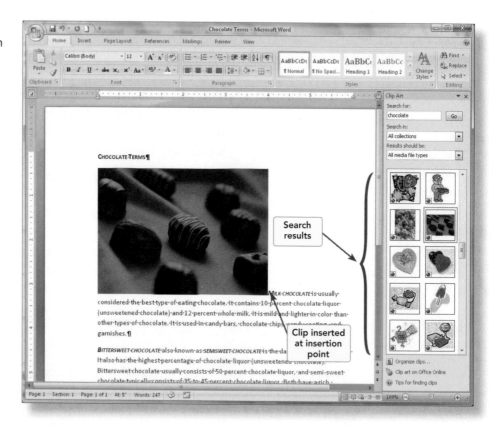

Exercise 17-2   FIND CLIPS BY BROWSING CATEGORIES

All clips in the Microsoft Office collection are organized by category. You can browse clips by category in the Microsoft Clip Organizer window.

1. Click **Organize clips** at the bottom of the Clip Art task pane. (The Microsoft Clip Organizer window appears.)

2. Under **Collection List**, click the plus sign next to **Office Collections** to expand the list of categories.

3. Click various category names to display the available clips. Expand a category, if necessary, to display subcategories.

4. To locate a special occasion picture, scroll to the **Special Occasions** category. Click the plus sign to expand the category, and then click **Special Occasions**.

5. Point to the heart picture selected in Figure 17-3. Click the down arrow that appears to the right of the picture. A pop-up menu appears with several options. For example, you can copy the clip, find clips of similar style, or preview a larger version of the clip.

Figure 17-3
Inserting a clip from the Microsoft Clip Organizer window

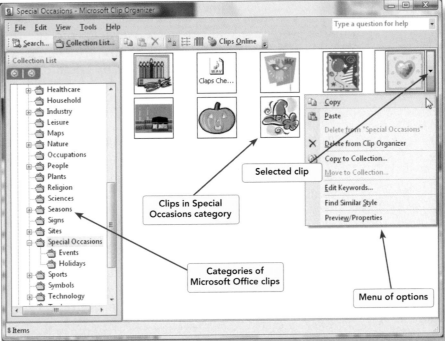

NOTE

You can drag the picture to the document.

REVIEW

Right-click where you want to paste the clip, and then choose Paste from the shortcut menu, use the Paste command, or press Ctrl+V.

6. Click **Copy** to copy the clip to the Clipboard.

7. Click within the document, and position the insertion point at the last paragraph mark. Paste the clip.

8. Save the document as *[your initials]*17-2 in a new folder for Lesson 17.

9. Close the Insert Clip Art task pane. Right-click the Microsoft Clip Organizer on the Windows taskbar and close it. Click **No** when asked if you want the clip to remain on the Clipboard. Leave the document open for the next exercise.

Exercise 17-3   INSERT A PICTURE FROM A FILE

In addition to the clip art images provided by Microsoft, you can insert pictures from a file.

1. Position the insertion point at the beginning of the paragraph that begins "White chocolate."

2. Click the **Insert** tab, and click the Picture button. The Insert Picture dialog box displays.

3. Locate the folder that contains the student data files, and double click **Chocolate - P1**. A third picture is inserted in your document.

4. Press Ctrl + Z to undo the insertion.

Moving and Formatting Clip Art

After you insert a clip in a Word document, there are many ways to manipulate it. You can change its size, trim it, change its position, and apply formatting options. To manipulate any graphic, you must select it first.

Exercise 17-4   SELECT CLIP ART

To select clip art, you click it. A selected graphic has a *selection rectangle* around it, formed by four small squares and four small circles at each side and corner of the object. These squares and circles are *sizing handles*, which you drag to resize the graphic.

1. Scroll to the picture near the top of the document.

2. Click the picture to select it. Notice the selection rectangle and the sizing handles. Also notice that the **Picture Tools Format** tab displays on the Ribbon.

Figure 17-4
Clicking a picture to
select it

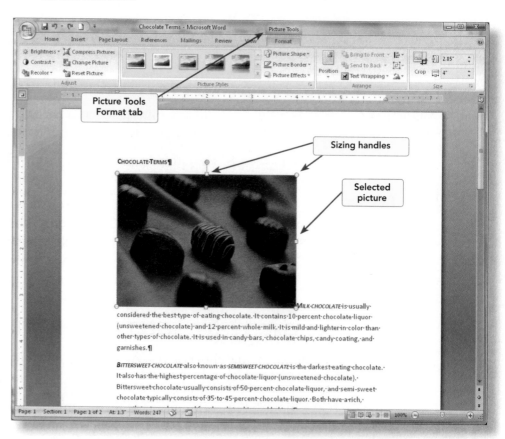

3. Click outside the borders of the picture to deselect it. The Picture Tools Format tab is no longer displayed on the Ribbon.

Exercise 17-5   SIZE CLIP ART

When you *size* a picture, you reduce or enlarge it. You can *scale* a picture to be a percentage of its original size. *Proportional sizing* resizes a picture while maintaining its relative height and width.

1. Click the chocolate picture to select it.

2. Move the pointer to the sizing handle in the top right corner until the pointer looks like this: ⤢.

3. Drag the sizing handle toward the center of the picture and notice that a transparent box appears. The box represents the new size.

Figure 17-5
Sizing a picture

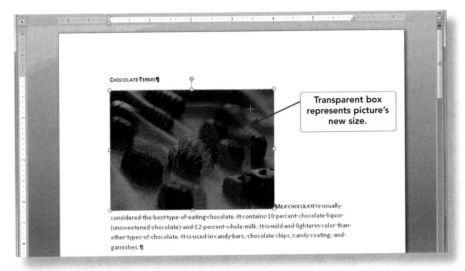

NOTE

The four corner (circle) sizing handles resize the image proportionately. The top center, bottom center, and side middle handles (square) distort the image's original proportions as the size changes.

4. Release the mouse button, and notice that the picture size changes proportionately.

5. Drag the right center sizing handle to the left, and release the mouse button. Notice that the picture size changes disproportionately.

Figure 17-6
Picture sized proportionately and disproportionately

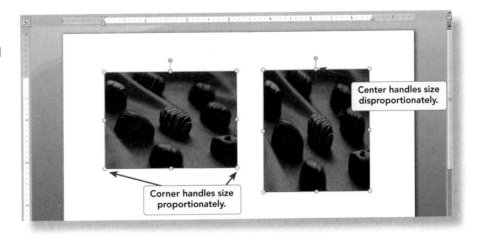

6. Click the Undo button  to undo the disproportionate resizing.

7. Select the heart picture. Press Ctrl and drag the lower-right sizing handle down and to the right. Notice that the center of the picture does not change. Release the mouse.

NOTE

When sizing or scaling a clip using the Size dialog box, be sure to read the original size measurements at the bottom of the dialog box. If the original size of the picture is large, avoid using the Reset button which would return the picture to its original size.

8. Select the heart picture again if necessary. Press Shift and drag the lower-right sizing handle down and to the right. Pressing Shift while you drag maintains the proportion of the picture.

9. Select the heart picture. Instead of using the sizing handles to size it, click the **Picture Tools Format** tab on the Ribbon.

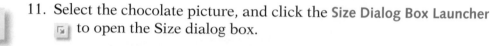

10. Locate the **Size** group and the Shape Height button. Change the height to **2** inches by clicking the down arrow.

11. Select the chocolate picture, and click the **Size Dialog Box Launcher** to open the Size dialog box.

12. Locate the **Scale** section, and change the **Height** to **50%**. Press Tab . The **Width** automatically changes to 50% because you are scaling proportionately.

Figure 17-7
Size dialog box: Size tab

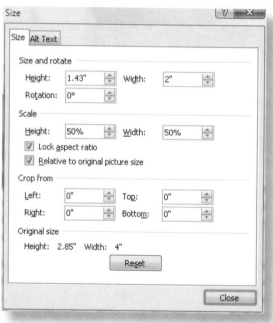

NOTE

In the Size dialog box, when the Lock aspect ratio box is checked, Word scales a picture proportionately, and when the Relative to original picture size box is checked, Word scales the picture from its original size. Use the Size dialog box to size a picture precisely by keying the desired measurements in the appropriate text boxes.

13. Click **Close**. The chocolate picture is half its original size. Click the Undo button to return the picture to its previous size.

Exercise 17-6   COMPRESS PICTURES

When a picture is inserted in a document, the file size of the document is increased. To save room on your storage medium (hard drive or removable storage device), you can compress pictures with little change in the quality of the image. It is important to note that all pictures cannot be compressed and maintain good image quality. The file format determines whether image data is lost during compression.

1. Select the chocolate picture.

2. Click the Compress Pictures button ⬚ Compress Pictures on the Picture Tools Format tab to display the Compress Pictures dialog box.

Figure 17-8
Compression
settings

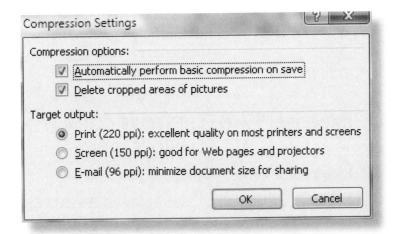

3. Click **Options**, and click to select **Automatically perform basic compression on save** and **Delete cropped areas of pictures**. Under **Target output**, click the **Print** option. Click **OK**.

4. Click to select the checkbox to **Apply to selected pictures only**. Click **OK**.

Exercise 17-7   CROP CLIP ART

When you trim, or *crop*, a picture, you hide part of the picture. For example, if you have a picture of a person standing next to a computer, you can crop either the person or the computer out of the picture. What you crop is neither displayed on screen nor printed, but remains part of the original image. The *outcrop* feature is used to add a margin to a picture.

1. Select the heart picture.

2. Click the Crop button ⬚ on the Picture Tools Format tab.

NOTE

The top, bottom, and side sizing handles crop those sides, respectively. The four corner sizing handles crop a picture from each respective corner. Press Ctrl and drag a corner cropping handle to crop a picture on all four sides. To crop a picture using exact measurements, click the Size Dialog Box Launcher, and key the measurements in the Left, Right, Top, and Bottom boxes.

Crop

3. Place the cropping tool over the bottom-middle sizing handle, and drag toward the top of the picture to remove the bottom border of the picture.

4. Release the mouse button, and notice that the graphic is cropped from the bottom.

5. Place the cropping tool over the right-center sizing handle, and press Ctrl. Drag inward, and notice that the picture is cropped equally on two sides.

6. Undo the cropping.

7. Select the picture, and click the Crop button ⬚. Drag a corner cropping handle outward from the center of the picture. A margin has been added to the picture. Press Esc to return to the normal pointer.

Exercise 17-8   RESTORE CLIP ART TO ITS ORIGINAL SIZE

1. Select the chocolate picture.

2. Click the **Picture Tools Format** tab, and locate the **Size** group. Click the **Size Dialog Box Launcher**, and click the Reset button ▭. Close the Size dialog box. The picture changes back to its original size, as it appeared when you first inserted it. Change the height to **1.5"** using the **Height** box in the **Size** group of the **Picture Tools Format** tab.

3. Select the heart picture. Click the **Picture Tools Format** tab, and locate the **Adjust** group. Click the Reset Picture button ▭ to reset the picture to its original size.

4. Change the height of the heart picture to 2 inches.

5. Save the document as *[your initials]***17-8** in your Lesson 17 folder.

Exercise 17-9   MOVE CLIP ART

You can move a picture by cutting and pasting or by dragging and dropping.

1. Select the heart picture and cut it, placing it on the Clipboard.

2. Paste the picture at the beginning of the paragraph that begins "Baking Chocolate."

3. Select the heart picture, point to it with the arrow pointer, hold down the left mouse button, and drag the picture back to the last paragraph

mark of the document. The pointer changes to the drag-and-drop shape ⌷, the pointer you use for dragging and dropping text.

Figure 17-9
Dragging a picture

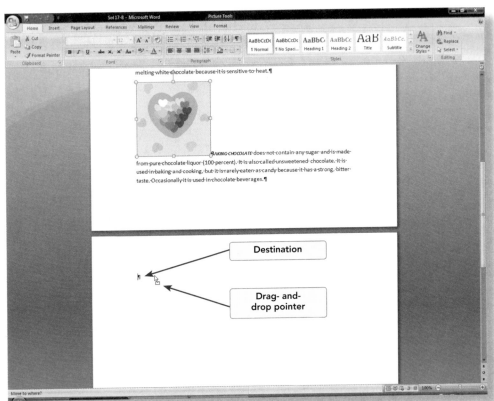

NOTE

To delete a picture, select it and press
Delete or Backspace.

4. Release the mouse button. The picture is positioned at the last paragraph mark. If it is not, click the Undo button and drag it again.

Exercise 17-10   CHANGE WRAPPING STYLE

When you insert a graphic, it appears in the document as an *in-line graphic*, by default. An in-line graphic is treated like a character and aligns with the current paragraph. You can change an in-line graphic to a *floating graphic*. A floating graphic is placed on the drawing layer of the Word document. You can move the floating graphic freely and layer it behind or in front of text or other objects, changing how text wraps around the graphic. This feature is called *text wrapping*.

1. Select the chocolate picture. The picture is an in-line graphic, treated by Word like any text object. It is left-aligned with its own paragraph mark.

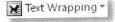

2. Click the **Picture Tools Format** tab on the Ribbon, and click the Text Wrapping button 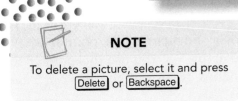. Notice the wrapping options available.

3. Choose **Square**. Text now wraps around the picture. Notice the anchor symbol and the selection handles around the picture.

Figure 17-10
Changing the wrapping style

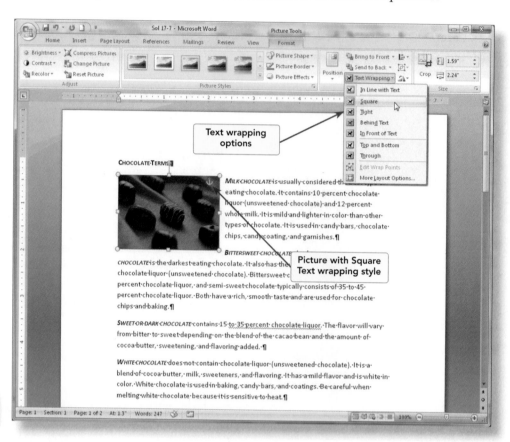

NOTE

The green circle above the picture is the rotation handle. You can drag this handle to rotate the picture either left (counterclockwise) or right (clockwise).

TIP

As you drag a floating picture, Word displays a transparent duplicate of the picture. You can use the top edge of the transparent picture as a positioning guide.

Use the Shift key to control movement either horizontally or vertically.

4. Move the pointer over the picture. The pointer is now a four-pointed arrow. You use this pointer to drag the floating picture freely on the page.

5. Using the four-pointed arrow, drag the picture to different locations in the document. Notice how the text wraps squarely around the picture.

6. Change the picture back to an in-line graphic by choosing the **In-Line with Text** wrapping style. The picture returns to the area where it was first inserted. If it appears on the same line as the first paragraph, click before "Milk Chocolate," and press Enter, leaving a blank area below the picture.

7. Select the picture, and click the Position button on the **Picture Tools Format** tab of the Ribbon. Move the mouse over the gallery of options. Notice there is one option for in-line graphics and nine options for floating graphics (graphics with a text-wrapping option selected.). Deselect the menu.

Word 2007

TIP

To align an in-line picture, use the Alignment buttons on the Ribbon, Paragraph group. To align a floating picture, click the Position command and choose an option, or choose More Layout Options to open the Advanced Layout dialog box and select the Picture Position tab.

TIP

To fine-tune the position of a floating graphic, use the arrow keys. To move a graphic by very small increments, hold down Ctrl while you press the arrow keys.

8. Select the picture if necessary, and click the Center button ≣ on the **Home** tab of the Ribbon to center-align the picture.

9. Select the heart picture, and change the wrapping style to **Top and Bottom**.

10. Move the picture around. Notice how text wraps only around the top and bottom and not the sides of the picture.

11. Change the wrapping style to **Tight**. This style is like Square, but the text wraps more closely around the contours of the picture.

12. Position the picture to the left of the last paragraph.

13. Format the document title as 16 points with 36 points spacing before and 24 points spacing after the paragraph. Center-align the title.

14. Save the file as *[your initials]***17-10** in your Lesson 17 folder and print it. Leave it open for the next exercise.

Figure 17-11
Preview of final document

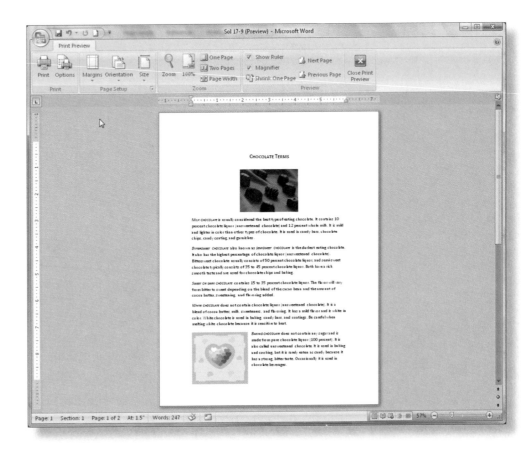

Exercise 17-11   ADJUST THE APPEARANCE OF A PICTURE

You can modify a picture by changing its brightness (how light or dark a color is), contrast (how dark and light an area is), or transparency (how much light can pass through). You can also apply a picture style to frame the selected image.

1. Select the heart picture. Click the **Picture Tools Format** tab, locate the **Adjust** group, and click the Brightness button .

2. Drag the mouse over each of the brightness options in the drop-down menu. Click **Picture Correction Options**. The Format Picture dialog box displays.

Figure 17-12
Adjusting the appearance of the picture

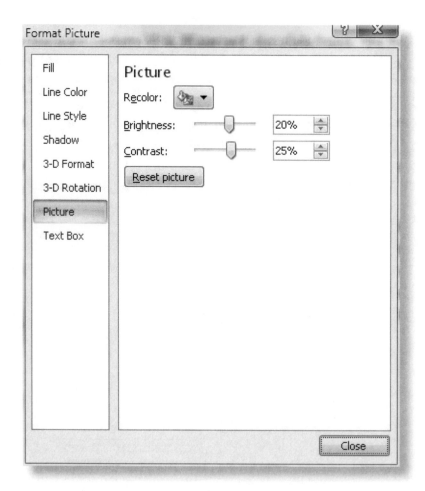

3. Drag the **Brightness** slider to **20%**, and change the **Contrast** value to **25%**. Click **Close**.

4. Click the Contrast button on the Ribbon, and click **-30%** in the drop-down menu.

5. Click the Recolor button 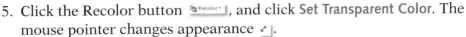, and click **Set Transparent Color**. The mouse pointer changes appearance ✐.

NOTE

The Set Transparent Color option is not available for all pictures.

 Reset Picture

6. Click one of the darker-colored, small hearts on the right side of the larger heart. Notice that the heart became the same color as the document background (white).

7. Select the chocolate picture. Locate the **Picture Styles** group, and click the More arrow ⬇ to display the Picture Styles gallery. Move the mouse over various styles, and observe the change in the frame around the selected picture. Click **Moderate Frame, Black**.

8. Select the heart picture, and click the Reset Picture button to return the picture to its original format. If necessary, change the height of the picture to 1.25 inches so that the document is one page, and drag the picture to the left of the last paragraph.

9. Save the document as *[your initials]*17-11 in your Lesson 17 folder. Submit the document, and leave the document open for the next exercise.

Exercise 17-12   ROTATE AND FLIP CLIP ART

You can rotate and flip clip art by using the Rotate options on the Ribbon, or you can manually rotate the image by dragging the rotate handle. You also can reverse or flip an object.

1. Click the heart picture. Click the **Picture Tools Format** tab, and locate the **Arrange** group.

2. Click the arrow beside the Rotate button to display the Rotate menu.

3. Move the mouse over each of the options, and observe the changes in the picture. Click **More Rotation Options** to open the Size dialog box. Change the rotation to **15** degrees. Click **Close**.

4. Select the heart picture, and notice the green rotation handle.

5. Place the mouse pointer on the green rotation handle, and drag the handle slightly to the left. Adjust the rotation if necessary.

Figure 17-13
Rotating the picture

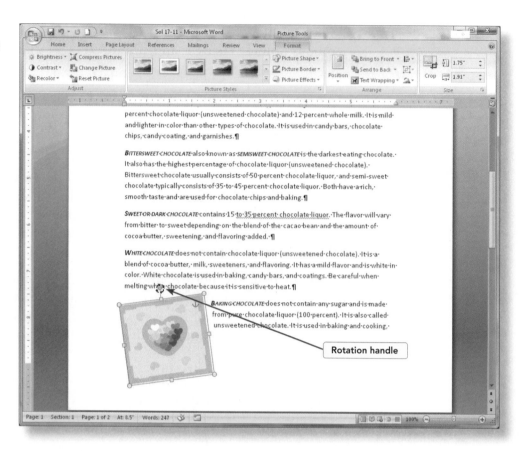

6. Right-click the heart picture, and choose **Text Wrapping** from the shortcut menu. Change the wrapping style to **Square**.

7. Save the document as *[your initials]*17-12 in your Lesson 17 folder. Submit the document, and keep it open for the next exercise.

Creating WordArt

WordArt is a drawing tool you can use to create special effects with text. You can choose from a variety of WordArt styles and then modify the object by editing the text or changing the shape, wrapping style, size, color, position, and so on.

Exercise 17-13 CREATE WORDART

1. Select the title text "Chocolate Terms" up to but not including the paragraph mark. (Because you will be creating WordArt from this text, not including the paragraph mark will retain the spacing before the title.)

2. Click the **Insert** tab, locate the **Text** group, and click the Word Art button. The WordArt Gallery appears, displaying a number of WordArt styles.

Figure 17-14
WordArt gallery

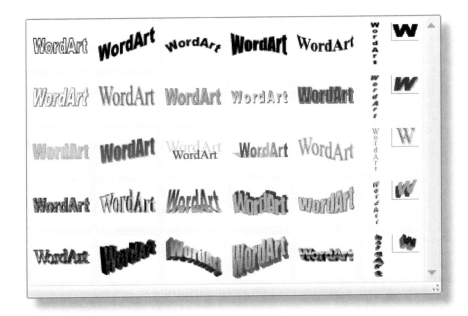

3. Choose one of the styles. The Edit WordArt Text dialog box appears. Click **OK**. You can key or paste text in the **Text** box when creating WordArt.

Figure 17-15
Edit WordArt Text
dialog box

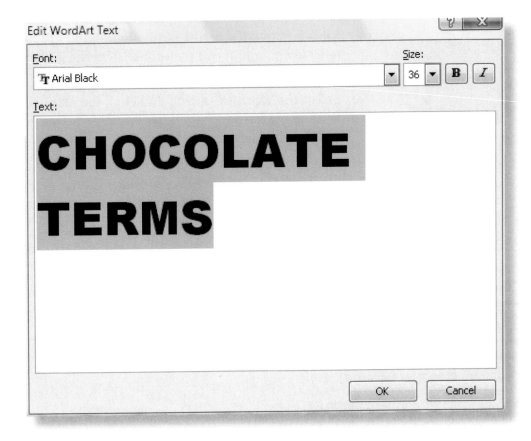

4. Click **OK**. The WordArt object is inserted in the document as an in-line graphic.

5. Click the WordArt object to select it. The WordArt Tools Format tab appears. Locate the **WordArt Styles** group, and click the More arrow to display the WordArt Styles gallery. Choose another style. Some styles are more readable than others, particularly for uppercase text.

NOTE

When you open the WordArt Styles gallery, move the mouse over each style to preview the change in your document.

6. Click the **WordArt Tools Format** tab on the Ribbon, if necessary, and view the WordArt Style group. Click the Change WordArt Shape button , and select a shape in the second row. Click the Undo button if you do not like the results.

7. Click the Position button, and click the **Position Top Center with Square Text Wrapping** option.

Exercise 17-14 FORMAT WORDART

You can change the appearance of WordArt objects, by changing the fill color and line color and by adding special effects such as shadows and reflections.

1. Select the WordArt object, and locate the **WordArt Styles** group on the Ribbon. Click the arrow beside the Shape Fill button. Point to **Gradient**, and move the mouse over the gallery of options. Select an option.

2. Select the WordArt object, and click the arrow beside the Shape Outline button in the WordArt Styles group. Select a color and weight for your WordArt object.

3. Select the WordArt object, and locate the **Shadow Effect** group on the Ribbon. Click the Shadow Effect button. Point to the various shadow styles, and choose one that is appropriate for your WordArt object. Notice that you can also select a **Shadow Color** from the gallery.

4. Change the shadow depth on your WordArt object, by selecting the object and using the Shadow On/Off button. Experiment with the **Nudge Shadow Right** feature and the **Nudge Shadow Down** option.

NOTE

As with any graphic object, there are many options for modifying a WordArt object. Practice the WordArt features using the WordArt Tools Format tab, on the Ribbon. To delete the WordArt object, select it, and press Delete.

Figure 17-16
Title text with a
WordArt style

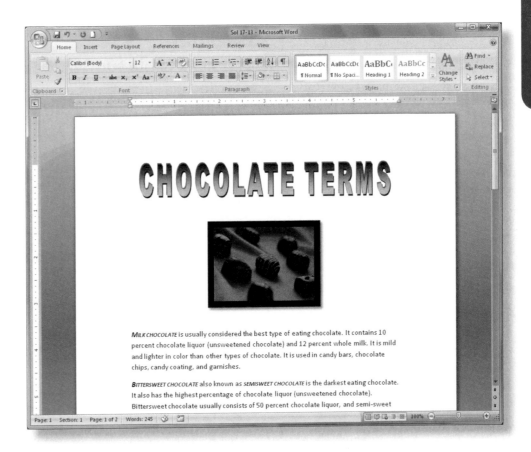

5. Save the document as *[your initials]*17-14 in your Lesson 17 folder.

6. Submit and close the document.

Working with Shapes and the Drawing Canvas

An easy way to add a graphic element to a document is to use the Insert tab, Illustrations group, to create a shape. You can draw simple geometric shapes or insert more complex predesigned shapes. There are six categories for shapes including lines, basic shapes, block arrows, flowchart, callouts, and stars and banners.

When you draw shapes, you can insert them directly into the document or place them in a *Drawing Canvas*, a bordered area in your document where you can size, move, and change the objects as a group. Use the Drawing Canvas when you plan to insert several shapes. The Drawing Canvas is an object you can modify. You can change its location and size and how text wraps around it.

Exercise 17-15 CREATE SHAPES

1. Start a new document. Click the **Insert** tab, and locate the **Illustrations** group.

2. Display the rulers if necessary by clicking the View Ruler button on the vertical scroll bar.

Figure 17-17
Shapes categories

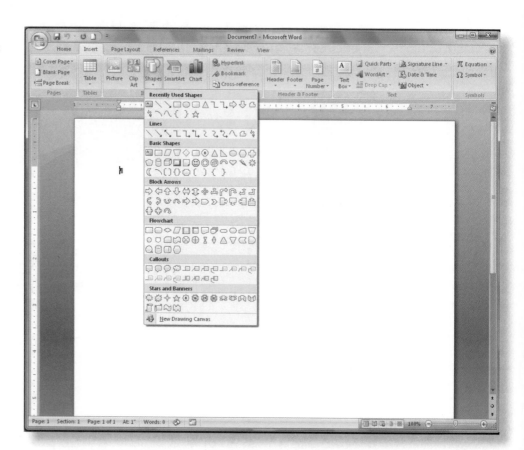

3. Click the Shapes button, and locate the **Basic Shapes** category. Click the Oval shape on the first row. The mouse pointer changes to a crosshair +.

4. Position the crosshair pointer in the upper left corner of the document. Drag to draw an oval that extends across the page and is about ½ inch high. Release the mouse button.

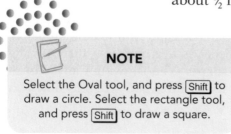

NOTE

Select the Oval tool, and press ⟨Shift⟩ to draw a circle. Select the rectangle tool, and press ⟨Shift⟩ to draw a square.

5. A selected oval appears in the document window. Press ⟨Delete⟩.

6. Display the **Insert** tab, and click the Shapes command again. Click the Oval shape. Press ⟨Shift⟩ and draw a circle approximately 2 inches in diameter. Press ⟨Delete⟩ to delete the circle.

7. Click the Shapes button on the Insert tab, and choose **New Drawing Canvas**. A Drawing Canvas appears in your document. The Drawing Canvas will be used to arrange and format several shapes.

8. Locate the **Insert Shapes** group, and click the Rectangle button ▢.

9. Position the crosshair pointer in the upper left corner of the Drawing Canvas. Drag to draw a rectangle that extends across the top of the Drawing Canvas and measures approximately ½ inch high.

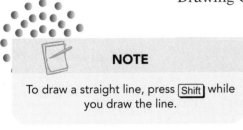

NOTE

To draw a straight line, press Shift while you draw the line.

10. Release the mouse button. The rectangle is displayed with eight sizing handles around its sides. An extra handle with a green circle extends from the top of the rectangle. You can use this handle to rotate an object. When you see an object's sizing handles, the object is selected. Deselect the rectangle by clicking below the rectangle in the Drawing Canvas.

Figure 17-18
Preparing to draw an object

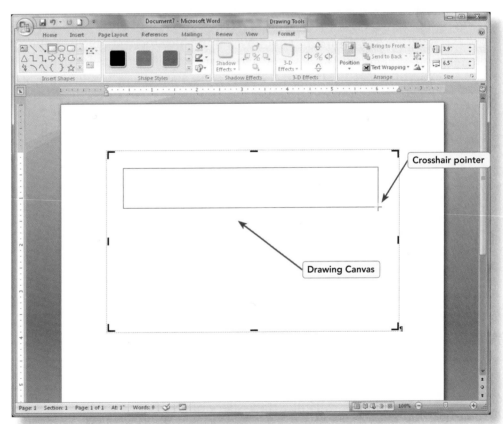

NOTE

To insert a shape with a predefined size without dragging to draw it, click the shape tool and click once in the document.

11. Click the Line button ╲. Press Shift, and draw a horizontal line ½ inch below the rectangle and the same length as the rectangle. Deselect the line.

12. Click the Oval button ◯ and then click anywhere on the Drawing Canvas. A 1-inch circle appears on the Drawing Canvas. Deselect the circle.

NOTE

Press Shift to maintain an object's width-to-height ratio as you draw. Press Ctrl to draw from the center point instead of from an edge.

13. Right-click the Rectangle button 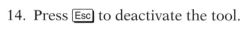, and choose **Lock Drawing Mode**. Press Shift and draw a small square on the canvas. Draw another square that slightly overlaps this square. Draw a third square.

14. Press Esc to deactivate the tool.

15. Click the **Home** tab, locate the **Editing** group, and click the Select button. Choose **Select All**, and press Delete. The document is blank.

Modifying Shapes

Exercise 17-16   RESIZE AND MOVE SHAPES

You can resize, rotate, flip, color, combine, and add text to shapes. To modify a shape, you must first select it by clicking it. To select multiple objects, press Ctrl or Shift and click each object, or click the Select Objects command on the Home tab and draw a box around the objects you want to select. A selected drawing object has sizing handles for reshaping.

To size a shape, place the mouse pointer on a sizing handle (the mouse pointer becomes a two-pointed arrow) and drag the handle. To move a shape, click anywhere inside the shape and drag with the four-pointed arrow. If a shape has a yellow diamond, you can change the contour of the shape by dragging the diamond.

NOTE

You can drag a shape from one Drawing Canvas to another.

1. Click the **Insert** tab, locate the **Illustrations** group, and click the Shapes button. Click **New Drawing Canvas**.

2. Right-click the Line button ↘, and choose **Lock Drawing Mode**. Draw a line across the top of the Drawing Canvas. Draw another line about 1 inch below and the same length as the first.

3. Press Esc to deactivate the drawing mode. Click to select the Drawing Canvas if necessary, and click the **Drawing Tools Format** tab on the Ribbon.

4. Locate the **Insert Shapes** group, and click the More arrow to display the gallery of shapes.

TIP

To insert a shape with a predefined size, click the desired shape button and then click in the document. To maintain a shape's width-to-height ratio, hold down Shift as you draw.

5. Choose **Basic Shapes**, and then click the Sun shape in the second row.

6. Draw a sun on the left side of the Drawing Canvas, between the two lines. Don't worry if the sun is not positioned exactly between the two lines; you will format the shape in the next exercise.

7. Right-click the Drawing Canvas, and choose **Fit**. The height of the Drawing Canvas now fits the height of the objects you have drawn.

8. Right-click the Drawing Canvas, and choose **Expand**. The Drawing Canvas expands slightly around the objects.

Figure 17-19
Adjusting the
drawing canvas

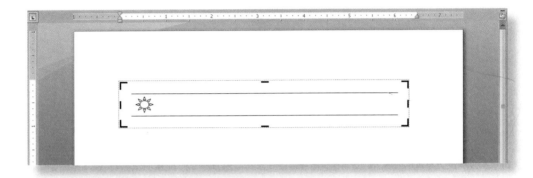

9. Right-click the Drawing Canvas, and click **Scale Drawing**. Move the mouse pointer to the bottom-right sizing handle of the Drawing Canvas. The mouse pointer turns to a diagonal two-pointed arrow .

10. Drag the handle diagonally up and to the left corner of the Drawing Canvas. The objects are scaled smaller.

11. Click the Undo button .

12. Click within the Drawing Canvas. Click the **Drawing Tools Format** tab, and click the Text Wrapping button 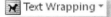. Click **Square**. Now you can move the Drawing Canvas and its contents freely on the page.

13. Move the pointer to the center of the sun shape. Use the four-pointed arrow to drag the shape to the center of the Drawing Canvas, positioned evenly between the two horizontal lines.

14. Point to the yellow diamond on the sun. When the pointer turns into a small arrowhead, drag the yellow diamond into the center of the shape. The sun now resembles a star shape.

Figure 17-20
Changing the shape
of an object

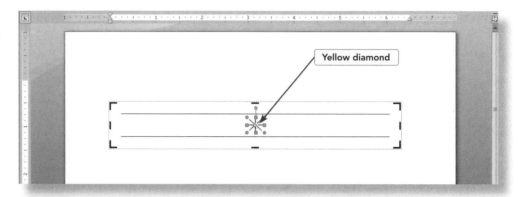

15. Move the mouse pointer to the left-pointing ray of the sun. The mouse pointer changes to a two-pointed arrow. Drag the ray to the left side of the Drawing Canvas. When you start to drag the ray, the mouse pointer becomes a crosshair +.

Figure 17-21
Resizing an object

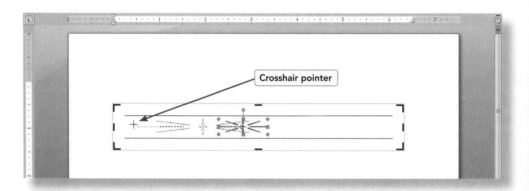

16. Drag the right-pointing ray to the right side of the Drawing Canvas. The shape should be centered and should extend from the left side to the right side of the Drawing Canvas.

Exercise 17-17   ROTATE AND FLIP SHAPES

You can rotate an object left or right 90 degrees, flip it horizontally or vertically, or turn the rotate handle on an object. The rotate handle extends from an object and has a green circle.

1. Select the shape, and click **the Drawing Tools Format tab**. Click the Rotate button and click **Rotate Right 90°**. The sun shape rotates 90 degrees to the right.

2. Click outside the Drawing Canvas to deselect the shape and the canvas.

Figure 17-22
Rotated shape

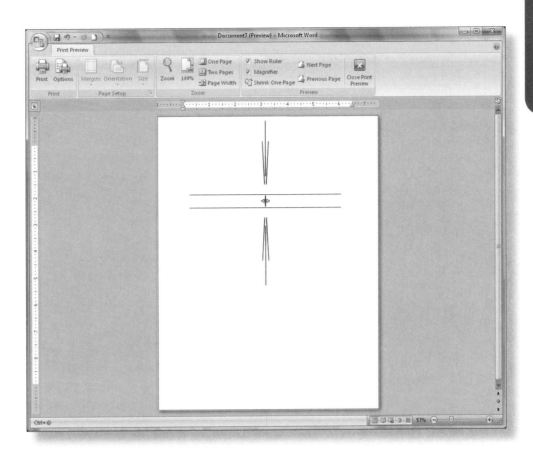

3. Preview the shape in Print Preview; then return to the document.

4. Select the sun shape by clicking its center or one of its rays.

5. Place the mouse pointer over the green circle on the rotate handle of the selected shape. Rotate the shape to the left, back to its original position between the two lines. The shape and the lines are now in the center instead of at the top of the Drawing Canvas.

6. Right-click the Drawing Canvas, and click **Fit**. The Drawing Canvas fits itself snugly to the objects. Drag the canvas back to the top of the document if necessary.

Exercise 17-18 FORMAT SHAPES

Document themes consist of colors, fonts, and effects and affect the overall appearance of a document. A *color set* in a theme includes four colors for text and background, six accent colors, and two colors reserved for hyperlinks. When you want to change the color of an object, the colors that display in the color gallery are determined by the document theme. When you change a document theme, the objects within the document are updated automatically.

Theme effects include three components: line style, fill, and special effects including shadow and 3-D. Galleries display the line and fill effects available. *Quick Styles* include various formatting options for objects and display as thumbnails in a gallery. When you move the mouse pointer over a thumbnail in the gallery, you can preview the color, line, and fill effects for selected shapes.

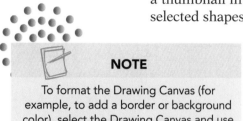

NOTE

To format the Drawing Canvas (for example, to add a border or background color), select the Drawing Canvas and use buttons on the Ribbon. Or right-click the Drawing Canvas, open the Format Drawing Canvas dialog box, and choose options.

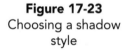

1. Select the sun shape. Click the Drawing Tools Format tab, and click the arrow beside the Shape Fill button 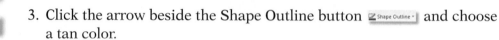, and choose Gradient. Click More Gradients to open the Fill Effects dialog box.

2. On the Gradient tab, click Two colors. Open the Color 1 list, and choose a light orange color. Open the Color 2 list, and choose yellow. Click From center under Shading Styles. Click OK. The sun's rays are colored with a gradient from orange to yellow.

3. Click the arrow beside the Shape Outline button 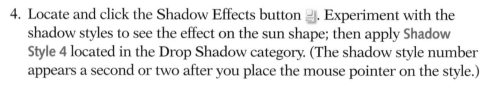 and choose a tan color.

4. Locate and click the Shadow Effects button. Experiment with the shadow styles to see the effect on the sun shape; then apply Shadow Style 4 located in the Drop Shadow category. (The shadow style number appears a second or two after you place the mouse pointer on the style.)

Figure 17-23
Choosing a shadow style

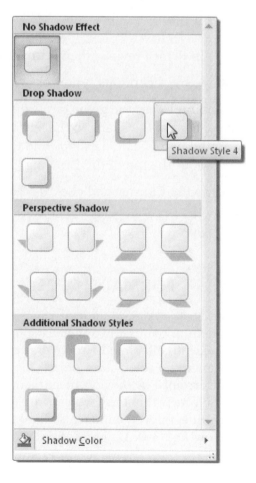

5. Point to the center of the Shadow On/Off button . The center of the button is used to turn the shadow effect on or off. The buttons surrounding the Shadow On/Off button are used to control the depth of the shadow.

Figure 17-24
Shadow settings

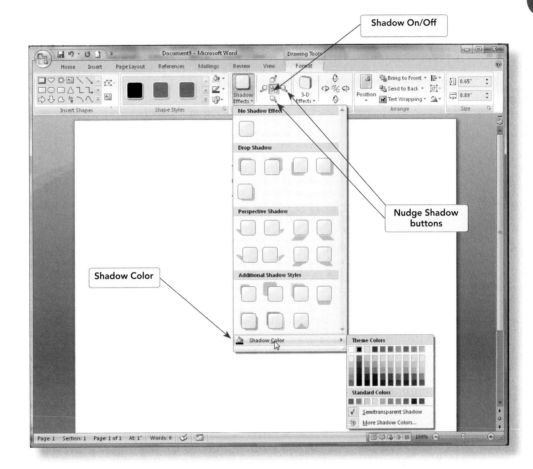

6. Experiment with the Nudge Shadow buttons—click each button once to nudge the shadow up, down, left, and right.

7. Click the Shadow Effects button and click **Shadow Color**. Choose light yellow.

8. Change the shadow to **Shadow Style 17**, and change the shadow color to the darkest orange color.

9. Click the 3-D Effects button , to display the 3-D options. Click **3-D Style 11**.

10. Click the 3-D On/Off button .

Figure 17-25
3-D settings

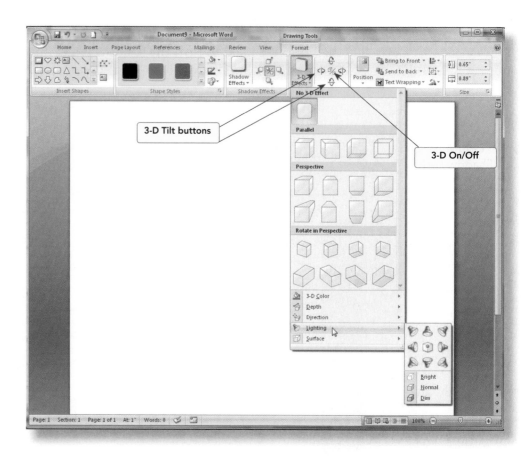

NOTE

After you rotate or format a shape, you might want to insert another shape just like it in your document. You can select the shape, copy it, and then paste it on the Drawing Canvas or in the document. Or after selecting the shape, you can press Ctrl and drag a copy of it somewhere else.

11. Click the Tilt Down button ⊖ once to shorten the object.

12. Click the 3-D Effects button 🔲 , and click **Lighting**. Point to each of the lighting options. Click the 0 Degrees 🔲 option.

13. With the modified sun object now extended out of the Drawing Canvas, right-click the Drawing Canvas, and click **Fit** to fit the canvas around the object.

Figure 17-26
Modified shape

14. Save the document as *[your initials]*17-18 in your Lesson 17 folder. Submit the document, and leave it open for the next exercise.

Exercise 17-19   CHANGE SHAPES

After you insert a shape in a document, you can change it to another shape.

1. Reopen the document *[your initials]*17-18 if necessary. Click the customized sun shape to select it.

2. Click the **Drawing Tools Format** tab, and click the Change Shape button .

3. Locate the Block Arrows group, and choose Quad Arrow ⊕ in the first row.

4. Drag the yellow diamond (the one inside the Drawing Canvas) toward the center of the shape.

5. Click the Change Shape button .

6. Choose **Basic Shapes** and then choose Sun ☼.

7. Drag the yellow diamond on the shape to the center of the shape.

8. Change the 3-D color to light blue.

Exercise 17-20   ADD TEXT TO SHAPES

Text added to a shape becomes part of the shape. If you delete the shape, you also delete the text.

1. Deselect the sun, but click within the Drawing Canvas to activate it.

2. Point to the top center resize handle (the short black line) on the Drawing Canvas. When the pointer changes to ⊥, drag the handle up until the canvas is about twice the height.

3. Click the **Drawing Tools Format** tab, and locate the **Insert Shapes** group. Click the Rounded Rectangle button ▭.

4. Draw a rounded rectangle on the Drawing Canvas, above the top horizontal line. Draw the rectangle the width of the line and about $\frac{1}{2}$ inch high.

5. Right-click in the rectangle, and choose **Add Text**. Key **Campbell's Confections**.

6. Center-align the text, and apply 11-point bold formatting.

7. Select the rectangle, and click the More arrow ▾ in the **Text Box Styles** group, and select the blue **Linear Up Gradient** option in the fifth row to create a gradient fill effect. Right-click the border of the rectangle, and choose **Format AutoShape** from the shortcut menu. Click the **Colors and Lines** tab, and click **Fill Effects**. Drag the **Transparency sliders** to **30%**. Change the **Shading styles** to **From center**; then click the variant with white in the center. Click **OK** twice.

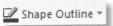

8. Click the Shape Outline button and choose **No Outline**.

Ordering, Grouping, and Aligning Shapes

A Word document is multilayered. When you insert a shape, the shape is placed on top of the text layer, which means it can obscure existing text. You can change the order of a shape by moving it to a different layer, such as behind text. You can also change the order of shapes on a single layer, so that one shape appears on top of or behind the others in the stack. You can group shapes into one object so they can be manipulated as a whole. Aligning shapes involves positioning them in relation to each other or in relation to the Drawing Canvas.

TIP

If you are unable to view graphics in a Word document, switch to Print Layout view, Web Layout view, or Print Preview.

Exercise 17-21   CHANGE THE ORDER OF SHAPES

1. In the current document, notice that the sun shape is in front of the bottom horizontal line you drew. Click the sun shape to select it.

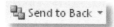

2. Click the **Drawing Tools Format** tab, and click the arrow beside the Send to Back button 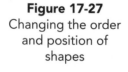. Click **Send to Back**. The sun shape is now behind the line.

3. Right-click the sun shape, point to **Order**, and then click **Bring to Front**. The sun shape is now in front of the line.

4. Select the rounded rectangle that contains the text. Using the four-pointed arrow, drag the shape down until it covers the top horizontal line and slightly overlaps the customized sun.

5. Right-click the rectangle's border (if you click the text, you will see an I-beam for editing text). Choose **Order, Send to Back**. Now the sun shape overlaps the rounded rectangle, but the top horizontal line is on top of the rectangle.

6. Move the rounded rectangle above the top horizontal line. Move the top horizontal line down, behind the top of the sun drawing, and then reposition the rounded rectangle as shown in Figure 17-27, behind the top of the sun shape.

Figure 17-27
Changing the order and position of shapes

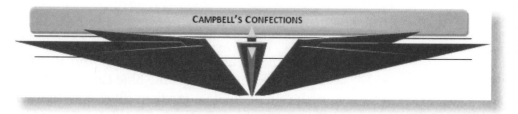

Exercise 17-22   GROUP SHAPES

1. Right-click the Drawing Canvas, and click **Expand** to expand the canvas well outside the edges of the objects.

2. Click the Select button and click **Select Objects**. Position the arrow pointer ↳ above and to the left of the "Campbell's Confections" text box (keeping inside the Drawing Canvas). Then drag down to draw a dashed selection box around all the objects.

Figure 17-28
Drag to draw a box around the objects

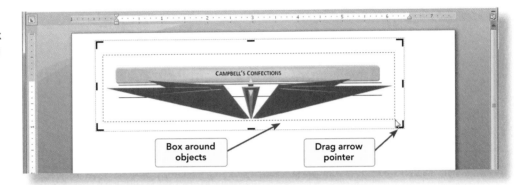

Box around objects

Drag arrow pointer

3. Release the mouse button. Each object is selected and has its own sizing handles.

4. Click the **Drawing Tools Format** tab, and click the arrow beside the Group button . Click **Group**. The objects become a single object, with a single set of sizing handles.

5. Place the mouse pointer in the center of the grouped objects, and drag the group around on the Drawing Canvas. The grouped objects move as one object.

6. Click the Undo button ↺ .

7. Click the arrow beside the Group button , and click **Ungroup**. The grouped object becomes individual objects again.

Exercise 17-23   ALIGN SHAPES

You can align shapes and distribute them evenly in a drawing by using the Align or Distribute options from the Arrange group on the Ribbon. You can align shapes in relation to each other or to the Drawing Canvas. For example, if you have three unevenly spaced shapes, you can align them to have equal space between shapes or align them to be equally spaced on the Drawing Canvas.

1. Deselect all the objects, and then select the top horizontal line. Press [Shift] and select the bottom line. With both lines selected, click the arrow beside the Align button .

2. Verify that **Align to Canvas** is not selected; then click Align Middle button. The lines are now aligned one on top of the other.

3. Press [Shift] and select the "Campbell's Confections" rectangle. Click the arrow beside the Align button 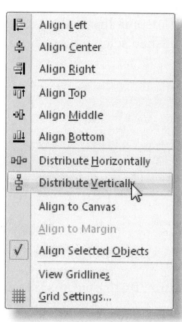 and click **Distribute Vertically**. The three objects are evenly spaced from each other.

Figure 17-29
Alignment options

⊫	Align Left
⊹	Align Center
⊒	Align Right
⊤	Align Top
⊹	Align Middle
⊥	Align Bottom
▯▯▯	Distribute Horizontally
⊹	Distribute Vertically
	Align to Canvas
	Align to Margin
✓	Align Selected Objects
	View Gridlines
⊞	Grid Settings...

4. Select all the objects on the Drawing Canvas, click **Align to Canvas**, and then click **Align Left**. The objects are aligned to the left edge of the Drawing Canvas.

5. With the objects still selected, click **Align Center**. The objects return to their position in the center of the Drawing Canvas.

6. Right-click the Drawing Canvas, and click **Fit**.

7. Save the document as *[your initials]* **17-23** in your Lesson 17 folder.

8. Preview, submit, and close the document.

Lesson 17 Summary

- Add ready-to-use pictures to your document in the form of drawings (clip art) or photographs.

- Search for clips by keyword, using the Clip Art task pane, or view collections of clips by category from the Microsoft Clip Organizer window (click the link at the bottom of the Clip Art task pane).

- Click a clip to select it. You can copy, paste, resize, crop, and format a selected clip.

- A selected clip is surrounded by a selection rectangle with sizing handles at each side and corner. Drag a corner sizing handle to make a clip larger or smaller while keeping the original proportions of the clip. Use the Size dialog box (Size tab) to resize a clip to exact measurements or a percentage of the original size.

- Crop a clip to hide part of it from view. Click the Crop command on the Picture Tools Format tab, Size group. Position the crop tool on a sizing handle, and drag until you have hidden the part of the picture you want cropped.

- You can undo any action applied to a clip. You can also restore a clip to its original size by clicking the Reset Picture command on the Picture Tools Format tab.

- By default, a clip is inserted in a document as an in-line graphic and treated like a character or word. To move a clip that is an in-line graphic, cut and paste the clip or drag and drop it. You can use the alignment buttons on the Home tab to change the horizontal alignment of a clip.

- To move a clip freely on the page, change it from an in-line graphic to a floating graphic by changing its wrapping style. Use the Text Wrapping command on the Picture Tools Format tab. You can drag a floating graphic to position it anywhere on the page, and have the document text wrap around the graphic. The square wrapping style wraps text around all sides of a graphic.

- Use the WordArt feature to create special effects with text. Choose from a variety of WordArt styles, and modify the WordArt object by using the WordArt Tools Format tab (to change shape, size, color, wrapping style, alignment, and so on).

- The Drawing Canvas is a bordered area in your document that contains objects you draw. You can size, move, and change the objects on the Drawing Canvas as a group.

- You can draw shapes such as rectangles, ovals, and lines by using the Insert tab, Shapes command. There are six categories including lines, basic shapes, block arrows, flowchart, callouts, and stars and banners.

- Click a shape to select it. To select multiple objects, hold down Shift and click each object, or use the Select Objects command on the Home tab to draw a box around the objects.

- A selected shape has eight sizing handles. Drag a sizing handle to make a shape larger or smaller. Move a shape by dragging it with the four-pointed arrow. Drag the yellow diamond in a shape to change its contour.

- Drag a shape's green rotation handle to manually rotate the object. You can also flip an object horizontally or vertically or rotate it 90 degrees left or right.

- Use the Format AutoShape dialog box or the Drawing Tools Format tab to apply formatting to shapes, including fill color, line color, shadows, and 3-D effects.

- After a shape is inserted in a document, you can change it to another shape by using the Change Shape command.

- You can add text to a shape—the text you add becomes part of the shape.

- Shapes can be placed on different layers of a document, such as in front of another shape or behind text. You can also group shapes into one object so they can be manipulated as a whole.

- You can align shapes and distribute them evenly in a drawing. You can also align shapes in relation to each other or to the Drawing Canvas.

LESSON 17 — Command Summary

Feature	Button	Command	Keyboard
Insert clip art		**Insert** tab, **Illustration** group, **Clip Art**	
Format picture		**Picture Tools Format** tab	
Crop picture	Crop	**Picture Tools Format** tab, **Size** group	
Resize picture		**Picture Tools Format** tab, **Size** group	
Reset picture	Reset Picture	**Picture Tools Format** tab, **Adjust** group	
Change wrapping style	Text Wrapping	**Picture Tools Format** tab, **Arrange** group, **Text Wrapping**	
Insert WordArt	WordArt	**Insert** tab, **Text** group	
Select drawing objects	Select	**Home** tab, **Editing** group	
Shapes	Shapes	**Insert** tab, **Illustration** group	
Line		**Insert** tab, **Illustration** group, **Shapes** command, **Lines** category	
Arrow		**Insert** tab, **Illustration** group, **Shapes** command, **Block Arrows** category	
Rectangle		**Insert** tab, **Illustration** group, **Shapes** command, **Basic Shapes** category	
Oval		**Insert** tab, **Illustration** group, **Shapes** command, **Basic Shapes** category	
Shape fill	Shape Fill	**Format** tab, **Styles** group	
Shape outline	Shape Outline	**Format** tab, **Styles** group	
Shadow effects		**Format** tab, **Shadow Effects** group	
3-D effects		**Format** tab, **3-D Effects** group	
Rotate or flip	Rotate	**Format** tab, **Arrange** group	
Change shape	Change Shape	**Format** tab, **Styles** group	
Change order	Bring to Front / Send to Back	**Format** tab, **Arrange** group	
Group shapes	Group	**Format** tab, **Arrange** group	
Align shapes	Align	**Format** tab, **Arrange** group	
Position shapes	Position	**Format** tab, **Arrange** group	

Concepts Review

True/False Questions

Each of the following statements is either true or false. Indicate your choice by circling T or F.

T F 1. You can search for clip art by keyword in the Clip Art task pane.

T F 2. You can change an existing star shape to a block arrow shape.

T F 3. The terms "size" and "crop" are used interchangeably in Word.

T F 4. The Drawing Canvas appears when you click a drawing tool, such as the Rectangle button.

T F 5. To select a WordArt object, point to the object and click.

T F 6. If an object has a yellow diamond, you can change the contour of the object.

T F 7. Theme effects include fill, shape, and special effects.

T F 8. You cannot apply a text-wrapping style to a picture.

Short Answer Questions

Write the correct answer in the space provided.

1. What is the name of the feature that displays various formatting options when you move the mouse pointer over a thumbnail in a gallery?

_____

2. What is the procedure to combine two colors in a gradient fashion and use them as the background in a shape?

_____

3. When you insert a picture, what is its default wrapping style?

_____

4. What is the procedure to insert WordArt?

_____

5. How do you make an object three-dimensional?

_____

6. Which group on the Ribbon is used to align, group, and rotate objects?

_____

7. How do you apply the square text-wrapping option to an inserted picture?

_____

8. How do you delete a shape you inserted in a document?

_____

Critical Thinking

Answer these questions on a separate page. There are no right or wrong answers. Support your answers with examples from your own experience, if possible.

1. Find three examples of clip art in newsletters, advertisements, letters, or other publications. Explain how the clip art helps communicate the message of the text.

2. Locate examples of various shapes in magazines, newsletters, and advertisements. When or where are shapes most likely to be used in a document (footer graphic, page number graphic, etc.)?

Skills Review

Exercise 17-24

Insert, size, move, crop, align, format, and change the wrapping style of clip art.

1. Start a new document, and open the Page Setup dialog box. Click the Paper tab, and change the Width and Height measurements to 3 inches. Click the Margins tab, and change the Orientation to Landscape, and change all margins to 0.5 inch.

2. Key the text in Figure 17-30, and format the text as shown. Center align and single space all lines.

Figure 17-30

Center Align	Strawberry Days — 12 pt Bold Small Caps, 0 Points Spacing After
	Arts & Music Festival — Bold
	June 12-14 — Bold Italic
	Enjoy our chocolate covered strawberries!
	Campbell's Confections — 12 pt Bold Small Caps

3. Insert a picture from a file at the top of the document by following these steps:

a. Position the insertion point at the top of the document. Click the **Insert** tab, and click the Picture button 🖼.

b. Locate the directory and folder for the student data files.

c. Select **Chocolate - P5**, and click **Insert**.

4. Size and crop the picture by following these steps:

a. Right-click the picture, and choose **Size**.

b. Change the **Height** to **.75**, and verify that **Lock aspect ratio** is checked.

c. Click **Close**.

d. Select the picture if necessary, and click the **Picture Tools Format** tab.

e. Drag the Zoom slider to **200%**.

f. Click the Crop button ✂.

g. Place the crop handle over the upper left corner, and drag to the center to crop the fork from the picture.

h. Press [Esc].

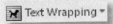

5. Select the picture, and click the Text Wrapping button 🖼Text Wrapping▾. Click **Square**.

6. Drag the strawberry to the upper left corner of the document.

7. Select the picture, and press [Ctrl]+[C] to copy the picture. Deselect the picture, and press [Ctrl]+[V] to paste the picture. Drag the picture to the lower left corner of the document.

8. Paste the picture two more times, and place a strawberry in each corner of the document.

9. Align the pictures by following these steps:

a. Click the picture in the upper left corner of the document. Press [Shift], and click the picture in the upper right corner of the document.

b. Click the Align button ⊟ Align▾, and choose **Align Top**.

c. Click the picture in the upper left corner, and press [Shift]. Click the picture in the lower left corner, and choose **Align Left** from the Align menu.

d. Click the picture in the lower left corner, press [Shift], and click the picture in the lower right corner. Choose **Align Bottom** from the Align menu.

e. Click the picture in the lower right corner, press [Shift], and click the picture in the upper right corner. Choose **Align Right** from the Align menu.

10. Open the Borders and Shading dialog box, and apply a thin, double-line page border.

11. Save the document as *[your initials]***17-24** in your Lesson 17 folder.

12. Submit and close the document.

Exercise 17-25

Insert, size, move, and change the wrapping style of clip art, and insert and format Word Art.

1. Open the file **Earth Day - 2**. Change the top margin to **1.5** inches.

2. Insert clip art by following these steps:

   a. Position the insertion point at the start of the paragraph that begins "In addition."

   b. Click the Insert tab, and click the Clip Art button ▯. The Clip Art task pane displays.

   c. Key earth in the Search text box. Verify that All collections is displayed in the Search in box and that All media file types is displayed in the Results should be box. Click Go.

   d. Select a clip showing a globe or a world map.

3. Resize the clip by following these steps:

   Figure 17-31
   World map clip art

   a. Click the clip to select it.

   b. Drag a corner handle slightly toward the middle of the clip to make the clip proportionately smaller.

   c. With the clip still selected, click the **Picture Tools Format tab** on the Ribbon. Locate the Size group, and click the **Size Dialog Box Launcher**. Click the Size tab.

   d. Under Size and rotate, change the height setting to **2** inches. Make sure the Lock aspect ratio box is checked. Press `Tab`. The width should be automatically adjusted. Click Close.

4. Move and align the clip by following these steps:

   a. With the clip selected, hold down the mouse button and drag the clip to the second paragraph. Release the mouse button.

   b. Click the Position button ▯ on the Picture Tools Format tab.

   c. Click the second option in the second row, **Position in Middle Center with Square Text Wrapping.**

5. Insert and format WordArt by following these steps:

   a. Position the insertion point at the top of the document.

   b. Click the Insert tab, and locate the Text group. Click the WordArt button ▯.

   c. Choose an option in the second row.

   d. Key Earth Day in the Edit WordArt Text dialog box. Click OK.

   e. Click the Shape Fill button ▭ and select a Theme Color to coordinate with your clip art.

   f. Click the Shape Outline button ▭, and select an outline color.

g. Click the Shadow Effects button , and select a **Drop Shadow** option in the second row.

h. Click **Shadow Effects**, and click **Shadow Color**. Select a color for the shadow that coordinates with your fill and line colors.

i. Use the Nudge Shadow buttons 🔲 to increase or decrease the depth of the shadow.

6. Click the WordArt object, click the Position button 🔲, and click **More Layout Options**. Click the **Text Wrapping** tab. Click **Top and Bottom**. Click **OK**.

7. Select the WordArt object, if necessary, and locate the Shape Height box [Height: 2.85"]. Change the height to **1** inch, and change the measurement in the Shape Width box 🔲 to **6** inches.

8. Close the Insert Clip Art task pane.

9. Save the document as *[your initials]*17-25 in your Lesson 17 folder.

10. Submit and close the document.

Exercise 17-26

Draw, move, format, and add text to a shape.

1. Open the file **Agenda - 3**.

2. Click the **Page Layout** tab, and click **Themes**. Choose the **Concourse** theme.

3. Insert a bevel shape by following these steps:

   a. Place the insertion point at the top of the document, and click the **Insert** tab.

   b. Click the Shapes button 🔲, and locate the **Basic Shapes** category.

   c. Click the Bevel shape 🔲 located in the second row, fourth icon.

   d. Click the document to insert a square bevel.

4. Modify the bevel object by following these steps:

   a. Right-click the shape, and choose **Format AutoShape** from the shortcut menu.

   b. Display the **Colors and Lines** tab. Click **Fill Effects**, and click the **Gradient** tab. Click **Two colors**, and click the **Diagonal Down** shading style. Click **OK**.

   c. Change the line weight to **2** points.

   d. Click the **Size** tab, and change the **Height** to **Absolute 1** inch, and change the **Width** to **Absolute 6.5** inches.

   e. Click the **Layout** tab, and click the **Center** option.

5. Drag the box so that the top edge of the box aligns with the ¹/₂-inch mark on the vertical ruler.

6. Add text to the shape by following these steps:

   a. Right-click the bevel shape.

   b. Choose Add Text from the shortcut menu.

   c. Key RISK MANAGEMENT in the shape.

   d. Format the text using the Mini toolbar. Apply 14-point bold formatting, with center alignment.

   e. Place 15 points spacing before the title.

7. Select the shape, and click the Text Box Tools Format tab. Open the Text Box Styles gallery by clicking the More arrow . Click the first shape in the sixth row, Diagonal Gradient - Dark.

8. Select the shape, and locate the yellow diamond handle. Drag the handle away from the shape to decrease the amount of bevel depth.

9. Draw a second bevel shape at the bottom of the document. Format the shape to match the first shape. Change the height to .5 inch. Key Sponsored by the Chamber of Commerce. Center the text.

10. Save the document as *[your initials]*17-26 in your Lesson 17 folder.

11. Submit and close the document.

Exercise 17-27

Insert, size, format, align, group, and add text to shapes.

1. Start a new document.

2. Insert a rectangle by following these steps:

   a. Click the Insert tab on the Ribbon, and click the Shapes button .

   b. Select the rectangle shape .

   c. Drag the cross-hair pointer down and across the top of the page creating a rectangle approximately 0.5 inch tall and 6 inches wide.

3. Select the rectangle, and locate the Shape Styles group on the Drawing Tools Format tab. Click the More arrow to display the Shape Styles gallery. Click the Blue, Colored Fill, White Outline–Accent 1 style (first row, second style).

4. Select the rectangle if necessary, and click the arrow beside the Shape Outline button . Click the Blue, Accent 1 color that appears in the first row, fifth column.

NOTE

The document theme determines the theme colors available.

5. Locate the Size group on the Drawing Tools Format tab. Change the Shape Height box to .5, and change the Shape Width box to 6.

6. Select the rectangle, and press Ctrl+C to copy the rectangle. Deselect the rectangle, and press Ctrl+V to paste. Drag the pasted copy of the rectangle directly below the first rectangle:

7. Select the second rectangle, and open the Shape Styles gallery. Click the red style in the first row (Colored Fill, White Outline–Accent 2).

8. Change the shape outline color to **Red, Accent 2** (first row, sixth column).

9. Use the Ctrl key plus the arrow keys to position the second rectangle below the first rectangle with a thin line of white between the two rectangles.

10. Right-click the first rectangle, and click **Add Text**. Key Campbell's Confections. Format the text using 14-point bold and small caps, with a white font color and right alignment. Select the text, and open the Paragraph dialog box. Change the line spacing to single, and add 6 points spacing before to center the text vertically in the shape.

11. Right-click the second rectangle, and click **Add Text**. Key the following text on two lines. Change the line spacing to single, and change the spacing before and after to **0**.

    25 Main Street • Grove City, PA 16127
    Telephone: 724-555-2025 • Fax: 724-555-2050

12. Format the text in the second rectangle using bold, white font color, and right alignment.

13. Select the first rectangle, press Shift, and click the second rectangle. Click the **Format** tab, and click the Align button ⬚ Align ▾. Click **Align Left**.

14. Group the rectangles as one object by following these steps:

    a. Click the first rectangle.

    b. Hold down Shift, and click the second rectangle.

    c. Click the **Format** tab if necessary, and click the Group button ⬚ Group ▾. Click **Group**.

15. Save the document as *[your initials]*17-27 in your Lesson 17 folder. Submit and close the document.

Lesson Applications

Exercise 17-28

Insert, position, and modify shapes.

1. Start a new document, and switch to landscape orientation. Verify that all margins are 1 inch.

2. Key the following text.

   Campbell's Confections
   Announces
   Chocolate Embossing for Greek Letters

3. Change the document theme to Trek.

4. Select the first line, and format using the Mini toolbar or the Font dialog box. Apply 20-point bold, small caps, and a brown accent color (first row, sixth column). Format the second line using 14-point bold, italic, brown font color, and small caps. Format the third line using 16-point bold, small caps, and brown font color. Center the three lines of text.

5. Click the Insert tab, and click Shapes. Click the line shape ⬊, and draw a line below the last line of text from the left margin to the right margin.

6. Right-click the line, and click Format AutoShape. Apply the following format:

   - Click the Size tab, and change the width to absolute 9 inches.
   - Click the Colors and Line tab, and change the line weight to 6 points. Change the line color to brown. Locate the Arrows section, and click the drop-down arrow for the Begin style. Click the second option in the second row . Click the down arrow for the End style, and click the second option in the second row.
   - Click the Layout tab, and click Center. Click OK.

7. Below the line draw a bevel shape ⬜ approximately 2.5 inches square.

8. Select the shape, and apply the following format:
   - Expand the Style gallery, and click the third style in the eighth row (Solid Fill, Compound Outline–Accent 2).
   - Drag the yellow contour handle outward to narrow the width of the outline.

9. Right-click the shape, and click Add Text. Click the Insert tab, and click Symbol, More Symbols. Change the Font in the Symbol dialog box to Symbol. Scroll to locate the uppercase Greek letter sigma (Σ), click the symbol to select it, and click Insert. Close the dialog box.

Figure 17-32
Chocolate square

10. Select the sigma symbol, and format the symbol using center alignment, bold, and 120 points (adjust the point size if necessary for your shape).

11. Copy the chocolate square, and paste the object two times. Drag each of the pasted squares to the right to form a row of three chocolate squares.

12. Change the Greek letter in the second square to a capital epsilon (E), and change the Greek letter in the third square to a capital delta (Δ). Verify that each letter is centered horizontally.

13. Click the Home tab, and click Select. Choose Select Objects. Position the mouse pointer slightly above and slightly to the left of the first square. Drag down and to the right to draw a selection rectangle to surround the three chocolate squares.

14. Locate the Arrange group on the Ribbon, and click the Align command. Click Distribute Horizontally to place an equal amount of space between the squares. Click Align again, and click Align Bottom.

15. Add a page border to the document. Select a geometric design from the art category that coordinates with the objects on the page. Change the color to brown, and adjust the width to 9 points.

16. Open the Page Setup dialog box, and change the vertical alignment to center.

17. Save the document as *[your initials]*17-28 in your Lesson 17 folder, and submit and close the document.

Exercise 17-29

Insert and format pictures; insert and format WordArt.

1. Open the file **Favors - 4**.

2. Position the insertion point at the start of the first paragraph that begins "Campbell's." Format the text from the first paragraph to the end of the document as two columns with 0.4 inch spacing between columns.

3. Format the list beginning with "wedding bells" through "other assorted shapes" as a bulleted list using the small black square bullet (■).

4. Apply the same bullet format to the list beginning with "solid milk chocolate" through "dark chocolate with mint filling."

5. Select the title "Favors." Click the Insert tab, and click the WordArt button ▲. Select a style in the first or second column. Click OK.

6. Right-click the WordArt object, and choose Format WordArt. Change the fill color and the line color. Change the size to an absolute width of 6.5 inches.

7. Keep the WordArt object selected, and click the WordArt Tools Format tab. Click Spacing and choose Loose. Click Change Shape, and select a style in the Wrap gallery. Click Shadow Effects, and choose Shadow Color. Select a color to coordinate with the fill and line color. Experiment with the Nudge Shadow buttons to create a shadow effect.

8. Click at the start of the paragraph that begins "Please check." Click the Insert tab, and click Clip Art. Key baby rattle in the Search for box and Enter.

9. Click a clip to insert it in the document.

10. Right-click the clip art, and choose Format Picture. Click Picture in the left pane, and drag the Brightness and Contrast sliders to create a special effect with your picture. Click Shadow in the left pane, and change the Preset, Color, Blur options. Click Close.

11. Change the Text Wrapping option to Top and Bottom. Change the shape height to 1.25 inches.

12. Add a blank paragraph before the paragraph that begins "Please check." Drag the picture to follow the first bulleted list (drag to the blank paragraph).

13. Insert a column break at the paragraph beginning "Please check."

14. Click in front of the paragraph in the second column that begins "The favor prices."

15. Key mascot in the Clip Art Search for box. Click a mascot to insert in the document.

16. Select the mascot if necessary, and click Picture Shape on the Picture Tools Format tab. Click the Oval shape. Click Picture Effects, and choose a glow style.

17. Change the Text Wrapping option to Tight, and change the shape height to 0.75 inch. Drag the picture to the middle of the paragraph that begins "In August." Use Ctrl and the arrow keys to move the picture in small increments.

18. Apply a page border to the document.

19. Save the document as *[your initials]*17-29 in your Lesson 17 folder.

20. Submit and close the document.

Exercise 17-30

Insert, size, position, format, and align clip art.

1. Start a new document, and open the Page Setup dialog box. Change the orientation to landscape, change all margins to 0.4 inch, and change the paper size to 4.5 inches wide and 3 inches high.

2. Key and format the text in Figure 17-33.

Figure 17-33

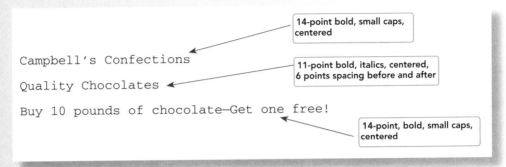

Campbell's Confections — 14-point bold, small caps, centered

Quality Chocolates — 11-point bold, italics, centered, 6 points spacing before and after

Buy 10 pounds of chocolate—Get one free! — 14-point, bold, small caps, centered

3. Draw a rectangle the width of the document and 0.25 inch high. Click **Shape Fill**, and apply a two-color gradient to the rectangle. Change the **Shape Outline** to coordinate with the fill color.

4. Copy and paste one copy of the rectangle.

5. Drag one rectangle to the top edge of the document, and drag one rectangle to the bottom edge of the document.

6. Insert a clip art of chocolate in the document.

7. Select the picture, and change the text wrapping to square. Right-click the picture, and click **Size** to open the Size dialog box. Deselect **Lock aspect ratio**, and change the height and width to 0.5 inch.

8. Select the picture if necessary, and click **Picture Shape**. Click the diamond shape in the Flow Chart group (◆).

9. Use the copy-and-paste feature to create two rows of pictures with each row containing five pictures.

Figure 17-34
Sample document with two rows of pictures

10. Use the Align, Group, or Distribute options to position the pictures. Refer to Figure 17-34 for a sample document.

11. Save the document as *[your initials]*17-30 in your Lesson 17 folder.

12. Submit and close the document.

Exercise 17-31 ◆ Challenge Yourself

Insert and format shapes.

1. Open the file **WV Stores**. Change the top margin to 1.5 inches.

2. Beginning with the first address, format the document as two columns with 1 inch spacing between.

3. Select each of the cities (Clarksburg, Fairmont, Morgantown, and Wheeling), and apply 14-point bold, italic, and small caps formatting.

4. Insert a column break at the end of the document.

5. Position the insertion point at the top of the second column, and use the Clip Art task pane to locate a map of West Virginia.

6. Change the width of the map to 2.5 inches, and lock the aspect ratio to maintain proportion.

7. Change the text wrapping to square, and drag the picture to the middle of the second column.

8. Open the Shapes gallery, and click the **Line Callout 2** shape ◿ (Callouts category, first row, sixth shape).

9. Point to the map of West Virginia, and draw a callout shape approximately 2 inches wide and 0.5 inch tall. Key **Clarksburg** in the callout. Draw three additional callout shapes for the map of West Virginia, and key a city name in each callout (Fairmont, Morgantown, and Wheeling).

10. Format the text in the callouts using appropriate character formatting. Size and format the callout shapes using an appropriate fill and line color. Apply shadow or 3-D effects if appropriate. Right-click the callouts, and choose **Format AutoShape** if you want to add an arrow style to the callout lines.

11. Use an atlas or the Internet to determine the location of each of these cities in West Virginia, and drag the callout to its approximate location.

12. Format the title using a WordArt design.

13. Save the document as *[your initials]***17-31** in your Lesson 17 folder. Submit and close the document.

On Your Own

In these exercises you work on your own, as you would in a real-life business environment. Use the skills you've learned to accomplish the task—and be creative.

Exercise 17-32

Log onto the Internet, and use Word's Clip Art task pane to search for a map of your home state. Insert the map, and use callouts to identify five cities. Format the objects, and add a title to the document using WordArt. Save the document as *[your initials]***17-32**. Submit the document.

Exercise 17-33

Create a design for a business card for yourself. Include a 3-D shape, and use rectangles or other shapes for your name and address. Insert clip art, and apply special effects if desired. Save the document as *[your initials]***17-33**, and submit it.

Exercise 17-34

Create a single-page recipe for your favorite dish. Include pictures of ingredients, and add shapes and lines for special effect. Experiment with the formatting effects on the Format tab. Save the document as *[your initials]***17-34,** and submit it.

Lesson 18

Text Boxes and Desktop Publishing

OBJECTIVES

MCAS OBJECTIVES

In this lesson:
WW 07 1.1.5
WW 07 3.2
WW 07 3.3.2
WW 07 3.4
WW 07 4.1.2
WW 07 4.1.3

After completing this lesson, you will be able to:

1. Apply page formatting.

2. Apply character and paragraph formatting.

3. Create and modify styles.

4. Create a newsletter-style column layout.

5. Insert text boxes.

6. Create a pull quote.

7. Link text boxes.

8. Work with a multisection layout.

Estimated Time: 1½ hours

In this lesson you use desktop publishing techniques to transform a document into a newsletter layout. You begin by changing the page background and applying paragraph and character formatting, specifying columns, inserting text boxes, and customizing clip art. Then you apply borders and shading and learn how to flow text between linked text boxes.

Applying Page Formatting

Page formatting consists of margins, orientation, headers, footers, page numbers, and page breaks. Special effects can be applied to pages, including watermarks, color, and borders.

A *watermark* is a transparent graphic or text placed behind text. A watermark adds dimension to the printed page by creating a layered effect. Watermarks are often used on stationery.

Exercise 18-1   CREATE A TEXT WATERMARK

You can insert a watermark from the watermark gallery, or you can create a custom watermark. To insert a watermark, use the Page Layout tab.

1. Start a new document.

2. Click the **Page Layout** tab, and locate the **Page Background** group. Click the Watermark button. A gallery of watermarks displays, including categories for confidential, disclaimers, and urgent.

3. Scroll to the **Urgent** category, and click the **Urgent 1** watermark. Notice the position and color of the watermark. Click Undo to remove the watermark.

4. Click the Watermark button, and click **Custom Watermark**.

5. Click the **Text watermark** option. Open the Text drop-down list to see the text options available. Close the list, and create your own watermark by keying **FOR REVIEW ONLY** in the text box. Notice that you can change the font, size, color, and layout (horizontal or diagonal) of the text watermark.

> **NOTE**
>
> To view a watermark as it will appear on the printed page, use Print Layout view or Print Preview.

Figure 18-1
Printed Watermark
dialog box

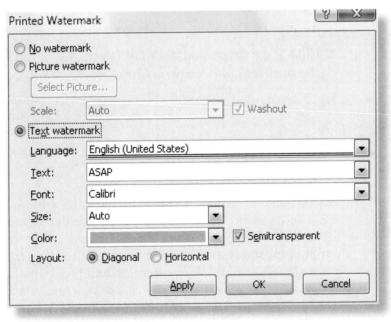

6. Click **OK**. The text appears diagonally on the page.

7. Click the Watermark button, and click **Remove Watermark**.

Exercise 18-2   CREATE A PICTURE WATERMARK

You can create a picture watermark using the Printed Watermark dialog box, or you can manually create a picture watermark using the brightness and contrast controls to create a washout effect and changing the picture's wrapping style to Behind Text.

NOTE

To use a shape as a watermark, insert the object in the document and use the Format AutoShape dialog box to control the object's contrast. Position and size the object.

1. Open the Printed Watermark dialog box, and click the **Picture watermark** option.

2. Click **Select Picture**, and locate the directory and folder for the student data files. Click the file **Chocolate - P1**, and click **Insert**.

3. Verify that the **Washout** option is checked. Click **OK**.

Exercise 18-3 CHANGE THE BACKGROUND COLOR

The background of a document can be customized by changing the color and adding a gradient, texture, or pattern. Background color or fill effects are usually reserved for Web pages or documents viewed online.

1. Click the **Page Layout** tab, and click the Page Color button ▓.

2. Point to several **Theme Colors**, and click a color that coordinates with the picture watermark.

3. Change the document theme to **Median**, and click **Page Color** on the Page Layout tab. Notice the change in theme colors. Select a different page color.

4. Click **Page Color**, and click **Fill Effects**. Click the **Texture** tab, and select the **Brown Marble** texture. Click **OK**.

5. Close the document without saving.

Applying Character and Paragraph Formatting

Basic character formatting involves choosing a font, a font style, and a font size. The choice of font is an important design decision. Fonts, also called "typefaces," should be readable and appropriate to the document. The title font should draw attention. The font for headings (often called "headlines" in newsletters) should draw attention and break up the body text. Document themes include two fonts—one for headings and one for body text. The fonts may be the same font or two different fonts. When selecting a theme, you may want to review the font(s) defined by the theme.

Headings are often *sans serif* (with no decorative lines projecting from the characters), and body text is *serif* (with decorative lines) in printed documents. Online documents often use sans serif fonts for body text.

- *Sans serif: Arial, with bold italic font style, used for headings*

- Serif: Times New Roman, used for body text

Paragraph formatting includes indents, spacing, alignment, borders, and shading. In this lesson you also apply styles, which provide a combination of character and paragraph formatting.

Exercise 18-4 CHOOSE A CHARACTER FORMAT FOR A TITLE

The newsletter title, or *nameplate*, is the most noticeable element on the page. You can design it in a drawing program or by using WordArt. Or you can choose a font that is appropriate for the title or the business name. In this exercise, you create the title, using a unique bold font.

1. Open the file **Chocolate News**. Change the top, bottom, left, and right margins to 0.75 inch.

2. On a new line at the top of the page, key the title Choc Talk.

3. Start a new line under the title and key Volume 1, Number 2.

4. On the same line, insert two spaces, and key the current month and year.

5. Format the title in 60-point Arial Narrow, with bold and italic.

6. Format the line under the title as 10-point Arial.

Figure 18-2
Matching fonts with business names

Lucida Calligraphy	*Magical Mystery Tour Co.*
Impact Italic	**North American School of Aviation**
Tahoma	Vision Consultants of Freemont
Monotype Corsiva	*Chez Pierre Catering*
Century Schoolbook	Smithfield Savings and Loan
Comic Sans MS	Westport Design Studios
Bodoni MT Black	World Gym

Exercise 18-5 WORK WITH CHARACTER SPACING

Just as a typographer does, you can change character spacing to improve the look of your document text. Some character-spacing features also help you create character effects and control the size of the document.

Using the Font dialog box (Character Spacing tab), you can control character spacing in the following ways:

• Stretch or compress text horizontally by a percentage of its original size.

• Add or delete space between letters by a specific number of points.

• Raise or lower selected text in relation to the baseline.

• Adjust *kerning,* or the amount of space between certain combinations of characters, so a word looks more evenly spaced.

1. Select the title text.

2. Open the Font dialog box, and display the Character Spacing tab.

3. Open the Spacing drop-down list, and choose Condensed. Notice the change in the Preview box. The text is condensed by 1 point.

4. Choose Expanded from the drop-down list, and click OK. The text is expanded by 1 point.

Figure 18-3
Changing Character
Spacing

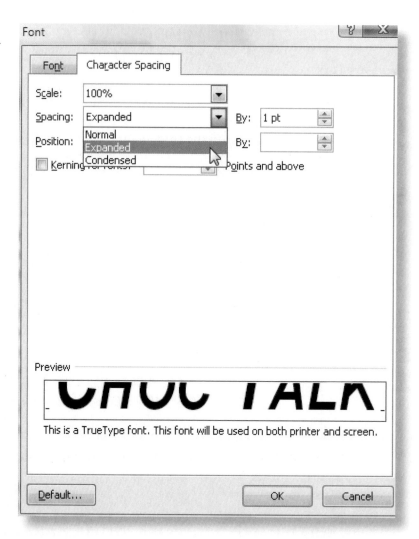

NOTE

You can change the number of points to expand or condense type to exaggerate the effect.

5. Change the **Spacing** setting back to **Normal**. Open the **Scale** drop-down list and choose **150%**. Click **OK**. This stretches each letter of text horizontally.

6. Reopen the **Font** dialog box and key **130%** in the **Scale** box. Click **OK**.

7. With the title selected, press Ctrl + Spacebar. All character formatting is removed.

8. Click the Undo button 🔄 (or press Ctrl + Z) to restore the formatting.

Exercise 18-6   APPLY PARAGRAPH FORMATTING

In this exercise you apply basic paragraph formatting (aligning, indenting, and paragraph spacing) to improve the text flow of the newsletter layout.

1. Center-align the title text, and right-align the line of text below the title.

2. Format the line below the title with 12-point spacing after paragraphs to provide more white space below it.

3. Select the text from the first heading ("Chocolate Terms") through the end of the document.

4. On the Home tab, Paragraph group, click the Line Spacing button and choose **1.0**. The selected text now has single spacing.

5. Select the text from the paragraph beginning "Chocolate Terms" through the end of the document if necessary, and verify that the spacing after is 10 points.

Exercise 18-7   APPLY BORDERS AND SHADING

1. To change the title to white text against a black background (sometimes referred to as *reverse* or *drop-out* text), select the title, including its paragraph mark. Click the **Home** tab, and click the arrow beside the **Borders and Shading** button . Click **Borders and Shading** to open the Borders and Shading dialog box. Display the **Shading** tab, click the **Fill** down arrow, click **Black** in the first row, second column, and click **OK**. Deselect the title.

Figure 18-4
Applying shading to the title

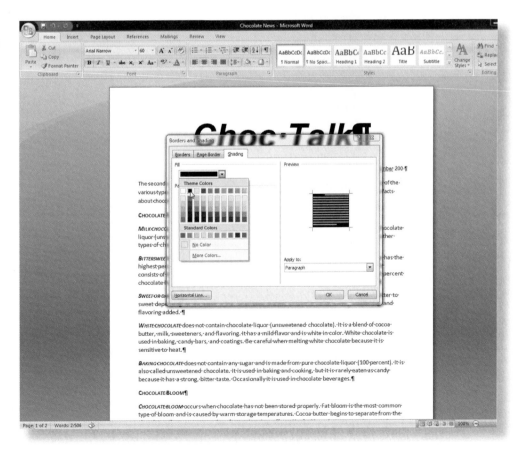

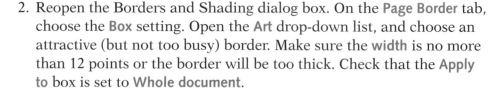

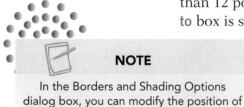

2. Reopen the Borders and Shading dialog box. On the **Page Border** tab, choose the **Box** setting. Open the **Art** drop-down list, and choose an attractive (but not too busy) border. Make sure the **width** is no more than 12 points or the border will be too thick. Check that the **Apply to** box is set to **Whole document**.

NOTE

In the Borders and Shading Options dialog box, you can modify the position of the page border from the margin to the edge of the page by adjusting the Top, Bottom, Left, and Right settings.

3. Click the Options button [Options...]. The Borders and Shading Options dialog box shows you that the border will appear, by default, 24 points (⅓ inch) from the top, bottom, left, and right edges of the page. Click **OK**. Click **OK** again to apply the page border.

Figure 18-5
Applying borders

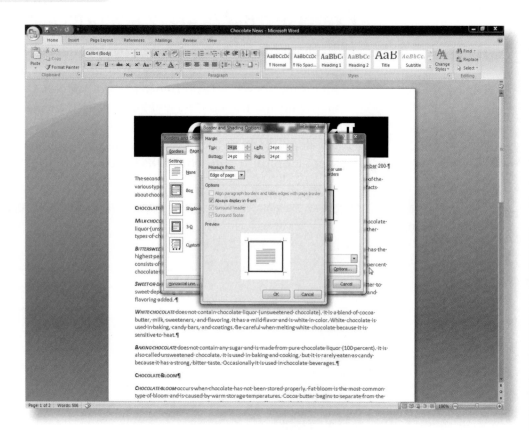

4. Save the document as *[your initials]***18-7** in a new folder for Lesson 18 documents. Leave it open for the next exercise.

Creating and Modifying Styles

A *style* consists of formatting characteristics that you apply to paragraphs, characters, tables, or lists to give a document a consistent look. Word provides predefined styles you can apply to text, such as heading styles for document titles and body text styles for paragraphs. In this lesson, you learn how to create and name your own styles and then modify them.

Exercise 18-8   CREATE PARAGRAPH AND CHARACTER STYLES

Paragraph styles include formatting related to such characteristics as text alignment, tab stops, line spacing, borders, and fonts. Character formatting affects selected text within a paragraph and can include fonts, font size, and bold and italic formats.

1. Display the Styles task pane by clicking the **Styles Dialog Box Launcher**. At the bottom of the task pane, click <u>Options</u> to display the Style Pane Options dialog box. Click the drop-down arrow for the **Select styles to show** box, and click **In use**. Click **OK**. This shows the formats currently used in the document, which is only the Normal style at this point.

2. Point to the Normal style in the Styles task pane to view its formatting instructions.

3. Click <u>Options</u> in the Styles task pane, and change the **Select styles to show** option to display **All styles**, and scroll through the list, which shows all of Word's predefined styles. A paragraph mark at the right of a style name indicates a paragraph style; an "a" indicates a character style.

4. Change the **Select styles to show** box to display **Recommended** (which shows both the formats you create and the Quick Styles). Click within the heading "Chocolate Terms." You are going to create a new paragraph style for the document headings.

REVIEW

The Normal style always appears as formatting in use in a document. It is the default paragraph style on which other styles are based. It is 11-point Calibri, left-aligned, 1.15 line spacing, and 10 points spacing after.

5. Click the **New Style** button at the bottom of the Styles task pane. In the New Style dialog box, make the following changes:

- In the **Name** box, key the style name *[your initials]*Paragraph Heading. The **Style type** box should be set to **Paragraph**. The **Style based on** box should be set to **Normal**.

- Under **Formatting**, change the font to Arial Narrow, 14-point bold.

- Click the **Format** button, and choose **Paragraph**. In the Paragraph dialog box, set the spacing before to 12 points and the spacing after to 6 points. Click **OK**.

Figure 18-6
Creating a paragraph
style

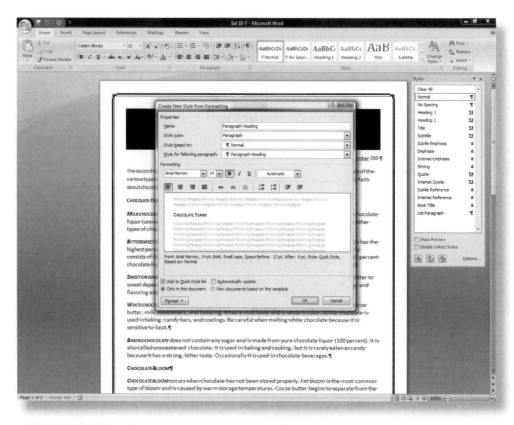

REVIEW

To clear paragraph formatting, place your
insertion point in the formatted paragraph
and press Ctrl+Q.

NOTE

You don't have to select text to apply a
paragraph style; simply place the insertion
point within the paragraph to which you
are applying the style.

6. Click **OK** in the New Style dialog box. The new style
   appears in the Styles task pane.

7. With the insertion point still in the heading
   "Chocolate Terms," click the new style, *[your
   initials]*Paragraph heading, in the task pane to apply
   the style.

8. Apply the new *[your initials]***Paragraph Heading**
   style to the following headings: "Chocolate Bloom"
   and "Storage."

9. In the paragraph beginning "Milk Chocolate,"
   select the text "Milk Chocolate." You will create a
   character style for this text, and to do so you need to
   select the text.

10. Click the New Style button and make the following changes in the
    New Style dialog box:

    - In the **Name** box, key the style name *[your initials]*Term.

    - Set the **Style type** to **Character**.

    - Click the **Format** button and choose **Font**. Change the font to Impact,
      no bold, no italic with 1.5 pt expanded character spacing. Click **OK**,
      and then click **OK** again.

11. Apply the new character style to the selected text and to the terms "Bittersweet Chocolate," "Semisweet Chocolate," "Sweet or Dark Chocolate," "White Chocolate," "Baking Chocolate," and "Chocolate Bloom."

TIP

To clear character formatting, select the formatted text and press Ctrl + Spacebar.

12. Position the insertion point in the first paragraph that begins "The second issue." Create a new paragraph style called *[your initials]*Newsletter body that is based on the Normal style. Use the font Book Antiqua, 12 points, single spacing, justified alignment, and 12 points spacing after.

13. Apply the new Newsletter body style to every paragraph except the three paragraphs formatted with the Paragraph Heading style. Notice that the applied paragraph style *[your initials]*Newsletter body does not affect the character style.

14. Save the document as *[your initials]***18-8** in your Lesson 18 folder.

Exercise 18-9   CREATE A STYLE FOR BULLET TEXT

You can create a style for a list of items and specify the numbering or bullet characters.

1. Position the insertion point at the end of the document.

2. Press Enter and key the following text. Press Enter after each sentence.

   Chocolate's flavonoids and antioxidants make it a "heart-healthy" food. Chocolate does not raise cholesterol because of a key ingredient, stearic acid. The darker the chocolate, the healthier it is for us because it has fewer calories but more antioxidants.

3. Click <u>Options</u> in the Styles task pane, and change the **Select styles to show** box to display **All styles**. Notice that the styles you created appear near the top of the list. Scroll the list of styles to view Word's predefined list styles.

4. Position the insertion point in the line that begins "Chocolate's flavonoids." Open the New Style dialog box, and create the following new style:

   - Name the style *[your initials]*Bulleted list, and change the style type to **Paragraph**.

   - Click the Format button [Format ▾] in the dialog box; then click **Numbering**. Click the **Bullets** tab.

   - Click **Define New Bullet** to choose a new symbol character, and click **Symbol** to open the Symbol dialog box.

   - Change the font to **Wingdings**, and choose a shadowed square symbol (❑). Click **OK** to close all open dialog boxes.

Figure 18-7
Choosing a symbol

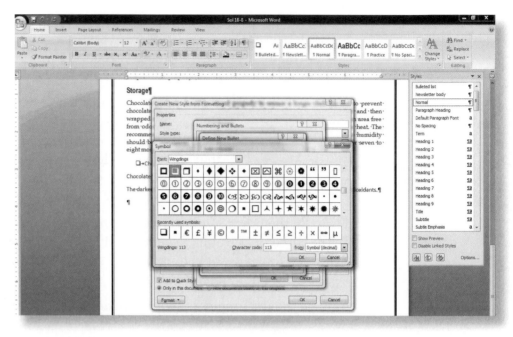

5. Apply the *[your initials]***Bulleted list** style to the three sentences that you keyed in step 2.

Exercise 18-10 MODIFY STYLES

After you create a style, you can modify it in a number of ways, such as renaming it or changing the formatting.

1. Right-click the style *[your initials]***Newsletter body** in the task pane and choose Modify.

TIP

You can create or modify a style so that a different style is assigned to the paragraph that follows once you press the Enter key. This means you can have styles applied automatically as you key text. This is useful for heading styles. In the New Style or Modify Style dialog box, open the drop-down list beside Style for following paragraph and choose the style you want to follow.

2. Change the font to Comic Sans MS, 11 points, left-aligned, with 6 points spacing after paragraphs. Click OK to close the Modify Style dialog box. The changes appear throughout the document.

3. Point to the style named *[your initials]***Paragraph heading** in the task pane, click its down arrow, and choose Modify.

4. Open the drop-down list for the box labeled Style for following paragraph. Choose Newsletter body and click OK.

5. Position the insertion point on page 2 at the end of the paragraph that begins "Chocolate products." Start a new paragraph and key Chocolate and Nutrition. Apply the *[your initials]***Paragraph heading** style to the text.

6. Press Enter to start a new paragraph. Notice the style Newsletter body is applied to the new paragraph. Key the following text:

The following list includes several interesting observations about chocolate.

7. Click <u>Options</u> in the bottom of the Styles task pane, and change the **Select styles to show** box to **In use** so you can see all the styles and formatting you have created for this document. Click to select the check boxes for **Paragraph level formatting**, **Font formatting**, and **Bullet and numbering** formatting. Selecting the check boxes allows you to see manual formatting applied to text in the document.

Figure 18-8
Style Pane Options
dialog box

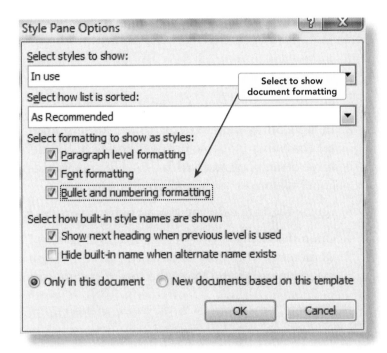

8. Click the first line in the document, the formatted newsletter title. Notice the format that is selected in the Styles task pane. Right-click the formatting description for the title in the Styles task pane, and choose **Modify Style**.

9. The selected format appears as the name of the style. Key the style name *[your initials]*Newsletter title. Click **OK**. Notice the formatting now has a style name in the task pane.

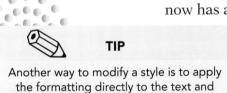

TIP

Another way to modify a style is to apply the formatting directly to the text and then right-click the formatting or style in the task pane and choose Update to Match Selection.

10. Follow the same procedure to modify the formatting for the line below the title, giving it the style name *[your initials]*Volume and adding 6 points of spacing before the paragraph.

11. Save the document as *[your initials]***18-10** in your Lesson 18 folder. Leave it open for the next exercise.

Creating a Newsletter-Style Column Layout

Newsletters typically use a column layout similar to a newspaper, in which text flows from the bottom of one column to the top of the next. When creating a newsletter, you need to determine the number, size, and placement of columns, all of which affect readability and the amount of white space on the page. After your document is in column layout, you can use Word's many tools to control the flow of text.

Exercise 18-11   CREATE A MULTICOLUMN LAYOUT

In this exercise, you create a multicolumn layout. You keep the existing one-column format for the text from the title through the first paragraph. You apply a three-column layout for all text beginning with the heading "Chocolate Terms."

1. Position the insertion point to the left of the bold paragraph heading "Chocolate Terms." Click the **Page Layout** tab, and click the Columns button ▣. Click **More Columns**.

2. In the Columns dialog box, under **Presets**, click **Three**. (You can also set the **Number of columns** text box to **3**.) By default, this layout has three 2-inch columns with 0.5-inch spacing between columns. (The **Equal column width** box should be checked.)

3. Check the **Line between** box to place a vertical line between columns.

4. Open the **Apply to** drop-down list, and choose **This point forward**. Remember, you want to start the three-column layout from the insertion point and leave the top of the page as one column.

Figure 18-9
Choosing column settings

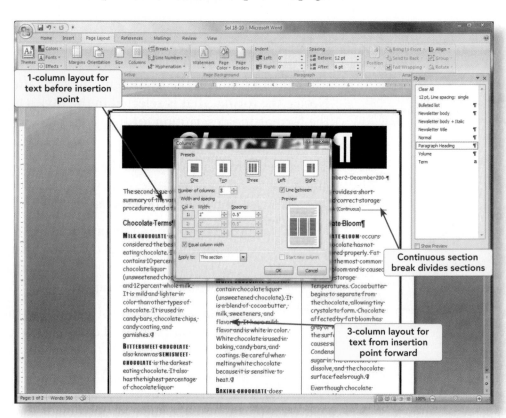

5. Notice the layout for the three-column format shown in the **Preview** box. This is the layout you will apply, but before doing so, click the other Presets (**Two**, **Left**, **Right**), and notice the layout changes.

6. Click **Three** again and click **OK**. The three-column text starts a new section. If necessary, click the Show/Hide ¶ button ⬚ to see the continuous section break.

7. Position the insertion point at the end of the first section (to the right of "nutrition!" and before the paragraph mark), and press Enter to add white space between the sections.

8. Format the heading "Chocolate Terms" with no spacing before the paragraph. This will align the heading with the text at the top of the second and third columns. (Do not modify the style; just change the formatting for that particular heading.)

9. Locate the paragraph in the third column that begins "Even though," and format the paragraph with a 0.25-inch first-line indent. Use this formatting to create a new style called "Newsletter indent." (Right-click the paragraph, and choose **Styles**. Click **Save Selection as a New Quick Style**. Key the style name *[your initials]*Newsletter indent, and click **OK**.)

10. At the end of the last paragraph in the document, insert a symbol of your choice from the font Wingdings or Webdings. This is often done in magazines to signify the end of an article.

11. Insert a symbol between "Number 2" and the month in the line after the title at the beginning of the document.

Exercise 18-12 BALANCE COLUMNS AND CONTROL TEXT FLOW

In a multicolumn layout, you can control how columns break. For example, you can insert a column break to force text to start at the next column, or you can insert a continuous section break to balance the length of columns.

For further control of how text flows in your layout, you can change text flow options in the Paragraph dialog box. For example:

- Make sure Word does not print the last line of a paragraph by itself at the top of a page (called a *widow*) or the first line of a paragraph by itself at the bottom of a page (called an *orphan*).

- Keep the lines of a paragraph together (preventing a page break within the paragraph).

- Keep one paragraph with another paragraph (preventing a page break between the paragraphs).

- Insert a page break before a paragraph.

Figure 18-10
Choosing text flow
options

1. Scroll to the end of the document.

2. To balance the length of the columns on page 2, position the insertion point at the end of the document (after the symbol).

3. Insert a continuous section break (**Page Layout** tab, **Breaks**). Word balances the length of the columns.

4. Scroll to page 2, and change the zoom to **Text Width**. Select the heading "Chocolate and Nutrition," and open the Paragraph dialog box. On the **Line and Page Breaks** tab, check the **Keep with next** option. (**Keep lines together** is used for lines in the same paragraph.) Click **OK**.

5. To change the line, column, and page breaks throughout the document, insert a picture—position the insertion point on page 1 at the beginning of the first paragraph ("The second issue"), and insert a picture related to chocolate.

NOTE

Notice that the Widow/Orphan Control option is turned on by default to prevent a paragraph's first line from appearing by itself at the bottom of a page (called an *orphan*) and to prevent a paragraph's last line from appearing by itself at the top of a page (called a *widow*).

6. Select the clip art, and change the text wrapping to square. Change the height to 1 inch. Scroll through the document, and notice the change in text flow in the columns.

7. Delete the continuous section break at the end of the document (click before the break and press Delete). The columns are no longer balanced.

8. Place the insertion point in the third column of the first page at the beginning of the paragraph that begins "Even though," and insert a continuous section break. Press Enter after "feels rough" if necessary to place the new section on page 2. Place the insertion point in the new section (page 2, section 3), open the Columns dialog box, and make the following changes:

   - Change the column measurements to unequal column widths.

   - Remove the line between columns for this section.

   - Set columns 1 and 2 to 2.3 inches wide with 0.25-inch space between them, and set column 3 to 1.9 inches. Click OK.

9. Click in the left column on page 1, reopen the Columns dialog box, and delete the line between columns for this section.

10. Save the document as *[your initials]*18-12 in your Lesson 18 folder.

11. Submit the document. Leave it open for the next exercise.

Inserting Text Boxes

In this section, you insert a photograph in a document, and add text to the layout. The easiest way to do this is by inserting a *text box*—a free-floating rectangular object. You can position a text box anywhere on a page and apply formatting to it.

Exercise 18-13   INSERT A TEXT BOX

You can create a text box from existing text or insert a blank text box and key text inside it (similar to drawing a shape and adding text to the shape).

1. Scroll to the bottom of page 2. Click the Insert tab on the Ribbon, and locate the Text group. Click the Text Box button.

2. A gallery of text box designs displays. Click Draw Text Box.

3. The pointer changes to a crosshair +. Draw a text box in the lower right corner by dragging the crosshair down and to the right until it measures approximately 2 inches wide and 3 inches tall.

Figure 18-11
Inserting text boxes

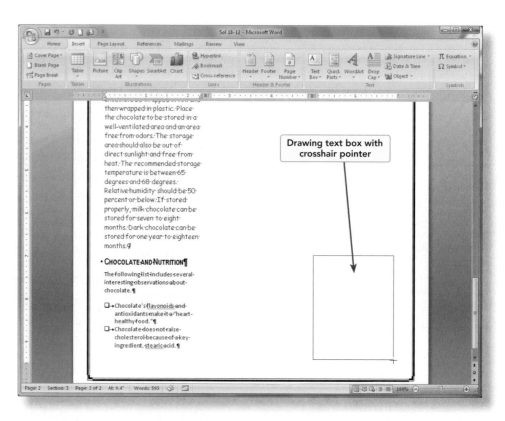

4. Select the paragraph mark, and open the Paragraph dialog box. Change the line spacing to single, and the spacing after to 0 points. Key the text in Figure 18-12, and apply the appropriate format.

Figure 18-12

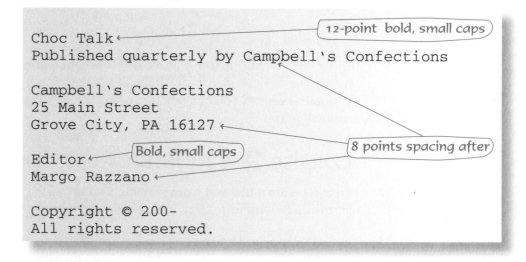

Exercise 18-14 SELECT AND SIZE A TEXT BOX

When you click within a text box, you activate it. The text box is then in Text Edit mode—you can add, edit, or format the text.

When you click the text box border, you select the text box. You can then move or format the text box. There is a subtle difference between the border of a selected text box and an activated text box.

NOTE

An activated text box has its own ruler, which you can use to change margins, indents, and tab settings for text within the text box.

NOTE

A text box does not expand automatically when you add or enlarge text. You must resize the text box.

NOTE

A *masthead* is an important newsletter element. It identifies the company producing the newsletter and may include names and titles (such as editor and contributing writers).

1. Click inside the text box containing text to activate it. Notice the border, made of dotted lines. You can add, edit, or format text in an activated text box.

2. Select the text "Published quarterly by." Apply italic formatting.

3. Point to the top-left resize handle of the text box. When you see the two-pointed arrow pointer, drag the handle diagonally up and to the left approximately 0.25 inch.

4. Use the middle-bottom handle to drag the bottom border up to fit the text. Notice that clicking on a text box border to resize it also selects the text box. The selected text box border has a solid line, rather than dotted lines.

5. Right-click the text box, and choose **Format Text Box**. Click the **Size** tab. Change the **Height Absolute** value to **2.5** inches, and change the **Width Absolute** value to **2** inches. Click **OK**.

6. Drag the selected text box until it is positioned in the lower right corner of the page.

7. Resize and position the text box as needed to resemble the one shown in Figure 18-13.

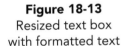
Figure 18-13
Resized text box with formatted text

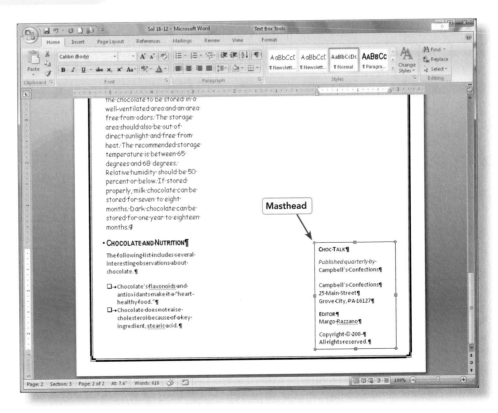

Exercise 18-15   FORMAT A TEXT BOX

As with other drawing objects, you can change the border, fill, and alignment of a text box and size the box to exact measurements. You can also change the internal text box margins. You can use the Text Box Tools Format tab on the Ribbon or use the Format Text Box dialog box.

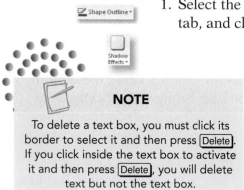

NOTE

To delete a text box, you must click its border to select it and then press Delete. If you click inside the text box to activate it and then press Delete, you will delete text but not the text box.

1. Select the text box by clicking the text box border. Click the **Home** tab, and click the Center button ≣ to center-align the text.

2. With the text box still selected, click the **Text Box Tools Format** tab, and click the Shape Outline button. Click **Weight**, and choose 1¹/2 pt.

3. Click the Shadow Effects button ⬛ and click the fourth style in the first row (**Shadow Style 4**).

4. Right-click the text box, and choose **Format Text Box**. Click the **Text Box** tab, and click **Center** under **Vertical alignment**. Click **OK**.

Figure 18-14
Choosing options in the Format Text Box dialog box

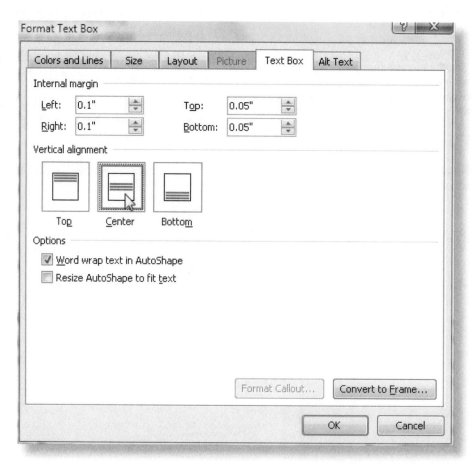

5. View the document in Print Preview.

6. Close Print Preview. Save the document as *[your initials]*18-15 in your Lesson 18 folder, submit the document, and leave it open for the next exercise.

Exercise 18-16   USE ADVANCED LAYOUT SETTINGS TO POSITION OBJECTS

Instead of dragging to position a picture, text box, or Drawing Canvas, you can specify the exact position by using advanced layout dialog box settings. For example, you can position a picture or text box exactly on the page in relation to a particular margin.

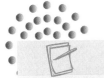

NOTE

Because all the margins are 0.75 inch, using "relative to margin" settings enables you to easily align the objects on the page exactly 0.75 inch from the edge of the page. The Absolute Position settings require you to enter an exact measurement in the text box. You can align or position an object in relation to the margin, page, column, or character. You can also choose Lock Anchor if you do not want the object to move along with the paragraph to which the object is anchored.

1. Right-click the text box, and open the Format Text Box dialog box. Display the **Layout** tab and click **Advanced**.

2. On the **Picture Position** tab, make the following changes:

   • Under **Horizontal**, click **Alignment** and set it to **Right relative to Margin**. This setting right-aligns the object with the right margin.

   • Under **Vertical**, click **Alignment** and set it to **Bottom relative to Margin**. This setting aligns the bottom of the object with the bottom margin. Click **OK** to return to the Format Text dialog box.

Figure 18-15
Choosing Advanced
Layout options

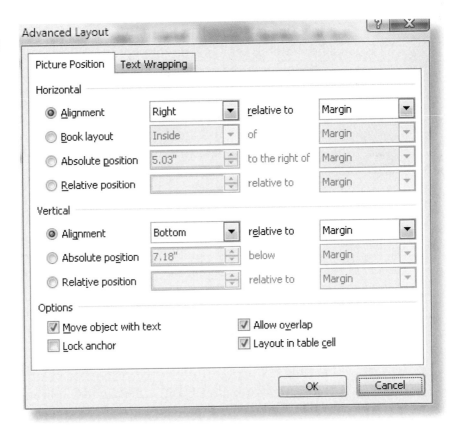

3. Save the document as *[your initials]***18-16** in your Lesson 18 folder. Submit the document, and leave it open for the next exercise.

Creating Pull Quotes

A *pull quote* is a sentence or quotation taken from a document and enlarged or set apart from the rest of the text for emphasis. When adding a pull quote, keep the following rules in mind:

- **Font, font style, and size:** Pull quotes should attract the reader's eye but not compete with headings or titles. The font should match other heading fonts.

- **Borders and shading:** Use these to enhance the pull quote, but remember not to compete with headings or titles.

- **Position:** Pull quotes should be placed within a column or in the white space next to a column, but not between columns, which interrupts text flow.

Exercise 18-17   CREATE PULL QUOTES

To create a pull quote, you copy the text, convert it to a text box, and position the text box on the page. You can then format the pull quote for added emphasis by changing the font and adding borders.

1. Scroll to page 2. Click the **Insert** tab. Click the Text Box button. Click **Draw Text Box**, and draw a text box approximately 1 inch high and 2 inches wide in the first column on page 2 above the heading "Chocolate and Nutrition." The text box is placed on top of the text in the column.

2. Scroll to the top of the second column on page 2, and locate the text "The darker the chocolate, the healthier it is for us." Copy the text, and paste the text in the text box.

NOTE

With both these settings checked, the text box is "locked" to the paragraph at which it is inserted. If you edit the document, the text box will not jump to another part of the document but will move with the paragraph as text flow changes.

3. Before moving the text box into position, right-click the text box, and choose **Format Text Box** from the shortcut menu. On the **Size** tab, change the width of the text box to **2.3** inches (the column width). On the **Layout** tab, go to advanced position settings and check the **Lock anchor** box. Make sure **Move object with text** is also checked. Click **OK**; then click **OK** again.

4. Select the text box if necessary, and change the text wrapping option to top and bottom. Use the ⬇ to move the text box above the heading "Chocolate and Nutrition." After positioning the text box, you can move it closer to the heading by holding down Ctrl as you press an arrow key.

5. Make the following changes to the text box:

   • Change the text style to italic and place a period at the end of the sentence.

   • Edit the text by starting the sentence with **Remember:**.

   • Remove the line around the text box (**Shape Outline, No Outline**), and add a top and bottom 1-point border. Resize the height of the text box to fit the text and borders. The text should fit on two lines. (To remove the line around the text box, select the text box, click the Shape Outline button on the Format tab on the Ribbon, and choose No Line.)

Figure 18-16
Using text boxes to create pull quotes

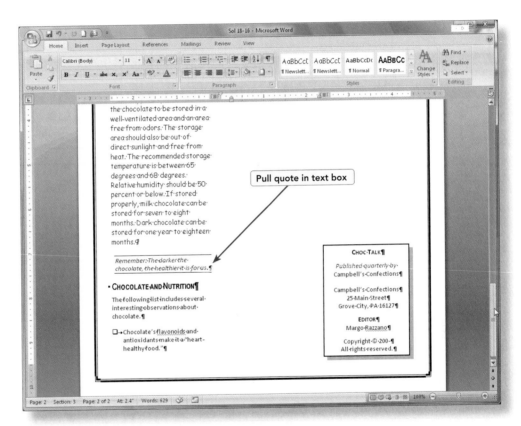

6. Save the document as *[your initials]***18-17** in your Lesson 18 folder.

7. Leave it open for the next exercise.

Linking Text Boxes

Newsletters often use linked text boxes in one of two ways:

• Flow an article from one text box into the other. For example, you can have an article in a text box on page 1 that continues in a text box on page 3. You do this by linking the two text boxes.

- Flow text in parallel text boxes from page to page. For example, you create two side-by-side text boxes on two pages. You link the right text boxes to each other and the left text boxes to each other. This is useful for pairing two similar text blocks, such as an article in Spanish on the right and the English translation on the left.

Figure 18-17
Ways to link text boxes

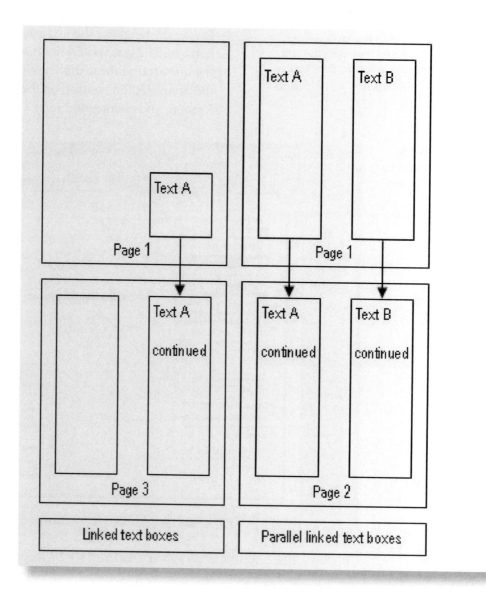

Exercise 18-18   INSERT AND LINK TEXT BOXES

In this exercise, you insert a text box in column 2 on page 2 and link it to a text box in column 3 on page 2 so text flows from one to the other.

1. Change the zoom to Whole Page, display page 2, and click within the page. Click the Insert tab, and click the Text Box button ▤. Click Draw Text Box; then draw a text box to cover the blank space in column 2.

2. Format the text box so it is 1.9 inches wide and 7 inches high, with square text wrapping. Right-click the text box, and open the Format Text Box dialog box. Click the Layout tab, and click Advanced. Position the text box horizontally left relative to the column and vertically aligned at the bottom margin.

REVIEW

To insert a file, click the Insert tab and click the down arrow beside Object. Choose Text from File. Select the appropriate directory and folder for the student data files, and click Insert.

3. Draw another text box in column 3 that begins at the top of the column and extends to the existing text box. Format the text box so that it is 1.9 inches wide and 6.5 inches high. Apply square text wrapping, and use advanced layout settings to align the text box horizontally with the right margin and vertically with the top margin.

4. Change the zoom to Page Width; then click in the text box in column 2, and insert the document file **Special Events**. Scroll to the bottom of the text box. There is more text in this file than can fit in this text box.

5. To flow the overflow text into the text box in column 3, click in the column 2 text box. Click the Text Box Tools Format tab, and locate the Text group. Click the Create Link button . The mouse pointer changes to a pitcher ▯.

6. Move the pitcher into the text box in column 3. The pointer changes to a pouring pitcher ▯.

NOTE

To break text box links, select the text box that precedes the text box you want to unlink. Then click Break Link on the Ribbon, Text Box Tools Format tab, Text group.

7. Click the column 3 text box. The text boxes are now linked. The text automatically flows from the first text box to the second text box.

8. Click the text box in the second column. Center the title, and apply 12 points spacing before and 24 points spacing after.

9. Select the store locations under each special event, and right-align the text.

Figure 18-18
Linking text boxes

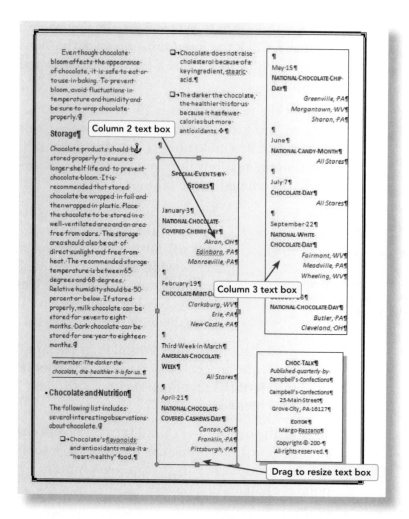

10. Change the Zoom level to **60%**, and adjust the text flow by resizing the height of the first text box. Drag the bottom-center sizing handle down to increase the height of the text box to accommodate all the text for the April 21 entry. If necessary, drag the text box slightly upward.

11. View the document in Print Preview. Make any adjustments and then save as *[your initials]***18-18** in your Lesson 18 folder.

12. Submit the document, and leave it open for the next exercise.

Creating a Multisection Layout

By creating a document with separate sections, you can format each section differently. For example, you can apply headers and footers to some but not all sections in a document, or you can change the vertical alignment of one section. In the following exercises, you add a new section to the newsletter to make it a self-mailer with one fold. You also add page numbers to certain pages and change the starting page number of sections.

Exercise 18-19 ADD A NEW SECTION WITH A DIFFERENT LAYOUT

After inserting a section break to create a new section, you can apply different formatting to the section: You use the Columns dialog box to change the column layout and the Page Setup dialog box to change the margins.

1. Go to the end of the current document ([Ctrl]+[End]), and insert a Next Page section break. If necessary, apply the Normal style to the blank paragraph mark.

2. Format the new section as one column and with no page border (verify that the **Apply to** box in the Borders and Shading dialog box is set to **This section**).

3. Open the Page Setup dialog box. Click the **Margins** tab, and change the left and right margins to 1 inch. Click **OK**.

4. At the paragraph mark in the new section, insert the picture file **Monogram**. Format the picture as follows:

   - Size: Scale height to 250%.

   - Text wrapping: Behind text.

   - Position: Centered horizontally relative to the page, positioned vertically 0.75 inch below the page.

   - Brightness: 80%.

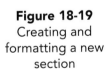

TIP

Hold down [Shift] as you draw to create a straight line.

5. Draw a horizontal line across the middle of the page, dividing the page in half. Assume that the newsletter will be folded at this line. Format the line as:

   - Size: 7 inches wide.

   - Position: Centered horizontally and vertically relative to the page.

Figure 18-19
Creating and formatting a new section

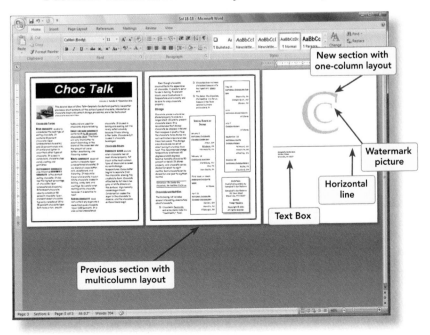

6. Below the line, draw a text box as shown in Figure 18-19. Copy Campbell's Confections' name and address from the masthead, and paste it in the text box. Format the text box as follows:

- Text: left aligned, 10 points with company name in bold.

- Right-click the text box, and open the **Format Text Box** dialog box. Click the **Text Box** tab, and click **Resize AutoShape to fit text**.

- Line: None (No color).

- Position: Below the line as shown and horizontally aligned left relative to the margin.

Exercise 18-20 UNLINK SECTION FOOTERS AND CHANGE STARTING PAGE NUMBERS

In this exercise you add page numbers in the footer area, but you do not want to number the last section. By default, the Link to Previous command is "on" when you work in the header or footer pane. As a result, the text you enter in the header or footer for the document is the same for every section. You can use the Link to Previous command to break the link between header and/or footer text from one section to another.

1. Go to the beginning of the document, and click the **Insert** tab. Click the Footer button 📄, and click **Blank**.

2. Notice that the pane is labeled "Footer–Section 1."

3. Press ⎯Tab⎯ twice to move to the right margin. Key the text **Page**, and key a space; then click the Quick Parts button 📄, and choose **Field**. Locate the **Field names** section, and click **Page**. Select the **1, 2, 3,** format, and click **OK**. Format the text as 11-point Arial Narrow, and align the text at the right margin by dragging the tab marker to the margin.

4. Click the **Header & Footer Tools Design** tab. Click the Next Section button 📑 Next Section to go to the next footer, which is on page 2. Notice the following:

- This section is labeled "Section 3" because page 1 contains two sections and page 2 starts as a new section.

- The Link to Previous button 📑 Link to Previous is turned on, which means this section is linked to the previous section, causing the same footer text to appear in this section.

5. Click the Next Section button 📑 Next Section to move to the next section, which is section 4, the last page. This part of the newsletter should not be numbered, so you need to unlink this section footer from the previous.

6. Click the Link to Previous button 📑 Link to Previous to unlink the section 4 footer; then delete the footer text:

Figure 18-20
Unlinking the section
footer

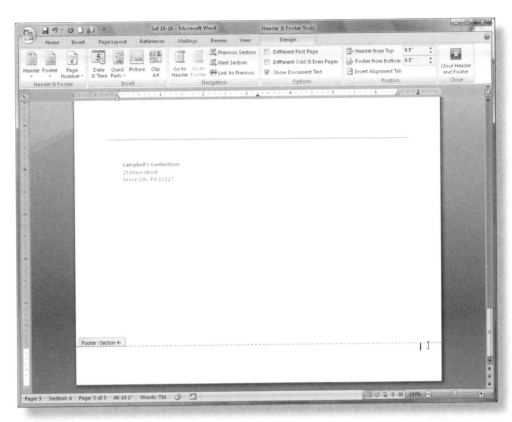

7. Go to the previous section footer to check that the page number is still there. Close the Header and Footer pane.

8. Check the document footers to verify that pages 1 and 2 are numbered correctly.

9. Save the document as *[your initials]***18-20** in your Lesson 18 folder. Submit and close the document.

Exercise 18-21 USE BUILDING BLOCKS TO FORMAT A DOCUMENT

Building blocks consist of AutoText entries, cover pages, headers, footers, page numbers, tables, text boxes, and watermarks. These items are reusable and are stored in galleries. You can insert building blocks through individual galleries such as footers and page numbers, or you can use the Building Blocks Organizer. One advantage of using built-in building blocks is the ability to create a document with a consistent design. In this exercise you create a framework for a document using built-in building blocks.

1. Start a new document.

2. Click the Insert tab, and click the Quick Parts button . Click **Building Blocks Organizer**. The Building Blocks Organizer displays.

Word 2007

Figure 18-21
Building Blocks
Organizer dialog box

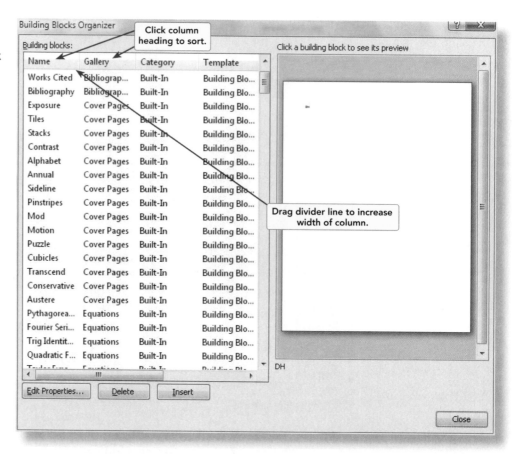

3. Click the **Name** column heading to alphabetize the list by name. Click the **Gallery** column heading to sort the building block entries by category.

4. Scroll to view the **Cover Pages** category, and click **Cubicles**. The cover page appears in the preview box. Click **Insert**.

5. Click the company name placeholder, and key **Campbell's Confections**.

6. Scroll to page 2, and click to position the insertion point at the top of the page. (Click Show/Hide ¶ if necessary.)

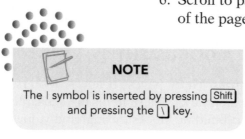

NOTE

The I symbol is inserted by pressing [Shift] and pressing the [\] key.

7. Open the **Building Blocks Organizer** dialog box, and scroll to the **Footers** category. Locate the **Cubicles** entry, and click **Insert**. Click the company address placeholder, and key **25 Main Street I Grove City, PA 16127**. Close the Footer pane.

8. Reopen the **Building Blocks Organizer** dialog box, and scroll to the **Text Boxes** category. Locate the **Cubicles Sidebar** entry, and click **Insert**. Read the information in the text box about the purpose of a side bar.

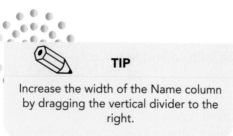

TIP

Increase the width of the Name column by dragging the vertical divider to the right.

9. Save the document as *[your initials]*18-21 in your Lesson 18 folder.

10. Submit and close the document.

Lesson 18 Summary

- A text box is a free-floating rectangular object that you can apply formatting to and position anywhere on a page.

- Size a text box by selecting it and dragging one of its sizing handles. Format a text box by changing its border, fill, alignment, size, and internal margins.

- Change text direction in a text box by rotating the text 90 degrees to the left or right.

- Use advanced layout settings to position any object precisely, horizontally and vertically.

- A watermark is a transparent graphic or text placed behind text.

- A newsletter generally begins with a title, or nameplate, that uses a font style appropriate for the publication. A newsletter might also contain a masthead (which lists the company and people who produce the publication).

- Important elements of newsletter design include proper paragraph formatting (aligning, indenting, and paragraph spacing), use of borders and shading, and allowing white space in a document, all of which help make the content more readable.

- Clip art includes drawings that can be inserted from the Clip Art task pane.

- A clip is inserted as an in-line graphic until you apply a wrapping style. Then you can move the clip freely on the page. You can also apply advanced text-wrapping options to control the distance of clip art from text.

- Newsletters typically have a multicolumn layout and often contain multiple sections, each with a different layout. For example, a newsletter can begin with a one-column section and then continue with a three-column section.

- Newsletter columns can be of equal or unequal width and can have a vertical line separating them. You can alter the space between columns.

- To balance columns, insert a continuous section break at the end of the column layout. To control how columns break, insert a column break to force text to start at the next column.

- A pull quote is a sentence or quotation copied from a document and enlarged or set apart from the rest of the text for emphasis. Pull quotes are contained in text boxes.

- A sidebar is a text box that is usually aligned on the right or left side of a page. It typically contains text that is related to but separate from the main document text.

- Linked text boxes are used in newsletters to flow text from one page to another. You insert text into one text box and then link the text to another text box where the text flow continues.

- Use the Styles task pane to see and reapply the formatting you have created in a document and to apply styles. To see all of Word's predefined styles, change the Select styles to show box to All styles.

- When you create a style, you can base it on another style so it will resemble that style's characteristics.

- After creating a style, you can modify it in many ways. For example, you can specify the style for the paragraph that follows the style and change the formatting (font, paragraph, tabs, borders, and so on).
- To control text flow, including line and page breaks, choose options from the Paragraph dialog box. For example, use the Keep lines together option to prevent a break between lines in the same paragraph and use the Keep with next option to prevent a paragraph (such as a heading) from being separated from the paragraph following it.
- By using the Font dialog box, you can change character spacing to alter the appearance of text. For example, you can stretch or compress text horizontally by a percentage of its original size or add or delete space between letters by a specific number of points.
- Use the Building Blocks Organizer to insert text boxes stored in a gallery.

LESSON 18		Command Summary	
Feature	**Button**	**Command**	**Keyboard**
Watermark	Watermark	Page Layout tab, Page Background group	
Page color	Page Color	Page Layout tab, Page Background group	
Character spacing		Home tab, Font group, Font dialog box, Character Spacing tab	
Remove character formatting		Home tab, Font group	Ctrl + Spacebar
Paragraph formatting		Home tab, Paragraph group	
Borders and shading		Home tab, Paragraph group,	
Remove paragraph formatting		Home tab, Paragraph group	Ctrl + Q
Create new style		Home tab, Styles group	
Columns	Columns	Page Layout tab, Page Setup group	
Insert text box	Text Box	Insert tab, Text group	
Link text box	Create Link	Text Box Tools Format tab, Text group	
Unlink text box	Break Link	Text Box Tools Format tab, Text group	
Link/unlink section header or footer	Link to Previous	Header & Footer Tools Design tab	
Building Blocks Organizer	Quick Parts	Insert tab, Text group, Quick Parts command	

Concepts Review

True/False Questions

Each of the following statements is either true or false. Indicate your choice by circling T or F.

T F 1. A newsletter title is sometimes called the nameplate.

T F 2. Times New Roman is an example of a sans serif font.

T F 3. You can create more white space on a page by decreasing the margins.

T F 4. A watermark is a transparent graphic or text placed behind text.

T F 5. "Condensed" is a paragraph spacing option.

T F 6. A pull quote is contained in a text box.

T F 7. By default, a two- or three-column layout has columns of equal width.

T F 8. Building Blocks are inserted using the Page Layout tab.

Short Answer Questions

Write the correct answer in the space provided.

1. Which task pane do you use to create a new style?

2. The pointer changes to 📋 after you click which button?

3. Which dialog box and tab contains options for controlling text flow?

4. To change text wrapping, which button do you use?

5. How do you insert vertical lines for separating columns in a three-column layout?

6. What is the name of the newsletter item that contains identifying information about the company (company name, editor, writers, and so on)?

7. What do you call text in a newsletter that is set apart for emphasis?

_____

8. What is white space?

_____

Critical Thinking

Answer these questions on a separate page. There are no right or wrong answers. Support your answers with examples from your own experience, if possible.

1. Choosing a font for a newsletter title is like designing a logo. Think of a title of a newsletter you might create. What type of font would be appropriate? Create a few versions of the title, using different fonts. Explain your choices.

2. What do you think are the most important ways to make a newsletter both attractive and readable? Which Word features would you incorporate to achieve that goal?

Skills Review

Exercise 18-22

Create a watermark, apply page formatting, and work with styles.

1. Open the file **Indiana**. Change the top margin to 2 inches, and create a memo heading. The memo is to "Store Managers" from Thomas Campbell. Use the current date, and the subject is "New Store."

2. Create a text watermark by following these steps:

   a. Click the **Page Layout** tab, and locate the **Page Background** group.

   b. Click the watermark button 🖼, and click **Custom Watermark**.

   c. Click **Text watermark**, and choose **Confidential** from the Text drop-down list. Verify that the **Diagonal** and **Semitransparent** options are selected. Click **OK**.

3. Add a page border and a page texture by following these steps:

   a. Click the **Page Layout** tab, and locate the **Page Background** group.

   b. Click the Page Border button 🖼. Select a double-line **style**, a dark blue **color**, and change the **width** to 1½ points. Click **OK**.

   c. Click the Page Color button 🖼, and click **Fill Effects**. Click the **Texture** tab and choose **Parchment**. Click **OK**.

4. Change the document style set, and modify the Normal style by following these steps:

   a. Click the **Home** tab, and locate the **Styles** group.

   b. Click the Change Styles button 🖼, and click **Style Set**. Select **Distinctive**.

c. Display the Styles task pane, and right-click Normal in the task pane. Click Modify. Change the font size to 11, and open the Paragraph dialog box. Change the spacing after to 0 points, and change line spacing to Single. Click OK twice.

5. Save the document as *[your initials]*18-22 in your Lesson 18 folder.

6. Submit and close the document.

Exercise 18-23

Create a newsletter-style column layout.

1. Start a new document.

2. Create a newsletter format by following these steps:

a. Click the Insert tab, and click the Quick Parts button. Click Building Blocks Organizer.

b. Click the Gallery heading to sort the gallery by type.

c. Scroll to the Footers category, and locate and click Pinstripes. Click Insert. Replace the placeholder text with Campbell's Confections. Apply italic formatting to the footer text. Close the Footer pane.

d. Open the Building Blocks Organizer dialog box. Scroll to the Text Boxes category. Insert the Pinstripes Sidebar building block.

3. Click the Sidebar text box, and insert the file **Bloom** (Insert tab, Text group, Object drop-down arrow command, Text from File).

4. Key the heading Bloom at the beginning of the sidebar text. Format the heading using 14-point bold and small caps, and 18 points spacing after.

5. Create a newsletter-style layout by following these steps:

a. Go to the beginning of the document, and open the Columns dialog box.

b. Change the Number of columns to 3, and the Spacing to .25. Click OK.

6. Insert the file **Chocolate Terms** at the beginning of the document.

7. Select the heading "Chocolate Terms," and format the heading as one column. Center the heading, and change the spacing after to 24 points. Change the font size to 14 points.

8. Select the text from "Milk Chocolate" to the end of the last paragraph ("Baking Chocolate"), and change the line spacing to single.

9. Insert a column break at the beginning of the paragraph beginning "White Chocolate."

10. Click the Insert tab, and click the Footer button. Select Edit Footer. Position the insertion point immediately after "Confections." Press Delete to delete the tab characters between the text on the left margin and the text on the right margin. When "Page 1" is beside "Confections," press Enter. (The page number is moved to the left margin because the formatted sidebar did not display the page number underneath.)

11. Insert a picture of chocolate in the blank text area of the sidebar.

12. Save the document as *[your initials]*18-23 in your Lesson 18 folder.

13. Submit and close the document.

Exercise 18-24

Work with text boxes and advanced layout settings.

1. Start a new document.

2. Insert a photograph, by following these steps:

   a. Click the Insert tab, and click the Picture button .

   b. Locate the directory and folder for the student data files, and select **Chocolate-P6**.

3. Change the text wrapping to square, and size the picture proportionally to 5.25 inches wide.

4. Center the picture ¹/₂ inch from the top of the page by following these steps:

   a. Select the picture, and click the Position button. Click More Layout Options from the Position menu.

   b. Click Alignment under Horizontal, and change the Alignment to Centered relative to Page.

   c. Click Absolute position under Vertical, and change the value to 0.5" below Page. Click OK. Deselect the picture.

5. Create a text box by following these steps:

   a. Click the Insert tab, and click the Text Box button . Click Draw Text Box.

   b. Below the picture, draw a text box approximately 2 inches square by pressing Shift when you draw. Key Chocolate Club in the text box.

   c. Locate the Text group on the Text Box Tools Format tab, and click the Text Direction button twice so that the text reads from bottom to top.

   d. Select the text, and format the text as 26-point Arial bold and italic.

   e. Center the text.

6. Size and position the text box by following these steps:

   a. Drag the text box over the bottom left corner of the picture.

   b. Use the top resize handle to drag the text box to the top of the picture. Use the right resize square handle to size the text box wide enough to fit the text. The text box should align with the left edge of the picture.

7. Remove the line and fill colors of the text box by following these steps:

   a. Select the text box, and select the Text Box Tools Format tab. Click the Shape Outline button , and click No Outline.

   b. Click the Shape Fill button , and click No Fill.

8. Select the text in the text box, and change the font color to white.

9. Draw a text box below the picture, about the same size as the picture.

10. Place the insertion point inside the text box, and insert the file **Club - 3**. Press Ctrl+A to select the text, and change the font size to 10. Change the height of the text box to fit the text.

11. Drag the box that contains the text file so it is about ¼ inch below the picture. Center the text box horizontally.

12. Select the text box, and change the shape outline weight to 4½ points, and select a pattern for the shape outline.

13. Save the document as *[your initials]*18-24 in your Lesson 18 folder.

14. Submit and close the document.

Exercise 18-25

Apply character and paragraph formatting, and link text boxes.

1. Start a new blank document. Change the top margin to *.75"*. Set the bottom, left, and right margins to **1"**.

2. At the top of the document, key the title Campbell's Connections, and press Enter two times.

3. Format the title in a 48-point font, appropriate to a title that fits on one line. Apply black shading to the title (the text color should automatically change to white). Center the text, and apply bold formatting (unless the font is already bold).

4. At the second paragraph mark, insert a page break (Ctrl+Enter).

5. Change the zoom to Whole Page.

6. Follow these steps to create side-by-side text boxes on both pages that you will use to flow parallel articles:

   a. On page 1, draw two text boxes to create two vertical columns. Size the text boxes **7"** high by **3"** wide.

   b. Position the left text box so it is horizontally aligned with the left margin and vertically aligned with the bottom margin.

   c. Position the right text box so it is horizontally aligned with the right margin and vertically aligned with the bottom margin.

   d. Draw two text boxes on page 2, each **9"** high by **3"** wide. Use the same alignment you used for the text boxes on page 1.

7. On page 1, in the left text box, insert the file **News - 1**. In the right text box, insert the file **News - 4**.

8. Link the two left text boxes and the two right text boxes by following these steps:

   a. Click the left text box on page 1. Click the Text Box Tools Format tab.

   b. Click the Create Link button ⊖ Create Link on the **Text Box Tools Format** tab.

⊖ Create Link

c. Using the pouring-pitcher pointer , click the left text box on page 2.

   d. Use the same method to link the right text boxes.

9. Create a footer using a building block by following these steps:

   a. Click the Insert tab, and click Footer.

   b. Click Blank in the footer gallery.

   c. Click the text placeholder, and click Quick Parts on the Header and Footer Tools Design tab.

   d. Click Building Blocks Organizer, and scroll to the Page Number Gallery. Select Bold Numbers 1. Verify that the selection is a footer with the format Page X of Y, and click Insert. Delete any blank paragraph marks that may appear in the footer pane. Close the footer pane.

10. Zoom to 100%. On page 1, in the left text box, format the title "Employee Newsletter" using 14-point bold and small caps. Select the text beginning with the paragraph "Remember" through the paragraph that begins "If your entry," and format it as a bulleted list.

11. At the end of the text in column 1 on page 2, insert the file **News - 2**. Select the text from "Name" through the "Date" line, and apply a box border to the text.

12. On page 1, in the right text box, format the title "Recipe of the Month" using 14-point bold and small caps. Select "Ingredients" and change the spacing after to 0 points. Select "Directions" and change the spacing after to 0 points. Select "Directions" on page 2, and change the spacing after to 0 points

13. On page 2, in the space at the bottom of the right text box, create a masthead by keying the following text (include your name as editor):

Campbell's Connections
Edited by:
[Your Name]
Published Monthly by:
Campbell's Confections
25 Main Street
Grove City, PA 16127
724-555-2025
www.campbellsconfections.biz

14. Increase the font size of "Campbell's Connections" in the masthead, and apply the font used for the newsletter title. Center all the masthead text, make it bold, and change it to white text against black shading.

15. On page 2, in the space at the bottom of the left text box, insert the file **News - 6**. If there is enough room after the Health Fair article, insert a health-related picture and format the picture height to 1 inch and center alignment.

16. Make any other adjustments to improve the appearance of the document; then save it as *[your initials]*18-25 in your Lesson 18 folder.

17. Submit and close the document.

Lesson Applications

Exercise 18-26

Insert and format text boxes.

1. Start a new document. Change to landscape orientation, change the top margin to **1.25"**, and change the left and right margins to **.75"**.

2. Draw a text box at the top of the page measuring approximately **1.5"** high and **9.5"** wide. Right-click the text box, and open the **Format Text Box** dialog box.

3. Click the **Colors and Lines** tab, and change the line color to dark blue and the weight to $2^{1}/_{4}$ points. Click the **Size** tab, and adjust the height to **1.5"** and the width to **9.5"**. Click the **Layout** tab, and click **Advanced**. Change the horizontal alignment to **Left relative to Margin**, and the vertical alignment to **Top relative to Margin**. Click the **Text Box** tab, and change all internal margin settings to **1"**, and select **Center** for the vertical alignment. Change the text wrapping to square.

4. Key **Chocolate-Covered Creams** in the text box.

5. Format the text using 48-point Arial Narrow bold. Change the font color to white.

6. Select the text box, and change the fill color to dark blue.

7. Draw a second box below the first text box. Format the text box as follows:
   - Change the line color to dark blue, the weight to $2^{1}/_{4}$ points, and the fill color to dark blue.
   - Change the size to measure 1 inch high and 9.5 inches wide.
   - Change the horizontal alignment to left relative to margin.
   - Change the internal margins settings to 0.1 inch, and change the vertical alignment to center.
   - Change the text wrapping to square, and drag the box approximately 3.5 inches below the first text box.

8. Key the following text in the second text box:

   Buy 10 pounds of chocolate, get one pound FREE!

9. Format the text using 24-point Arial Narrow bold, with small caps and center alignment.

10. Draw a third text box measuring 3.5 inches high and approximately 4.7 inches wide. Format the text box as follows:
    - Change the line color to dark blue, the weight to $2^{1}/_{4}$ points, and the fill color to white.
    - Change the size to measure 3.5 inch high and 4.7 inches wide.
    - Change the horizontal alignment to right relative to margin.
    - Change the internal margins settings to 0.1 inch, and change the vertical alignment to center.

- Change the text wrapping to square, and drag the box approximately directly below the first text box and aligning with the right border of the first text box.

11. Key the following text in the third text box. Use single spacing.

Figure 18-22

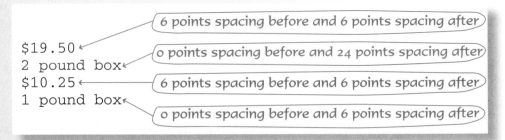

12. Format the text using 36-point Arial Narrow bold, with center alignment. Change the spacing before and the spacing after as indicated in Figure 18-22.

13. Insert a picture of chocolate creams using the Clip Art task pane. Size the picture to 3.5 inches high, and maintain proportion of the picture. Change the text wrapping to square. Add a 2¼-point outline to the picture.

14. Drag the picture to align with the left margin directly below the first text box.

15. Refer to Figure 18-23 for proper placement of the picture and text boxes.

Figure 18-23
Sample placement of picture and text boxes

16. Change the zoom to whole page to view the text boxes and picture placement.

17. Press Ctrl and the arrow keys to nudge the boxes into correct placement.

18. Save the document as *[your initials]*18-26 in your Lesson 18 folder.

19. Submit and close the document.

Exercise 18-27

Apply character and paragraph formatting, create styles, and link text boxes.

1. Open the file **History - 4**.

2. Insert a cover page using the Pinstripes design.

3. Key Campbell's Confections as the title and Background and Services as the subtitle. Key today's date and your name in placeholders below the subtitle. Delete extra paragraph marks or placeholders on the cover page.

4. Scroll to page 2, and insert a text box from the text box gallery. Choose the Pinstripes Sidebar option.

5. Click in the sidebar text box, and insert the file **Wholesale**.

6. Format the text box to center text vertically, and change internal margins to 0.2 inch on all sides. Select the text box, and add an outline to the text box. Choose an appropriate color and weight.

7. Edit the footer text to include the word "Page" in front of the page number. Change the alignment to left.

8. Locate the heading "Tours" on page 3. From this point forward, change the document format to 3 columns with 0.5 inch spacing between columns, and a vertical line between columns.

9. Scroll to page 3, and insert a text box approximately 1 inch high and 2.5 inches wide. Change the text wrapping to top and bottom, and drag the text box to the middle of column 3. Format the text box with an outline and fill color.

10. Scroll to page 4, and locate the paragraph that begins "To experience" in the first column. Copy the sentence, and paste the text in the text box on page 3. Format the text.

11. Insert a clip art picture of chocolate coins in the middle column of page 4. Place the picture at the start of the paragraph that begins "If you want." Change the text wrapping of the picture, and size the picture.

12. Insert a clip art picture of a candy foil-wrapped heart in the first column of page 5. Change the text wrap, and size the picture. Position the heart so that it is at the bottom of the first column.

13. Go to page 6. Open the Building Block Organizer dialog box, and select the Pinstripe Quote from the text box gallery.

14. Drag the text box to the middle of the second column, and key The most popular fundraising products are six quality chocolate bars. Center the text.

15. Insert the picture file **Chocolate - P7** (student data file) at the bottom of the third column on page 6. Size the picture, and change the text wrapping to top and bottom.

16. Go to the end of the document, and insert a continuous section break to balance the columns.

17. Insert the picture file **Chocolate - P6** at the end of the third column on page 7. Format and size the picture. Change the picture shape to a rounded rectangle.

18. Open the Styles task pane, and change the Normal style font to Cambria.

19. Preview the document; then save it as *[your initials]*18-27 in your Lesson 18 folder.

20. Submit and close the document.

Exercise 18-28

Apply character and paragraph formatting, create styles, and link text boxes.

1. Start a new document, and change the top, left, and right margins to 0.75 inch.

2. Key the title Choc Talk at the top of the document, and press Enter.

3. Format the title as 72 points, using a font that fits on one line. Apply a dark shading color, and change the font color to white.

4. At the blank paragraph insert a page break, and switch the Zoom to Whole Page.

5. Create a two-page layout to be used for linked text boxes. On page 1, draw two text boxes to create two vertical columns. Size the text boxes 7 inches high by 3.25 inches wide. Position the text boxes as follows:

   - Left text box: Horizontally aligned with the left margin, vertically aligned with the bottom margin.
   - Right text box: Horizontally aligned with the right margin, vertically aligned with the bottom margin.

6. Draw two text boxes on page 2. Each should measure 9 inches high by 3.25 inches wide. Use the same alignment used for the text boxes on page 1.

7. On page 1, in the left box, insert the file **News - 8**.

8. Create a forward link from the left text box on page 1 to the left text box on page 2.

9. Change the zoom to Page Width, and verify that the text flows from the left text box on page 1 to the left text box on page 2.

10. On page 1, in the right box, insert the file **News - 4**. Create a forward link from the right text box on page 1 to the right text box on page 2.

11. Go to page 1, and position the insertion point to the immediate left of the "Chocolate Fudge Frosting" heading. Press Enter to move the "Chocolate Fudge Frosting" heading to the top of page 2.

12. Go to page 2. Insert a horizontal line below each of the articles. The horizontal line will serve as a divider line between two articles.

13. Insert the file **News - 9** below the divider line in the left text box on page 2.

14. Insert the text file **News - 7** below the News - 9 article on page 2 in the left column.

15. Apply dark blue shading (or the color used in the title) to the heading paragraph of the **News - 7** article, "Vote Today!" Change the font color to white.

16. Select the text "Candy-Making Classes" at the beginning of the first article on page 1. Create a paragraph style named Article Head and include the following font format: Cambria, 14-point bold, small caps,

and shadow. Verify that the paragraph formatting includes 0 points spacing before, 15 points spacing after, and single spacing.

17. Apply the Article Head style to the following headings: "Recipe of the Month," "Open House," and "Chocolate Fudge Frosting."

18. Delete blank paragraphs that may appear as a result of the new style.

19. Go to the bottom of page 1, and draw a rectangle that slightly overlaps both text boxes at the bottom of the page. Add the text Continued on page 2. Format the text using 9-point Arial Narrow italic. Center the text. (See Figure 18-24.)

Figure 18-24
The continued line

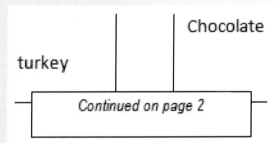

20. Format the document with a page number positioned in the bottom right corner. The page number should not appear on page 1. Include the word "Page" in front of the number.

21. Key a masthead at the bottom of the right text box on page 2. Use font and paragraph formatting to match your newsletter title and text. Use the text in Figure 18-25 for the masthead.

Figure 18-25

```
Choc Talk
Published quarterly
By
Campbell's Confections
25 Main Street
Grove City, PA 16127
724-555-2025
www.campbellsconfections.biz

Editor
Margo Razzano

Copyright © 200-
All rights reserved.
```

22. Preview the document, and then save it as *[your initials]***18-28** in your Lesson 18 folder.

23. Submit, and close the document.

Exercise 18-29 ◆ Challenge Yourself

Insert a text box, a line, and a watermark to create a letterhead.

1. Start a new document. Change the top margin to 0.75 inch.

2. Insert the picture file **Chocolate P-8** from your student data files.

3. Format the picture as follows;
   - Two inches wide.
   - Square wrapping style.
   - Brightness at 70 percent.
   - Right-aligned with the right margin and top-aligned with the top margin with the Move object with text option turned off. (Click the Position button and click More Layout Options.)

4. Apply the picture style in the third row, first option—Center Shadow Rectangle.

5. Draw a text box over the picture, sized slightly smaller than the picture.

Figure 18-26
Business letterhead

6. Key the Campbell's Confections text shown in Figure 18-26 using 10-point Arial Narrow bold, with 0 points spacing after and single spacing.

7. Right-align the text, and apply small caps formatting to the first line.

8. Change the spacing before for the telephone number line so that the last two lines of text align at the bottom of the text box. (Refer to Figure 18-26.)

9. Draw a horizontal line below the text box, from the left margin to the right margin. Press Shift as you draw to ensure a straight line.

10. Format the line as follows:
    - Six inches wide.
    - Three-point black line color.
    - Behind text wrapping style.
    - Centered horizontally on the page; positioned vertically 2 inches below the page.

11. Add a text watermark with text Sample Letterhead.

12. Save the document as *[your initials]*18-29 in your Lesson 18 folder.

13. Submit and close the document.

On Your Own

In these exercises you work on your own, as you would in a real-life business environment. Use the skills you've learned to accomplish the task—and be creative.

Exercise 18-30

Design the first page of a newsletter for an organization in which you are interested. Create the nameplate and the general layout. Use real headings with your own created style and text for the content. Save the document as *[your initials]*18-30 in your Lesson 18 folder, and submit it.

Exercise 18-31

Open any document that has at least one full page of text, apply a 3-column layout, and create two pull quotes. Format the pull quotes attractively. Make one of the pull quotes the width of a column and the other one the width of two columns. Save the document as *[your initials]*18-31 in your Lesson 18 folder, and submit it.

Exercise 18-32

Draw three text boxes on one page, positioned randomly (not overlapping). Link the first text box to the second, and the second to the third. Key text in the first box (key a poem, a paragraph from a book, or other text). When the text fills the last text box, format and position the boxes attractively on the page. Consider changing the text boxes to a different Shape. Save the document as *[your initials]*18-32 in your Lesson 18 folder, and submit it.

Lesson 19

SmartArt and Charts

OBJECTIVES

After completing this lesson, you will be able to:

1. Create SmartArt.
2. Create charts.
3. Edit chart data.
4. Modify chart types.
5. Add and modify chart options.
6. Format charts and chart elements.

MCAS OBJECTIVES

In this lesson:
WW 07 3.1.1
WW 07 3.2.5

Estimated Time: 1¼ hours

Word provides two graphics tools to display information visually—SmartArt graphics and charts. SmartArt graphics are helpful when presenting conceptual ideas. Charts show numerical data in a graphical way. Word uses Microsoft Excel to create charts. Chart tools are used to modify and format charts.

After you create a chart, you can customize it. You can change the chart's type—for example, from a bar chart to a column chart. You can add information to a chart, such as titles and gridlines, and control the chart's appearance, including fonts, colors, sizes, and shading.

Creating SmartArt

Using Word's SmartArt tools, you can insert seven types of SmartArt:

- *List* illustrates groups and subgroups of information or blocks of information in a vertical or horizontal format.

- *Process* illustrates a progression or sequential steps toward a goal.

- *Cycle* illustrates a process that has a continuous cycle.

- *Hierarchy*, sometimes called *org chart*, illustrates the top-down relationship of members of an organization.

- *Relationship* illustrates the relationship of objects to a main object.

- *Matrix* illustrates relationships of objects to a whole in quadrants.

- *Pyramid* illustrates foundation-based relationships.

Exercise 19-1 CREATE A SMARTART GRAPHIC

To insert a SmartArt graphic, click the Insert tab and locate the Illustrations group. Click the SmartArt command and select a type (category) and layout.

1. Start a new document and key the title Campbell's Confections—Ohio Stores. Center the text and change it to 14-point Arial Black, with small caps. Change the spacing after to 24 points. Press Enter.

2. Click the Insert tab, and click the SmartArt button ⊞ to open the Choose a SmartArt Graphic dialog box.

Figure 19-1
SmartArt Graphic
dialog box

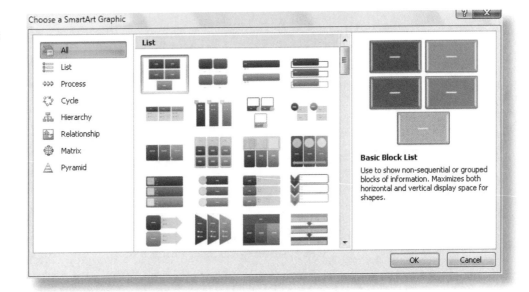

3. Click the Cycle type, and click the Basic Radial layout (third row, second graphic). Click OK. The Basic Radial graphic is inserted in the document. The graphic displays with a drawing space and a nonprinting border. Inside the border are sizing handles. The text pane also appears.

4. Select the innermost circle in the Basic Radial diagram, if it is not already selected. To select a circle, point to the circle's edge and click when you see the four-pointed arrow pointer. The selected circle has round selection handles.

Word 2007

Figure 19-2
Inserting a Basic
Radial diagram

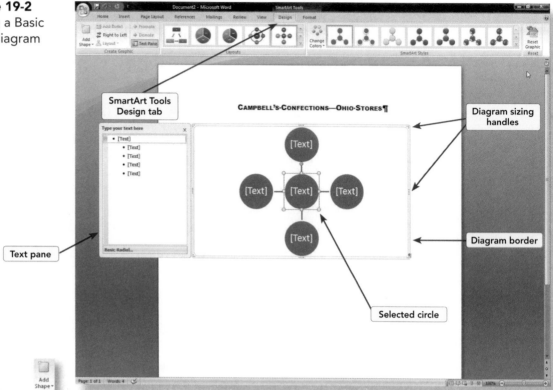

NOTE

Click the arrow under the Add Shape command to display a list of options for inserting shapes. Choices include Add Shape After, Add Shape Before, Add Shape Above, Add Shape Below, and Add Assistant (available for organizational charts). The position of the insertion point in the text pane or the graphic object selected determines the placement of the new object.

5. Click the **SmartArt Tools Design** tab on the Ribbon. Click the innermost circle to select it, and locate the **Create Graphic** group. Point to the Add Shape button, and notice the button displays two colors. Clicking the top half of the button automatically inserts a shape to the outer circle. Clicking the bottom half of the button displays a list of options for inserting a new shape. Click the top of the Add Shape button. The Basic Radial diagram should now have five outer circles.

Exercise 19-2   ADD TEXT TO A SMARTART GRAPHIC

You can add text to a SmartArt graphic by clicking a shape and then keying the text, or you can click **[Text]** in the text pane and key the text. The copy and paste commands can be used to add text to a SmartArt graphic.

TIP

To display the text pane, click the SmartArt Tools Design tab, and click the Text Pane command.

1. Click inside the center circle, and key **Ohio**. The text should automatically resize. Notice the text pane displays "Ohio" at the top of the pane.

2. Click in the topmost circle to select it, and notice that [Text] is selected in the text pane. Key **Akron**.

3. Moving clockwise, key the following cities, one per circle, in each of the remaining circles: Canton, Cleveland, and Massillon.

4. Click the last bullet item in the text pane, and key Warren. Press Enter to add a sixth circle to the SmartArt graphic. Key Youngstown.

Exercise 19-3   FORMAT A SMARTART GRAPHIC

There are two ways to change the appearance of a SmartArt graphic. One is to click the SmartArt Tools Design tab and change the layout, colors, or SmartArt style for the graphic. You can also click the SmartArt Tools Format tab, and change the Shape Fill, Shape Outline, Shape Effect, and other text effects. The colors and effects available are determined by the selected theme.

NOTE

To add a shape before an existing shape in a SmartArt graphic in the text pane, position the insertion point before the text where you want the new shape inserted. Key the text; then press Enter. To add a shape after an existing shape, place the insertion point at the end of the text where you want the new shape inserted, and press Enter. To indent the new shape, press Tab.

1. Click the SmartArt graphic border. Click the **SmartArt Tools Design** tab. Click the Change Colors button .

2. Select a Gradient Range Accent color. Remember that you can move the mouse over the various options to preview their effect on the SmartArt graphic.

Figure 19-3
Changing colors

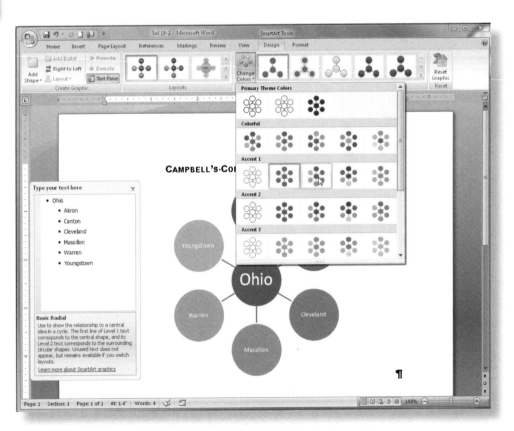

3. Locate the **SmartArt Styles** group, and click the More arrow to display the SmartArt Styles gallery. Click the **3-D Flat Scene** style from the gallery.

4. Locate the **Layouts** group, and click the More arrow to expand the Layouts gallery. Click the **Diverging Radial** layout.

5. Click the **SmartArt Tools Format** tab. Click the Size button. Change the **Height** to **4** inches, and change the **Width** to **6** inches.

6. Click the Shape Fill button, and select an accent color for the background of the drawing canvas. Click the Shape Outline button, and select an appropriate color for the outline of the drawing canvas.

7. Right-click the SmartArt graphic, and click **Format Shape** to open the Format Shape dialog box.

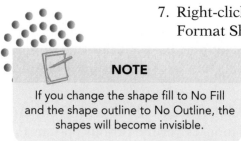

NOTE

If you change the shape fill to No Fill and the shape outline to No Outline, the shapes will become invisible.

8. Click **Text Box**, and verify or change the following settings: **Vertical alignment: Middle**, **Text direction: Horizontal**, **Internal margin: 0.03** inch for all sides. Click **Close**.

Figure 19-4
Format Shape dialog box

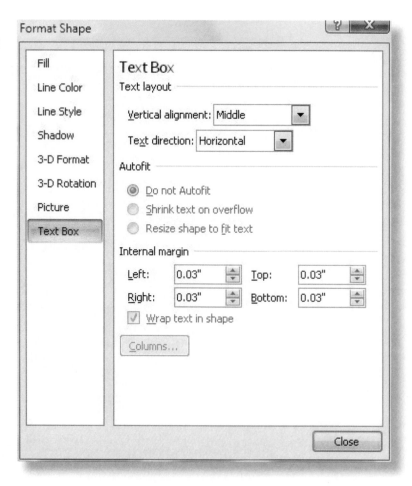

9. Click the Ohio shape. Click the **SmartArt Tools Format** tab, and click the Shape Fill button ![Shape Fill]. Click **Picture**, and locate the directory and folder for the student data files. Click the file **Chocolate - P1**, and click **Insert**. Notice the picture within the shape. Click Undo ![Undo].

10. Center the document vertically on the page (**Page Setup, Layout** tab).

11. Save the file as **[your initials]19-3** in your Lesson 19 folder.

12. Submit and close the document.

Creating Charts

A chart is a visual representation of numeric data. Charts often make values in a table easier to understand. You can usually look at a chart and quickly grasp the meaning of the numbers.

You create a chart in a Word document by inserting a generic chart as an embedded object. The chart data are stored in an Excel worksheet. When you first create the chart, the worksheet contains sample data, and the chart is displayed in a column graph format. You replace the sample data with your own numbers and column labels.

Exercise 19-4 INSERT A CHART IN A DOCUMENT

1. Open the file **Mills**. Add the current date. The letter is from Lynn Tanguay, vice president. Include your reference initials and an enclosure notation.

2. Position the insertion point in the blank line below the paragraph that begins "As you requested."

3. Click the **Insert** tab, and locate the **Illustration** group. Click the Chart button ![Chart]. The Insert Chart dialog box displays.

4. Click **Column**, and click the first chart in the first row. Click **OK** to insert the Column chart. A sample chart is inserted in the document between the second and third paragraphs, and the Word document window and the Excel worksheet window appear side by side. The chart is based on the sample data in the Excel worksheet. You will replace this data with your own labels and numbers in the next exercise.

Figure 19-5
Inserting a chart

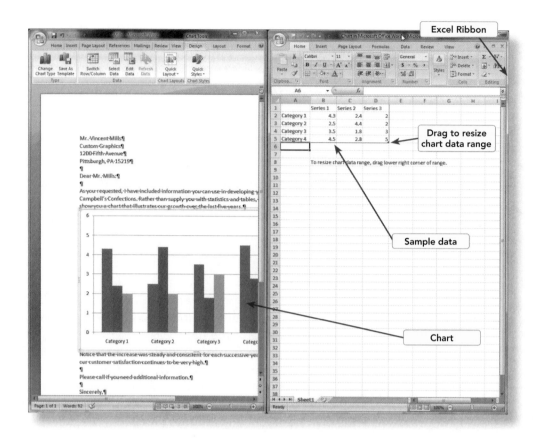

5. Drag the lower right corner of the data range to column F, row 4. Notice the change in the chart.

6. Click anywhere in the Word document and maximize the document window.

7. Click the chart once to select it. The Word Ribbon displays the Chart Tools Design, Layout, and Format tabs. Notice the chart selection handles. Word treats the chart as an in-line graphic object. You can move or resize it. To edit the chart, you can click the Edit data button on the Chart Tools Design tab or click the Microsoft Excel button ![Microsoft Excel - Bo...] on the Windows taskbar.

Exercise 19-5   KEY DATA IN THE WORKSHEET

1. Click the **Chart Tools Design** tab, and click the Edit Data command. The worksheet displays.

2. Verify that the data range is A1 through F4.

3. Click the upper left box of the worksheet (to the left of column A) to select the entire worksheet (or press Ctrl + A).

TIP

You can change the width of worksheet columns to display text that might be hidden. Move the pointer to the divider line between the columns until the two-pointed arrow appears; then hold down the mouse button and drag to the desired width (or double-click the divider line). If the worksheet is too small to show all the data, point to the side or bottom border of the datasheet window and then use the two-pointed arrow pointer to drag to a larger size.

4. Press Delete. This deletes the sample data. The entire worksheet is now blank and ready for you to key new data. Notice the change in the chart when you erase the sample data.

5. Key the data and headings shown in Figure 19-6. The chart grows as you key the data. Notice that you cannot see the entire row 1 label "Total Revenues" after you enter the value in the adjacent column—this does not affect how the label is displayed on the chart.

6. Press Enter after keying the last figure to make sure it is entered in the chart. Data are not entered until you move to another cell.

Figure 19-6
Worksheet with new data

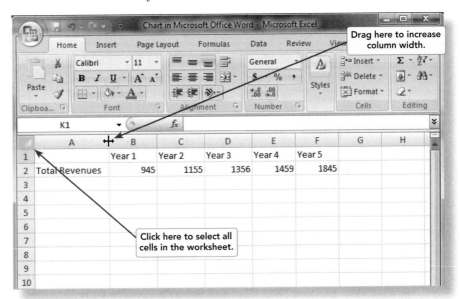

7. Click anywhere in the document to redisplay the Word Ribbon.

8. Save the document as *[your initials]*19-5 in your Lesson 19 folder. Leave it open for the next exercise.

Editing Chart Data

After you create a chart, you might need to edit the data. Numbers in a chart can be changed only on the worksheet.

Exercise 19-6   EDIT CHART DATA

1. In the document *[your initials]*19-5, click the Chart Tools Design tab, and click the Edit Data button .

2. Change the Year 5 total revenue to **2155** (press Enter after keying the text to enter the value). Notice that the chart changes with the new value.

3. Add two new rows of data to the datasheet for "New Business" and "Repeat Business," as shown in Figure 19-7. Adjust the width of the first column to accommodate "Repeat Business."

Figure 19-7
Worksheet with two new rows

	A	B	C	D	E	F
1		Year 1	Year 2	Year 3	Year 4	Year 5
2	Total Revenues	945	1155	1356	1459	2155
3	New Business	661	742	762	808	816
4	Repeat Business	284	413	594	651	1339

Exercise 19-7   **SWITCH DATA SERIES FROM ROWS TO COLUMNS**

Data are plotted in a chart in groups of *data series*, which are collections of related data points. These values are usually found within the same column or row in the worksheet. Each data series is distinguished by a unique color. Sometimes it is hard to know in advance if it is better to arrange your data in rows or in columns on the datasheet. You can enter it either way and switch back and forth.

TIP

Depending on the type of data in your chart, switching data series between row and column orientations is often a good idea. Sometimes a different view can emphasize and improve chart data in a way you didn't anticipate.

Switch Row/Column

Text Wrapping

NOTE

The Word Ribbon groups and commands change appearance based on the size of the document window. If you do not see the Text Wrapping command, click the Arrange command.

Position

1. Select the chart, and click the **Chart Tools Design** tab.

2. Click the Switch Row/Column button. The graph columns are grouped by column data instead of row data. Notice that the data are now grouped into three categories, showing the yearly changes within each of the three categories.

3. Click the Switch Row/Column button to change the data series groupings back to a row orientation.

4. Click anywhere in the document to redisplay the Word document.

5. Click the chart once to select it. If necessary, resize the chart (by dragging its border) to display the year labels on one line.

6. Click the chart to select it. Click the **Chart Tools Format** tab, and click the Text Wrapping button. Click **Top and Bottom**.

7. Click the Arrange button if necessary. Click the Position button, and click **More Layout Options** to open the Advanced Layout dialog box. Click

the **Picture Position** tab, and change the **horizontal alignment** to **Centered relative to Page**.

NOTE

Charts are inserted in-line with text by default. Change the text-wrapping option to move a chart freely on the page, or use the Align command.

8. Create a letterhead for the document by keying the following information in the header pane, formatted as 10-point Arial, right-aligned.

CAMPBELL'S CONFECTIONS
25 Main Street
Grove City, PA 16127
724-555-2025
www.campbellsconfections.biz

9. Change the top margin to 1.5 inches and the bottom margin to 0.5 inch.

10. Preview the document; then save it as *[your initials]***19-7** in your Lesson 19 folder.

Figure 19-8
Document with modified chart and letterhead

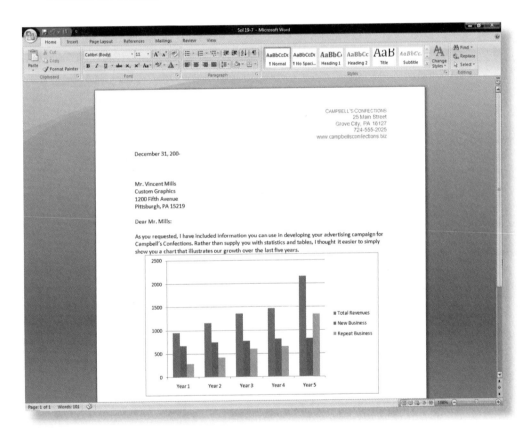

11. Submit the document.

Modifying Chart Types

After creating a chart, you might want to change the way the data are displayed. Microsoft Excel offers a wide variety of chart types, each designed for a specific purpose.

Many charts can be displayed with a 3-D visual effect, and you can combine different types within a single chart, such as column and line. Table 19-1 summarizes the available chart types.

TABLE 19-1 Chart Types

Type	Definition
Area	Shows the relationship of parts to a whole and emphasizes the magnitude of change (includes 3-D effects).
Bar	Illustrates comparisons among items or shows individual figures at a specific time (includes 3-D effects).
Bubble	Compares sets of three values. They are like scatter charts, with the third value displayed as the size of the bubble marker (includes 3-D effects).
Column	Shows variation over a period of time or demonstrates a comparison among items (includes 3-D effects).
Doughnut	Compares the sizes of parts of a whole. Each chart can show more than one data series.
Line	Shows trends in data over a period of time at the same intervals, emphasizing the rate of change over time (includes 3-D effects).
Pie	Compares the sizes of parts of a whole. Each chart shows only one data series (includes 3-D effects).
Radar	Show changes or frequencies of data relative to a center point and to other data points. Each category has its own value axis radiating from the center point. Lines connect all values in the same series (includes 3-D effects).
Stock	Requires three series of values in high, low, and close order. They are frequently used to illustrate stock prices. Also known as "high-low-close charts."
Surface	Displays optimum combinations between two sets of data. They can show relationships between large amounts of data that would otherwise be difficult to see (includes 3-D effects).
XY (Scatter)	Compares trends over uneven time or measurement intervals plotted on the category axis. Scatter charts also display patterns from discrete x and y data measurements.

Exercise 19-8   CHANGE A CHART TYPE

1. In the Word document *[your initials]*19-7, select the chart to activate the graph-editing tools.

2. Click the **Chart Tools Design** tab.

 3. Click the Change Chart Type button. Choose **Line**, and click the fourth option in the fourth row. Click **OK**. The chart changes, and each of the data series ("Total Revenue," "New Business," and "Repeat Business") is represented as a line. Along each line, a marker indicates the series' value for each of the five years.

Figure 19-9
Change Chart Type
dialog box

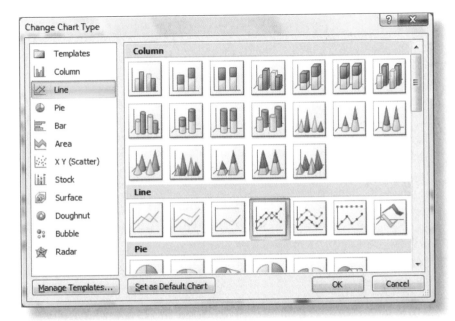

4. Click the Change Chart Type button again, click **Area**, and click the first option in the first row. Click **OK**. Notice that this chart type shows the trend over time of each of the three series combined together, or "stacked." Although the area chart creates a dramatic effect, determining the individual values of each series at any given time is difficult.

5. Open the **Change Chart Type** dialog box, and click **Line**. Seven subtypes are available for line charts.

6. Click the last subtype, which is the **3-D Line** chart (or "ribbon" chart). Click **OK**. The dialog box closes, and the chart changes to the new type. Like the stacked area chart, the 3-D line chart provides an interesting effect. It also allows readers to see the upward trend in all the data categories. But some of the data are hidden because of the 3-D effect. This chart type might work better with data categories that have more widely varying values.

7. Reopen the **Change Chart Type** dialog box. Click **Column** from the Chart type list.

8. Choose the second subtype on the first row, **Stacked Column**. Click **OK**. Notice that this subtype shows the contribution of each value to a total across five years.

9. Reopen the **Change Chart Type** dialog box, and click **Column**. Click **Clustered Column**, the first subtype, and click **OK**. The chart type is changed to a simple two-dimensional column chart.

10. Click anywhere in the document to return to Word. Notice that removing the 3-D effect has made the chart easier to read.

11. Leave the document open for the next exercise.

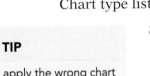

TIP

If you accidentally apply the wrong chart type to the chart, you can use the Undo command to restore the chart to its previous state. Or reopen the Chart Type dialog box, and choose another chart type.

Exercise 19-9   COMBINE CHART TYPES

Microsoft Excel enables you to combine certain chart types in a single chart. Each data series can be assigned its own chart type.

1. Select the chart.

2. Click one of the "New Business" columns (the red columns). The "New Business" data series is selected.

3. Click the Change Chart Type button .

4. Click the **Line** type. Click the fourth subtype, which is the **Line with Markers** at each data value. Click **OK**. The "New Business" data series now appears as a line.

> **NOTE**
>
> Some chart types cannot be combined with one another. For example, a column chart cannot have one data series with 3-D effects and another without.

5. Select the "Repeat Business" data series by clicking one of the green columns.

6. Reopen the **Change Chart Type** dialog box, and click the **Area** chart type.

7. Select the first subtype and click **OK**. The "Repeat Business" data series appears as an area chart.

8. Click anywhere in the document to redisplay the Word document.

Figure 19-10
Combined chart types

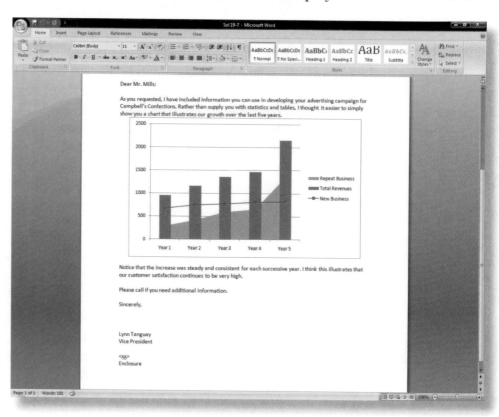

9. Save the document as *[your initials]*19-9 in your Lesson 19 folder. Submit the document and leave it open.

Adding and Modifying Chart Options

After you create a chart, you can add and modify various options in the chart. Besides the numeric data from the datasheet, charts can include other elements that you can select and modify individually:

- The *category axis* is the horizontal (or *x*) axis along the bottom of most charts; it frequently refers to time series.

- The *value axis* is the vertical (or *y*) axis against which data points are measured.

- The *plot area* is the rectangular area bounded by the two axes; it includes all axes and data points.

- A *data marker* is an object that represents an individual data point. It can be a bar, area, dot, picture, or other symbol that marks a single data point or value.

- A *legend* is a guide that explains the symbols, patterns, or colors used to differentiate data series.

- A *tick mark* is a division mark along the category (*x*) and/or value (*y*) axis.

- A *data point* is a single piece of data.

- A *data series* is a collection of related data points. These values are usually found within the same column or row in the datasheet.

- The *chart title* gives the name of the chart. Titles can also be assigned to the axes.

Figure 19-11
Chart elements

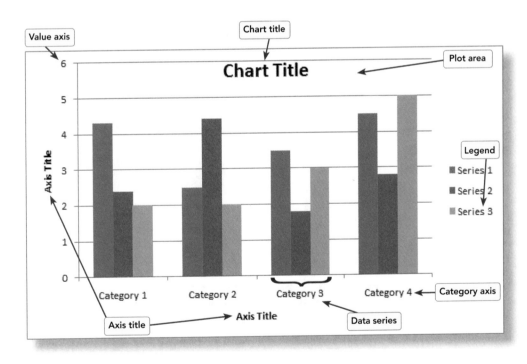

Exercise 19-10 ADD CHART TITLES AND GRIDLINES

1. Select the chart to activate the chart-editing tools. Maximize the Word document window.

2. Position the pointer over the legend, and notice that a ScreenTip appears. Move the pointer to the white area above the legend, and notice that this is identified as the chart area. Move the pointer around the different areas of the chart, and notice the ScreenTips.

3. Click the **Chart Tools Layout** tab, locate the **Labels** group, and click the Chart Title button.

4. Click **Above Chart**. Drag to select the text in the Chart Title box, and key **Growth at Campbell's Confections**. Deselect the chart title box.

5. Click the **Chart Tools Layout** tab, and click the Axis Titles button. Click **Primary Vertical Axis Title**, and click **Rotated Title**. Drag to select the text in the Vertical Axis Title box, and key **(Thousands)**. Deselect the title.

6. Select the chart if necessary. Click the Gridlines button. Click **Primary Vertical Gridlines**, and click **Major Gridlines**. The gridlines are added to the chart. Notice that the plot area has been compressed to compensate for the additional text. You will resize the chart later in the lesson.

NOTE

You can also add chart titles by displaying the Chart Tools Design tab, and selecting a Chart Layout that contains titles.

Figure 19-12
Adding chart titles
and gridlines

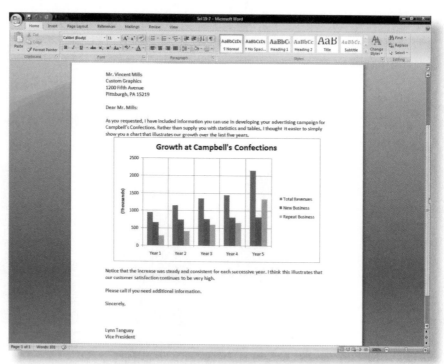

Exercise 19-11 ADD A SECONDARY AXIS

The addition of a secondary value axis can enhance a chart when there are data series representing widely different numeric values.

1. Select the chart; then select the "**Repeat Business**" data series.

Format Selection

2. Click the **Chart Tools Format** tab. Click the Format Selection button Format Selection , and click **Series Options**. Click **Secondary Axis**. Click **Close**. A secondary value axis appears in the chart. This axis will represent the "New Business" and "Repeat Business" values. You will need to add an axis label to reflect this change.

Axis
Titles ▼

3. Select the chart if necessary. Add a secondary vertical axis title by clicking the Axis Title button 🔲, and clicking **Secondary Vertical Axis Title** and **Rotated Title**. Drag to select the text. Key **New & Repeat Business**. Press Enter and key **(Thousands)**. A second value axis appears in the chart. Because "New Business" and "Repeat Business" refer to the same axis, the chart would be clearer if both data series used the same chart type.

4. Right-click anywhere in the "Repeat Business" data series, and choose **Change Series Chart Type** from the shortcut menu.

5. Click the **Line** type, and click the fourth subtype. Click **OK**. The "New Business" and "Repeat Business" data series are both line charts.

6. Right-click the "New Business" data series, and choose **Format Data Series** from the shortcut menu.

NOTE

When adding a second value axis, make sure that each data series is plotted against the correct axis.

7. In the Format Data Series dialog box, click **Series Options**, and click **Secondary Axis**. Click **Close**. The "New Business" data series is now plotted on the correct axis. Check to make sure the "Repeat Business" data series is also plotted on the secondary value axis.

8. Click anywhere in the document to return to Word.

9. Resize the chart, making it wider.

Figure 19-13
Chart with second
value axis added

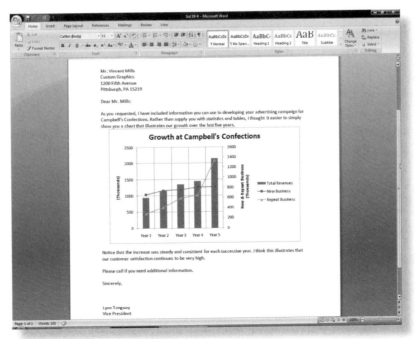

10. Save the document as *[your initials]*19-11 in your Lesson 19 folder.

11. Submit the document. Leave it open for the next exercise.

Formatting Charts and Chart Elements

Charts have a wide variety of formatting options. You can change the colors and patterns of the data markers, for instance, and control the fonts used throughout a chart. You can reposition the legend or even eliminate it. You can also format the numbers on the value axis.

> **NOTE**
>
> You can select a chart element by using the Chart Tools Layout tab, Current Selection group. Click the arrow next to the Chart Elements box, and click the appropriate chart element. When you select a chart element, the label on the button changes to reflect the selection. For instance, when you select the chart, the label changes to "Chart Area."

Exercise 19-12   CHANGE COLORS AND PATTERNS

Colors and patterns add interest to your chart. You can change the color of individual columns or an entire group of columns. Even the background color can be changed to achieve a special effect.

1. Select the chart.

2. Right-click one of the "Total Revenue" columns, and click **Format Data Series** from the shortcut menu. The Format Data Series dialog box appears.

Figure 19-14
Format Data Series
dialog box

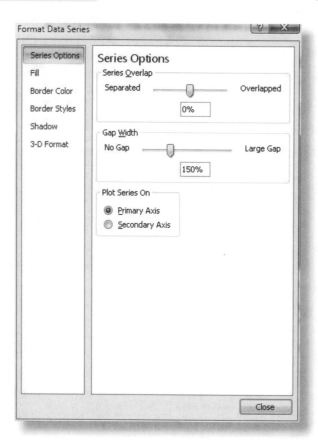

NOTE

To change an individual column, first select the entire data series, and then click the individual column whose color you wish to change. This selects only that column in the data series. When you right-click, you'll display the Format Data Point dialog box, which is similar to the Format Data Series dialog box.

TIP

Press Ctrl + 1 to open a Format dialog box for selected chart elements.

3. Click Fill. Click Gradient fill. Click Close.

4. Right-click the plot area, and choose Format Plot Area from the shortcut menu. The Format Plot Area dialog box appears.

5. Click Fill, and select a coordinating color for your chart. Adjust the Transparency level if desired. Click Close.

6. Right-click the "Repeat Business" data series, and choose Format Data Series from the shortcut menu.

7. Click Line Color, and click Solid line. Select a line color. Click Marker Fill, and click Solid fill. Click Close.

Figure 19-15
Chart with new colors for the data series and plot area

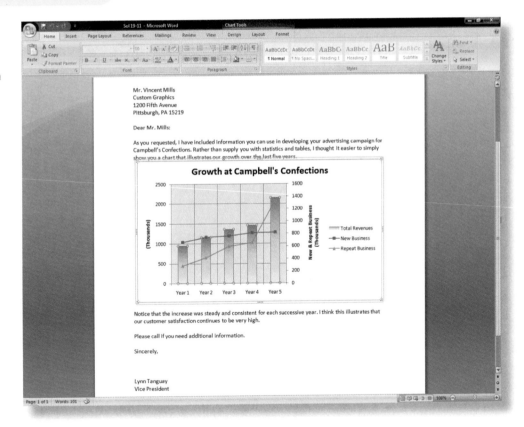

Exercise 19-13 FORMAT THE LEGEND

You can change the placement, font, and appearance of a chart's legend.

1. Right-click the legend. Choose Format Legend from the shortcut menu. The Format Legend dialog box appears.

2. Click Legend Options, and choose Bottom. This moves the legend under the chart.

3. Click **Border Color**. Click **No line**. This removes the box around the legend. Notice that you can use the Fill options to change the background color and patterns of the legend box. For now, leave these unchanged. Click **Close**.

4. Select the legend, and use the Mini toolbar to make sure the font size is 10 points. The legend is reformatted, and the chart area adjusts to accommodate the additional space now available on the right.

5. Use the left and right sizing handles to expand the legend box width. This provides more space between the items and makes them easier to read.

Figure 19-16
Chart with
reformatted legend

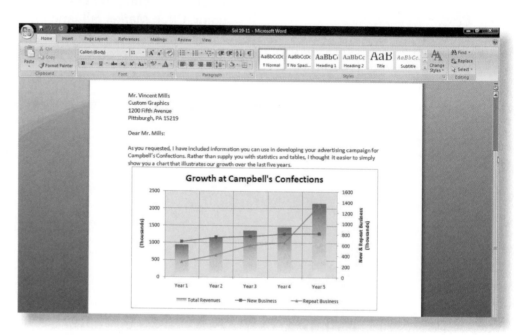

Exercise 19-14 FORMAT THE AXES

1. Right-click the value axis (the numbers along the left edge of the chart), and select **Font**. The Font dialog box appears.

2. Click the **Font** tab and change the font to 9-point bold. Close the Font dialog box.

3. Right-click the secondary value axis (the numbers along the chart's right edge). Change the font to 9-point bold.

4. Right-click the category axis (the row of years along the chart's bottom), and change the font to 9-point bold. With a smaller font for the three axes, the legend now appears too large. Change the legend font to 9 points if necessary.

Exercise 19-15 FORMAT CHART TITLES

You can format titles by using dialog boxes, or you can edit them directly in the chart.

1. Select the primary value axis title "(Thousands)" by clicking it once.

2. Move the pointer inside the selected title. The pointer changes to an insertion point. Drag over the word "(Thousands)."

3. Change the font size to 8 points and apply bold italic formatting. Click **OK**.

4. Click anywhere in the chart area.

5. Right-click the secondary value axis title, and change the font size to 8 points.

6. Right-click the secondary value axis, and click **Format Axis Title**. Click **Alignment**. Click the drop-down arrow beside **Text direction**, and click **Rotate all text 90°**. This reverses the orientation of the text.

7. Click **Close**. Notice that you cannot edit text or format individual parts of the text in the dialog box. To italicize the "(Thousands)" portion of the axis title, you will need to edit it directly.

8. Select the secondary axis title.

9. Apply italic formatting to "(Thousands)" and then click anywhere in the chart area. The "(Thousands)" portion of the title appears in italic.

10. Click anywhere outside the chart to return to Word.

Figure 19-17
Chart with
reformatted titles

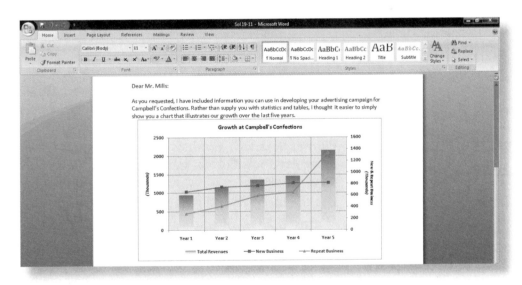

11. Save the document as *[your initials]*19-15 in your Lesson 19 folder.

Exercise 19-16   CHANGE THE LAYOUT OR STYLE OF A CHART

You can format a chart very easily by using the predefined styles and layouts provided. Once a style or layout is selected, you can customize it by manually changing the format.

1. Select the chart.

2. Click the **Chart Tools Design** tab, and locate the **Chart Layouts** group. Click the More arrow ⬛ to see the Quick Layout gallery. Click **Layout 1**, and notice the changes in the position of the chart and chart elements.

3. Open the **Quick Layout** gallery, and click **Layout 3**.

NOTE

A custom format cannot be saved, but you can save the chart as a chart template. To save a chart as a chart template, click the Chart Tools Design tab, and click the Save As Template command.

4. Select the chart if necessary, and click the **Chart Tools Design** tab. Locate the **Chart Styles** group.

5. Click the More arrow ⬛ to open the Chart Quick Styles gallery.

6. Select a style.

7. Save the document as *[your initials]*19-16 in your Lesson 19 folder.

8. Submit and close the document.

Lesson 19 Summary

- Use Word's SmartArt feature to insert seven different types of SmartArt graphics. Add text to a SmartArt graphic by clicking a shape or clicking a text placeholder in the text pane.

- Format SmartArt graphics by using the Smart Tools Design tab or the SmartArt Tools Format tab on the Ribbon. You can change the layout, colors, style, fill, outline, and effects of the graphic.

- Use the Insert tab, Illustration group to insert a chart.

- Microsoft Excel offers 11 types of charts. (See Table 19-1.) Each chart type also has multiple subtypes available in the Change Chart Type dialog box. You can modify the chart type after a chart is created.

- If a chart uses multiple data series, you can apply a different chart type to each series.

- A chart is made up of many separate elements, such as axes, data markers, gridlines, legend, and more. Each element's attributes (such as its size, color, font, placement, and so on) can be modified. For example, you can change the color of data series columns or the plot area. You can change the position and formatting of the legend. You can also add or delete chart elements, such as a chart title or a secondary axis title.

- To format a chart element, right-click the element, and open the Format dialog box.

- To format a text element of a chart, such as the chart title, click the title and then select the text. Use any of Word's text-formatting tools to change the text's font, size, alignment, and other options. Click outside the title when you have finished editing.

LESSON 19		Command Summary	
Feature	**Button**	**Command**	**Keyboard**
Create SmartArt graphics	SmartArt	Insert tab, Illustrations group	
Create a chart	Chart	Insert tab, Illustrations group	
Chart type	Change Chart Type	Chart Tools Design tab, Type group	
Format selected chart object		Chart Tools Design, Layout, or Format tabs	Ctrl + 1

Concepts Review

True/False Questions

Each of the following statements is either true or false. Indicate your choice by circling T or F.

T F   1. SmartArt graphics are best used to present numerical data.

T F   2. You right-click a chart to activate the chart-editing tools.

T F   3. You can add or delete shapes from a SmartArt graphic.

T F   4. Pie charts can show only one data series.

T F   5. Every chart type has a corresponding 3-D version.

T F   6. Every chart type can be combined with every other chart type.

T F   7. The sample data of a chart display in a Word table.

T F   8. You cannot change the color of an individual column in a chart.

Short Answer Questions

Write the correct answer in the space provided.

1. When a chart is inserted in Word, where are the sample data located?

_____

2. Which chart axis is the vertical (or *y*) axis?

_____

3. Which chart axis is the horizontal (or *x*) axis?

_____

4. Each chart type has several different versions. What are these versions called?

_____

5. What shortcut menu command would you choose to change the color of a selected data series?

_____

6. What is the procedure to change a chart type?

_____

7. What is the name for the guide in a chart that explains the symbols, patterns, or colors used to differentiate data series?

_____

8. What type of SmartArt graphic illustrates the top-down relationship of members in an organization?

Critical Thinking

Answer these questions on a separate page. There are no right or wrong answers. Support your answers with examples from your own experience, if possible.

1. How would you decide if a chart would be a useful addition to your document? When would you use a chart instead of a simple table? Explain your answer.

2. You have seen the number of details and elements that can be added to a chart. Is there a point at which you can have too much detail in a chart? Explain how you would decide what amount of detail is appropriate for the message you want to communicate.

Skills Review

Exercise 19-17

Insert and format a SmartArt graphic.

1. Start a new document.
2. Change the document orientation to landscape.
3. Key Campbell's Confections—Holiday Favorites. Press Enter. Format the title by centering it and using 18-point bold, small caps.
4. Create a SmartArt graphic by following these steps:
   a. Click the Insert tab, and locate the Illustrations group.
   b. Click the SmartArt button .
   c. Click the List type, and click the second row, second style (Picture Accent List).
   d. Click OK.
5. Click the rotated <Text> placeholder for the left rectangle, and key Halloween. Click the rotated <Text> placeholder for the middle rectangle, and key Valentines. Key Easter in the third rotated <Text> placeholder.
6. Key the following text as bullet text in each of the rectangles.

Halloween rectangle	Valentine rectangle	Easter rectangle
Chocolate Bars	Gift Box Chocolates	Solid-chocolate Rabbits
Chocolate Suckers	Novelty Chocolates	Chocolate Eggs

7. Format the SmartArt graphic by following these steps:

   a. Select the SmartArt graphic border.

   b. Click the SmartArt Tools Design tab. Click the Change Colors button, and select a color from the Change Colors gallery.

   c. Click the SmartArt Tools Format tab, Click the Shape Fill button, and select a color for the background. Click the Shape Outline button, and select a color and weight for the line border.

   d. Click the Arrange button if the Arrange group does not display. Click the Position button, and click the Position in Middle Center with Square Text wrapping option.

   e. Click the Size button, and change the Width to **8** inches.

8. Insert a picture by following these steps:

   a. Click the picture placeholder for "Halloween." Locate and insert the picture file **Chocolate - P7**.

   b. Click the picture placeholder for "Valentines," and insert the picture file **Chocolate - P2**.

   c. Click the picture placeholder for "Easter," and insert the picture file **Chocolate - P3**.

9. Add a page border using a 3-point double-line format.

10. Save the document as *[your initials]*19-17 in your Lesson 19 folder.

11. Submit and close the document.

Exercise 19-18

Create a chart and edit chart data.

1. Open the file **Memo - 5**. Key the current date in the memo heading.

2. Insert a chart by following these steps:

   a. Position the insertion point at the end of the document. Click the Insert tab, and locate the Illustrations group.

   b. Click the Chart button.

   c. Click the Pie type, and click the second style, Pie in 3-D. Click OK.

3. Key the following data in the Excel worksheet.

Cell	Data
A2	Chocolate Nuts
A3	Chocolate Creams
A4	Chocolate Melt-a-ways
A5	Other
B2	38
B3	34
B4	26
B5	2

4. Edit chart data by following these steps:

   a. Select the chart, and click the **Chart Tools Design** tab.

   b. Click the Edit Data button ▣.

   c. Change the value 38 to **36**, change the value 26 to **24**, and change the value 2 to **6**.

5. Click anywhere outside the chart to return to Word.

6. Key your reference initials at the end of the document.

7. Save the document as *[your initials]***19-18** in your Lesson 19 folder.

8. Submit and close the document.

Exercise 19-19

Add chart titles, gridlines, and a secondary axis.

1. Open the file **Gift Sales**. Set the top margin to **2** inches.

2. Key your name in the "From" line.

3. Insert a properly formatted Date field to show the current date.

4. Select the chart.

5. Add a chart title and gridlines by following these steps:

   a. Click the **Chart Tools Layout** tab.

   b. Click the Chart Title button ▣, and click **Above Chart**. Key **Gift Sales** in the Chart Title box.

   c. Select the chart if necessary, and click the Gridlines button ▣ on the Chart Tools Layout tab. Click **Primary Vertical Gridlines**, and click **Major Gridlines**.

6. Add a secondary value axis by following these steps:

   a. Select the chart, and select the "Figurines/Collectibles" data series.

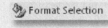

   b. Click the **Chart Tools Layout** tab, and click the Format Selection button 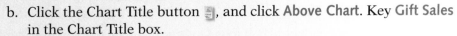 . Click **Series Options**, and click the **Secondary Axis** option. Click **Close**.

7. Click outside the chart to deselect it.

8. Save the document as *[your initials]***19-19** in your Lesson 19 folder.

9. Submit, and close the document.

Exercise 19-20

Add and format chart titles, change chart colors, format the legend, and format axes.

1. Open the file **Market - 1**. Select the chart by clicking it once.

2. Resize the chart, dragging the right sizing handle until it is even with the right margin.

3. Select the chart.

4. Change the chart type by following these steps:

   a. Click the **Chart Tools Design** tab, and click the Change Chart Type button ![icon].

   b. Click **Column** for the chart type, and click **Clustered Column** for the layout.

5. Key the chart title **Specialty Chocolate Sales**.

6. Change the chart area color by following these steps:

   a. Move the pointer into the chart area.

   b. Right-click, and choose **Format Chart Area** from the shortcut menu.

   c. Click **Fill**, and select a color. Click **Close**.

7. Format and resize the legend by following these steps:

   a. Right-click the legend, and choose **Format Legend** from the shortcut menu.

   b. Click **Legend Options**, and click **Top Right**. Click **Close**.

   c. Change the format of the legend text to 9-point bold and italic.

8. Format the value axis by following these steps:

   a. Right-click the value axis, and choose **Format Axis** from the shortcut menu.

   b. Click **Number**. In the Category list, click **Number**. Set **Decimal places** to **0**, and select the **Use 1000 Separator** check box.

   c. Click **Axis Options**. Change the value in the **Maximum** box to **Fixed** and **250**. Click **Close**.

   d. Format the text using 9-point bold and italic.

   e. Add minor gridlines to the value axis (with the **Chart Tools Layout** tab).

9. Format the chart title by following these steps:

   a. Select the chart title.

   b. Format the title using 14-point bold and italic.

10. Change the color of a data series by following these steps:

   a. Right-click one of the green columns.

   b. Click **Format Data Series** from the shortcut menu.

   c. Click **Fill**. Click **Gradient fill**.

11. Click outside the chart to deselect it. Key your initials at the bottom of the document.

12. Select the chart. Click the **Chart Tools Format** tab, and change the **Height** to **3.5** inches. Change the bottom margin to .5 inch.

13. Make any final adjustments to improve the layout, if needed, and then save the document as ***[your initials]*19-20** in your Lesson 19 folder.

14. Submit and close the document.

Lesson Applications

Exercise 19-21

Create a chart, change the chart type, and add and modify chart elements.

1. Create a new document, and change the orientation to landscape.

2. Insert a chart using the bar type, and the 100% Stacked Bar in 3-D layout.

3. Key the text from Figure 19-18 in the Excel worksheet. (Drag to resize the chart range to include only the column and row data.)

Figure 19-18

	A	B	C	D	E	F
1		Chocolate Bars	Gift Box	Novelty	Dark	Sugar-Free
2	Retail	540.4	953.3	347.8	168.6	69.5
3	Wholesale	216.7	383.7	124.6	134.6	74.4

4. Change the chart type to Column, and change the layout to Clustered Column.

5. Change the color of the plot area to light blue, and change the color of the "Novelty" data series to yellow.

6. Format the legend box, removing its border and moving it to the bottom of the chart. Change the font to 9-point regular. After repositioning the box, manually widen it so its width is the same as the plot area.

7. Key a chart title with the text Chocolate Sales by Division.

8. Change the height of the chart to 6 inches and the width to 8 inches. Click the Chart Tools Layout tab, click Data Labels, and click Center.

9. Apply a 3-point dark blue outline to the chart.

10. Change the font for both the category and value axes to 9-point bold.

11. Center the chart vertically and horizontally on the page.

12. Add a primary vertical axis title using the Rotated Title option. Key (Thousands) in the title box.

13. Format the value axis using the following settings: Minimum: Fixed 0; Maximum: Fixed 1000; Major unit: 200.

14. Make any final adjustments to improve the layout, if needed, and then save the document as *[your initials]*19-21 in your Lesson 19 folder.

15. Submit and close the document.

Exercise 19-22

Edit chart data; modify the chart type; and add, modify, and format chart elements.

1. Open the file **Revenue - 2**, and select the chart.

2. Switch to the worksheet, and change the number "161" to 116.

3. Change the chart type to Stacked Column.

4. Key the chart title Revenue Comparison. Format the title as 16-point bold and italic.

5. Format the value axis as 10-point bold and italic, with a currency number format and no decimal places. Format the category axis as 10-point bold and italic.

6. Format the legend as 9-point bold and italic, and place it at the bottom of the chart. Manually widen the legend box, adding more space between the text and symbols.

7. Resize the chart by using the bottom sizing handle.

8. Change the 2007 data series color.

9. Change the color of the plot area.

10. Apply a black border to each data series.

11. Add a border to the chart.

12. Save the document as *[your initials]*19-22 in your Lesson 19 folder. Submit the document.

13. Select the chart, and change the chart type to Clustered Column.

14. Save the document as *[your initials]*19-22b in your Lesson 19 folder.

15. Submit and close the document.

Exercise 19-23

Insert and modify a SmartArt graphic.

1. Start a new document and create a memo heading. The memo is to "Store Managers" from Lynn Tanguay. Use today's date, and the subject is "Setting Goals."

2. Key the following text below the memo heading.

   The following diagram illustrates our new approach to improving sales and productivity at Campbell's Confections. Please use this model to create your goals and objectives for the new fiscal year. We will meet next Thursday to discuss company goals and individual store goals.

3. Insert a SmartArt graphic using the Cycle type and the Nondirectional Cycle style (first row, fourth style).

4. Key Customer in the first shape. Move in a clockwise direction, and key the following terms in the shapes.

New Products
Technology Innovations
Marketing and Sales
Leadership Skills

5. Select the SmartArt graphic, and apply a 3-D SmartArt style. Change the color of the graphic.

6. Click the SmartArt Tools tab, and apply a fill and line color to the graphic.

7. Change the height of the graphic to 4 inches, and center the SmartArt graphic horizontally.

8. Key your reference initials at the end of the document.

9. Save it as *[your initials]*19-23 in your Lesson 19 folder.

10. Submit and close the document.

Exercise 19-24 ◆ Challenge Yourself

Change a chart's type, and add and modify chart elements.

1. Open the file **WV Sales**.

TIP

To change the data's grouping, click the Chart Tools Design tab and click the Switch Row/Column command. If the Switch Row/Column button is not active, click the Select Data command, verify the data range, and click OK.

2. Select the chart and switch the row and column data to change the data series groupings. (There should be four groups of two columns.)

3. Change the chart width to 6.5 inches.

4. Change the color of the plot area to light blue. Change the colors of both the 2007 and 2008 data series to complementing shades of blue using a solid fill color.

5. Format the scaling in the value axis so the major unit is 10,000. Change the font to 9-point bold and italic.

6. Key the chart title WV Sales. Format the title as 14-point bold.

7. Adjust the sizing and placement of the chart so it is balanced and centered horizontally on the page.

8. Save the document as *[your initials]*19-24 in your Lesson 19 folder.

9. Submit and close the document.

On Your Own

In these exercises you work on your own, as you would in a real-life business environment. Use the skills you've learned to accomplish the task—and be creative.

Exercise 19-25

Visit the Web sites of three popular computer manufacturers. Check the price that each one charges for a PC that is "perfect" for you. Create a Word document that uses a chart to show the different prices. Include a SmartArt graphic in the document to display the list of manufacturers. Save your document as *[your initials]*19-25 and submit it.

Exercise 19-26

Create a Word document that summarizes your personal expenses. Use a pie chart to show what percentage of your total expenses goes toward clothing, food, and other expenses. Save your document as *[your initials]*19-26 and submit it.

Exercise 19-27

Go online and look up the average high temperature and average rainfall of your four favorite places during the month of July. Create a chart that uses different chart types for these two data series. Save your document as *[your initials]*19-27 and submit it.

Unit 5 Applications

Unit Application 5-1

Create a flyer using clip art, pictures, and WordArt.

1. Start a new document, and change the orientation to landscape.

2. Key the text in Figure U5-1.

Figure U5-1

```
Introduction to Candy Making
Saturday, September 21
9 a.m. to 4 p.m.
Campbell's Confections—Auditorium
Instructor: Patricia Hoover
Registration: $25

Topics:
Temper, dip, decorate, and mold chocolate.
Taste factors—flavor and texture.
Master the techniques for making cream centers.
Where to buy chocolate-making ingredients, supplies, and
equipment.
```

3. Center the text and apply appropriate formatting for emphasis.

4. Add a page border to the document, and change the color to a chocolate-brown. Enhance the page with a light fill color or a light texture.

5. Move to the top of the document, and insert a table with 1 row and 9 columns.

6. Placing one letter in each cell, key **Chocolate** in the table. Format the text using 48-point bold, with either small caps or all caps. Select a display font for the text.

7. Change the row height for the table to 0.4 inch, center the table horizontally, and center the text in the cells vertically. Center the text in the table horizontally.

8. Delete the letter "o" from the two cells in the table, and replace the letters with a clip art of chocolate. Change the text wrapping of the clip art to square, and size the clip to fit in the cell. Change the picture shape to a circle. Refer to Figure U5-2 for an example.

Figure U5-2

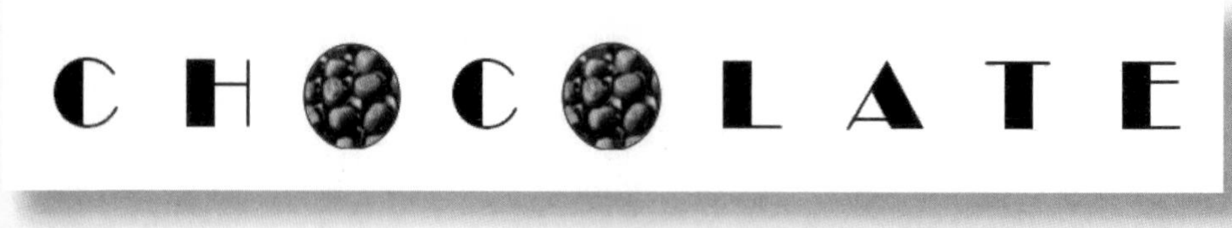

9. Preview the document and make adjustments to the format or placement of the text.

10. Save the document as *[your initials]*u5-1 in a new folder for Unit 5 applications.

11. Delete the table at the top of the document, and replace the table with a WordArt object. Format and size the WordArt object.

12. Save the document as *[your initials]*u5-1b in your Unit 5 folder.

13. Submit and close the document.

Unit Application 5-2

Create a one-page newsletter using clip art, pictures, and text boxes.

1. Start a new document. Change the top margin to 0.75 inch.

2. Click the Insert tab on the Ribbon, and open the Text Box gallery. Click the Exposure Sidebar style.

3. Key Campbell's Connections in the sidebar.

4. Format the title in a 48-point (or bigger) font. The title should fill the text box but not wrap to a new line. Center the text, and apply bold formatting if the font is not already bold. Select the text box, and apply dark blue shading to the title to create reverse text. Change the font color of the title to white.

5. Position the insertion point at the paragraph mark at the top of the document, and format the document from this point forward with three columns of unequal width. The first column is reserved for the sidebar, and the second and third columns are for the newsletter articles. Choose appropriate widths for the columns.

6. Insert the file **New Products** at the beginning of the second column. (If necessary, insert a column break to place the insertion point at the beginning of the second column.)

7. Format the title of the article. Select the last two paragraphs of the article, and format the paragraphs with a 0.25-inch first-line indent.

8. Insert a column break at the end of the second column, and insert the file **Volunteers**.

9. Format the title of the article using the same format applied to the first article. Select the last paragraph, and format with a 0.25-inch first-line indent.

10. At the beginning of the last paragraph of the second article, insert a clip art of a chocolate heart. Change the text wrapping to tight, and change the height to 0.75 inch. Drag the heart into the first paragraph.

11. Draw a text box at the bottom of the second column measuring 2.5 inches wide and 3.75 inches high.

12. Draw a second text box at the bottom of the third column measuring 2.5 inches wide and 5 inches high.

13. Select the text boxes and add a shape outline. Choose a 2-point dark blue color. Align the boxes using the Align Bottom option.

14. Insert the file **Survey Results** in the text box in the third column. Format the title to match the other articles. Select the column headings for the tabbed text, and format the headings.

15. Position the insertion point in the text box at the bottom of the second column. Key the title Chocolate Resources. Format the title.

16. Use the Internet or a local library to list the names of two or three resources related to chocolate. For books, include the title, author, publication date, cost, and ISBN number. For magazines or periodicals, include subscription information.

17. Preview the document and make final adjustments.

18. Save the document as *[your initials]u5-2* in your Unit 5 folder.

19. Submit and close the document.

Unit Application 5-3

Create and format a chart.

1. Start a new document.

2. Set a 2-inch top margin, and add a memo heading to the document. The memo is to "Store Managers" from Glenn Moore. Use the current date, and the subject is "Chocolate Sales."

3. Key the following text below the memo heading.

The following chart reflects the change in consumer preferences for chocolate. As a result of the increase in dark chocolate sales, we will modify our dark chocolate production schedules. Please use the new point-of-sale software to continue tracking chocolate preferences for the next six weeks.

4. Create a column chart using the information in Figure U5-3.

Figure U5-3

	A	B	C	D	E
1		Q1	Q2	Q3	Q4
2	Milk Chocolate	299	350	385	418
3	Dark Chocolate	60	65	73	85

5. Switch the row and column format if necessary to place the quarters along the *x*-axis.

6. Edit the chart data. Change the text in B3 to **45**.

7. Key the chart title **Chocolate Sales**.

8. Format the legend text using 10-point bold and italic.

9. Center the chart horizontally.

10. Add vertical gridlines, and format the chart area using a gradient fill.

11. Save the document as *[your initials]***u5-3** in your Unit 5 folder.

12. Submit and close the document.

Unit Application 5-4 ◆ Using the Internet

Design and create a newsletter with a multisection layout.

1. Use the Internet to research information about one of your hobbies. Include information concerning special training or education required, supplies and equipment needed, and professional resources available to learn more about the hobby. Write a minimum of four articles related to your hobby. Locate clip art related to your topic.

2. Create a two-page multisection newsletter.

3. Include the following elements in your newsletter:

   • Nameplate

   • Masthead

   • Multicolumn format

   • Pull quote using copied text from one of your articles

4. Create a style for the body text and a style for the article headings.

5. Include the following additions or modifications to the newsletter:

   • Change the document theme.

   • Change the font of the body text and headings.

   • Add horizontal lines.

   • Add bullets.

   • Insert clip art images.

6. Adjust text flow (line breaks, column breaks, page breaks), paragraph spacing, and character spacing as needed.

7. Add page numbers.

8. Save the document as *[your initials]***u5-4** in your Unit 5 folder.

9. Submit and close the document.

unit 6

ADVANCED TOPICS

Mail Merge

OBJECTIVES

After completing this lesson, you will be able to:

1. Create a main document.

2. Create a data source.

3. Insert merge fields into a main document.

4. Perform a mail merge.

5. Use data from other applications.

6. Edit an existing main document.

7. Sort and filter a data source.

8. Create mailing labels.

MCAS OBJECTIVES

In this lesson:
WW 07 4.5.1
WW 07 4.5.2
WW 07 4.5.3

Estimated Time: 1½ hours

Businesses and organizations often want to send the same letter to several people. *Mail merging* combines a document such as a form letter with a list of names and addresses to produce individualized documents. Using this process, you can create hundreds of personalized letters with just two documents:

- The *main document*, which contains special merge fields that act as placeholders for the recipient's name and address.

- The *data source*, which lists the specific recipient information (including the name, address, and any additional data such as the phone number) to be inserted in the merge fields.

You can also create mailing labels or envelopes by using Word's mail merge feature.

Creating a Main Document

The mail merge process involves the following steps for completing a mail merge:

1. Create or identify the main document.

2. Create or identify the data source.

3. Refine the list of recipients through sorting and filtering.

4. Insert merge fields (placeholders) in the main document.

5. Merge the data source with the main document.

You can create the main document and data source during the mail merge, or you can use existing files. The first step is to identify the main document.

Exercise 20-1   SELECT A STARTING DOCUMENT

You can mail-merge different types of documents, including letters, e-mail, envelopes, and labels. In this exercise, your main document will be a business letter.

NOTE

The documents you create in this course relate to the case study about Campbell's Confections, a fictional candy store and chocolate factory (see the Case Study in the frontmatter of the book).

1. Start a new document. Select the paragraph mark at the beginning of the document, and change the spacing after to 0 points, and change the line spacing to Single.

2. Format the current document as a business letter. Set a 2-inch top margin. Insert a date field at the top of the document, using the third format in the Date and Time dialog box. Make sure Update automatically is checked. Press ⏎Enter four times.

3. Insert a blank header, and create a letterhead for Campbell's Confections within the header by keying the following text. Center the text, and apply bold and small caps to the first line. To separate the phone and fax numbers, insert a symbol, such as the bullet character shown. Format the last line of the letterhead with a single-line bottom border.

Campbell's Confections
25 Main Street
Grove City, PA 16127
Telephone: 724-555-2025 • Fax: 724-555-2050
www.campbellsconfections.biz

4. Click the Mailings tab on the Ribbon. Notice the four groups associated with mail merge: Start Mail Merge, Write and Insert Fields, Preview Results, and Finish.

5. The first step in mail merge is to select the document type. Click the Start Mail Merge button 📄, and click **Letters**.

Figure 20-1
Mailings tab on the ribbon

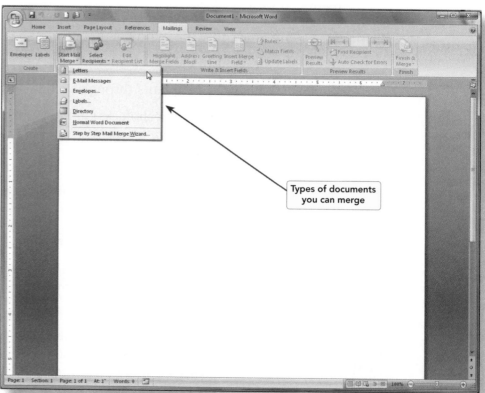

Types of documents you can merge

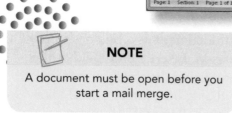

NOTE

A document must be open before you start a mail merge.

6. Save the document as *[your initials]*20-1main in a new folder for Lesson 20.

Creating a Data Source

A data source is a file that contains information, such as names and addresses. The information is organized in a table. Each column of the table represents a category of information, such as last name. The column heading of each category is called a *field name*. Each row of the table represents a *record*, which is usually a person's name and his or her contact information. Each piece of information in a record is a *field*.

To perform a mail merge, you can use a preexisting data source in the form of a Word table, an Excel worksheet, an Access table, or an Outlook contact list. Or you can create your own data source during the mail merge process, which creates an Access database file. To do this, you first define the data (fields) you need for each record (person), such as title, name, and address, and then you enter each item of information.

Figure 20-2
Sample data source
table

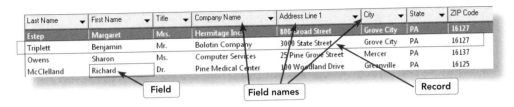

Exercise 20-2 CREATE A DATA SOURCE

When you click the Select Recipients button 📇, you have three choices: you can use an existing list, such as an Excel or Access data file; you can select from contacts you might have entered in Outlook; or you can type a new list.

1. Click the Select Recipients button 📇, and click **Type New List**. Word opens the New Address List dialog box. You will create your own data source by entering the data needed for this mail merge, which creates a database file.

Figure 20-3
New Address List
dialog box

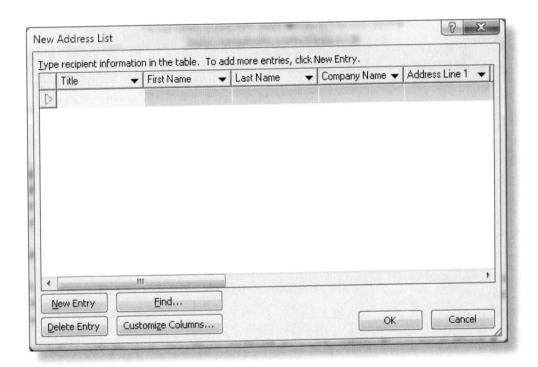

2. Use the scroll bar in the dialog box to see a list of commonly used field names. Because you won't be using many of these fields, you will customize this address list to include only the fields you need.

3. Click the Customize Columns button [Customize Columns...] in the New Address List dialog box to open the Customize Address List dialog box where you can delete, add, or rename field names and change their order.

Figure 20-4
Customize Address
List dialog box

NOTE

Check that you have only the field names shown in Figure 20-5. If you don't, click Cancel and start again.

4. Select **Address Line 2**. Click **Delete**. Click **Yes** when Word asks if you are sure you want to delete the field. The field name is removed from the list.

5. Using the same technique, remove the following fields from the list: **Country or Region** and **Home Phone**.

Figure 20-5
Customizing the
list of address
information

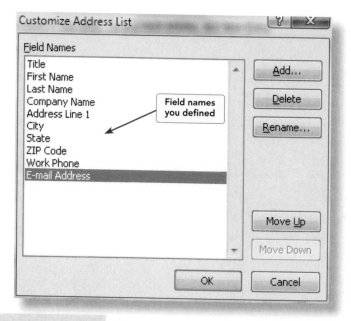

NOTE

When preparing to enter data, it is best to customize the address list so you can quickly key each line of data and move from record to record without worrying about a missed or blank field.

6. Click **OK** to close the Customize Address List dialog box. The New Address List dialog box lists only the fields you will need for your mail merge letters. You are now ready to enter data.

Exercise 20-3 ENTER RECORDS IN A DATA SOURCE

After defining field names for your data source, you can create records for mail merging.

1. In the New Address List dialog box, key **Mrs.** in the **Title** field and press `Tab`.

2. Key the information shown in Figure 20-6 in the appropriate text boxes, pressing `Tab` after each field entry. After you key the ZIP Code, you will need to press `Tab` three times to move to the next record, or you can click the New Entry button `New Entry`.

>
>
> **TIP**
>
> To move from field to field within a record, press `Tab` to move to the next field and press `Shift`+`Tab` to move to the previous field. You can also click the mouse.

Figure 20-6
Entering data

Title ▼	First Name ▼	Last Name ▼	Company Name ▼	Address Line 1 ▼	City ▼	State ▼	ZIP Code ▼
Mrs.	Margaret	Estep	Hermitage Inc.	800 Broad Street	Grove City	PA	16127
Mr.	Benjamin	Triplett	Bolotin Company	3000 State Street	Grove City	PA	16127
Ms.	Sharon	Owens	Computer Services	25 Pine Street	Mercer	PA	16137
Dr.	Richard	McClelland	Pine Medical Center	100 Woodland Drive	Greenville	PA	16125

Click to sort by last name.

3. Click the **Last Name** column heading (not the down arrow to the right of the column heading) to sort the list alphabetically by last name.

4. Click **OK** to close the New Address List dialog box.

5. In the Save Address List dialog box, open your Lesson 20 folder, key *[your initials]***20-3data** as the file name, and click **Save**.

> **NOTE**
>
> You can add or remove a recipient to include in your mail merge by selecting or clearing the check box next to the recipient's last name.

Figure 20-7
Save Address List dialog box

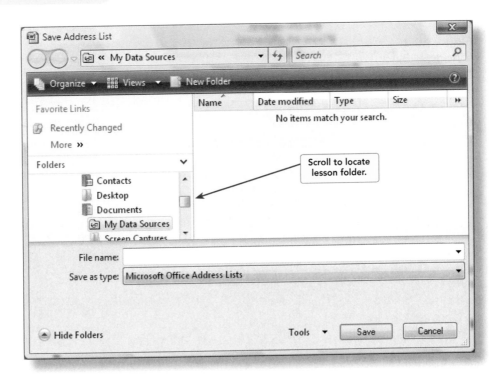

Inserting Merge Fields into a Main Document

Now that you have created a data source, you can complete the main document by keying text and inserting placeholders for data called *merge fields*. Merge fields appear in the main document as *field codes*, which show the field name, such as «Title». Mail merging replaces these fields with information from your data source, changing «Title» to "Mr.," for example.

When a field name has a space in its title (such as "Last Name"), Word displays the merge field in the document as «Last_Name», with an underscore for the space.

Exercise 20-4   INSERT MERGE FIELDS INTO THE MAIN DOCUMENT

When you return to your main document, you are ready to key the body of the letter and add field placeholders. Word provides two mail merge fields—address block and greeting—that insert fields automatically. You can also insert individual fields.

1. Position the insertion point four lines below the date. Click the Address Block button 🗐. The Insert Address Block dialog box opens.

2. The **Preview** box shows the field elements for the address block: title, first and last names, company, street address, city, state, ZIP Code, and country. Click **OK**. The address block is inserted in the document and contains the recipient's name and address.

Figure 20-8
Insert Address Block dialog box

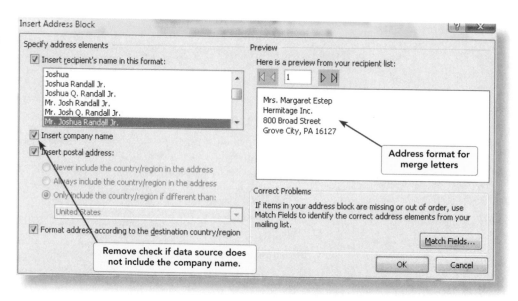

3. Position the insertion point two lines below the address block, and then click the Greeting line button. The Insert Greeting Line dialog box opens.

4. Change the comma in the greeting line format to a colon. The Preview box shows how the greeting will appear in your letters. The greeting includes "Dear," followed by the title field, the last name, and a colon. Click **OK**.

Figure 20-9
Insert Greeting Line
dialog box

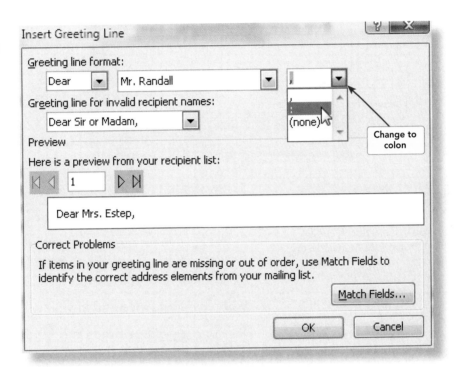

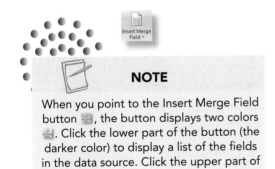

NOTE

When you point to the Insert Merge Field button, the button displays two colors. Click the lower part of the button (the darker color) to display a list of the fields in the data source. Click the upper part of the button to open the Insert Merge Field dialog box.

5. Key **Thank you,** two lines below the greeting line.

6. Click the top half of the Insert Merge Field button, and click the "FirstName" field. Click **Insert**. Type a comma, and key the following opening paragraph:

for agreeing to serve on the Western Pennsylvania Charity Foundation Steering Committee. We are looking forward to an exciting year, and we have high expectations for our annual fundraising campaign.

Figure 20-10
Insert Merge Field
dialog box

TIP

When you insert fields in a main document, make sure to include the correct spacing and punctuation.

NOTE

To create the most attractive letters, *The Gregg Reference Manual* recommends adjusting margins to suit the length of a letter and positioning the date either 2 inches from the top of the page or, as in this case, 0.5 inch from the bottom of the letterhead.

7. Press [Enter] twice to start a new paragraph.

8. Key the following closing paragraph.

   An agenda for our first planning meeting is enclosed. Please let me know if you cannot attend. Once again, thank you for your support.

9. Press [Enter] twice and key Sincerely.

10. Press [Enter] four times and key Thomas Campbell. Key President on the next line. Add your reference initials, followed by an enclosure notation.

11. Click the Preview Results button. The fields in the letter are replaced by the information from the first record.

12. Change the left and right margins to **1.25** inches and change the header distance from the page to **1** inch. Add three blank lines before the date.

13. Click the Save button to save these changes to the main document.

Performing a Mail Merge

Now that you have created both the main document and the data source, you can begin the mail merge. The mail merge will create one copy of the main document customized for each record. In each copy, the merge fields will be replaced by data from one record in the data source.

The simplest way to perform the mail merge is to:

- Preview the merged letters on-screen to see how they look with the merged data.

- Complete the merge by merging directly to the printer or merging to a new document that you can save and print later.

Exercise 20-5 PREVIEW AND COMPLETE THE MERGE

After you preview the merged letters and are satisfied with the results, complete the mail merge. You can merge all the records or a certain range of records, such as records 2 through 4.

Figure 20-11
Moving in a merged document

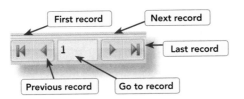

1. Locate the **Preview Results** group on the **Mailings** tab, and click the Next Record button . The fields display the information from the second record.

2. Continue to click the Next Record button to review each merged letter.

3. Click the Finish and Merge button. You can choose to edit individual documents, print document, or send e-mail messages.

4. Click **Print Documents**. The Merge to Printer dialog box displays. In the Merge to Printer dialog box, you can choose to print all merged letters or specific records.

Figure 20-12
Merge to Printer dialog box

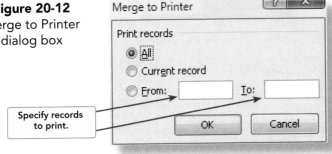

5. Key **1** in the **From** box and key **2** in the **To** box to print just the first two merged letters. Click **OK**.

6. Click **OK** in the Print dialog box. Word prints records 1 and 2 as merged letters.

7. Click the Finish and Merge button, and click **Edit Individual Documents**.

8. In the Merge to New Document dialog box, choose **All** and click **OK**. Word creates a new document, temporarily called Letters1, containing four merged letters. Scroll through the document to check the letters. Each letter appears as a separate section.

9. Save the merged document as **[your initials] 20-5merged** in your Lesson 20 folder.

10. Print pages 3–4 so you have a complete printout of all four letters.

11. Close the merged document and the main document, saving changes.

REVIEW

Because each letter is a separate section, key **s3-s4** in the Pages box of the Print dialog box.

Using Data from Other Applications

A data source can be a different file type, such as a Word table, an Excel worksheet, or an Outlook contact list. When you create a data source using the Mailings tab on the Ribbon, you create a database file automatically.

Exercise 20-6 USE DATA FROM A WORD DOCUMENT

1. Open the file **Tour Names**. This is a Word table that will be used as a data source in a mail merge.

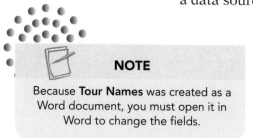

NOTE

Because **Tour Names** was created as a Word document, you must open it in Word to change the fields.

2. Insert a column on the far left of the table. In the top cell of the new column, key Title. This is a new field name you are adding to the data source file **Tour Names**.

3. Key Mr. as the title for the first record, Mrs. for the second record, and Ms. as the title for the last record. (Remember to press ⎀, not Enter, when going to the next cell in the column.)

Figure 20-13
Using and editing a word data source file

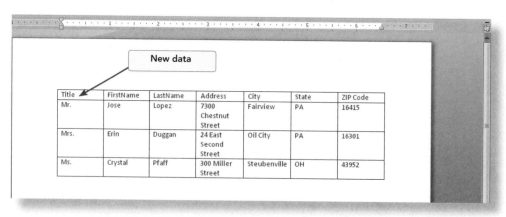

4. Save the revised data source as **[your initials]20-6data** in your Lesson 20 folder. Close the document.

5. Open the file **Tour Info**. This is a document that will serve as the main document in a mail merge, but it is missing merge fields.

6. Replace "[xx]" with your reference initials.

7. Click the Mailings tab, and click the Start Mail Merge button. Click Letters.

8. Click the Select Recipients button, and click Use Existing List. The Select Data Source dialog box opens.

9. Locate the directory and folder for *[your initials]*20-6data file. Click Open. The file is now open for use with the **Tour Info** main document, but it is not visible.

10. Position the insertion point on the fourth blank line below the date. Click the Address Block button. Click OK.

11. Press Enter twice, and click the Greeting Line button. Change the comma (,) to a colon (:).

12. Check that there is one blank line above and below the Greeting Line merge field and three blank lines between the date and the Address Block merge field.

13. Click the Preview Results button to view the first record of the mail merge.

14. Click the Finish and Merge button. Click Edit Individual Documents to open a new document.

15. Click OK to close the Merge to New Document dialog box.

16. Scroll through the document to view the three letters.

17. Save the merged document as *[your initials]*20-6merged in your Lesson 20 folder. Open the Print dialog box, and change the Pages per sheet option to 4. Close the merged document.

TABLE 20-1 Mail Merge Buttons

Button	Description	Function
	Start Mail Merge	Formats a main document for a specific type of mail merge, such as letters or labels, or restores the document to a normal Word document.
	Select Recipients	Attaches an existing data source to the active document, making the active document a mail merge main document if it is not one already.
	Edit Recipient List	Displays a dialog box where you can sort, search, filter, add, and validate mail merge recipients.
	Highlight Merge Fields	Applies background shading to mail merge fields in a main document to make them more visible.
	Address Block	Provides different address formats (including title, name, and address) to insert into a main document for a mail merge.
	Greeting Line	Provides different greeting line formats (including salutation, name, and punctuation) to insert into a main document for a mail merge.

continues

TABLE 20-1 Mail Merge Buttons *continued*

Button	Description	Function
Insert Merge Field	Insert Merge Field	Inserts merge fields from your data source or from a list of standard address fields into the main document.
Rules	Rules	Inserts into the main document Word fields, such as Ask and Fill, to control how Word merges data.
Match Fields	Match Fields	Displays a dialog box where you can match fields from a data source to fields in a main document that have different field names.
Update Labels	Update Labels	Copies the field codes for one label into the rest of the labels in a mail merge main document.
Preview Results	Preview Results	Displays the main document merged with information from the associated data source.
First Record	First Record	Displays the main document merged with information from the first record in the data source, if the View Merged Data button is clicked.
Previous Record	Previous Record	Displays the main document merged with information from the previous record in the data source, if the View Merged Data button is clicked.
1	Go to Record	Shows the currently merged record number. To display the main document merged with a specific record, key the record number and press [Enter].
Next Record	Next Record	Displays the main document merged with information from the next record in the data source, if the View Merged Data button is clicked.
Last Record	Last Record	Displays the main document merged with information from the last record in the data source, if the View Merged Data button is clicked.
Find Recipient	Find Recipient	Searches the database for text contained in a specified mail merge field.
Auto Check for Errors	Auto Check for Errors	Reports errors in the main document or data source that prevent merging.
Finish and Merge	Finish and Merge	Completes the mail merge.

Exercise 20-7   USE AN EXCEL WORKSHEET AS A DATA SOURCE

1. With **Tour Info** still open, click the Select Recipients button ⬛, and click **Use Existing List**. The Select Data Source dialog box opens.

2. Locate and open the Excel file **Group Names**. This is an Excel workbook that contains fields necessary for use with **Tour Info**. Click **Open**.

NOTE

The field names in this letter match the field names in the data source. If you tried to merge this main document with a data source that had different field names, you would get errors. You could correct these errors through a matching fields process, but it is best to match a main document with the correct data source. Naming fields consistently is also a good idea.

3. In the Select Table dialog box, click OK to use data from the first worksheet in the Excel workbook. The file is now open for use with **Tour Info**, but it is not visible.

4. Click the Edit Recipient List button ⊞. The Mail Merge Recipients dialog box displays the data from the Excel worksheet.

5. Click OK to close the Mail Merge Recipients dialog box.

6. Click the Finish and Merge button ⊞. Click Edit Individual Documents, and click OK to merge all records.

7. Preview the merged document.

8. Save the merged document as *[your initials]*20-7merged in your Lesson 20 folder. Submit and close the document.

Editing an Existing Main Document

After you have created a main document, you can edit and reuse it. In the main document, you might want to change the text or add a new field from the data source. When you open a main document that is associated with a data source, the following dialog box may appear. Click Yes to continue. If the associated data source is not located, it may be necessary to browse to locate the file.

Figure 20-14
Alert message

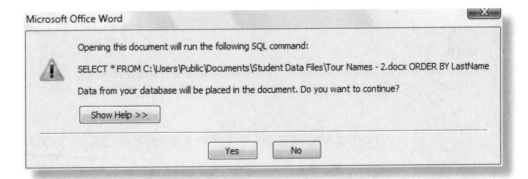

Exercise 20-8   EDIT AN EXISTING MAIN DOCUMENT

1. Reopen *[your initials]*20-7merged.

2. Click Yes to continue.

3. Position the insertion point in the first paragraph after the first sentence (after "tours.").

4. Key the following sentence.

> The factory that produces Campbell's Confections is located on Monroe Street in Grove City, Pennsylvania, just two blocks from the main retail candy store on Main Street.

5. Save the document as *[your initials]*20-8main in your Lesson 20 folder. Submit and close the document.

NOTE

If you discover an error in the merged document during a preview of the completed merge, edit the main document so that the changes will appear in all the merged documents.

Sorting and Filtering a Data Source

At times you might want to sort your data source before merging with your main document. You can also filter the data so that only records with certain characteristics are merged.

Exercise 20-9   SORT A DATA SOURCE

1. Open **Tour Info**.

2. Click the Select Recipients button , and click **Use Existing List**. Locate and open the file **Tour Names - 2**.

3. Click the Edit Recipient List button.

4. Click the **"LastName"** column heading (not the down arrow to the left of the column heading) to sort the list alphabetically by last name.

5. Click the <u>Sort</u> link to open the Filter and Sort dialog box.

6. In the **Then by** drop-down list, choose **FirstName**. Notice that the default order is **Ascending**.

7. Click **OK**. The records are sorted first by last name and then by first name.

Exercise 20-10   FILTER A DATA SOURCE

1. Click the <u>Filter</u> link to open the Filter and Sort dialog box with the Filter Records tab selected.

NOTE

You can click the down arrow next to any of the field names and click (Advanced) to access the Filter and Sort dialog box. Also, you can click the down arrow next to a field name and choose one of the fields listed. This filters the data based on the field you choose.

2. In the first **Field** text box, choose **LastName** from the drop-down list.

3. Make sure the **Comparison** text box is set to **Equal to**.

4. In the **Compare to** text box, key **Steele**.

5. In the text box below and to the left of **LastName**, choose **And** from the drop-down list if it is not selected. (See Figure 20-15.)

6. In the **Field** text box to the right of **And**, choose **ZIP_Code** from the drop-down list.

7. In the **Comparison** text box, choose **Greater than**.

8. In the **Compare to** text box, key **15500**.

Figure 20-15
Filtering data by
using comparisons

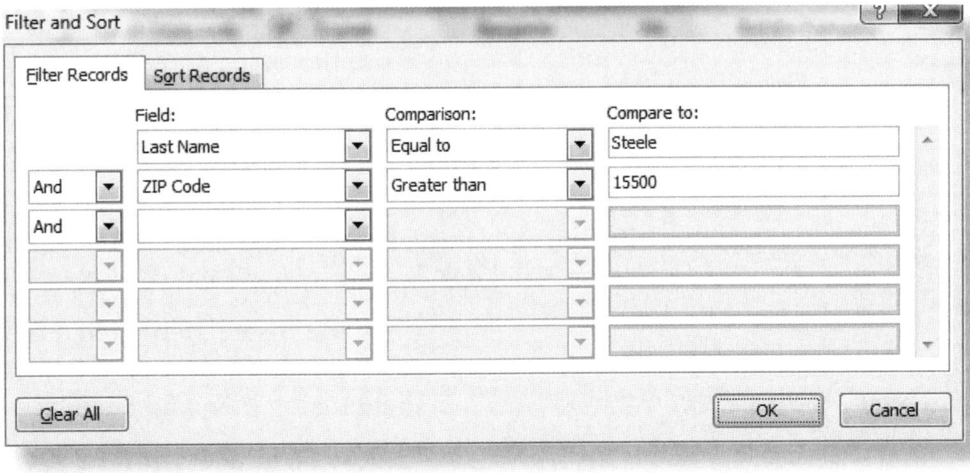

9. Click **OK** to filter the data—Word looks for records with the last name "Steele" and a postal code greater than "15500" and finds one record. Click **OK** again to accept the filtered data.

10. Add your reference initials to the letter, and make "Enclosure" plural (more than one item will accompany the letter).

11. Save the document as *[your initials]*20-10main in your Lesson 20 folder.

12. Click the Finish and Merge button ⬚. Click **OK**. The record for "Raymond Steele" is merged with the main document to create a new document.

13. Save the document as *[your initials]*20-10merged in your Lesson 20 folder.

14. Submit the letter and close all open documents, saving changes if prompted.

Creating Lists and Mailing Labels

You can merge data from a data source to create a list or a directory. You can also create mailing labels from a document to address envelopes and packages. Word enables you to designate the style of the label and insert the merge fields for the addresses.

Exercise 20-11   CREATE A LIST FROM A DATA SOURCE

To create a list from a data source, you use the Mailings tab on the Ribbon.

1. Start a blank document and click the Mailings tab on the Ribbon.

2. Click the Start Mail Merge button .

3. Choose Directory from the list.

4. Click the Select Recipients button ⟨⟩, and click Use Existing List. Locate and open **Tour Names - 2** as a data source.

5. Open the Mail Merge Recipients dialog box by clicking the Edit Recipient List ⟨⟩, and sort the data source alphabetically by last name. Click OK.

> **NOTE**
>
> If you click the lower part of the Insert Merge Field button, you can insert the fields automatically by clicking the field name. Click the upper part of the Insert Merge Field button to open the Insert Merge Field dialog box.

6. Click the Insert Merge Field button ⟨⟩, choose LastName from the list of fields in the Insert Merge Field dialog box, and click Insert.

7. Choose ZIP_Code from the list, click Insert, and click Close. Both fields are inserted in the document.

8. Press Tab between the fields. Set a left tab at 1.5-inch mark on the ruler. Insert a new paragraph mark after the ZIP_Code field.

9. Click the Finish and Merge button ⟨⟩, click Edit Individual Documents, and click OK to allow all the records to be merged.

> **NOTE**
>
> You must insert a paragraph mark after the ZIP_Code field or the last field in the paragraph. Otherwise, each record will be listed one after the other in one paragraph.

10. Save the merged list as *[your initials]***20-11merged** in your Lesson 20 folder and submit it.

11. Close only the merged document.

Exercise 20-12   CREATE A CATALOG-TYPE MAIN DOCUMENT

Not only can you merge data to create a list, but you can also create more extensive catalog-type documents or directories.

1. With your insertion point directly after the LastName field, click the lower part of the Insert Merge Field button ⟨⟩.

2. Choose FirstName from the list.

3. Insert the field State by clicking the lower part of the Insert Merge Field button ⟨⟩.

Exercise 20-13   ADD FORMATTING TO A CATALOG-TYPE MAIN DOCUMENT

1. Insert tab characters before each of the fields except the first field.

2. Select the paragraph containing the fields, clear the 1.5-inch tab, and set 1.75-inch, 3.75-inch, and 5.0-inch left tabs.

3. Select the «LastName» field and apply bold formatting.

4. Apply numbering to the paragraph containing the fields by clicking the Numbering button on the Home tab.

5. Apply double-line spacing to the paragraph containing the fields.

6. Set a 2-inch top margin, and apply a single-line page border to the document.

7. Save the document as *[your initials]*20-13main in your Lesson 20 folder.

8. Click the Finish and Merge button, click Edit Individual Documents, and click OK to allow all the records to be merged.

9. Key a title at the top of the catalog directory: Catalog Directory of Customer Requests. Format it as 14-point bold, with small caps and centered.

10. Change the spacing after to 12 points.

11. Save the merged catalog directory as *[your initials]*20-13merged in your Lesson 20 folder and submit it.

12. Close all open documents, saving changes if prompted.

Exercise 20-14   CREATE MAILING LABELS

Creating labels follows the same process as creating form letters. Identify the main document, and select recipients.

The process of creating mailing labels requires that you:

- Create a mailing label main document.

- Choose a data source.

- Specify label size and type.

- Insert merge fields.

- Merge the main document and the data source.

TIP

To create envelopes instead of labels, choose Envelopes as the document type and then follow the mail merge steps.

1. Start a blank document.

2. Click the Mailings tab.

3. Click the Start Mail Merge button, and click Labels. The Label Options dialog box displays.

4. Select Avery US Letter in the Label vendors box.

5. Scroll the **Product number** list and choose **5160**. Click **OK**. The document is now formatted for labels.

6. Click the Select Recipients button , and click **Use Existing List**.

7. In the Select Data Source dialog box, locate and open **Tour Names - 2**. Word adds the merge field «Next Record» to your labels.

8. Click the Edit Recipient List button , and display the last column and click the column heading, **ZIP_Code**. The records are now sorted by ZIP Code.

9. Click **OK**.

Address Block

10. Click the Address Block button , and click **OK**. Word adds the «Address Block» field to the first label.

Figure 20-16
Adding the Address Block field

 Update Labels

11. Click the Update Labels button . Word automatically adds the «Address Block» field to each label.

Preview Results

12. Click the Preview Results button . Word merges the data from **Tour Name - 2** with your label document. Show table gridlines (click the **Table Tools Layout** tab) if they do not already appear.

Finish & Merge · Finish

13. Click the Finish and Merge button , and click **Edit Individual Documents**. Click **OK** to merge to a new document.

14. Save the merged labels as *[your initials]*20-14labels in your Lesson 20 folder.

15. Prepare your printer with the correct label sheet or use a blank sheet of paper, and print the document.

16. Close and save the document.

Lesson 20 Summary

- Mail merging combines a main document (such as a form letter) with a data source (such as a list of names and addresses) to produce individualized documents. The main document contains merge fields. The data source is a table—column headings are field names and rows are records. Each cell of a record is a field that appears in the matching merge field of the main document.

- The main document is a Word document; the data source can be a table in Word, an Excel worksheet, an Access database, or an Outlook contact list.

- Use the Mailings tab to create mail merge documents.

- You can create a new data source by keying records into a data form called the New Address List dialog box. You can customize the fields in this dialog box to match the fields you will use in your main document. A data source created by using the New Address List dialog box produces a database file.

- You insert merge fields in a main document individually or as field blocks, such as Word's built-in Address Block.

- You can preview the data merged into your main document before performing the merge. Complete the merge by merging directly to a printer (or merging to e-mail addresses or fax numbers) or to a new document.

- At any point before or after merging, you can edit mail merge documents. Edit the main document or the data source file (if it is a Word table) as you would any Word document.

- You can sort and filter data source files to produce only the merged files you want. Use more than one field for advanced sorting capability.

- You can merge data from a data source to create a list or a catalog-type document or directory.

- You can create mail merge envelopes or mailing labels. Choose envelopes or labels as the main document type, choose or create a data source, choose envelope or label options, insert merge fields into the main document, and then perform the merge.

LESSON 20		Command Summary	
Feature	**Button**	**Command**	**Keyboard**
Identify main document		Mailings tab, **Start Mail Merge** group	
Create or select data source		Mailings tab, **Start Mail Merge** group	
Sort or filter data source		Mailings tab, **Start Mail Merge** group	
Insert merge fields		Mailings tab, **Write & Insert Fields** group	Alt + Shift + F
Preview merge		Mailings tab, **Preview Results** group	
Merge data		Mailings tab, **Finish** group	Alt + Shift + N

Concepts Review

True/False Questions

Each of the following statements is either true or false. Indicate your choice by circling T or F.

T F   1. Field names are the column headings in a data source table.

T F   2. A field contains several pieces of unrelated information.

T F   3. Mail merging inserts the information from the merged document into copies of the data source.

T F   4. Each record in a data source table must contain the same number of fields.

T F   5. A row in a data source table is called a record.

T F   6. You cannot edit an existing main document.

T F   7. When you create a data source by using the Mailings tab, you create a database.

T F   8. Data source files can only be Word documents.

Short Answer Questions

Write the correct answer in the space provided.

1. What serves as a placeholder in the main document for information found in the data source?

   _____

2. List an example of a document type for a mail merge main document.

   _____

3. What are the two major documents used in mail merging?

   _____

4. What does a record contain?

   _____

5. Which button in the New Address List dialog box is used to add or delete field name columns in the New Address List dialog box?

   _____

6. What is the procedure for sorting a list of names in the New Address List dialog box?

   _____

7. What is the mail merge field called that contains a salutation, a name, and punctuation for letters?

_____

8. Which button on the Mailings tab do you click to create a new document containing all merged letters?

_____

Critical Thinking

Answer these questions on a separate page. There are no right or wrong answers. Support your answers with examples from your own experience, if possible.

1. Businesses use a mail merge process to send personalized letters for fundraising or sales promotions. For a business, what are the advantages and disadvantages of sending personalized mail of this type?
2. Have you or a member of your family ever received a personalized mailing from a business? Describe the reaction you had to receiving it.

Skills Review

Exercise 20-15

Create a main document and a data source, insert merge fields, and perform a mail merge.

1. Create a memo main document by following these steps:
   a. Create a new blank document, and change the top margin to 2 inches, and set a 1-inch left tab.
   b. Click the Mailings tab.
   c. Click the Start Mail Merge button , and choose Letters.
2. Key the memo heading shown in Figure 20-17. Press Enter after keying the subject line.

Figure 20-17

```
MEMO TO:

FROM:      Lynn Tanguay

DATE:      [Current Date]

SUBJECT:   Visitation Schedule
```

3. Create a data source by following these steps:

 a. Click the Select Recipients button .

 b. Click **Type New List**.

 c. Click **Customize Columns**.

 d. With the first field name selected (**Title**), click **Delete** and click **Yes** to verify the deletion.

 e. Select the third field name (**Company Name**), click **Rename**, and key **Quarter**. Click **OK**.

 f. Delete the following fields: **Address Line 1**, **Address Line 2**, **City**, **ZIP Code**, **Country or Region**, **Home Phone**, **Work Phone**, and **E-mail Address**.

 g. Click to select the **State** field, and click **Move Up** to place the **State** field above the **Quarter** field.

 h. Click **OK**.

 i. Key the data shown in Figure 20-18.

Figure 20-18

FirstName	LastName	State	Quarter
Elizabeth	Veritz	Pennsylvania	First
Jackson	Sigmon	Ohio	Second
Patrick	Donaldson	Ohio	Second
Vince	Teague	West Virginia	Third

 j. Click **OK** to return to the main document.

4. Save the data source as *[your initials]*20-15data in your Lesson 20 folder.

5. Key the body of the memo as shown in Figure 20-19. Use correct spacing after the subject line and between paragraphs. Insert merge fields in place of field names by using the Insert Merge Field button . Include spaces around merge fields where needed.

Figure 20-19

The quarterly visitation schedule for the retail stores has been completed. Your store is scheduled for a visit during the second week of the «quarter» quarter. Our plan is to visit all stores in Pennsylvania during the first quarter, Ohio stores in the second quarter, and West Virginia stores in the third quarter.

Please let me know if you are aware of any conflicts with this schedule.

6. Add your reference initials, and format the subject line with 24 points spacing after.

7. After the heading "TO:" insert the FirstName and the LastName merge fields.

8. Save the main document as *[your initials]*20-15main in your Lesson 20 folder.

9. Preview the merged data by following these steps:
    a. Click the Preview Results button .
    b. Click the Next Record button ▶ to see the next record.
    c. Make any corrections to the main document that might be needed, and resave the document.
10. Complete the merge by following these steps:
    a. Click the Finish and Merge button.
    b. Click **Edit Individual Documents** to merge the data to a new document.
    c. In the Merge to New Document dialog box, choose **All** and click **OK**.
11. Save the merged document as *[your initials]***20-15merged** in your Lesson 20 folder and print 4 pages per sheet.
12. Close all open documents, saving changes if prompted.

Exercise 20-16

Use and edit a data source from Word, edit an existing main document, sort and filter data, and merge the documents.

1. Edit an existing Word data source and add a new record by following these steps:
    a. Open the file **Contributors**. This is a Word table that will be used as a data source.
    b. Change the abbreviation "Rd." to **Road**, "St." to **Street**, and "Dr." to **Drive**.
    c. Change the "City" of Ms. Merita Loy-Jones to **Mercer**.
    d. Insert a new row to the bottom of the table.
    e. Key the data shown in Figure 20-20.

Figure 20-20

```
Title:          Ms.
FirstName:      Linda
LastName:       Del-Reo
Address:        12 East Main Street
City:           Harrisville
State:          PA
PostalCode:     16038
```

2. Add a new field by following these steps:
    a. Insert a new column before the "Address" column. Key the column heading **Company** at the top of the new column.
    b. Key the company names shown in Figure 20-21 directly into the table.

Figure 20-21

LastName	Company
Little	Liberty Cable Works
Loy-Jones	Millcreek Consultants
Abadini	Oakwood Planning Association
Del-Reo	B&G Enterprise

3. Center the table horizontally on the page. Save the file as *[your initials]*20-16data in your Lesson 20 folder. Submit and close the document.

4. Open the file **Gala**.

5. Insert the date field at the top of the document, with three blank lines below it. Set a 2-inch top margin and 1.5-inch left and right margins.

6. Click the Mailings tab, and click the Start Mail Merge button 📧, and click **Letters**.

7. Open an existing data source by following these steps:

   a. Click the Select Recipients button 📧, and click **Use Existing List**.

   b. Locate and choose *[your initials]*20-16data as the data source file.

8. Modify the main document by following these steps:

   a. Position the insertion point at the beginning of the first paragraph, and click the Address Block button 📧. Click **OK**, and press ⏎ two times.

   b. Position the insertion point at the beginning of the first paragraph, click the Greeting Line button 📧, and change the punctuation from a comma to a colon. Click **OK**. Press ⏎ two times.

   c. Add your reference initials to the main document, and add an enclosure notation.

9. Save the document as *[your initials]*20-16main in your Lesson 20 folder.

10. Sort and filter data by following these steps:

   a. Click the Edit Recipient List button 📧.

   b. Click the LastName column heading to sort by last name.

   c. Click the down arrow to the right of LastName and choose (**Advanced**).

   d. Click the Sort Records tab and click **Descending**. Make sure the **Then by** text box is empty. Click **OK**.

   e. Click the <u>Filter</u> link at the bottom of the dialog box.

   f. In the first Field text box, choose City from the drop-down list.

   g. In the Comparison text box, choose Equal to if it is not selected.

   h. In the Compare to text box, key Grove City.

   i. In the text box below and to the left of the City, choose Or from the drop-down list.

   j. In the Field text box next to Or, choose Zip_Code from the drop-down list.

   k. In the Comparison text box, choose Less than.

   l. In the Compare to text box, key 16100.

   m. Click OK twice.

11. Preview and complete the merge by following these steps:

    a. Click the Preview Results button 🔍 to see the data merged with the main document.

    b. Click the button again to see the fields.

    c. Click the Finish and Merge button 📄, and click **Edit Individual Documents**.

    d. With **All** selected, click **OK** to merge the record.

12. Save the merged document as *[your initials]***20-16merged** in your Lesson 20 folder.

13. Submit the letter and close all open documents, saving changes if prompted.

Exercise 20-17

Create and format a directory-type main document.

1. Create a catalog-type main document by following these steps:

    a. Start a blank document.

    b. Click the Start Mail Merge button 📄.

    c. Choose **Directory** from the list.

    d. Locate and select the data file **Managers** as a data source.

    e. Click the Edit Recipient List button 📄, and click the **LastName** field to sort alphabetically. Click **OK**.

    f. Click the Insert Merge Field button 📄, choose **LastName**, and click **Insert**.

    g. Choose **FirstName** from the list and click **Insert**.

    h. Choose **City** from the list, click **Insert**, and then click **Close**.

    i. Press ⏎Enter to insert a blank paragraph mark after the last field.

2. Format the document by following these steps:

    a. Set 2-inch and 4-inch left tabs in the fields line.

    b. Insert a tab before the «FirstName» and «City» fields.

    c. Apply numbering to the field paragraph.

    d. Apply 1.5-line spacing to the field paragraph.

    e. Format the «City» field using small caps.

3. Save the document as *[your initials]***20-17main** in your Lesson 20 folder.

4. Click the Finish and Merge button 📄, click **Edit Individual Documents**, and allow all the records to be merged.

5. Key a title at the top of the catalog directory: **Pennsylvania Store Managers**. Format the title using 14-point bold, with small caps and centered. Change the spacing after to 18 points.

6. Set a 1.5-inch top margin.

7. Save the merged catalog directory as *[your initials]***20-17merged** in your Lesson 20 folder and submit it.

8. Close all open documents, saving changes if prompted.

Exercise 20-18

Create labels.

1. Create a main document for labels that will be used as a name tag by following these steps:

   a. Start a new document.

   b. Start the mail merge by clicking the Mailings tab and choosing Labels as the starting document.

   c. Choose Avery US letter from the Label vendors drop-down box.

   d. Choose 5383 - Name Tag from the Product number drop-down list, and click OK.

2. Locate and select the data source **Managers**.

3. Insert merge fields for a name tag by following these steps:

   a. Scroll in the main document to the top left label, and click to position the insertion point.

   b. Insert the fields «FirstName» and «LastName». (Be sure to place a space between the fields.)

   c. Click the Update Labels button .

4. Preview the merge.

5. Select the text in the table, and format it as 24-point bold, with small caps. Use the table align option to center the text vertically and horizontally in the cell. Apply the All Borders option from the Borders drop-down list.

6. Save the merged document as *[your initials]***20-18merged** in your Lesson 20 folder.

7. Submit the document. Close all open documents without saving.

Lesson Applications

Exercise 20-19

Create a main document and a data source, and merge the documents.

1. Create a new form-letter main document with a 2-inch top margin. Change the left and right margins to 1.25 inches.

2. Create a data source with the following field names: SalesRep, Date, Contact, Hotel, and Comment.

3. Key the two records shown in Figure 20-22. In the "Date" row, key today's date for both records.

Figure 20-22

Field name	Record 1	Record 2
SalesRep	Doris Simms	Korey Walters
Date	[today's date]	[today's date]
Contact	Ethel Lewis	Mark Hunter
Hotel	Plaza Hotel	Premium Hotels
Comment	Dark chocolate sales are increasing.	Seasonal chocolates are very popular.

4. Save the data source as *[your initials]***20-19data** in your Lesson 20 folder.

5. Key the following heading in the main document followed by three blank lines:

   Campbell's Confections
   25 Main Street
   Grove City, PA 16127

6. Format the heading as 14-point bold, centered, small caps, and 6 points spacing after, with a 1-point shadow paragraph border and light gray shading.

7. Key CALL REPORT as uppercase, bold, and centered below the document heading.

8. Change the paragraph spacing for "Call Report" to 18 points spacing before and 18 points spacing after.

9. Position the insertion point at the paragraph mark below "Call Report," and set a 2.25-inch hanging indent.

10. Key the text, press Tab, and insert the merge field codes shown in Figure 20-23. Apply small caps to the headings on the left margin. The merge field codes should align at the 2.25-inch indent.

Figure 20-23

```
Sales Representative:        «SalesRep»
Date of Contact:             «Date»
Name of Contact:             «Contact»
Hotel:                       «Company»
Comment:                     «Comment»
```

11. Save the main document as *[your initials]*20-19main in your Lesson 20 folder.

12. Preview the merged data. Correct the main document and data source, if necessary, and save any changes.

13. Complete the merge by merging both records to a new document.

14. Save the new document as *[your initials]*20-19merged in your Lesson 20 folder.

15. Print 2 pages per sheet. Close all open documents, saving changes if prompted.

Exercise 20-20

Create a directory-type document.

1. Create a new document, and change the top margin to 1.5 inches. Change the left and right margins to 2 inches.

2. Click the Mailings tab, and start a mail merge by choosing Directory as the main document type.

3. Locate and open the file **Directory - 3** document as a data source.

4. Sort the data source alphabetically by department.

5. Set left tabs at 2 inches and 4 inches. Insert the following fields in the document: Name, Department, and Extension. Place a tab character between the fields, and press Enter at the end of the line.

6. Save the document as *[your initials]*20-20main in your Lesson 20 folder and submit it.

7. Finish the merge by merging to a new document and selecting all records.

8. Key the title Corporate Telephone Extensions by Department at the top of the document. Apply 14- point bold, with small caps and center alignment. Change the spacing after to 18 points.

9. Save the document as *[your initials]*20-20merged in your Lesson 20 folder. Submit the directory.

10. Close all documents, saving any changes.

Exercise 20-21

Edit existing mail merge documents, filter data, and perform a mail merge.

1. Open the file **Invoice**.

2. Format the first six lines (the heading) as bold and centered. Under the heading, change the word "Invoice" to 14-point uppercase and centered with 18 points spacing before and after.

3. Edit the rest of the document as follows:

   - Replace each colon (:) with a tab character.
   - Convert the paragraphs from "Date" to "Total Due" (including the tabs) into a two-column table by selecting the text and clicking the Table button on the Insert tab.
   - Format the first column to be 1.75 inches wide and the second column 2.5 inches wide.
   - Apply bold and small caps formatting to the first column.
   - Change the row height for all rows to at least 0.4 inch.
   - Center the table horizontally on the page, and center the cell contents vertically.
   - Apply 1-point gridlines inside the table and a 3-point double-line (one thick, one thin) outside border to the table.
   - In the first row, second column, insert the date as an automatically updating field, using the December 25, 200-, format.

4. Save the document as *[your initials]*20-21main in your Lesson 20 folder.

5. Open the file **Accounts**. This file will be the data source for the main document. Edit the table as shown in Figure 20-24. Change the page orientation to landscape to make space for the extra columns created by reorganizing the data in the Address2 field. (Hint: To avoid rekeying data, create the new columns and drag and drop data to the new cells).

Figure 20-24

AcctNo	InvNo	Name	Address1	Address2	Total
2037L	797411	Nicole R. Sanchez	798 Armden Drive	Manchester, OH 45144	$598.00
2943L	1856429	Emery Ellis	2720 Summer ~~Dr.~~ Street	Chillicothe, OH 45601	$875.00
1243S	617831	Sara O'Neill	83 Morris Boulevard	Sunbury, OH 43074	$458.00

Add two columns to the table. Separate the Address2 column information into three columns—City, State, and ZIP_Code. Change the column headings.

6. Use the AutoFit Contents option to set the width of the columns.

7. Save the data source as *[your initials]***20-21data** in your Lesson 20 folder and submit it. Close the document.

8. Switch to your main document, and choose *[your initials]***20-21data** as its data source.

9. Edit the main document to insert the appropriate merge fields from the data document into the second column of the table.

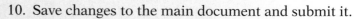

|←→| **REVIEW**

You do not have to use the Filter and Sort dialog box to filter the data. You can simply choose the city name from the list of fields under "City."

10. Save changes to the main document and submit it.

11. Filter the data source to define "Sunbury" as the city.

12. Merge to create a new document. Save the new document as *[your initials]***20-21merged** in your Lesson 20 folder and submit it.

13. Close all open documents, saving changes.

Exercise 20-22 ◆ Challenge Yourself

Use an Excel worksheet as a data source, sort the data, create and edit the main document, merge the documents, and create mailing labels.

1. Open the file **Campaign**. This file will be the main document of a mail merge.

2. Use the Excel file **Campaign Data** (Sheet1$) as the data source.

3. Create a two-level sort of the recipients by last name and then by first name.

4. Make the following changes to the main document to format it as a letter:
   - Set a 2-inch top margin.
   - Insert the date as an updating field, using the correct date format.
   - Insert the Address Block.
   - Insert the Greeting Line. Make sure to change the greeting line punctuation to a colon.
   - Insert your reference initials.

5. In the last sentence of the first paragraph, edit the text as follows: «SalesRep», one of our.

6. Save the main document as *[your initials]***20-22main** in your Lesson 20 folder.

7. Preview the merged data; then merge to a new document.

8. Save the new document as *[your initials]***20-22merged** in your Lesson 20 folder, and print 4 pages per sheet.

9. Close the merged document and main document, saving changes.

10. Create mailing labels. Use the 5160 product number and the data source you used earlier for this exercise. Use the Address Block field in the labels.

11. Merge the labels to a new document. Format the label text as 14-point Arial Narrow bold.

12. Save the labels as *[your initials]*20-22labels in your Lesson 20 folder.

13. Submit the labels and close the file. Close the main label document without saving.

On Your Own

In these exercises you work on your own, as you would in a real-life business environment. Use the skills you've learned to accomplish the task—and be creative.

Exercise 20-23

Create a main document that is a form letter you will send to five friends, family members, or business contacts. Create a data source for the contacts. Include at least one merge field in the body of the form letter. Save the main document and the data source with appropriate file names. Merge the documents to a new file called *[your initials]*20-23 and submit it.

Exercise 20-24

Increase the size of the data source created in the previous exercise, or create a new data source as a Word table that contains 10 records. Create name tag labels that contain just the first and last name, formatted attractively. Save the merged labels as *[your initials]*20-24 and submit it.

Exercise 20-25

Launch Internet Explorer, and research five or more companies where you would like to work. Write a form letter that you will send to these companies, and attach your résumé to the form letter. Your database should include a contact name, title, and department. Your form letter should include a few merge fields in the body of the letter to further customize the letter for each company. Save the main document and the data source with appropriate file names. Merge the documents to a new file called *[your initials]*20-25 and submit it.

Fields and Forms

After completing this lesson, you will be able to:

1. Insert fields.

2. View, edit, and update field codes.

3. Understand bookmarks.

4. Create a template to use as a form.

5. Insert content controls and form fields.

6. Protect and save a form.

7. Use and edit a form.

MCAS OBJECTIVES

In this lesson:
WW 07 1.1.1
WW 07 1.3.4
WW 07 4.1.4

Estimated Time: 1 hour

A *field* is a placeholder for information that can change in a document. You can insert most fields into a document by using familiar Ribbon commands and buttons, such as inserting a page number in a header or footer or inserting a date in a letter. Other examples of fields that are automatically inserted are those for creating tables of contents and indexes.

This lesson explains how to insert fields and how to modify those fields by adding options to change the way the fields are displayed. You will also learn how to create electronic forms, which can be used over and over. Electronic forms are based on a custom template.

Inserting Fields

You can use many different types of fields in a Word document. Fields are used to insert basic document information, such as a date, page number, document filename, or document author. There are special fields that are used with mail merge operations and form fields that are used to gather information on an electronic form. Fields are inserted automatically through built-in commands or inserted manually.

When you choose a field, the *field code syntax* is displayed in the Field dialog box along with a text box that displays the actual characters in the field and a description of the selected field's purpose. The field code's syntax is shown in a format similar to a diagram, indicating optional and required information and the required order for inserting that information.

Exercise 21-1 SET FIELD CODE VIEW OPTIONS

Field codes might be displayed differently on different computers, depending on the selected options. To begin this lesson, you verify the display options for field codes.

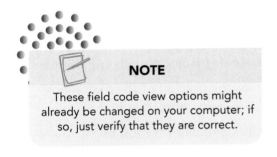

NOTE

These field code view options might already be changed on your computer; if so, just verify that they are correct.

1. Open the file **Promotion**.

2. Open the Word Options dialog box, click Advanced, and display the Show document content group.

3. Locate the option Show field codes instead of their values, and make sure the check box is clear. This will keep the codes from displaying in your document—the field results will show instead.

4. Locate the Field shading option. Open the Field shading: list box and choose Always. This will highlight fields with light gray shading. The shading will display on your screen but will not print.

Figure 21-1
Setting view options for field codes

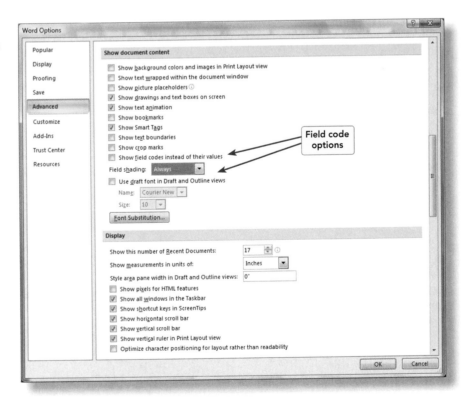

5. Click OK to close the Word Options dialog box.

Exercise 21-2   USE VARIOUS DATE FIELDS

When you insert a date field by using the **Date and Time** command on the **Insert** tab, you insert the current date in text form. If you choose the **Update automatically** option, a date field is inserted and updated to reflect the current date each time you open the document. Other date and time fields are available that display the date the document was created, the date it was last printed, or the date it was last saved.

1. Place the insertion point to the right of the text "Date Created:" and press ⌷Tab⌷.

2. Click the **Insert** tab, click the Quick Parts button 📋, and click **Field** to open the Field dialog box.

3. Open the **Categories** drop-down list and choose **Date and Time**. From the **Field names** list, choose **CreateDate** if it is not already highlighted.

4. Click the Field Codes button ⌷Field Codes⌷ at the bottom of the dialog box. Notice the field code syntax under the **Field codes:** text box.

5. Make sure the **Preserve formatting during updates** option in the lower portion of the dialog box is checked. This option ensures that any formatting you apply to the field—such as bold or underline—will be preserved if the field's result or value changes.

Figure 21-2
Field dialog box

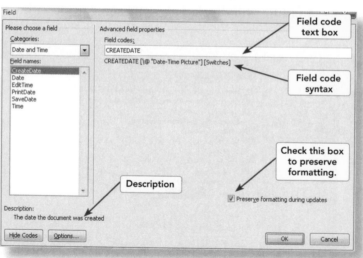

TIP

If you see codes instead of a date and time, remember to change the settings for field codes in the Word Options dialog box.

6. Click **OK**. The date and time that the document was first created appears. It is shaded, indicating that it is a field rather than text. Remember that the shading will not print.

7. Insert a tab character after the words "Date Last Revised:" and then reopen the Field dialog box.

8. Choose **SaveDate** from the **Date and Time** category, and then click **OK**. The date and time that the document was last saved appears.

9. To insert the **PrintDate** field on the line with the text "Date Last Printed:," follow steps 1 through 6 again.

Exercise 21-3 EXPLORE OTHER TYPES OF FIELDS

1. Insert a tab character after the words "Number of Pages:" and then reopen the Field dialog box.

2. Choose the Numbering category. The field names for the numbering category include BarCode and Page.

3. Choose another category and examine its list of field names.

4. Choose the Document Information category, choose NumPages, and then click OK. The number of pages contained in the document is displayed.

Viewing, Editing, and Updating Field Codes

While editing your document, it is sometimes convenient to see which options you have added to a field and to edit them directly in the document. You can easily toggle between the field code and the field result when necessary.

The date codes you inserted display the date and time in the default date format. You can choose other field properties in the Field dialog box to change the field format. The field code options available depend on the field code you choose. Some field codes enable you to choose more than one option at a time. When you choose one or more options, they are added to the field code text box, preceded by a backslash (\). These added options are called *switches*.

Exercise 21-4 CHANGE FIELD PROPERTIES

The Field properties section of the Field dialog box lets you change formatting and other features of the fields in your document. For example, you can change a date from a short format to a long format, and you can change case and number formats if appropriate for that field.

1. Drag the I-beam over the date on the "Date Created" line, but do not select the paragraph mark. The entire date is selected.

Figure 21-3
Selecting a field

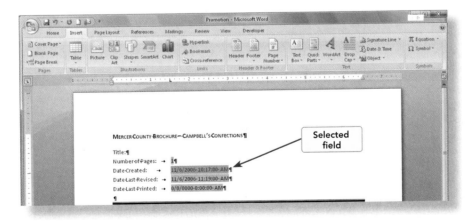

Word 2007

2. Click the Insert tab, click the Quick Parts button 📄, and click **Field** to open the Field dialog box.

3. Choose **CreateDate** from the **Date and Time** category.

4. From the **Date formats** list, choose the fifth date format. The text **"yyyy-MM-dd"** appears in the **Date formats** text box. This format is for a four-digit year, two-digit month, and two-digit day. It does not display the time.

[Field Codes]

5. Click the **Field Codes** button [Field Codes] and notice the "\@ "yyyy-MM-dd" switch (option) that is added to the end of the field code in the **Field codes:** text box.

[Hide Codes]

6. Click the **Hide Codes** button [Hide Codes] to return to the previous version of the dialog box.

7. Click **OK** to insert the changed field in your document.

8. Using steps 1–7, change the formatting of the other date fields to match. (Use the **SaveDate** field for "Date Last Revised:" and the **PrintDate** field for "Date Last Printed.")

TABLE 21-1 Useful Field Code Options

Field Result	Option	Switch	Result Example
Date or time	M/d/yy	\@ "M/d/yy"	1/9/09
	MM/dd/yyyy	\@ "MM/dd/yyyy"	01/09/2009
	MMMM d, yyyy	\@ "MMMM d, yyyy"	January 9, 2009
	dddd,MMMM d, yyyy	\@ "dddd,MMMM d, yyyy"	Sunday, January 9, 2009
	h:mm am/pm	\@ "h:mm am/pm"	11:30 pm
Numbering	1, 2, 3, . . .	* Arabic (default)	21
	I, II, III, . . .	* Roman	XXI
	One, Two, Three . . .	* CardText	twenty-one
	First, Second, Third . . .	* OrdText	twenty-first
	Dollar Text	* DollarText	twenty-one and 00/100
	0.00	\# "0.00"	21.00
	0%	\# "0 %"	21%
	$#,##0.00;($#,##0.00)	\# "$#,##0.00;($#,##0.00)"	$21.00
Text	Uppercase	* Upper	CAMPBELL
	Lowercase	* Lower	campbell
	Title case	* Caps	Campbell
	First capital	* FirstCap	Campbell conf.

Exercise 21-5   APPLY MULTIPLE OPTIONS TO A FIELD CODE

1. Select the field to the right of "Number of Pages:" (now displaying the numeral "1").

2. Open the Field dialog box. Choose **NumPages** from the **Document Information** category and choose **One, Two, Three** from the **Format** list.

3. Click **Field Codes**. Notice the switch "* **CardText**" appears in the **Field codes** text box, indicating that cardinal numbers will be displayed as text.

4. Click **Options** to open the Field Options dialog box.

5. Under the **Formatting** options list, scroll to the bottom and choose **Uppercase**; then click the **Add to Field**. Notice the switch "*Upper" is added to the field code in the **Field codes** text box. Now there are two options (switches).

6. Click **OK** twice to return to your document. The text "ONE" is displayed.

7. On a new line under the "Date Last Printed" line, key **Filename:** and press [Tab]. Create a hanging indent that aligns with the tab.

8. Open the Field dialog box. From the **Document Information** category, choose **FileName**.

9. Click **Field Codes** and then click **Options**.

10. Click the **Field Specific Switches** tab. With **\p** highlighted, click **Add to Field**.

11. Click **OK** twice. The filename along with the file path is now included in the document.

Exercise 21-6 VIEW AND EDIT FIELD CODES IN A DOCUMENT

When you display a field code in a document, the field code name and the options you selected are enclosed in curly braces. If you selected the Preserve formatting during updates option, the option (or switch) "* MERGEFORMAT" appears as part of the code. Also, field codes will not print automatically. You must set print options to print field codes.

Figure 21-4
Anatomy of a field code

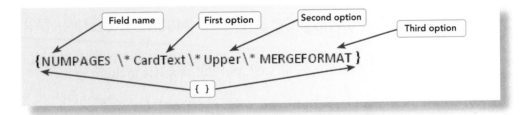

NOTE

If you were to print the document now, the field result would print instead of the field code. You must set print options to print field codes.

1. Right-click the **NumPages** field (displayed as "ONE"), and choose **Toggle Field Codes** from the shortcut menu. (Or click the field and press [Shift]+[F9].) The field code appears.

2. Select the text "Upper" within the code and replace it with **FirstCap**.

NOTE

When you edit field codes directly within a document, you must be absolutely sure you have the correct syntax. It is usually best to make changes by using the dialog boxes.

3. Right-click the field code again, and choose Toggle Field Codes from the shortcut menu. The field result is once again displayed, but the text is still uppercase. You must manually update the field code to see the new result. Field codes are automatically updated when you first open a document, but changes that you make while editing a field are not displayed in the current document until you manually update it.

Exercise 21-7 UPDATE FIELD CODES

1. Right-click the field containing "ONE," and choose Update Field from the shortcut menu. (Or click the field and press F9.) The capitalization is changed to "One."

2. Format the six lines below the title "Mercer County Brochure" (beginning with the "Title" line) in 10-point type.

3. Save the document as *[your initials]*21-7 in a new folder for Lesson 21.

4. Press Ctrl+A to select the entire document.

5. Right-click anywhere in the document, and choose Update Field. Now all the fields contain the most current information.

6. Resave the document.

Understanding Bookmarks

A *bookmark* is a named location in a document. It can be a group of characters or words, a graphic or other object, or simply an insertion point position. You can use bookmarks to jump to a place you designate in a document.

Exercise 21-8 INSERT A BOOKMARK

Bookmark names can include all letters of the alphabet and many other characters as well, but they cannot include spaces.

1. Select the heading below the horizontal line "Campbell's Confections" (do not include the paragraph mark in the selection).

2. Click the Insert tab, and locate the Links group. Click the Bookmark button to open the Bookmark dialog box. Two bookmarks have already been inserted in this document.

Figure 21-5
Inserting a bookmark

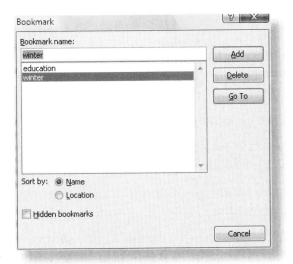

3. Under **Bookmark name**, key **BrochureTitle**. Do not key a space between the words.

4. Click **Add**. The bookmark is inserted, but the document might not indicate that anything has changed.

5. Open the **Word Options** dialog box. Click **Advanced**, and scroll to **Show document content**.

6. Click to select the **Show bookmarks** option.

7. Click **OK**. Deselect the bookmarked text, which is now contained in brackets. The brackets will not print, but they will help you see what you have bookmarked in the document.

Exercise 21-9 GO TO A BOOKMARK

Bookmarks provide a convenient way to navigate through a long document. Insert bookmarks at the beginning of important sections or chapters. Then use the **Go To** command to move quickly to the bookmarked locations.

1. Press ⌨Ctrl+⌨G. The Find and Replace dialog box opens, with the **Go To** tab selected.

2. Under **Go to what**, choose **Bookmark**.

3. Under **Enter bookmark name**, click the down arrow to see a list of bookmarks in this document.

4. Choose **winter** and then click **Go To**. The dialog box remains open, but the area of the document that includes "winter" is displayed. (The "winter" bookmark was inserted in the document previously.)

5. Open the bookmark name list again and choose **BrochureTitle**.

6. Click **Go To**. Now the bookmark you created is selected. (You might need to drag the Find and Replace dialog box out of the way to see it.)

7. Click **Close** to close the Find and Replace dialog box.

Exercise 21-10   USE A BOOKMARK IN A FIELD

Another use for a bookmark is to insert it as part of a field. For example, the Ref field syntax requires a bookmark. The bookmark's text will appear where you insert the Ref field.

1. Insert a tab character after the text "Title:" at the top of the document.

2. Click the **Insert** tab, click the Quick Parts button 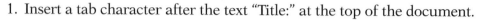, and click **Field** to open the Field dialog box.

3. Choose **Links and References** from the **Categories** list, and then choose the field name **Ref**.

4. Click **Field Codes**. Notice the field code syntax "**REF Bookmark [Switches]**". The name of the field is "**Ref**," and the bookmark name must follow the field name. "**Switches**" is enclosed in brackets to indicate that switches are not required, but if you use them, they must appear after the bookmark.

5. Make sure the **Preserve formatting during updates** check box is checked.

6. Click **Options**. The Field Options dialog box has three tabs.

7. Click the **Bookmarks** tab. All the bookmarks contained in the document are listed.

8. Choose **BrochureTitle** and then click **Add to Field**. The bookmark name is inserted after the field name Ref.

9. Click the **General Switches** tab. Under **Formatting**, choose **Title case**. Click **Add to Field**. The text "*Caps" is added to the field code.

Figure 21-6
Inserting a bookmark
in a field

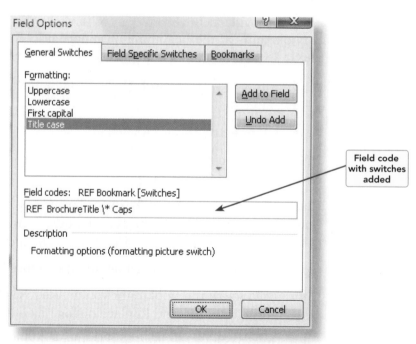

10. Click **OK** twice to close the dialog boxes and insert the field into the document. The text "Campbell's Confections" now appears in two places in the document-in the bookmarked text and in the **Ref** field you just created.

11. Right-click the **Ref** field, and choose **Toggle Field Codes** from the shortcut menu.

Figure 21-7
Completed REF field
code

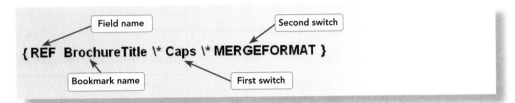

12. Verify that the field code is the same as Figure 21-7. If not, you can either edit it directly or delete the code and re-create it.

13. Toggle the field code again to display the field result.

NOTE

The type size of the text "Campbell's Confections" in the Ref field is 12 points even though the type size for the field code when you toggle it is 10 points. The field result takes on the type size of the bookmark text. A little later you will change the field result type size to match the field code type size.

Exercise 21-11 MAKE CHANGES TO BOOKMARK TEXT

You can change the text inside a bookmark if you do not delete all the characters between the brackets. Always leave at least one space or other character. If all the characters are deleted between the brackets, the bookmark will be deleted and you will need to create a new one in its place. (Remember, if you do not see the brackets, open the Word Options dialog box to turn them on.)

1. Position the insertion point in the bookmark below the horizontal line, between the words "Campbell's" and "Confections."

2. Key **Chocolate** and add a space where necessary. Notice that the **Ref** field you created at the top of the document still contains the text "Campbell's Confections."

3. Right-click the **Ref** field containing the text "Campbell's Confections," and then choose **Update Field** from the shortcut menu. The text in the field changes to reflect the change you made to the bookmark.

4. Select the **Ref** field result "Campbell's Chocolate Confections," and change the font size to 10 points.

Figure 21-8
Completed
document with field
results displayed

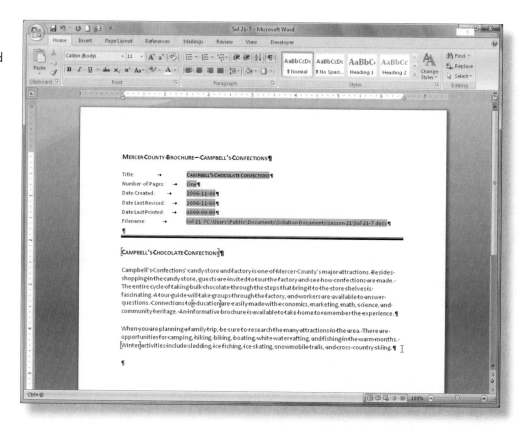

Exercise 21-12 USE PRINT OPTIONS FOR FIELD CODES

You can set print options to print field codes or to update fields automatically each time you print a document. If you set the option to print field codes, be sure to clear that option before printing the final document with the field results.

1. Save the document as *[your initials]21-12* in your Lesson 21 folder.

2. At the top of the document, update the filename field.

3. Open the Word Options dialog box, and click Advanced.

4. Scroll to the Print group.

5. Click to select the option Print field codes instead of their values. Click OK.

6. Print the document.

7. Open the Word Options dialog box, and click Advanced.

8. Scroll to the Print group.

9. Click to deselect the option Print field codes instead of their values. Click OK.

10. Open the Print dialog box, and click Options.

11. Click to select the option **Update fields before printing**. This assures that when you print the document, all fields will contain the most current information.

12. Click **OK** twice to print the document.

13. Save the document again, and then close it.

Creating a Template to Use as a Form

When creating an electronic form, you start with a template. The person filling out the form creates a new document based on your template form. When you base your form on a template, the template form remains unchanged and is available for use the next time the form needs to be completed.

Exercise 21-13 CREATE A TEMPLATE TO USE AS A FORM

1. Click the Microsoft Office Button, and click **New** to open the New Document dialog box.

2. Click **My templates** to open the New dialog box. Click the **Blank Document** icon.

Figure 21-9
Creating a new
blank template

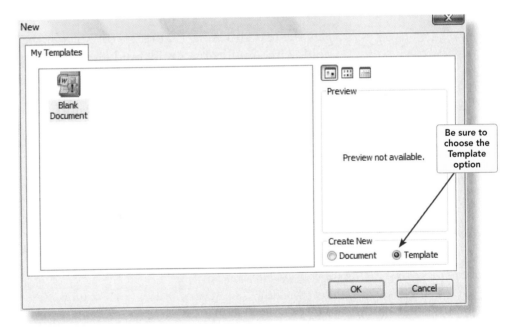

3. Under **Create New**, choose **Template** (in the lower right corner). Click **OK**. A new template, based on the Normal template, appears on your screen. Its temporary filename is Template1 (or another number).

4. Open the Font dialog box. Display the **Font** tab and choose **+Body**, **Regular**, **12** points.

5. Click **Default** in the lower left corner; then click **Yes** to change the default font. The default font is changed for all documents based on this new template. The Normal template's default font remains unchanged.

Exercise 21-14   KEY TEXT IN A FORM

When you create a form, a good idea is to create a rough draft or layout sketch first, including the text and the fields the form will contain. As you create the form, you key the standardized text and insert regular fields and content controls where needed. Keep the following in mind to decide what kind of field to use:

- Use a content control wherever you want the person using the form to key information.

- Use document information fields and other fields discussed previously when you want the form to insert the information automatically.

1. Key the text shown in Figure 21-10. Format the first line as 16-point bold, with small caps. Apply bold and small caps to the second line. Center the first two lines. Apply bold formatting to lines 3 through 6, and set a left tab at 1.75 inches. Change the paragraph spacing and line spacing where indicated in the figure. Set a left tab at 1.75 inches for the seventh line.

Figure 21-10

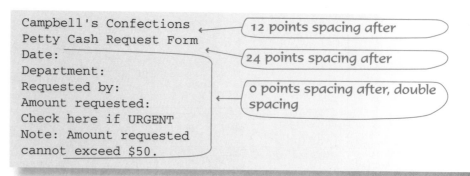

```
Campbell's Confections          12 points spacing after
Petty Cash Request Form
Date:                           24 points spacing after
Department:
Requested by:                   0 points spacing after, double
Amount requested:               spacing
Check here if URGENT
Note: Amount requested
cannot exceed $50.
```

2. Press Tab after the text "**Date:**," and then click the **Insert** tab. Click the Quick Parts button, and click **Field**.

3. Choose **CreateDate** from the **Date and Time** category, and then choose the third **Date format** option. Close the Field dialog box.

Insert Content Controls and Form Fields

Content controls and form fields enable users to key information in forms and to control the type of entry the user can make. Content controls are found on the Developer tab. Table 21-2 shows the seven content controls.

TABLE 21-2

Button	Description	Purpose
Aa	Rich text	Short paragraphs. Formatting can be saved.
Aa	Text	Plain text paragraph.
	Picture	Drawing, shape, chart, table, clip art, or SmartArt.
	Combo box	List that can be edited.
	Drop-down list	List of restricted choices.
	Date picker	Calendar control for entering date.
	Building Block gallery	Displays gallery options.

Exercise 21-15 INSERT A CONTENT CONTROL

1. Open the **Word Options** dialog box, and click **Popular**. Click to select the option **Show Developer in the Ribbon**. Click **OK**.

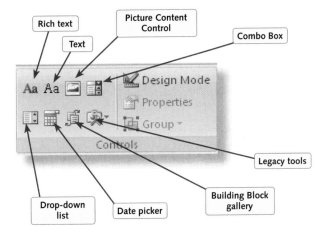

Figure 21-11
Controls group

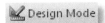

2. Click the **Developer** tab, and click the Design Mode button .

3. Position the insertion point after the text "Requested by:," and press Tab.

4. Locate the **Controls** group, and click the Rich Text content control button Aa . A content control is inserted at the insertion point. Notice the placeholder and the instructional text.

5. Position the insertion point after the text "Amount requested:," and press Tab. Insert another Rich Text content control.

Exercise 21-16   WORK WITH CONTENT CONTROL PROPERTIES

You can set or change properties for content controls. For example, you can change the style of the content control to format the contents.

To help people understand the kind of information you expect to be entered in your form, you can edit the instructional text.

1. Click within the **Requested by:** content control. The field is highlighted, indicating that it is selected.

2. Edit the placeholder text to read **Key first and last name**.

3. Click within the **Amount requested** content control, and change the instructional text to read **Key amount in currency format ($0.00)**.

4. Right-click the content control for **Requested by**, and click **Properties**. Key **Name** in the Title text box. Click **OK**. Right-click the content control for **Amount requested**, and click **Properties**. Key **Amount** in the **Title** text box. Click **OK**.

Figure 21-12
Setting content control properties

Exercise 21-17   INSERT A CHECK BOX FORM FIELD

A check box field works just like the check boxes you often use in dialog boxes. The person filling out your form can click to put an X in the box, or click again to remove the X.

1. Position the insertion point at the end of the line "Check here if URGENT." Press Tab.

2. Click the Legacy Tools button 🔲 to display Legacy Forms and Active X Controls. Click the Check Box Form Field button ☑ under **Legacy Forms**.

3. Right-click the Check Box Form Field, and choose Properties. The Check Box Form Field Options dialog box displays.

4. Under Check box size, click Exactly, and increase the size to 12 points. Click OK.

Exercise 21-18   INSERT A DROP-DOWN CONTROL

1. Click at the end of the line with the text "Department:" and press Tab.

2. Click the Drop-Down List content control button ⊞ . A Drop-Down List content control is inserted.

3. Click the Properties button ⟦ Properties ⟧ in the Control group on the Ribbon to open the Content Control Properties dialog box.

4. Key Department in the Title text box.

5. Click the Add button ⟦ Add... ⟧ .

6. Key Retail Sales in the Display Name text box, and click OK. Key each of the following entries for the Drop-Down List content control. Click Add (or press Enter) for each, key the name, and click OK or press Enter.

Wholesale Sales

Fundraising

Customer Service

Accounting

Human Resources

TIP

After you key an entry for the drop-down list, the OK button is automatically highlighted. Pressing Enter accepts the entry and returns you to the Content Control Properties dialog box with the Add button automatically selected. Press Enter to add a second entry. Consequently, it is not necessary to click the Add button and OK button.

Figure 21-13
Adding items to a drop-down form field

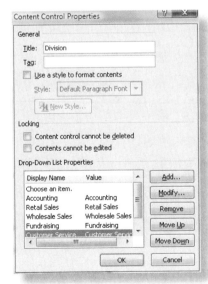

7. In the list of drop-down items, click Accounting, and then click the Move Up button ⟦ Move Up ⟧ four times. "Accounting" is now the first entry in the list.

8. Use the Move Up button or the Move Down button to alphabetize the list of departments. Click OK to close the dialog box. The first entry in the list becomes the default entry. You will see the entire list with a drop-down arrow when a document based on this form is created a little later in this lesson.

Protecting and Saving a Form

Before saving a form, you should protect it by locking it. When you *lock* a form, the person filling out the form has access only to the form fields. The other text, regular fields, and elements such as graphics are locked and cannot be changed by the user. This ensures that all documents created from the form will be uniform in layout and content.

Because a form is actually a special-purpose template, you save it in the same way you save a template.

Exercise 21-19 PROTECT A FORM

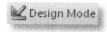

1. Click the Design Mode button to turn off Design Mode.

2. Click the Protect Document button ⬜. The Restrict Formatting and Editing task pane displays.

3. Locate the **Editing restrictions** section. Click the check box to **Allow only this type of editing in the document**. Click the drop-down arrow and choose **Filling in forms**. This option locks everything on the form except the content controls and the form fields.

Figure 21-14
Protecting a form

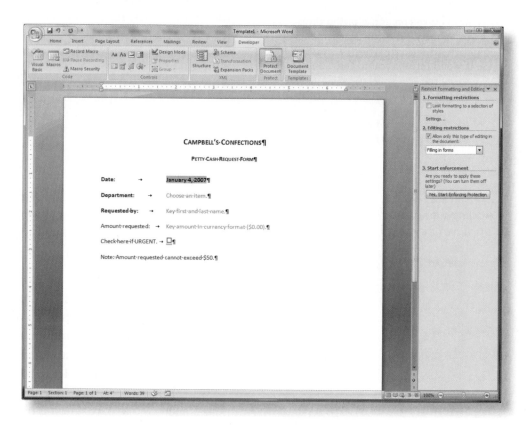

TIP

A password would prevent a user from unprotecting a document based on your form. Avoid passwords if you can, but if one is necessary, keep a duplicate copy of your form without a password in a safe place out of circulation. If you forget the password you used for the template and need to make changes later, you are out of luck unless you have an unprotected backup copy.

NOTE

By default, Word saves a new template (or form template) in the Templates folder on your hard disk. Before proceeding, ask your instructor where you should save your forms. If you use the default location (or a subfolder below it) or the Workgroup Templates file location (if one is specified), you can create new documents based on your form template by using the Templates dialog box. If you save your form in your Lesson 21 folder, you will use My Computer or Windows Explorer to create a new document.

4. Click **Yes, Start Enforcing Protection** in the Restrict Formatting and Editing task pane. Click **OK** to close the Start Enforcing Protection dialog box. Do not enter a password. Notice that the Protect Document button on the Ribbon displays a lock symbol, indicating that the form is now protected. Also notice the change in the Restrict Formatting and Editing task pane. Close the task pane.

5. Double-click the text **Campbell's** on the first line of the form. Notice that you cannot select it, because the form is protected.

6. Click the field to the right of "Department:" containing the text "Choose an item." A drop-down arrow and list appear.

7. Choose **Customer Service**. Notice that the text box expands to accommodate all the characters.

8. Click the Protect Form button on the Ribbon. Click **Stop Protection** to unprotect the form. Then click **Yes, Start Enforcing Protection**, and click **OK**, to protect it.

Exercise 21-20   SAVE A FORM

1. Check to make sure the form is protected.

2. Open the Save As dialog box. A folder named **Templates** should appear in the **Save in** box.

3. Save your form as a document template named *[your initials]***Form21-20** in your Lesson 21 folder (unless your instructor advises you to save in the default Templates folder).

4. Submit the form, and close the template.

Using and Editing a Form

A form is a special type of template. You use a form by starting a new document based on the form template. Depending on where you saved the template, you start the new document in one of the following ways:

NOTE

To create a new document based on your form, you can also right-click the template file and choose New from the shortcut menu. If you choose Open from the shortcut menu, the form template will open.

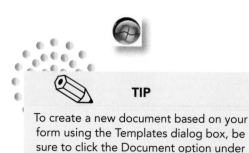

TIP

To create a new document based on your form using the Templates dialog box, be sure to click the Document option under Create New.

- If you saved the form template in the Templates folder, in a subfolder under the Templates folder, or in the Workgroup Templates folder, use the New dialog box to access the template you created.

- If you saved the form template in your Lesson 21 folder, right-click the Windows Start button and use the Windows Explorer to find and use your form template.

Exercise 21-21 CREATE A DOCUMENT BASED ON A FORM

1. Right-click the Windows Start button , and choose **Explore** from the shortcut menu.

2. In the **Folders** list, navigate to your Lesson 21 folder and click to open it.

3. In the Lesson 21 folder (on the right side of the Explorer window), locate the form template *[your initials]*Form21-20.

Figure 21-15
Creating a new document based on your form template

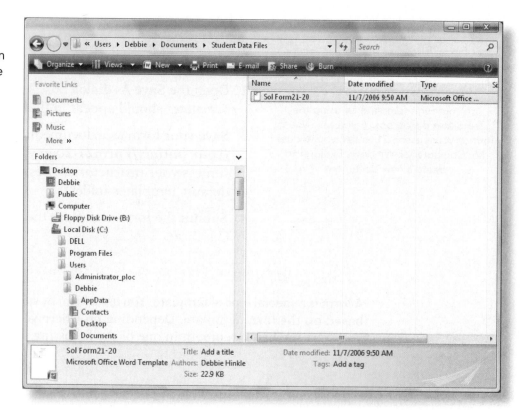

4. Double-click the file to start Word and a new document based on the form template.

Word 2007

Exercise 21-22 ENTER INFORMATION IN THE FORM DOCUMENT

When you create a document based on a form that has been protected, the first content control or form field is automatically selected and ready for you to enter information. You can navigate around a form document by clicking a content control or form field or by pressing Tab.

1. Click the content control next to "Department:" and choose Accounting from the drop-down list.

2. Press Tab to move to the next content control. Key Glenn Moore.

3. Click the Amount requested content control.

4. Key $40.00.

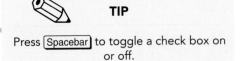

TIP

Press Spacebar to toggle a check box on or off.

5. Click the check box on the next line to place an "X" in the box, or press Spacebar to toggle the check box on.

6. Save the document as *[your initials]*21-22 in your Lesson 21 folder.

7. Submit the document and close it.

Exercise 21-23 CREATE A NEW FORM BASED ON AN EXISTING FORM

When you want to make changes to a form or to create a new form based on an existing one, you open the form and edit it in the same way as a document file, but with the following additional steps:

- You must change the Files of type setting in the Open dialog box to either Document Templates or All Files. If the setting is different, you will not see your form in the list of files.

- You must unprotect the document before you can edit it.

After opening an existing form, a good idea is to save it with a new name before making any changes. That way, you won't accidentally save to the existing form the changes intended for a new form.

1. Display the Open dialog box, and choose All Word Templates from the Files of type drop-down list.

2. Navigate to your Lesson 21 folder (or follow your instructor's directions).

3. Choose the form template *[your initials]*Form21-20, and then click Open.

4. Save the form as a template with the new name *[your initials]*Form21-23.

5. Click the **Developer** tab, and click the Protect Document button 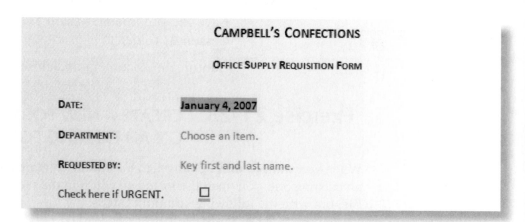. Click **Stop Protection**.

6. Make the following changes to the form (refer to Figure 21-16):

   • Delete the text "Petty Cash Request Form," and key in its place **Office Supply Requisition Form**. Verify that the text is bold and small caps.

   • Delete the line containing the text "Amount requested:" (including the content control.

   • Delete the last line that begins "Note."

   • Apply small caps formatting to "Date," "Department," and "Requested by."

Figure 21-16
Edited form

CAMPBELL'S CONFECTIONS
OFFICE SUPPLY REQUISITION FORM
DATE: January 4, 2007
DEPARTMENT: Choose an item.
REQUESTED BY: Key first and last name.
Check here if URGENT.   ☐

7. Insert a table at the end of the document measuring 4 columns by 12 rows. Refer to Figure 21-17 for content and column width. Select a table style that includes banded rows. Center the table horizontally, change the row height to 0.4 inch, and center the cell text vertically. Change the line spacing to single.

Figure 21-17
Sample table format

QTY.	ITEM NO.	DESCRIPTION	UNIT PRICE
[1" wide]	[1.25" wide]	[2" wide]	[1" wide]

8. Save the form. Submit and close the document.

Lesson 21 Summary

- A field is a placeholder for information that can change in a document. You can insert most fields into a document by using familiar Ribbon commands, such as inserting a page number in a header or footer or inserting a date in a letter.

- Every field contains a field code—text and instructions that will produce the field result.

- You can change field properties, such as changing the date format for a date code. You can also apply one or more field code options to some fields. These options are added to the field code text, preceded by a backslash (\) or switch. See Table 21-1.

- You can edit field codes directly in the document. To do this you toggle between the field result and the field code.

- When you display a field code in a document, the field code name and the options you selected are enclosed in curly braces. If you selected the Preserve formatting during updates option, the option (or switch) "* MERGEFORMAT" appears as part of the code.

- Field codes are automatically updated when you first open a document, but changes you make while editing a field are not displayed in the current document until you manually update it.

- A bookmark is a named location in a document. It can be a group of characters or words, a graphic or other object, or simply an insertion point position. Insert bookmarks at the beginning of important sections or chapters; then use the Go To command to move quickly to the bookmarked locations.

- You can change the text inside a bookmark if you do not delete all the characters between the brackets. Always leave at least one space or other character. If all the characters are deleted between the brackets, the bookmark will be deleted and you will need to create a new one in its place.

- If you have dollar amounts or other numerical values in a document, you can perform calculations on them by using the formula field and bookmarks.

- You can set print options to print field codes or to update fields automatically each time you print a document. If you set the option to print field codes, be sure to clear that option before printing the final document with the field results.

- There are two basic types of forms: (1) a paper form that you create by using normal editing tools and then print for someone to fill in by hand and (2) an electronic form that is based on a custom template and that a user completes in Word.

- When creating an electronic form, you start with a template. The person filling out the form starts a new document based on the template form.

- Before creating a form, create a rough layout sketch, including the text and the fields the form will contain. When you create the form in Word, you key the standardized text and insert regular fields and content controls where needed.

- Use a text control wherever you want the person using the form to key information. Use document information fields and other fields when you want the form to insert the information automatically.

- You can set content control options to control the formatting and the type of entry the user can make. To help people understand the kind of information you expect to be entered in your form, you can edit the instructional text that appears with the content control.

- Before saving a form, you should protect it by locking it. When a form is locked, the person filling out the form only has access to the content controls and form fields. The user cannot change the other form elements.

- You use a form by starting a new document based on the form template. Depending on where you saved the template, you create the new document by using the New dialog box or Windows Explorer.

- When you create a document based on a protected form, the first form field is automatically selected and ready for you to enter information. You can navigate around a form document by clicking a form field or by pressing Tab.

LESSON 21		Command Summary	
Feature	**Button**	**Command**	**Keyboard**
Insert a field		Insert tab, **Text** group, **Quick Parts**, **Field**	Ctrl + F9 (empty field)
Update selected field(s)		Shortcut menu, **Update Field**	F9
Toggle field codes		Shortcut menu, **Toggle Field Codes**	Shift + F9
Insert a bookmark	Bookmark	Insert tab, **Links** group, **Bookmark**	
Protect/unprotect a form	Protect Document	Developer tab, **Protect** tab	

Concepts Review

True/False Questions

Each of the following statements is either true or false. Indicate your choice by circling T or F.

T F 1. Fields can be created only in the Field dialog box.

T F 2. If you toggle field codes to see code rather than the result, the codes will always print.

T F 3. A field's syntax is the set of rules that describes how to construct the field.

T F 4. When you add an option to a field, it must be preceded by a backslash.

T F 5. Forms must always be saved in the Templates folder.

T F 6. Bookmark names cannot contain a space.

T F 7. Use the Text content control when formatting must be saved.

T F 8. When you protect a form, you must assign a password.

Short Answer Questions

Write the correct answer in the space provided.

1. What is a placeholder for information that can change in a document?

_____

2. What dialog box do you need to open to change the shading of a field code?

_____

3. How do the switches "* CardText * Upper" format a numerical field?

_____

4. What must you do to update a field code?

_____

5. If you open a protected form template, what must you do before you can edit the form?

_____

6. How do you insert a bookmark?

_____

7. How do you jump to a bookmark in a document?

_____

8. What is the result of the SaveDate field?

_____

Critical Thinking

Answer these questions on a separate page. There are no right or wrong answers. Support your answers with examples from your own experience, if possible.

1. The CreateDate field inserts the date a document was first created (or saved with a new name). The Date field displays the current date each time you open the document. When is the Date field appropriate to use in a document, and when should you instead use the CreateDate field?

2. When creating a report, are bookmarks something you would consider helpful? When might you use bookmarks in either a long or short document?

Skills Review

Exercise 21-24

Insert fields, change field properties, toggle the field code view, apply field options, and update fields.

1. Open the file **Inventory**.
2. Position the insertion point three lines below the table in the document. Key **Revision date:** and press [Spacebar].

3. Insert the date the document was last saved by following these steps:
   a. Click the **Insert** tab, click the Quick Parts button 📄, and click **Field**.
   b. Open the **Categories** list and choose **Date and Time**. Choose **SaveDate** from the **Field names** list.
   c. Choose the third date format from the **Date formats** list. "MMMM d, yyyy" should appear in the **Date formats** text box. Click **OK**.
4. Toggle to view the date's field code by following these steps:
   a. Right-click the date field.
   b. Choose **Toggle Field Codes** from the shortcut menu. Review the field code.
   c. Right-click the date field again.
   d. Choose **Toggle Field Codes** from the shortcut menu.

5. On a new line below "Revision date" line, key **File name:** and press
   Spacebar.

6. Insert the **Filename** field with the path option by following these steps:

   a. Click the **Insert** tab, click the Quick Parts button ⧉, and click **Field**.

   b. Click the **Document Information** category, and then click **FileName**
   from the **Field names** list.

   c. Click the **Field Codes** button and then click **Options**.

   d. Click the **General Switches** tab if it is not active, and then choose
   Lowercase.

   e. Click **Add to Field**.

   f. Click the **Field Specific Switches** tab.

   g. With the **\p** switch highlighted, click **Add to Field**.

   h. Click **OK** twice to close both dialog boxes.

7. Save the document as *[your initials]*21-24 in your Lesson 21 folder.

8. Update the fields by following these steps:

   a. Select the last two lines (which contain the fields).

   b. Right-click the selection, and choose **Update Field** from the shortcut
   menu.

9. Format the two lines containing fields as 10-point italic.

10. Add a right-aligned footer to the document. Key **Page** and then add the
    page number field.

11. Save the document again, submit the document, and close it.

Exercise 21-25

Change field display options; view, edit, and update field codes.

1. Open the file **Class**.

2. The date at the top of the letter is a field. If it is not shaded, follow these
   steps to display shaded fields:

   a. Open the **Word Options** dialog box.

   b. Click **Advanced** and scroll to the **Show document content group**.

   c. Locate **Field shading:**, and choose **Always**. Click **OK**.

3. Toggle to view the date's field code.

4. Modify the date format to eliminate the name of the day by following
   these steps:

   a. Select "dddd" within the field code and press Delete.

   b. Delete the comma and space that followed "dddd."

   c. Examine the resulting code, and make any necessary editing changes
   so it matches the following:

   { CREATEDATE \@ "MMMM dd, yyyy"* MERGEFORMAT }

   d. Use the shortcut menu to update the field.

5. Change the field name from "CREATEDATE" to "SAVEDATE" by following these steps:

   a. Display the date's field code.

   b. Double-click **CREATEDATE** within the field code to select it.

   c. Key **SAVEDATE**.

6. Insert your reference initials at the end of the document; then save the document as *[your initials]*21-25 in your Lesson 21 folder.

7. Update the field once more. Then save, submit, and close the document.

Exercise 21-26

Insert and go to bookmarks.

1. Open the file **Community - 2**.

2. Create a bookmark by following these steps:

   a. Select the text "Community Involvement" at the top of page 1. Be careful not to select the paragraph mark at the end of the line.

   b. Click the **Insert** tab, and click the Bookmark button .

   c. In the **Bookmark name** text box, key **DocTitle**. Be sure not to key a space between the words.

   d. Click **Add**.

3. Display the brackets surrounding the bookmark by following these steps:

   a. Open the **Word Options** dialog box.

   b. Click **Advanced** and scroll to **Show document content**. Click to select **Show Bookmarks**. Click **OK**.

4. Create bookmarks for the following terms, and name them appropriately. Remember not to key a space between words.

   United Way
   March of Dimes
   Humane Society
   Susan G. Komen Foundation
   Grove City Charitable League

5. Go to a bookmark by following these steps:

   a. Press Ctrl+G.

   b. Under **Go to what**, choose **Bookmark**.

   c. Under **Enter bookmark name**, click the down arrow to see a list of bookmarks in this document.

   d. Choose **DocTitle** and then click **Go To**.

6. Change the title to 18-point bold and italic.

7. Save the document as *[your initials]*21-26 in your Lesson 21 folder.

8. Add a right-aligned footer to every page. Key **Page** and then add the page number field.

9. Submit the document.

Exercise 21-27

Create a form template, insert content controls, and protect and save the form.

1. Create a template form by following these steps:

   a. Open the file **Telephone Order**.

   b. Open the Save As dialog box, and change the Save as type to Word Template.

   c. Save the document as *[your initials]*Form21-27 in your Lesson 21 folder.

2. Insert content controls by following these steps:

   a. Display the Developer tab by opening the Word Options dialog box, and clicking Popular. Click to select Show Developer tab in the Ribbon.

   b. Click the Developer tab, and click the Design Mode button 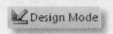.

   c. Position the insertion point to the right of "Date:" and press [Spacebar] two times.

   d. Click the Date Picker control button .

   e. Change the instructional text to read Enter today's date.

3. Click to the right of "Sold by:" and press [Spacebar] two times. Click the Rich Text control button . Change the instructional text to read Sales Associate.

4. Insert a Rich Text control to the right of each heading item under "Billing Information" and to the right of each heading item under "Shipping Information."

5. Add a title to the content controls by following these steps:

   a. Select the "Date" control, and right-click. Click Properties from the shortcut menu.

   b. Key Date in the Title text box, and select the third date format. Click OK.

NOTE

When you insert the content controls for the city, state, and zip code, the content control text may wrap to the next line.

6. Select each control in the Billing Information section and the Shipping Information section, and change the title for each. Use the shortcut menu or click the Properties button  on the Ribbon.

7. Insert a Drop-Down List control by following these steps:

   a. Click to the right of "Type of chocolate," and press [Spacebar] two times.

   b. Click the Drop-Down List control button .

   c. Right-click the control and click Properties.

   d. Click the Add button , and key Milk Chocolate in the Display Name text box. Click OK.

   e. Add Dark Chocolate and White Chocolate to the Drop-Down List Properties.

   f. Click OK to close the dialog box.

8. Insert a Drop-Down List control to the right of "Chocolate." Add the following items to the control properties:

   Nuts
   Creams
   Melt-a-ways
   Assorted

9. Insert a Rich Text control to the right of "Quantity," "Account No.," and "Expiration Date."

10. Insert a Check Box Form Field by following these steps:

    a. Click to the right of "Check."

    b. Click the Legacy Tools button , and click the Check Box Form Field button ✓.

11. Insert a Drop-Down List control to the right of "Credit Card." Add the following items to the control properties:

    Visa
    MasterCard
    Discover
    American Express

12. Protect the form by following these steps:

    a. Click the Design Mode button 🖊Design Mode to turn off the design feature.

    b. Click the Protect Document button 📄.

    c. Click to select the check box to Allow only this type of editing in the document.

    d. Click the drop-down arrow and click Filling in forms.

    e. Click Yes, **Start Enforcing Protection**. Click **OK**.

13. Save the template.

14. Submit and close the document.

Lesson Applications

Exercise 21-28

Insert fields inside a text box and change field properties.

1. Open the file **Tempering**.

2. Save the document as *[your initials]*21-28 in your Lesson 21 folder.

3. Scroll to the end of the document, and press [Enter]. Draw a text box approximately 2 inches wide by 2 inches tall.

4. Position the text box in the lower left corner of the document, aligned horizontally with the left margin and vertically with the bottom margin.

5. With the insertion point inside the text box, insert the FileName field from the Document Information category with the lowercase and path options.

6. Insert a new line in the text box. Key Revision Date: and press [Spacebar].

7. To the right of "Revision Date," insert the SaveDate field, using an appropriate date format of your choice.

8. Insert a new line in the text box. Key Word Count: and press [Spacebar].

9. To the right of "Word Count," insert the DocProperty field from the Document Information category. Choose Words from the Property list box. Click OK.

10. Format all the text inside the text box as 9-point italic.

11. Add your reference initials on a new line in the text box. Adjust the height and width of the text box to fit the text.

12. Save, submit, and close the document.

Exercise 21-29

Create a bookmark, insert fields, change field properties, view and edit fields, go to a bookmark, and update fields.

1. Open the document **Glossary**.

2. Save the document as *[your initials]*21-29 in your Lesson 21 folder.

3. Create a bookmark named Date for the date in the date line of the letter.

4. Format the document for a different first page for headers and footers, and change the header margin to 1 inch from the edge.

5. On page 2, create a continuation page header:

   - Key Mrs. Doris Forman as the first line of the header.

   - On a new second line, key the word Page and press [Spacebar]. Then insert the page number field.

- On a new third line of the header, insert the first type of date format for the CreateDate field.

- Insert two blank lines to make the header five lines long.

6. Display the field code in the header for the CreateDate field showing the date. Then change the date format to \@ "MMMM d, yyyy".

7. Update the field code, and then close the header pane.

8. Go to the "Date" bookmark, and replace the entire bookmark with a CreateDate field which has the same date style as the header.

9. Add your reference initials to the end of the document. Resave, submit, and close the document.

Exercise 21-30

Insert, view, edit, and update fields; insert and update formula fields that use bookmarks; and print field codes.

1. Open the file **Mercer**.

2. Replace the date with a CreateDate field, using the fourth date format.

3. Toggle the field code view for the date field.

4. Edit the date field switch to \@ "MMMM d, yyyy".

5. Update the field.

6. Create the following bookmarks for the dollar amounts in the first paragraph:

Amount	Bookmark name
$480	Deposit
$720	Total

7. Key the following sentence at the end of the first paragraph: Please send your final payment in the amount of.

8. Press Spacebar and open the Field dialog box. Display the Equations and Formula category, click the Field name =(Formula). Click Formula to open the Formula dialog box. Click the Paste bookmark down arrow, and click Total. Type a minus (−), and click the Paste bookmark down arrow, and click Deposit. Select the third format in the Number format drop-down list. Click OK.

9. Key the following after "$240": 30 days after the date of your invoice.

10. Change the total amount from "$720" to $840. (Do not delete the bookmark brackets.)

11. Update the formula field.

12. Add your reference initials at the end of the document.

13. Save the document as *[your initials]*21-30 in your Lesson 21 folder.

14. Update the date field again.

15. Submit the document, showing the field codes.

16. Submit the document again without the field codes, resave, and close it.

Exercise 21-31 ◆ Challenge Yourself

Create a form template that includes fields and content controls, and protect and save the form.

1. Open a new blank template; then key the form sketched in Figure 21-18. Format the heading attractively, choosing fonts and aligning text to make an attractive arrangement.

Figure 21-18

```
            Mid-Atlantic Confections Association
                    Annual Conference
                     Sponsored by
             The Nut and Fruit Plantation
              Conference Evaluation Form

1. Who was your group leader?      [Insert a drop-down list]

2. Please rate the registration process:

   The registration              ❏  Smooth
   process was:                   ❏  OK
                                  ❏  Tedious

   The registration              ❏  Helpful and efficient
   personnel were:               ❏  OK
                                  ❏  Not helpful

3. Please rate the information    ❏  Very useful
   presented:                     ❏  Somewhat useful
                                  ❏  Not at all useful

4. Please state briefly what you enjoyed the most (or least)
   about the conference:

   _____

   _____

5. Your name (optional): _____
```

2. Insert a drop-down form field at the end of question 1 where indicated on the figure. Include the following names in the drop-down list:

   Eddie Martin
   Jodie Berger
   Melissa Alvarez
   Jon McGill

3. Insert check box form fields where the figure indicates for questions 2 and 3.

4. Insert a Rich Text control in place of the line below question 4 and another Rich Text control to the right of question 5.

5. Protect the form, and then save it as a template named *[your initials]* **Form21-31** in your Lesson 21 folder (or follow your instructor's directions). Print the form and close it.

6. Open a new document based on the form, choosing **Melissa Alvarez** as your group leader and choosing whichever check boxes you want.

7. In the text form field for question 4, key the following: Ms. Alvarez was knowledgeable, presented her material clearly, and was very patient with all my questions.

8. In the text form field for question 5, key Your name.

9. Save the document as *[your initials]***21-31** in your Lesson 21 folder; then submit and close it.

On Your Own

In these exercises you work on your own, as you would in a real-life business environment. Use the skills you've learned to accomplish the task—and be creative.

Exercise 21-32

You are a volunteer at an animal shelter and have been asked to create a business letter form template for possible adopters, thanking them for their interest in a specific animal. Use Date, Rich Text, and Drop-Down content controls to complete the task. Format the letter appropriately, save the template as *[your initials]***Form21-32**, and submit it.

Exercise 21-33

You have been charged with keeping a current list of supplies on hand at your school's computer lab. Create a template using Drop-Down List and Rich Text content controls to make your job easier each month. Save the template as *[your initials]***Form21-33** and submit it. Use the template to create a current list of supplies. Save the document as *[your initials]***21-33** and submit it.

Exercise 21-34

Use the Internet to research three automobiles that interest you. Create a table with Rich Text and Drop-Down List content controls and check box fields to compare the features of each car. Record information on class of car, interior and exterior features, price, reliability and safety records, and other features that you want to include. Save the table as a template with the name *[your initials]***Form21-34** and submit it. Open the template as a new document and record your findings. Save the document as *[your initials]***21-34** and submit it.

Lesson 22

Macros

After completing this lesson, you will be able to:

1. Create a macro.

2. Run a macro.

3. Edit a macro.

4. Copy, rename, and delete macros.

5. Customize the Quick Access toolbar.

MCAS OBJECTIVES

In this lesson:
WW 07 1.4.1
WW 07 6.1.1
WW 07 6.2
WW 07 6.3

Estimated Time: 1¹⁄₂ hours

A Word *macro* enables you to quickly perform repetitive tasks involving command sequences and keystrokes. With a macro, you can save a sequence of tasks as a single command. Then you can execute one command to perform the entire sequence automatically. A macro can include Ribbon commands, formatting options, keystrokes, and dialog box selections. For example, you can create a macro that automatically converts text to an attractively formatted table.

Creating a Macro

When you create macros, you store them in either a document or a template. By default, Word stores macros in the Normal template; however, it is usually best to store special-purpose macros in a special-purpose template. You can attach the template to a document when you need to use its stored macros, AutoText, or styles.

Sometimes it is better to use styles or AutoText instead of a macro. Here are some guidelines for deciding:

- Use AutoText to save standard text paragraphs, sometimes called *boilerplate* text. Use a macro to automate the insertion of AutoText.

- Use paragraph or character styles to save special formatting.

- Use AutoText to save specific text that is formatted in a special way.

- Use a macro to combine several Ribbon and dialog box choices that you use regularly—for example, inserting a sequence of AutoText entries or applying special formatting to a table.

Exercise 22-1 CREATE AN AUTOTEXT ENTRY TO USE WITH A MACRO

REVIEW

To create the AutoText entry, select all the lines, starting with "Sincerely" and ending with your reference initials. Click the Insert tab, and click the Quick Parts command. Click Save Selection to Quick Part Gallery. Key Signature in the Name box. Select AutoText in the Gallery box. Select Campbell Letter - 1 in the Save in box. Click OK.

1. Display the Open dialog box. Change the type of file box to Word Macro-Enabled Template. Open the template **Campbell - Letter 1** from the folder and directory holding the student data files. This template contains a letterhead and a date field. Two AutoText entries are also stored in the template.

2. On the last line of the template, create a signature block using Sincerely as the closing, Tamara Robbins, Fundraising Department as the author, and your reference initials.

3. Create an AutoText entry from the signature block. Name it Signature and store it in the **Campbell Letter - 1** template.

4. Delete the signature block you just created. (Remember that it is now an AutoText entry.)

5. Save the template as *[your initials]***LetterTemplate1** in a new folder for Lesson 22.

Exercise 22-2 PREPARE TO RECORD A MACRO

NOTE

When naming a macro, be careful not to use names of existing built-in Word macros. If you do, your macro actions will replace the built-in Word macro actions. To see a complete list of built-in macro names, click the Developer tab on the Ribbon, and locate the Code section. Click the Macros button 🔲, and select Word Commands in the Macros in list box.

Before beginning a macro recording, you should plan the steps you want the macro to perform, choose a name for it, and decide where it will be stored.

The macro created in this exercise will be stored in the currently open template. It will insert a boilerplate closing paragraph and the signature block AutoText entry you created in the previous exercise.

1. Display the Developer tab on the Ribbon by clicking the Microsoft Office Button and clicking Word Options. Click Popular, and click Show Developer in the Ribbon. Click OK.

Word 2007

2. Click the Record Macro button . In the **Macro name** text box, key **LetterClosing1**. Like merge-field names, macro names must not contain spaces and must begin with an alphabetic character.

NOTE

If you attempt to record a macro by using an invalid macro name, you will get an error message stating "Invalid procedure name." If this happens, click **OK** and start with step 1 again, remembering to key a macro name that does not contain spaces.

3. Under **Store macro in**, choose **Documents Based On** *[your initials]***LetterTemplate1**.

4. In the **Description** box, key **Inserts closing paragraph 1 and the signature block for Tamara Robbins**.

Figure 22-1
Record Macro
dialog box

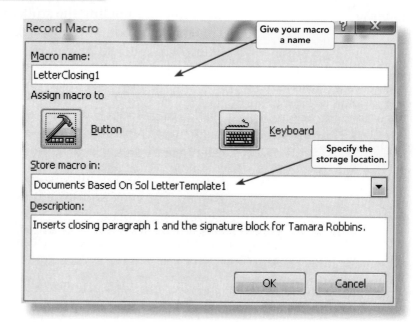

5. Click the **Keyboard** icon. This opens the Customize Keyboard dialog box, where you can assign a keyboard shortcut to your macro.

TIP

To avoid conflicts with built-in Word keyboard shortcuts, choose a keyboard combination that uses Alt plus a letter or number character.

6. With the insertion point in the **Press new shortcut key** text box, press Alt + 1. The message "**Currently assigned to: [unassigned]**" appears under the **Current Keys** text box. If you choose a key combination that is already assigned to a Word command, delete your choice and try a different key combination.

7. Under **Save changes in**, choose *[your initials]***LetterTemplate1**, if it is not active.

Figure 22-2
Customize Keyboard
dialog box

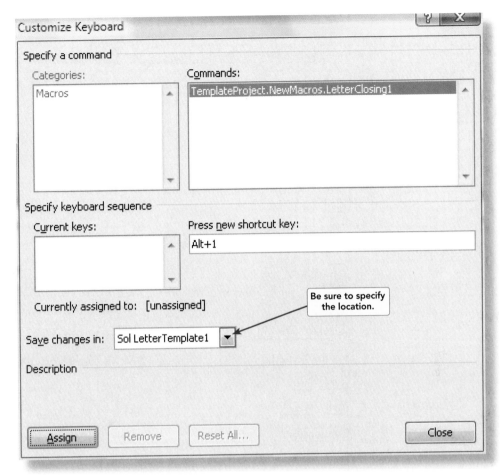

8. Click **Assign** to assign the shortcut keys. The key combination Alt + 1 now appears in the **Current keys** list.

9. Click **Close**. The Stop Recording toolbar appears, and the mouse pointer changes to the recording pointer.

Exercise 22-3　RECORD A MACRO

When you see the recording pointer ⌕, every action you take with the mouse or the keyboard is being recorded in your macro.

You cannot use the macro pointer to select text or move the insertion point. It is not possible to record mouse movements in a macro. Use the macro pointer to select Ribbon commands and to move within a dialog box. Use keyboard equivalents for selecting text or repositioning the insertion point.

TABLE 22-1 Shortcut Keys for Navigating, Selecting, and Deleting in a Document

Keystroke	Result
←	Move one character to the left.
→	Move one character to the right.
Ctrl + ←	Move one word to the left.
Ctrl + →	Move one word to the right.
Ctrl + ↑	Move one paragraph up.
Ctrl + ↓	Move one paragraph down.
↑	Move up one line.
↓	Move down one line.
End	Move to the end of a line.
Home	Move to the beginning of a line.
Ctrl + Page Down	Move to the top of the next page.
Ctrl + Page Up	Move to the top of the previous page.
Ctrl + End	Move to the end of a document.
Ctrl + Home	Move to the beginning of a document.
Backspace	Delete one character to the left.
Ctrl + Backspace	Delete one word to the left.
Delete	Delete one character to the right or delete selected text.
Ctrl + Delete	Delete one word to the right.
Shift + →	Select one character to the right.
Shift + ←	Select one character to the left.
Ctrl + Shift + →	Select to the end of a word.
Ctrl + Shift + ←	Select to the beginning of a word.
Shift + End	Select to the end of a line.
Shift + Home	Select to the beginning of a line.
Shift + ↓	Select one line down.
Shift + ↑	Select one line up.
Ctrl + Shift + ↓	Select to the end of a paragraph.
Ctrl + Shift + ↑	Select to the beginning of a paragraph.
Ctrl + Shift + Home	Select to the beginning of a document.
Ctrl + Shift + End	Select to the end of a document.
Ctrl + A	Select to include the entire document.

1. Using the recording pointer, click the **Insert** tab, and click the Quick Parts button ▣. Click **Building Blocks Organizer**, and click the entry for **ClosingParagraph1**. Click **Insert**. The paragraph is inserted into the template.

2. Click the Quick Parts button ▣. Click **Building Blocks Organizer**, and click the entry for **Signature**. Click **Insert**. The signature block is now inserted below the closing paragraph.

3. Click the **Developer** tab, and click the Stop Recording button  on the Ribbon. The mouse pointer returns to its normal shape, indicating that the recording is completed.

4. Delete the paragraph and signature block you inserted while recording the macro. Your template should have a letterhead, date, and four blank lines below the date.

5. Resave the template.

> ✏️ **TIP**
>
> You can record a macro even if you do not have any documents open on the screen. This enables you to record in a macro the steps to open a document.

Running a Macro

If you assigned a shortcut key to a macro when you recorded it, the easiest way to run the macro is to press the shortcut key combination. You can also run a macro from the Macros dialog box, in which you can list all the macros in the current template, the normal template, or the Word built-in macros.

Exercise 22-4 SET MACRO SECURITY

Security settings for macros are located in the Trust Center. To view or change settings, open the **Word Options** dialog box and either click **Trust Center** and then **Trust Center Settings** or click the Macro Security command in the Code group of the Developer tab. There are four settings for macros:

- Disable all macros without notification.

- Disable all macros with notification (default).

- Disable all macros except digitally signed macros.

- Enable all macros (not recommended; potentially dangerous code can run).

Figure 22-3
Trust Center dialog
box

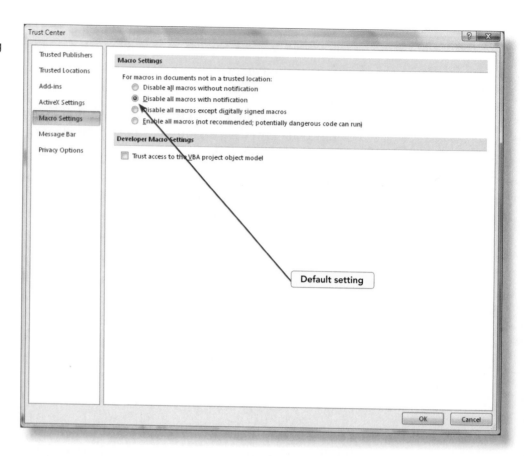

You may have occasion to work with documents containing macros that were created by another user. Since macros can threaten the security of your computer and contribute to the spread of a virus, you should exercise caution when running macros. The Trust Center settings determine what happens on your machine when you run a macro. A security dialog box may appear with options to enable the macro or to leave it disabled. Do not enable the macro unless you know it is from a trustworthy source.

NOTE

Digitally signing a macro and recording trusted sources is an advanced topic. If you are interested, you can learn more about it using the Help feature.

Macros may include a digital signature, which is an encrypted stamp of authentication. The signature ensures that the macro originated from the signer and has not been altered. Digital signatures are issued by a commercial organization. When macros are not signed, the identity of the macro publisher cannot be verified by the Trust Center. It is possible to create your own digital certificate.

1. Display the **Developer** tab, and click the Macro Security button ⚠ Macro Security.

2. Click **Macro Settings**.

3. View the **Macro Settings**, and verify that **Disable all macros with notification** is selected. Click **OK**.

4. Close the template, resaving it if necessary.

Exercise 22-5 RUN A MACRO

1. Reopen the template you just created. Be sure to open the template and not a new document based on the template.

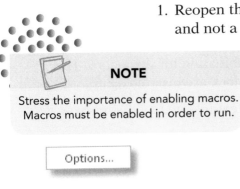

NOTE

Stress the importance of enabling macros. Macros must be enabled in order to run.

Options...

2. Notice the security warning that appears below the Ribbon indicating that macros have been disabled.

3. Click the Options button Options... to open the Microsoft Office Security Options dialog box shown in Figure 22-4, allowing you to choose to enable or disable macros.

Figure 22-4
Microsoft Office Security Options dialog box

Microsoft Office Security Options

Security Alert - Macro

Macro
Macros have been disabled. Macros might contain viruses or other security hazards. Do not enable this content unless you trust the source of this file.

Warning: It is not possible to determine that this content came from a trustworthy source. You should leave this content disabled unless the content provides critical functionality and you trust its source.

More information

File Path: C:...lic\Documents\Solution Documents\Lesson 22\Sol LetterTemplate1.dotm

○ Help protect me from unknown content (recommended)

○ Enable this content

Open the Trust Center   OK   Cancel

4. Click **Enable this content**, and click **OK**. Move the insertion point to the end of the template.

5. Click the **Developer** tab, and click the Macros button . Verify that *[your initials]***LetterTemplate1** is selected from the **Macros in** list box. **LetterClosing1** is the only macro listed.

6. Select **LetterClosing1** and click **Run**. The closing paragraph and the signature block are inserted at the insertion point.

7. Click the Undo button 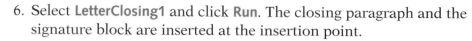 twice to remove the signature block and closing paragraph from the template.

8. Press Alt+1, the shortcut key combination for the macro. The closing paragraph and signature block are inserted again.

9. Press Ctrl+Z twice to remove the text inserted by the macro.

Exercise 22-6   CREATE A MACRO THAT CONVERTS TEXT TO A TABLE

1. With the insertion point four lines below the date, insert the file **AddrText**. A tab-delimited address list is inserted.

2. Select all the text in the address list.

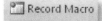

3. Click the **Developer** tab, and click the Record Macro button. The Record Macro dialog box opens.

4. Key **MakeTable** in the **Macro name** text box.

5. Under **Store macro in**, choose **Documents Based On *[your initials]*LetterTemplate1**.

6. Under **Description**, key **Converts selected tab-delimited text to a formatted table.**

7. Click the **Keyboard** button. Under **Press new shortcut key**, press Ctrl+Shift+T.

8. Under **Save changes** in, choose *[your initials]*LetterTemplate1, if it is not active.

9. Click **Assign** and then click **Close**.

10. With the recording pointer, click the **Insert** tab, and click the Table button. Choose **Convert Text to Table**. The Convert Text to Table dialog box opens.

11. Under **Separate text at**, make sure **Tabs** is chosen. Click **OK**.

12. Click the **Table Tools Design** tab, and click the More arrow to display the Table Styles gallery.

13. Click a style in the second row of the Built-In styles. Locate the Table Style Options group on the Table Tools Design tab, and verify that the **First Column** option is not checked.

Figure 22-5
Choosing a table
style

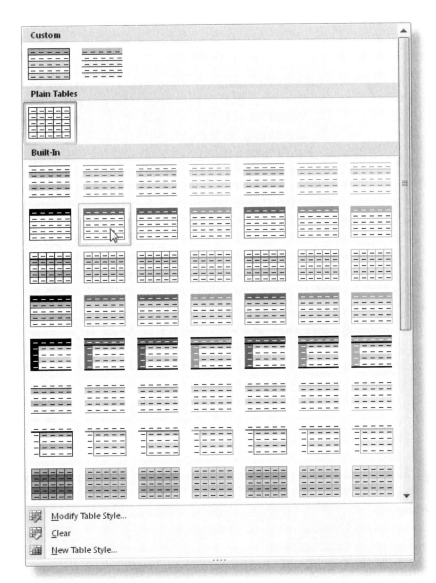

14. Click the **Table Tools Layout** tab, and click the AutoFit button . Click **AutoFit Contents**.

15. Click the Properties button and click the **Table** tab.

16. Under **Alignment**, choose **Center** and click **OK**. The table is now horizontally centered on the page.

17. Press ⬇ once to deselect the table.

18. Click the **Developer** tab, and click the Stop Recording button . The address list is now a formatted table.

19. Click the Undo button five times to change the table back to a tab-delimited list. (Pressing Undo will not remove the macro.)

20. Make sure all the text in the list is selected, and then press Ctrl+Shift+T (the keyboard shortcut you assigned) to run the MakeTable macro.

Editing a Macro

When you record a Word macro, a computer program is created that uses Visual Basic for Applications. Even if you do not understand Visual Basic programming, you can do simple editing to change your macro—if you are careful.

The Visual Basic Editor is made up of several windows that you can display or hide, depending on the task you are performing. When you edit a recorded macro, the Project Explorer window and the Code window are displayed. *Code* is programmer terminology for the text written in the Visual Basic language (or other programming language) that makes up a macro or program.

The MakeTable macro will be successful only for tables that are six columns wide. The number of columns and the number of rows are *hard-coded*, meaning that the exact number of rows and columns is written into the program. You can safely delete the part of the program that specifies the number of columns and the number of rows to make the macro work for any number of rows and columns.

Exercise 22-7   EDIT A MACRO

1. Click the Macros button or press [Alt]+[F8] to open the Macros dialog box.

2. In the **Macros in** text box, choose **LetterTemplate1 (template)**, choose **MakeTable**, and then click **Edit**. The Microsoft Visual Basic Editor window opens.

Figure 22-6
Microsoft Visual Basic window

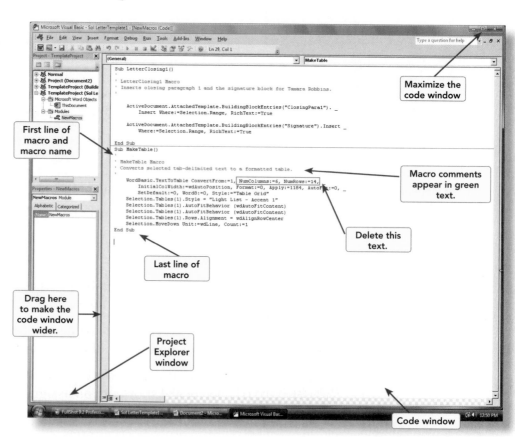

NOTE

Your screen might look slightly different from the figure. For instance, your Project Explorer window might not appear when the Visual Basic window opens.

NOTE

Comments are not part of the actual macro program. A comment can contain any text that identifies the macro or makes it easier to understand. Each comment line must begin with an apostrophe.

TIP

If a line of code turns red while you are editing, there is an error in the code. If you can't figure out how to fix it, press Ctrl + Z to undo the editing and try again.

3. If necessary, maximize the Code window and drag its left edge to make it wide enough to display the entire width of the code (text).

4. Using Figure 22-6, locate the various parts of the MakeTable macro: the first line and macro name, "Sub MakeTable()"; the last line, "End Sub"; and the comments, which are the green lines beginning with an apostrophe.

5. In the MakeTable macro, locate the text "WordBasic. TextToTable." TextToTable is a Word built-in macro. When working in a document, if you choose Table, Convert, Text to Table, Word automatically runs the TextToTable macro. The code that follows on the next several lines of the macro specifies various table settings.

6. Notice that many lines end with a space and an underscore (_). The underscore is a symbol that represents a line continuation. In other words, the complete command with all its settings is too long to fit on one line. When editing, make sure you do not delete an underscore and the space before it.

7. In the MakeTable macro, select the text "NumColumns:=6," (including the space before and the comma after) and delete it. Use Figure 22-7 to help you locate the text. This part of the code tells Word to make the table six columns wide. If the number of columns is not specified, Word will adjust the number of columns to the number of tabs in a row of selected text.

8. Select the text "NumRows:=14," and delete it.

Figure 22-7
MakeTable macro
after editing

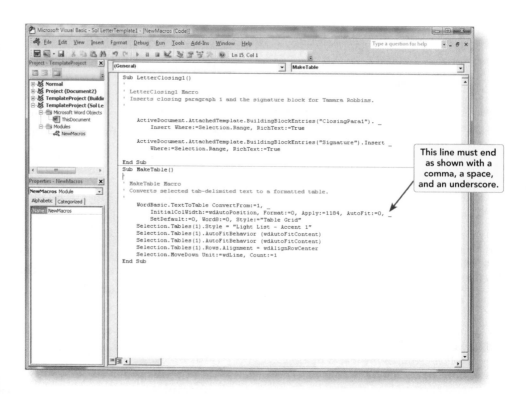

NOTE

When you record a macro that inserts AutoText, the default is to insert the AutoText as unformatted text. This will not be apparent until you actually run a macro that inserts AutoText that has special formatting. To force your macro to insert the AutoText with its formatting intact, add the text "Richtext:=True" to the end of the line that inserts an AutoText entry.

9. Click the Save button  on the Visual Basic Editor's toolbar; then click **File** and **Close and Return to Microsoft Word** (or press Alt+Q) to close the Visual Basic Editor window.

Exercise 22-8   TEST CHANGES MADE TO A MACRO

To test the MakeTable macro, try it on a tab-delimited list that requires a number of columns other than six.

1. Move to the bottom of the template, below the table, and insert two blank lines.

2. Insert the file **Fund 3** at the insertion point.

3. Select all lines of the inserted text.

4. Press Ctrl+Shift+T to run the MakeTable macro. A formatted table appears.

5. Delete both tables from the template, and make sure there are only four blank lines below the date. Resave the template. It should now contain a letterhead, a date, and four blank lines below the date.

6. Open the Print dialog box, and choose **Key assignments** from the **Print what** drop-down list. Print the key assignments, and then close the template.

Exercise 22-9 CREATE A LETTER BY USING MACROS

1. Start a new document based on *[your initials]***LetterTemplate1**.

2. Click **Options** in the Security Warning area, and **Enable this content**. The new document based on your template opens.

3. Key the text in Figure 22-8, formatting it as a standard business letter.

Figure 22-8

```
Mr. Robert Briggs
543 Hermitage Road
Transfer, PA 16154

Dear Mr. Briggs:

Thank you for your recent letter regarding Campbell's
Confections Fundraising Program. The following table lists
several order options including cost and profit.
```

REVIEW

To open a document based on a template saved in your Lesson 22 folder, use Windows Explorer or My Computer to navigate to the folder. Locate the file *[your initials]***LetterTemplate1**, and double-click it (or right-click it and choose New from the shortcut menu).

4. On the second line below the paragraph you keyed, insert the file **Fund 3**.

5. Select all the tabbed text, and press Ctrl+Shift+T to run the MakeTable macro.

6. Position the insertion point two lines below the table, and then press Alt+1 to run the LetterClosing1 macro.

7. Save the document as *[your initials]***22-9** in your Lesson 22 folder. Submit and close the document, saving changes.

Copying, Renaming, and Deleting Macros

You can edit, rename, or delete macros by using the Macros dialog box. Simply select the macro and click the appropriate button. To copy macros from one document or template to another, use the Organizer. You might already be familiar with using the Organizer for moving or copying styles from one template to another. In the same way, you can move and copy macros from one template to another.

Exercise 22-10 COPY MACROS

When you record a macro, it is stored in a *module*. In Word, a module is a container attached to a document or template, where macros and other program code is stored. All recorded macros are stored in a module named "NewMacros." If you want to copy macros from one template to another, you copy the NewMacros module. All macros contained in the module are copied to the new template.

1. Open the template file **Letterhead 3**. This template contains two AutoText entries similar to the ones in the file *[your initials]*LetterTemplate1, but it contains no macros.

2. Press Alt + F8 to open the Macros dialog box. Notice that there are no macros listed. You will copy macros from LetterTemplate1, so you can use the LetterClosing1 macro created earlier in this lesson.

3. Click the Organizer button to open the Organizer dialog box.

4. Click the Macro Project Items tab. The left side of the dialog box lists modules in the current template or document—in this case, **Letterhead 3**. The right side lists the document or template you will use to copy modules to or from, currently Normal.

5. On the right side of the dialog box, click Close File. The Normal template closes, and the Close File button changes to Open File.

6. Click Open File on the right side of the dialog box and navigate to your Lesson 22 folder.

7. Choose *[your initials]*LetterTemplate1 and click Open. The module NewMacros appears in the list on the right.

Figure 22-9
Copying the
NewMacros module

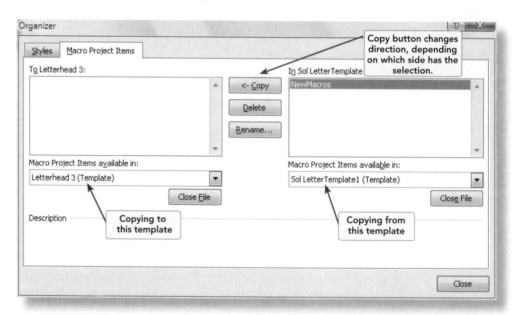

8. Make sure NewMacros is selected in the list on the right side, and then click Copy to copy all the macros in the NewMacros module to the list on the left side. Click Close.

9. Save the template as *[your initials]*LetterTemplate2 in your Lesson 22 folder. Be sure to choose Word Macro-Enabled Template from the Save as type list box.

10. Press Alt + F8 to reopen the Macros dialog box. Two macros now appear in the list.

Exercise 22-11 COPY AN INDIVIDUAL MACRO

You can copy and paste a macro within a module. This can be convenient if you have a useful macro that can serve a different purpose with a few changes.

To copy a macro, select the macro name in the Macros dialog box and then click **Edit**. In the Visual Basic Editor window, select all of the macro's text and then click **Copy**. Place the insertion point at the beginning of the first line of an existing macro, or place it on a new line at the end of the module; then click the **Paste** button.

1. If necessary, reopen the Macros dialog box.

2. Select **LetterClosing1** and click **Edit**. The Visual Basic Editor opens, with the LetterClosing1 macro displayed at the top of the code window.

3. Select all the text in the macro, beginning with "Sub LetterClosing1()" and ending with "End Sub," as shown in Figure 22-10.

4. Click the Copy button 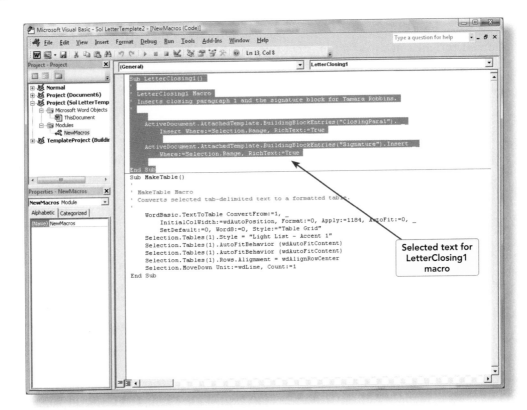 on the Visual Basic toolbar.

Figure 22-10
Copying an
individual macro

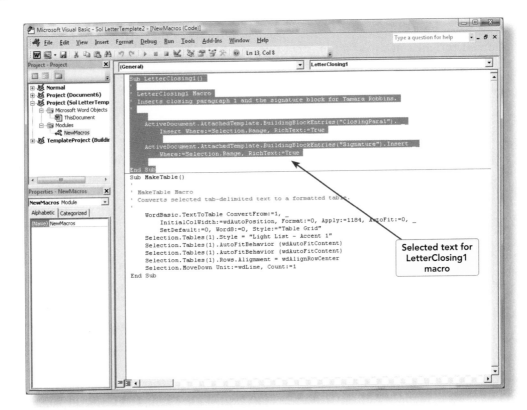

5. Scroll to the bottom of the code window, and position the insertion point on a blank line below the MakeTable macro.

6. Click the Paste button on the Visual Basic Standard toolbar. A copy of LetterClosing1 appears.

Exercise 22-12   RENAME A MACRO

Because a module cannot contain two macros with the same name, you must rename the copy of LetterClosing1. To do that, you edit the text after the word "Sub" on the first line of the macro.

1. On the first line of the pasted macro, change the text "Sub LetterClosing1()" to **Sub LetterClosing2()**.

2. In the green comment text, change "LetterClosing1 Macro" to **LetterClosing2 Macro**. Change "paragraph 1" to **paragraph2** and change "Tamara Robbins" to **Lydia Hamrick**.

3. On the first line below the green text, change the Building Block name from "ClosingPara1" to **"ClosingPara2"** (be sure to enclose the AutoText name in quotes). After editing, the end of the line should read: Building BlockEntries("ClosingPara2").

Be sure to include the parentheses, quotation marks, period, space, and underscore. The renamed and edited macro should agree with Figure 22-11.

Figure 22-11
Copied and renamed macro after editing

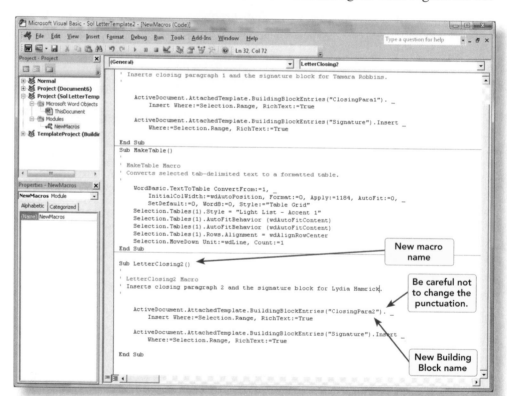

4. Click the Save button on the Visual Basic toolbar to resave the template.

5. Choose **Print** from the Visual Basic **File** menu, and then click **OK** to print a copy of your macro code. Close the Visual Basic window and return to Word.

6. Press Alt + F8 to open the Macros dialog box. Notice that three macros are now listed.

7. Select **LetterClosing2**. In the **Description** box, key **Inserts closing paragraph 2 and signature block for Lydia Hamrick**. Do not close the Macros dialog box.

Exercise 22-13 DELETE A MACRO

The easiest way to delete a macro is in the Macros dialog box.

TIP

You can also delete a macro in the Visual Basic Editor. Be careful to select the entire macro and nothing else. Then press Delete.

1. Reopen the Macros dialog box if it is not already open.

2. Select **LetterClosing1**.

3. Click **Delete** and then click **Yes**.

4. Click **Close** to close the Macros dialog box.

Exercise 22-14 ASSIGN A KEYBOARD SHORTCUT TO A COPIED MACRO

1. Open the **Word Options** dialog box, and click **Customize**. Near the bottom of the dialog box, locate the section **Keyboard Shortcuts**.

2. Click the **Customize** button at the bottom of the dialog box. The Customize Keyboard dialog box opens.

3. Under **Categories**, scroll to the bottom of the list and choose **Macros**.

4. Make sure *[your initials]*LetterTemplate2 is selected from the **Save changes in** list box.

5. Under **Macros**, choose **LetterClosing2**, if it is not active.

6. In the **Press new shortcut key** box, press Alt + 2.

7. Click **Assign** and then click **Close**.

8. Click **OK** to close the Word Options dialog box.

9. Resave the letter template and close it.

Customizing the Quick Access Toolbar

By now you have probably found several Ribbon commands that you use over and over again. You can add a Ribbon command to the Quick Access Toolbar. You can also assign a macro to the Quick Access Toolbar and change its position.

Exercise 22-15   ADD A COMMAND TO THE QUICK ACCESS TOOLBAR

The Quick Access Toolbar displays three commands by default. You can add additional commands, by customizing the Quick Access Toolbar. Use the Word Options dialog box or click the Customize Quick Access Toolbar button to add commands to the Quick Access Toolbar. You can also right-click selected buttons on the Ribbon to open the Word Options dialog box.

1. Create a new document.

2. Click the Customize Quick Access Toolbar button ⬇ located on the right side of the Quick Access Toolbar. A list of commands displays.

Figure 22-12
Quick Access Toolbar command list

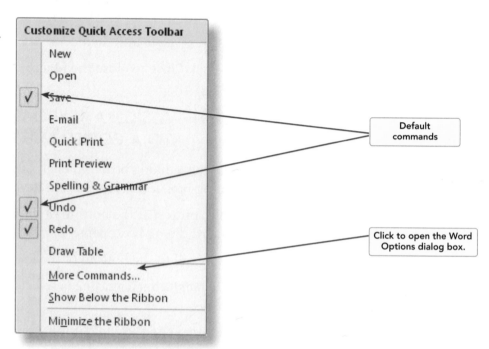

3. Notice that the three default commands are selected as indicated by the checkmarks.

4. Click **Print Preview**. The Print Preview button appears in the Quick Access toolbar.

Figure 22-13
Customized Quick Access Toolbar

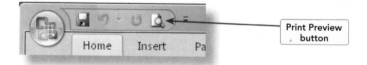

5. Click the Customize Quick Access Toolbar button ⬇, and click **More Commands**. The **Word Options** dialog box opens with **Customize** selected.

Figure 22-14
Word Options:
Customize

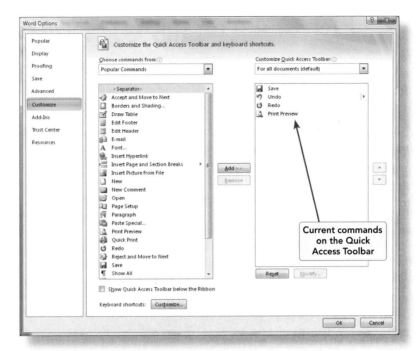

6. Click the down arrow to open the drop-down list box for **Choose commands from**. Select the **Popular Commands** category. Drag the scroll box to locate the **Spelling and Grammar** command. Click the command to select it, and click the Add button 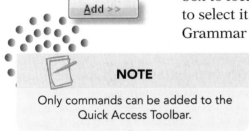. The Spelling and Grammar command is added to the Quick Access Toolbar. Click **OK**.

NOTE

Only commands can be added to the Quick Access Toolbar.

7. Notice the appearance of the Quick Access Toolbar with the additional button.

8. Open the File menu, and right-click **Print**. Click **Add to Quick Access Toolbar**. The Print command is added to the Quick Access Toolbar.

Figure 22-15
Shortcut menu to customize the Quick Access Toolbar

Exercise 22-16   MOVE THE QUICK ACCESS TOOLBAR

The default location for the Quick Access Toolbar is beside the Microsoft Office Button. You can change its position by placing it below the Ribbon.

1. Click the Customize Quick Access Toolbar button ⛌, and click **Show Below the Ribbon**.

2. Click the Customize Quick Access Toolbar button ⛌ again, and click **Show Above the Ribbon**.

Exercise 22-17   ASSIGN A MACRO TO THE QUICK ACCESS TOOLBAR

When you record a macro, you can assign the macro to appear on the Quick Access Toolbar.

1. Click the **Developer** tab, and click the Record Macro button .

2. Key **InsertPageNumber** in the **Macro name** box. Remember not to insert spaces between the words. Click the down arrow for the **Store macro in** box, and click **Document1 (document)**. (Your document number may differ from Document 1.)

3. Click Button ▨.

4. Locate the heading **Choose commands from** in the Word Options dialog box. Click **Project.NewMacros.InsertPageNumber**.

5. Locate the heading **Customize Quick Access Toolbar** on the right side of the Word Options dialog box. Select **For Document1** (or the document number that appears).

6. Click **Add**. Click **OK**.

7. Record the macro by following these steps:

8. Click the **Insert** tab, and click the **Footer** button. Scroll through the footer style gallery, and click **Pinstripes**. Close the Header and Footer pane. Click the **Developer** tab, and click the Stop Recording button ▣ Stop Recording . Notice the macro button on the Quick Access Toolbar.

Exercise 22-18   RESET THE QUICK ACCESS TOOLBAR

1. Open the Word Options dialog box, and click **Customize**.

2. Click **Reset**. Click **Yes** to restore the Quick Access Toolbar. Click **OK**.

3. Close the document without saving.

Lesson 22 Summary

- A Word macro enables you to quickly perform repetitive tasks involving command sequences and keystrokes. With a macro, you can save a sequence of tasks as a single command.

- When you create macros, you store them in either a document or a template. By default, Word stores macros in the Normal template, but it is best to store special-purpose macros in a special-purpose template.

- Before beginning a macro recording, plan the steps you want the macro to perform, choose a name for it, and decide where it will be stored.

- When you see the recording pointer 📄, every action you take with the mouse or the keyboard is being recorded in your macro.

- You can assign a macro to a button, the Quick Access Toolbar, or to a keyboard shortcut key, which you can then use to run the macro. You can also run a macro from the Macros dialog box.

- When you record a Word macro, a computer program is created that uses Visual Basic for Applications. You can change the macro by carefully editing the Visual Basic code.

- You can use the Macros dialog box to edit, rename, or delete macros.

- You use the Organizer to copy macros from one document or template to another.

- You can customize the Quick Access Toolbar by adding and deleting commands.

LESSON 22		Command Summary	
Feature	**Button**	**Command**	**Keyboard**
Open the Macros dialog box	Macros	**Developer** tab, **Code** group	Alt + F8
Close the Visual Basic Editor		**File, Close and Return to Microsoft Word**	Alt + Q
Set macro security	Macro Security	**Developer** tab, **Code** group	
Edit a macro	Macros	**Developer** tab, **Code** group	Alt + F8
Customize the Quick Access Toolbar		**Customize Quick Access Toolbar, More Commands**	

Concepts Review

True/False Questions

Each of the following statements is either true or false. Indicate your choice by circling T or F.

T F   1. The pointer 📃 indicates that a macro is being recorded.

T F   2. When a macro is being recorded, you can use the special mouse pointer to select text.

T F   3. You should never use the [Shift] key when assigning shortcuts to macros.

T F   4. Unless you are an advanced programmer, you should never delete the underscore (_) at the end of a line when editing a macro.

T F   5. The code for a macro always ends with the words "End Sub."

T F   6. By default, macros are saved in a separate file named NewMacros.

T F   7. You can key anything you want in comments, as long as each line begins with an apostrophe.

T F   8. You can use the Word Options dialog box to customize the Quick Access Toolbar.

Short Answer Questions

Write the correct answer in the space provided.

1. What dialog box do you use to copy a macro module from one template to another?

_____

2. What do you do to tell Word you have finished recording a macro?

_____

3. What color are comment lines?

_____

4. If a line in a macro you are editing turns red, what does it mean?

_____

5. What do you call the container where macros are stored?

_____

6. On what line of a macro do you find the macro's name?

_____

7. What dialog box must be open before you can remove a command from the Quick Access Toolbar?

_____

8. How do you rename a macro?

_____

Critical Thinking

Answer these questions on a separate page. There are no right or wrong answers. Support your answers with examples from your own experience, if possible.

1. Describe briefly three word-processing tasks you think a macro could simplify.

2. Which buttons would you include on a customized Quick Access Toolbar and why?

Skills Review

Exercise 22-19

Create and run macros.

1. Start a new template.

2. Save the template as *[your initials]*LetterTemplate3 in your Lesson 22 folder. Select Word Macro-Enabled Template in the Save as type box.

3. Start a macro recording by following these steps:

   a. Click the Developer tab, and click Record Macro .
   b. In the Record Macro dialog box, under Macro name, key InsertLogo.
   c. Under Store macro in, select Documents Based On *[your initials]*LetterTemplate3.
   d. Under Description, key the description Inserts letterhead logo.

   e. Click the Keyboard button to open the Customize Keyboard dialog box.
   f. Under Press new shortcut key, press Ctrl + Alt + Shift + L.
   g. Under Save changes in, make sure *[your initials]*LetterTemplate3 is selected.
   h. Click Assign and then click Close. The recording pointer appears.

4. Record the steps to insert the logo, as follows:

    a. Click the **Insert** tab, and click **Picture**.

    b. Locate the folder for the student data files, and click the file **Letterhead Logo**.

    c. Click **Insert**, and click the Stop Recording button ⬛ Stop Recording .

    d. Delete the logo.

    e. Press Ctrl + Alt + Shift + L to test-run the macro. Press Ctrl + Z.

5. Create a macro to insert a watermark by following these steps:

    a. Click the **Developer** tab, and click the Record Macro ⬜Record Macro .

    b. In the Record Macro dialog box, under **Macro name**, key InsertWatermark.

    c. Under **Store macro in**, select **Documents Based On *[your initials]*LetterTemplate3**.

    d. Under **Description**, key the description **Inserts corporate watermark**.

    e. Click the **Keyboard** button to open the Customize Keyboard dialog box.

    f. Under **Press new shortcut key**, press Ctrl + Alt + Shift + W.

    g. Under **Save changes in**, make sure *[your initials]*LetterTemplate3 is selected.

    h. Click **Assign** and then click **Close**. The recording pointer appears.

6. Record the steps to insert the watermark, as follows:

    a. Click the **Page Layout** tab, and click **Watermark**.

    b. Click **Custom Watermark**, and click **Select Picture**. Locate the folder for the student files, and click the file **Monogram**. Click **Insert**. Verify that **Washout** is checked, and click **OK**.

    c. Click the Stop Recording button ⬛ Stop Recording .

    d. Undo the watermark.

    e. Press Ctrl + Alt + Shift + W to test-run the macro.

    f. Undo the watermark.

7. Resave the letter template, and print the key assignments by following these steps:

    a. Working in the document window, open the **Print** dialog box.

    b. Under **Print what**, choose **Key assignments**. Click **OK**.

8. Close the template.

9. Start a new document based on *[your initials]*LetterTemplate3. Enable the macros by clicking **Options**.

10. Press Ctrl + Alt + Shift + L to run the InsertLogo macro.

11. Insert a CreateDate field below the logo with appropriate format.

12. Save the document as *[your initials]*22-19 in your Lesson 22 folder. Submit and close the document, saving changes.

⬛ Stop Recording

Exercise 22-20

Create an AutoText entry and create a macro that uses the AutoText entry.

1. Open the template file **Letterhead3**.

2. On the last line of the template, create a signature block keying Sincerely, and press Enter four times.

3. Key Lynn Tanguay, then press Enter and key Vice President. Press Enter two times, and key your reference initials.

4. Save the template as a Word Macro-Enabled Template named *[your initials]*Campbell Letterhead in your Lesson 22 folder, but do not close it.

5. Select the entire signature block, including your reference initials.

6. Create an AutoText entry for the signature block, and name it SignatureBlock. (Be sure to select AutoText for the Gallery and *[your initials]*Campbell Letterhead as the location for storing the AutoText entry.)

7. Delete the signature block from the template.

TIP

To create an AutoText entry, click the Insert tab, click Quick Parts, and click Save Selection to Quick Part Gallery.

8. Start a macro recording named SignatureBlock that is stored in *[your initials]*Campbell Letterhead. Enter an appropriate description for inserting a signature block. Assign the keyboard shortcut Ctrl+Shift+Alt+S.

9. Record the macro by following these steps:

   a. Click the Insert tab, and click Quick Parts. Click Building Blocks Organizer.

   b. Choose SignatureBlock.

   c. Click Insert.

   d. Click the Developer tab, and click the Stop Recording button 🔲 Stop Recording .

10. Delete the signature block; then resave the template and close it.

11. Start a new document based on the *[your initials]*Campbell Letterhead template. Enable macros.

12. Use the following information for an inside address and a salutation:

    Ms. Elizabeth Craemer
    Harold James Keller Group
    182 South Street
    Ganister, PA 16693

13. For the body of the letter, insert the file **Craemer**.

14. Run the SignatureBlock macro.

15. Add an enclosure notation, and change the bottom margin to .5.

16. Save the document as *[your initials]*22-20 in your Lesson 22 folder. Submit and close the document, saving changes.

Exercise 22-21

Copy a macro module to a different template, rename a macro, and delete a macro.

1. Open the template file **Retail Addresses**. This template contains AutoText entries, but it has no macros.

2. Copy a macro module from a different template by following these steps:

    a. Press Alt + F8 to open the Macros dialog box.

    b. Click the Organizer button to open the Organizer dialog box. Display the Macro Project Items tab.

    c. On the right side of the dialog box, click Close File.

    d. Click the Open File, navigate to your student disk or folder, and then select **Ohio Logos**. Click Open.

    e. Select NewMacros in the Ohio Logos list box, and click Copy.

    f. Click Close to close the Organizer dialog box.

3. Save the template as *[your initials]*OhioLogos in your Lesson 22 folder.

4. Rename a macro by following these steps:

    a. Press Alt + F8 to open the Macros dialog box.

    b. Select AkronLogo and click Edit.

    c. Locate the text "Sub AkronLogo()" and change it to Sub AkronLetterhead().

    d. Click Save, and then close the Visual Basic window to return to Word.

5. Assign keyboard shortcuts to all the macros by following these steps:

    a. Open the Word Options dialog box, and click Customize.

    b. Click the Customize button to open the Customize Keyboard dialog box.

    c. Under Categories, choose Macros (at the bottom of the list).

    d. Make sure *[your initials]*OhioLogos is selected in the Save changes in list box.

    e. From the Macros list, select AkronLetterhead.

    f. In the Press new shortcut key box, press Ctrl + Alt + Shift + A.

    g. Click Assign, but do not close the dialog box.

    h. Assign an appropriate keyboard shortcut for ClevelandLogo.

    i. Click Close to close the Customize Keyboard dialog box. Then click OK to close the Word Options dialog box.

6. Delete a macro by following these steps:

    a. Press Alt + F8 to open the Macros dialog box.

    b. Select CantonLogo from the list of macros.

    c. Click **Edit**.

    d. Select all the text for the CantonLogo macro, starting with the line "Sub CantonLogo()" and ending with the line "End Sub."

    e. Press Delete.

    f. Click **Save**.

7. Print the macro code by following these steps:

    a. Still working in the Visual Basic Editor, choose **File** and **Print**.

    b. Click **OK**, and then close the Visual Basic Editor window.

8. Print key assignments and close the template.

9. Start a new document based on the template *[your initials]***OhioLogos**. Enable macros.

10. Using the key assignments you printed, run a logo macro of your choice.

11. Imagine you work for Campbell's Confections. Create a business letter to include a date, an inside address, salutation, and one paragraph.

12. Include a closing, and use your name as the writer.

13. Save the document as *[your initials]***22-21** in your Lesson 22 folder. Submit and close the document, saving changes.

Exercise 22-22

Copy a macro, edit a macro, print macro code, and customize the Quick Access Toolbar.

1. Open the template file **Candy Classes**. This template contains three special styles: CompanyName, ClassName, and Quarter.

2. Key the following text on three lines:

    Campbell's Confections
    Candy Making Classes
    Fall Schedule

3. Save the template as *[your initials]***CandyClasses** in your Lesson 22 folder.

4. Start recording a new macro named ClassHeading with the description Formats the first three lines of a document as a centered heading. Assign the keyboard shortcut Ctrl + Shift + Alt + H. Make sure the macro will be stored in the *[your initials]***CandyClasses** template.

5. Record the steps to apply styles to each heading line, as follows:

    a. Press Ctrl + Home to move the insertion point to the top of the document.

    b. Apply the style CompanyName to the first line.

    c. Press ↓ once to move to the second line, and then apply the style ClassName.

    d. Press ⬇ once again to move to the third line, and then apply the style **Quarter**.

    e. Stop recording.

6. Customize the Quick Access Toolbar by following these steps:

    a. Click the Customize Quick Access Toolbar button , and click **More Commands**.

    b. Click the down arrow for the **Choose Commands from** box, and click **Commands Not in the Ribbon**.

    c. Scroll to locate **Small Caps**. Click to select **Small Caps**, and click **Add**. Scroll to **Quick Print**, and click to select the command. Click **Add**.

    d. Click **OK**. The Quick Access Toolbar displays two new buttons.

7. Create three new styles for the three lines of text. Name them **Favorite1**, **Favorite2**, and **Favorite3**. Choose appropriate font and paragraph formatting for each style.

8. Remove the new commands from the Quick Access Toolbar by following these steps:

    a. Open the **Word Options** dialog box.

    b. Click **Customize**.

    c. Click the **Reset** button. Click **Yes** when the Reset Customizations message box displays.

    d. Click **OK** to close the Word Options dialog box.

9. Resave the template.

10. Copy an individual macro by following these steps:

    a. Press [Alt]+[F8] to open the Macros dialog box.

    b. Make sure ***[your initials]*CandyClasses** (template) is selected in the **Macros in** list box and **ClassHeading** is selected in the **Macro name** list box.

    c. Click **Edit**.

    d. Select all the macro code in the code window, and copy it to the Clipboard.

    e. Press ⬇ to move to the last line in the code window.

    f. Click the Paste button.

11. Edit the copied macro by following these steps:

    a. Change the macro name from "ClassHeading" to **FavoriteHeading**. Remember to change the comment lines as well.

    b. Locate the three style names "CompanyName," "ClassName," and "Quarter." Change the style names to **Favorite1**, **Favorite2**, and **Favorite3**.

12. Save the macro code and then print it. Close the Visual Basic window to return to Word.

13. Assign the keyboard shortcut [Ctrl]+[Shift]+[Alt]+[F] to the FavoriteHeading macro and [Ctrl]+[Shift]+[Alt]+[C] to the ClassHeading macro.

14. In the Macros dialog box, enter an appropriate description for the FavoriteHeading macro.

TIP

Be careful to make sure each style has the correct punctuation. Example: ActiveDocument.Styles("Favorite1").

15. To test the macro, press [Ctrl]+[Shift]+[Alt]+[C] to apply the ClassHeading macro. Then press [Ctrl]+[Shift]+[Alt]+[F] to apply the FavoriteHeading macro.

16. Delete all the text in the template, and then apply the Normal style to the remaining paragraph mark.

17. Resave the template, print the key assignments, and then close the template.

18. Start a new document based on the *[your initials]***CandyClasses** template. Enable macros.

19. Key the following text on three separate lines:

    Campbell's Confections
    Chocolate Tempering
    Winter Schedule

20. Save the document as *[your initials]***22-22** in your Lesson 22 folder.

21. Run the ClassHeading macro, save, and submit the document.

22. Run the FavoriteHeading macro and save the document as *[your initials]***22-22b** in your Lesson 22 folder

23. Submit and close the document.

Lesson Applications

Exercise 22-23

Create a macro that changes page orientation to landscape and another macro that changes to a two-column format.

1. Start a new template.

2. Create a letterhead of your own design, using the following information:

   Campbell's Confections
   25 Main Street
   Grove City, PA 16127
   Phone 724-555-2025
   www.campbellsconfections.biz

3. Insert four blank lines below the letterhead.

4. On the third line below the letterhead, key Chocolates.

5. Select "Chocolates," center it, and format it as 14-point Arial, with bold, italic, and small caps.

6. Save the template as a macro-enabled template *[your initials]*Chocolates in your Lesson 22 folder.

7. Record a macro named Landscape, and store it in the *[your initials]*Chocolates template. Enter appropriate descriptive text in the description box. Assign the keyboard shortcut Ctrl + Shift + Alt + L. In this order, change the orientation to landscape, set 0.5-inch top and bottom margins, and set 1-inch left and right margins.

8. When the macro is completed, change the page orientation back to portrait with 1-inch top and bottom margins and 1-inch left and right margins. Resave the template.

9. Record a second macro named TwoColumns, and store it in *[your initials]*Chocolates with an appropriate description. Assign the keyboard shortcut Shift + Ctrl + Alt + C. This macro should create a two-column layout with 0.5-inches between columns that is applied from the insertion point to the end of the document.

10. When the macro is completed, click the Undo button to change the number of columns back to one. Then resave the template.

11. Print the template's key assignments, and close the template.

12. Create a new document based on *[your initials]*Chocolates. Enable macros.

13. Position the insertion point three lines below "Chocolates," and insert the file **Chocolate Terms**.

14. Position the insertion point at the beginning of the first line of inserted text ("Chocolate Terms").

15. Run the Landscape macro and the TwoColumns macro. (Press Ctrl + Shift + Alt + L and then Ctrl + Shift + Alt + C, but remember to run the TwoColumns macro from the beginning of the inserted text.)

16. Insert a column break at the beginning of the line with the text "White Chocolate." Delete the heading "Chocolate Terms." Select the text, and apply 12 points spacing after.

17. Save the document as *[your initials]*22-23 in your Lesson 22 folder. Submit and close the document, saving changes.

Exercise 22-24

Create a macro that inserts an AutoText picture; copy the macro, rename it, and edit it to insert a different AutoText picture.

1. Open the file **ChocPic** as a template. This template contains a letterhead and a picture from the Microsoft Clip Gallery that has been formatted to be behind the text and to allow overlapping.

2. Select the picture, and then click the **Picture Tools Format** tab. Click the Brightness button ⚹ Brightness and click **+40%**.

3. Save the template as *[your initials]*ChocPic in your Lesson 22 folder.

4. With the background picture selected, create an AutoText entry named ColorBackground in the template *[your initials]*ChocPic.

5. Click the Recolor button on the Picture Tools Format tab, and change the background picture to Grayscale. Click the Brightness button ⚹ Brightness and click **+40%** to make the image lighter.

6. With the background picture selected, create a second AutoText entry named GrayscaleBackground in *[your initials]*ChocPic.

7. Delete the background picture so only the letterhead is displayed.

8. Record a macro named ColorPicture in *[your initials]*ChocPic that inserts the ColorBackground AutoText entry. Add an appropriate description.

9. When you finish recording the macro, delete the background picture.

10. Open the Visual Basic Editor by selecting the macro in the Macros dialog box and clicking **Edit**.

11. Copy the entire macro and then paste a copy below it.

12. Change the name of the copied macro to GrayscalePicture, editing the comments where necessary.

13. In the macro code, change the text "("ColorBackground")" to ("GrayscaleBackground"), the name of the other AutoText entry.

14. Save the file and print the macro code. Close the Visual Basic Editor.

15. Working in the Word document window, open the Macros dialog box and change the description for the GrayscalePicture macro.

16. Assign the keyboard shortcut Ctrl + Shift + Alt + G to the GrayscalePicture macro and Ctrl + Shift + Alt + C to the ColorPicture macro.

TIP

Key the text before running the background picture macro. Keying text on top of a graphic can be difficult.

17. Resave the template, print the key assignments, and then close the template.

18. Create a new document based on the template; then key the text shown in Figure 22-16, formatting and arranging it attractively on the page. Adjust line breaks if needed to enhance your design.

Figure 22-16

```
You are cordially invited to attend

A presentation and lecture

"Chocolate Enrobing"

Presented in our auditorium

By world-renowned chocolatier

Jenna Bergen

8 p.m. on Thursday, October 12, 20—
```

19. Run the GrayscalePicture macro by pressing Ctrl + Shift + Alt + G. Save the document as *[your initials]*22-24gray then submit the document.

20. Delete the background picture, and then run the ColorPicture macro by pressing Ctrl + Shift + Alt + C.

21. Save the document as *[your initials]*22-24color in your Lesson 22 folder. Close the document, saving changes.

Exercise 22-25

Create macros to change page orientation and to format a table. Copy the table macro, and edit the macro to create a second table format.

1. Start a new template.

2. Save the new template as macro-enabled template *[your initials]*Tables in your Lesson 22 folder.

3. Record a macro that changes page orientation to portrait with 1-inch margins for the top, bottom, left and right. Name it PortraitPage, and assign the keyboard shortcut Ctrl + Shift + Alt + P. Store the macro in the *[your initials]*Tables template.

4. Create another macro that changes page orientation to landscape with 1-inch top and bottom margins and 1.25-inch left and right margins. Name it LandscapePage and assign the keyboard shortcut Ctrl + Shift + Alt + L. Store it in *[your initials]*Tables and insert an appropriate description.

5. With the page orientation set to landscape, insert the file **Nutrition Table**.

6. Select the table.

7. Start recording a macro named TableStyleGrid. Store it in the *[your initials]*Tables template with an appropriate description for applying the Light Grid style. Do not assign a keyboard shortcut at this time.

8. With the recording pointer, choose AutoFit from the Table Tools Layout tab; then choose AutoFit Contents.

9. Click the Table Tools Design tab, and expand the Table Styles gallery. Then choose a Light Grid style from the third row of built-in styles. Deselect the First Column option in the Table Styles Options group.

10. Click Properties from the Table Tools Layout tab. On the Table tab, click the Options button. In the Table Options dialog box, change the Top and Bottom default cell margins to 0.05 inch. Make sure the Automatically resize to fit contents box is checked. Click OK.

11. In the Table Properties dialog box, make sure Preferred width is unchecked. Choose Center alignment.

12. Click the Cell tab of the Table Properties dialog box, and click Center.

13. Click OK to close the dialog box, press ⬇ once to deselect the table, and then stop recording.

14. Press Ctrl + Shift + Alt + P to change the page orientation to portrait.

15. Copy the macro code for the TableStyleGrid macro, and paste it at the end of the macro code. Name the copy TableStyleShading. Edit the copied macro so it applies a different table style—Colorful Shading – Accent 1. Be sure to edit the comments as well. (Hint: Locate the text Style = "Light List – Accent 1," and change it to Style = "Colorful Shading – Accent 1".)

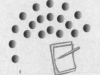

16. Save and print the macro code. Close the Visual Basic window, and return to Word.

17. Assign the keyboard shortcut Ctrl + Shift + Alt + S to the TableStyleList macro, and change its description in the Macros dialog box. Assign the keyboard shortcut Ctrl + Shift + Alt + C to the TableStyleGrid macro.

18. Delete the table from the template, and resave the template.

19. Print the key assignments for the template. Close the template.

20. Start a new document based on the template. Enable macros.

21. Insert the file **Nutrition Table**. If there are extra blank lines at the bottom of the table, delete them.

22. Apply the LandscapePage macro; then select the table and run the TableStyleShading macro. Center the table vertically on the page.

23. Save the document as *[your initials]*22-25a in your Lesson 22 folder, and then submit it.

24. Apply the PortraitPage macro; then select the table and run the TableStyleGrid macro. Center the table vertically on the page.

25. Save the document as *[your initials]*22-25b in your Lesson 22 folder. Submit and close the document.

Exercise 22-26 ◆ Challenge Yourself

Create a template with a customized Quick Access Toolbar, create AutoText entries and macros to insert the AutoText entries, and compose letters using the AutoText entries.

1. Start a new template. Save it as macro-enabled *[your initials]*PittLetter in your Lesson 22 folder.

2. Customize the Quick Access Toolbar to include Print Preview, Spelling and Grammar, and Print.

3. Design a letterhead using character and paragraph formatting. The letterhead should read as follows:

   Campbell's Confections
   40 Station Square
   Pittsburgh, PA 15219
   Telephone: 412-555-2025
   Fax: 412-555-2050
   www.campbellsconfections.pitt.biz

4. Create an AutoText entry for the letterhead. Store it in *[your initials]*PittLetter, and name it LetterheadSimple.

5. Delete the letterhead, and design a second letterhead for the Pittsburgh store using WordArt, clip art, text boxes, or other graphic elements. Group graphic elements, and set appropriate word-wrap and overlap properties. (Use the Drawing Canvas to group the elements.)

6. Create an AutoText entry for the new letterhead. Name it LetterheadFancy.

7. Delete the letterhead and resave the template.

8. Compose a generic closing paragraph that thanks the customer for doing business with Campbell's Confections. Create an AutoText entry for it, naming it ThanksForBusiness. Be sure to store it in *[your initials]*PittLetter.

9. Compose a second generic closing paragraph that asks the customer to contact the company if he or she wants to know more about ordering gourmet chocolate or custom gift boxes. Create an AutoText entry for it, naming it CallMe.

10. Create another AutoText entry for a signature block, using your name and reference initials sm. Name it Signature.

11. Record a macro that inserts the LetterheadSimple AutoText entry. Name it SimpleLetter. Be sure to store it in *[your initials]*PittLetter.

12. Copy and paste the SimpleLetter macro. Edit the pasted macro so it inserts the LetterheadFancy AutoText entry instead. Name the macro FancyLetter and save it.

13. Assign [Ctrl]+[Shift]+[Alt]+[S] for the SimpleLetter macro and [Ctrl]+[Shift]+[Alt]+[F] for the FancyLetter macro.

14. Record a macro named CallMeClose that inserts the CallMe and Signature AutoText entries. Store it in *[your initials]*PittLetter.

15. Copy and paste the CallMeClose macro. Name the pasted macro ThankYouClose, and edit it so it inserts the ThanksForBusiness AutoText entry instead of the CallMe entry. Save the new macro.

16. Assign the keyboard shortcut [Ctrl]+[Shift]+[Alt]+[C] for the CallMeClose macro and [Ctrl]+[Shift]+[Alt]+[T] for the ThankYouClose macro.

17. Delete all the text and graphics from the template, and then resave it.

18. Print the key assignments, and then close the template.

19. Create a new document based on the template you just created. Enable macros. Run the macro to insert the simple letterhead. Create a business letter addressed to anyone you choose. Compose a first paragraph that tells your customer you have a new line of gourmet chocolate and custom gift boxes.

20. As a second and closing paragraph, run the CallMeClose macro.

21. Save the document as *[your initials]*22-26a in your Lesson 22 folder; then print and close it.

22. Create a second letter based on the same template. For the second document, use the macro that inserts the fancy letterhead. Address the letter to the same person as the first letter. Compose a paragraph confirming a recent order for one of the products you mentioned in the first letter. Run the ThankYouClose macro.

23. Save the document as *[your initials]*22-26b in your Lesson 22 folder. Submit and close the document.

On Your Own

In these exercises you work on your own, as you would in a real-life business environment. Use the skills you've learned to accomplish the task—and be creative.

Exercise 22-27

Create a letter template for an announcement or invitation that you want to send to several family members or friends. Include macros that insert AutoText entries for the body of the letter and the closing. Save the template as *[your initials]*22-27a. Open a new document based on the letter, and create a letter for one family member or friend. Save the document as *[your initials]*22-27b and submit it.

Exercise 22-28

Design a birthday party announcement—customize the Quick Access Toolbar containing formatting buttons that do not appear on the Ribbon, and then use the toolbar to apply formatting to the announcement. Save the document as *[your initials]*22-28 and submit it. Reset the Quick Access Toolbar.

Exercise 22-29

Research the Internet for great prices on supplies you want for your favorite hobby. Create a list of the supplies that you will convert to a table by using a macro you have created in a template file named *[your initials]*22-29a. In the macro include a table style. Save the new document based on the template as *[your initials]*22-29b and submit it.

Unit 6 Applications

Unit Application 6-1

Create a main document and a data source, edit the data source, and merge the documents.

1. Start a new document based on the Metro theme.

2. Create a letterhead design using the company address listed below.

   Campbell's Confections
   25 Main Street
   Grove City, PA 16127
   724-555-2025
   www.campbellsconfections.biz

3. Display the Styles task pane, and modify the Normal style to font size 12 points, 0 points spacing before, and 0 points spacing after, and apply single spacing.

4. Insert the date as an automatically updated field using business letter format, and identify the letter as a main document for a mail merge.

5. For the data source, key the data in Figure U6-1. Customize the list of field names as needed.

Figure U6-1

Title	First Name	Last Name	High School	Address	City	State	Zip
Mr.	Gary	Hines	Elk High School	1115 Sunset Drive	Arden	NY	10910
Ms.	Donna	Albert	Armstrong High School	12 Avon Lane	Nichols	NY	13812
Mr.	Paul	Green	Somerset High School	55 Elm Street	Newbury	NH	03255
Ms.	Lucy	Chin	Clearfield High School	154 Fourth Avenue	Highland Park	NH	08904
Ms.	Gina	Saxion	Clinton High School	55 Lincoln Avenue	Camden	NJ	08105
Mr.	Raymond	Steele	Greene High School	667 Washington Boulevard	Glenwood	NJ	07418

TIP

It may be necessary to match fields in the Insert Address Block dialog box. Match the High School field with Company.

6. Save the data source as *[your initials]*u6-1data in a new folder for Unit 6 Applications.

7. Check the recipient list against Figure U6-1 for errors, and then sort the list by ZIP Code.

8. Three blank lines below the date, insert the Address Block followed by the Greeting Line block. Specify a colon in the Greeting Line dialog box rather than a comma. Verify correct spacing between the parts of the letter.

9. For the body of the letter, key the text shown in Figure U6-2.

Figure U6-2

```
Enclosed is the fundraising information you requested. You
will notice from the enclosed brochure that we have six
quality chocolate bars.

The chocolate bar flavors include:

Solid milk chocolate

Milk chocolate with almonds

Milk chocolate with caramel filling

Milk chocolate with peanut butter filling

Milk chocolate with double chocolate filling

The individual bars are 2.5 ounces and are priced at $1. A
case contains 36 bars, and the cost per case is $36. Your
profit is 50 percent, or $18 per case.

Please let us know if you would like one of our sales
representative to meet with you or your students to discuss
fundraising strategies.
```

10. Key an appropriate complimentary closing. The letter is from Tamara Robbins, Fundraising Department. Add your reference initials and an enclosure notation.

11. Edit the last paragraph that begins "Please" to read as follows:

    Please let us know if you would like one of our sales representatives to visit «High School» to meet with you or your students. . . .

12. Preview the letter with the merged data, making sure the letter fits on one page.

13. Sort alphabetically the list of chocolate bars, and format as a bullet list.

TIP

Click Edit Recipient List on the Mailings tab, and click the name of your file under Data Source. Click Edit to open the Edit Source dialog box.

14. Save the main document as *[your initials]*u6-1main in your Unit 6 Applications folder and print it.

15. Edit the data source to change Mr. Raymond Steele to Mr. Harold Steele and add a new record for Mr. Allen Jones, 34 Sky Road, Allegheny High School, Park Ridge, NJ 07656. Sort the list by ZIP Code.

16. Complete the merge, merging all data to a new document.

17. Save the new document as *[your initials]*u6-1merged in your Unit 6 Applications folder.

18. Print the document, four pages per sheet.

19. Use the data source created in this application to create mailing labels. Use the **5160 - Address** product number. Save the merged labels to a new document.

20. Format the label text as 11-point with 0 points spacing after. Save as *[your initials]*u6-1labels. Submit the labels.

21. Close all documents, saving changes when prompted.

Unit Application 6-2

Create an electronic form with content controls.

1. Start a new template to use as an electronic form. Save the template as *[your initials]*FieldForm in your Unit 6 Applications folder.

2. Create a form that Campbell's Confections employees can use to schedule field trips to the factory. The form should include the following information:

Figure U6-3

```
                    Campbell's Confections
                Field Trip Planning Worksheet
                     (For internal use only)

Group Name:

Type:

Contact:

Telephone:

E-mail:

Anticipated number in group:

Requested date:

Time of arrival:
```

3. Format the document as follows:

- Format the first three lines as a document heading. You may include clip art, shapes, borders, or a watermark.

- Insert Rich Text controls for the following: Group Name, Contact, Telephone, Email, Requested date, and Time of arrival.

- Add titles for the Rich Text controls, and edit the instructional text.

- Set a tab to align the Rich Text controls.

- Insert a Drop-Down List control for "Type." The list should include:

  School
  Civic
  Tourists
  Other

- Insert a Drop-Down List control for "Anticipated number in group." The list should include:

  10–15
  16–20
  >20

4. Format the form headings.

5. Save the form.

6. Protect and resave the form. Submit and close the form.

7. Create a document based on the form inserting text for each Rich Text control and selecting an item from each of the drop-down lists. Save the document as *[your initials]*u6-2 in your Unit 6 Applications folder and submit it. Close the document.

Unit Application 6-3

Create a template, record document format macros, and customize the Quick Access Toolbar.

1. Start a new template. Save the macro-enabled template as *[your initials]*BusinessDocuments in your Unit 6 folder.

2. Create a business letter format macro using the following guidelines:

   - Insert the picture file **LetterheadLogo**, and format the picture as follows: Top and bottom text wrapping, horizontally centered on the page, and positioned vertically 0.5 inch from the top of the page. Select the picture, create an AutoText entry named **Logo**, and store it in your **BusinessDocuments** template.

   - Record a new macro named **LetterFormat**, and store it in your **BusinessDocuments** template.

   - Create a header, and insert the Logo AutoText entry.

   - Change the top margin to 2 inches. Change the font size to 12, change the spacing after to 0 points, and apply single spacing.

   - Insert an automatically updated date field, and select the third date format.

   - Press [Enter] four times, and stop recording the macro.

   - Delete all text in the template including the logo in the header.

3. Create a memo format macro using the following guidelines:

   - Record a new macro named **MemoFormat**, and store it in your **BusinessDocuments** template.

   - Change the top margin to 2 inches.

   - Set a 1-inch left tab. Change the spacing after to 0 points, and apply single spacing.

   - Turn on Caps Lock, and key the following:

     MEMO TO: [Tab] [Enter] [Enter]

     FROM: [Tab] [Enter] [Enter]

     DATE: [Tab] «Date field» [Enter] [Enter]

     SUBJECT: [Tab] [Enter] [Enter] [Enter]

   - Stop recording the macro.

   - Delete all text in the template.

4. Open the Word Options dialog box, and click Customize. Select Macros in the Choose commands from list box. Select your *[your initials]*BusinessDocuments template in the Customize Quick Access Toolbar list box.

5. Select each of the macros, and click Add. Click OK to close the Word Options dialog box.

6. Save and close the template.

7. Create a new document based on the *[your initials]*BusinessDocuments template. Enable macros.

8. Run the macro to create a business letter format by clicking the Letter Format button on the Quick Access Toolbar.

9. Save the document as *[your initials]*u6-3a. Submit and close the document.

10. Create a new document based on the *[your initials]*BusinessDocuments template. Enable macros.

11. Run the macro to create a memo format by clicking the Memo Format button on the Quick Access Toolbar.

12. Save the document as *[your initials]*u6-3b. Submit and close the document.

Unit Application 6-4 ◆ Using the Internet

Design a template that includes AutoText and creates a form.

1. Use the Internet to locate a graphic or graphics you will use in creating a letterhead template and form for a business or school organization. Save each graphic as a file in your Unit 6 Applications folder.

2. Create a new template, and save it as *[your initials]***u6-4LetterA** in your Unit 6 Applications folder. Perform the following actions in relation to the new template:

   - Create a letterhead that includes the following information: name of business or school organization, complete address, phone and fax numbers, and Web address.

   - Format the letterhead text by applying character and paragraph attributes.

   - Create an AutoText entry for the letterhead text, and store the entry in the template.

   - Save and submit the template.

3. Perform these additional actions with the template:

   - Add a graphic to the letterhead. Position the graphic and text to create an attractive design.

   - Create an AutoText entry for the graphic, and store the entry in your *[your initials]***U6-4LetterA** template.

   - Save the letterhead and graphic as a new template named *[your initials]***u6-4LetterB** in your Unit 6 Applications folder.

   - Submit and close the template.

4. Design and create a form to be used by your company or school organization, using one or both of the AutoText entries for the letterhead text and letterhead graphic. Save the template as *[your initials]***u6-4Form** in your Unit 6 Applications folder.

   - Record a macro to insert one of the AutoText entries.

   - Assign a shortcut key for the macro, and then resave the template. Print the key assignments.

   - Include Rich Text and Drop-Down List controls and appropriate options. Protect and resave the form. Print the form with field codes displayed. Close the document.

unit 7

LONG DOCUMENTS AND DOCUMENT SHARING

footnotes and Endnotes

OBJECTIVES

After completing this lesson, you will be able to:

1. Add footnotes and endnotes.

2. View footnotes and endnotes.

3. Edit and format footnotes and endnotes.

4. Move, copy, and delete footnotes and endnotes.

5. Change the placement of footnotes and endnotes.

6. Change the numbering of footnotes and endnotes.

7. Create a bibliography.

MCAS OBJECTIVES

In this lesson:
WW 07 2.1.4
WW 07 4.4.1
WW 07 4.4.2
WW 07 4.4.3
WW 07 4.4.4

Estimated Time: 1 hour

Text references that appear at the bottom of the page in a report, book, or other document are called *footnotes*. They are used for two purposes: to credit the source of information or to offer additional explanation. Text references assembled at the end of a document are called *endnotes*.

Adding Footnotes or Endnotes

Adding a footnote or endnote to a document is a two-part process. First, you insert a *reference mark* within the document text, which can appear as a number or a character (such as an asterisk). You then enter the corresponding footnote or endnote text in a separate pane.

Begin by working with footnotes. By default, Word automatically numbers footnotes and provides space for them at the bottom of the page by adjusting page breaks.

Exercise 23-1 ADD FOOTNOTES TO A DOCUMENT

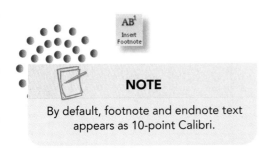

Use Print Layout view to insert footnotes. You can add a footnote by clicking the Insert Footnote command or by launching the Footnote and Endnote dialog box.

1. Open the file **Ordering**.

2. On page 1, in the paragraph that begins "The goal," place the insertion point immediately after the period at the end of the paragraph (after "areas.").

3. Click the **References** tab, and locate the **Footnotes** group. Click the Insert Footnote button. A superscript reference mark appears above the document text, and a separator line is inserted at the bottom of the document with a superscript reference mark.

Figure 23-1
Inserted footnote

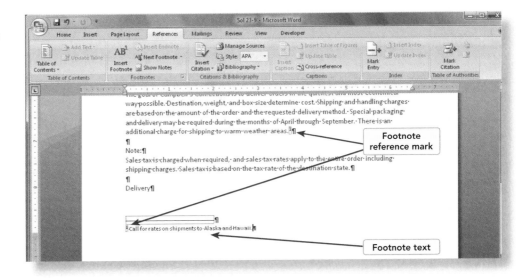

4. Key **Call for rates on shipments to Alaska and Hawaii.**

5. Double-click the reference mark (the number 1) in the footnote pane to return to the reference mark in the document.

6. Click the Show/Hide ¶ button to hide nonprinting characters, if they are showing. This makes the reference mark easier to see.

7. Locate the sales tax paragraph, and position the insertion point at the end of the paragraph following "destination state."

8. Click the Footnote and Endnote Dialog Box Launcher. The Footnote and Endnote dialog box opens.

Figure 23-2
Footnote and
Endnote dialog box

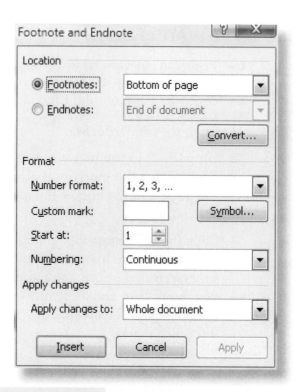

TIP

The keyboard shortcut to insert a footnote is Ctrl + Alt + F.

NOTE

It is important to use the correct form for footnotes or endnotes that refer to published material. For magazine articles, include author, article title, magazine name, date, and page number(s). For books, include author, book title, publisher, place of publication, year of publication, and page number(s).

NOTE

Your instructor might prefer a style other than the Word default and direct you to modify footnotes and endnotes accordingly.

9. Make sure **Footnotes** is selected. Under **Format**, note that the default numbering of footnotes is 1, 2, 3, and so on.

10. Click **Insert**. Notice that Word automatically numbered the footnote with a superscript 2.

11. Key the following footnote text: **Candy sales are subject to sales tax.**

12. Double-click the reference mark (the number 2) to return to the reference mark in the document.

You have inserted two consecutively numbered footnotes in the document. To create endnotes, you follow similar steps: After placing the insertion point in the desired position, open the Footnote and Endnote dialog box, choose Endnotes (or press Alt + Ctrl + D), and key the note text in the endnotes pane. You can also use the Insert Endnote command.

You can format footnotes and endnotes in many different styles. For example, American Language Association (ALA) style differs from *The Gregg Reference Manual* style, and both differ from Word's default style. Figure 23-3 compares *Gregg* and Word styles. This book uses Word's default style—its automatic formatting is easy to use and ensures consistency.

Figure 23-3
Two common
footnote and
endnote styles

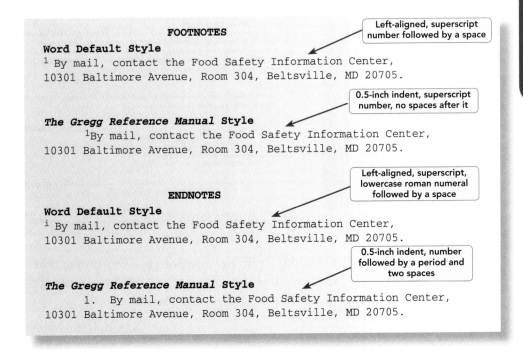

Viewing Footnotes or Endnotes

You can view footnotes or endnotes in a document in three ways:

- Point to the reference mark to display a ScreenTip containing the note text.

- Switch to Draft view, and click the Show Notes command in the Footnotes group.

- Use Print Preview or Print Layout view to see how footnotes and endnotes will appear on the printed page.

To locate footnotes or endnotes in a document, use the Next Footnote command. You can also use the Go To command or set the Select Browse Object button ⊙ to browse by footnotes or endnotes.

Exercise 23-2   VIEW FOOTNOTES

1. Point to the superscript reference mark for footnote 1. A ScreenTip displays the footnote text.

2. Double-click the reference mark in the document. The insertion point moves to the footnote.

3. Scroll to the bottom of page 1. Word reduced the number of text lines on the page and placed the two footnotes above the 1-inch bottom margin. Separating the footnotes from the document text is a 2-inch horizontal *note separator*.

Figure 23-4
Page 2 footnotes in
Print Layout view

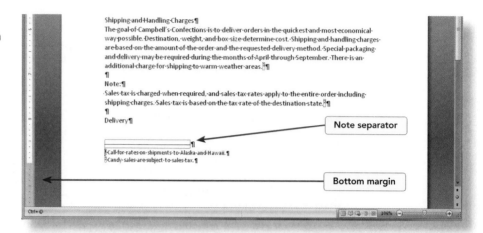

4. Click the Draft view button , and notice that footnotes are not displayed. Draft view does not display footnotes, headers, columns, and other page layout features.

Figure 23-5
View Footnotes
dialog box

5. Click the Show Notes button ![Show Notes], and click **View footnote area** if necessary. The footnote pane appears at the bottom of the page.

6. Click within the footnote 1 text in the footnotes pane. Notice that the text in the document window scrolls to display the corresponding reference number.

Figure 23-6
Footnote pane

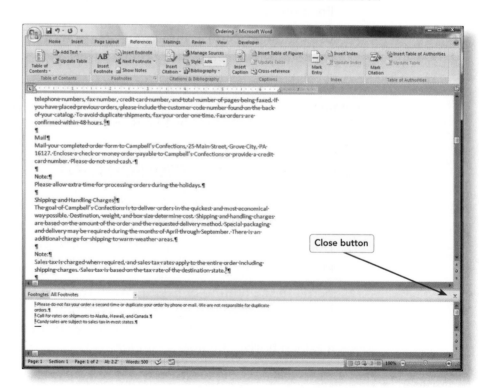

Figure 23-7
Setting the Select
Browse Object button

Browse by Footnote

7. Click the Close button ⊠ to close the footnote pane.

8. Click the Select Browse Object button ⊙, and set it to browse by footnote.

9. Click the Previous Footnote ⬆ and Next Footnote ⬇ buttons to scroll from footnote to footnote. In a long document, this is an easy way to scroll between footnotes.

10. Switch to Print Preview. Magnify the footnote area of page 1 to see how the note text appears with the note separator, and then close Print Preview.

Editing and Formatting Notes

You edit and format footnotes and endnotes the same way as any other text. For example, you can cut, copy, and paste note text. You can also change fonts, font sizes, styles, and paragraph formatting. You can make these changes in the footnotes area or on the endnotes page or in Print Layout view.

Exercise 23-3 **EDIT AND FORMAT FOOTNOTES**

1. Move the insertion point to the end of the paragraph heading "Fax." Press Alt+Ctrl+F to insert a footnote.

2. Key the following text for the footnote: **Please do not fax your order a second time or duplicate your order by phone or mail. We are not responsible for duplicate orders.**

3. Place the insertion point in the text for footnote 2, and edit the text as follows: **Call for rates on shipments to Alaska, Hawaii, or Canada.**

4. Edit footnote 3 to read **Candy sales are subject to sales tax in most states.**

5. Select all the text in the footnotes pane, and change the size to 9 points.

Figure 23-8
Edited footnotes in
Print Preview

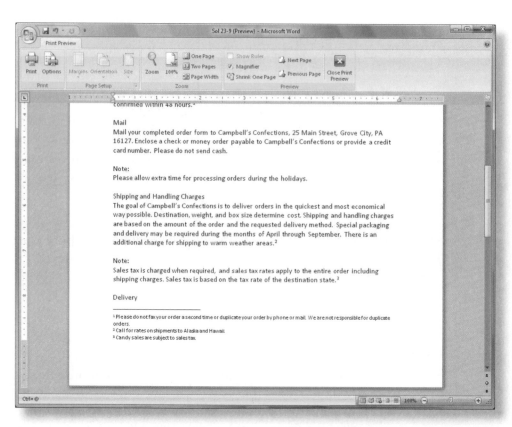

Moving, Copying, and Deleting Notes

You can move, copy, or delete footnotes or endnotes. To do so, you work with
the reference mark, not the actual footnote or endnote text. For example, you
move a footnote by selecting the reference number and cutting and pasting it
(or dragging it) to another location in the document. When you move, copy,
or delete a note, Word automatically renumbers the remaining notes.

Exercise 23-4 MOVE FOOTNOTES

1. Click the Show/Hide ¶ button ¶ to display nonprinting characters.

2. Select the reference mark for footnote 1 (after "Fax").

3. Click the Cut button ✂ to cut the number. Notice
that the note text disappears.

4. Move to the end of the paragraph under the "Fax"
heading (after "48 hours"), and paste the reference
number. The footnote text appears in the footnote
area of the document.

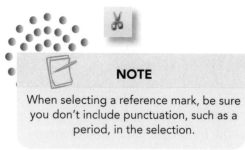

NOTE

When selecting a reference mark, be sure
you don't include punctuation, such as a
period, in the selection.

5. Select reference number 2 in the document. Use the arrow pointer to
drag it to the end of the "Shipping and Handling Charges" heading.

Exercise 23-5 COPY AND DELETE FOOTNOTES

1. Select and copy reference number 2 in the document.

2. Scroll to page 2, and paste the reference mark after "toll-free number." You copied the footnote, and Word automatically assigns the next value to the footnote.

3. Select the copied reference mark (number 4) in the document.

4. Press Delete or Backspace to delete the reference mark and the footnote text. Close the footnotes pane.

5. Save the document as *[your initials]*23-5 in a new folder for Lesson 23.

6. Submit the document. Leave it open for the next exercise.

TIP

Another way to copy footnotes is to use the Ctrl method: Select the reference mark, hold down Ctrl, and drag the mark to the new location.

Changing the Placement of Notes

You can insert footnotes in a document at either of two locations:

- The bottom of the page (the default setting)

- Immediately below the last line of text on the page

Likewise, you can place endnotes at either of two locations:

- The end of the document (the default setting)

- The end of a section

Another way to change the placement of note text is to convert footnotes to endnotes or endnotes to footnotes.

Exercise 23-6 CHANGE THE PLACEMENT OF FOOTNOTES

1. Scroll to the footnotes at the bottom of page 1. Click within the footnote text for the third note, and notice the position of the text on the status bar (approximately 9.8 inches from the top of the page).

2. Scroll to the paragraph that begins "Note:" followed by the "Sales tax" paragraph at the bottom of page 1, and insert a hard page break at the beginning of the "Note" paragraph. Notice that footnote 3 moved to the bottom of page 2.

TIP

If the position 9.8 inches does not appear in the status bar, right-click the status bar and click Vertical Page Position.

3. On page 2, at the end of the paragraph that ends, "toll-free number," insert a new footnote by clicking the Footnotes Dialog Box Launcher.

4. Open the **Footnotes** drop-down list and change the location from **Bottom of page** to **Below text**. Check that the **Apply changes to** option is set to **Whole document**.

5. Click **Insert**. Notice that the existing footnote on page 2 is now positioned just below the last paragraph on the page. Scroll to see how much space is now available on the page.

6. Next to the number 4, key the new footnote text **Web site: www. campbellsconfections.biz or call 800-555-2025.**

7. Format the new footnote as 9 points.

8. Click the arrow beside the Next Footnote button 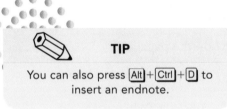 and click **Previous Footnote** to look at the footnotes on page 1. The change you made in footnote placement applies to all footnotes in the document.

Exercise 23-7   CONVERT ALL FOOTNOTES TO ENDNOTES

TIP

You can also press [Alt]+[Ctrl]+[D] to insert an endnote.

NOTE

Switch to Draft view and click Show Notes if you do not see the footnotes/ endnotes pane.

TIP

Use the selection area to select note text. Position the pointer to the left of the note. When the arrow is pointing to the text, press [Ctrl] and click to select all the text in the pane.

1. Before converting all footnotes to endnotes, insert one endnote. Position the insertion point on page 2 at the end of the last paragraph, and click the Insert Endnote button .

2. Key the endnote text **Policies and Procedures Manual (Campbell's Confections, 2006) 25.** (Remember to key the period at the end of the note.) Notice that endnotes are numbered in lowercase roman numerals by default. Turn off nonprinting characters to see the numbers better.

3. Format the endnote as 9 points.

4. In the endnotes pane, open the **Endnotes** drop-down list and choose **All Footnotes**. Use the scroll bar, if necessary, to see the footnotes.

5. Select all the footnote text in the footnotes pane.

6. Click the right mouse button, and choose **Convert to Endnote** from the shortcut menu.

Figure 23-9
Converting footnotes
to endnotes

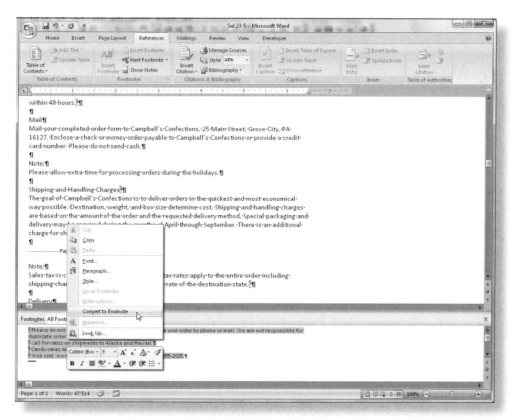

7. Scroll through the endnotes pane. All the footnotes are now endnotes, numbered in the order they are referenced in the document.

8. Close the pane, and look at the last page of the document in Print Layout view. Insert a blank line after each note and check that all note text is 9 points.

Exercise 23-8 CONVERT INDIVIDUAL ENDNOTES TO FOOTNOTES

You can convert individual footnotes to endnotes, or endnotes to footnotes, by using the same method. In this document, you will keep the source note (the note that refers to a specific publication) as an endnote and change the remaining notes into footnotes.

1. Still in Print Layout view, scroll to page 2 to display the endnotes. Right-click endnote "i." Choose **Convert to Footnote** from the shortcut menu. This moves the endnote from the pane and renumbers the remaining notes.

2. Repeat step 1 for endnotes "i" through "iii." There should only be one endnote.

3. Scroll toward the beginning of the document. The document now has footnotes and endnotes. The four endnotes you converted to footnotes are numbered 1 through 4, using the default footnote-numbering style.

Exercise 23-9 PLACE ENDNOTES ON A SEPARATE PAGE

Endnotes are usually placed with a centered title on a separate page at the end of the document. The title begins 2 inches from the top of the page, and two blank lines separate the title and the notes. The separator can be formatted so a title and spacing are inserted automatically.

1. Switch to **Draft** view. Open the endnotes pane by clicking the Show Notes button , and click **View endnote area** from the View Footnotes dialog box. Click **OK**.

2. Choose **Endnote Separator** from the drop-down list in the endnotes pane. Now you can edit, delete, or format the separator.

3. Display nonprinting characters, if they are not showing.

4. With the insertion point at the beginning of the separator line in the pane, press [Enter] four times.

5. Select the separator line and press [Delete].

6. Key **NOTES** in bold uppercase, and click the Center button ≣ to center-align the text.

7. Press [Enter] twice. Four paragraph marks should appear above the title and two below it.

8. Close the separator pane.

9. Press [Ctrl]+[End] to go to the end of the document, and insert a page break.

10. Change to Print Layout view to see the new endnotes page.

TIP

You can also edit, delete, or format the footnote separator. For example, you can center the separator so it is not left-aligned, or you can delete it and insert a double-line bottom border in its place.

Figure 23-10
Endnote page

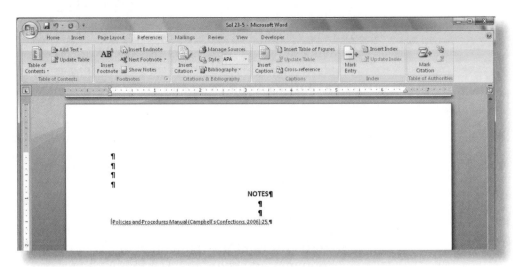

11. Save the document as *[your initials]*23-9 in your Lesson 23 folder. Submit the document.

Changing Numbering of Reference Marks

Instead of using cardinal numbers for footnotes and lowercase roman numerals for endnotes, you can choose a different type of number formatting. Another option is to choose your own custom reference mark. For example, you can use any symbol key on the keyboard or choose one from the Symbol font. For a more graphical symbol, you can choose an image from the Wingdings font.

In the current document, you change the footnotes to asterisks and the endnotes to cardinal numbers.

Exercise 23-10 CHANGE FOOTNOTE REFERENCE MARKS TO SYMBOLS

1. Still in Print Layout view, use the Go To feature to locate the second footnote. (Press F5, choose **Footnote**, enter the number 2, click **Go To**, and close the dialog box.)

2. Right-click the footnote text, and choose **Note options** from the shortcut menu to open the Footnote and Endnote dialog box.

NOTE

Be careful you don't click Insert in the Footnote and Endnote dialog box, or you will insert another note.

3. Open the **Number format** drop-down list, and choose the last format (the one that begins with an asterisk). This format starts by applying the asterisk, applies the next symbol to the next footnote, and so on.

4. Open the **Numbering** drop-down list, and choose **Restart each page**. This option will start numbering each page of footnotes with the asterisk.

Figure 23-11
Choosing footnote options

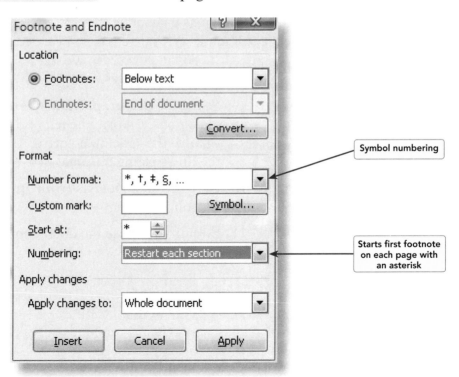

5. Click **Apply**. The footnotes are now marked with asterisks.

Exercise 23-11   CHANGE THE NUMBER FORMAT FOR ENDNOTES

1. In Print Layout view, display page 3 (the endnote).

2. Right-click the endnote number, and choose **Note options** from the shortcut menu.

3. In the Footnote and Endnote dialog box, change the **Number format** to **1**, **2**, **3**, and click **Apply**. The new numbering appears in the document.

4. Add page numbers to the bottom right of the document. Do not number the first page.

5. Format the title on page 1 ("How to Place an Order") with 72 points of space before the paragraph and 24 points spacing after. Center, bold, and apply 16-point small caps. Apply the Heading 2 style to the document side headings (do not style the "Note" headings).

6. Apply italic and 6 points spacing before to the "Note" paragraphs. Delete the blank paragraph marks, and review the document page breaks.

7. Position the insertion point at the end of the paragraph on page 2 that begins "Our customer service," and press ⏎Enter.

8. Key the following paragraph below the "Customer Service" paragraph.

   Campbell's Confections guarantees that your orders and gifts will arrive in perfect condition when using our recommended method of shipping. If you are not satisfied with your order, we will be glad to replace or exchange the products or issue a refund.

NOTE

Format long quotations (four or more lines) using single spacing and indent the text a half inch from the left and right margin. A blank line should precede the text, and do not use quotation marks to enclose the text.

9. Select the paragraph, and open the Paragraph dialog box. Change the left and right indents to .5. Change the spacing before to 12 points, and change the line spacing to single.

10. Save the document as *[your initials]*23-11 in your Lesson 23 folder.

11. Submit and close the document.

Create a Bibliography

A *bibliography* is a list of sources that identifies references consulted or cited in a report or manuscript. A bibliography usually appears at the end of a formal report.

Word generates a bibliography automatically using document citations and formats the bibliography based on the style you select.

Exercise 23-12 ADD A CITATION

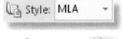 Style: MLA

1. Open the file **Books**.

2. Click the **References** tab, and click the arrow beside the Style button Style: MLA. Click **MLA**.

3. Locate the list of books at the end of the memo, and position the insertion point at the end of the first book (Chocolate: A Bittersweet Saga of Dark and Light).

4. Click the Insert Citation button, and click **Add New Source**. The Create Source dialog box appears.

Figure 23-12
Create Source
dialog box

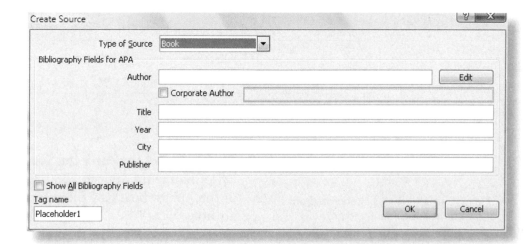

5. Key the following information in the dialog box.:

Author:	Mort Rosenblum
Title:	Chocolate: A Bittersweet Saga of Dark and Light
Year:	2004
Publisher:	North Point Press

6. Click **OK**.

7. Create three citations for the other books listed using the information in Figure 23-13.

Figure 23-13

Author	Chloe Doutre-Roussel	Maricel Presilla	Sophie D. Coe
Title	The Chocolate Connoisseur	The New Taste of Chocolate: A Cultural and Natural History of Cacao with Recipes	True History of Chocolate
Year	2006	2001	1999
Publisher	Tarcher	Ten Speed Press	Thames & Hudson

8. Click the Manage Sources button  to open the Source Manager dialog box.

Figure 23-14
Source Manager
dialog box

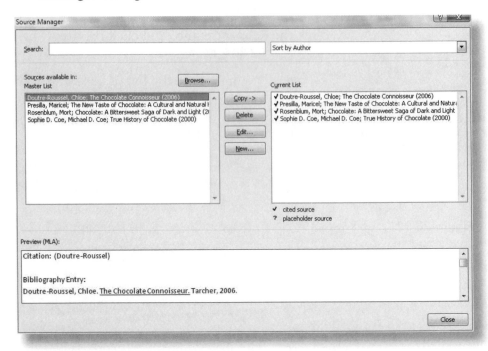

9. Click to select the entry for Sophie D. Coe, and click **Edit**. Change the year to 2000. Click **Edit** to the right of the **Author** box. Key the information for a second author, Michael D. Coe, in the appropriate text boxes. Click **OK** twice; then click **Close**.

10. Go to the end of the document, and insert a page break. Key BIBLIOGRAPHY and press Enter twice. Format the title using 12-point bold and uppercase letters. Center the title.

11. Position the insertion on below the title, and click the Bibliography button , and click Insert Bibliography.

12. Save the new document as *[your initials]*23-12 in your Lesson 23 folder.

13. Save, submit, and close the document.

Lesson 23 Summary

- Text references can appear at the bottom of the page as footnotes or at the end of a document as endnotes. By default, footnotes and endnotes are preceded by a 2-inch horizontal note separator.

- To insert a footnote or endnote, first insert a reference mark in the document text and second key the note text in a separate pane. Word automatically numbers footnotes and endnotes.

- To view footnotes or endnotes, point to the reference mark in the document to display a ScreenTip containing the text or open the footnotes or endnotes pane. You can also see footnotes and endnotes in Print Layout view or Print Preview.

- You can edit and format note text as you would any other text. By default, note text is 10-point Calibri, single-spaced.

- To move, copy, or delete footnotes or endnotes, work with the reference mark in the document, not the actual note text.

- Footnotes can be placed at the bottom of the page or below the last line of text on the page. Endnotes can be placed at the end of the document or section.

- You can convert existing footnotes to endnotes or endnotes to footnotes. You can convert all notes or individual notes.

- By default, footnotes are numbered with cardinal numbers (1, 2, 3) and endnotes are numbered with roman numerals (i, ii, iii). You can change either footnotes or endnotes to cardinal numbers, roman numerals, letters, or symbols.

- Change note options (for example, location and format) in the Footnote and Endnote dialog box. A quick way to open the dialog box is to right-click the note text and choose Note options from the shortcut menu.

- To insert a citation, select a format style, and key the bibliography field information. Use Manage Sources to edit or locate a source.

- To create a bibliography, position the insertion point at the end of the document, and click the Bibliography command. Select a format for the bibliography.

LESSON 23		Command Summary	
Feature	**Button**	**Command**	**Keyboard**
Insert footnote	AB¹ Insert Footnote	**References** tab, **Footnotes** group	Alt + Ctrl + F
Insert endnote	Insert Endnote	**References** tab, **Footnotes** group	Alt + Ctrl + D
Open footnotes or endnotes pane	Show Notes	Draft view, **References** tab, **Footnotes** group, **Show Notes**	
Select browse object	○		
Insert citation	Insert Citation ▾	**References** tab, **Citations & Bibliography** group	
Manage Sources	Manage Sources	**References** tab, **Citations & Bibliography** group	
Bibliography	Bibliography ▾	**References** tab, **Citations & Bibliography** group	

Concepts Review

True/False Questions

Each of the following statements is either true or false. Indicate your choice by circling T or F.

T   F   1. Every footnote corresponds to a reference mark.

T   F   2. A reference mark must be either a number or a letter.

T   F   3. You can insert a footnote by pressing Alt + Ctrl + F.

T   F   4. Footnotes display by default in either Draft or Print Layout view.

T   F   5. Book titles and magazine names should be italicized in footnotes or endnotes.

T   F   6. The note separator is a 2-inch vertical line that divides note text from document text.

T   F   7. The footnote separator line is three inches in length.

T   F   8. You can add a placeholder to insert a citation at a later time.

Short Answer Questions

Write the correct answer in the space provided.

1. What is the default placement for footnotes?

   _____

2. When you point to a footnote reference mark in a document, what does Word display?

   _____

3. What is the default numbering format for endnotes?

   _____

4. With a document in Draft view, which button do you use to display the footnotes pane?

   _____

5. By default, footnotes are placed immediately above what part of a page?

   _____

6. What would you insert at the end of a document to make endnotes print on a separate page?

   _____

7. What setting for footnotes is the alternative to the default placement?

_____

8. What feature is used to create a list of sources?

_____

Critical Thinking

Answer these questions on a separate page. There are no right or wrong answers. Support your answers with examples from your own experience, if possible.

1. Do you prefer using footnotes or endnotes? Why?

2. In this lesson you learned that there are differing styles for footnotes and endnotes. Compare the differences in style between footnotes and/or endnotes for three professional associations. Which do you prefer? Why? How close are these styles to the Word default style?

Skills Review

Exercise 23-13

Add and view footnotes.

1. Open the file **Community - 2**.
2. Add the footnotes shown in Figure 23-15 by following these steps:
   a. Position the insertion point after "United Way" in the second paragraph below the heading.
   b. Click the References tab on the Ribbon.
   c. Click the Insert Footnote button .
   d. Key the first footnote in the figure. Do not press Enter after the text—you will single-space these footnotes.
   e. Position the insertion point after "March of Dimes."
   f. Press Alt+Ctrl+F, and key the second footnote.
   g. Add the third footnote after "Humane Society," and add the fourth footnote after "Foundation."

Figure 23-15

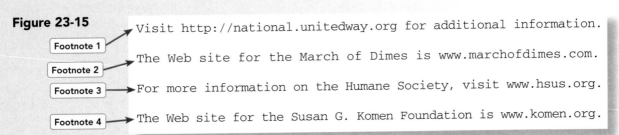

Footnote 1 → Visit http://national.unitedway.org for additional information.

Footnote 2 → The Web site for the March of Dimes is www.marchofdimes.com.

Footnote 3 → For more information on the Humane Society, visit www.hsus.org.

Footnote 4 → The Web site for the Susan G. Komen Foundation is www.komen.org.

3. Switch to Print Preview to see the footnotes. Close Print Preview.

4. Save the document as *[your initials]*23-13 in your Lesson 23 folder. Submit and close the document.

Exercise 23-14

Edit footnotes in a document.

1. Open the file **Tax Update**.

2. Position the insertion point in the first line of the memo heading and add 72 points spacing before.

3. Double-click the reference mark (the superscript 1) in the second paragraph of the memo.

4. Edit the footnote in the footnote pane by following these steps:

    a. Delete the text "Publication 15."

    b. Underline the text "(Circular E), Employer's Tax Guide."

    c. Change the font for the footnote text to Arial.

5. Add a new footnote by following these steps:

    a. Position the insertion point after "W-3" at the end of the first paragraph.

    b. Press Alt+Ctrl+F.

    c. Key You must provide registration information to file electronically.

    d. Insert a blank line between the footnotes.

6. Save the document as *[your initials]*23-14 in your Lesson 23 folder. Submit and close the document.

Exercise 23-15

Move, copy, and delete footnotes.

1. Open the file **Promote**.

2. Move a footnote by following these steps:

    a. Scroll within the document to the paragraph that begins "Most stores carry."

    b. Select the reference mark for footnote 3. Cut the reference mark, placing it on the Clipboard.

    c. Move the insertion point to the end of the paragraph that begins "Campbell's Confections encourages," and paste the Clipboard contents. Delete the space character that is inserted to the left of the reference mark.

3. Copy a footnote by following these steps:

    a. Double-click the second footnote in the footnotes pane to locate the reference mark in the document pane.

    b. Select the reference mark (number 2) in the document pane, copy it, and paste it to the end of the last paragraph. Delete the space character that Word inserts.

4. In the footnotes pane, edit footnote 3 by changing "Della Shawley" to **Kim Abbington**, "Chocolate Sensations" to **Candy-Making**, "March" to **October**, and 21 to **4**.

5. Delete footnote 1 by selecting the reference mark (the number 1) in the document pane and pressing [Delete].

6. Change the top margin to 1.5 inches.

7. Save the document as *[your initials]***23-15** in your Lesson 23 folder. Submit and close the document.

Exercise 23-16

Insert citations and create a bibliography.

1. Open the file **Email**.

2. Go to the end of the document, and insert three citations by following these steps:

    a. Click the Insert Citation button .

    b. Click **Add New Source**.

    c. Refer to Figure 23-16 and key the text for the first entry in the appropriate text boxes. Click **OK**.

    d. Repeat for each book.

Figure 23-16

> Tom Antion, *The Ultimate Guide to Electronic Marketing for Small Business: Low-Cost/High Return Tools and Techniques That Really Work*, John Wiley & Sons, Inc., 2005.
>
> Herschell Gordon Lewis, *Effective E-mail Marketing*, AMACOM, 2002.
>
> Chet Meisner, *The Complete Guide to Direct Marketing: Creating Breakthrough Programs That Really Work*, Kaplan Publishing, 2006.

3. Create a bibliography by following these steps:

    a. Insert a page break at the end of the document.

    b. Key **BIBLIOGRAPHY**, and press [Enter]. Format the heading using 14-point bold and all caps. Center the heading, and apply 24 points spacing after.

    c. Position the insertion point on the blank line below the title. Select **MLA** from the **Style** drop-down list.

    d. Click the Bibliography button , and click **Insert Bibliography**.

4. Save the document as *[your initials]***23-16** in your Lesson 23 folder. Submit and close the document.

Lesson Applications

Exercise 23-17

Add, view, and edit footnotes.

1. Open the file **OH Stores**.

2. Format the title with the Heading 1 style, and apply 36 points spacing before.

3. Format each of the store names with the Heading 2 style.

4. Indent all the document text so it is centered horizontally on the page.

5. Delete the blank paragraph marks.

6. Add the footnote text in Figure 23-17 to the document, and place the reference mark to the right of the appropriate store name. Use the default autonumbering and placement. Include the corrections and formatting shown in the figure.

Figure 23-17

Double space between footnotes.

The akron store will host National Chocolate Covered Cherry Day on in January 3

The Canton store will host National Chocolate Covered Cashews Day on April (12)

The Youngstown store will host Chocolate Day on July 7

7. Change the footnote font to 10-point Arial, and view the footnotes in Print Preview. Close Print Preview.

8. Save the document as *[your initials]*23-17 in your Lesson 23 folder. Submit and close the document.

Exercise 23-18

Locate, format, move, and delete endnotes.

1. Open the file **College**.

2. Apply the following formatting changes to the document:

   • Change the top margin to 2 inches.

   • Apply the Heading 2 style to all the names of colleges and universities on page 2.

3. Use the Go To command to locate the reference number for endnote 1. Move the reference number to the end of the previous sentence, and delete the extra space Word inserts to the left of the number.

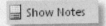

4. Switch to Draft view, and click the Show Notes button [Show Notes].

5. Click endnote iv in the pane to locate the text reference, and delete the note.

6. Display the endnote separator by clicking ↓. Add four blank lines before it.

7. Close the pane, and switch to Print Layout view.

8. To all endnote text, apply paragraph spacing of 6 points after and increase the font size by 1 point.

9. Save the document as *[your initials]*23-18 in your Lesson 23 folder. Submit and close the document.

Exercise 23-19

Add, move, and format footnotes; convert footnotes to endnotes; and change the endnote number format.

1. Open the file **Candy Making - 2**.

2. Add 72-point spacing before the title on page 1.

3. Convert footnote 2 to an endnote by using the shortcut menu.

4. Right-click the endnote, and open the Note Options dialog box. Change the endnote numbering format to A, B, C.

5. Switch to Draft view, and display the footnote/endnote pane. Replace the endnote separator line with the word NOTES. Format the "NOTES" heading as 12-point bold, uppercase, and centered. Insert four blank lines before the word and two blank lines after it. Switch to Page Layout view.

6. Insert a page break at the end of the document to place the endnotes on a new page.

7. On page 2, locate the paragraph that begins "Centers." Insert the following endnote: Norma Crawford, "Perfect Centers," *Food Today*, February 2006: 47.

8. Locate footnote 3, and move it to the end of the line beginning "Pour out."

9. Format all the footnote text as 9 points.

10. Format all the endnote text as 10 points with one blank line between notes.

11. Create a header on pages 2 and 3 only, to print the page number in the upper right corner with the text Page immediately preceding the number.

12. Save the document as *[your initials]*23-19 in your Lesson 23 folder. Submit and close the document.

Exercise 23-20 ◆ Challenge Yourself

Add and format footnotes, convert footnotes to endnotes, and change the endnote number format.

1. Open the file **Background**.

2. Go to the end of the paragraph on page 1 that begins "You will find."

3. Insert a footnote at the end of this paragraph.

   Campbell's Confections sponsors educational programs at the auditorium in Grove City and also through educational displays and learning centers in all retail stores.

4. Go to the bulleted list on page 4. At the end of the last bullet, "other assorted shapes," insert a new footnote with the text We have recently added Greek letters and mascots to our line of embossed chocolates.

5. Go to page 6, and locate the "E-Commerce" paragraph. Above the heading, at the end of the preceding paragraph, insert the following footnote: Call the Fundraising Department to schedule a visit from one of our sales associates.

6. Go to page 1, and position the insertion point after the first sentence in the paragraph that begins "There are," and insert a footnote: A new store is scheduled to open in Indiana, Pennsylvania.

7. Review the document and apply Line and Page Break controls where necessary.

8. Create a header as follows:

   - Include the text Campbell's Confections aligned at the left margin; include the page number (and the word Page) aligned at the right margin. Add two blank lines below the header line.

   - Format the header text as 10-point italic.

   - The header should appear on every page except the first.

9. Switch to Draft view, display the footnotes pane, and format all the footnote text as 9 points. Switch to Print Layout view.

10. Add a footer on every page except the first. Insert the field name for the filename in the footer in 10-point italic and center it.

11. Adjust page breaks that separate paragraphs from headings or for paragraphs that look unattractive.

12. Save the document as *[your initials]*23-20a in your Lesson 23 folder.

13. Submit the document.

14. Convert all the footnotes that refer to a publication to endnotes.

15. Place the endnotes on a separate page. Format the endnote separator by replacing the line with the word NOTES in bold uppercase letters and center it. Add 24 points spacing after to the text.

16. Change the number format for the endnotes to **1, 2, 3**.

17. Format the endnotes with 12-points spacing after, and increase the font size to 11 points.

18. Adjust page breaks if necessary.

19. Save the document as *[your initials]*23-20b in your Lesson 23 folder.

20. Print the page with the endnotes (page 8), and close the document.

On Your Own

In these exercises you work on your own, as you would in a real-life business environment. Use the skills you've learned to accomplish the task—and be creative.

Exercise 23-21

Research using the Internet or *The Gregg Reference Manual* to learn about the use of footnote or endnote abbreviations such as "ibid." and "op cit." Write a short document describing their use and create some examples. Save the document as *[your initials]*23-21 and submit it.

Exercise 23-22

Key at least six lines of poetry from a famous author. Add footnotes to at least three of the lines, giving your interpretation or insight into the poem's meaning. Change the placing of the footnotes to appear below the text. Format the document attractively, save it as *[your initials]*23-22, and submit it.

Exercise 23-23

Using a report (in the form of a Word document) you created for another class, add at least three footnotes that relate to the report content and at least three endnotes that cite your information sources. Place the endnotes on a separate page at the end of the document, under the bold heading "NOTES." Change the endnote numbering format to uppercase letters. Add an appropriate header to the document. Insert citations and create a bibliography. Save it as *[your initials]*23-23 and submit it.

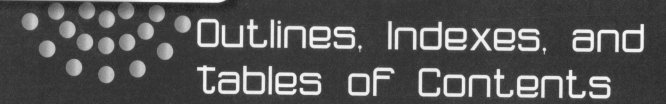

Lesson 24

Outlines, Indexes, and tables of Contents

OBJECTIVES

MCAS OBJECTIVES

In this lesson:
WW 07 1.3.1
WW 07 1.3.2
WW 07 4.4.5

After completing this lesson, you will be able to:

1. Create an outline

2. Identify index entries.

3. Format and compile an index.

4. Edit and update an index.

5. Create a table of contents.

6. Format a table of contents.

7. Edit and update a table of contents.

Estimated Time: 1½ hours

Outlining is a powerful way to organize ideas. Writers typically use an outline to help them decide what to say and in what order to say it. With a good outline, it is easier to develop a document that is orderly and logical. In Word, you can build a document by creating an outline and assigning various levels to headings and body text. You can also outline an existing document. After a document is outlined, you can use Word's outline features to review and reorganize the document quickly and easily.

An *index*, typically found at the back of a book or the end of a document, directs readers to the pages where specific words, phrases, or topics are located. You create an index in Word by using field codes to identify the text you want to include in the index. After you identify all the entries, you compile the index. If you change your document by adding or removing pages, you can update the index to include the new page numbers. A *table of contents (TOC)* is usually found at the beginning of a book or document. It is a list of topics with their page numbers, arranged in the order in which they appear in the document.

Creating an Outline

The process of creating an outline involves determining the content and order of the final document. An outline generally consists of the following:

- **Headings**: The major points.
- **Subheadings**: The topics under the headings (and under other subheadings).
- **Body text**: The text under a heading or subheading.

You create an outline in Outline view, where you can assign different levels to your text as you key it. For example, you can *promote* a heading (raise it to a higher outline level) or *demote* a heading (move it to a lower outline level). Word allows as many as nine levels in an outline. You can also apply heading styles to text in Draft view or Print Layout view to create an outline or to outline an existing document. You can then use Outline view to reorganize the outline.

Exercise 24-1   CREATE AN OUTLINE

1. Start a new document, and click the Outline view button 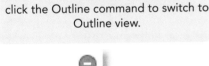 on the status bar. The Outlining tab displays in the Ribbon.

> **NOTE**
>
> Click the View tab on the Ribbon and click the Outline command to switch to Outline view.

2. Key the heading Theobroma tree. It is automatically assigned the Heading 1 style (14-point Cambria, bold). A selection symbol shaped like a large minus sign in a circle ⊖ appears to the left of the text. It indicates that no *subtext* (any lower-level heading or body text) appears below the heading.

Figure 24-1
Keying the first heading in Outline view

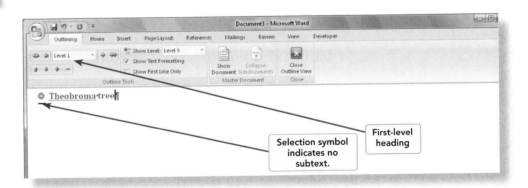

Selection symbol indicates no subtext.

First-level heading

3. Press Enter and click the Demote button . This demotes the new blank paragraph one level so it becomes a level-2 heading. Notice that the first heading now has a selection symbol shaped like a plus sign indicating that subtext follows.

4. Key the subheading Varieties and press Enter. Notice that the subheading is assigned the Heading 2 style (13-point Cambria, bold). Press Tab to demote the subheading.

5. Key Criollo. Heading 3 is applied. Press Enter.

6. With the insertion point on the blank line, click the Demote to Body Text button ⇥, and key the text shown in Figure 24-2.

Figure 24-2

> The Criollo variety has a smaller yield per tree, but provides 10 percent of the world crop. It is used for premier chocolate.

7. Press Enter. Your outline now includes first-, second-, and third-level headings and body text. Body text is assigned the Normal style and is indicated in the outline by the small circle • to the left of the paragraph.

Figure 24-3
Outline with level-1, -2, and -3 headings and body text

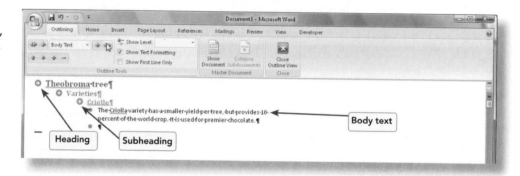

8. Switch to Print Layout view. In Print Layout view you can see all the style characteristics, including paragraph formatting. Notice that the text is not indented in the actual document—indents appear in Outline view only to make viewing the outline structure easier.

9. Switch back to Outline view to continue your outline. With the insertion point still on the last blank line of the document, click the Promote button to create a level-3 heading and key Forastero.

10. Press Enter, click the Demote to Body Text button ⇥, and key This variety provides 80 percent of the world crop.

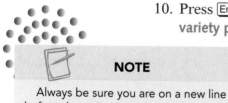

NOTE

Always be sure you are on a new line before demoting or promoting a heading so you do not change the level of an existing heading by accident.

11. Press Enter and click the Promote button ⇤. Key Trinitario.

12. Press Enter, click the Demote to Body Text button ⇥, and key This variety is the easiest to cultivate, and it provides 10 percent of the world crop.

TABLE 24-1 Outlining Tab Buttons and Keyboard Shortcuts

Button	Function	Keyboard
Promote to Heading 1	Promotes any text to a level-1 heading	
Promote	Promotes one heading level	Alt + Shift + ←
Body Text ▾ Outline Level	Assigns an outline level to text	
Demote	Demotes one heading level	Alt + Shift + →
Demote to Body Text	Demotes any heading to body text	Ctrl + Shift + N
Move Up	Moves heading up in document	Alt + Shift + ↑
Move Down	Moves heading down in document	Alt + Shift + ↓
Expand	Displays subheadings and body text	Alt + Shift + +
Collapse	Hides subheadings and body text	Alt + Shift + −
Show Level ▾ Show Level	Displays selected heading levels	
☐ Show First Line Only	Displays first line only of body text	Alt + Shift + L
☑ Show Text Formatting Show Formatting	Displays character formatting in Outline view	/ (on numeric keypad)

Exercise 24-2 COLLAPSE AND EXPAND AN OUTLINE

You can *collapse* an outline so only the main headings appear and *expand* it again to display your subtext. You can also collapse an outline to display headings and only the first line of text paragraphs. When you collapse an outline, you can see the "main points" of the document, which makes it easier to rearrange the text in a more logical sequence.

1. To collapse the outline, open the **Show Level** drop-down list on the **Outlining** tab and choose **Level 3**. This tells Word to display only headings that are level 3 or higher; all other text is hidden, or "collapsed." A gray line appears under all headings that have collapsed text.

Figure 24-4
Outline with body
text collapsed

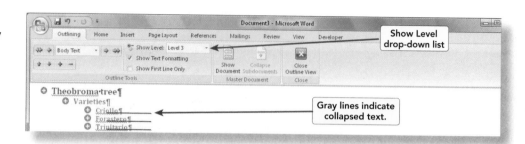

2. Open the **Show Level** drop-down list and choose **Level 2**. Word displays only level-1 and level-2 headings and collapses level-3 headings.

3. Choose **Level 3** from the drop-down list again. All three heading levels are displayed again.

4. Position the insertion point in the level-2 heading, "Varieties." Click the Collapse button ⊟ to collapse the subheadings for that heading. Click the Expand button ⊕ to display the subheadings once again.

5. Position the pointer on the selection symbol for the first heading, "Theobroma tree." When the pointer changes to a four-headed arrow, double-click to collapse all text below the heading.

Figure 24-5
Double-click
selection symbol to
collapse text

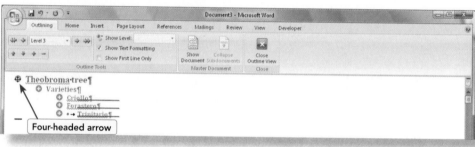

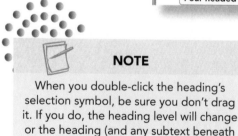

NOTE

When you double-click the heading's selection symbol, be sure you don't drag it. If you do, the heading level will change or the heading (and any subtext beneath it) will be repositioned.

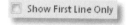

6. Double-click the selection symbol to expand the outline completely. Notice that double-clicking a selection symbol selects both the heading and all its subtext.

7. With the entire outline expanded and selected, click the Show First Line Only check box ☐ Show First Line Only. Now only the first line of each text paragraph is displayed.

8. Click to deselect the Show First Line Only button ☐ Show First Line Only again to expand all the body text. Click within the outline to deselect it.

9. Save the document as *[your initials]*24-2 in a new folder for Lesson 24.

10. Submit and close the document.

Exercise 24-3 NAVIGATING IN AN OUTLINE

When you modify an outline, you need an efficient way to move around if the outline extends beyond the length of your screen. You can collapse the outline, find a certain heading or section, and then expand it, but this is cumbersome in a large outline or when you have several changes to make. Instead, you can set the Select Browse Object button to move the insertion point from heading to heading. Or, you can use a feature called the *Document Map*—a separate pane on the left side of the screen that shows the headings of your document.

TIP

You do not have to be working on an outline to use the Document Map. This feature is useful for navigating in any document with headings. Note, however, that your headings must have a heading style applied before they will appear in the Document Map.

NOTE

The Next and Previous buttons "remember" which object you last selected with the Select Browse Object button.

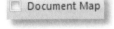

1. Click in the first heading, "Theobroma tree." Click the Select Browse Object button ⊙ near the bottom of the vertical scroll bar.

2. Click the Browse by Heading button ▤. The insertion point moves to the beginning of the next heading, "Varieties."

3. Click the Next Heading button ⬇ just below the Select Browse Object button. The insertion point moves to the next heading, "Criollo."

4. Click the Previous Heading button ⬆ two times to move back to the first heading, "Theobroma tree."

5. Click the **View** tab on the Ribbon. Click to select the Document Map button 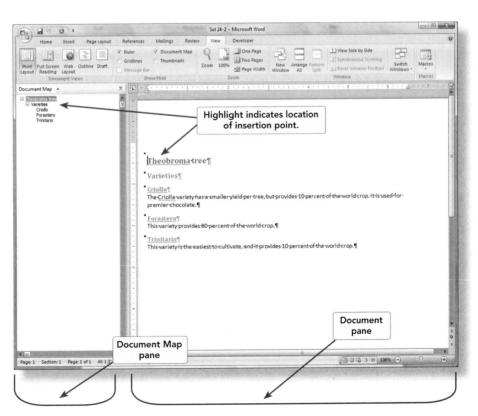. A new pane opens on the left side of your screen, displaying each heading in your outline.

Figure 24-6
Document Map

NOTE

You can expand and collapse the headings in the Document Map by clicking the plus and minus signs to the left of each heading.

6. Click the heading "Trinitario" in the Document Map. The heading scrolls to the top of the document pane and the insertion point moves to the beginning of the heading.

7. Click the heading "Theobroma tree" in the Document Map pane to return to the beginning of the outline.

8. Click the **View** tab on the Ribbon if necessary. Click to deselect the Document Map button .

9. Close the document.

Identifying Index Entries

The first step in creating an index is to identify (or mark) the text you want indexed and—at the same time—indicate how you want the entries to be worded in the index itself. An index entry can be an individual word, phrase, symbol, or range of text. Word gives you three ways to identify an entry for inclusion in an index:

- Mark the text by selecting it; then open the Mark Index Entry dialog box.

- Place the insertion point where you want the entry to be; then key the entry into the Mark Index Entry dialog box.

- Create a concordance file, and use the AutoMark command in the Index and Tables dialog box. This method lets you mark many entries at once.

Exercise 24-4 **MARK TEXT TO IDENTIFY INDEX ENTRIES**

NOTE

Always create an index *after* you make all changes and revisions in your document. This approach ensures accuracy in the index page-number references.

1. Open the file **Ordering - 2**. The file has been previously formatted using Word's built-in styles.

2. Select the heading "Online."

3. Click the **References** tab on the Ribbon, and locate the **Index** group.

Figure 24-7
Index group

NOTE

You can key or edit text in the Main entry text box.

4. Click the Mark Entry button . The Mark Index Entry dialog box appears with "Online" displayed in the **Main entry** text box. Click **Mark** to mark "online" for the index. The index entry appears in the document as a field, enclosed in braces and quotation marks. In the field, **XE** stands for index entry. Do not close the Mark Index Entry dialog box.

Figure 24-8
Mark Index Entry
dialog box

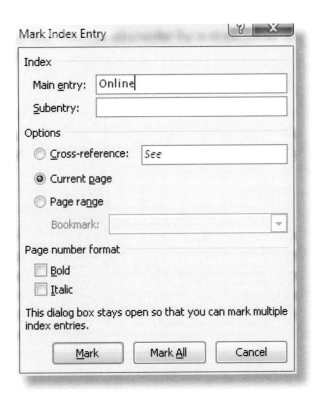

TIP

You can use the keyboard shortcut [Alt]+[Shift]+[X] to open the Mark Index Entry dialog box.

NOTE

The Mark Index Entry dialog box remains open while you mark index entries in your document. You can even use the Find and Replace commands to locate and index other topics while the dialog box remains open.

5. Drag the Mark Index Entry dialog box to the lower right portion of the document window so you have space to view your document.

6. Select the heading "Telephone." Click the title bar of the Mark Index Entry dialog box. The selection appears in the **Main entry** text box.

7. With "Telephone" displayed in the **Main entry** text box, click **Mark**.

8. Select "E-mail" in the last sentence of the first paragraph.

9. Activate the Mark Index Entry dialog box by clicking its title bar. Then click **Mark** to mark this selection as an index entry (see Figure 24-9).

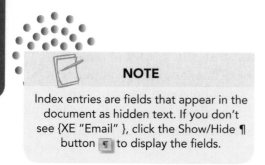

NOTE

Index entries are fields that appear in the document as hidden text. If you don't see {XE "Email" }, click the Show/Hide ¶ button ¶ to display the fields.

Figure 24-9
Index entry

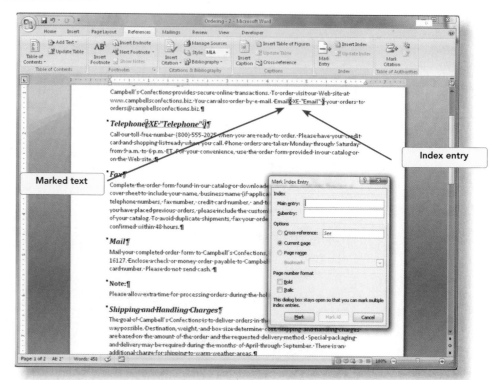

Exercise 24-5   MARK MULTIPLE-LEVEL INDEX ENTRIES

You can also create *subentries* that are subordinate to the main index entries. This is useful when a topic has subtopics that are located in different places in the document.

1. Select "Rush delivery" in the first sentence of the paragraph under "Delivery." Press Alt+Shift+X to activate the Mark Index Entry dialog box.

2. Edit the **Main entry** to read **Delivery**. Click in the **Subentry** text box and key **Rush delivery** as the subentry.

3. Click **Mark**. Word inserts a new index field. This index field has the main entry ("Delivery") followed by a colon and the subentry ("Rush delivery").

Figure 24-10
Creating a subentry

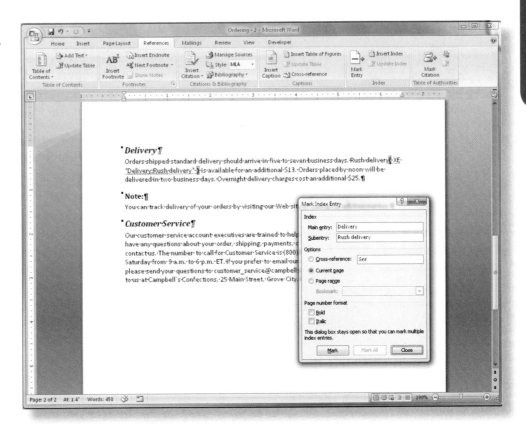

TIP

You can select and reformat the text contained within the field code brackets of your document and edit or delete your index entries with the Mark Index Entry dialog box closed, much as you would edit ordinary text. Any changes you make to index entries will be included in your index the next time you update it.

4. Select "Overnight delivery" in the paragraph below the "Delivery" heading, and activate the Mark Index Entry dialog box. Key **Delivery** in the **Main entry** text box, and key **Overnight delivery** in the **Subentry** text box. Click **Mark**. Now two headings are in your index under "Delivery" ("Rush delivery" and "Overnight delivery"), with page numbers for each one.

5. Close the Mark Index Entry dialog box.

Exercise 24-6 MARK A RANGE OF PAGES AS AN INDEX ENTRY

Sometimes an index refers readers to a range of pages (rather than to just one page) if the topic extends beyond one page. To do this, you need to create a bookmark for the text to be indexed and then use the bookmark to mark the text for the index.

1. Select all the text from the heading "Shipping and Handling Charges" to "our toll-free number" (the end of the "Note" paragraph following the "Delivery" paragraph).

2. Create a bookmark named **Shipping and Handling**. The selected paragraphs are now marked as a bookmark.

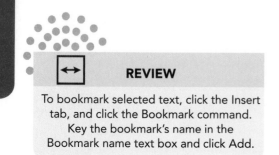

3. Place the insertion point at the end of the section you just bookmarked (after "toll-free number").

4. Press Alt+Shift+X to open the Mark Index Entry dialog box. Key **Shipping** in the **Main entry** text box. This will be the entry in the index you create.

5. Click **Page range**. Click the down arrow next to the **Bookmark** text box to display the list of bookmarks. Choose the bookmark you created in step 2 (Shipping).

Figure 24-11
Using a bookmark to mark an index entry

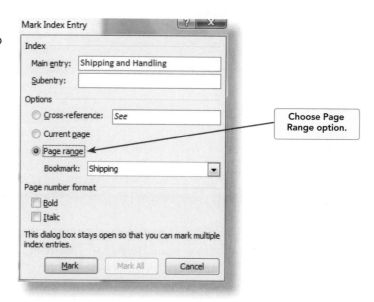

6. Click **Mark**. The field code for the index entry is inserted at the end of the bookmarked section. Now when you create the index, the page number for this entry will be "1–2" instead of just "1."

Exercise 24-7 ADD A CROSS-REFERENCE

You use a cross-reference when you want readers who look up one entry in the index to be referred to another entry. There is an option for creating a cross-reference in the Mark Index Entry dialog box.

1. With the Mark Index Entry dialog box still open, scroll to the bottom of page 1. Select the word "sales tax" in the first sentence under the heading "Note."

2. Click the **Cross-reference** option in the Mark Index Entry dialog box. The selected text appears in the **Main entry** text box, and the insertion point is in the **Cross-reference** text box, one space after "*See*."

3. Key **Shipping and Handling Charges** and click **Mark**. The cross-reference appears in your index entry in the document. "See Shipping and Handling Charges" will now appear under "Sales tax" in your index.

Word 2007

Figure 24-12
Creating a cross-reference

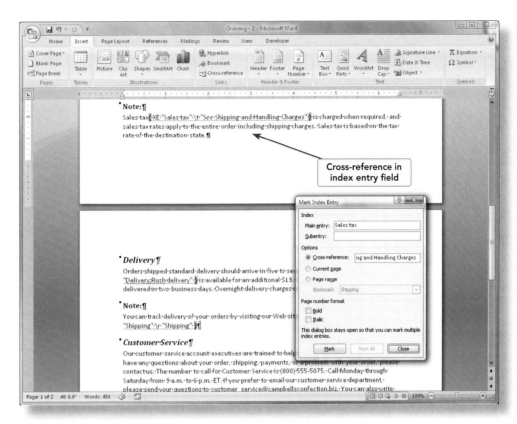

4. Close the Mark Index Entry dialog box.

Formatting and Compiling an Index

After you mark all the index entries in your document, you are ready to create the index. Generally, an index is placed at the end of a document, on a separate page.

You can control the basic layout of the index. For example, you can choose the number of columns and specify one of several styles with which to format the index text.

Exercise 24-8   FORMAT AND COMPILE AN INDEX

1. Position the insertion point at the end of the document. Press Enter twice and click the **References** tab. Locate the **Index** group, and click the Insert Index button . The Index dialog box appears.

2. On the **Index** tab, click the **Run-in** option to the right of **Type**. Notice the change in the **Print Preview** window. Click the **Indented** option and notice the difference.

3. Open the **Formats** list box, and click each index format, examining each style in the **Print Preview** window.

4. Choose the **From template** format, which uses styles from the default template attached to the document. Notice that the index is set for two columns.

5. Click the **Right align page numbers** check box. Notice the change in the **Print Preview** window. (By default, this number style includes a dotted tab leader.) Click the check box again to clear it.

6. Click **Modify**. The Style dialog box appears.

7. Click the various styles (**Index 1** through **Index 9**) in the **Styles** list, noticing the effect in the **Preview** box. Instead of using one of these preset choices, you can modify each style.

8. Choose the **Index 1** style and click **Modify**. The Modify Style dialog box appears.

Figure 24-13
Modify Style dialog box

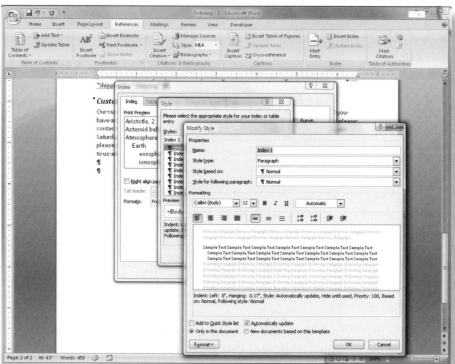

9. Change the font size to 11 points. Click **OK** to close the Modify Style dialog box.

10. Click **OK** to close the Style dialog box; then click **OK** to compile the index. The index is inserted at the bottom of the document.

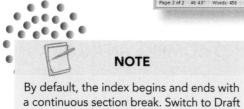

NOTE

By default, the index begins and ends with a continuous section break. Switch to Draft view to see the continuous section breaks.

Editing and Updating Indexes

To edit your index, change the text contained in the index entry (XE) fields of the document and then update the index.

After editing the index entry, you have three ways to update the index:

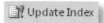

- Click the Update Index button on the Ribbon.

- Press F9.

- Use the shortcut menu.

Exercise 24-9 EDIT AND UPDATE AN INDEX

1. Locate the bold index entry "Online" in the first heading of your document (*not* in the index). In the index entry field (the text in brackets—not the heading itself), change the uppercase "O" to lowercase.

2. Place the insertion point in the index.

3. Click the Update Index button . Word recompiles and replaces your old index with a new one.

4. Check the index, and verify that the index listing "online" is lowercase.

5. Change the "online" entry to uppercase.

6. Place the insertion point in the index, and press F9. The index is instantly updated.

7. In the first paragraph of the document, locate the index entry for "E-mail." Drag the pointer over the entire index entry to select it (including the brackets), and press Delete.

8. Place the insertion point in the index, and right-click. Click **Update Field** from the shortcut menu.

Figure 24-14
Using the shortcut menu to update an index

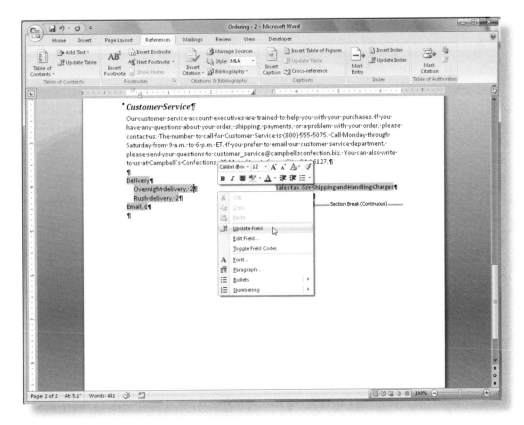

9. Switch to Draft view. Place the insertion point just above the index, at the end of the previous section. Insert a page break to start the index on a new page.

10. On the new page, on a blank line above the index, key **INDEX** and press Enter. Apply the Heading 1 style to the word and center it. Switch to Print Layout view.

Figure 24-15
Index in Print Layout view

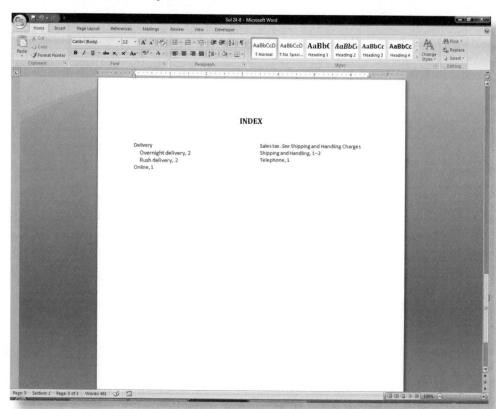

11. Save the document as *[your initials]*24-9 in your Lesson 24 folder.

Creating a Table of Contents

The easiest way to generate a table of contents is to use Word's heading styles (Headings 1–9) for your document headings. Word can then search for the heading styles, record the associated page numbers, and create the table. After the table of contents is created, you can update it periodically to reflect changes in the document.

TIP

Create the index before you create a table of contents, and give your index a heading that will appear in the table of contents. In this way, your index will be listed in your table of contents.

Exercise 24-10 CREATE A TABLE OF CONTENTS

1. Move to the top of the document, and click the Styles Dialog Box Launcher to display the Styles task pane. Notice that the title of the document is formatted using the Heading 1 style.

NOTE

You can click one of the built-in table of contents styles listed in the drop-down list or you can click Insert Table of Contents for more options.

2. Click in the "Online" heading, and notice that it is formatted using the Heading 2 style.

3. Position the insertion point in one of the "Note" paragraphs, and modify the Heading 3 style. Change the font size to 12 points.

4. Position the insertion point at the beginning of the document, and insert a page break. (The table of contents usually appears at the front of a document, on a separate page.)

5. Move to page 1, and click the **References** tab on the Ribbon. Click the Table of Contents button. Click **Insert Table of Contents**. The Table of Contents dialog box appears. Click **OK** to accept the default settings. The table of contents is inserted at the beginning of the document on the new page.

Figure 24-16
Table of Contents

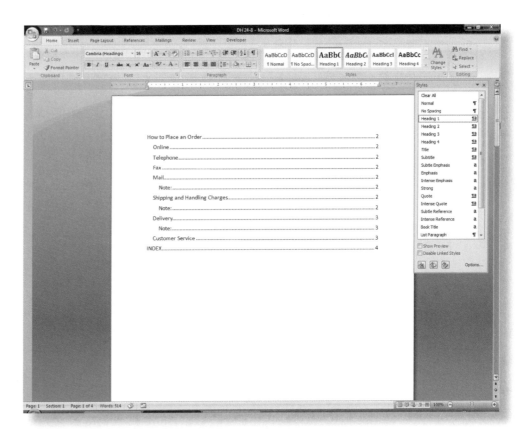

Formatting a Table of Contents

To format the table of contents, you can choose from several styles and formatting options in the Table of Contents dialog box.

Exercise 24-11   FORMAT A TABLE OF CONTENTS

1. Click once anywhere in the table of contents to select it. Notice that the selected text is highlighted in gray.

2. Click the Table of Contents button 🔲, and click **Insert Table of Contents**. The Table of Contents dialog box displays.

3. Open the **Formats** list box. Click each choice to see how the format looks in the **Print Preview** window.

4. Choose the **Classic** format. By default, this format right-aligns page numbers.

5. Open the **Tab leader** list and choose the solid line leader.

NOTE

This dialog box displays a Print Preview and a Web Preview window. If you use Word to create Web pages, you can include a table of contents to help visitors navigate your pages.

Figure 24-17
Formatting the Table of Contents

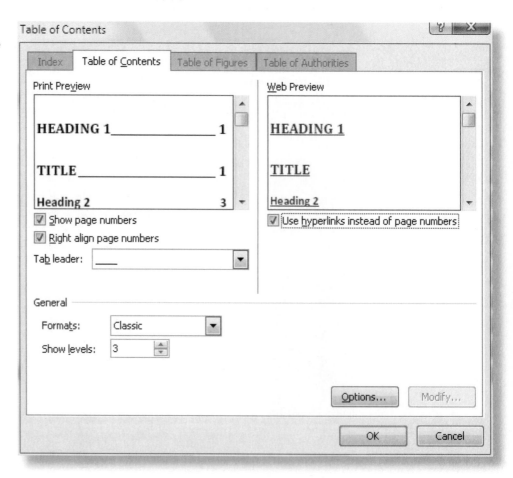

6. Locate **Show levels** in the **General** section. Verify that **3** displays in the box. This feature determines how many heading levels appear in the table of contents.

7. Click **OK**. When you are prompted to replace the selected table of contents, click **OK**.

Editing and Updating a Table of Contents

To edit the table of contents, change the headings in the document and then update the table of contents.

NOTE

If you make changes to the table of contents itself, your changes will be lost the next time you update it unless you make the same changes to the headings in the document.

After you edit the document's headings, you can update the table of contents by using the Update Table button 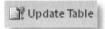, pressing [F9], or using the shortcut menu.

Exercise 24-12 EDIT AND UPDATE A TABLE OF CONTENTS

1. Press [Ctrl] and click the text "Shipping and Handling Charges" in the table of contents. Word moves the insertion point directly to that heading in the document.

2. Position the insertion point at the end of the "Note" paragraph that follows "Shipping and Handling," and press [Enter].

3. Key the following text:

   Payment
   We accept checks, money orders, and Visa, MasterCard, Discover, and American Express credit cards.

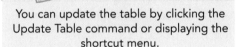

4. Select "Payment" and click the Add Text button 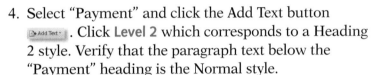. Click **Level 2** which corresponds to a Heading 2 style. Verify that the paragraph text below the "Payment" heading is the Normal style.

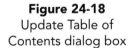

NOTE

You can update the table by clicking the Update Table command or displaying the shortcut menu.

5. Press [Ctrl]+[Home] and press [F9]. When you are prompted to update the table of contents, click **Update entire table** and click **OK**.

Figure 24-18
Update Table of Contents dialog box

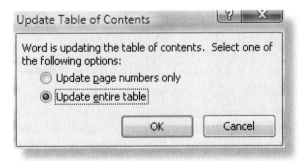

6. Click the Show/Hide ¶ button [¶] to hide the field codes.

Figure 24-19
Completed Table of Contents

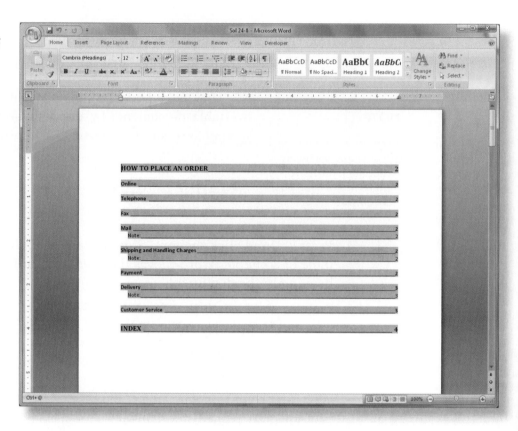

HOW TO PLACE AN ORDER	2
Online	2
Telephone	2
Fax	2
Mail	2
Note:	2
Shipping and Handling Charges	2
Note:	2
Payment	2
Delivery	3
Note:	3
Customer Service	3
INDEX	4

7. Click below the table of contents to deselect it.

8. Apply page numbers to the lower right corner of every page of the document.

9. Update the index because page references have changed since you added the table of contents (and hide the index field codes).

10. Save the document as *[your initials]*24-12 in your Lesson 24 folder.

11. Submit and close the document.

Exercise 24-13 CREATE, MODIFY, AND UPDATE A TABLE OF FIGURES

A table of figures is used to create a list of captions within a document. Captions can be added to figures, tables, equations or other objects. The Table of Figures dialog box contains many of the same options found in the Table of Contents dialog box. You can choose to show page numbers, select a tab leader option, and select a format for the table. You can also select a caption label.

1. Open the file **Figures**, and click the References tab.

2. Position the insertion point in the first row of the first table, and click the Insert Caption button to open the Caption dialog box.

Figure 24-20
Caption dialog box

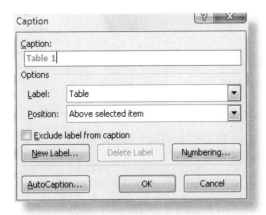

3. Click **OK** to accept the default settings.

4. Insert a caption for each table in the document, accepting default settings for each. Verify that you have five captions in the document.

5. Go to the end of the document, and insert a page break.

6. Key **TABLE OF FIGURES** at the top of the new page, and press Enter.

🗋 Insert Table of Figures

7. Click the Insert Table of Figures button 🗋 Insert Table of Figures to display the Table of Figures dialog box.

Figure 24-21
Table of Figures
dialog box

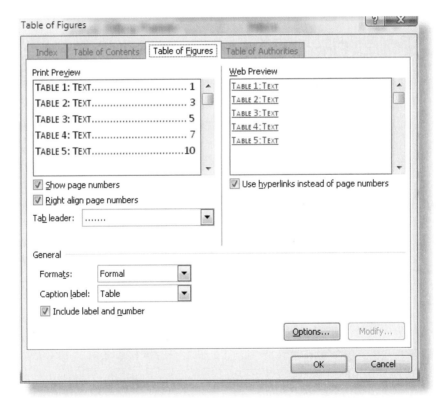

8. Click the down arrow for **Formats**, and click **Formal**. Select the dotted leader format for the **Tab leader**. Click **OK**.

9. Format the heading for the table of figures using 14-point bold, with small caps and 24 points spacing after, and center it.

10. Select the caption, all rows of the third table, and the blank line following the table. Press [Ctrl]+[X] to cut the table.

11. Position the insertion point at the top of the document to the left of the caption for Table 1.

12. Press [Ctrl]+[V] to paste the table.

13. Select the caption for the first table in the document, and right-click to display the shortcut menu. Click **Update Field** to renumber the caption.

14. Select and update each of the remaining captions.

15. Go to the table of figures, and right-click it. Click **Update Field**. Click **OK**.

16. Select the caption and all rows of the third table. Apply the **Keep with next** paragraph formatting option.

17. Select the caption and all rows of the fifth table, and apply the **Keep with next** option.

18. Update the entire table of figures.

19. Save the document as *[your initials]*24-13 in your Lesson 24 folder.

20. Submit and close the document.

Exercise 24-14　CREATE, MODIFY, AND UPDATE A TABLE OF AUTHORITIES

A table of authorities is used to cite references to cases, statutes, and other legal documents. To create a table of authorities, you mark citations and then insert the table of authorities. The procedure is very similar to creating an index or a table of contents.

1. Open the file **Email - 2**, and click the **References** tab.

2. Go to page 2, and select the text "§ 7661."

3. Click the Mark Citation button to open the Mark Citation dialog box.

Figure 24-22
Mark Citation dialog box

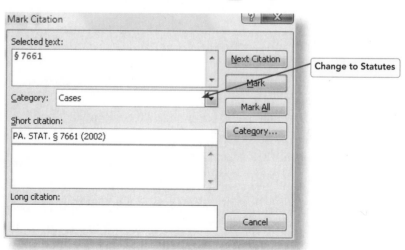

NOTE

To insert the symbol for a section, click the Insert tab. Click Symbol and click More Symbols. Click the drop-down arrow for the Font box, and click (normal text). Scroll to locate the symbol for section. Click Insert and Close the dialog box.

4. Change the **Category** to **Statutes**, and edit the **Short citation** text box to read PA. STAT. § 7661 (2002).

5. Click **Mark** and **Close** the dialog box.

6. Select the text "§ 2250.1" in the second legal reference, and press Shift + Alt + I . Edit the **Short citation** to read PA. STAT. § 2250.1 (2002). Click **Mark**.

7. Click **Next Citation** in the Mark Citation dialog box to move to the next section mark. Click in the document and select "§ 7702." Click in the **Selected text** section of the Mark Citation dialog box to update the selection.

8. Edit the **Short citation** to read 15 U.S.C. § 7702, and click **Mark**.

9. Click **Next Citation**, and expand the selection to "§ 7703." Click in the Mark Citation dialog box, and edit the **Short citation** to 15 U.S.C. § 7703. Click **Mark**.

10. Click **Next Citation**, and expand the selection to "§ 2701." Click in the Mark Citation dialog box, and edit the **Short citation** to 18 U.S.C. § 2701. Click **Mark**.

11. Click **Next Citation**, and expand the selection to "§ 1030." Click in the Mark Citation dialog box, and edit the **Short citation** to 18 U.S.C. § 1030. Click **Mark**, and click **Close**.

12. Insert a page break at the end of the document, and key TABLE OF AUTHORITIES. Press Enter , and format the title using 14-point bold, with center alignment. Change the spacing before to 72 points and the spacing after to 24 points.

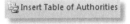

13. Click the Insert Table of Authorities button 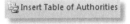 to open the Table of Authorities dialog box.

Figure 24-23
Table of Authorities dialog box

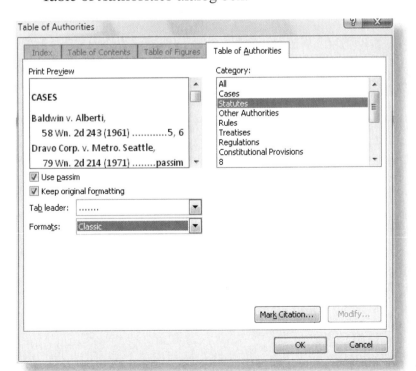

14. Click **Statutes** under **Category**, and click **Classic** in the **Formats** drop-down list.

15. Click **OK** to insert the table.

16. Save the document as *[your initials]*24-14 in your Lesson 24 folder.

17. Submit and close the document.

Lesson 24 Summary

- You create an outline to determine the content and order of a final document. An outline consists of styled headings, subheadings, and body text. To create an outline, switch to Outline view. Then type headings, and apply the appropriate styles by using the Outlining toolbar's buttons. See Table 24-1.

- You assign different levels to your outline text. For example, you can promote a heading (raise it to a higher outline level) or demote a heading (move it to a lower outline level). Word allows as many as nine levels in an outline.

- The easiest way to rearrange text in an outline is to first collapse the outline to show only the headings and body text you want. After rearranging the outline text, you can expand the outline to display all subtext. To collapse or expand an outline so that only the desired heading levels are visible, use the Show Level drop-down list.

- To navigate an outline by jumping from one heading to another, set the Select Browse Object to browse by heading; then click Next Heading or Previous Heading on the vertical scroll bar.

- Another navigation tool for outlines is the Document Map: a separate pane on the left side of the screen that shows the headings of your document. Click a heading in the Document Map, and Word jumps to that heading in the document pane.

- To move text in an outline, collapse the outline to show the heading levels you want. Select a heading; then click the Move Up button ⬆ or the Move Down button ⬇ to move the heading and its subtext to a new location. You can also move a selected heading by dragging it up or down in the outline.

- To move text by using the Clipboard, select the heading you want to move, copy it, place the insertion point where you want the text to appear, and paste it. Then delete the original heading and its subtext.

- To delete a heading and its subtext in an outline, select the heading and press Delete.

- Indexes and tables of contents are common features in long documents. An index usually appears at the end of the document and lists the pages where specific words, phrases, or topics can be found. The table of contents usually appears at the beginning of the document and lists topics and their page numbers in the order in which they appear in the document.

- To create an index, you first identify, or mark, the text you want indexed. You use the Mark Index Entry dialog box to mark text. Marking the text inserts field codes in the document.

- When a topic has subtopics that are located in different parts of a document, you can create subentries that are subordinate to the main index entry. You do this in the Mark Index Entry dialog box.

- To mark several entries automatically, you can create a concordance file—a list of words, in the form of a two-column Word table, to be located and indexed in a document. Column 1 contains the words you want to locate in the document; column 2 contains the words as they should appear in the index. You use the AutoMark command in the Index dialog box (Index tab) to mark the document with your concordance file.

- When a topic extends beyond one page and you want the index to refer readers to a range of pages, you create a bookmark for the text to be indexed and then use the bookmark to mark the text.

- When you want readers who look up one entry in the index to be referred to another entry, you use the cross-reference option in the Mark Index Entry dialog box.

- After you mark all the index entries in a document, you use the Index dialog box (Index tab) to compile the entries and create the index. The dialog box also contains formatting options.

- To edit an index, make changes to any of the index entry fields in the document. After editing index entries, update the index by clicking within the index and then pressing [F9].

- To create a table of contents, apply heading styles to the document headings. Word can then search for the heading styles, record the associated page numbers, and create the table. Use the Table of Contents dialog box (References tab). The dialog box also contains formatting options.

- If you make changes to the document that affect headings or pagination, update the table of contents by selecting it and then pressing [F9].

- To create a table of figures, insert captions in your document and use the Table of Figures dialog box to format and number the table of figures.

- To create a table of authorities, mark citations in the document, and use the Table of Authorities dialog box to insert the table in the document.

LESSON 24		Command Summary	
Feature	**Button**	**Command**	**Keyboard**
Outline view		**View** tab, **Document Views** group	Alt + Ctrl + O
Promote a heading		**Outlining** tab, **Outline Tools** group	Alt + Shift + ←
Demote a heading		**Outlining** tab, **Outline Tools** group	Alt + Shift + →
Demote a heading to body text		**Outlining** tab, **Outline Tools** group	Ctrl + Shift + N
Show selected heading levels	Show Level:	**Outlining** tab, **Outline Tools** group	
Show only first line of body text	Show First Line Only	**Outlining** tab, **Outline Tools** group	Alt + Shift + L
Document Map	Document Map	**View** tab, **Show/Hide** group	
Mark index entry	Mark Entry	**References** tab, **Index** group	Alt + Shift + X
Insert index	Insert Index	**References** tab, **Index** group	
Update index	Update Index	**References** tab, **Index** group	F9
Insert table of contents	Table of Contents	**References** tab, **Table of Contents** group	
Update table of contents	Update Table	**References** tab, **Table of Contents** group	F9
Insert a caption	Insert Caption	**References** tab, **Captions** group	
Insert table of figures	Insert Table of Figures	**References** tab, **Captions** group	
Mark a citation	Mark Citation	**References** tab, **Table of Authorities** group	Alt + Shift + I
Insert table of authorities	Insert Table of Authorities	**References** tab, **Table of Authorities** group	

Concepts Review

True/False Questions

Each of the following statements is either true or false. Indicate your choice by circling T or F.

T   F   1. An index can contain subentries.

T   F   2. The plus sign symbol in outline view indicates a heading with subtext.

T   F   3. When you mark index entries, Word marks each occurrence of an index entry in each paragraph.

T   F   4. You can use the [F9] key to update an index.

T   F   5. You need to create a bookmark before you can mark index entries.

T   F   6. The most reliable way to add an entry to an index is to key it into the index list and then add a page number.

T   F   7. The easiest way to create a table of contents is to create your own heading styles.

T   F   8. A selected table of contents is shaded gray.

Short Answer Questions

Write the correct answer in the space provided.

1. What is the name of an index entry that is subordinate to a main entry?

   _____

2. Which selection symbol in Outline view indicates a heading with no subtext?

   _____

3. What is the keyboard shortcut to mark an index entry?

   _____

4. If index entry fields are not visible in a document, which button should you click to display them?

   _____

5. Within the brackets of an index entry field, which two letters appear first?

   _____

6. Which key should you press when you click a heading in a table of contents if you want to jump to that section of the document?

   _____

7. Which command can you choose from the shortcut menu to update your index or table of contents?

8. Which dialog box displays a preview of the table of contents formats?

Critical Thinking

Answer these questions on a separate page. There are no right or wrong answers. Support your answers with examples from your own experience, if possible.

1. Some people find Outline view useful for building reports, term papers, and other business or school documents. Others write these documents using Print Layout view. Which do you prefer? Why?

2. Some people prefer to use an index to locate subject matter, and others prefer to find topics by using the table of contents and then skimming the topic to locate specific subject matter. Which do you prefer? Why?

Skills Review

Exercise 24-15

Create an outline.

1. Start a new document, and switch to Outline view.
2. Key the heading CAMPBELL'S CONFECTIONS FALL RETREAT AGENDA.
3. Create a level-2 heading by following these steps:
   a. Press Enter, and click the Demote button ⇨.
   b. Key Objectives.
4. Create three level-3 headings by following these steps:
   a. Press Enter, and click the Demote button ⇨.
   b. Key Year-to-Date Performance Analysis. Press Enter.
   c. Key Strategy for Next Year. Press Enter, and key Five-Year Plan.
5. Press Enter, and click the Promote button ⇦, and key the following level 2 headings.
   Staff to Attend
   Dates and Location
   Activities Planned
6. Key the following lines as level 3 headings under "Activities Planned."
   Business
   Leisure

7. Add body text to the level-1 heading by following these steps:

   a. Position the insertion point at the end of the first line, and press Enter.

   b. Click the Demote to Body Text button 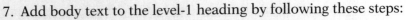, and key This fall, we will refresh our spirits and plan for the future at our favorite resort in western Pennsylvania.

8. Switch to Print Layout view to view the document.

9. Save the document as *[your initials]*24-15 in your Lesson 24 folder.

10. Submit and close the document.

Exercise 24-16

Identify single and multiple index entries and compile an index.

1. Open the file **Computer Use Policy**. Make sure the Show/Hide ¶ button ¶ is turned on.

2. Mark computer terms as index entries by following these steps:

   a. Select "Computer theft" in the first paragraph.

   b. Click the References tab, and click the Mark Entry button.

   c. Click Mark in the Mark Index Entry dialog box. Drag the dialog box to the lower right corner of the window so you can see the document area.

   d. Select the next computer term, "Computer trespass." Click Mark in the Mark Index Entry dialog box.

   e. Repeat step D for each of the following terms in the document.

   Computer invasion of privacy

   Password

   Pirated software

3. Mark a main entry with two subentries by following these steps:

   a. Select the text "disruption of computers" in the paragraph that begins "State and federal."

   b. Activate the Mark Index Entry dialog box, and make sure "Disruption of computers" is in the Main entry text box. In the Subentry text box, key invasion of privacy and click Mark.

   c. Place the insertion point after the text "steal computer services." In the Main entry text box, key Disruption of computers, and in the Subentry text box, key steal computer services. Click Mark.

   d. Place the insertion point after the text "commit fraud." In the Main entry text box, key Disruption of computers, and in the Subentry text box, key commit fraud. Click Mark.

   e. Close the Mark Index Entry dialog box.

4. Add 72 points of spacing before the title "Computer Use Policy."

5. Compile the index, using the default index format settings, by following these steps:

   a. Click the Show/Hide ¶ button ¶ to hide the field codes.

   b. Place the insertion point at the end of the document.

   c. Press Enter and insert a page break.

   d. Key INDEX and press Enter twice. Format the word "INDEX" as 14-point bold and centered.

   e. Move the insertion point to the second blank line after the title "Index."

   f. Click the References tab, and click the Insert Index button 📄 Insert Index . Click OK.

📄 Insert Index

6. Save the document as *[your initials]*24-16 in your Lesson 24 folder. Submit and close the document.

Exercise 24-17

Mark index entries by using a concordance file; mark a range of pages; compile, edit, and update an index.

1. Open the file **Health Events**.

2. Create a concordance file for health topics by following these steps:

   a. Start a new document and insert a 2-column by 1-row table.

   b. Key the text shown in Figure 24-24 pressing Tab after keying each item.

   c. Save the concordance file as *[your initials]*24-17a in your Lesson 24 folder. Submit and close the file.

NOTE

A concordance file is used to generate several index entries at one time. The file contains a list of words to be located in the document and is formatted as a two-column table. The first column contains the words you want to locate in your document. The second column contains the words as they should appear in the index.

Figure 24-24

Height and weight	Height and weight
BMI	Body mass index
Body composition analysis	Body composition analysis
Obesity and weight loss	Obesity and weight loss
Blood pressure	Hypertension monitoring
Blood typing	Blood typing
Diabetes screening	Diabetes screening
Cholesterol ratios	Cholesterol ratios
Glaucoma screening	Glaucoma screening
Allergy screening	Allergy screening
Asthma screening	Asthma screening

3. Use the concordance file to mark index entries automatically by following these steps:

   a. Click the Show/Hide button ¶ [¶] to display nonprinting characters, if they are not already showing.

   b. Click the **References** tab on the Ribbon, and click the Insert Index button [Insert Index].

   c. On the **Index** tab, click **AutoMark**.

   d. Choose the file *[your initials]24-17a* you created in step 2. (If necessary change the type of file to All Files.)

   e. Click **Open**.

4. Use a bookmark to mark a range of text by following these steps:

   a. Select the sessions on page 2 beginning with "Board Room No. 1" and ending with "Fatigue."

   b. Click the **Insert** tab; click the Bookmark button [Bookmark]; key **Seminars** in the **Bookmark name** text box; and click **Add**.

   c. Place the insertion point at the end of the document, and press [Alt]+[Shift]+[X] to open the Mark Index Entry dialog box.

   d. Click **Page Range**, and click the **Bookmark** drop-down arrow. Click **Seminars**. Click **Mark**.

   e. Close the Mark Index Entry dialog box.

5. Insert centered page numbers at the bottom of the page, and number page 1.

6. Format and compile the index by following these steps:

   a. Move to the end of the document, and insert a page break.

   b. Key **INDEX TO HEALTH EVENTS**. Apply the Heading 1 style, center the text, and add 24 points spacing after. Press [Enter].

   c. Click the Insert Index button [Insert Index], and choose **Modern** from the **Formats** list.

   d. Select the **Right align page numbers** check box.

   e. Choose leader dots from the **Tab leader** list, and click **OK**.

7. Edit an index entry and update the index by following these steps:

   a. On page 1, locate the index entry for "Cholesterol ratios."

   b. Insert the words **and triglycerides** after "ratios" in the index entry field.

   c. Click the Show/Hide ¶ button [¶] to hide the field codes.

   d. Right-click anywhere within the index, and choose **Update Field** from the shortcut menu.

8. Save the indexed document as *[your initials]24-17b* in your Lesson 24 folder. Submit and close the document.

Exercise 24-18

Create, format, edit, and update a table of contents.

1. Open the file **Guidelines - 3**.

2. Insert page numbers aligned at the bottom right margin.

3. Create and format a table of contents by following these steps:

   a. Place the insertion point at the top of the document, insert a page break, and click within the page break.

   b. Click the References tab, and click the Table of Contents button. Click Insert Table of Contents.

   c. Open the Formats drop-down list, and choose the Distinctive format. (This format right-aligns page numbers and includes an underline tab leader.) Click OK.

4. Change the left and right margins for the document to 1.25 inches.

5. Locate the heading "Corporations." Change the style to Heading 3.

6. Update the table of contents by right-clicking it and then choosing Update Fields from the shortcut menu. Update the entire table.

7. On a new line above the table of contents, key the heading TABLE OF CONTENTS. Apply the Normal style to the heading, and change the formatting to 14-point bold, centered, with 72 points spacing before and 24 points spacing after.

8. Save your document as *[your initials]*24-18 in your Lesson 24 folder. Submit and close the document.

Lesson Applications

Exercise 24-19

Outline a document.

1. Open the file **Marketing Plan**, and switch to Outline view.

2. Apply the level-1 heading style to the first line.

3. Apply the level-2 heading style to the following lines:

   Purpose/Mission
   Analysis
   Marketing Strategy/Objectives
   Promotion
   Budget & Implementation

4. Apply the level-3 heading style to the following lines:

   Analyze Product
   Analyze Target Market
   Analyze Competitors
   Financial Analysis
   Market Growth
   Financial Objectives
   Market Share
   Advertising
   Sales Promotion
   Personal Selling
   Public Relations
   Performance Analysis
   Timelines
   Spending by Product/Segment

5. Apply the level-4 heading style to the remaining lines in the document.

6. Delete blank lines in the document.

7. Switch to Print Layout view.

8. Save the document as *[your initials]*24-19 in your Lesson 24 folder. Submit and close the document.

Exercise 24-20

Mark index entries, mark a range of text, and compile an index.

1. Open the file **Leave Policy**.

2. Change the left and right margins to 1.25 inches, and add 72 points spacing before the title.

3. Mark an index entry for each heading beginning with "Eligibility" and ending with "Leave without Pay."

4. Find the text "medical leave of absence" in the second paragraph below the heading "Family & Medical Leave," and mark an index entry.

5. Select the table on page 1, and create a bookmark for this text, naming it "AnnualLeave." Mark the text as an index entry, using "Annual Leave" as the main entry.

6. Insert page numbers on all pages, centering the numbers at the bottom of the page.

7. Turn off the display of hidden text.

8. Add a page break at the end of the document.

9. Key INDEX below the page break, and press Enter. Format "INDEX" as 14-point bold and centered. Change the spacing after to 24 points.

10. Position the insertion point below "Index," and insert the index. Use the default format (From template) with right-aligned page numbers and dotted leaders.

11. Save the document as *[your initials]*24-20 in your Lesson 24 folder. Submit and close the document.

Exercise 24-21

Create and format an index and a table of contents.

1. Open the file **History - 4**.

2. Apply the Heading 1 style to the first line of the document. Modify the Heading 1 style to 18 points with 24 points spacing before and 3 points spacing after.

3. Add a footer that starts on page 2. Use the text Campbell's Confections aligned at the left margin and Page plus the page number aligned at the right margin. Change the footer text to 10 points.

4. Go to page 1, and locate the paragraph under the heading "Background." Mark an index entry for "retail," "wholesale," and "fundraising."

5. Mark as index entries the text listed in Figure 24-25.

Figure 24-25

```
Tours
Chocolate Club
Corporate Gifts
Favors
Fountains
Gift Cards
Fundraising
E-commerce
Gourmet Chocolate
```

6. Select "Internet" in the E-commerce paragraph. Click in the Mark Index Entry dialog box, and create a cross-reference. Key E-commerce after "See."

7. Insert the index on a separate page at the end of the document, under the heading INDEX (apply Heading 1 style to the index heading and center the heading). Use the Formal style with right-aligned numbers and a dotted tab leader, and change the number of columns to 1.

8. Go to the top of the document, and insert a page break. At the top of the document, before the page break, key the heading TABLE OF CONTENTS. Apply the Normal style to the heading to separate it from the table of contents. Format the heading as 18-point bold, with all caps and 24 points of spacing after, and center it.

9. Turn off the display of hidden characters; then insert a table of contents below the heading you just created. Use the Formal style.

10. Save the document as *[your initials]*24-21 in your Lesson 24 folder. Submit and close the document.

Exercise 24-22 ◆ Challenge Yourself

Insert, edit, and update an index and a table of contents.

1. Open the file **Ordering - 3**.

2. Apply the Heading 1 style to the first line.

3. Apply the Heading 2 style to the following headings: Online, Telephone, Fax, Mail, Shipping and Handling Charges, Delivery, and Customer Service. Delete the blank paragraph marks before each Heading 2 paragraph.

4. Mark an index entry for each of the Heading 2–styled paragraphs.

5. Locate the text "Sales tax," and create a cross-reference to "Shipping and Handling."

6. Select the text from "Delivery Chart" through the last line of the tabbed text, and create a bookmark named DeliveryChart.

7. Mark an index entry for the bookmarked text.

8. On a new page at the end of the document, key the index heading Index to Ordering. Apply the Heading 1 style to the index heading, apply all caps, and center the heading. Apply 24 points spacing after to the heading.

9. Insert the index below the index heading. Use a format of your choice.

10. Mark one additional index entry, and update the index.

11. At the beginning of the document, key Table of Contents, and insert a table of contents below the heading. Use an appropriate format.

12. Format the table of contents heading as 16-point bold, with all caps and 24 points spacing after, and center it.

13. Turn off the display of hidden characters, and adjust page breaks as needed.

14. Update the table of contents and the index.

15. On every page of the document, add a footer that includes Campbell's Confections aligned at the left margin and the page number aligned at the right margin. Use the format "Page 1" for the page numbering. Format the entire footer as 10 points.

16. Save the document as *[your initials]*24-22 in your Lesson 24 folder. Submit and close the document.

On Your Own

In these exercises you work on your own, as you would in a real-life business environment. Use the skills you've learned to accomplish the task—and be creative.

Exercise 24-23

Create a detailed outline for a document that describes a hobby or one of your interests. Use headings to introduce categories of information, and include a minimum of three heading levels and one occurrence of body text. Save the file as *[your initials]*24-23 and submit it.

Exercise 24-24

Using a report you created for another class, add a table of contents and an index. Format the table of contents and the index so they match and are consistent in style with the rest of the document. Save the file as *[your initials]*24-24 and submit it.

Exercise 24-25

Use the Internet to research three popular tourist destinations in the United States. Look up facts such as population, most popular tourist attractions, restaurants, and other information. Write a three-page report on these destinations, using headings to indicate various levels of information. Add a table of contents and an index of the most frequently used terms in the document. Save the file as *[your initials]*24-25 and submit it.

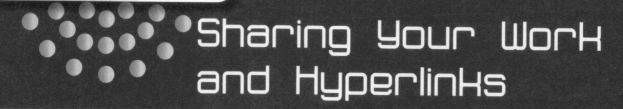

Sharing Your Work and Hyperlinks

OBJECTIVES

After completing this lesson, you will be able to:

1. Create comments.

2. Use the Track Changes feature.

3. Compare and merge documents.

4. Review a document and secure document content.

5. Insert hyperlinks.

Estimated Time: 1½ hours

MCAS OBJECTIVES

In this lesson:
WW 07 1.3.4
WW 07 1.4.1
WW 07 5.2
WW 07 5.3
WW 07 5.4
WW 07 6.1.3
WW 07 6.2
WW 07 6.3

In most offices, more than one person works on a document. A document might have a primary author and several editors. Word provides tools that make it easy to collaborate with others—on your computer instead of on paper—to produce a finished document. After you have a finished document, you might take it one step further—sharing it with others on the World Wide Web. You will also learn to work with hypertext to link documents.

Creating Comments

Comments are notes or annotations you add to a document. Each person who adds a comment is called a *reviewer*. Comments are color-coded by reviewer. Word refers to comments and any other type of document revision marks as *markup*. You can display, hide, or print markup.

In Print Layout view, you insert, edit, and view comments in the *Reviewing pane*—a narrow horizontal or vertical pane that opens at the bottom or left side of the screen, or you can enter, edit, and view comments in *markup balloons* that appear in the document margin with a line leading to where the comment was inserted.

Exercise 25-1 ADD COMMENTS TO A DOCUMENT

The easiest way to add a comment to a document is to use the Review tab on the Ribbon. You can also use the keyboard shortcut Alt+Ctrl+M.

1. Open the file **CruiseFAQs**.

2. Click the **Review** tab, and locate the **Comments** group.

3. Open the Word Options dialog box, and click **Popular**. Review the information in the **Personalize your copy of Microsoft Office** section.

4. Enter your name and initials in the appropriate data fields. Click **OK**.

5. Position the insertion point at the beginning of page 2.

6. Click the New Comment button 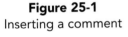 on the Ribbon. A balloon appears in the margin displaying your reference initials and an insertion point. A line leads from the balloon to the position of the comment insertion.

7. Key the following text in the balloon: **Verify the number of employees and family members planning to attend the sales conference.**

> **TIP**
>
> If you review a document by using another person's computer, your comments will be attributed to the person whose name appears in the User Information section. Make sure to change the User Information to your name when you insert comments, and then change back to the original user's name when you are finished.

Figure 25-1
Inserting a comment

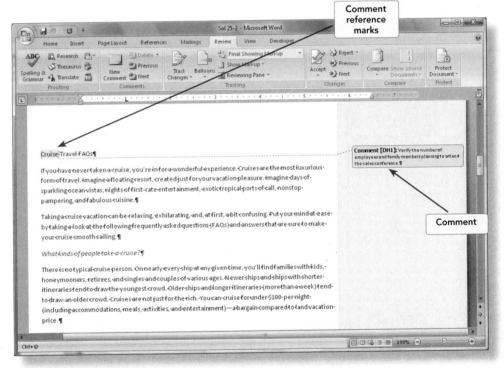

8. Click the Reviewing Pane button 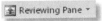. Click **Reviewing Pane Horizontal**. The Reviewing pane opens, showing your name, followed by the date and time you are inserting the comment.

NOTE

When you comment on a selected word, sentence, or paragraph, the text is enclosed by two comment reference marks. You can also position the insertion point at a particular location and insert a comment.

NOTE

You can also key comments in the Reviewing pane. Click the insertion point in the Reviewing pane, and key the comment text.

The entry in the Reviewing pane is color-coded to the reviewer. *Comment reference marks* also appear in the document where you insert the comment. The reference marks are color-coded to the reviewer.

9. Scroll within the document to the paragraph below *"Is a cruise good for families with kids?"* Select "programs" in the first line, and click the New Comment button to insert another comment. A second balloon displays with an insertion point for keying the new text.

10. Key **Request a copy of the activities planned for children for our cruise.** Notice the comment reference marks around "program" in the document.

11. Move the mouse pointer over a balloon. A ScreenTip displays the name of the reviewer and the time and date when the reviewer entered the comment.

Figure 25-2
Comments displayed in the Reviewing pane

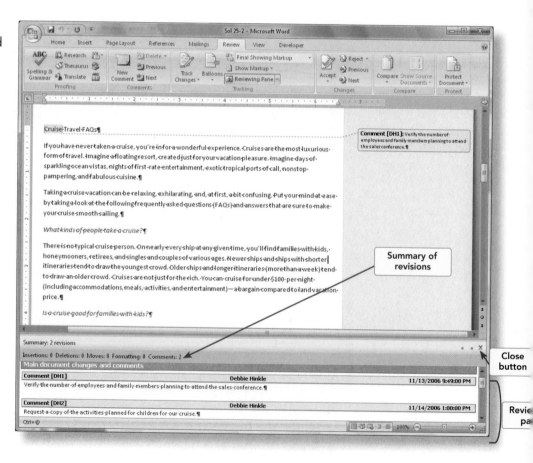

12. Click the Close button ⊠ on the Reviewing pane to close the Reviewing pane.

13. Locate the paragraph below the text *"What documentation is needed?"* Select the entire paragraph (which starts "This depends").

14. Press Alt + Ctrl + M to insert a new comment. Word inserts a balloon in the right margin area.

15. Key the comment Verify the documentation that we will need. The document now has three comments.

TIP

The Next and Previous buttons are helpful for jumping from one comment to another, particularly in a long document. The insertion point moves to the next or previous comment.

NOTE

You can also delete a comment by right-clicking the comment balloon and choosing Delete Comment from the shortcut menu. To delete all comments, click the arrow on the Delete command and choose Delete All Comments in Document.

NOTE

You can insert a comment in an existing comment balloon. Click in the balloon, click the New Comment command, and key the text.

Exercise 25-2 EDIT AND DELETE COMMENTS

You can edit and delete comments by working directly with the balloon text in Print Layout view or by using the Reviewing pane.

1. Click the comment in the first balloon. The comment appears highlighted (the balloon's background color darkens and the dotted connector line becomes solid).

2. Key total before "number." Increase the zoom level if necessary to key the text.

3. Click the Next button on the Review tab. The second comment mark is highlighted. Click the button again to move to the third comment.

4. Click the Delete button on the Ribbon. The comment is removed from the document.

5. Click the Reviewing Pane button to display the Reviewing pane. The two remaining comments are listed.

6. Edit the second comment to read: Verify the total number of adults and children planning to attend the sales meeting.

Figure 25-3
Edited text of two remaining comments

TIP

You can set the Select Browse Object button on the vertical scroll bar to browse by comments. Then the double-arrow scroll buttons become the Previous Comment and Next Comment buttons.

NOTE

Word sets the zoom level and page orientation to best display the comment balloons in your printed document.

TIP

From the Print what drop-down list in the Print dialog box, choose Document to print a document without comments, choose Document showing markup to print a document with its comments in balloons, or choose List of markup to print the document's comments only.

7. Close the Reviewing pane.

8. Save the document as *[your initials]*25-2 in a new folder for Lesson 25.

Exercise 25-3 PRINT COMMENTS

You can print a document with its balloon comments, as they appear in Print Layout view, or you can print just a list of a document's comments. You can also print a document without comments.

1. Verify that the document displays in Print Layout view.

2. Print the document. The document prints with comments.

3. Open the Print dialog box. Notice that **Print what** is automatically set to **Document showing markup**. This setting will appear when you print from any view that displays balloon comments. Click **Cancel**.

4. Switch to Draft view. Notice that balloon comments are not displayed.

5. Open the Print dialog box. Notice that **Print what** is set to **Document**. With this setting, the document would print without comments.

6. Open the **Print what** drop-down list box, and choose **List of markup**. Click **OK**. Word prints your comments as a list, similar to how comments appear in the Reviewing pane.

7. Close the document, saving changes.

Using the Track Changes Feature

When the job of revising a document is shared by more than one person, you can use the Track Changes feature to mark each person's changes. When this feature is turned on, Word tracks changes as you edit the document. These *tracked changes*, also called *markup*, are revision marks that show where deletions, insertions, and formatting changes were made. When you review the document, you can either accept the changes or return to the original wording.

Word displays tracked changes in the following way:

- **Underline:** New text is underlined.

- **Strikethrough:** Deleted text has a horizontal line through it.

- **Revision bar:** A vertical bar appears in the margin next to revised text.

To show tracked changes in the text and also in *markup balloons* in the document margin, change the balloons setting by clicking the Balloons command and clicking Show Revisions in Balloons. Balloons make it easy to see and respond to document changes, additions, deletions, and comments.

Exercise 25-4　USE THE TRACK CHANGES FEATURE TO ENTER REVISIONS

To track changes in a document, turn on Track Changes by clicking the Track Changes command. When you point to the Track Changes command, you see a divider line. Click the upper part of the button to turn on and to turn off Track Changes. Click the lower portion of the button to display options for Track Changes.

Figure 25-4
Track changes button

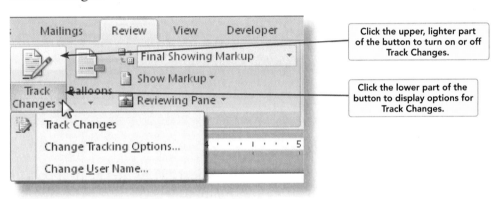

1. Open the file **Wholesale - 2**. Tracked changes already appear in the document, indicating that another reviewer has edited the document. You are going to make additional revisions to the document.

 2. Make sure the Show/Hide ¶ button ¶ is turned on.

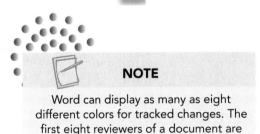

3. Right-click the status bar, and click Track Changes. The status bar shows the status of Track Changes. Click the Balloons button ▤ and click Show Revisions in Balloons.

4. In the first paragraph, change the beginning of the second sentence to read Contracts were negotiated with two large hotel chains. The new words appear underlined and in another color, and the deleted word appears in a balloon in the margin.

5. Select the heading "Wholesale," and change the font size to 14 points. The revision bar displays to the left of the heading, and a balloon displays the formatting change.

Figure 25-5
Tracked changes in Print Layout view

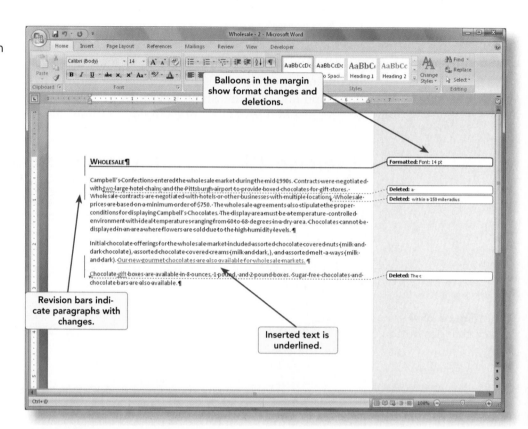

NOTE

To see tracked changes for formatting revisions, you must be in Print Layout view. When you change the Balloons setting to Show All Revisions Inline, you will not see formatting revisions.

REVIEW

When you are making changes to a document that will be reviewed by others, a good idea is to insert comments to explain why you made specific changes. To add a comment, click the New Comment command. You can also use the keyboard shortcut Alt + Ctrl + M.

6. Select "$750" in the first paragraph, and apply italics.

7. Select the last sentence in the first paragraph, and press Delete to remove it. The sentence appears in a balloon.

8. Select the last paragraph, and cut the selection.

9. Position the insertion point before the sentence that begins "Our new gourmet," and paste the cut text. Vertical bars appear to the left of the paragraphs to show they were changed.

10. Click the lower part of the Track Changes button to display Track Changes options. Click **Change Tracking Options**. The Track Changes Options dialog box displays.

Figure 25-6
Track Changes
Options

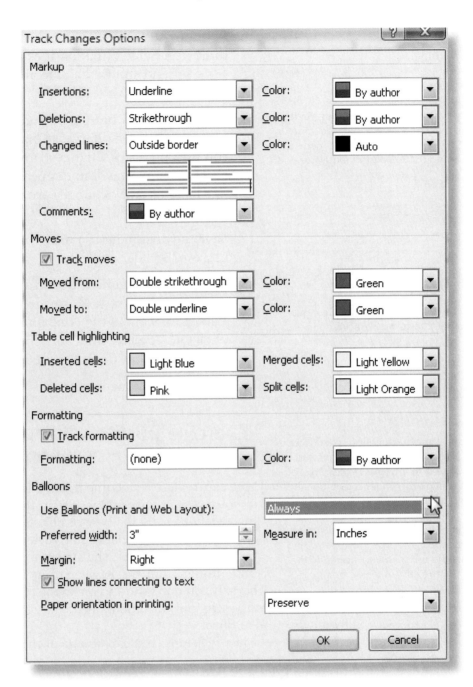

11. Locate the Markup section of the Track Changes Options dialog box.
    The default settings for Insertions, Deletions, and Changed lines are
    displayed. Locate the Balloons section. Notice the default settings for
    Preferred width, Margin, and Show lines connecting to text. Locate the
    section for Moves. Study the default settings.

12. Click the down arrow for the Color drop-down list for Insertions.
    Notice the colors available for reviewers.

13. Click Cancel to close the dialog box without making changes.

14. Point to any revision you have made in the document. A ScreenTip
    identifies your name, the date, and the type of revision.

NOTE

Not only can you track changes made to the main body of a Word document, but you can also track changes made to headers and footers and to footnotes and endnotes.

Track Changes: On

TIP

You can also click the Track Changes command to turn off Track Changes.

NOTE

Switch the page orientation to landscape when printing tracked changes and balloon text to improve readability. You can change the Paper orientation in printing tracked changes by opening the Track Changes Options dialog box and changing the Preserve default setting to Force Landscape. The Preserve setting prints the orientation specified in the Page Layout dialog box.

15. Point to the revision marks "within a 150 mile radius." A ScreenTip identifies Lynn Tanguay as the reviewer and shows the date and type of revisions she made.

16. Click the Track Changes button `Track Changes: On` on the status bar to turn off Track Changes mode. When you turn off Track Changes, any changes you make to the document will not appear as tracked changes. The existing track changes are not removed from the document.

17. Save the document as *[your initials]*25-4 in your Lesson 25 folder.

18. To print the document with tracked changes, open the Print dialog box. Make sure **Document showing markup** appears in the **Print what** drop-down list box. Click **OK**. Tracked changes appear on the printed page just as they do in Print Layout view.

19. Leave the document open for the next exercise.

Exercise 25-5 ACCEPT AND REJECT REVISIONS

You can review a document after it is edited and decide if you want to accept or reject the revisions. You can review changes by the type of change made or review only changes made by a particular reviewer. If you accept the revisions, Word deletes the strikethrough text, removes the underlining from the new text, and removes the revision bars. If you don't want to make the revisions, you can reject them and restore the original document. You can accept or reject changes individually or all at once.

To accept or reject revisions, you can do one of the following:

- Use the Ribbon.

- Use the Reviewing pane.

- Right-click the revision, and use the shortcut menu.

You can also merge revised files from other reviewers into the same document. Then you can protect the document from revisions and allow only the author to turn off the tracking or accept or reject revisions.

Reviewing Pane ▾

1. Click the Reviewing Pane button `Reviewing Pane ▾` to display the Reviewing Pane.

2. Review the summary information, and notice the total number of revisions and the breakdown by insertions, deletions, and formatting.

3. Point to the Accept and Move to Next button . Notice this button has a divider line. When you point to the upper half of the button, the revision is accepted, and you move to the next change. If you click the lower half of the button, a list of options appears.

Figure 25-7
Accept button

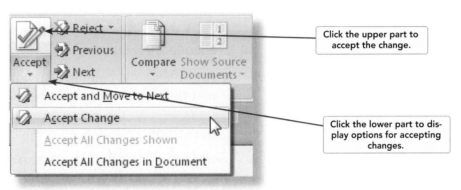

4. Select the title at the beginning of the document. Click the Accept and Move to Next button on the Ribbon to accept the change. The text in the next balloon is highlighted.

5. Click the Show Markup button , and deselect the **Insertions and Deletions** option, leaving the **Formatting** option checked. Now only the changes to formatting appear in the document.

> **NOTE**
>
> You can leave the Comments option turned on because there are no comments in the document. The Markup Area Highlight option shades the markup area.

Figure 25-8
Show markup options

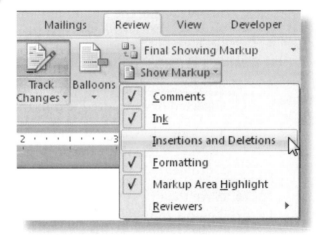

6. Click the Next button , if necessary, to move to the next formatting change in the document.

7. Click the Reject and Move to Next button  on the Ribbon to reject the formatting change. Click **Cancel** if a Word question box displays. Notice the change in the Summary information in the Reviewing pane.

8. Click the Show Markup button , and choose **Insertions and Deletions**. Now the other changes you made to the document appear.

9. Click the inserted word "two" in the first paragraph. Click the Accept and Move to Next button. The change is accepted.

10. Right-click the balloon that contains the deleted text that begins "Chocolates cannot." Click **Reject Deletion**, and the sentence appears at the end of the paragraph.

11. Click the Next button to select the next revision. Click the Accept and Move to Next button to accept the change.

12. Repeat this process to accept the remaining revisions. When you reach the end of the document, click **OK** to continue searching from the beginning of the document. Accept all remaining changes, and click **OK** when the message box appears indicating, "**The document contains no comments or tracked changes.**" Review the **Summary** section of the Reviewing pane indicating there are no revisions.

13. Close the document without saving it, and then reopen *[your initials]25-4*.

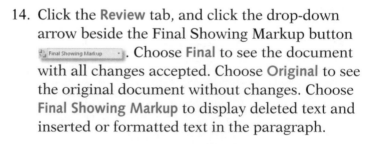

14. Click the **Review** tab, and click the drop-down arrow beside the Final Showing Markup button. Choose **Final** to see the document with all changes accepted. Choose **Original** to see the original document without changes. Choose **Final Showing Markup** to display deleted text and inserted or formatted text in the paragraph.

15. Click the down arrow on the Accept and Move to Next button. Choose **Accept All Changes in Document**.

16. Save the document as *[your initials]25-5* in your Lesson 25 folder.

17. Open the **File** menu, and click the arrow beside **Prepare**. Click **Inspect Document**. The Document Inspector dialog box opens and is used to check documents for comments, revisions, hidden text, and other content.

Figure 25-9
Document Inspector
dialog box

18. Verify that **Comments, Revisions, Versions, and Annotations** is checked. Deselect all other options. Click **Inspect**. Review the results. If necessary, remove all tracked changes. Click **Close**.

19. Click the **Microsoft Office Button**, and click **Prepare**. Click the **Mark as Final** option.

20. Click **OK** to mark the document as final and to save it. Click **OK** to close the information box.

21. Submit and close the document.

Comparing and Merging Documents

Suppose you have two similar documents—an edited copy of a document and the original document. You can use the Compare and Merge feature to compare the edited document with the original. Word will show the differences as tracked changes.

When comparing two documents, use the *legal blackline* feature, which compares the documents and creates a third document that shows the changes. Law firms use this feature to maintain records of all document revisions and versions.

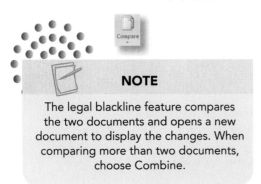

Word 2007

NOTE

The legal blackline feature compares the two documents and opens a new document to display the changes. When comparing more than two documents, choose Combine.

Exercise 25-6 COMPARE AND MERGE DOCUMENTS

1. Start a new document. Click the Review tab on the Ribbon. Click the Compare button, and click Compare to open the Compare Document dialog box.

2. Click More to expand the dialog box.

Figure 25-10
Expanded Compare Documents dialog box

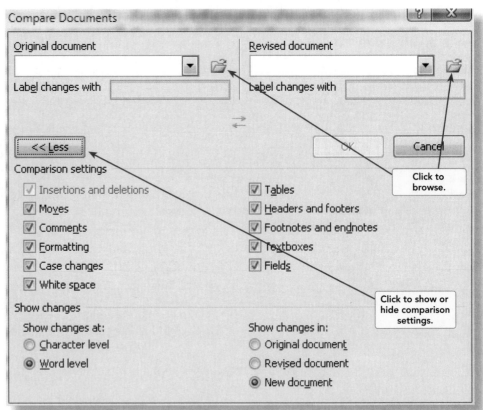

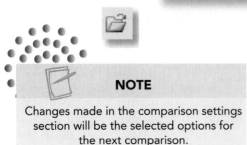

NOTE

Changes made in the comparison settings section will be the selected options for the next comparison.

3. Click the down arrow for the Original document text box, and select the file **Club - 2**. Click the down arrow for the Revised document text box, and click **Club - 3**. (It may be necessary to click the Browse button to locate your student data files.)

4. Verify that Word level is selected in the Show changes section and that New document is selected in the Show changes in section.

NOTE

Click the Show Source Document command to specify which document(s) to view. You can hide the source documents, show both source documents, show the original, or show the revised document. If the Reviewing Pane does not display, click the Reviewing Pane command and click Reviewing Pane Vertical.

5. Click **OK** to create a new document. Click **Yes** to continue with the comparison. Word opens a new document that compares the edited file **Club - 3** with the original file **Club - 2** in the Compared Document pane. All changes appear as revision marks. Deleted text appears as strikethrough text; new text is underlined. Revisions are color-coded by reviewer. A revision bar appears to the left of each line with a revision. The **Reviewing** pane displays the number and type of revisions. The Original Document pane displays the **Club - 2** file, and the **Revised Document** pane displays the **Club - 3** file.

Figure 25-11
Merged documents showing revision marks

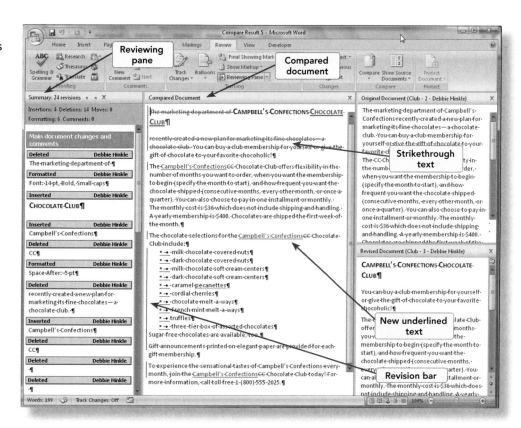

6. Drag the scroll box in the Compared Document pane, and notice that the text in the Original Document pane and the Revised Document pane scroll too.

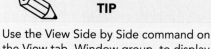

7. Click the Show Source Documents button [icon], and click **Hide Source Documents**. Close the Reviewing pane.

TIP

Use the View Side by Side command on the View tab, Window group, to display two documents side by side to compare content and not merge changes.

8. Save the document as *[your initials]25-6* in your Lesson 25 folder.

NOTE

Printing a document with revision marks is a good way to keep a record of changes made to a document.

9. Submit, print, and close the document. Word prints the document with the revisions, changing the zoom level to best display the revision balloons.

Exercise 25-7 COMBINE REVISIONS FROM MULTIPLE USERS

1. Start a new document. Click the **Review** tab on the Ribbon. Click the Compare button 🔄, and click **Combine** to open the Combine Document dialog box.

2. Click **More** to expand the dialog box if necessary.

3. Click the Browse for Original button 📖 in the **Original document** section and locate the file **Club - 2**. Click the Browse for Revised button 📖 in the **Revised document** section and locate the **Club - 3** file.

4. Verify that **Word level** is selected in the **Show changes** section, and that **Original document** is selected in the **Show changes in** section.

5. Click **OK** to combine the documents.

6. Click **The other document (Club - 3)** and click **Continue with Merge**. Word combines the documents and all changes appear as revision marks.

7. Click the Compare button 🔄, and click **Combine**.

NOTE

Only one set of formatting instructions can be stored at a time. You may be prompted to choose formatting from the original document or to use formatting from the edited document. You can also choose not to track formatting changes by clearing the Formatting check box in the Comparison settings section.

8. Click the down arrow for the **Original document** text box, and select the file **Club - 2**.

9. Click the Browse for Revised button 📖 in the **Revised document** section and locate the **Club - 4** file.

10. Click **OK** to combine the documents.

11. Click **The other document (Club - 4)** and click **Continue with Merge**. Word combines the documents and all changes appear as revision marks.

12. Click the Compare button 🔄, and click **Combine**.

13. Click the down arrow for the **Original document** text box, and select the file **Club - 2**.

14. Click the Browse for Revised button 📖 in the **Revised document** section and locate the **Club - 5** file.

15. Click **OK** to combine the documents.

16. Click the Accept and Move to Next button 🔄 and click **Accept All Changes in Document**.

17. Save the document as *[your initials]*25-7 in your Lesson 25 folder.

18. Submit and close the document.

Exercise 25-8 PROTECT A DOCUMENT FROM REVISIONS

You can protect a document from changes in several ways. One is to require a password to open or modify the document. Another way is to designate the document as a *read-only* file. *Read only* allows a user to open or copy a file but not to change the file. Another way is to allow users to insert comments, or you can ensure that any changes appear only as tracked changes.

1. Open the file **Club - 3**.

2. Click the **Review** tab.

3. Save the document as *[your initials]*25-8 in your Lesson 25 folder.

4. Turn on Track Changes, and verify that you are in Print Layout view.

5. Click the Protect Document button 🖹. The Restrict Formatting and Editing task pane displays.

Figure 25-12
Restrict formatting and editing task pane

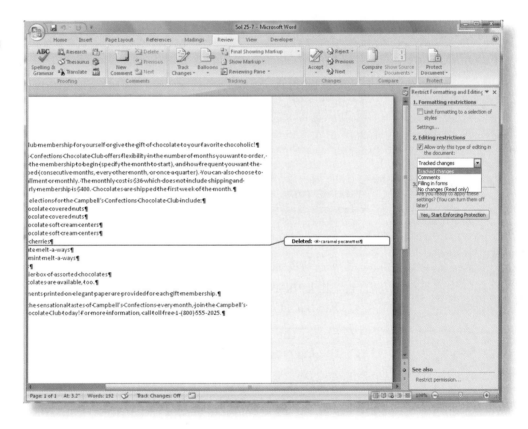

6. Click the check box under **Editing Restrictions**, and choose **Tracked changes** from the drop-down list.

7. Click the **Yes, Start Enforcing Protection** command. Do not enter a password, but click **OK** to apply the editing restrictions.

8. Locate the text "caramel pecanettes" in the bulleted list and delete it. The deletion appears as a tracked change.

9. Right-click the markup balloon. Notice that the **Accept Deletion** and **Reject Deletion** options are not available. As long as the protection is turned on, revisions cannot be accepted or rejected.

NOTE

The Accept and Move to Next command and the Reject and Move to Next commands are not available on the Ribbon.

Figure 25-13
Revision attempt with protection enabled

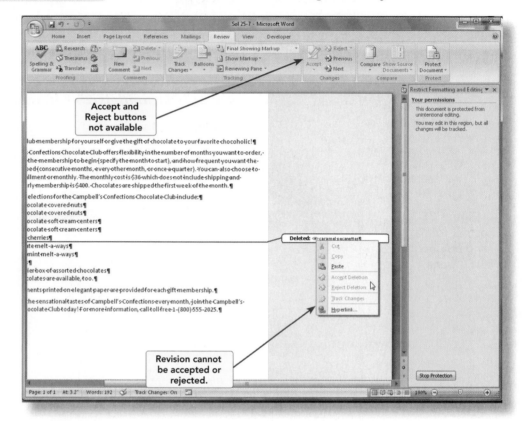

10. Click the **Stop Protection** command in the Restrict Formatting and Editing task pane.

11. Click the down arrow in the Editing restrictions section of the Restrict Formatting and Editing task pane, and choose **Comments**.

12. Select the first and second paragraphs of the document, and select the **Everyone** check box in the **Groups** section.

NOTE

Words, sentences, or paragraphs in a document can be designated as unrestricted for editing. You can also specify which individuals have permission to modify the unrestricted areas of the document. Click the More users link to enter the names of the users who have permission to edit the document.

13. Click **Yes, Start Enforcing Protection**. Do not enter a password, and click **OK**. The unrestricted area of the document is highlighted.

14. Delete the text "You can," in the first paragraph. Capitalize "buy."

15. Select the last paragraph of the document. Press [Delete]. The status bar displays a message indicating that you cannot modify this paragraph. Click **Stop Protection**.

16. Close the document without saving.

17. Reopen *[your initials]*25-8.

18. Click the Review tab, and click the Protect Document button 🗎.

19. Click the check box under Editing Restrictions, and choose No changes (Read only). Click Yes, Start Enforcing Protection. Click OK.

20. Save, close, and reopen the document. Word displays a message in the status bar indicating the document is protected.

21. Open the File menu and click Save As. The Save As dialog box appears. Locate and click the Tools down arrow ⬛. Click General Options. The General Options dialog box appears. Use the General Options dialog box to set a password to open or modify a document or to apply the Read-only option.

Figure 25-14
General Options
dialog box

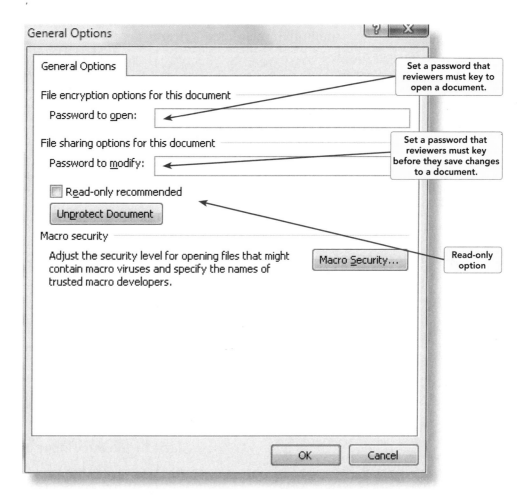

22. Click the Read-only recommended option and click OK. Save, close, and reopen the document. Word displays a prompt to open the file as read only. Click Yes. Notice the change in the document name in the title bar. Close the document.

Review a Document

When a document has been revised and reviewed several times, you can choose Reading Layout view to read the document and to verify its accuracy and content. Reading Layout view hides the Ribbon and displays the Document Map.

There are two ways to switch to Reading Layout view:

- Click the **View** tab, **Document Views** group.

- Click the Full Screen Reading view button.

Exercise 25-9   REVIEW A DOCUMENT

1. Open the file **History - 5** and save the document as *[your initials]*25-9.

2. Click the **View** tab, and click to select Document Map [Document Map]. Click the Full Screen Reading button [].

Figure 25-15
Full Screen Reading view

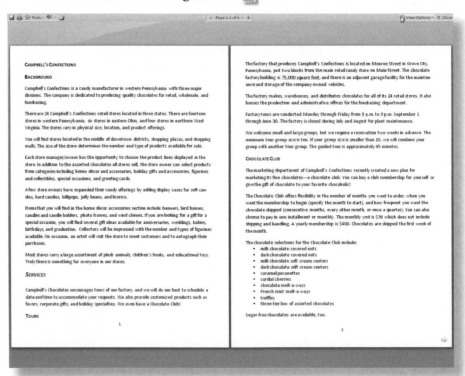

TIP

Press Ctrl+→ or Ctrl+← to move one screen at a time. Press Home to move to the first screen, and press End to move to the last screen.

3. To navigate in the document by page, click the Next arrow → or the Previous arrow ← in the lower corner of the page, press PageUp or PageDown, or click the navigation arrows at the top of the screen [◄ Page 1-2 of 6 ▾ ►].

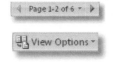

4. To navigate in the document by screen, click the arrow beside the View Options button [View Options ▾]. Click **Show One Page** to read one page at a time, or click **Show Two Pages** to read two pages at a time. Click the **Increase Text Size** option to display text in a larger size.

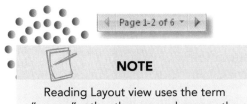

NOTE

Reading Layout view uses the term "screen" rather than pages because the screens do not display an entire page of text. The document does not display as it would in Print Layout view.

5. Click the down arrow beside the navigation arrows at the top of the screen, and click **Thumbnails**. The Document Map pane displays on the left of the screen. *Thumbnails* are miniature representations of each page.

6. Scroll through the thumbnails, and click on screen 4. The thumbnail is highlighted and displays in an enlarged view.

7. Click the down arrow beside **Thumbnails** in the pane, and choose **Document Map**. The Document Map displays headings in the document. Click a heading to move that part of the document. Click the Gourmet Chocolate heading to move to the end of the document. Click the Campbell's Confections heading to return to the top of the document.

8. Click the arrow beside the Tools button and notice that you can insert comments, highlight text, or find text in Full Screen Reading view. Close the list. You can also display the Research task pane to use reference books. Close the list.

9. Click the arrow beside the View Options button, and notice that you can track changes and show comments in Full Screen Reading view.

10. Click the first option, **Don't Open Attachments in Full Screen**. This option prevents e-mail attachments from opening automatically.

11. Click the Close button to return to Print Layout view. Click the **View** tab, and deselect **Document Map**.

Exercise 25-10   ATTACH DIGITAL SIGNATURES

You can digitally sign an Office document to ensure the signer of the document is who he/she claims to be, the content has not been altered since it was digitally signed, and to verify the origin of the signed content. A *digital signature* is used to authenticate documents, e-mail messages, and macros. The digital signature must be valid, current, and signed by a trusted person or organization. There are two ways to use a digital signature.

- Add a visible signature line to the document.

- Add an invisible digital signature to the document.

A visible signature line resembles a signature line in a business letter and includes information about the signer of the document. Once a document is digitally signed, it becomes read-only. An invisible signature provides authenticity but is not visible within the document. A document with an invisible signature displays a Signatures button on the status bar.

1. Go to the end of the document.

2. Click the **Insert** tab, and locate the **Text** group. Click the arrow beside the Signature Line button, and click **Microsoft Office Signature Line**. Click **OK** in the message box.

3. Key [your name] in the **Suggested signer** text box. Key **Customer Service Representative** in the **Suggested signer's title** text box. Click **OK** to insert the signature line in the document.

4. Double-click the signature line. Click **OK** to close the message box. Click to select the option to **Create your own digital ID**. Click **OK**.

5. Key [your name] in the Name text box, the [name of your school] in the **Organization** text box, and the [city and state] where you live in the **Location** text box.

Figure 25-16
Create a Digital ID
dialog box

Create a Digital ID

Enter the information to be included in your digital ID.

Name:

E-mail address:

Organization:

Location:

Create   Cancel

6. Click **Create** to open the Sign dialog box.

7. Key [your name] in the signature text box, and click **Sign**. Click **OK** to close the **Signature Confirmation** dialog box.

8. The Signatures task pane displays and indicates the document is signed.

Figure 25-17
Signatures task pane

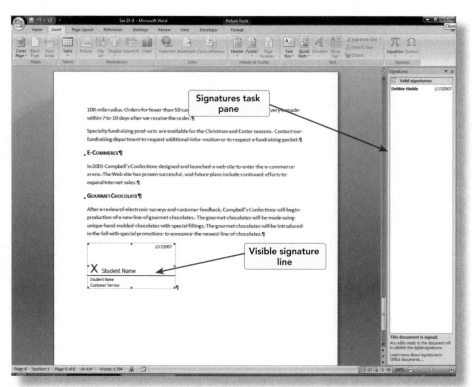

9. Submit the document.

10. Click the down arrow beside your name in the Signatures task pane, and click **Remove Signature**. Click **Yes** to remove the signature. Click **OK** to close the **Signature Removed** dialog box.

NOTE

You can select a digital image of your signature or write a signature using the ink feature of a Table PC.

11. Click to select the digital signature box in the document. Press Delete to remove the signature box from the document. Click **OK** if asked to verify the deletion. Close the **Signatures** task pane.

12. Click the **Microsoft Office Button** and click **Prepare**. Click the option to **Add a Digital Signature**. Click **OK** to close the message box.

13. Key **Authenticate document content.** in the Sign dialog box.

Figure 25-18
Sign dialog box

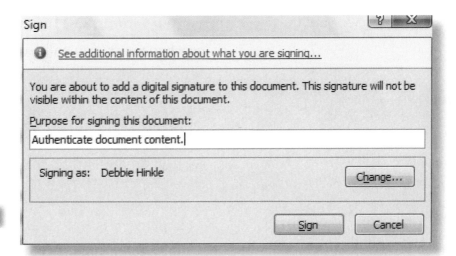

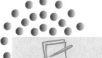

NOTE

Click the Signature button on the status bar to display or hide the Signatures task pane. Click the drop-down arrow beside the signature name in the Signatures task pane to view Signature Details. Click the Microsoft Office Button, click Prepare, and click View Signatures to verify the digital signature.

14. Click **Sign**, and then click **OK**. The Signatures task pane appears, and the status bar displays a button to indicate that the document contains a digital signature.

15. Close the Signatures task pane and close the document.

Creating Hyperlinks

A hypertext link, called a *hyperlink*, is text you click to move to another location. The location to which you move can be within the same document, in another document, or somewhere on the World Wide Web or your company's intranet. Readers use hyperlinks to jump to related information. You can create a series of hyperlinks, thereby creating your own "web" of locations.

In a document, hypertext links can be a word or phrase. Hypertext links are usually blue and underlined.

Word 2007

Exercise 25-11   CREATE A HYPERLINK WITHIN
THE SAME DOCUMENT

In a long document, you can use a hyperlink to jump quickly from one page
to another. You can do this in one of three ways:

- Create a bookmark at a particular location in the document, and then
  insert a hypertext link to the bookmark.

- Apply a heading style to text in the document, and then insert a
  hypertext link to the styled text.

- Copy text in the document, and then use the **Paste as Hyperlink**
  command.

1. Open the file **History - 4**.

2. Save the document as *[your initials]***25-11** in your Lesson 25 folder.

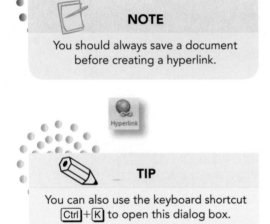

NOTE

You should always save a document
before creating a hyperlink.

TIP

You can also use the keyboard shortcut
Ctrl + K to open this dialog box.

3. Using a bookmark, you will create a hyperlink
   from the text "corporate gifts" on page 1 to the
   description of corporate gifts on page 3. Scroll to
   the top of page 3. Position the insertion point to the
   left of the heading "Corporate Gifts," and insert a
   bookmark named **CorporateGifts**. (Click the **Insert**
   tab and click **Bookmark**. Remember, bookmark
   names cannot have spaces.)

4. Below the heading "Services" on page 1, select the
   text "corporate gifts."

5. Click the **Insert** tab, and click the Hyperlink button
   to open the Insert Hyperlink dialog box.

6. Under **Link to**, click the **Place in This Document**.

7. Click **CorporateGifts** under Bookmarks to choose this
   bookmark as the "jump to" location.

Figure 25-19
Creating a hyperlink
to a bookmark

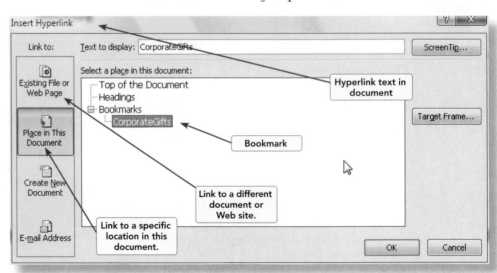

8. Click **OK**. The words "corporate gifts" are blue and underlined, indicating you have created a hyperlink.

9. Point to the blue hyperlink text. A ScreenTip displays the bookmark name with the instructions "**CTRL + click to follow link.**" Press Ctrl, and the pointer changes to a pointing hand 👆.

10. Test the hyperlink by clicking it. The insertion point jumps to the description of corporate gifts on page 3.

11. Scroll to the hyperlink text on page 1. Notice the change in color, indicating you have used the hyperlink.

12. On page 1, below the "Services" heading, select the text "Chocolate Club" at the end of the paragraph.

13. Open the Insert Hyperlink dialog box. Click the heading **Chocolate Club**, and then click **OK**.

NOTE

In a document with many hyperlinks, this change in color helps you remember which hyperlink locations you have already visited.

NOTE

To hyperlink to a heading, verify that the heading is styled.

Figure 25-20
Creating a hyperlink to a heading

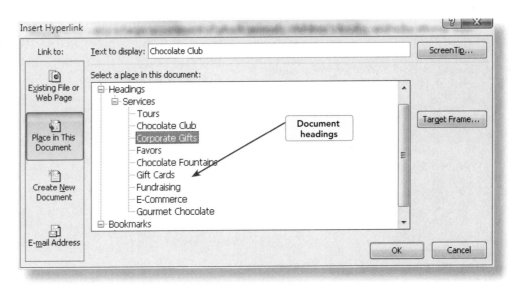

14. Press Ctrl, and click the hyperlink to test it. The insertion point jumps to the heading "Chocolate Club" on page 2.

15. Locate the heading "Gourmet Chocolate" on page 6. Select and copy the heading (but not the paragraph mark). In the following steps, you create a hyperlink in this heading by using the **Paste as Hyperlink** command.

16. Return to the beginning of the document. Find and select the text "gourmet chocolate" (in the paragraph under the heading "Services" that begins "Campbell's Chocolates").

TIP

Instead of scrolling back and forth to create hyperlinks within a document, you can split the document and display the appropriate text within each pane. Click the View tab, and click Split (or double-click the split bar on the vertical scroll bar).

> **NOTE**
>
> You can also drag and drop to insert hyperlinks. Select the text to which you want to jump, drag it to another location by using the right mouse button, and then choose Create Hyperlink Here to insert the text as a hyperlink.

> **NOTE**
>
> After creating a hyperlink, you can change the blue hyperlink text as well as the link destination. To change the text, right-click the hyperlink, click Select Hyperlink from the shortcut menu, and then key different text. To change the hyperlink destination, right-click the hyperlink, choose Edit Hyperlink, and then choose a different heading or bookmark in the document to which you want to link. To remove a hyperlink, right-click the hypertext and choose Remove Hyperlink.

17. Click the **Home** tab, and click the Paste button. Click **Paste as Hyperlink**. Word replaces the selected text with hyperlink text.

18. Press Ctrl, and click the hyperlink to jump to the gourmet chocolate heading on page 6.

19. Save, submit, and close the document.

Exercise 25-12 CREATE A HYPERLINK TO ANOTHER DOCUMENT

You can create hyperlinks to another Word document or to Office documents such as an Excel worksheet or a PowerPoint presentation.

1. Start a new document. Create a memo to **Store Managers** from **Lynn Tanguay**. Key **January 10** for the date. The subject is **Risk Management Seminar**. For the body of the memo, key the text shown in Figure 25-18.

Figure 25-21

> The agenda for the Risk Management seminar has been finalized.
>
> Participants should receive their materials by Friday.

> **NOTE**
>
> To jump to a specific area of the linked document, you would click Bookmark and use the Select Place in Document dialog box. In this case, however, because the linked document is short, you don't need to select a more specific location.

2. Add your reference initials to the memo, and save it as *[your initials]*25-12 in your Lesson 25 folder.

3. Select "agenda" in the first paragraph.

4. Click the Insert Hyperlink button or press Ctrl+K.

5. In the Insert Hyperlink dialog box, under **Link to**, click **Existing File or Web Page**.

6. Click **Current Folder** if it is not active.

7. In the **Look in** text box, locate and click the file **Risk** on the student disk. The filename appears in the **Address** text box.

Figure 25-22
Linking to another
document

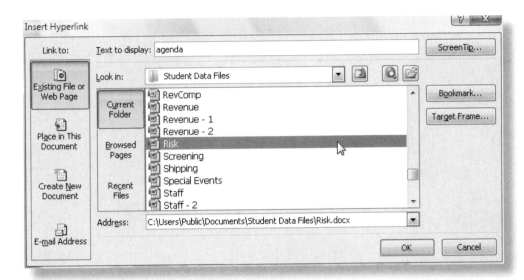

NOTE

After inserting a hyperlink to another document, you can select the hyperlink text and modify it. You can also change the document or location to which you want to link. Right-click the hyperlink, choose Edit Hyperlink, and choose a different location.

8. Click **OK** in the Insert Hyperlink dialog box. The text "agenda" is blue and underlined, indicating you have created a hyperlink.

9. Press Ctrl, and click the hyperlink to test it. Word opens the linked document. Close **Risk**.

10. Save the document and close it.

Exercise 25-13 CREATE A HYPERLINK TO A WEB SITE

In addition to creating hyperlinks between documents, you can create a link to a location on the World Wide Web. For example, suppose you are sending an e-mail memo to the store managers about upgrading software and hardware. You can include a hyperlink to a Web site that lists up-to-date information on features and pricing.

NOTE

You cannot link to the Web without an Internet connection. Your computer must be equipped with appropriate hardware and software for navigating the Internet.

To link to a Web site, you need to know the site's "address," or *URL* (Uniform Resource Locator). A URL is a combination of characters that is recognized by the Internet. For example, the Web address for Microsoft is **http://www.microsoft.com**. The prefix **http://** (which stands for Hypertext Transfer Protocol) is used for Web addresses but is understood and is no longer necessary when keying a Web address.

1. Start a new document. Create the memo shown in Figure 25-23. When you key the Web address www.microsoft.com, Word will automatically apply the hyperlink character formatting.

Figure 25-23
Creating automatic hypertext as you type

MEMO TO: Store Managers

FROM: Lynn Tanguay

DATE: [Current Date]

SUBJECT: Upgrades

Please check the Microsoft Web site, www.microsoft.com, periodically to learn the projected release date of the operating system update. We are planning to implement a two-year replacement schedule for our computers and software.

NOTE

If you receive an error message, ask your instructor how to proceed.

TIP

Instead of using a Web address as a hyperlink in a document, you can use any word or phrase in the document. Simply select the document text, open the Insert Hyperlink dialog box, and enter the URL in the Address text box (just as you entered the path to link a document).

2. Add your reference initials to the memo, and save it as *[your initials]*25-13 in your Lesson 25 folder.

3. Press Ctrl, and click the new hyperlink to test it. Word jumps to the Microsoft home page on the Web if your Internet connection is activated. If it is not, you might be asked to sign on.

4. Scroll to the bottom of the Web page. Notice that the Web page contains both text and graphics. Scroll back to the top of the Web page.

5. Try two or three links on the Web page.

6. Close the Internet connection.

7. Use the taskbar to return to the document and to submit and close it.

Lesson 25 Summary

- Use comments to insert notes in a document. Comments are color-coded by reviewer. Make sure your name and initials appear in the text boxes in the Popular section in the Word Options dialog box before inserting your comments.

- Comments appear in the Reviewing pane or as balloons in the margins.

- Edit comment text in either the comment balloon or the Reviewing pane. Use the Next command and the Previous command on the Ribbon to move from comment to comment.

- To delete a comment, click within the comment text and click the Delete command, or right-click the comment text and choose Delete Comment from the shortcut menu.

- To print comments with a document, use the Print command from Print Layout view or Print Preview. Or open the Print dialog box and choose Document showing markup from the Print what drop-down list. Word scales the document text of the printed document to make room for the comment balloons.

- To print comments separate from a document, open the Print dialog box and choose List of markup from the Print what drop-down list.

- The Track Changes feature makes it easy to collaborate with others when revising documents.

- Tracked changes appear as revision marks that show where deletions, insertions, and formatting changes were made. In Draft view, inserted text appears underlined, deleted text has a horizontal line through it, and a revision bar appears to the left of every revised paragraph. In Print Layout view, tracked changes appear in the text and also in balloons in the right margin. Formatting changes only appear in Print Layout view. Changes also appear in the Reviewing pane.

- You can review a document after it is edited and decide if you want to accept or reject the revisions. Use the Ribbon to accept or reject revisions, or right-click a revision mark and use the shortcut menu.

- You can review changes by the type of change made. You can also review only the changes made by a particular reviewer.

- To accept all revisions at once, click the arrow on the Accept and Move to Next command and choose Accept All Changes in Document.

- When several people have reviewed a copy of a document, you can use the Compare feature to consolidate revisions into one file.

- You can compare two documents, such as an edited copy of a document and the original document. Open the Compare Documents dialog box, browse for the original document, and browse for the revised document. Select appropriate comparison settings and options for showing changes, and click New document under Show changes in. Click OK. Word opens a new document that shows the differences as color-coded revision marks.

- When you compare more than two documents, select Combine from the Compare drop-down list. Word combines the documents and displays the differences as color-coded revision marks.

- To review the content of a document, switch to Full Screen Reading view. The document appears as a series of screens for easier readability. You can change the view of the document and navigate through the screens.

- You can protect a document from changes by requiring a password to open or modify the document. You can also designate the document as a read-only file.

- Use digital signatures to authenticate documents, e-mail messages, or macros. You can add a visible signature line or an invisible digital signature to a document.

- A hypertext link, called a hyperlink, is text you click to move to another location. The location to which you move can be within the same document, in another document, or somewhere on the World Wide Web or your company's intranet.

- In a long document, you can use a hyperlink to jump quickly from one page to another. You can do this by creating a bookmark in a document and inserting a hypertext link to the bookmark, by inserting a hypertext link to a heading, or by using the Paste as Hyperlink command.
- You can create hyperlinks to another Word document or to Office documents such as an Excel worksheet or a PowerPoint presentation.
- In addition to creating hyperlinks between documents, you can create a link to a location on the World Wide Web. To link to a Web site, you need to know the site's "address" or URL (Uniform Resource Locator). A URL is a combination of characters that is recognized by the Internet.

LESSON 25 — Command Summary

Feature	Button	Command	Keyboard
Comments	New Comment	Review tab, Comments group	Alt + Ctrl + M
Print comments		File, Print, Print what	
Track changes	Track Changes	Review tab, Tracking group	Ctrl + Shift + E
Accept change	Accept	Review tab, Changes group	
Reject change	Reject	Review tab, Changes group	
Compare and combine documents	Compare	Review tab, Compare group	
Full screen reading	Full Screen Reading	View tab, Document Views group	
Document Map	Document Map	View tab, Show/Hide group	
Protect a document	Protect Document	Review tab, Protect group	
Visible digital signature	Signature Line	Insert tab, Text group	
Insert a hyperlink	Hyperlink	Insert tab, Links group	Ctrl + K

Concepts Review

True/False Questions

Each of the following statements is either true or false. Indicate your choice by circling T or F.

T F 1. In Draft view, comments appear in balloons.

T F 2. You can access the Reviewing pane from the View tab.

T F 3. You can print a document with or without revision marks.

T F 4. Comments and revision marks both appear in Print Preview.

T F 5. A hypertext link is usually blue and underlined.

T F 6. Use the legal blackline feature to compare two documents.

T F 7. When you protect a document from revisions, no one can add a revision to the document without entering a password.

T F 8. You can turn off tracked changes by clicking Track Changes on the status bar.

Short Answer Questions

Write the correct answer in the space provided.

1. When checking revisions, which command is used when you do not want to accept the changes?

   _____

2. Which feature is used to authenticate documents and e-mail messages?

   _____

3. When you point to a comment balloon in Print Layout view, what does the ScreenTip display?

   _____

4. Where are comments displayed if you want to view them in Draft view?

   _____

5. How do you use the shortcut menu to delete a comment in Print Layout view?

   _____

6. Which view displays document pages as a series of screens?

   _____

7. Which Ribbon tab do you use for comments and tracked changes?

_____

8. What does the mouse pointer change to when you point to a hyperlink and press Ctrl?

_____

Critical Thinking

Answer these questions on a separate page. There are no right or wrong answers. Support your answers with examples from your own experience, if possible.

1. Think of a scenario when three of the new features introduced in this lesson could be helpful. Discuss comments, track changes, and compare documents. Include advantages and disadvantages for using each feature.

2. What are the advantages of attaching digital signatures to a document?

Skills Review

Exercise 25-14

Insert, delete, edit, and print comments.

1. Open the file **Email - 3**.
2. Prepare the document for the insertion of comments by following these steps:
   a. Open the Word Options dialog box, and click Popular.
   b. Make sure your name and initials are in the appropriate data fields.
   c. Click OK.

   d. Click the Review tab on the Ribbon. Click the lower part of the Track Changes button. Click Change Tracking Options. Locate the Comments box in the Markup section, and click the down arrow to display the list of colors. Select Blue.
   e. Verify the balloon options. The preferred width should be 3 inches and balloons should display on the right margin.
   f. Click OK to close the Track Changes dialog box.
3. Add comments by following these steps:
   a. Select e-mail marketing in the first bullet item.
   b. Click the New Comment button on the Ribbon.
   c. Key Purpose could be to advertise, improve customer service, and/or send an e-mail newsletter. in the Comment balloon.

  d. Select "Tracking" in the third bullet item, and click the New Comment button . Key the comment Tracking includes analyzing bounces, delivered e-mail, click rates, and open rates. in the Comments balloon.

  e. Create a comment for "Risks" in the last bullet item, keying the text Investigate breach of confidentiality, legal liability, and damage to the IT system.

4. Delete the "e-mail marketing" comment by clicking within the balloon and clicking the Delete button .

5. Edit the comment text for "Risks" by clicking within the balloon and typing potential before "damage."

6. Save the document as *[your initials]*25-14 in your Lesson 25 folder.

7. Print the comments as balloons with the document text and as a separate list by following these steps:

  a. Open the Print dialog box.

  b. Make sure that the Print what drop-down list box is set to Document showing markup. Click OK.

  c. Open the Print dialog box again.

  d. Change the Print what drop-down list box to List of markup. Click OK.

8. Submit and save the document.

Exercise 25-15

Track changes in a document.

1. Open the file **Hawaii**.

2. Click the Review tab, and click the Track Changes button to turn on Track Changes.

3. Position the insertion point to the immediate left of "macadamia" in the first sentence of the first paragraph, and key three.

4. Locate the text "instead of using" in the first paragraph. Key our before "present."

5. Add the following paragraph after the first paragraph.

 Since this nut is one of the hardest nuts to crack, I am somewhat dubious of these claims. It would certainly be a most profound development if the process works.

6. Delete the sentence that begins "Good luck" in the last paragraph.

7. Go to the top of the document, and click the Next button in the Changes group.

8. Click the Accept and Move to Next button to accept the insertion of "three." Click Next , and accept the insertion of "our."

9. Move to the next change, and reject the addition of the paragraph.

10. Accept the deletion of the sentence in the last paragraph.

11. Save the document as *[your initials]*25-15 in your Lesson 25 folder.

12. Submit and close the document.

Exercise 25-16

Merge three revisions of the same document and protect a document.

1. Start a new document.
2. Compare the **Email Marketing - 2** file with the original and the Email Marketing - 3 file by following these steps:

   a. Click the Review tab.

   b. Click the Compare button , and click Combine. In the Combine Documents dialog box, click the Browse for original button 🖼 to locate and select the original file **Email Marketing**. In the Revised document box, locate and select the file **Email Marketing - 2**.

   c. Click More to display the Comparison settings. Locate the Show changes in section, and click Original document.

   d. Click OK.

   e. Click the Compare button ☝, and click Combine.

   f. Locate and select the file **Email Marketing** for the Original document box. Locate and select the file **Email Marketing - 3** for the Revised document box.

   g. Verify that Original document is selected under Show Changes in, and click OK.

   h. Click the Show Source Document button ☝, and click Hide Source Documents. Close the Reviewing pane if necessary.

3. Right-click each balloon, and click Reject Deletion.

   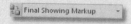

4. Click the Display for Review button [📋 Final Showing Markup ▾], and click Final.
5. Protect the document from further revisions by following these steps:

   a. Click the Review tab. Click the Protect Document button 📄.

   b. In the Restrict Formatting and Editing task pane, click the check box below Editing Restrictions to select it. Choose Tracked changes from the drop-down list, and click Yes, Start Enforcing Protection.

   c. Click OK in the Start Enforcing Protection dialog box. Close the Restrict Formatting and Editing task pane.

   d. In the last paragraph, delete the word "filtering." Check the document protection by attempting to accept the revision.

6. Save the document as *[your initials]*25-16 in your Lesson 25 folder.
7. Submit the document with revision marks; then close the document.

Exercise 25-17

Create hyperlinks, within a document, to another document and to a Web site.

1. Open the file **Community - 2**.
2. Save the document as *[your initials]*25-17 in your Lesson 25 folder.

3. Create a link between the word "schools" on page 1 and a paragraph on page 2 by following these steps:

   a. Go to the paragraph that begins "Last year." Select the text "Campbell's Confections Educational Foundation."

   b. Click the Insert tab, and click the Bookmark button . Key **Foundation** for the bookmark name.

   c. Go to page 1, and select "schools" in the second line of the paragraph that begins "Another way."

   d. Click the Insert tab, and click the Hyperlink button 🌐.

   e. Click **Place in This Document** if it is not active. Locate and select the bookmark **Foundation**, and click **OK**.

   f. Press Ctrl, and click the hyperlink to test it.

4. Create a hyperlink to the file **Power** by following these steps:

   a. Select the word "communities" in the last sentence of the first paragraph. Press Ctrl+K to open the Insert Hyperlink dialog box.

   b. Click **Existing File or Web Page**.

   c. Click **Current Folder** if it is not active.

   d. In the **Look in** text box, locate the file **Power** on your student data disk and click **OK**.

   e. Test the hyperlink.

   f. Close **Power**.

5. Create a hyperlink to a Web site by following these steps:

   a. Locate the text "Humane Society" in the paragraph that begins "It is not just."

   b. Open the Insert Hyperlink dialog box. In the **Address** text box, key the URL **www.hsus.org**. Click **OK**.

   c. Make sure your Internet connection is active, and click the hyperlink to test it.

   d. Close the Web page.

6. To all pages in the document, add a footer that contains the file name left-aligned, and "Page" followed by the page number, right-aligned. Update the file name field.

7. Review the document in Full Screen Reading view by following these steps:

   a. Click the Full Screen Reading view button on the status bar.

   b. Switch the Navigation window by clicking the down arrow beside **Document Map** and selecting **Thumbnails**.

   c. Close Full Screen Reading view by clicking the Close button ✕ Close.

8. Save the document.

9. Submit and close the document.

Lesson Applications

Exercise 25-18

Create comments, track changes, and accept revisions.

1. Open the file **Minutes**.

2. Turn on Track Changes.

3. Select the first line of the document, and change the font size to 14 points.

4. Position the insertion point at the end of the attendance paragraph (after 1:30 p.m.), and key the following comment: Bryson Clark from the Sharon store was not present.

5. At the end of the "Old Business" paragraph, insert the following: The official date for shipping the gourmet chocolates is April 10.

6. Change February 20 to February 16.

7. Change "Internet and e-mail policy" to computer use policy.

8. Edit the "Attendance" paragraph to include the comment text, and delete the comment.

9. Accept all revisions.

10. Save the document as *[your initials]*25-18 in your Lesson 25 folder.

11. Submit and close the document.

Exercise 25-19

Create a hyperlink from one document to another.

1. Open the file **Chamber**.

2. Verify that the top margin is 2 inches and key your reference initials.

3. Spell-check the document, and save it as *[your initials]*25-19 in your Lesson 25 folder.

4. Create a hyperlink between the text "PowerPoint presentation" and the file **Power**.

5. Test the hyperlink. Submit the **Power** document and close it.

6. Save, submit, and *[your initials]*25-19.

Exercise 25-20

Review a document, and protect a document from revisions.

1. Open the file **Handbook**.

2. Save the document as *[your initials]*25-20 in your Lesson 25 folder.

3. Click the Review tab, and protect the document from any changes (read only). Enforce the protection, and do not assign a password.

4. Save and close the document. Reopen the document.

5. Switch to Full Screen Reading view, and display two pages. (If necessary close the Document Map.)

6. Click the Tools button [Tools ▾], and click Find. Key leave in the Find what text box. Close the Find and Replace dialog box.

7. Return to Print Layout view.

8. Close the document.

Exercise 25-21 ◆ Challenge Yourself

Merge two revisions of the same document, track revisions, and accept revisions.

1. Open the file **Marketing Plan**.

2. Save the document as *[your initials]*25-21 in your Lesson 25 folder. Close the document.

3. Start a new document.

4. Compare the document *[your initials]*25-21 (original document) with **Marketing Plan - 2** (revised document) using the Show changes at the Word level and Show changes in the original document comparison settings.

5. Accept all revisions in the document.

6. Switch to Outline view, and turn on Track Changes mode, making sure the revision marks appear.

7. Change "Purpose/Mission" to Purpose and Mission.

8. Change the entries under "Analysis" to the following:

   Product Analysis

   Target Market Analysis

   Competitor Analysis

9. Turn off Track Changes mode, and accept all revisions in the document.

10. Switch to Print Layout view.

11. Modify the Heading 2 style to a left indent of 0.25 inch, modify the Heading 3 style to a left indent of 0.5 inch, and modify the Heading 4 style to a left indent of 0.75 inch.

12. Save the document.

13. Submit and close the document.

On Your Own

In these exercises you work on your own, as you would in a real-life business environment. Use the skills you've learned to accomplish the task—and be creative.

Exercise 25-22

Read and summarize an article from a book or magazine you find interesting. Insert at least five comments. They can be humorous or insightful, or they can simply describe how you feel about the text. Practice editing, deleting, and navigating through the comments. Save the document as *[your initials]*25-22 in your Lesson 25 folder. Submit the document with comments displayed.

Exercise 25-23

Create a one-page rough draft report on a current electronic device. Save the document, and edit the document to create a final copy. Save the final copy using a different filename. Compare the two documents. Insert a comment describing your results. Save the new document as *[your initials]*25-23 in your Lesson 25 folder, and submit it with revision marks displayed.

Exercise 25-24

Go to the Internet, and research digital certificates and the procedure to obtain a digital certificate. Write a report (at least two pages, double-spaced) about the topic. Insert hyperlinks to locations within the document and to Web sites. Test the hyperlinks. Use Full Screen Reading view to review the content. Save the document as *[your initials]*25-24 in your Lesson 25 folder, and submit it.

Unit 7 Applications

Unit Application 7-1

Compare two documents, track changes, and insert comments.

1. Compare the **Summary** file and the **Summary 2** file, merging both documents into a new document.

2. Review the tracked changes, and accept the formatting changes. Reject the chart deletion.

3. Save the revised document as *[your initials]*u7-1 in your Unit 7 folder.

4. Insert a comment at the end of the document. Key the text Add a concluding paragraph.

5. Insert a comment on page 1 after the first paragraph that ends "strongest gain." Key the text Add a chart for net income.

6. Add a three-line header to page 2 only to include the following text:

   Year-End Summary
   Page *[Insert page number]*
   January 7, 200-

7. Save the document.

8. Submit and close the document.

Unit Application 7-2

Insert footnotes and create an index and table of contents.

1. Open the file **Catalog**.

2. Save the document as *[your initials]*u7-2 in your Unit 7 folder.

3. Use the Find command to locate the first occurrence of "MAW."

4. Insert a footnote, and key the text MAW is the abbreviation for Melt-a-Way.

5. Position the insertion point after "Product Catalog" at the top of the document, and insert a footnote. Key the text This is a partial listing. It does not include specialty candies or sugar-free candies.

6. Mark index entries for the following using the first occurrence of each under boxed chocolate.

   Choice Assorted
   Nut Assorted
   Cream Assorted
   Light & Dark Assorted
   Light & Dark Creams
   Light & Dark Nut
   Dark Assorted
   Dark Nut Assorted
   Dark Cream Assorted
   Bark
   Candy Bar

7. Mark index entries for the following using the first occurrence of each under "bulk chocolate."

   Creams
   Nuts
   Turtles
   Break Up
   Clusters

8. Create an entry for **MAW** with a subentry for "Boxed Chocolate" and a subentry for "Bulk Chocolate."

9. Create an index on a separate page at the end of the document. Select an appropriate format, and key the heading **INDEX**.

10. Add page numbers to the bottom margin aligned at the right. Number each page and format the text using 10-point italic.

11. Go to the top of the document, insert a page break, and create a table of contents with an appropriate format and the heading **TABLE OF CONTENTS**.

12. Save the document and submit it. Close the document.

Unit Application 7-3 ◆ Using the Internet

Work with footnotes and create a table of contents and an index.

1. This is a group exercise. The class as a whole chooses a specific theme, such as:

   • A current event

   • A popular movie

   • A book

Each class member will create a short document that discusses one aspect of the selected theme. For example, if the class selects a movie as the major topic, one student could write a document about the film's plot, another student could write about the director, and others could write about the actors. Students should look for interesting topics to cover. For example, if the movie was based on a book or another movie, someone could discuss this. Was the film based on a real-life event? Did reviewers give the movie favorable or unfavorable reviews, and was attendance affected by their comments? If so, there's another interesting topic to discuss.

2. Log onto the Internet to research your specific topic. Find as much detailed information as you can in the time allotted by your instructor.

3. When you finish your research, create your document in Word. The document should have a Heading 1–style heading, body text, and lower-level headings as appropriate. The document should also include a footnote attached to the main heading, containing your name and identifying you as the document's author. Save your document as *[your initials]***u7-3** in a location your instructor specifies.

NOTE

Ask your instructor where to save the file so it is available to all students in the class. You'll insert your classmates' files to create a long document.

4. Copy your document and your classmates' documents into your Unit 7 Applications folder. Open your document, and insert each of your classmates' documents into a single document.

5. Format the document attractively, using consistent styles. Change the font and font size of the footnotes. You might also include clip art or other graphics (avoid altering your heading styles).

6. Create an index and a table of contents for the document. Format them appropriately. Create a title page for the document.

7. Save and submit the document.

appendixes

Proofreaders' Marks

Proofreaders' Mark		Draft	Final Copy
⌗	Start a new paragraph.	ridiculous! If that is so	ridiculous!
			If that is so
⌒	Delete space.	to gether	together
#	Insert space.	Itmay be	It may not be
⌒	Move as shown.	it is (not) true	it is true
∩	Transpose.	beleivable	believable
		is it so	it is so
⬯	Spell out.	(2) years ago	two years ago
		16 Elm (St.)	16 Elm Street
∧	Insert a word.	How much is it?	How much is it?
℘ OR —	Delete a word.	it may not be true	it may be true
∧ OR ⋏	Insert a letter.	temperature	temperature
⌒ OR ⊇	Delete a letter and close up.	committment to buuy	commitment to buy
℘ OR —	Change a word.	but and if you won't can't	but if you can't
(Stet)	Stet (don't delete).	I was very glad	I was very glad
/	Make letter lowercase.	Federal Government (Stet)	federal government
≡	Capitalize.	Janet L. greyston	Janet L. Greyston
∨	Raise above the line.	in her new book*	in her new book*
∧	Drop below the line.	H2SO4	H_2SO_4
⊙	Insert a period.	Mr. Henry Grenada	Mr. Henry Grenada
∧	Insert a comma.	a large old house	a large, old house
∨	Insert an apostrophe.	my childrens car	my children's car
⩔	Insert quotation marks.	he wants a loan	he wants a "loan"
= OR ∧	Insert a hyphen.	a first rate job	a first-rate job
		ask the coowner	ask the co-owner
─M─	Insert an em dash.	Here it is cash!	Here it is—cash!
─N─	Insert an en dash.	Pages 1 5	Pages 1–5
—	Insert underscore.	an issue of Time	an issue of Time
(ital)	Set in italic.	(ital) The New York Times	*The New York Times*

Proofreaders' Mark	Draft	Final Copy
(bf) Set in boldface.	(bf) the Enter key	the **Enter** key
(rom) Set in roman.	(rom) the _most_ likely	the most likely
⟨ ⟩ Insert parentheses.	left today⟨May 3⟩	left today (May 3)
⌐ Move to the right.	$38,367,000 ⌐	$38,367,000
⌐ Move to the left.	⌐Anyone can win!	Anyone can win!
(ss) Single-space.	(ss) I have heard / he is leaving	I have heard / he is leaving
(ds) Double-space.	(ds) When will you / have a decision?	When will you / have a decision?
(+ 1 line) Insert 1 line space.	Percent of Change / (+ 1 line) 16.25	Percent of Change / 16.25
(− 1 line) Delete (remove) 1 line space.	Northeastern / (− 1 line) regional sales	Northeastern / regional sales

Standard Forms for Business Documents

Reference manuals, such as *The Gregg Reference Manual*, provide a variety of letter and memorandum styles, as well as styles for reports and other documents. Many businesses also have their own styles for documents. This appendix includes two basic styles—a business letter and a memorandum. It also shows the most common format for a continuation page (used for either letters or memos).

TABLE B-1 Parts of a Letter

Part of Letter	Location/Description
Heading	
Letterhead or return address	Often appears on preprinted stationery; can also be created in Word. Includes the company name, address, and other contact information.
Date line	Two inches from the top of the page on letterhead stationery or on the third line below a Word letterhead. Use date format shown in Figure B-1.
Opening	
Inside address	Starts on the fourth line below the date; consists of name and address (and possibly company name and job title) of person to whom you are writing.
Salutation	On the second line below the inside address; typically includes a courtesy title (Mr., Mrs., Ms., Miss) and ends with a colon.
Body	
Message	Content of the letter, single-spaced with one blank line between paragraphs.
Closing	
Complimentary closing	On the second line below the last line of the body of the letter. Common closings are "Sincerely" or "Sincerely yours" followed by a comma.
Writer's identification	On the fourth line below the closing, to leave space for a signature; includes the writer's name and job title (and sometimes the department).
Reference initials	On the second line below the writer's name and title; consists of the typist's initials in small letters.
Enclosure notation	On a new line below the reference initials if letter has an enclosure. Specify the number of enclosures. Can also use "Attachment" if enclosure is attached.
Optional features	Filename notation—indicates document name for reference purposes; delivery notation—method of delivery (other than regular mail); copy notation—people who will receive copies of the letter (usually begins with "c:" or "cc:")

Figure B-1
Business letter style

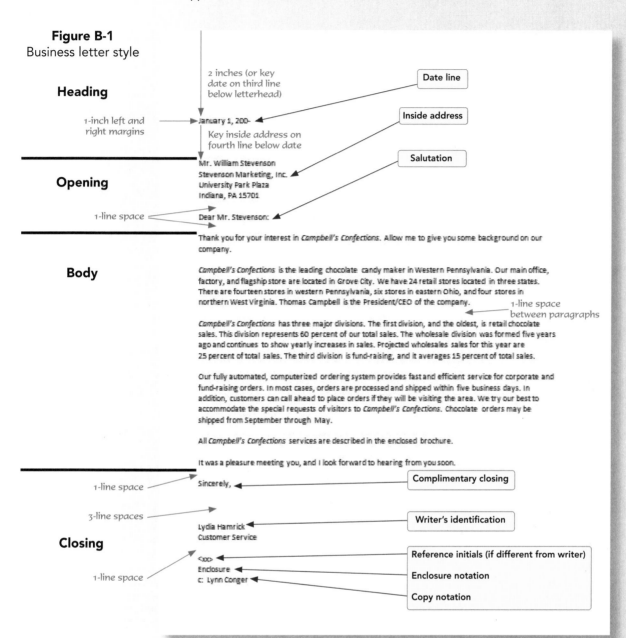

Heading

1-inch left and right margins

2 inches (or key date on third line below letterhead)

Date line

January 1, 200-

Key inside address on fourth line below date

Inside address

Opening

Salutation

Mr. William Stevenson
Stevenson Marketing, Inc.
University Park Plaza
Indiana, PA 15701

1-line space

Dear Mr. Stevenson:

Thank you for your interest in *Campbell's Confections*. Allow me to give you some background on our company.

Body

Campbell's Confections is the leading chocolate candy maker in Western Pennsylvania. Our main office, factory, and flagship store are located in Grove City. We have 24 retail stores located in three states. There are fourteen stores in western Pennsylvania, six stores in eastern Ohio, and four stores in northern West Virginia. Thomas Campbell is the President/CEO of the company.

1-line space between paragraphs

Campbell's Confections has three major divisions. The first division, and the oldest, is retail chocolate sales. This division represents 60 percent of our total sales. The wholesale division was formed five years ago and continues to show yearly increases in sales. Projected wholesales sales for this year are 25 percent of total sales. The third division is fund-raising, and it averages 15 percent of total sales.

Our fully automated, computerized ordering system provides fast and efficient service for corporate and fund-raising orders. In most cases, orders are processed and shipped within five business days. In addition, customers can call ahead to place orders if they will be visiting the area. We try our best to accommodate the special requests of visitors to *Campbell's Confections*. Chocolate orders may be shipped from September through May.

All *Campbell's Confections* services are described in the enclosed brochure.

It was a pleasure meeting you, and I look forward to hearing from you soon.

1-line space

Sincerely,

Complimentary closing

3-line spaces

Lydia Hamrick
Customer Service

Writer's identification

Closing

<xx>

Reference initials (if different from writer)

1-line space

Enclosure

Enclosure notation

c: Lynn Conger

Copy notation

Figure B-2
Continuation page header for two-page (or longer) letter or memo

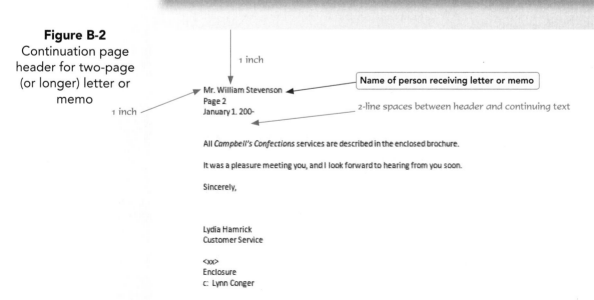

1 inch

1 inch

Mr. William Stevenson
Page 2
January 1. 200-

Name of person receiving letter or memo

2-line spaces between header and continuing text

All *Campbell's Confections* services are described in the enclosed brochure.

It was a pleasure meeting you, and I look forward to hearing from you soon.

Sincerely,

Lydia Hamrick
Customer Service

<xx>
Enclosure
c: Lynn Conger

TABLE B-2 Parts of a Memo

Part of Memo	Location/Description
Heading	Starts 2 inches from top of page using plain paper or letterhead stationery or on third line below memo letterhead. Consists of guide words ("MEMO TO," "FROM," "DATE," and "SUBJECT") in capital letters followed by a colon. Entries after guide words align at a 1-inch left tab setting. Use the date format shown in Figure B-3.
Body	Starts on the third line below the memo heading; contains the message, single-spaced with one blank line between paragraphs.
Closing	On the second line below the last paragraph; includes reference initials (the typist's initials in small letters). Might also include an enclosure notation, a file name notation, and a copy notation or distribution list.

Figure B-3
Memorandum style

Heading

Body

Closing

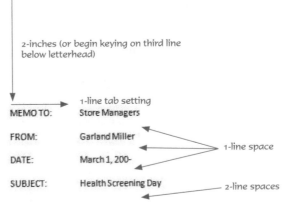

2-inches (or begin keying on third line below letterhead)

1-line tab setting

MEMO TO: Store Managers

FROM: Garland Miller   — 1-line space

DATE: March 1, 200-

SUBJECT: Health Screening Day   — 2-line spaces

In an effort to keep our health premiums low and our health benefits high, Campbell's Confections is planning a "Health Screening Day." We hope to have a high turnout, and if the day is successful, we may plan a Health Screening Day each year.

1-line space between paragraphs

All reports and research studies that we have analyzed have convinced us that the more workers know about their health, the more likely they are to take the initiative to improve it. If we empower our employees regarding their health habits, the more likely we will reap the benefits of fewer health insurance claims. Even more noticeable should be a lower absenteeism rate and fewer sick days accrued.

We are tentatively studying the following categories:

- Height and weight
- BMI (body mass index) and weight loss
- Body composition analysis (to determine safe levels of body fat percentages)
- Obesity and weight loss
- Blood pressure and pulse for hypertension monitoring
- Blood typing
- Diabetes screening
- Cholesterol ratios and triglycerides
- Flexibility analysis
- Reflex time
- Glaucoma screening
- Allergy screening
- Asthma screening

Download the Health Screening worksheet from the Web site, and poll all employees to record their interest level. Fax the completed worksheet to me by March 17. Thank you for your assistance.

<xx>   — 1-line space

Microsoft Office Objective Domain

TABLE C-1 Microsoft Office Word 2007 Activities Related to Lessons

Code	Activity	Lesson
WW 07 1	**Creating and Customizing Documents**	
WW 07 1.1	Create and format documents	1
WW 07 1.1.1	Work with templates	13, 21, 22
WW 07 1.1.2	Apply Quick Styles to documents	12
WW 07 1.1.3	Format documents using themes	12, 18
WW 07 1.1.4	Customize themes	12
WW 07 1.1.5	Format document backgrounds	5, 18
WW 07 1.1.6	Insert blank pages or cover pages	11
WW 07 1.2	Layout documents	
WW 07 1.2.1	Format pages	9, 10, 11, 18
WW 07 1.2.2	Create and modify headers and footers	11
WW 07 1.2.3	Create and format columns	16, 18
WW 07 1.3	Make documents and content easier to find	
WW 07 1.3.1	Create, modify, and update tables of contents	24
WW 07 1.3.2	Create, modify, and update indexes	24
WW 07 1.3.3	Modify document properties	2
WW 07 1.3.4	Insert document navigation tools	21, 24, 25
WW 07 1.4	Personalize Word 2007	
WW 07 1.4.1	Customize Word options	4, 22, 25
WW 07 1.4.2	Change research options	4
WW 07 2	**Formatting Content**	
WW 07 2.1	Format text and paragraphs	
WW 07 2.1.1	Apply styles	3, 12, 18
WW 07 2.1.2	Create and modify styles	12, 15
WW 07 2.1.3	Format characters	3, 18
WW 07 2.1.4	Format paragraphs	5, 18, 23
WW 07 2.1.5	Set and clear tabs	6
WW 07 2.2	Manipulate text	
WW 07 2.2.1	Cut, copy, and paste text	7

TABLE C-1 (*continued*)

Code	Activity	Lesson
WW 07 2.2.2	Find and replace text	8
WW 07 2.3	Control pagination	
WW 07 2.3.1	Insert and delete page breaks	10
WW 07 2.3.2	Create and modify sections	10, 16, 18
WW 07 3	**Working with Visual Content**	
WW 07 3.1	Insert Illustrations	
WW 07 3.1.1	Insert SmartArt graphics	19
WW 07 3.1.2	Insert pictures from files and clip art	17, 18
WW 07 3.1.3	Insert shapes	17
WW 07 3.2	Format Illustrations	
WW 07 3.2.1	Format text wrapping	17, 18, 19
WW 07 3.2.2	Format by sizing, cropping, scaling, and rotating	17, 18, 19
WW 07 3.2.3	Apply Quick Styles	17, 19
WW 07 3.2.4	Set contrast, brightness, and coloration	17
WW 07 3.2.5	Add text to SmartArt graphics and shapes	17, 19
WW 07 3.2.6	Compress pictures	17
WW 07 3.3	Format text graphically	
WW 07 3.3.1	Insert and modify WordArt	17
WW 07 3.3.2	Insert Pull Quotes	18
WW 07 3.3.3	Insert and modify drop caps	3
WW 07 3.4	Insert and modify text boxes	
WW 07 3.4.1	Insert and modify text boxes	18
WW 07 3.4.2	Format text boxes	18
WW 07 3.4.3	Link text boxes	18
WW 07 4	**Organizing Content**	
WW 07 4.1	Structure content by using Quick Parts	
WW 07 4.1.1	Insert building blocks in documents	4, 11, 18
WW 07 4.1.2	Save frequently used data as building blocks	4, 18
WW 07 4.1.3	Insert formatted headers and footers from Quick Parts	11, 18
WW 07 4.1.4	Insert fields from Quick Parts	11, 21
WW 07 4.2	Use tables and lists to organize content	
WW 07 4.2.1	Create tables and lists	5, 14, 15
WW 07 4.2.2	Sort content	6, 14

TABLE C-1 (*continued*)

TABLE C-1 (continued)

Code	Activity	Lesson
WW 07 4.2.3	Modify list formats	5
WW 07 4.3	Modify tables	
WW 07 4.3.1	Apply Quick Styles to tables	14, 15
WW 07 4.3.2	Modify table properties and options	14, 15
WW 07 4.3.3	Merge and split table cells	14, 15
WW 07 4.3.4	Perform calculations in tables	15
WW 07 4.3.5	Change the position and direction of cell contents	14, 15
WW 07 4.4	Insert and format references and captions	
WW 07 4.4.1	Create and modify sources	23
WW 07 4.4.2	Insert citations and captions	15, 23
WW 07 4.4.3	Insert and modify bibliographies	23
WW 07 4.4.4	Select reference styles	23
WW 074.4.5	Create, modify, and update tables of figures and tables of authorities	24
WW 07 4.5	Merge documents and data sources	
WW 07 4.5.1	Create merged documents	20
WW 07 4.5.2	Merge data into form letters	20
WW 07 4.5.3	Create envelopes and labels	9, 20
WW 07 5	**Reviewing Documents**	
WW 07 5.1	Navigate documents	
WW 07 5.1.1	Move through a document quickly using the Find and Go To commands	8, 10
WW 07 5.1.2	Change window views	7, 10, 24, 25
WW 07 5.2	Compare and merge document versions	
WW 07 5.2.1	Compare document versions	25
WW 07 5.2.2	Merge document versions	25
WW 07 5.2.3	Combine revisions from multiple authors	25
WW 07 5.3	Manage track changes	
WW 07 5.3.1	Display markup	25
WW 07 5.3.2	Enable, disable, accept, and reject tracked changes	25
WW 07 5.3.3	Change tracking options	25
WW 07 5.4	Insert, modify, and delete comments	25

TABLE C-1 (continued)

Code	Activity	Lesson
WW 07 6	**Sharing and Securing Content**	
WW 07 6.1	Prepare documents for sharing	
WW 07 6.1.1	Save to appropriate formats	1, 2, 22
WW 07 6.1.2	Identify document features not supported by previous versions	2
WW 07 6.1.3	Use compatibility checker	25
WW 07 6.1.4	Remove inappropriate or private information using Document Inspector	25
WW 07 6.2	Control document access	
WW 07 6.2.1	Restrict permissions to documents	21, 25
WW 07 6.2.2	Mark documents as final	25
WW 07 6.2.3	Set passwords	25
WW 07 6.2.4	Protect documents	25
WW 07 6.3	Attach digital signatures	
WW 07 6.3.1	Authenticate documents using digital signatures	25
WW 07 6.3.2	Insert a line for a digital signature	25

TABLE C-2 Lessons Related to Microsoft Office Word 2007 Objective Domains

Lesson		Code
1	Creating a Document	1.1, 6.1.1
2	Selecting and Editing Text	1.3.3, 6.1.1, 6.1.2
3	Formatting Characters	2.1.1, 2.1.3, 3.3.3
4	Writing Tools	1.4.1, 1.4.2, 4.1.1, 4.1.2
5	Paragraph Formatting	1.1.5, 2.1.4, 4.2.1, 4.2.3
6	Tabs and Tabbed Columns	2.1.5, 4.2.2
7	Move and Copy Text	2.2.1, 5.1.2
8	Find and Replace	2.2.2, 5.1.1
9	Margins and Printing Options	1.2.1, 4.5.3
10	Page and Section Breaks	1.2.1, 2.3.1, 2.3.2, 5.1.1, 5.1.2
11	Page Numbers, Headers, and Footers	1.1.6, 1.2.1, 1.2.2, 4.1.1, 4.1.3, 4.1.4
12	Styles and Themes	1.1.2, 1.1.3, 1.1.4, 2.1.1, 2.1.2
13	Templates	1.1.1
14	Create a Table	4.2.1, 4.2.2, 4.3.1, 4.3.2, 4.3.3, 4.3.5

TABLE C-2 (continued)

Lesson		Code
15	Advanced Tables	2.1.2, 4.2.1, 4.3.1, 4.3.2, 4.3.3, 4.3.4, 4.3.5, 4.4.2
16	Columns	1.2.3, 2.3.2
17	Graphics	1.1.4, 3.1.2, 3.1.3, 3.2.1, 3.2.2, 3.2.3, 3.2.4, 3.2.5, 3.2.6, 3.3.1
18	Desktop Publishing and Text Boxes	1.1.5, 1.2.1, 1.2.3, 2.1.1, 2.1.3, 2.1.4, 2.3.2, 3.1.2, 3.2.1, 3.2.2, , 3.3.2, 3.4.1, 3.4.2, 3.4.3, 4.1.1, 4.1.2, 4.1.3
19	SmartArt Graphics and Charts	3.1.1, 3.2.1, 3.2.2, 3.2.3, 3.2.5
20	Mail Merge	4.5.1, 4.5.2, 4.5.3
21	Fields and Forms	1.1.1, 1.3.4, 4.1.4, 6.2.1
22	Macros and Customizing Word	1.1.1, 1.4.1, 6.1.1
23	Footnotes and Endnotes	2.1.4, 4.4.1, 4.4.2, 4.4.3, 4.4.4
24	Outlines, Indexes, and Tables of Contents	1.3.1, 1.3.2, 1.3.4, 4.4.5, 5.1.2
25	Sharing Your Work and Hyperlinks	1.3.4, 1.4.1, 5.1.2, 5.2.1, 5.2.2, 5.2.3, 5.3.1, 5.3.2, 5.3.3, 5.4, 6.1.3, 6.2.1, 6.2.2, 6.2.3, 6.2.4, 6.3.1, 6.3.2

( ) denotes Lesson number where term can be found.

Active window   Window in which you are currently working that shows the title bar and taskbar button highlighted. (7)

Antonym   Word that is opposite in meaning to another word. (4)

Ascending sort order   Arrangement that places items in first-to-last or lowest-to-highest order, such as from A to Z or 0 to 9. (6) (15)

Attribute   Setting, such as boldface or italics, that affects the appearance of text. (3) (12)

AutoComplete   Automatic Word feature that suggests the completed word when you key the first four or more letters of a day, month, or date. (4)

AutoCorrect   Automatic Word feature that corrects commonly misspelled words as you key text. (4)

AutoFormat   Word feature that automatically changes formatting as you key text or numbers. (3)

AutoRecover   Word feature that automatically saves open documents in the background. The backup version of the document can be recovered in case the original is lost or damaged in a power failure or because of a system problem. (2)

Autoshapes   Ready-made shapes that are grouped by category: lines, basic shapes, block arrows, flow chart symbols, callouts, and stars and banners. (17)

AutoText   Word feature you can use to insert text automatically. (4)

Background pagination   Automatic process of updating page breaks and page numbers that occurs while you are creating or editing a document. (11)

Bar tabs   Used to make tabbed columns look more like a table with gridlines. A bar tab inserts a vertical line at a fixed position, creating a border between columns. (6)

Bibliography   List of sources that identifies references consulted or cited in a report or manuscript. (23)

Boilerplate   Standardized text used in business documents. (22)

Bookmark   Item or location in a document that you name so you can refer to it later. (21)

Border   Line, box, or pattern placed around text, a graphic, or a page. (5)

Building Blocks   AutoText entries, cover pages, headers, footers, page numbers, tables, text boxes, and watermarks that are stored in galleries to be inserted in documents. (4) (11)

Bulleted list   List of items, each preceded by a bullet (•). Each item is a paragraph with a hanging indent. (5)

Caption   Label that identifies a part of a document, such as a figure or table. A caption can include a number and usually includes text that describes the object, such as "Table 1. Delivery Schedule." (15)

Category axis   Horizontal (or x) axis along the bottom of most charts; frequently refers to time series. (19)

Cell   Portion of a table that is formed by the intersection of rows and columns. (14)

Character style   Formatting applied to selected text within a paragraph; includes font, font size, and font style. (12)

Chart title   Label that appears at the top of a chart and identifies the chart. (19)

Check Box Form Field   A field that can be selected or cleared. (21)

Click and type   Insert text or graphics in any blank area of a document. Position the insertion point anywhere in a document, click, and then type. Word automatically inserts paragraph marks before that point and also inserts tabs, depending on the location of the insertion point. (5)

Clip art   Ready-to-use drawings that can be inserted into a document. (17)

Clipboard   Temporary storage area in the computer's memory used to hold text or other information that is cut or copied. (7)

Clips   Multimedia files that can be clip art, photographs, movies, or sound files. (17)

Code   Text written in a programming language to create a macro or other computer program. (22)

Collapse   To hide body text and subheadings under a heading in Outline view. (24)

Color set   Feature for applying color. It includes four colors for text and background, six accent colors, and two colors reserved for hyperlinks. (12)

Comment   Electronic note that you add to a document. In Visual Basic and other programming languages, text that is not part of the macro or program and identifies the macro or makes it easier to understand. In Visual Basic, comment lines must always begin with an apostrophe. (22) (25)

Comment reference mark   Vertical line that appears where a reviewer has inserted a comment; the mark is color-coded to reviewer. (25)

Concordance file   Two-column table of words to be located and indexed in a document. (24)

Contiguous text   Any group of characters, words, sentences, or paragraphs that follow one another. (2)

Crop   Trim a picture so that only a portion of the original shows. (17)

Cut and paste   Method for moving text or other information by removing it from a document, storing it on the Clipboard, and then placing it in a new location. (7)

Cycle SmartArt graphic   Illustrate a process that has a continuous cycle. (19)

Data marker Object that represents individual data points in a chart. (19)

Data point Single piece of datum in a chart. (19)

Data series Group of related data points plotted in a chart, originating from the datasheet rows or columns. Each data series is distinguished by a unique color. (19)

Data source Variable information in a mail merge, such as names and addresses, to use in personalizing the main document. (20)

Demote To move a heading to a lower level in Outline view. (24)

Descending sort order Arrangement that places items in last-to-first or highest-to-lowest order, such as from Z to A or 9 to 0. (6) (15)

Destination document File that displays information stored in a different file. For example, a Word document that displays a linked Excel worksheet. (15)

Document Map Separate pane that displays a list of headings in a document; used to quickly navigate through the document and keep track of your location. (24) (25)

Document theme Feature that includes colors, fonts, and effects which affect the overall appearance of a document. (12)

Drag and drop Method for moving or copying text or other objects short distances by dragging them. (7)

Drawing canvas Rectangle graphic object in which you can draw multiple shapes and then size and format them as a group. (17)

Drawing objects Shapes, such as squares, circles, stars, banners, arrows, that you can draw and modify in Word. (17)

Drop cap Large letter that appears below the text baseline, usually applied to the first letter in the word of a paragraph. (3)

Drop-Down List Control A field that controls the choices that can be selected. (21)

Em dash Dash twice as wide as an en dash and used in sentences where you would normally insert two hyphens. (5)

Embedded worksheet Worksheet that exists only in the Word document or other file in which it is embedded. There is no corresponding Excel file. (15)

En dash Dash slightly wider than a hyphen. (5)

Endnote Text reference at the end of a document to credit the source of information or to offer additional explanation. (23)

End-of-cell marker Character that indicates the end of the content of each cell in a table. (14)

End-of-row marker Character to the right of the gridline of each row in a table; indicates the end of the row. (14)

Expand To display body text and subheadings under a heading in Outline view. (24)

Facing pages Document with a two-page spread. Right-hand pages are odd-numbered pages, and left-handed pages are even-numbered pages. (9)

Field Hidden code that tells Word to insert specific information, such as a date or page number. In a data source table, each item of information contained in a record. (4) (9) (20) (21)

Field code Merge field that appears in the main document as a placeholder for data from a data source. (20)

Field code syntax Field code text shown in a diagramlike format, indicating optional and required information and the required order for inserting that information. (21)

Field name In a data source table, the column heading of each category of information. (20)

Filename Unique name given to a document saved in Word. (1)

Find Command used to locate text and formatting in a document. (8)

First-line indent Indent for the first line of a paragraph. (5)

First-line indent marker Top triangle on the left side of the ruler. Drag the indent marker to indent or extend the first line of a paragraph. (5)

Floating graphic Graphic inserted in the drawing layer of a document so it can be positioned freely on the page, in front of or behind text and other objects. (17)

Font The design applied to an entire set of characters, including all letters of the alphabet, numerals, punctuation marks, and symbols. (3)

Footer Text that appears in the bottom margin of a page throughout a section or document. (11)

Footnote Text reference that appears at the bottom of a page to credit the source of information or to offer additional explanation. (23)

Form Standardized document used to request specific information. (21)

Formatting mark Symbol for a tab, paragraph, space, or another special character that appears on the screen, but not in the printed document. (2)

Function Predefined mathematical operation that can be used within a formula to process numerical data in a table. (15)

Gallery List of design options for modifying elements of a page. (11)

Gridlines Lines that mark the boundaries of cells in a table. (14)

Gutter margins Extra space added to the inside or top margins to allow for binding. (9)

Hanging indent Indentation of the second and subsequent lines of a paragraph. (5)

Hanging indent marker Bottom triangle on the left side of the ruler. Drag the marker to indent the second and subsequent lines in a paragraph. (5)

Hard page break Page break inserted manually. Does not move, regardless of changes in the document. (10)

Hard-coded Number, color, font, or other property that is specified exactly in a computer program. (22)

Header   Text that appears in the top margin of a page throughout a section or document. (11)

Header row   First or second row (if the table has a title row) of a table, in which each cell contains a heading for the column of text beneath it. (14)

Hierarchy SmartArt graphic   Graphic that illustrates the top-down relationship of members of an organization. (19)

Hyperlink   Text or graphic you click to move to another location. (25)

Hyphenation   The process of dividing a word that cannot fit at the end of a line or of joining two words. (16)

I-beam   Shape of the mouse pointer when it is positioned in the text area. (1)

Indent   Increase the distance between the sides of a paragraph and the two side margins (left and right). (5)

Indent marker   On Word's horizontal ruler, small box or triangle that you drag to control a paragraph's indents. (5)

Index   Lists the page numbers where specific words, phrases, or subjects occur in a printed document. (24)

Inline graphic   Graphic inserted in a line of text, on the same layer as the text. (17)

Insert mode   Mode of text entry that inserts text without overwriting existing text. (1)

Insertion point   Vertical blinking bar on the Word screen that indicates where an action will begin. (1)

Kerning   Adjusting the amount of space between certain combinations of characters so a word looks evenly spaced. (18)

Key Tips   Letters that appear over commands after you press the Alt key. Press the letter of the command you want to activate. The Key Tips may also be called *badges*. To turn off the Key Tips, press Alt again. (1)

Landscape   Page orientation setting in which the page is wider than it is tall. (9)

Leader characters   Patterns of dots or dashes that lead the reader's eye from one tabbed column to the next. (6)

Left and right indent   Indent left and right sides of paragraph (often used for quotes beyond three lines). (5)

Left indent   Indent paragraph from left margin. (5)

Left indent marker   Small rectangle on the left side of the ruler. Drag the marker to indent all lines in a paragraph simultaneously. (5)

Legal blackline   Word feature that lets you compare and merge two documents. The differences between the two documents appear in a new document as revision marks. (25)

Legend   In a chart, guide that explains the symbols, patterns, or colors used to differentiate data series. (19)

Line break character   Character that starts a new line within the same paragraph. Insert by pressing Shift+Enter. (2)

Line space   Amount of vertical space between lines of text in a paragraph. (5)

Link   Relationship between the data in a destination file and its source file, so that when the data are changed in one file, the other file is updated automatically to reflect the change. (15)

Linked style   Paragraph formatting applied to selected text. (12)

List SmartArt graphic   Graphic that illustrates groups and subgroups of information or blocks of information in a vertical or horizontal format. (19)

List style   Formatting instructions applied to a list, such as numbering or bullet characters, alignment, and fonts. (12)

Lock   To protect a form document, so the person filling out the form can have access only to the form fields. (21)

Macro   Automated procedure consisting of a sequence of word processing tasks. You can create a macro by recording mouse commands and keystrokes or you can write one by using Visual Basic editor. (22)

Mail merge   Process of using information from two documents (a main document and a data source) to produce a set of personalized documents, such as form letters or mailing labels and envelopes. (20)

Main document   Document in a mail merge to be merged with a data source and sent to many people or printed on envelopes or labels. The main document is information that is constant (it does not change). (20)

Margins   Spaces at the top, bottom, left, and right of the document between the edges of text and the edges of the paper. (9)

Markup   Comments and tracked changes, such as insertions, deletions, and formatting changes. (25)

Markup balloon   Comment or tracked change in the margin of a document in Print Layout view. (25)

Masthead   Part of a newsletter that contains publication information, such as the address, telephone number, editorial staff names, frequency of publication, and so on. (18)

Matrix SmartArt graphic   Graphic that illustrates relationships of objects to a whole in quadrants. (19)

Merge fields   In a mail merge, placeholders inserted in a main document that indicate where to insert information from the data source. (20)

Microsoft Office Button   Button that displays the File menu which lists the commands to create, open, save, and print a document. (1)

Mirror margins   Inside and outside margins on facing pages that mirror one another. (9)

Module   In Word, a container attached to a document or template and containing macro code. (22)

Multilevel list   Numbering sequence used primarily for legal and technical documents. (5)

Nameplate   Publication title with a distinctive typeface and graphic design. (18)

Negative indent   Extends a paragraph into the left or right margin areas. (5)

Nested table Table that is contained within a single cell of another table. (15)

Nonbreaking hyphen Hyphen used in a hyphenated word or phrase that should not be divided at a line break. (16)

Nonbreaking space Space between words, defined by a special character, that prevents Word from separating two words. Insert by pressing `Ctrl`+`Shift`+`Spacebar`. (2)

Noncontiguous text Text items (characters, words, sentences, or paragraphs) that do not follow one another, but each appears in a different part of a document. (2)

Nonprinting character Symbol for a tab, paragraph, space, or another special character that appears on the screen, but not in the printed document. (2)

Normal style Default paragraph style with the formatting specifications 11-point Calibri, English language, left-aligned, 1.15 line spacing, 10 points spacing after, and widow/orphan control. (12)

Note separator Short horizontal line that separates text from footnotes. (23)

Numbered list List of items preceded by sequential numbers or letters. Each item is a paragraph with a hanging indent. (5)

Optional hyphen Indication where a word should be divided if the word falls at the end of a line. (16)

Ordinal number Number indicating an order or position, for example, 1st, 2nd, or 3rd. (3)

Organizer Feature that lets you copy styles from one document or template to another or copy macros from one template to another. (13)

Orientation Setting to format a document with a tall, vertical format or a wide, horizontal format. (9)

Orphan First line of a paragraph that remains at the bottom of a page. (10) (18)

Outcrop Process of adding a margin to a picture. (17)

Outline Summary of a document based on heading levels. (24)

Overtype mode Mode of text entry that lets you key over existing text. (1)

Pagination Process of determining how and when text flows from the bottom of one page to the top of the next page in a document. (10)

Pane Section of a window that is formed when the window is split. A split window contains two panes. (7)

Paragraph Unique block of text or data that is always followed by a paragraph mark. (5)

Paragraph alignment Determines how the edges of a paragraph appear. (5)

Paragraph mark On-screen symbol (¶) that marks the end of a paragraph and stores all formatting for the paragraph. (1) (5)

Paragraph space Amount of space (measured in points) before and after a paragraph; replaces pressing `Enter` to add space between paragraphs. (5)

Paragraph style Formatting instructions applied to a paragraph; includes alignment, line and paragraph spacing, indents, tab settings, borders and shading, and character formatting. (12)

Parent table Table containing one or more nested tables. (15)

Placeholder text In a template (or a new document based on a template), text containing the correct formatting, which you replace with your own information. (13)

Plot area Rectangular area bounded by two axes in a chart; includes all axes and data points. (19)

Point Measure of type size; 72 points equals 1 inch. (3)

Portrait Page orientation setting in which the page is taller than it is wide. (9)

Positive indent Indentation between the left and right margins. (5)

Process SmartArt graphic Graphic that illustrates a progression or sequential steps toward a goal. (19)

Promote To move a heading or body text to a higher level in Outline view. (24)

Proofreaders' marks Handwritten corrections to text, often using specialized symbols. (1) (Appendix A)

Property Any information, such as the filename, date created, or file size, that describes a document. (2)

Proportional sizing Resizing an image while maintaining its relative height and width. (17)

Pull quote Sentence or quotation that is taken from a document and enlarged or set apart from the rest of the text for emphasis. (18)

Pyramid SmartArt graphic Graphic that illustrates foundation-based relationships. (19)

Quick Access Toolbar Toolbar containing frequently used commands and which is easily customized. (1)

Quick styles Various formatting options for text and objects that display as thumbnails in a gallery.

Record In a data source table, a row of related information (such as name, address, city, state, and ZIP Code) for one person or business. (20)

Reference mark Number or other symbol marking text that is accompanied by a footnote or endnote. (23)

Relationship SmartArt graphic Graphic that illustrates the relationship of objects to a main object. (19)

Replace Command used to replace text and formatting automatically with specified alternatives. (8)

Reverse text White text on a colored background. (14) (18)

Reviewer Person who adds a comment or tracked change to a document. (25)

Reviewing pane Narrow horizontal or vertical pane that opens at the bottom or side of the screen to display revisions and comments. (25)

Revision bar Black vertical line that appears to the left of each line containing a revision. (25)

Revision mark Mark that Word applies to text that has been changed while the Track Changes feature is turned on. (25)

Ribbon Seven default tabs, each tab containing a group of related commands. (1)

Rich Text Control A field where users can enter information. (21)

Right indent Indent paragraph from right margin. (5)

Right indent marker Triangle on the right side of the ruler; drag the marker to indent the right side of a paragraph. (5)

Ruler Part of the Word window that shows placement of indents, margins, and tabs. (1)

Sans serif Font characteristic in which the font has no decorative lines, or serifs, projecting from its characters, such as Arial. (3) (18)

Scale Change the size of an image as a percentage of its original size. (17)

ScreenTip Brief explanation or identification or an on-screen item such as a Ribbon command. (1)

Scroll bar Bar used with the mouse to move right or left and up or down within a document to view text not currently visible on screen. (1)

Section Portion of a document that has its own formatting. (9)

Section breaks Double-dotted lines that appear on screen to indicate the beginning and end of a section. (9)

Selection Area of a document that appears as a highlighted block of text. Selections can be formatted, moved, copied, deleted, or printed. (2)

Selection rectangle Box formed by the sizing handles of a selected object. (17)

Serif Font characteristic in which the font has decorative lines projecting from its characters, such as Times New Roman. (3) (18)

Shading Applying shades of gray, a pattern, or color to the background of a paragraph. (5)

Shortcut menu Menu that opens and shows a list of commands relevant to a particular item that you right-click. (3)

Sidebar Text box that is usually aligned on the right or left side of a page. It typically contains text that is related to but separate from the main document text. (18)

Size Change the size of an object. (17)

Sizing handles Squares or circles that appear around the border of a selected object and are used for resizing the object. (17)

Smart tags Feature that recognizes dates, addresses, and user-defined data types, all of which you can use to perform actions in Word that you would normally open other programs, such as Microsoft Outlook, to do.

SmartArt graphic Visual representation of ideas. (18)

SmartQuotes Quotation marks that curl in one direction (") to open a quote and curl in the opposite direction (") to close a quote. (5)

Soft page break Page break automatically inserted by Word and continually adjusted to reflect changes in the document. (10)

Sort To arrange items in a particular order, such as alphabetical or numerical order. Sorting is often done on tables and lists but can also be performed on text paragraphs within a document. (6) (14) (15)

Source document File containing information to be linked to another file. For example, an Excel worksheet that contains information to be displayed in a Word document. (15)

Special characters Characters such as the trademark symbol ™ or those used in foreign languages. (5)

Split bar Horizontal line that divides a document into panes. (7)

Split box Small gray rectangle located just above the vertical scroll bar. You can drag it down to split a document into two panes. (7)

Status bar Bar located at the bottom of the Word window that displays information about the task you are performing, shows the position of the insertion point, and shows the current mode of operation. (1)

Style Set of formatting instructions that you apply to text. (12) (18)

Style set List of style names and their formatting specifications. (12)

Subentries Index entries that are subordinate to the main index entries. (24)

Subtext Any heading or body text beneath a heading. (24)

Switches Parameter that controls the field display. Switches (or options) are inserted at the end of the field code and preceded by a back slash (\). (21)

Symbol Special character, such as the copyright symbol ©. (5)

Synonym Word that is similar in meaning to another word. (4)

Tab Paragraph-formatting feature used to align text. (6)

Tab character Symbol on the horizontal ruler that indicates a custom tab setting. (6)

Tab characters Nonprinting characters used to indent text. (2)

Tab marker Symbol on the horizontal ruler that indicates a custom tab setting. (6)

Tab stop Position of a tab setting. (6)

Table Grid of rows and columns that intersect to form cells. (14)

Table of authorities List of case, statutes, and other references that appear in a legal document. (24)

Table of contents List of topics contained in a document, arranged numerically by the page numbers where the topics appear. (24)

Table of figures List of captions and the pages where they appear in a document. (24)

Table style   Formatting instructions applied to a table, such as borders, shading, alignment, and fonts. (12)

Table template   Table based on a gallery of preformatted table designs. Usually contains sample data. (14)

Task pane   Pane to the right of the text area that provides access to a variety of functions. (4) (7) (12) (17)

Template   File that contains formatting information, styles, and text for a particular type of document. (13)

Text box   Free-floating rectangle that contains text. (18)

Text wrapping   Graphic option that lets text flow around an object or that positions the object behind or in front of text. (17)

Theme   Set of formatting instructions for the entire document. (12)

Thesaurus   Tool you can use to look up synonyms for a selected word. (4)

Thumbnail   Miniature representation of a page in Reading Layout view. (25)

Tick mark   Division mark in a chart along the category (x) and value (y) axes. (19)

Title bar   Bar that displays the name of the current document at the top of the Word window. (1)

Tracked changes   Revision marks that show where an insertion, deletion, or other editing change occurred. (25)

Value axis   Vertical (or y) axis in a chart, against which data points are measured. (19)

Watermark   Transparent graphic or text placed behind text, adding dimension to the printed page by creating a layered effect. Often used on stationery. (18)

White space   Unused space in a page layout that provides the necessary contrast for text and graphics. (18)

Widow   Last line of a paragraph that remains at the top of a page. (10) (18)

Wildcard   Symbol that stands for missing or unknown text. (8)

Wingding   Font that includes special characters, such as arrows. (5)

Workgroup templates   Templates that are stored centrally on a network server. (21)

Index

Borders—*Cont.*
   manual application of, 145
   for page decoration, 139–143
   for paragraphs, 139–141, 145,
      565–566
   for pull quotes, 580
   ScreenTips for, 139
   selections for, 141
   for tables, 403, 421–422
   for text, 141–143
   at top, 581
Borders and Shading dialog box, 139
Borders button, 139
Bottom alignment, vertical, 296
Bound documents, 261
Break(s), 286–293
   automatic, 286
   column, 231, 494–496, 573
   within column layout, 494–496
   continuous section, 293, 786
   on even pages, 293
   hard page, 286, 288–290
   for indexes, 786
   line, 34, 35, 231, 290–293, 575
   manual line, 231
   on next page, 293
   for odd pages, 293
   page, 257, 286–292
   paragraph, 290–293
   in Print Layout view, 257
   section (*see under* Section breaks)
   Show and Hide button for, 291
   soft, 286–287, 289
Break dialog box, 293
Brightness, of picture, 526
Bubble charts, 614
Building block(s), 587–588
Building Block gallery button, 685
Building Blocks Organizer, 101, 587
Built-in keyboard shortcuts, 708
Built-in styles, 347, 348, 350
Bullet(s), 146
   changing graphic of, 148, 149
   defining new, 149
   picture, 149
   selection by, 148
Bulleted lists, 146–150
   AutoFormat for, 149–150
   automatic creation of, 149–150
   changing, 148–149
   closing, 149
   continuing format for, 149
   creating, 146–150
   defined, 146
   selecting, 148
   styles for, 569–579
Business documents, 324
By box (character spacing), 74

C

Calculations, 454–458
Calibri (font), 63
Cambria (font), 63, 270
Capitalization
   in cells, 94
   correcting improper use of, 94
   of days, 94
   of sentences, 94

   small, 72
   of weekdays, 94
Caps Lock, 12, 94
Captions
   defined, 450
   for Excel worksheets, 461–462
   in tables, 450
Case (text)
   changing, 76–77
   correcting, 94
   matching, 222–223
Catalog-type document
   creating, 656
   formatting, 657
   mail merge for, 656–657
Categories, clip art, 516–517
Category axis, 617
Cell(s), 409–415
   borders for, 421–422
   capitalization in, 94
   content formatting for, 419–425
   defined, 402
   deleting, 413–414
   inserting, 413
   margins of, 418, 445–446
   merging, 415
   movement in, 409
   moving, 414
   nonprinting characters in, 445
   selecting, 409–412
   shading for, 421–422
   sorting text in, 420–421
   splitting, 415
   text formatting in, 420
   width of, 417
Cell Margins button, 445
Center alignment
   of tables, 417
   of tabs, 165
   vertical, 296
Change All option, 107
Change option, 107
Character(s)
   leader, 169
   for line breaks, 34, 35
   selecting, 41
   special, 151, 153, 229–231
   symbols, 151–152
   tab, 34, 35
Character (font) effects
   with Font dialog box, 70–73
   highlighting, 77–78
   keyboard shortcuts for, 73
Character formatting, 62–80, 562–564
   applying, 66–68
   AutoFormat features for, 79–80
   basic, 65–68
   case changing, 76–77
   clearing, 569
   copying, 75, 76
   drop caps, 78–79
   Find and Replace for, 231–232
   font basics for, 62–65
   Font dialog box for, 68–75
   with Format Painter button, 75, 76
   highlighting text, 77–78
   with keyboard shortcuts, 67
   with mini toolbar, 68
   purpose of, 62

   removing, 67–68
   with Repeat command, 75
   with ribbon, 66–67
   for title, 563
Character spacing, 563–564
   changing, 73–74
   with Font dialog box, 73–74
Character Spacing tab (Font dialog
   box), 73
Character styles, 341, 346–347,
   567–569
Chart(s), 609–624
   alignment of, 613
   area, 614
   axes of, 618–620, 622
   bar, 614
   bubble, 614
   colors for, 620–621
   combining, 616
   custom format for, 624
   data series formats in, 612–613
   defined, 604
   doughnut, 614
   editing data in, 611–613
   formatting, 620–624
   gridlines of, 618
   inserting, into document, 609–610
   key data in, 610–611
   layout for, 624
   legend of, 621–622
   line, 614
   options for, 617–620
   patterns for, 620–621
   pie, 614
   position of, 613
   radar, 614
   scatter, 614
   secondary axis of, 618–620
   stock, 614
   style of, 624
   surface, 614
   titles of, 617, 618, 623
   tools for, 604
   types of, 613–616
   undoing type selection, 615
   worksheets, 610–611
   XY, 614
Chart titles, 617, 618, 623
Chart Tools Layout tab, 620
Check boxes
   form field, 686–687
   toggle for, 691
Circle (four corner) sizing, 519
Citations, in bibliography, 763–764
Clear Formatting button, 144
Clearing
   formatting, 144, 569
   tabs, 169–170
Click and Type, 130–131
Clip(s), 514
   Paste for, 517
   scaling, 519, 520
   sizing, 520
Clip art, 514–528
   appearance adjustments for,
      526–527
   categories for, 516–517
   compressing, 521
   cropping, 521–522